MANAGEMENT RESEARCH METHODOLOGY

MANAGEMENT RESEARCH METHODOLOGY

Integration of Principles, Methods and Techniques

K. N. Krishnaswamy
Consultant and Former Professor
Department of Management Studies
Indian Institute of Science
Bangalore

Appa Iyer Sivakumar
Associate Professor
School of Mechanical and Aerospace Engineering
Nanyang Technological University
Singapore

M. Mathirajan
Principal Research Scientist
Department of Management Studies
Indian Institute of Science
Bangalore

Pearson

ISBN 978-81-7758-563-6

First Impression, 2007
Seventeenth Impression, 2018
Eighteenth Impression, 2023

Published by Pearson India Education Services Pvt. Ltd, CIN: U72200TN2005PTC057128.

Head Office: 15th Floor, Tower-B, World Trade Tower, Plot No. 1, Block-C, Sector-16,
Noida 201 301, Uttar Pradesh, India.

Registered Office: 7th Floor, SDB2, ODC 7, 8 & 9, Survey No.01 ELCOT IT/ ITES - SEZ,
Sholinganallur, Chennai - 600119, Tamilnadu, India.
Phone: 044-66540100
Website: in.pearson.com, Email: companysecretary.india@pearson.com

Laser typeset by Tej Composers, Delhi.

Printed in India at Sai Printo Pack Pvt Ltd

Management Research Methodology/Krishnaswamy

This book is dedicated to

My esteemed parents, the late K. Chokkammal and the late Kalkunte Narasimha Iyengar
—KNK

My beloved mother, the late A. I. Sakunthala
—AIS

Meena, Madhu, Keerthna and Shankar for their loving support
—MMR

Preface

This book is designed as an introductory textbook on management research methods. Research is a creative process and the topic of research methodology is complex and varied. The writing of a book like this is beset with over-structuring and simplification. The basic premise for writing this book is that research methods can be taught and learnt. The emphasis is on developing a research outlook and a frame of mind for carrying out research. Competence in mathematical and statistical techniques of analysis is not necessary for understanding this book; however, some competence is required for carrying out research in management.

To present the overall research process as a unitary whole, and then explain it by breaking it into small pieces, is a difficult task. We have attempted such a task in this book so that the student can see the whole and then take time to grasp the details in order to get a proper perspective of the subject.

Management research has three predominant approaches: First, there is the quantitative empirical approach in which the design provides for obtaining data that can be treated by rigorous statistical analysis. In this, hypothesis testing and multivariate analysis procedures are used. This is predominant in marketing management, organization theory and decision theory. Second, the mathematical modelling approaches use mainly logical thinking and operations research models in decision making situations, especially in the areas of operations, manufacturing, logistics, inventory and finance. These two provide solutions to problems on the lines of positive science. The third approach is the qualitative analysis approach of organizational theorists who emphasize studying and understanding particular problems and situations based on voluminous empirical data. They prefer depth of understanding of the particulars to the generalizations of the other two approaches. The book tries to integrate all these approaches and present to the student a blend of the general and the specific methods.

The book is organized into the following six parts:

- **Part A—Scientific Method in Management Research** consists of principles of scientific method and overview of management research. It provides insight into the basics of scientific method in research and discusses the way in which it is currently viewed in contemporary management research.
- **Part B—Research Problem** deals with methods of problem solving, research problem identification and formulation, and project proposal. The emphasis is on a mix of creative, logical and systems approaches particularly in problem identification and formulation.
- **Part C—Research Design Strategy** details the various types of researches, namely, experimental, *ex post facto* and modelling research. Modelling approaches in research design are elaborated along with experiment and *ex post facto* approaches. This is a new dimension in the treatment of management research methodology.
- **Part D—Research Design Tactics** discusses measurement and sample design as the final phase of planning of research before the research study is dealt with.
- **Part E—Data Acquisition and Preparation** encompasses data collection procedures and preliminary data analysis as research tools. The technical aspects of executing a research study are detailed in this part.
- **Part F—Data Analysis and Reporting** is devoted to methods of data analysis as tools of research and reporting as a means of communication of results of research.

Each chapter of the book contains learning objectives; a summary of the chapter; an annexure, in which the longer research examples or cases are provided; suggested readings; and questions and exercises that are considered useful for students.

The book is an outcome of several years of teaching in management in the form of teaching courses at the graduate level and through participation in workshops and seminars, guest lectures, management development programmes at the Indian Institute of Science, Bangalore and many in-house programmes of a number of industrial units in Bangalore and Singapore. In addition, the feedback from the students has helped the authors in structuring the book. This book, therefore, blends the needs of the research students on the one hand and the practising managers on the other.

This book is intended for students of MBA programmes and researchers at masters and doctoral levels. It can also be used by undergraduate management students, practising managers, and scientific professionals of R&D-sponsoring organizations.

This book contains some special features that will be of particular interest to research students:

- The material in the book is supplemented by a number of schematic diagrams for clear communication. Particularly, in the depiction of research process, they are intended to give a total picture of the flow of research to enable the student to get an integrated perspective of the details to be provided later.
- The text contains illustrations from research, consultancy, personal research, and Ph.D. and M.Sc. theses of the authors, their students and from research literature.
- Chapter 3 is intended to enhance the student's appreciation of a variety of problem-identification and problem-formulation approaches. It also makes the student aware of different kinds of thinking required in the various stages of research. The present education system seems to neglect training in creativity and to promote only logical and analytical thinking. The authors believe that the initial phase of identifying and formulation of the research problem, being fuzzy, is the most difficult phase of research and will be facilitated by making the student aware of these approaches.
- A separate section is devoted to qualitative research methods.
- A basic and thorough treatment of mathematical formulation (principles of modelling) is another aspect which distinguishes this book from others. Structural modelling and patterns of modelling are presented. Further, analytical, heuristic and simulation approaches are detailed. Some AI approaches are outlined for the awareness of the student. This will be of special interest to those interested in operations/manufacturing management, logistics and financial management.
- The composite modelling methodology, seldom mentioned in other books on the subject, will be useful to doctoral students.
- Preliminary data analysis, with data mining for analysing qualitative data, is another special feature of this book. This will aid in preliminary analysis of large public databases that are becoming increasingly available to the students.
- The statistical analysis procedures are so presented that the students can learn their appropriate choice, appreciating the conditions under which they have to be used and also their strengths and weaknesses. The mathematical and statistical aspects are kept to the maximum and only the interpretations are emphasized. They are demonstrated using software.
- The principle of thesis writing and qualitative and research reporting are also special features. It will be beneficial to the students while developing their theses.
- The current issues and controversies of management research are outlined in detail.

ACKNOWLEDGEMENTS

We acknowledge with thanks:

- The chairman, faculty, staff and students of the Department of Management Studies, Indian Institute of Science, Bangalore, for providing support and encouragement during the preparation of the manuscript.
- JNCASR, IISc, for providing a project assistant to prepare the initial draft of the manuscript.
- The Centre for Continuing Education, IISc, for the preparation of the first draft of the manuscript.
- The MIT–Singapore alliance of Nanyang Technological University for developing the second draft of the manuscript.

We also thank the following authors and publishers for permitting us to reproduce material from their works:

- Thompson Hampshire, UK, for Fig. 3.3 (p. 50) from Michael J. Hicks' *Problem Solving in Business and Management* (1991).
- Professor Paul Finlay for Fig. 4.8 (p. 90) from *Mathematical Modelling for Business Decision Making* (1985), Croom-Helm, London.

- INFORMS for Exhibit 4.3 (p. 98) from Terry Connolley, Leonard M. Jessup and Joseph S. Valacich's "Effects of Anonymity and Evaluative Tone on Idea Generation in Computer Mediated Groups" (1990), *Management Science*, Vol. 36(6), pp. 689–703 and for Exhibit 4.4 (p. 100) from George P. Benson, Jayant V. Saraph and Roger G. Schroeder's "The Effects of Organizational Context on Quality Management: An Empirical Investigation" (1991), *Management Science*, Vol. 37(9), 1107–1124.
- *The ASQ Journal* for Fig. 6.13 (p. 141) from Gerald I. Susman and Roger D. Evered's "An Assessment of Scientific Merits of Action Research" (1978), *Administrative Science Quarterly*, Vol. 23(4), pp. 582–602.
- Thompson Hampshire, UK, for Exhibits 7.1–7.3 (p. 176) from *Management Research Handbook* by Paul Dainty and Craig Smith.
- Professor Peter Checkland for Fig. A-1 (p. 488) from the *Journal of System Engineering*, Vol. 3(2), 1972.
- The American Statistical Association for Table D-4 (pp. 524–25) from "The Kolmogorov–Smirnov Test for Goodness of Fit" by F. J. Massey Jr., *Journal of the American Statistical Association*, pp. 68–78, Vol. 46, No. 253, March 1951.

A large number of individuals, including our M.Tech., MS and Ph.D. students, have helped us to complete this book. Their help is acknowledged with thanks. In particular, mention must be made of the following:

- The late Prof. B. G. Raghavendra of the Department of Management Studies, IISc, for reading the initial proposal and making valuable corrections and suggestions.
- Prof. A. K. N. Reddy, former Chairman of the Department of Management Studies, IISc, for support and encouragement.
- Prof. N. J. Rao, Chairman of the Department of Management Studies, IISc, for his support.
- Prof. M. H. Bala Subrahmanya of the Department of Management Studies, IISc, for meticulously correcting the final draft and making suggestions.
- Prof. K. S. P. Rao, Prof. B. S. Chetty, Dr G. Balaji, Dr Mukund Mohan, Sri Prince Vijayakumar, Dr G. Karthikeyan, Dr Suchitra Mouly, Prof. Madan Mohan, Dr Avvari Mohan, Sri K. V. Narssimha Murthy, and Dr B. V. Vasumathi, all ex-research scholars of the Department of Management Studies, IISc, for their contribution to the book.
- Mrs G. Bhanumathy for rendering invaluable services in typing, in creating tables and many figures, in composing the mathematical and statistical formulae, and meticulously incorporating the corrections.
- Mr Saleem Ahmed of the Department of Management Studies, IISc, and Mr Narayan of the Metallurgy Department, IISc, for drafting the manuscript and Ms K. Ramya for checking the final version of the manuscript.
- Mr Sanjay Singh, Mr Raza Khan, Mr Vikas Kanchan, and Mr J. Saravanan of Pearson Education India for helping us in bringing out the book.

K. N. Krishnaswamy

Appa Iyer Sivakumar

M. Mathirajan

- SPORTS: [illegible] Anonymity and [illegible] Bulletin of [illegible] [illegible] Management Science, Vol. [illegible]
- The LSD [illegible] Stanton and Young D. Edwards, "An Assessment of Scientific Merit of [illegible] Research" (1973). [illegible] Vol. [illegible]
- Thompson, [illegible] Paul Dainty and [illegible]
- Professor Peter Checkland for Fig. [illegible] Systems Engineering, Vol. [illegible]
- [illegible] Vol. 40, [illegible]

A large number of [illegible] Their help is acknowledged with thanks. In particular, mention may be made of the following:

- The late Prof. B. [illegible] of the Department of Management Studies, IISc, for reading the initial draft and making valuable corrections and suggestions.
- Prof. A. K. N. Reddy, [illegible] Chairman of the [illegible] for the support and encouragement.
- Professor [illegible] Chairman of the Department of Management Studies, IISc, for the support [illegible]
- Prof. M. [illegible] of the Department of Management Studies, IISc, [illegible] correcting the final draft and making suggestions.
- [illegible] Prof. [illegible] Dr [illegible] Dr Mukund [illegible] Karthikeyan [illegible] Mohan [illegible] and Dr [illegible] Narasimhan [illegible] of the Department of Management Studies, IISc, for their contribution to the book.
- Mr C. Shanmugam for rendering invaluable services in typing, illustrating tables and figures, in [illegible] the mathematical and statistical formulae [illegible]
- Mr Saleem Ahmed of the Department of Management Studies, IISc and Mr Nagaraj [illegible] the manuscript.
- Mr Sanjay Singh, Mr Rajat Khanna [illegible] Pearson Education India [illegible] in bringing out this book.

K. N. Krishnaswamy

Appa Iyer Sivakumar

M. Mathirajan

About the Authors

K. N. Krishnaswamy is a consultant and former professor at the Department of Management Studies, Indian Institute of Science, Bangalore. He has nearly three decades of teaching and research experience in management. Before joining the faculty at IISc, he was a manager at the Directorate General of Ordnance Factories, Ministry of Defence, Government of India, for over six years. He has a BE in electrical engineering from Mysore University and an ME in aeronautics and a Ph.D. in management, both from IISc. He has authored over 100 research papers on management science and three books. His research interests are production/operations management, industrial engineering, research methods, operations research/decision support systems/expert systems applications in operations management, R&D and technology management.

Appa Iyer Sivakumar is Associate Professor at the School of Mechanical and Aerospace Engineering, Nanyang Technological University, Singapore and a fellow of the Singapore–Massachusetts Institute of Technology Alliance (SMA). He was also associated with the Gintic Institute of Manufacturing Technology, Singapore. His research interests include operations research, manufacturing systems, logistics, supply chain, simulation, scheduling, and research methodology. He has several years of industrial and research experience in the UK. He held various management positions, including technical manager and project manager, for nine years at Lucas Systems and Engineering and Lucas Automotive, UK. During this period he was responsible for manufacturing re-engineering projects and was involved in the introduction of IT systems. He received a BE degree and a Ph.D. in manufacturing systems engineering from the University of Bradford, UK. He has presented several papers at international conferences and his articles have appeared in various journals. He has also trained and supervised a number of Ph.D. students. He was the technical chair and co-editor of the proceedings of the 3rd and 4th International Conferences on Computer Integrated Manufacturing, Singapore.

M. Mathirajan is Principal Research Scientist at the Department of Management Studies, Indian Institute of Science, Bangalore. He received his M.Sc. degree in mathematics from Madurai Kamaraj University and a postgraduate diploma in operations research from Anna University. He received another M.Sc. (engineering) degree in applied operations research and a Ph.D. in operations management from IISc. He was a postdoctoral fellow at the Singapore–Massachusetts Institute of Technology Alliance at Nanyang Technological University, Singapore. He was also a visiting consultant at Sultan Qaboos University, Oman. He was selected to present a paper in the 1999 Fall Annual Conference of the Operational Research Society of Japan in Tokyo. His Ph.D. thesis was adjudged the best thesis and was awarded the

M. N. Gopalan Award of 2002 at the annual convention of the Operational Research Society of India. His research interests include mathematical modelling and heuristic methods for production planning and scheduling, personnel scheduling, routing and scheduling in logistics, container terminal logistics, distribution in supply-chain management and research methods. He has published over 25 research articles in both national and international journals and also presented over 30 research papers, both at national and international conferences. He is the co-author of two books and a monograph. He has guided a number of research students at the management studies department in IISc.

Contents

Part B Research Problem

Part C Research Design—Types of Research

Part A

Scientific Method in Management Research

1. Scientific Method
2. Overview of Research in Management

CHAPTER 1

Scientific Method

- Introduction
- Scientific Method
- Issues of Management Research

The Cone of Science

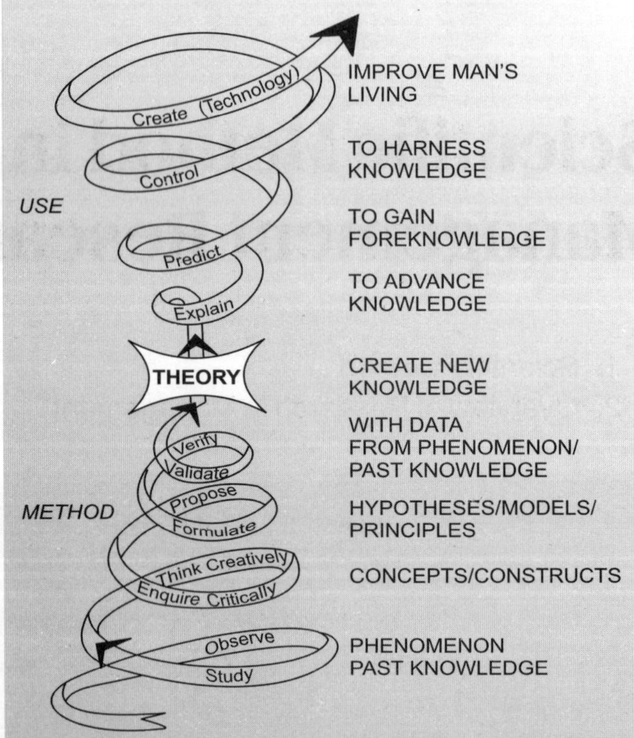

Learning Objectives

Upon completion of this chapter, you will be able to:

- ✓ Study the nature of management research
- ✓ Understand the process of scientific enquiry
- ✓ Develop definitions and hypotheses
- ✓ Appreciate the principles of formal science
- ✓ Study empiricism in scientific method
- ✓ Understand the logic of scientific method
- ✓ Study the inductive method for hypothesis generation
- ✓ Study the deductive method for hypothesis testing
- ✓ Study the hypothetico-deductive approach as the core of scientific method
- ✓ Appreciate scientific attitude
- ✓ Understand the current objections to the use of scientific method in management research
- ✓ Enumerate alternatives to scientific method in management research

Introduction

Management initiates and determines the activities of an enterprise. It makes plants, offices, computers, materials, and equipment productive through human effort. It gives competence and effectiveness to organisations in rendering goods and services to society. The aims of the management are to motivate the employees in the organisation to achieve a high degree of work performance in competitive situations, utilise resources efficiently, and to provide high quality goods and services. In trying to achieve these aims, the manager faces many hurdles and problems, which he needs to overcome and solve. He does this by taking appropriate decisions.

In this book, we assume the management to be synonymous with decision making, with respect to all activities in an organisation, in all areas pertaining to an enterprise and its environment. These activities encompass human resources, technology, supply chain, production, marketing, accounting and finance, public relations, policies and strategies of the firm. They also include managerial functions like organising, staffing, planning, controlling, and innovating.

A decision-making situation is one in which a manager is faced with a number of possible courses of action to solve a problem and a number of possible states and conditions of problem situations, which arise with uncertainty. The manager, in order to be effective, has to choose the course of action which is the most suitable against a set of criteria (like minimum cost and maximum profit in a particular situation though in practice there may be other criteria). The procedures for decision making in an organisation range from simple rules to complex analysis, individual decision-making to group decision making, from application of precedence and experience to considerable amount of enquiry and investigation.

management
Management is synonymous with decision-making with respect to all activities in an organization : planning, organizing, controlling, staffing, coordinating and innovating.

decision-making
Choosing from a number of possible courses of actions a course of action, which is the best against a set of criteria.

In practice, managers base their decisions on theories of organisation, which draw upon judgments and assumptions of well known and successful practitioners and research on leadership organisation and management, in addition to their own experience and judgment. In recent times, however, as management decision making is becoming more complex, there is a shift in most organisations from experience and judgment to analysis and research in decision-making. Management may be construed as both an art and a science. It is an art in sofar as it relies on individual experience and judgment, and a science insofar as it is based on findings of analysis and research. In recent times, quantitative research, which is valid and verifiable, has been rapidly adding to the body of knowledge on management and organisation. Traditional principles and practices are being looked at skeptically by the modern manager and research oriented knowledge is being preferred. But with the vast amounts of information available, it is necessary for the manager to understand what the evidence is and how one proceeds, to be better able to take good decisions. Until all such understanding is gained, management will remain an art as well as a science and research into management decision-making practices will continue to exist.

Defining Research

research
Research is a systematic, self-critical enquiry

Research is defined as a systematic, self-critical enquiry. The enquiry is aimed at understanding a thing or phenomenon or solving a problem. When an enquiry is aimed at understanding, it is termed as basic or fundamental research, which pursues knowledge, and may or may not have practical or commercial use. When the enquiry is aimed at applying the available knowledge for practical or commercial use, or for solving a problem faced in practice, it is termed as applied research.

scientific research
Research which employs scientific method is scientific research.

Research is a systematic enquiry, whether scientific or otherwise. Scientific research, on the other hand, employing scientific method, (to be dealt with later in the chapter) has well defined objectives and methods, generates dependable data, reliable and unambiguous findings, and justifiable conclusions.

management research
Management research is an applied research directed to aid the manager in his decision-making and in understanding the decision-making process. Management research may be reporting, descriptive, explanatory or predictive.

Management research Research in management is primarily applied research, in the sense that it is directed towards aiding the manager in his decision-making. Research is carried out in the enterprise to solve managers' immediate problems or help them in their predictive efforts for determining the future course of action or tackling an anticipated problem.

However, management research may be carried out in universities and research institutions where the primary objective of the researcher is to understand the phenomena of decision-making processes and their environments. In this case, research tends to be basic or fundamental.

The manager himself may carry out management research in the enterprise when he makes systematic enquiries. Data/information is collected and analysed, depending upon his own background and experience. Such research may not be scientific but would be useful in decision-making. However, more often, a hired outside specialist (management scientist or consultant), in collaboration with the manager, carries out the research. Research in such cases is more scientific and also gives practically useful results. The manager tends to check on the objectives, methods, and the terms of research to make it more useful to the firm, and within this framework the scientist makes a scientific enquiry to derive valid results. In either of these cases, the research process follows the same general steps. However, in the latter, some problems may arise between the manager and the scientist in the conduct of research. (This aspect will be discussed in Chapter 4).

descriptive research
Descriptive research describes a single event or characteristic or relates a few events or variables through statistical analysis.

explanatory research
Explanatory research answers why and how of the phenomenon through hypotheses and theories.

predictive research
Predictive research constructs and uses models to forecast the occurrence of an event or events.

Management research may comprise studies, which are reporting, descriptive, explanatory, or predictive (Cooper & Schindler 2000). **Reporting** type of research consists of furnishing data, information, or statistics. It may involve considerable skill in obtaining data from sources, abstracting the information from it, and evaluating the information thus obtained. In **descriptive** type of research, the researcher may try to describe a single event or characteristic through distributions or may try to relate a few events or variables through statistical analysis. The results cater to broader decision interests in the organisation, relating to policy, administration, and the like. **Explanatory** research explains the phenomenon. Hypotheses and theories mark this kind of research. Statistical or Operations Research (OR) modelling may be used in analysis. **Predictive** research uses the type of modelling done in explanatory research to forecast the occurrence of an event or events under certain conditions arising in the future; for example, when a capacity addition/expansion of a plant would be desirable with the current trends of demand continuing or changing because of technological changes. Predictive research is particularly useful in planning the activities of a firm.

Whether the manager himself researches or depends on an outside scientist, he should have a good understanding of the processes of management research. It would be ideal if he is carrying out the research himself, in order to get good and reliable results. If he is collaborating with a scientist, it would be fruitful for both to interact closely.

Whether the management research is basic or applied, many diverse disciplines like social science, economics, psychology, administration, statistics, and mathematics merge into a theory of management and decision-making. Therefore, research in management tends to be complex. The rigorous natural science modes of investigation tend to become more difficult to apply in management research. There are also other factors that impede management research.

The competence and effectiveness of any firm is dependent upon the quality of its human resources. Managing the human component of an enterprise is the most important and central task of management (Likert 1967). In this context, social relations in an enterprise present many difficulties in the application of natural science methods. Severe problems arise in measurement, which cannot be rigorously carried out. Motivation, attitude, stress, loyalty, cooperation, and so on, are not amenable to precise measurement. Further, the openness of results, which is so essential in natural science, becomes well nigh impossible, as considerable resistance of organisations and customers, coupled with patenting problems, exists. Public funding for management research is not generally as widespread as for physical, biological, and engineering sciences. For these reasons, the application of scientific method in management research has lagged considerably behind other disciplines.

The main objective of this chapter is to outline the scientific thinking and method necessary for good management research. It also highlights the concerns of many researchers and practitioners who seem to advocate alternate perspectives for management research. Research processes, methods, and techniques are elaborated in subsequent chapters.

Scientific Enquiry

Definition of science Since science is dynamic, its definition, if one is attainable, must change over time. Therefore, it is more useful to obtain a common understanding of some agreed characteristic of science, rather than to attempt to define it rigorously.

Science is at once a body of knowledge and the process of generating that knowledge. Science as a process is one of enquiry. It is different from common sense enquiry in that it is controlled (Ackoff, 1962). Science is "... trained and organised common sense" (Huxley, 1953). Further, scientific enquiry has goals of improving the method of conducting the enquiry itself, of answering questions, and of solving problems.

science
Science is a body of knowledge and also the process of generating that knowledge. Its goals are advancing knowledge, mapping patterns, and improving its own process.

The central goal of science is the enhancement of knowledge. Bunge (1967) proposes the following goals:

1. Advancement of knowledge and prediction
2. Mapping the patterns of various domains of facts (conceptual mappings)
3. Continuous improvement of its products through a set of partial models, using logical and empirical analysis
4. Metascience, which is the science of science itself.

Science, in the main, aims at developing more and more true patterns of reality gradually. It starts with simple and partial models representing different aspects of reality—first its components, then the relationships among them. It then adds on more and more territories and features. Another major objective of science is to sharpen and improve its own methodology and techniques for gaining knowledge of reality and of predicting it. This is referred to as metascience by Bunge (1967).

Process of scientific enquiry Science deals with nature and has grown out of natural philosophy. Bwad (1923) identifies two models of philosophical activities as a means of enquiry—speculative and critical (analytical). Speculative activity depends much on broad experience and imagination. Analytical activity, on the other hand, requires thoroughness, insight, and concentration on detail. It is clear that each must complement the other. In science, as in metaphysics, both the modes are necessary. There is, however, a dominance of analytical activity in scientific enquiry and method.

scientific enquiry
Scientific enquiry is a mental activity both speculative and critical in which critical (analytical) activity dominates.

Analysis is concerned with the language in which thinking is expressed, and can be done in three ways, namely, through the method of redefinition, the method of explication, and the method of illustration in use (Caws, 1965).

In the method of redefinition, terms and statements are made more carefully in a language that classifies their meaning and can be communicated without distortion. Consider, for example, the term quality. When controlling production in a plant it may be defined as the proportion of acceptance (that is, the quality of production is high when rejections are low). When the quality of a product is specified, the customer redefines quality as the degree of acceptance. The lexical definition is *degree of excellence*.

In explication, concepts are specified in a symbolic language so that they are unambiguous and precise, for instance, proportion is often denoted by % (percentage) as in

Worker percentage = (Workers/Total number of employees) * 100 = w%

Percentage annual interest = (Interests per year/Investment) * 100 = i %

The third method, that of illustration, holds that the meanings of terms and concepts are to be according to 'use'. Sometimes terms or concepts are defined for a specific study or research. For example, the term 'worker' in this research means an employee of a factory, who is eligible for workman's compensations under the Workman's Compensation Act.

However, sometimes the only way of classifying the meaning of a term or concept is to stipulate one. For example, conditional reflex is a reflex action that has been induced by habit or training to follow a stimulus that is not naturally associated with it. These are usually terms that form part of the jargon of a particular discipline.

Science uses explanation as a way of understanding some aspect of the world. But science is not just explanation; it encompasses the ability to predict the behaviour of things and to obtain control over them.

The classical view of Victorian scientists' empiricism and positivism was that the central characteristic of science was argued as the use of induction, as propounded by Francis Bacon and John Stuart Mill (Whitney, 1961, page 2 & 220). The strategy was that of accumulating facts and that broader laws and theories would emerge automatically by the sheer volume of data. The risk of being misled by false theories was considered to be minimal.

Subsequently, simple induction gave place to the hypothetico-deduction, that facts would lead to hypothesis (theory) and further investigations would lead to testing the hypothesis, thus, rendering science as a progressive process. Popper (1959) introduced the concept of falsification which engendered that scientists should strive to disprove every theory advanced, that is, science falsifies wrong theories but does not prove any theory once and for all. In other words, a theory holds until it is disproved. Further, Kuhn (1970) believed that science operates without much change over periods within paradigms in which implications of current theories are researched. As anomalies build up, the new progressively destroy old theories in a revolutionary manner. Thus a theory, is possibly only relative.

Science is knowledge, which is the ability to make true statements and to defend them. A truth corresponds with facts and is coherent with other truths, which are already established. The former gives science an empirical base and the latter a systematic structure, fitting it with other truths.

scientific knowledge
Scientific knowledge is the knowledge gained systematically through a cycle of process: observation, perception, language, thought, concepts, classification, definition, constructs, principles, hypotheses, laws and theory and verification.

Scientific knowledge is gained systematically rather than by direct experience. However, the origin of scientific knowledge is the experience of the scientist or the communication of the experience of others. Knowledge originating from experience generally goes through a cycle of scientific processes—like observation, perception, thought, language, concepts, classification, definition, constructs, theory and verification—before it is accepted as scientific knowledge (Fig. 1.1).

The processes of enquiry (Fig. 1.1) involved in the transformation of experiential knowledge to scientific knowledge is now briefly outlined.

Observation Much of what we know is derived from observation, either systematic or haphazard. The starting point of research is often an observation. Observation of phenomenon undertaken as a part of scientific enquiry is scientific observation. It is purposeful, related to scientific properties, systematically carried out in a phased way, and is subject to checks with regard to validity and reliability. Observation may be direct (as in the case of studying individual behaviour) or indirect (as in interviews and questionnaires).

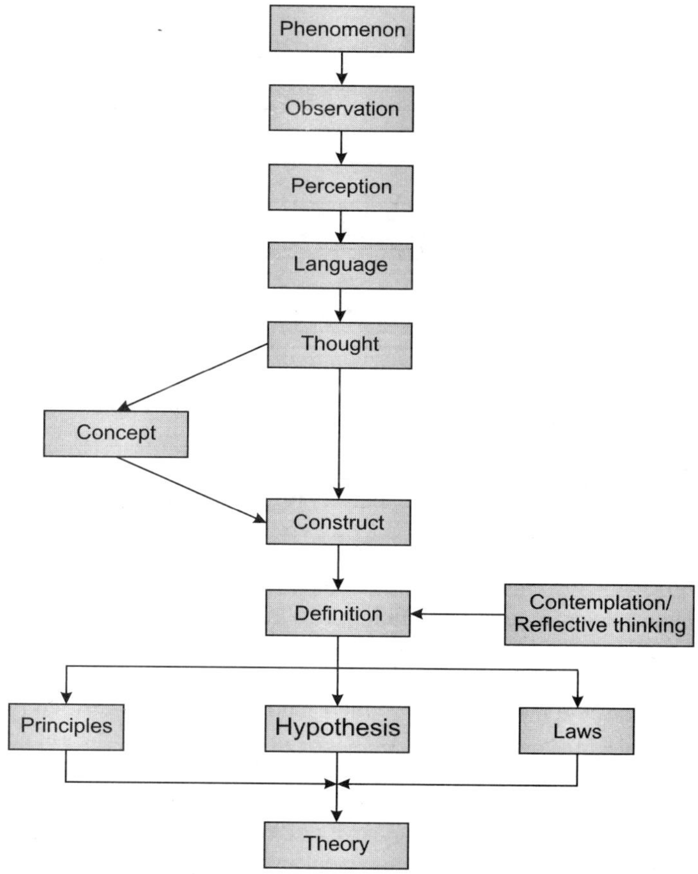

Fig. 1.1 Scientific knowledge acquisition

Concept Concepts are the basic building blocks of thought and communication. Any phenomenon is contemplated by using concepts but a concept represents only one aspect of reality. Concepts help in organising an observation and experiential knowledge. When carrying out scientific enquiry, concepts have to be precise. Values, leadership, costs, and a machine centre are all concepts. A machine centre, for example, can be thought of as a means of conversion in a process, as a demand for investment in financial considerations, and as a source of failure in system maintenance. Each one of these concepts, when investigated, would require different tools of analysis or methods of investigation. Concepts are, thus, products of experience and perception and are, therefore, inventions of the human mind. They make it possible to think about the same phenomenon in different ways.

concept
A concept is a basic building block of thought and communication which helps in organizing an observation or an experiential knowledge. It is a product of an experience and perception representing a degree of abstraction.

Concepts also represent different degrees of abstraction. Consider the human resource concept of a manufacturing company. At the highest level of abstraction we have the human resource concept and at the lowest level we may consider a lathe operator [Fig. 1.2]. There are many other types of machine operators like millers, press operators, and so on. A higher level of abstraction is a machine operator. There are skilled workers in the company like assemblers, inspectors, viewers, and so on. The next higher level of abstraction is a skilled worker. Further, we have supervisors to supervise these skilled workers, engineers and designers, who are technically qualified, to support them. Thus, the next higher abstraction is technical manpower. In addition to technical manpower, we have administrative, legal, human relations, purchase, and selling manpower. This sums up the human resource of the organisation at the highest level of abstraction. In management, concepts are particularly useful in providing insights and understanding of perceptions, roles, and viewpoints of various actors in an organisation.

Classification No two objects are identical, but they may bear likeness to one another. This adds to the complexity of a phenomenon. A fundamental philosophy of science is to reduce this

Fig. 1.2 Human resource concept—an example

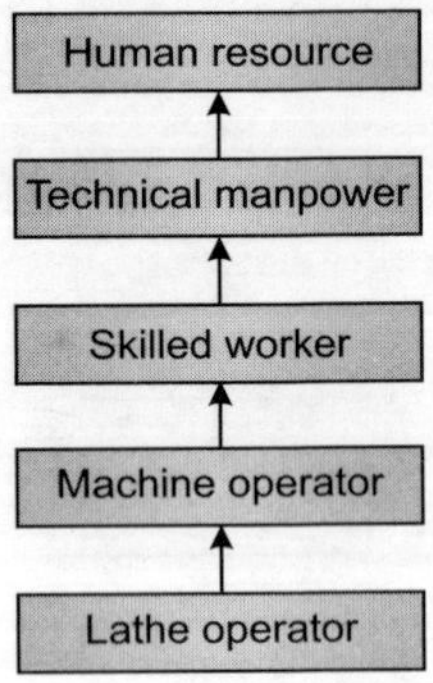

complexity so that a few general fundamental principles can explain them. To reduce this complexity, objects are classified together based on what they have in common, such as genetic similarity (having similar origin, for instance, sea foods, and cotton textiles), structural similarity (having similar constituent parts, for example, process layouts, and line organisations), or fundamental similarity (having similar behaviour, like schizophrenia).

definition

A definition is a statement whose truth is asserted but not considered liable to empirical challenge. A definition can be descriptive or lexical or operational or mathematical.

Definition With each classification obtained, the members of the classification will provide a definition of the term denoting that classification. When a definition aims at showing the meaning of a term by indicating the application to which it refers, but not through other terms, it is called ostensive definition. For example, we may ask which companies, from a list of companies, have good industrial relations between their management and staff, and get it marked by a trade union leader. By its very aim, ostensive definition is of the lowest form and leaves room for ambiguity. Some definitions are internal, in the sense that they belong to the same language system, for example, the language of statistics. When the definition extends outside the language system it becomes external. All ostensive definitions are, thus, external. Definitions that depend upon intentions are internal. Ostensive definitions are not generally useful in scientific research but may be used in the initial stages. Whether or not internal to a language system, a statement whose truth is asserted but not considered liable to empirical challenge is a definition.

Definitions have several functions (Caws, 1965): (1) Grounding concepts in general observation, (2) Describing relationship between concepts and properties, (3) Indicating substitutability with other concepts, (4) Introducing metrical considerations, and (5) Mathematically linking different concepts.

The above definitions can be descriptive or lexical, operational or mathematical. Table 1.1 briefly outlines the functions, value, and use of various definitions.

Table 1.1 Definitions

Type	*Function*	*Nature*	*Use*	*Remarks*
Ostensive definition	To explain meaning	External	General communication of thought	Ambiguous and vague, lowest form
Descriptive definition	To describe properties and relations	Internal if within a discipline, otherwise external	Grounding concept in observation; communication	
Operational definition	To introduce metrical considerations	Internal if within a discipline, otherwise external	Measurement	Clear precise and unambiguous
Lexical definition	To substitute one concept for another	External	Enrichment of concepts	Ambiguity in highly abstract definition but unambiguous in definitions at lower abstraction levels
Mathematical definition	To substitute in a mathematical sense, that is, equation	External	In all physical sciences and where mathematical methods can be used	Precise and logical

Descriptive definition: When one term is defined using other terms, the definition is verbal. Concepts may be defined in terms of other concepts. Such definitions are descriptive definitions, for example, a vendor is a person or organisation supplying goods and services to an establishment. Concepts may be defined in terms of other concepts at a lower level or a higher degree of abstraction, but usually definitions using lower level concepts are more useful and meaningful. In lexical definitions too concepts are defined in terms of other concepts (synonyms) at the same level of abstraction. For example, Firm – partnership for carrying out business; factory building – buildings with plant for manufacturing, and so on.

Operational definitions: These are mostly used in research and help in making measurements. They are stated in terms of criteria for measurements so that they are unambiguous and precise. They must be capable of being counted or measured, or it must be possible to gather information on them in some way. The object to be defined may be physical (amount of investment) or highly abstract (attitude), the first may be measured in monetary terms and the second may require a set of questions to measure the multidimensional construct.

operational definition
An operational definition is stated in terms of criteria for measurement so that it is unambiguous and precise, which is mostly used one in research.

Mathematical definitions: are expressed in terms of symbolic expressions.

For example: Inventory holding cost for an item = $(Q \times c \times i/2)$

Where Q = quantity purchased in a cycle

c = cost per unit of the item

i = interest rate on capital locked up in the inventory.

A conceptual scheme, a precise language, and definitions are required to enable scientific observation and classification of information collected. But all these operate together and in a cyclic manner.

Construct Refinements and redefinitions of familiar concepts to suit a particular discipline in order to describe the operations of the phenomena relevant to the discipline, lead to 'constructs'. Thus, constructs of a particular discipline are concepts, which are clear and precise after being shorn of ambiguity and vagueness by rigorous redefinitions and refinements. Constructs linked to the perception of scientists are called observables. Observables can be enhanced and enriched by instruments used for extending the range of perception of the scientist (for example, a telescope for an astronomer or a motion picture camera for making time and motion studies in industrial engineering). A construct may not have a direct link to perception or observation and may be purely speculative. Such constructs are termed theoretical constructs.

construct
A refined and redefined familiar concept to suit a particular discipline is called a construct. It is clear and precise. A construct not directly linked to perception or observation, is termed theoretical construct.

Hypothesis Based on enquiry or insight or a limited observation of phenomena, a scientist may make a proposition. A proposition is the meaning of a declarative sentence used for the assertion of some relationship between concepts.

If a series of observations are made on objects O, in order to determine whether or not the objects in this class exhibit property P, and if in each case of O and so on, that is, O1, O2, O3, and so on, the property P is observed, the scientist moves from a declarative statement with respect to each observation of O to a universal statement about class P, like all Os are P. Such a jump is known as generalisation.

Hypothesis is any declarative sentence in which at least one empirical generalisation follows but whose contradiction does not take the form of a protocol sentence. Hypothesis is a proposition that typically states the existence, size, form, or distribution of some variable (Emory 1976). In this form, a proposition can be tested and becomes a hypothesis. If a declarative sentence whose consequences, when tested empirically, result in reality not leading to them it becomes necessary to reject it. What is scientific is, therefore, relative to the status of knowledge at the time of making the hypothesis. Hypotheses are rejected not because they are false but because they are irrelevant. Usually, generalisations that are not confirmed are called hypotheses. They are only tentative, need to be confirmed, and are only just 'working hypotheses'. Generalisations emerge but hypotheses have to be invented (Caws, 1965). In any case, a hypothesis that is confirmed indicates confidence in the repeatability of observations.

hypothesis
A hypothesis is a declarative sentence or proposition in which at least one empirical generalization follows and states the existence of the size, form, or distribution of some variables. The relationship between a fact and its cause is expressed as hypothesis, which must be capable of being experimentally verified and must have a definite practical consequence.

Any statement whose truth can be tested by observing the world is an empirical proposition. A hypothesis is a proposition that can be experimentally verified, and has a definite practical consequence. Most hypotheses have the following features (Weatherall, 1968).

1. Logical relationships like

   All, some, or none

   If, unless

   Greater than, equal to, less than

   Proportional to

2. Quantitative relationship
3. Spatial relationship
4. Generality
5. Simplicity.

Descriptive hypotheses: These describe properties.

1. "Current unemployment in India is greater than 15 per cent."
2. The marketing manager and the financial manager of a firm do not agree on the quantity of finished products to be maintained as safety stocks.

Relational hypotheses: These describe the relationship between two variables.

1. "Parents with higher education spend more on the education of their children," while an associative relationship is implied, a cause-effect relationship is not implied.
2. The greater the employee welfare measures provided by the management of a company, the smaller the labour turnover of skilled workers.

Explanatory hypotheses: These indicate a cause-effect relationship. The direction of relationship is important and should be interpreted properly.

When the salaries of government employees increase, their families spend more on their clothing. The direction of relationship is: increase in salary → purchase of clothing. But the reverse is not true, that is, it cannot be said that by purchasing more clothing salaries can be increased. But in all cases the direction of relation is not so obvious.

Generally, good hypotheses and associated experiments are designed to win both ways. Hypotheses may be defective because they are indefinite, narrow, semantically faulty, logically faulty, and related to unattainable conditions. In developing hypotheses, argument by analogy is a great spur to imagination, but has no justification (cf. inductive inference).

In confirming a hypothesis, tests of statistical significance measure the strength of evidence that a difference between the hypothesised and actual relationship is not fortuitous. However, it gives no information about the importance of the difference. The errors that are usually associated with hypothesis testing are Type I error-insignificant is taken as significant or Type II error—lack of significant difference is taken as evidence of no difference.

Laws An empirical generalisation, either affirmative or conditional, accepted as true becomes a law. Laws are based mostly on partial and intermittent observations and, therefore, a certain inexactitude is the price to be paid if the law covers a wide territory. A statement whose truth is asserted and is empirically significant is a principle if it has theoretical terms or else it becomes a law. Principles are *a priori* to the scientific system like in physics but they may be feasible in sciences like the social sciences. Principles and hypotheses are accepted as suitable starting points of theoretical work but are not observable. All generalisations accepted as true are laws and all hypotheses accepted as true are principles.

theory
A theory is a set of asserted universal propositions communicated in a set of universal sentences (by several researchers) which are derived by observation and empirical evidence capable of agreement and corroboration.

Theory Theory is a set of asserted universal propositions communicated in a set of universal sentences. Each scientist may have his own set of propositions. However, several sets of assertions of several scientists will be fully or partially isomorphic with each other. Therefore, a union of such sets would be a theory in an all-inclusive sense. A theory is nothing but an outlook, systematically acquired and derived by observation and empirical evidence, capable of agreement and corroboration.

Hypotheses, laws, and theories play a vital part in the scientific enterprise of explanation. This is depicted in Fig. 1.3. Scientific knowledge develops through theory building. Theory and empirical evidence constitute every scientific effort. Theory as a set of definitions, constructs, and hypotheses, which are systematically related and are used for explaining and predicting phenomena through testing against observable data. The inferences thus drawn provide the necessary evidence to accept the theory, modify it, or add to it as further research adds hypotheses and constructs to the existing ones. A theory, generally, constantly changes as new laws and new propositions replace old ones. At any point of time a theory serves as a guideline for the useful ways in which phenomena can be investigated.

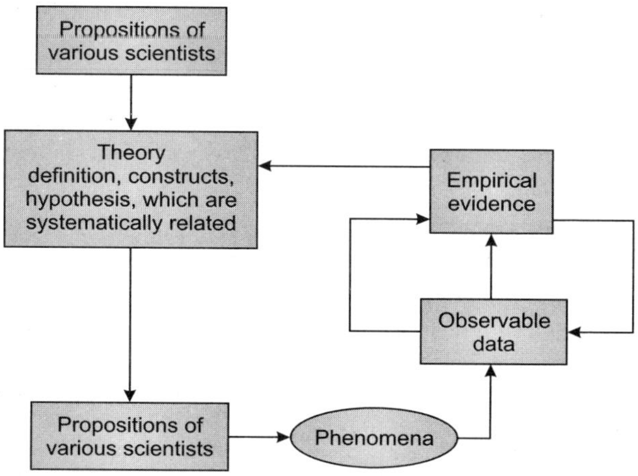

Fig. 1.3 Theory development process

Consider, for example, the business systems theory. Ludwig Von Bertanalaffy (1969) set forth concepts of open systems and a general systems theory. He based his theory on living systems. A living system is not a conglomeration of separate elements but a definite system having organisation and wholeness. It is an open system maintaining a constant state, while matter and energy, that enter it keep changing (called dynamic equilibrium). The organism is influenced by and influences its environments and reaches a state of dynamic equilibrium. This is analogous to a business organisation, which is a manmade system and has dynamic interactions with its environments, customers, competitors, labour organisations, suppliers, government, and technology.

A business organisation is a system of interrelated parts working together with each other in order to achieve business goals and individual goals. Compare a business organisation to a human body, the skeletal and muscular systems correspond to operating elements, the circulatory system to staff function, the nervous system to the communication system in an organisation, and the brain to the top management. Such a viewpoint of business theory could provide a framework for rational decision-making, as propounded by Simon (1960), and would indicate the desired focus for scientific enquiry on proper points for decision-making, for the benefit of both the organisation and the individual (Johnson et al, 1980).

SCIENTIFIC METHOD

Formal Science and Empirical Science

Formal science (for example, mathematical sciences) is based on the axiomatic method. An axiom is postulated as true and further axioms are deduced from it. Thus, an axiom is an analytical truth. The only truths that logical terms deal with are analytical and a science embodying only such terms is called a formal science. In formal science some of the following terms are relevant.

formal science
A formal science is a mathematical science based on axiomatic method (an axiom is an analytical truth). It embodies only logical and analytical terms and also has theorems.

Logical calculus is a system within which formal properties and relationships can be calculated. (for example, Calculus). A **deductive system** is one that has interrelated statements out of which some follow from the others deductively. An **axiomatic system** is either an axiom (not following deductively from any statement) or an axiom has to result in a useful calculus and must be independent. Axioms, in general, should be consistent. A **theorem** is a sentence arrived at by using a set of axioms put together by means of acceptable transformation rules, inference rules, formation rules, or rules for specification of terms. A series of sentences starting with axioms and ending with a theorem is the proof of the theorem. (Bullock Alan, et al. (1990), pp.64-65

empirical science
A science based on facts is an empirical science. It draws inspiration from natural sciences (physics, chemistry, astronomy, etc.).

Empirical science draws inspiration from natural sciences (like physics, chemistry, geology, astronomy, and so on) and is based on facts. The scientific method used in developing scientific laws and theory uses the hypothetico deductive procedure (Popper, 1959). This procedure inductively evokes hypothesis by experience or by the study of a phenomenon and tests it deductively using information from the phenomenon. Science, in this sense, has empirical meaning.

scientific method
Scientific method is one that uses hypothetico-deductive method for developing laws and theories, evoking hypotheses inductively and testing them deductively.

The scientific method uses, both descriptive terms and logical terms, and axioms both logical, like in formal science, and syntactical (axioms that are empirical). Arguably, the best way to go about science is to separate the mathematical form and the empirical meaning and argument (Braithwaite, 1973).

Logic of Scientific Method

A satisfactory scientific explanation is one that logically classifies the relationships between facts and not one that is merely psychologically acceptable. Logic has two values, like simple switches, connoting either a Yes or a No. In a logical system, deriving logical truth from one sentence to another is called inference. In logical inference there is a need to start with a true sentence. The relationship, which can be inferred in such a process, is called implication.

deductive logic
Inferences drawn from a general principle to particular conclusion constitute deductive logic. The set of sentences deriving conclusion is called an arguments. Conclusions are true inferences. Deductive logic is the study of validity and not of truth,

Deductive logic If the inferences in a logical system are certainties, they are called demonstrative, and if they are probable, they are called non-demonstrative. Demonstrative inferences are deductive—drawing particular conclusions (true inferences) from general principles. The set of sentences deriving conclusions (last sentences) from other sentences is called an argument. The set of sentences, reasons, or premises must be true for the conclusion to be true, then the argument is valid. Propositions are true or false; reasoning or argument is valid or invalid. Deductive logic is the study of validity and not of truth. The following examples illustrate this.

1. All managers take decisions — Premise 1 (P1) True (T)
   Raman is a manager — Premise 2 (P2) True (T)
   Therefore ↓ (argument) (A) — Valid (V)
   Raman takes decisions — True (T)

   Both the premises are true and the argument is valid and, therefore, the deduction is True.

2. All industrial organisations manufacture goods — (P1) (F)
   India Systems is an industrial organisation — (P2) - (T)
   Therefore ↓ A — valid
   India Systems manufacture goods — False (F)

The first premise is false (because an industrial organisation may produce goods or services. The second premise is true. The argument is valid but the deduction is false. (Note that India Systems may not produce goods but may produce only services).

3. All factories are organisations — (P1) True
   All offices are organisations — (P2) True
   Therefore ↓ (A) — Invalid
   All factories are offices — False

Therefore, it can be seen, in general, that all premises must be true and the argument must be valid for the deduction to be true. We know the truth of the premises. They provide evidence for the conclusion, but not complete evidence—they render the conclusion probable to a degree (see example, 2 above). Whenever we take samples and base our conclusions on them, we argue inductively.

One of the most important applications of deductive logic is in the testing of hypotheses. If we know that the consequences of hypothesis are true then the hypothesis is true.

h > g	g follows from h is true
g/h	if g is true then h is true

This is the most frequently used argument in testing scientific hypothesis. But this argument suffers from the fallacy of affirming the consequence (the consequence of one hypothesis may be the consequence of another).

h > g	g follows from h is true
g/h	but g is false, therefore, h is false

Inductive logic Francis Bacon introduced the use of inductive logic. In induction, empirical evidence or fact is the starting point. Inference is drawn from the evidence in the form of conclusions, which explain the evidence or facts. An inductive conclusion may be one of the many possible explanations of the fact and is, therefore, only tentative. It may also explain facts other than those observed as evidence. Therefore, it is usual to refer to the relation between evidence and inductive conclusion as supporting, that is, the evidence supports the conclusion. When contradictory new evidence is observed, the conclusion has to be abandoned. Take for instance the following example:

inductive logic
In inductive logic inference is drawn from the evidence in the form of conclusions, which explain the evidence or facts. Inductive conclusion is one of the many possible explanation of the facts and therefore only tentative.

Statement: If productivity is high then the workers are motivated.

Deduction: Productivity is high in organisation X, therefore, the workers in organisation X, are motivated. (1)

Induction: Workers are motivated in organisation X, therefore, the productivity is high in organisation X. (2)

The argument in (1) implies that unless workers are motivated, productivity cannot be high. In (2), however, it does not follow that if workers are motivated, the productivity will be high. There may be other reasons (premises) in the organisation, like low quality material or old machines, which may result in low productivity.

Inductive-deductive thinking Any research effort uses both inductive and deductive thinking. The formulation of a hypothesis, not much emphasised in scientific method, involves the limited observation of a fact (evidence) and inference from that tentative cause. The relationship between fact and presumed cause is expressed in the form of a hypothesis that should be rigorously checked and confirmed through the hypothetico deductive procedure. In this procedure, deductive thinking is predominant. This is well treated by Emory (1976) as 'double movement thinking'. Thus, scientific knowledge is accumulated and science progresses through cycles of inductive-deductive thinking.

inductive and deductive thinking
Hypotheses are developed by scientific method inductively using a limited observation of facts. The hypothesis is rigorously checked through the procedure of deductive thinking.

Explanations can be analogical, tautological, probabilistic, genetic, or deductive. The deductive mode is most often used in science, the other are quasi-deductive. **Analogy** relates to the use of a logical form of a well established relation to the one under consideration. **Tautology** relates to future conditions; probability relates to a number of possible consequences of a given law under given conditions. **Genetic mode** highlights how the given events occur from other events as a result of a process spread over time. To identify pseudo science, which may give explanations using the deductive or **quasi-deductive** procedures to appear as science, it becomes necessary to test it through prediction, which is the hallmark of true science. Prediction can demonstrate other phenomena, not merely the one on which the prediction rests (Caws, 1965).

Thus, while a hypothesis cannot be verified with reference to consequences, it can be falsified or rejected. This enables one to reject an alternative hypothesis so that one has more confidence in one's hypothesis. Thus, sets of principles, propositions, or hypotheses, are put together to form scientific theories derived from observation.

hypothetico-deductive method
This is a process of operations of raising precise questions converting the questions into hypotheses. The logical consequences of the hypotheses are obtained. They are tested and verified.

Hypothetico-deductive Method

The objective of science is to seek knowledge. Scientific method leads to three detailed objectives, namely, classification, explanation, and prediction. Scientific activities include collection and classifying facts about phenomena—a descriptive activity which lays down the observational foundation for science and for further research. The search for relationships (hypotheses) between facts and their discovery leads to explanation, which gives an understanding of phenomena. Prediction is the anticipation of future events, which gives control over the facts for their practical use. Really, all the three objectives merge into explanation. An unsatisfactory explanation of phenomena causes a strong motivation for research. Non-acceptance or total absence of a theoretical explanation of facts causes the progress of science. Thus, scientific method is characterised by hypothesis, deduction, and test.

Every scientific investigation involves a method, which is a combination of a general method common to every scientific investigation, and special methods or techniques unique to the problem being investigated or to the territory of knowledge in which it is located. It is the general method that distinguishes the scientific method from the non-scientific. The eight hallmarks of scientific research, according to Sekharan (2000), are purposiveness, rigour, testability, repeatability, precision and confidence, objectivity, generalizability, and parsimony.

Scientific investigation or research using a hypothetico deductive process is a cycle of operations, as depicted below. Study of the body of present available knowledge coupled with observations of the phenomena being investigated leads to the following.

1. Raising of completely formulated and precise questions, that are practically useful and form a theoretical framework.
2. The questions are converted into conjectures or hypotheses, which are well grounded in theory and can be tested.
3. Logical consequences of the hypotheses are obtained.
4. Techniques or instruments of testing and verifying the hypothesis are designed.
5. Validity and reliability of the testing techniques/instruments are established.
6. Using these techniques, evidence or data collected is tested rigorously, the results are interpreted, and explanations are deduced for generalising.
7. The areas in which the hypotheses are relevant are stated. They raise questions, leading to new knowledge and new problems are enumerated.

Testing and verification are central to the scientific method, which is based on the above hypothetico-deductive process. Thus, the range of scientific method stretches from enquiry, which is qualitative, speculative, inductive, and generative to rigorous measurement and testing, which is quantitative, logically deductive, explanative, and verificative. The end product of any significant research is a well conceived and rigorously verified theory.

model
A model is a representation of phenomenon while theory tries to explain it. Model represents the structure, function and process of a phenomenon. The main features of the model: description, explication and simulation.

Models

The term "model" is currently very popular and is ubiquitously used to define relationships among variables, concepts, and constructs. Consequently, it is necessary to define models with precision. Some view organisation charts and maps as models. Others feel they should be more meaningful than a mere static representation. There is a difference between models and theories. Models are a representation of phenomena. While the theory tries to explain phenomena, a model tries to represent its structure, function, and process. Description, explication, and simulation are the three features of a model (Cooper & Schindler 2000). Descriptive models describe the behaviour of a system; simulation models are those that study the dynamic behaviour of systems, enable experimentation with the models, and predict alternate scenarios for decision-makers. Models are discussed extensively in Chapter 8.

Scientific Attitude

scientific attitude

People with scientific attitude have a firm conviction in the order of things subject to laws. These people are devoted to facts and accurate empirical data close to the phenomenon. They search for theories, appreciate the possibility of errors and are open to criticism and corrections.

Scientific method is more a mental attitude than a method. Scientific attitude has to be inculcated in order to conduct good research. The attitude of scientifically-oriented people differs from the traditional attitude, as per Lewin (1951), in the following ways:

1. A scientist should have a firm conviction that there exists an "order of things", which is subject to laws. There may be doubts regarding the nature of this order but not on the existence of some order.
2. A scientist should be devoted to facts, accurate empirical data, and to being in close touch with phenomena. He must never lose sight of the empirical nature of science.
3. A scientist should search for theories (webs of principles and laws to tie up the facts together) that are refutable. He should be clear about what evidence will make him give up a hypothesis or theory.
4. There must be an appreciation of the possibility of error and, therefore, in the tentativeness of scientific conclusions.
5. Science is open to public criticism and correction. The public can conduct enquiries regarding scientific progress.
6. Widely accepted views of important variables, theories, and the basic nature of discipline serve as a model (paradigm) for further scientific work in the area.

ISSUES OF MANAGEMENT RESEARCH

Use of Scientific Method

The scientific method of research, which was outlined in the earlier section, is based on the model of research in the natural sciences where (1) procedures are public, (2) definitions are precise, (3) data collection is objective, (4) findings are replicable, (5) the approach is systematic and cumulative, and (6) the purpose is explanation, understanding, and prediction (Luthans, 1973). Many researchers often question the applicability of this method to management research, particularly organisational behaviour on the grounds that organisations and individuals making them up differ from the phenomena in natural sciences (Glaser and Strauss, 1967; Bheling and Shapiro, 1974; Argyris, 1976; Lundberg, 1976 and Gummesson, 2000). The main objections seem to be with reference to rigour, precision, exorcism of value laden questions, and dominance of verification and proof. They also hold that the openness towards hypothesis generation stage should really extend beyond it. Their key objections (Smith and Dainty, 1991) are:

- Uniqueness—each organisation, group, or person, to some degree, is different from all others; generalisations are impossible
- Instability—phenomena are transitory in organisations, the facts and laws governing them change over time
- Sensitivity—individuals in an organisation behave differently from inert entities common in natural sciences, and react to research
- Lack of realism—variable manipulation in phenomena in experiments changes them and is different from the real ones
- Epistemological differences

However, they hold that these are not insurmountable and that the natural science method is useful in management research.

Alternative Perspectives of Management Research

The current trends in management research, particularly organisational research, indicates a general proclivity for the use of methods and approaches of natural science. There are, however, exceptions like Kaplan (1964) who emphasise human values in scientific research. Evered and Louis (1981) present two paradigms of enquiry—inquiry from outside, which is dominant in natural sciences research and inquiry from within, which is assuming increasing importance in social science and management research. The differences between the two

nomothetic knowledge
This emphasizes the generalization as in natural science. Management science approach relies predominantly on model building and is nomothetic.

idiographic knowledge
This emphasizes the importance of the knowledge of the particular. Organizational enquiries like 'action research' and 'situational learning' emphasizes the idiographic approach.

modes of enquiry are highlighted in Table 1.2. The role of the researcher shifts to one of an organisational actor, through an empirical data analyst, who is an unobtrusive and participating observer in the enquiry from within, from that of a purely rationalistic model builder in the enquiry from the outside.

There is little scope in most natural/physical science research for participant observation or acting a part of the phenomena and hence these modes of research are not developed in physical sciences. In organisational and social science research, however, where they can be afforded, a powerful mode of research is used. Another important distinguishing feature is the dominant emphasis of generalisation in natural science research tending to nomothetic knowledge, whereas in social sciences and management there is growing emphasis on idiographic knowledge stressing the importance of knowledge of the particular.

It should be noted, however, that both these methods find complementary utilities in management research. The management science (operations research) approach relies predominantly on the model-building approaches of natural science and organisational enquiries rely heavily on case study, action research, and situational learning in addition to the statistically oriented positive approaches. A student of management research can mix these approaches judiciously and optimise his research results, just as a manager in decision-making would optimise the performance of his system by judiciously mixing rational approaches and judgment based on experience.

Table 1.2 Difference Between Two Ways of Enquiry

Enquiry from without		*Enquiry from within*
Researcher detached, neutral	⟷	Researcher immersed in setting
Validation by measurement and logic	⟷	Validation by experiment
Researcher is an observer	⟷	Researcher is a participant
Categories made a priori	⟷	Categories emerge interactively
Aimed at universality and generalizability	⟷	Aimed at situational relevance
Acquired knowledge is nomothetic	⟷	Acquired knowledge is idiographic
Data is factual and context free	⟷	Data is contextually embedded and interpreted

SUMMARY

Science is a systematic and rigorous way of acquiring accurate knowledge of the facts, structure, processes, and behaviour of any phenomenon. It is a cyclic process involving observation, conceptualisation, generalisation (hypothesisation), and verification. Science proceeds in steps, with Popperian pessimism. Often Kuhenian revolutions take place in scientific knowledge, destroying old concepts and setting up new ideas.

Logic, both inductive and deductive, is an essential part of scientific method. Induction works backwards from facts or phenomena; deduction works forward from the researcher's own perception of phenomena based on earlier work. The hypothetico deductive method, in which hypotheses are carefully formulated and rigorously verified, forms the backbone of scientific method. In order to do good scientific work on these lines, the researcher must possess certain attitudes like objectivity, openness of mind, pessimism about results, rigorousness in analysis, and honesty in effort, to get at the truth.

These aspects of scientific method are derived from the positive scientific approaches of physical and natural sciences. However, these are considered by many social scientists as not wholly applicable to research in management and social sciences. The main arguments proposed by these scientists are that human behaviour and organisational phenomena cannot always be objectively analysed. Both inside perspective and objectivity of positive science are required to successfully research and analyse management problems and organisational phenomena.

Suggested Readings

- Bentz, Valerie Malhotra and Jeremy J. Shapiro (1998). *Mindful Inquiry in Social Research.* New Delhi: Sage Publications.
- Braithwaite, A. R. (1973). *Scientific Explanation.* Cambridge: Cambridge University Press.
- Easterby, Smith Mark, Richard Thorpe and Andy Love. (2000). *Management Research* (2d ed.). London: Sage Publications.
- Evered, R. and M. R. Lewis (1981). "Alternative Perspectives in the Organizational Sciences: Inquiry from the Inside and Inquiry from the Outside", *Academy of Management* Review, vol. 6(3), pp. 385–95.
- Gummesson Evert (2000). *Qualitative Methods in Management Research* (2d ed). London: *Sage Publications.*
- Popper Karl (1972). *The Logic of Scientific Discovery.* London: Hutchinson.

QUESTIONS AND EXERCISES

1. Apply Dewey's steps in problem solving to the following (Refer to Emory, 1976):
   (a) General decline of educational standards.
   (b) Lowered employment opportunity in industries due to automation.
   (c) Should only applied research be encouraged in India?
2. Is the hypothetico deductive method the only way of research? Discuss.
3. Since management is decision-making, should management research aim only at decision problems?
4. Illustrate a research problem that is not likely to use the Dewey's steps in problem solving.
5. Give at least two operational definitions of the following terms and state in what way their use may differ.
   (a) Innovation effort
   (b) Production performance
   (c) Technology
   (d) Skill
6. In what situations do you think the procedure of formal science fails to yield useful results in management research? What is the alternative?
7. The distinction between false and trustworthy knowledge is not possible without deductive formulation of theory. Discuss this statement giving examples.
8. Why do you think the idiographic method of research is more useful in management research than the nomothetic method? What do you have to say about operations research applications in management in this regard?
9. Some authors do not attach much importance to hypothesis testing in scientific method. What is the case against hypothesis testing?
10. Do you think a total objectivity is realisable in practical research? Explain and discuss your answer.
11. Select a few outstanding research works in your area of interest in management. Try to find the hallmarks of research as proposed by Sekharan (2000). Briefly write your findings. What do you conclude?
12. Explain the concepts (a) Deduction, (b) Induction, (c) Decision, (d) Pseudo science, (e) Scientific enquiry, (f) Formal science, (g) Hypothesis, (h) Operational definition, and (i) Hypothetico-deductive method.

CHAPTER 2

Overview of Research in Management

- Scientific Research in Management
- Research Problem Identification
- Research Problem Definition
- Research Design
- Research Design Process
- Decisional Research with Mathematical Models
- Some Philosophic Issues of Management Research
- Errors in Research

The decision maker is a man at the moment of choice, ready to put his foot on one or another of the routes that lead from the cross roads.

Learning Objectives

Upon completion of this chapter, you will be able to:

- ✓ Perceive research as a cycle of exploration, investigation, and verification
- ✓ List the various stages of a typical research process
- ✓ Enumerate the several paths to identification and definition of a research problem
- ✓ Understand the importance of theoretical framework in problem formulation
- ✓ Learn to use variables as the skeletons of theory
- ✓ See that hypotheses and models are two ways to problem formulation
- ✓ Understand the need of exploration in all types of research
- ✓ Understand the meaning and intricacy of research design
- ✓ Understand the reasons for classifying research literature, experiments, *ex post facto*, and modelling
- ✓ Understand research design process
- ✓ Study mathematical modelling as a research design
- ✓ Gain knowledge of the views alternative to the positive scientific approach

Scientific Research in Management

The objective of this chapter is to take an overall look at the process of scientific research in relation to the management discipline. After a brief discussion of the setting of management research, its process is outlined. Each step of the process is briefly presented in the subsequent sections for the reader to get a feel of the total picture, in other words, to see the forest and not the trees. In the subsequent chapters, each one of these steps is detailed for a deeper understanding of the subject. In such an approach, the reader is introduced to definitions, concepts, and techniques that will be explained later in the text.

scientific research
It is epistemologically a critical enquiry in a cyclical process, of idea generation, exploration, investigation and verification.

In practice, a manager either solves a problem, makes a decision, or answers a question to understand the system under his control. Whether or not scientific method is preferred in doing so depends upon the cost and time needed to acquire the knowledge or make the decisions. In emergencies and in situations where the information required for analysis is not readily available and costs overweigh benefits of knowledge, scientific method may not be preferred. However, management pursues the ideal of acquiring more knowledge through better methods. Such a pursuit is possible through scientific research.

Epistemologically speaking, scientific research can be thought of as a critical enquiry in the cyclical process of idea generation, exploration, investigation, and verification. In the idea generation stage, the scientist, out of his/her own experience in research, or as a result of an observation, may conceive an idea or develop a concept. In order to check the validity of such a concept arrived at subjectively, it becomes necessary for him/her to initially explore a little bit more the phenomenon to which the concept relates. The nature of this exploration is again cyclic, as mentioned above, but at this stage the attitude is one of inquisitiveness, investigation, and verification. Processes tend to become tentative and not rigorous. Once the idea is accepted as tentatively valid, further investigation will be necessary. In this, the researcher will lay down the detailed steps of the investigation, accurate data will be collected, and statistical or logical procedures will be used to verify the idea or concept in the form of a declaration, a hypothesis, or a model.

investigation
It starts with the identification of a decision problem. In investigation, the researcher lays down the detailed steps of research, collects accurate data, uses statistical and logical procedures to verify the concepts in the form of hypothesis or model.

A manager, in contrast, deals with a goal-oriented system of people and other resources like money, equipment, information, and material. He sets objectives for the organisation, which he consciously builds up. In the process of accomplishing these objectives, he generally meets with problems or choices. Thus, the management can be considered as making choices or

research process

A typical research process has the following stages: research problem identification, research problem definition, theoretical framework (that is, identification of variables and development of hypothesis or model), research design, data collection, analysis of data and reporting.

solving problems. In practice, whether or not a manager understands a problem situation he will have to find a solution to the problem and, in most cases, as quickly as possible. In a rational decision-making process, the manager will have several alternative courses of action from which he has to choose the best one, that is, the optimal. The manager would be highly effective if he were capable of making an optimum choice every time he was faced with a decision-making problem. The research approach or investigative approach aims at this effectiveness. Since decision-making is a problem-solving process in an organisational context, the research process starts with the identification of a decision problem.

Research process The typical research process is succinctly represented in the diagram given in Fig. 2.1. Scientific research process outlined in Fig. 2.1 has typically the following stages:

Problem identification: Sources of a research problem are: (1) A manager who is faced with a problem to be solved or who needs improvement in some aspect of his decision-making. (2) Research literature, consisting of theses, research journal articles, books, general observations in conferences and seminars, and opinions of experts in the field of interest. (3) Considerable personal experience of the above researcher in the field of research interest. (4) A scientific observation of a phenomenon or a managerial set up.

In problem identification (a) the problem faced in practice by a manager or organisation is translated into a research problem or examined for application of standard methods of solution

Fig. 2.1 Research process

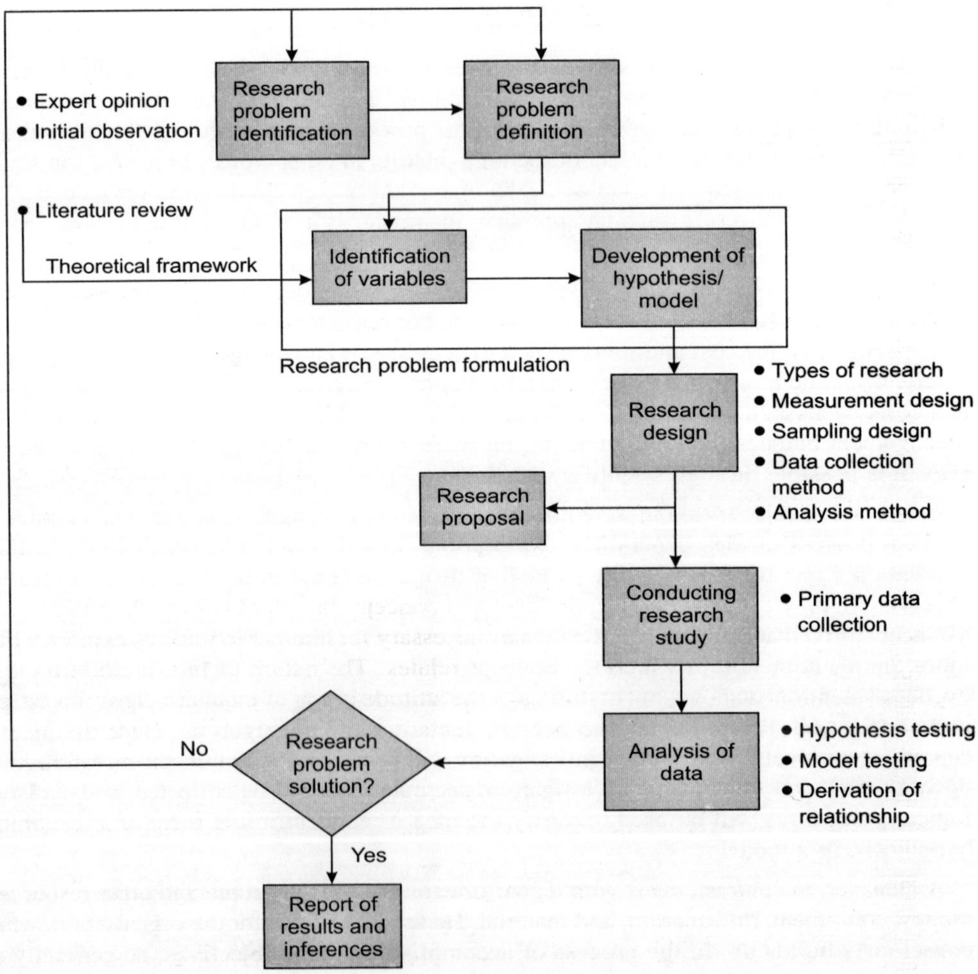

available, or (b) inadequate treatment of a problem is improved, or (c) new problem ideas are creatively generated.

Research problem definition: The tentative and general statements of problems obtained in the identification phase are converted into researchable questions and propositions. Clear and unambiguous statements of the problem are made and the information required for research is stated.

Theoretical framework: Variables required for solving the problem are identified, partly from literature and partly by the researcher for defining the problem. The problem is related to the existing research—theories, constructs, and hypothesis in a theoretical framework that will ensure step-by-step progress of knowledge (as in pure research) or a strong basis for the current problem solving (as in applied research).

Tentative hypothes/models development: The problem definitions/propositions are converted into hypotheses or models, which are in testable form to ascertain whether they can be verified statistically or are feasible for solution procedures. (Hypothesis and theoretical framework are termed research problem formulation.)

Research planning (design): This involves the following steps: (i) Determining the type of research to be carried out for data collection—secondary data, experiment, ex *post facto*, or model building; (ii) Selection of the measurement and scaling of the variables that is, whether questionnaires, or observations or interview techniques are used; (iii) Selection of the representative sample: specification of how many respondents, and what kind of respondents or objects to measure; (iv) Selection of the appropriate method/techniques of analysis of data; and (v) Preparation of a research proposal. In addition to the above steps in research design specification of the time schedule of research, cost estimates and usefulness of the research are summarised in a research project proposal. This serves as a means of communication to the sponsorer or the administration of a university for obtaining funds or approval.

Execution of research study: Data is collected as per the sampling plan using the instrument developed as per the specification in the design phase.

Data preparation and analysis: The raw data collected in the earlier step is converted into data usable for research by carrying out coding, transformation, and performing descriptive analysis, as required. This converted data is used for verifying hypothesis, deriving significant relationships, or testing models, as required, and inferences are drawn from the study and results are analysed.

Reporting results: The results obtained in the research are presented in the form of a written report, thesis, or in an oral presentation.

The research process outlined above requires substantial information about the particular situation and the decision-making system. However, very often the manager takes decisions with incomplete knowledge of the situation. The incompleteness of knowledge is either due to a lack of understanding of the system under his control or an inability to recognise a possible course of action to solve his decision problem. In the former case, there is a need for carrying out research to enhance his knowledge and understanding of the system. This would be the domain of pure research. In the latter case, the identification of a new course of action, which was not known to the manager earlier, would be the researcher's objective. This falls under the category of developmental research according to Ackoff (1962).

The domain of research, which applies to problem solving, is, in the majority of instances, applied research. The cycle of processes described earlier refers to pure research. The processes that are used for applied research are generally not different from the above. The objective of application of scientific method to management research is to solve the decision-making problem rather than to acquire knowledge, which is the objective of a pure researcher. Not all

research problem identification

There are three modes of problem identification: (a) extraction from a manager's practical problem in a dialogue, (b) cognitive identification of an experienced researcher in the area of his expertise, (c) a two-step research process by a novice (scholar): literature search and pilot study.

research problem definition

Broadly, there are two types of problem definition: generation of hypotheses and formulation of models. A literature gap and/or an unanswered research question, and/or an unsolved problem and/or reflective enquiry helps in generating a hypothesis or formulating an appropriate model.

research design

Research design is a multidimensional concept. It is a plan of research to determine the type of research (that is, experiment, ex post facto and modelling), measurement method, type of sampling, data collection methods and methods of analysis.

applied research is necessarily aimed at application only. Sometimes, as a by product of an application-oriented management research a situation is encountered in which sufficient knowledge is not available in some basic disciplines like psychology, economics, or organisation theory for solving the problem. This may lead to pure research. Therefore, basic research in management is relevant in such situations. The following case illustrates the point (Madan Mohan, 1991).

> In a study of technological development in Indian manufacturing organisations, the initial objective of the study was to measure the difference in the technological levels among firms belonging to electronic and precision engineering industries. After working with several definitions of technology and partial measures developed by earlier researchers, it was noticed that no comprehensive measures of technological levels were available. The motive behind the research objective was that if an executive is interested in upgrading technology or raising the technological level, it would be of considerable interest and use to him to have a measure of change in technological levels. This clearly would not be achieved without a knowledge of measuring technological level or the difference in technological levels that may arise over a period of time. The research objective had to be reoriented towards discovering variables/factors, that would determine the level of technology. Since the direct measurement of technological levels would not be of much use because generalisations across different kinds of technologies would become impossible (electronics versus precision engineering; chemical products versus metallurgical products, and so on), it became necessary to define technological change in terms of organisational, managerial, and environmental variables and some generalised technological variables. Moreover, the concept of a support system for technology was developed and was substantiated using factor analysis and discriminant analysis.

Notwithstanding this difference, both applied and basic research are important for the development of the management discipline.

RESEARCH PROBLEM IDENTIFICATION

Ackoff (1962) describes three phases of the research process, namely, observation, generalisation, and experimentation as relevant to pure research. The process, however, is not a linear sequence, but proceeds in a cyclical manner. Applied research, on the other hand, takes place generally as a two-stage process. The first is the exploration for problem identification and the second is the plan of research or research design. A simplistic view of the research process is one that has four stages, namely, problem identification and definition, research design, data collection, and analysis of data for problem solution. This sequence is common to most research, but may tend to become different depending upon the researcher's experience and origin of the problem. Some of the more common modes of management research problem identification and definition are as follows:

1. A manager uses the services of a management scientist or consultant for solving an organisational problem. The manager poses the problem in terms of difficulties felt and symptomatically presents the issues. The researcher, during the interactive dialogue digs out the research problem from the practical one stated by the manager.
2. An experienced management researcher has a deep understanding of the ongoing research work of other researchers and cognitively identifies a potential research problem and works on it.
3. A research scholar is initiated into research. He acquires knowledge in a broad area of interest and makes a systematic study of research literature. With the guidance of his supervisor, he selects a problem area after narrowing down various possibilities and arrives at the broad structure of the problem. He may consciously adopt a two-step process in research problem definitions using a pilot study (see Chapter 4).

RESEARCH PROBLEM DEFINITION

Depending upon whether the type of research involves hypothesis testing of a statistical relationship or a mathematical model building, the research problem definition may follow two patterns: (i) generation of hypotheses, and (ii) formulation of the problem. (This view is ours and is a convention. It is maintained throughout the text.)

Generation of Hypotheses

This is the most difficult phase of research. It is primarily a creative process and, therefore attempting well structured approaches to this would be self defeating. However, there are some general approaches culled out of the experience of many researchers, which may be useful to a student. A broad problem is stated on the basis of a limited observation or a quick review of research literature as well as secondary sources of data, discussions with executives, and so on.

Usually tentative propositions or declarative statements regarding the description or relations are first generated, which are later converted into hypotheses. Hypotheses are built on the basis of theoretical work that has already been done. Examples of such work are the existence of a research gap, an unanswered research question, or an unsolved research problem. Hypothesis generation will be facilitated by broad knowledge of the area and good knowledge of research techniques. Individual reflective enquiry can lead to hypothesis. Group techniques like ISM (Interpretive Structural Modeling) and brainstorming can be used for purposes of generating hypotheses. It should be ensured that hypotheses are well grounded in the cultural setting of the decision-making system. Analogy with problems in other disciplines is a useful method for generating hypotheses. Before generating hypothesis, it is necessary to identify the relevant variables related to the problem. A list of variables generally used in hypothesis generation is given below:

1. *Independent variable (resultant variable):* A manipulated variable in an experiment (treatment).
2. *Explanatory (causal) variable:* Independent variable that influences the dependent variable.
3. *Dependent variable (criterion variable):* The effect in an experiment.
4. *Extraneous variable (non-observable):* Independent variable other than the one manipulated in an experiment, (independent variables that are not related to the purpose of the study), which affects the result. Unless controlled, they become sources of errors.
5. *Moderating variable:* Values that are not variable, which directly influence the dependent variable but modify or moderate the influence on one or more independent variables on the dependent variables.
6. *Mediating variable:* Values that affect the relationship between independent and dependent variable but is not causal with respect to dependent variables.
7. *Discrete variable:* Values that the variable can take are non-continuous (for example, integer variable).
8. *Continuous variable:* Values that the variable can take are continuous.
9. *Dummy variable:* Used in algebraic manipulations, but is a variable in a technical sense only.

Formulation of Research Problems

In the model building context, the researcher needs to make a study of the system in which the decision-making problem resides. This will help in correctly diagnosing the problem and transforming the management problem into a research problem. The objectives of the decision maker, the constraints in the system, and alternative courses of action available are studied in depth. A measure of effectiveness is developed and mathematically expressed in terms of variables and parameters of the system.

In problem formulation, it is necessary to edit the objectives and the alternatives carefully and to transform all the relevant variables to the same dimension (usually this is done in monetary terms). The formulation will enable the researcher to offer the best course of action to the executive.

The typical variables considered in problem formulation in the modeling context are the following:

1. *Exogenous variables* Variables that reside outside the system in which the problem resides, for example, demand in an inventory control model.
2. *Endogenous variables* Variables of the system under consideration.
3. *Controllable variables* Variables that can be controlled by the manager, for example, the order quantity in a purchasing system or a batch in production.
4. *Uncontrollable variables* Variables that cannot be controlled by the manager of the system, for example, due dates stipulated by the customer for order delivery.
5. *Discrete variables* Variables that assume only discrete values, for example, the number of jobs completed in a period.
6. *Continuous variables* Variables that assume continuous values, for example, price of a commodity or the total cost of a policy.

In addition, there are system parameters to be considered. Parameters are generally the cost factors like holding costs, repair costs, cost of a work package, and so on. These are estimated and the influence of the errors in their estimation on the model performance is an important aspect of model management and is termed as sensitivity analysis.

RESEARCH DESIGN

The research design phase deals with the detailing of procedures that will be adopted to carry out the research study. The kind of research that is carried out, whether the study is carried out in the field or in the laboratory, are decided. The details of data collection procedures and the schedule of analytical procedures to be used in order to accomplish the research objectives (set in the earlier stages of research process) are also dealt with in research design.

Classification of Designs

There are many types of research designs defined in research literature. The definitions of research design suggest that the researcher faces a number of crucial design choices. These can be summarised in a categorisation of research design types, but unfortunately there is no satisfactory single classification. Various writers on research advance different classification schemes, some of which are given below:

- The experimental, the historical, and the inferential (American Marketing Association).
- Exploratory and descriptive designs that permit inferences about causality (Selltiz, Jahoda, Deutsch, and Cook).
- Experimental and ex *post factò* (Kerlinger).
- The historical method, descriptive method, and case and clinical studies (Goode and Hatt).
- Sample surveys, field studies, experiments in field settings and laboratory experiments (Festinger and Katz).
- Exploratory, descriptive, and causal (Green and Tull).
- Exploratory and conclusive research. Conclusive research, in turn, consists of descriptive studies (case and statistical studies).
- Experimental studies (Boyd and Westfall).

This confusing array exists because research design is a complex concept, which cannot be described in a simple manner. A more useful way of looking at a classification would be to ascertain several dimensions of research design and then place any particular research on these dimensions. Whitney (1958) gives eight dimensions that are useful in classifying schemes, and these are:

dimensions of research design
There are eight dimensions that are useful in deciding the design for a research study. They are: objective, area of thinking, locus of location, relationship sought, method of gathering evidence, kind of data, the procedure and time.

1. The *objective* of research may be fact finding, exploring, or evaluatory.
2. The area of *thinking* would indicate the broad disciplinary area of the research, like sociology, economics, management, and so on.
3. The locus of *location* is whether the research is primarily located in a library, in archives and records, in a field of activity, or in a laboratory.
4. The *relationship sought* would include associative relationship, comparison, or causal relationship.
5. The method of gathering *evidence* itself gives certain special features of research. For example, a questionnaire may be used, as in the surveys, interviews may be held, or participant observation may be used.
6. The *kind of data* collected profoundly influences the kind of research. The data may be either qualitative, which may either allow generalisation on arguments and description or it could be quantitative, which may lead to rigorous quantitative analysis and definitive conclusions.
7. The *procedure* may be comparison of data, descriptive measures of data, or in-depth analysis of an incident, or it may be an evaluation of a policy.
8. The *time* dimension of study is important from the point of view of whether the study is cross-sectional or longitudinal. In the first, the status of systems or phenomenon is analysed, whereas in the second, the developmental aspects of several variables of the phenomenon will be investigated over time.

From the above it is clear that in a research design, a particular subset of these dimensions may be emphasised and the other dimensions may have a minor role to play or may not exist at all. The following is an example—library research, as a precursor to hypothesis generation, using a perfunctory exploratory research followed by either a laboratory experiment or a field experiment or a field study. A possible relationship among various classifications is represented in Fig. 2.2. *Ex post facto* research is shown at the start of the diagram, because most research starts with an observation of some kind of the phenomenon. This observation is generally backed up by the results of earlier research, hypotheses, experiment, historic generalisation, and so forth. In a particular study, some exploration takes place to relate this current research efforts to this earlier research through library search. Working hypothesis generated either in exploratory or descriptive research is treated in ongoing research (i) through hypothesis testing or a mathematical model as an estimator, if the hypothesis is correlational or descriptive, or (ii) through experimental research if it is causal.

If the system is small and the variables of causal relationship can be highly controlled physically, a laboratory experiment is planned. If the physical control can only be partial then a field experiment is proposed. If the control is infeasible, or when a high degree of control is possible but the system is complex and physical control becomes impossible, a model of the system is simulated on a computer in an experimental framework to make inferences. Generalisations and theory building go on with the addition of new knowledge. The relationships and the strength of a field of research develop and the research in that particular area matures.

The two broad classifications of *ex post facto* and experimental are taken primarily because they indicate the degree of control by the researcher and would be the simplest in a classification scheme, that is, low and high. All the eight dimensions, which have been earlier discussed, can be incorporated with this classification and sub-classifications generated accordingly.

A useful way of depicting the two major research designs, *ex post facto* and experimental, would be to indicate the importance or relevance of certain research/analysis approaches in these designs. This is shown in Table 2.1.

The table is self explanatory and gives a general understanding of the attributes of research under the two broad headings of *ex post facto* and experiments. However, some comments are in order. (Further comments can be derived similarly.)

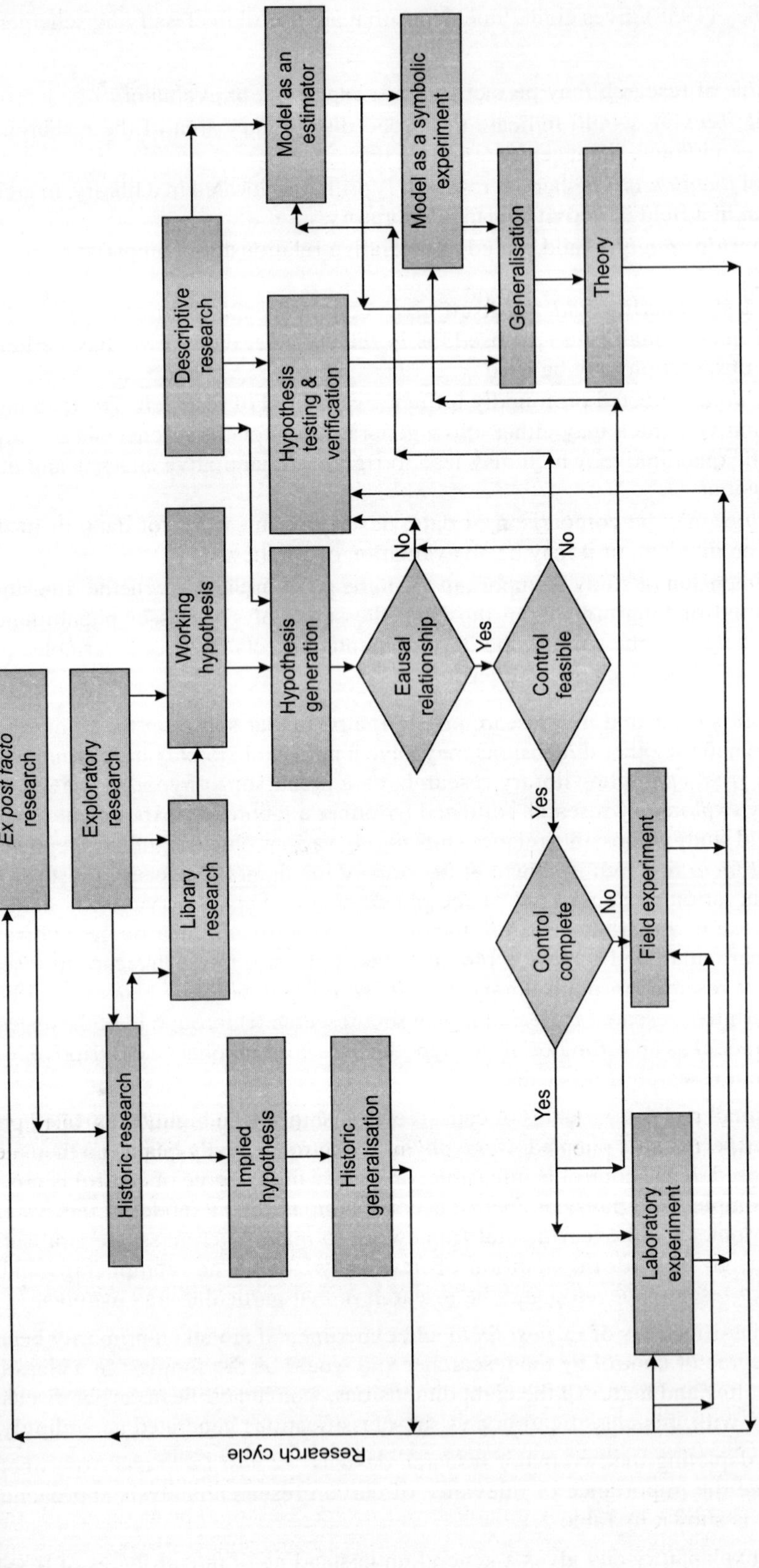

■ **Fig. 2.2** Classification of research

Table 2.1 Attributes of the Various Types of Research

	Types of Research			
	Ex post facto		*Experiments*	
Attributes	*Survey*	*Field studies or case in depth*	*Laboratory experiments*	*Field experiments or quasi experiments*
Qualitative	Y	Y	-	-
Quantitative	Y	-	Y	Y
Descriptive	Y	Y	-	-
Causal	Y	Y	Y	Y
Exploratory	Y	Y	-	Y
Formal	Y	Y	Y	Y
Case	-	Y	-	-
Statistical	Y	-	Y	Y
Understanding Theoretical	-	Y	Y	Y
Applied Problem	Y	Y	-	Y
Analytical	-	-	-	-
Empirical	Y	Y	Y	Y
Longitudinal	Y	Y	-	Y
Cross-Sectional	Y	Y	Y	Y
Participatory	-	Y	-	Y
Non-Participatory	Y	Y	Y	Y

- *Ex post facto* surveys can produce generalisations through development and testing of all three types of hypothesis, but cannot give the depth of understanding of managerial phenomena, that can be derived by in-depth field studies and case studies for a particular situation.
- Theory producing qualitative research is almost always in depth field studies over extended periods of time generating large amounts of data/number of hypotheses. But in recent research, complex procedures are used for data analysis and have quantitative connotations (Ref. Kelle, Udo 1995).
- Neither research type is analytical, they are only empirical. But mathematical model building in decision-making environments is analytical. It is infact more quasi-analytical as current modelling is moving away from purely analytical to heuristic, simulation, and AI approaches. These approaches are well grounded in some form of empiricism (see Chapter 9).
- Participation of the researcher can be present in both designs, but only in the field setting, to reflect the alternate perspective of insider approach, as explained in Chapter 1.

Issues of Research Design

The basic research design issue involved in determining the kind of research strategy is whether the study is a field study or a laboratory study. The considerations in such a determination are the following (Whitney, 1958).

issues of research design
Issues in determining the research strategy are: richness of the research in the discipline, degree of problem clarity, degree of control obtainable, the time scale, unit of study, kind of relationship, and type of model.

1. The *richness of the research* in the discipline is evaluated depending on whether the discipline is in the initial stages of exploration and classification or a mature subject leading to considerable amounts of application in practice.
2. The *degree of clarity* of the problem should be judged. The higher the degree of clarity, the more rigorous the research design, tending towards experimental research.
3. The *degree of control* that can be obtained over a variable should be evaluated. If this is negligible, then field studies are preferred and the relationships or hypotheses tend to become somewhat weak.

4. The *time scale* with respect to phenomenon to be studied should be determined. If a phenomenon can be studied effectively, considered only over a period of time, then longitudinal studies will be required.
5. The objectives set forth should be related to the *units of study*, that is, the individuals, groups, organisations, or an economy/society. The research design will considerably vary as the domain of research gets enlarged.
6. The *kind of relationship* that is implied by the objective or hypothesis is important. This will considerably influence the type of techniques that will be used for analysis.
7. Whether the research implies a statistical model dependent heavily on phenomenological world or a conceptual (theoretical) mathematical model influences the design. The problem of verification and testing will become considerably more difficult in these situations.

The research carried out will be a field study for most management problems (Fig. 2.3). However, there are instances of experimental research, especially in the areas of organisation theory and market research, where the researcher intervenes with the phenomena in some way. Such cases are mostly field experiments. The simulation experimentation is a classic example of how the data and knowledge acquired in the field study is used for carrying out laboratory experiments.

The field study or experimental study may generate data for the purpose of hypothesis testing or verification of a conceptual mathematical model related to a decision. There are two broad ways in which the research may proceed.

A. Hypotheses are tested using statistical hypothesis testing procedures and accepted or rejected.
B. A hypothesis or a conceptual model may lead to a mathematical decision model* or a relational statistical model.
    - The statistical relational model will be analysed using bivariate or multivariate statistical procedures, as required, and the relation is established and validated using the data generated.
    - The decisional mathematical model will be an analytic model, a heuristic model, or a simulation model. It is logically validated when a solution is derived from the model and is tested and verified empirically.
    - If an analytical solution is not possible, a heuristic procedure may be used to derive an acceptable solution after validating it.
    - When a simulation model of the decision problem is used, it is verified and validated using the research data and the solution to the problem is derived.
    - When the hypothesis or objective of the study is to explore the dimensions of a construct, then the data generated will be subject to factor analysis or cluster analysis to obtain them.

A truly scientific research is believed by most physical science researchers to be one of experimentation. Experimental type of research will be carried out when the problem clarity is very high and the casual relationships between variables are investigated rigorously. When the problem clarity is low, usually exploratory kind of research will be undertaken. In exploration the researcher may try to discover factors and authenticate the variables with which he starts the research, thereby, obtaining a greater understanding of the phenomena, whereas when the problem clarity is comparatively moderate, a field study may be attempted. The study is usually carried out with the help of a questionnaire, which seeks to get information to test relationships between variables. Correlational analyses are the popular mode of analysis of field study, but sometimes casual relationships are also obtained using statistical procedures, wherein the researcher is a little more confident and well supported by earlier research. The point is that a research design may combine many of these features.

**Note:* Some of the models mentioned here are treated later. The reader may consult the glossary of terms at the end of the textbook for quick reference.

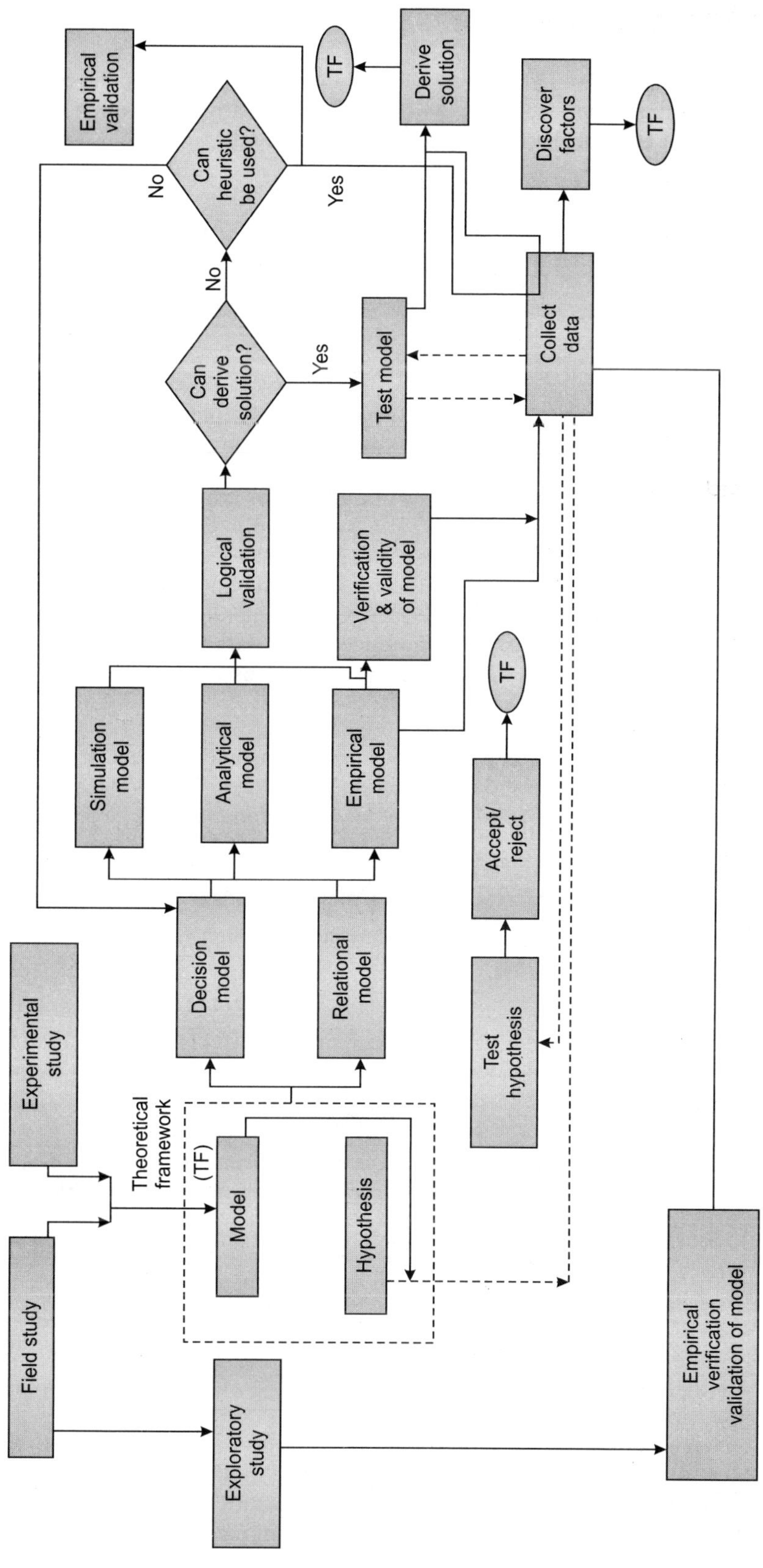

■ **Fig. 2.3** Research design

RESEARCH DESIGN PROCESS

Once the objective of research is clear, the research process enters the research design phase. In this phase, the researcher will have to detail a plan in which alternatives are going to be chosen at each of the following stages of research.

1. Selection of the type of research.
2. Selection of the measures and the measurement techniques.
3. The kind and the number of subjects sampled, that is, sample design.
4. Selection of the data collection procedures.
5. The selection of methods of analysis of data.

Selection of the Type of Research

The type of research determines the strategy of collecting research data and information directly from the respondents by one of the following methods.

field survey research
In field survey research information is obtained from a general study of large respondents using questionnaire.

Field survey research In this method data/information are obtained from a general study of a large number of respondents (large sample), eliciting direct responses to specific questions. The responses may be collected orally, in face-to-face meetings, or remotely, through mail in written form or telephone in oral form. The data obtained can be generalised and is representative of a large population. These surveys are generally carried out at a particular point of time and are cross sectional. They produce 'thin' data (not deep). They are generally used for descriptive analysis, correlational type hypothesis testing, and often for exploration.

field study
It is an in-depth study of a single or very small number of respondents in the field setting.

Field study This is an in-depth study of a single respondent or a very small number of respondents to obtain rich (deep) data of specific instances by using methods of probing. It uses combinations of several data collection procedures. It provides greater understanding of specific instances but its results cannot be easily generalised like research survey results.

experiment
Experiment is a controlled manipulation of independent variables to find their effects on one or more dependent variables. Experiments are done in laboratory or in field or by simulation.

Experiment In an experiment there is controlled manipulation of one or more independent variables so that its effects on one or more dependent variables can be measured.

There are two major types of experimental designs.

1. **Basic design:** This considers the effects of manipulating only one independent variable.
2. **Statistical design:** This considers the effects of manipulating concomitantly more than one independent variable.

There are three kinds of experiments.

1. *Laboratory experiments (Equivalent Physical system):* Experiments in which manipulation of independent variables is carried out in an artificial environment away from the location of phenomena.
2. *Simulation experiments (Equivalent Symbolic System):* Here, selective manipulation of independent variables of a model of the (phenomena) system is carried out.
3. *Experiments in field setting:* The manipulation of independent variables is carried out in the natural setting but control is not as rigorous as in laboratory experiments.

Experiments are used for finding cause-effect relationship, which is one of the major objectives of scientific research.

mathematical model
A decision problem is represented by a mathematical model and conclusions are drawn from the solution.

Mathematical models of phenomena Another type of research assuming great importance in management problems is the mathematical modeling approach (as contrasted with statistical models used for analysis of research data) in which the decision problem is represented by a mathematical model, solutions are obtained, and conclusions are drawn from them. A high degree of understanding of the systems is necessary to model them. In this sense, they are close to experiments in traditional research. They are only representative and are approximate, and they have to be verified, tested, and validated before drawing any inferences from them. The data collection procedures are similar to the ones in other types. Secondary and primary data are used for modelling purposes*.

Measurement and Measurement Techniques

Measurement is defined as the assignment of numbers to characteristics of objects, persons, states, or events according to rules (Tull & Hawkins, 1987). The most critical aspect of measurement is the development of rules for assigning numbers to the characteristics. This problem is particularly tricky and difficult in social science and organisational research in which the definition of concepts and variables are often neither easy nor direct. To overcome this difficulty, many techniques of measurement have been developed by social science researchers. These are very relevant in management research too.

measurement
Measurement is assignment of numbers to characteristics of objects, persons, states, or events according to rules. There are four measurement techniques: questionnaires, attitude scales, observation sheets and depth interview schedules.

Techniques of measurement Based on the research design characteristics and the kind of variables defined, a suitable measurement technique is selected. In general, there are four techniques available to a researcher—questionnaires, attitude scales, observation sheets, and depth interview schedules.

Questionnaire: This is a set of questions, used as an instrument for seeking relevant information directly from respondents. The questions pertain to one or more of characteristics of the respondent, like behaviour, demographic characteristic, knowledge, opinions, attitudes, beliefs, and feelings. Generally a question or a set of questions represents a variable used in research. These are usually specially designed for a particular research and then suitably validated before use. However, in many studies standard inventories/tests designed and tested by others may also be used.

Attitude scales: These scales elicit self-reports of beliefs and feelings towards an object. There are different types of attitude scales: (i) Rating Scales that require the respondent to place the object at some point on a continuum that is numerically ordered; (ii) Composite scales require a respondent to express a degree of belief with regard to several attributes of an object; (iii) multidimensional scales and scales developed using conjoint analysis are mathematically developed scales to be used for inferring specific aspects of an individual's attitude towards an object as against direct evaluation of the respondents (as in the first two scaling methods).

Observation: This is the direct examination of behaviour or results of behaviour.

Depth interviews: These are interviews in which individuals are made to express their feelings freely and without fear of dispute or disapproval. The details are recorded in specifically designed sheets.

Errors of measurement A number of errors tend to vitiate a measurement. The researcher has to ensure that the desired accuracy levels are achieved by conducting suitable tests. The errors in measurement can be systematic or variable. Systematic errors, which are consistent, constitute the bias in measurement. Validity refers to bias and is the degree to which measurement is free from systematic error. The variable error is associated with each replication of measurement and the term reliability refers to variable errors. It is defined as the extent to which a measurement is free of variable errors.

errors of measurement
Systematic errors constitute bias in measurement and validity refers to bias. Variable errors occur in replication of measurement and reliability refers to variable errors.

Therefore, unless a pre-evaluated and reliable instrument is used for data collection, the validity and reliability of a measurement technique or instrument designed by the researcher must be established.

Selection of Sample

The next step in research design is the selection of a sample of subjects for study. In most cases of research, sampling is needed. Sampling is a necessary and an inescapable part of any human

*Note: Primary research empirical data is generated in the first three types of research.

sampling
Sampling is an inescapable part of research, since populations are large and resources are limited. Sampling is aimed at obtaining representativeness and determining size of the sample.

activity like purchasing commodities, selection of a television programme to watch or even a book to read. If the population is small enough, instead of sampling a census can be carried out. But usually, populations are large and there is limited time and resources available with the researcher for data collection. Therefore, selecting a sample becomes necessary. Further, sampling by reducing the data collection effort makes data collection more efficient and accurate.

Inspite of statistical methods being used in the selection of a sample, judgment is central to all stages of sampling. Sampling designs are aimed at two major objectives: (i) the sample is representative of the population, and (ii) the size of the sample is adequate to get the desired accuracy. In general, the sampling process consists of:

- A definition of the target population in terms of elements, sampling units, domain, and period;
- Specification of a frame of sampling if probability sampling is used (for example, telephone directory, map, or listings);
- Specifying sampling units (for example, a firm, department, group, or an individual that is addressed in the sample);
- The sampling method (for example, probability versus non-probability, single versus cluster, stratified versus non-stratified, single stage versus multistage);
- Determination of sample size, which is the number of elements in the sample, using statistical methods but often moderated by judgment based on other considerations like availability, cost, and accessibility;
- Implementation of the sampling plan by ensuring the various controls required in the field to attain the sampling objectives and by contacting the sample members.

Selection of Data Collection Procedures

data collection
Data collection consists of identification of sources of data and the use of instrument and sampling to acquire data. There are two sources of data: *primary data* which are specially generated in a research study and *secondary data* which are already available.

The data collection phase itself is considerably developed in contemporary research. Data collection will involve the development of the instruments for data collection, identification of sources of data, and the context in which the sampling has to be done. The sources of data are usually people and existing records. To get information from people, it is either necessary to use interviews, where the information may be given readily, or questionnaires, where the information may have to be given after careful reflection on the part of the respondent. There are several procedures of data collection available to the researcher. Depending on the problem, he may choose one or a combination of more than one procedure.

There are two sources of data—secondary data and primary data.

Secondary data This kind of data is generated for purposes other than for solving the problem under study. There are three methods of obtaining secondary data:

1. The data is available in published research journals, reports, and books open to the public in libraries.
2. Search of data generated within the organisation through reports, log books, records of unions, minutes of meetings, proceedings, accounting documents, home journals, and so on.
3. Computer search of databases and the World Wide Web.

Primary data The procedures used for collecting primary data in a research study are those of the research types already discussed. They are, (a) questionnaire mail surveys, (b) interviews of several kinds, (c) observation of phenomena/subjects, and (d) special techniques like video/audio recording/projective methods.

In general a researcher may use a pure strategy (one single type research) or a combination of a few types as in mixed design. For example, cross-sectional research may be repeated at many points of time in a longitudinal study. An exploration may be used before a descriptive study or a field study or an experiment.

Selection of Methods of Analysis

Data is useful only after analysis. Data analysis deals with the conversion of a series of data gathered into information statements (i) which descriptively state the information in terms of means, percentages, classification or distribution, or (ii) which make assertions about relationships conjectured prior to data collection, or (iii) which provide estimates for the purposes of prediction. The selection of methods or techniques of analysis must generally precede the collection of data in any good research. Dummy data (intuitional responses) may be used with the designed instrument and subjected to analysis as per the selected methods to test whether the results provide the desired information for the solution of the problem at hand.

There are a large number of statistical methods available for analysing the research data collected. In this book we deal with the more common ones that are used and their importance in research design has been broadly outlined.

Data analysis methods in general

methods of data analysis

There are three levels of data analysis methods. They are *univariate analyses, bivariate analyses* and *multivariate analyses*. Data analysis yields information in terms of means, percentages, classifications, distributions, assertions, relationship and estimates.

- Data analysis aims at the levels of variables and their variability when a single variable is used in the analysis. Univariate hypothesis testing is a typical analysis. An important aspect is when small samples of data are used, non-parametric tests are used, and parametric tests are used on large samples.
- It aims at associations in the case of two variables. Correlation and regression analysis are performed and the significance of regression or correlation coefficient are tested to confirm the results.
- It aims at dependence relationships (in general a set of independent variables) or interdependence relationships (a set of independent variables are present but there is no dependent variable). The former are more useful in establishing relationships and the latter in developing concepts and constructs.

Four basic procedures are involved. They are as follows:

A. ***Data reduction*** This includes the following steps—

1. Field controls to minimise errors in data collection
2. Editing to ensure readable and accurate data
3. Coding to categorise the edited data
4. Transferring data to usable media, like tapes
5. Generation of new variables by aggregation, scale changing, and data transformation and
6. Calculating summary statistics like the mean, standard deviation, proportion, and so on.

B. ***Hypothesis testing*** This includes—

1. Hypothesis testing requiring interval data; tests for single sample—sample mean and sample proportions; tests for multiple samples involving differences in means, difference in proportions of both independent and related samples
2. Hypothesis testing using ordinal data
3. Hypothesis testing using nominal data
4. Multivariate hypothesis testing, including hypothesis tests of difference between groups to test interaction effects, for example, ANOVA in experimental situations.

C. ***Bivariate measures of association*** This constitutes—

1. Simple correlation and regression analysis using ratio/interval data
2. Rank correlation analysis using ordinal data
3. Contingency coefficient determination for nominal data

D. ***Multivariate measures of association*** The flow diagram in Fig. 2.4 relates to the choice of various multivariate measures of association. The diagram is self explanatory. The key questions to be answered in order to make the choice of a particular technique are: (1) The number of independent variables (two or more), (2) Whether there is a dependent variable, (3) The level of measurement; nominal (category) ordinal (Ranked)

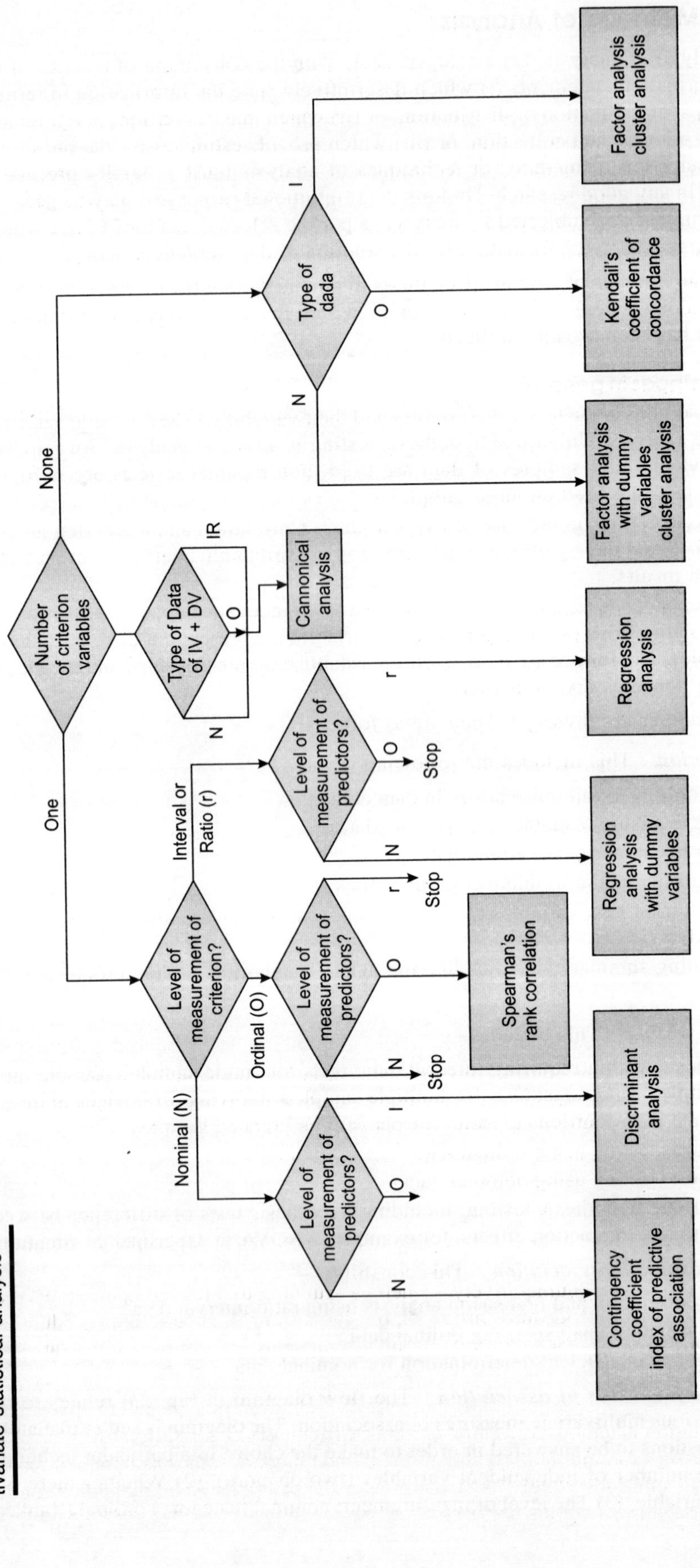

Fig. 2.4 Choosing a multivariate statistical analysis

or Internal or ratio, with respect to independent variables in the analysis of dependence relationships, and (4) The level of measurement, nominal, ordinal or interval of the independent variables whose interdependence is to be analyzed. A brief outline of each technique is given below.

- *Multiple regression analysis* examines relationships between two or more intervally scaled predictor variables and one intervally scaled criterion variable (ordinal data that are near interval can also be used). This is an extension of the bivariate regression analysis.
- *Discriminant analysis* is used in place of regression analysis when the criterion variable is nominally scaled and the predictor variables are intervally scaled. The objective is to group the criterion variables into two or more categories like good or bad, high risk or low risk, and so on.
- *Path analysis* is a technique for refining causal relationships in theory building or understanding influencing factors. It uses a series of regression analyses con ducted simultaneously to determine if a set of proposed causal relationships exist in a sample data.
- *Factor analysis* is helpful in summarising a large number of original variables into a smaller number of factors (synthetic variables) in order to achieve parsimony in representing phenomena. It can help (i) in determining underlying dimensions of data, (ii) in condensing and simplifying data, and (iii) in hypothesis testing and the structuring of data, that is, if a set of variables come from a specified factor. It does not use criterion and predictor variables or their relationships. It determines the relationship among a set of variables.
- *Cluster analysis* is useful in segregating objects into groups such that the groups are relatively homogeneous. Examples are grouping of products and market segmentation.

DECISIONAL RESEARCH WITH MATHEMATICAL MODELS

Whenever hypothesis is a part of the theoretical framework, the collected data will be used for testing the hypothesis (accepting it or rejecting it). This enhances the researcher's knowledge and adds to the theoretical framework. When the theoretical framework is mainly dependent upon a model, the model takes the form of either a mathematical decision model, for example, inventory models or a relational model, for example, regression models. Relational models are empirically validated and tested after the relevant data is collected.

Decision models fall into three major categories, namely, (i) Analytical models (ii) Heuristic models, and (iii) Simulation models (Fig. 2.3). In operations research, we find that a large number of analytical models are employed for solving problems. The models are usually verified only for inbuilt logic, but are tested for relevance to the phenomena or the system by collecting data and replicating the model using the data. The results of the model replication are compared with the actual phenomena for existence of closeness or of serious divergence.

decision model
There are three categories of decision models. They are: *analytical models*, *heuristic models* and *simulation models*. Decision models are usually verified for inbuilt logic and tested for the relevance for the tested phenomenon.

If, however, a mathematical model cannot be solved analytically by the existing knowledge in mathematical fields, heuristic procedures are attempted. In recent developments in the field of OR a large number of problems involving thousands and tens of thousands of variables are being investigated for solutions on the computers. These problems are called combinatorial problems. Even with high speed computers these problems require enormous amounts of computational time if solved enumeratively, sometimes running to a few computational years. In these cases too heuristic procedures are used, but the aim of the heuristic procedure is to reduce computational time to practical limits. Heuristics are classic examples of the satisficing procedure enunciated by Ackoff and Sasieni (1963).

Heuristics will not yield optimal solutions, but will give solutions that are practically satisfactory where computation is tedious, or optimisation is difficult or not possible. When heuristics are used, it is necessary to empirically validate them and compare solutions obtained through them with the actual solutions used by the executive or the solutions given by approximations or optimisation procedures (Merbach 1981).

When analytical solutions are not possible due to the extreme complexity of a problem, computer simulation is usually undertaken. In simulation, the phenomenon/system is broken down into smaller elements and connected by logical relations, as observed. A model will be built and replicated on a computer. The advantage of simulation models as against analytic and empirical models is that various parameters of the system and various environmental conditions can be assumed in the model and alternate solutions obtained without actually disturbing the system. Simulation is thus experimentation with the model of the system and is very useful as a tool where results can be obtained in a compressed time frame [Law & Kelton (1991)].

Two illustrations of research design are provided from actual research undertaken, one with hypothesis generation and testing and the other with model building and simulation. Only an outline sequence of the design of research is provided for each case in Annexure 2.1.

SOME PHILOSOPHIC ISSUES OF MANAGEMENT RESEARCH

Paradigms

Kuhn (1962) in his model of research in social science, has stressed the importance of the conscious judgment of a community of research practitioners in addition to limited objective scientific evidence in order to validate scientific ideas. A large number of social scientists and organisational theorists contend that natural science methods using positivistic approaches have serious limitations in social science or management research. This has led to paradigm thinking in research methodology for management. The contention is that other approaches more appropriate to social science and management research would need to be developed and used for obtaining useful research results.

paradigms of research
There are two basic paradigms: *enquiry from within a phenomenon* in which the researcher is experientially involved and having no a priori analytical framework, and *enquiry from outside* in which data is gathered systematically according to a predetermined procedure and analysed to draw conclusions.

There are two basic paradigms of research, as practiced by organisation theorists. In one the researcher is experientially involved with the phenomena and has the objective of understanding a particular situation. He is immersed in the phenomena psychologically and physically. He approaches the problem with an open mind without having an *a priori* analytical framework. The enquiry is subjective and ethnographic. It is called 'enquiry from within' (Evered and Louis, 1991, Creswell, 2002).

The other paradigm is characterised by gathering data from the system according to a predetermined procedure and design in order to unearth knowledge in the form of generalisations. This is more in line with the natural science approach. This is called 'enquiry from outside'. Both of these paradigms are practiced in management and social sciences research. The first has richness of data and understanding and specificity to a situation, but its weakness is difficulty in generalisation. The second is strongest in terms of knowledge that can be generalised, but tends to be shallower than the first.

Social theories (Hassard, 1979) consider four paradigm models of social theory. On the subjective side, we have radical humanist and interpretive theories, and on the objective side, functionalist and radical structurist theories. These paradigms are based on assumptions about the social world, in the former, and on grounds of scientific knowledge, in the latter, or in other words, human nature and methodology. In the radical humanist approach, the assumption is that people in an organisation are tied down by the society they have created. In the interpretive paradigm, the assumption is that the social world (in an organisation) is best understood by the actors and, therefore, encourages participation of the researcher in organisational activities in order to do fruitful research. In the functionalist paradigm, the society or organisation is considered to have a systematic character and is believed to produce order and regulation and is value free. Thus, objectivity and distanced observation is held appropriate for research into the social world. The radical structural approach has a materialistic concept of society, which inherently possesses contradictions, and tensions, which have their own existence.

In management research optimising multiple paradigms in management and organisation is considered very useful by many researchers in the systematic analysis of rich and voluminous data that can be generated. In developing research designs, it is important to consider whether it is fruitful to focus on a single paradigm (single issue related to management and organization) or multiple paradigms (where several issues are interlinked). However, the multiple paradigm analysis has been criticised on the grounds that the same issues may be looked at from different angles in such studies, but the use of system methodology is not evident. From a purely theory development angle, the multiple paradigm analysis may not be acceptable to a group of researchers. The researcher may be in a dilemma if he has to adjust to several viewpoints as a researcher is generally nurtured only on a single viewpoint.

Paradigmic thinking, as described above, has broad connotations for management research. The concept can be gainfully extended to research at greater levels of detail. The first essential principle of these paradigms is enquiry from within and enquiry from outside. The second principle is that certain patterns of phenomenon (process/structure) are recognisable in any problem situation. Using these two principles it is possible to do useful and relevant management research in a cultural situation (either social culture or economic culture), which is different from the one in which the paradigms were propounded. For example, in determining the innovations of firms several authors from developed countries like the United States of America, Germany, and Great Britain have identified patterns of management and organisational and technological processes that have led to the understanding of the innovative success of firms in these countries. In a recent study, these paradigms/patterns were identified in Indian firms. The first signs of relevance of these paradigms in the Indian context have been understood as a combination of several of these paradigms rather than as a single pure pattern. The admixture of such paradigms serves to throw more light on the existing technological development efforts of Indian firms. Thus, technology push observed in the United States of America is found in Indian companies in conjunction with choice of technology. Management philosophy of technology development is a tool for meeting a need or solving a problem rather than for exploiting an opportunity. (The latter would be the case in the United States of America).

Consultative Approach to Management Research

consultative approach
In consultative approach, a consultant is regarded as having greater understanding of organisational/ managerial problems and regarded as sharing experiences interactively. A consultant's role is considered as most appropriate for management research.

Easterby et al (2002) raise further questions on the philosophy of research design in management. The researcher can understand the real problems of management and their origins only by sharing experiences interactively with the people in the organisation, understanding their perceptions of the problem, and their collective feelings for the solution. Analysis of stories, narrations, incidents, and discussions yield a better understanding than surveys and even experiments of the organisational realities (socialist construction viewpoint). In this regard, a consultant has a far greater understanding of the organisational/managerial problems. Eking out patterns from data [grounded theory by Glaser (1998)] yields a true picture of concepts through familiarisation, reflection, and cataloguing. Analysing historical artefacts using content analysis, conversation analysis, and discourse analysis are held to provide far richer information than those obtained by quantitative analysis of data obtained in a distant/unfamiliar mode characteristic of positive scientific research in management. However, Locke (2001) feels grounded theory data accessibility is limited and Staruss and Corbin (1998) contend that prior research is needed to structure the process of enquiry on grounded theory data. A consultant's role is held appropriate for an academician to carry out management research as it increases "accessibility to the inner folds of information in the managerial and organisational world".

However, Easterby et al (2002) caution against combining research designs from different paradigms and structuring compromise designs of management research to suit the structures of different disciplines in management. However, they hold that no single approach may be adequate and a combination of approaches is necessary to realise the true objective of research—to understand managerial/organisational processes.

ERRORS IN RESEARCH

errors in research
There are nine major errors in research: errors in identification, variable selection, surrogate information, measurement, experimental, subject selection, sampling, selection and non-response.

Errors may creep in at any stage of the research process outlined in Section 2.1.1. The researcher has to be wary of them and must deliberately provide means of minimising these errors. These errors are outlined here and will be discussed in detail later at appropriate junctures.

- *Identification error:* This error occurs when the researcher is unable to recognise the correct problem and finds solutions to wrong ones.

- *Variable selection error:* These errors are Type I and Type II, that is, omitting a relevant variable and including an irrelevant variable, respectively, for the purposes of formulation of problems or development of hypotheses.
- *Surrogate information errors:* The respondents introduce this error while answering the researchers' questions. The information required is different from the information sought for.
- *Measurement errors:* The difference between the researcher's requirement of the information and what the instruments provide is measurement error.
- *Experimental errors:* These are errors due to extraneous variables in an experiment and the actual impact of the independent variables on the dependent variables is different from the impact attributable in the experiment to the independent variables.
- *Errors of subject selection:* This error is due to two reasons: (a) the population required is different from population actually selected, (b) The population specified is different from populations listed in a frame. It is also called frame error.
- *Sampling error:* Sampling error is the difference between a truly representative sample and a probability sample.
- *Selection error:* This indicates errors due to the difference between a truly representative sample and a non-probability sample. It largely constitutes bias errors.
- *Non-Response error:* Errors introduced by the lack of response of certain respondents in a sample.

For each one of the above errors there is a method to reduce or eliminate it, and these are important from the point of view of the validity and reliability of the research results.

SUMMARY

Research in management and organisation demands a grasp of the decision-making process and its environments. The research problem is identified in the background of the manager's experience of decision related problems. A system study is carried out in order to formulate the problem. The other modes of research problem identification are when an experienced researcher investigates a gap or controversy in the area, or when a student sets out on research based on literature review and the classical two-step research process. The first step involves exploration through pilot studies, and firming up the instruments and the hypotheses. In the second step, the student carefully collects and rigorously analyses the data. The components of such rigorous study are outlined as research design in which the method of research, whether experimental, non-experimental, or mathematical model building, is decided upon. The associated measurement techniques and instruments are designed, sampling methods and size of samples are set forth, and the kinds of analysis required and kind of solution to mathematical models are laid down. In decisional research, the model building approach is of importance, in particular, heuristics and simulation procedures. The importance of qualitative research and analysis has been stressed in recent literature. Errors in research design, measurement, and data acquisition have to be carefully reduced.

ANNEXURE 2.1

Research Design Illustration 1 (Chetty, 1995)

Research literature revealed that there is a need to understand the relationship of managerial, organisational, and environmental variables with manufacturing, planning, and control (MPC) and how the performance of the manufacturing system is influenced by MPC. The objectives of the research were to attempt a better understanding of the

Contd.

MPC system through the identification of (a) natural factors underlying MPC construct, (b) variables that discriminate high MPC performing firms the low MPC performing firms and to generate and test hypotheses related to MPC in batch manufacturing firms.

Both manufacturing system and MPC systems were redefined using a theoretical framework derived from several earlier research studies and the following research design was adopted for achieving the objectives (See Exhibit 2.1 for flow chart).

- The study will be a cross-sectional study.
- A two-tier design (that is, case study comprising the first tier and survey statistical analysis in the second) will be employed.
- Combining the results of the pilot study with the definitions of MPC variables obtained in research literature, a set of variables will be redefined and selected for the first survey of a sample of about 150 organisations to carry out a descriptive study of MPC practices (the questionnaire developed by the Global Business, United States of America and Prof Ramdass and validated in Europe, Japan, Korea and China on MPC practices will be adopted with modifications). In addition, variables identified in literature will be scaled and included. The questions in the questionnaire are a mix of multiple choice questions scaled high to low, dichotomous questions (Yes/No) and open-ended questions. These questions, will be scrutinised by experts who are practicing managers and academicians (Questionnaire 'A').

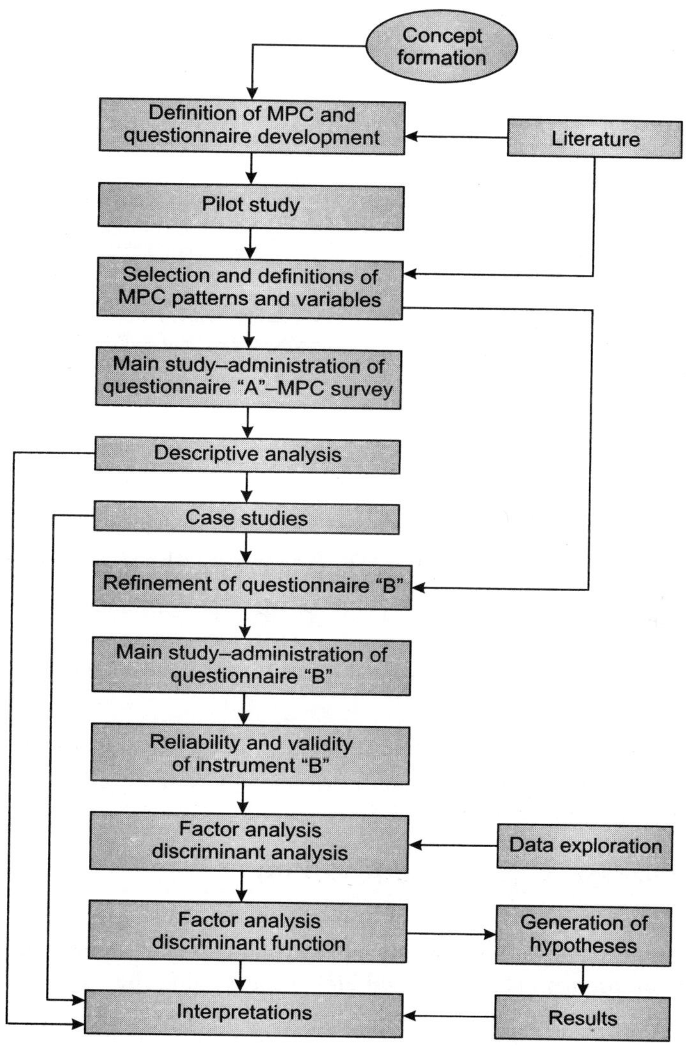

Exhibit 2.1 Flowchart of research design adopted for analysing MPC

Contd.

- A set of case studies (ten numbers) will be conducted in batch manufacturing firms to confirm or modify the variables used in the descriptive study mentioned above and the questionnaire will be refined.
- Using the refined questionnaire (Questionnaire 'B'), the questions in the questionnaire will be rated on 1–5 rating scale and a second main study will be carried out. Its validity and reliability will be tested with the data generated by a sample of companies. The data thus generated will be subjected to the following statistical analyses (See Exhibit 2.2).

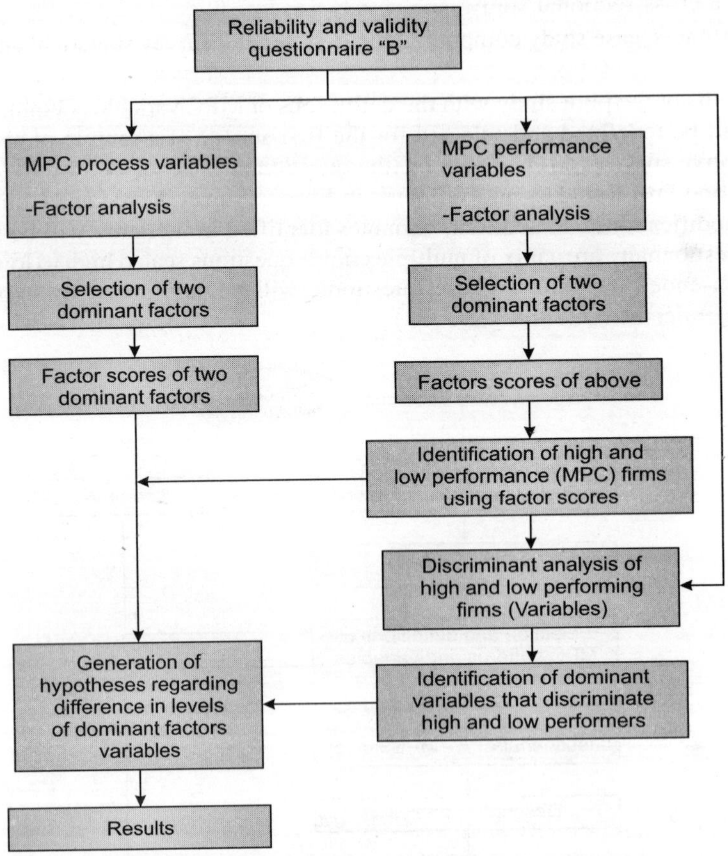

Exhibit 2.2 Details of statistical analysis

- Data on both MPC process variables and MPC performance variables will be explored using factor analysis.
- Two dominant factors, each of the MPC process and the MPC performance, will be used to identify the high and low performance of MPC.
- A discriminant analysis will be used to extract variables of MPC (process), which discriminates high/low MPC performers.

Using the dominant variables of MPC (process) from the last but one step above, hypotheses will be generated regarding difference in levels of variables/factors that discriminate between high and low performing batch manufacturing units, and these will subsequently be tested.

Research Design Illustration 2 (Vasumathi, 2000)

An analytical study of the silk reeling operations in Karnataka, India, was carried out with the objective of understanding cocoon market dynamics and getting insights into the operations of reeling units in order to manage better the sick industry. The research problem was identified and defined using the combination of the researchers personal knowledge of the system, literature and discussion with experts in the sericulture industry.

From the point of view of silk reeling, it is necessary to study the reeling industry at a micro level to grasp the real problems of the individual reeler and the literature does not reflect such attempts. A broader study of the total reeling sector as attempted by some of the authors would not yield this understanding. In order to study silk reeling at the

Contd.

micro level, that is a typical reeling unit, two pre-requisites are to be met. The first is a clear measure of cocoon quality. Second is the establishment of the relationships among cocoon price, quality and quantity, as also between cocoon price and raw silk price. The research design adopted for carrying out the study to fulfill these requirements is shown as a flow chart in Exhibit 2.3. From Exhibit 2.3, it can be seen

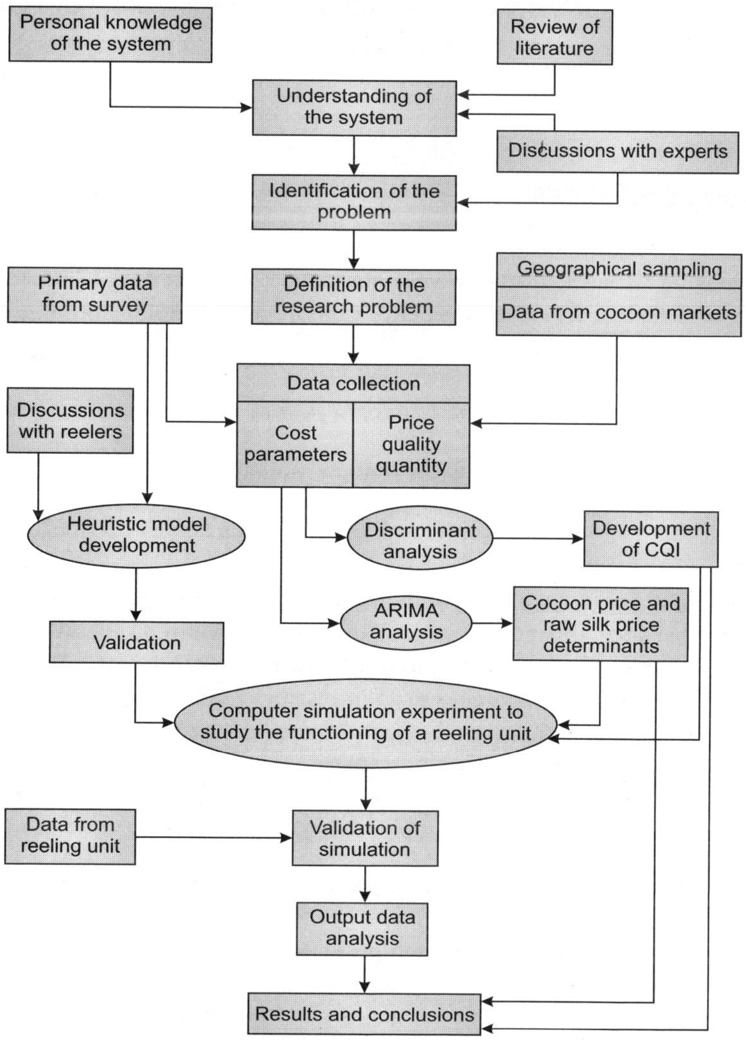

Exhibit 2.3 Details of statistical analysis

- Using geographic sampling, the secondary data will be collected from cocoon markets on price quality and quantity for a period of 2 years (40,000 lots of cocoons). Two analyses are made on this data.
  - By using discriminant analysis on cocoon quality parameters collected from the major cocoon markets of Karnataka, a Cocoon Quality Index (CQI) will be developed as a measure of the quality of cocoons.
  - By using the ARIMA model on CQI, cocoon price, cocoon quantity, and raw silk price, their causal relationships will be established.
- From a survey (about 20 reelers) primary data will be collected on the cost parameters and operations of several reeling units and the decision-making heuristics will be derived. Further, a heuristic model of the operations of a typical reeling unit will be developed using the internal dialogue of reelers, their operational strategies and other constraints, and it will be validated.
- Using the heuristic model above, cocoon price, CQI raw silk price along with their interrelationships and primary data on cost parameters, simulation experiments will be conducted. Real world data will be used to validate the model and the outputs. Simulation output will be analysed for insights into the operations.
- The outcome of the three models will be presented subsequently along with discussions.

Suggested Readings

- Creswell, John W. (2002). *Research Design: Quantitative and Qualitative Methods*. New York: John Wiley.
- Easterby-Smith, Mark, Richard Thrope, and Andy Lowe (2002). *Management Research*, 2nd ed. London: Sage.
- Sekaran, Uma (2000). *Business Research Methods: A Skill-Building Approach*, 7th ed. New York: John Wiley.

QUESTIONS AND EXERCISES

1. Discuss the term decision variable. Illustrate your answer with some examples.
2. How can managers and researchers obtain a better rapport while implementing a research model into the organisation?
3. Suggest how you would carry out what are specified as
   (a) Exploratory, one time observational, descriptive, *ex post facto* case studies of professional training effectiveness.
   (b) A formalised longitudinal, descriptive, ex *post facto*, statistical survey of professional training effectiveness.
   (c) One time, causal, field survey, case study, experiment of consumer reactions to 'food store advertising' (Emory, 1976).
4. What does replication of research have to do with its ability to be generalised? Explain.
5. What is the difference between a management problem and a research problem?
6. How do exploratory research, descriptive research, and casual research differ from each other?
7. What are the four basic measuring techniques used in research?
8. What are the methods of minimising potential research error?
9. Prepare a research design using the following procedure:
   (a) Select an area of research (after discussing with your research guide).
   (b) Select five to six research papers on the topic, or a particular aspect of the topic, published in reputed research journals.
   (c) Combine the information obtained from (b) above into an integrated literature.
   (d) Find gaps in the literature review as in (c).
   (e) Develop a hypothesis or formulate a research problem.
   (f) Develop a research design for (e).
10. Choose a good research paper on a topic of your interest and expertise. Note down the objectives and hypotheses of the study and the background that the author develops to justify the research problem. Without studying the paper in detail, develop your own research design and a procedure for solving the research problem, indicating methods of analysis. Discuss your design in detail with the research guide. Study the paper and the design explained in it. Discuss, compare and present the differences between the two designs.
11. What are the fundamental characteristics of a decision problem?
12. Explain the concepts: (a) Problem identification and (b) Verification.
13. Given the following decision problems, identify the research problems:
    (a) Whether expansion of current warehouse facilities is required.
    (b) Whether changing current inventory control procedures is required.
    (c) Whether introducing a new production planning model in place of the existing rule of thumb method is advisable.
    (d) Whether the demand and production capacity are matched.
14. Give an example of:
    (a) Pure research (research problem).
    (b) Applied research (research problem).
    (c) Action research (research problem).

Part B

Research Problem

CHAPTER 3

Problem Solving

- General Problem Solving
- Logical Approach
- Soft System Approach
- Creative Approach
- Development of Creativity
- Group Problem Solving Techniques for Idea Generation

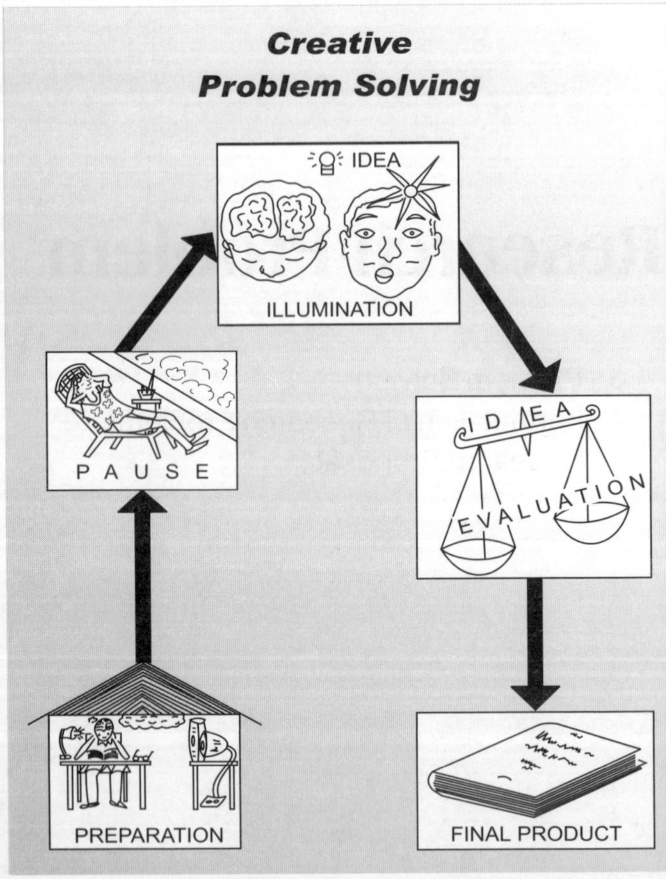

LEARNING OBJECTIVES

Upon completion of this chapter, you will be able to:

- ✓ Appreciate the meaning of a problem
- ✓ Enumerate categories of problems in research
- ✓ Get an overview of the problem-solving process
- ✓ Broadly understand the three basic approaches of problem solving
- ✓ Appreciate intense questioning as the root of all methods of problem solving
- ✓ Understand why creativity should be studied
- ✓ Appreciate the difference in thinking strategies needed at different phases of research
- ✓ Look at the overall creative problem-solving process
- ✓ Get a feel for various ways of improving creativity
- ✓ Appreciate a few group problem-solving techniques

GENERAL PROBLEM SOLVING

In Chapter 1, management research was defined as applied research whose objective is to solve the immediate problems of the manager. It has also been observed that the manager may take the decision to solve a problem in a rational way based on research or investigation; or he may prefer to depend upon his own or collective experience and judgment. Some managers react individually to problem situations. A manager's decision-making behaviour depends upon his abilities, background, training, and the organisational environment. This leads us to several questions: What are the kinds of problem-solving approaches available to a decision maker? What are their characteristics? In which situations is each of these appropriate?

Scientifically based education and training programs emphasise rational procedures where logical approach dominates. In areas related to products, inventory, logistics, manufacturing, and finance, where human intervention is low, analytical approaches of operations research are widely used and implemented. There is a need to look at total systems and the decision makers' preferences to certain aspects of the system and of the accomplishment of different performance objectives. Here the logical approach dominates.

In complex management problems where several organisational entities interact, and have interest in solving a common/shared problem, their viewpoints will generally be different. There will be multiple pressures on the problem solver. Further, in management problems related to broader issues of policies and strategies, long range concerns and questions of consensus and conflicting viewpoints dominate. A system viewpoint is imperative. One of the emerging approaches for such situations is the soft system methodology, which is a qualitative system approach.

In academic research, whether there is emphasis on adding on to the existing knowledge or creating new knowledge, there is a need for generation of new ideas for theory building. There is also a need for looking at phenomenon or theory or even a single fact in new and novel ways while solving a particular problem that is extremely difficult, complex, and ill-structured. This is in the domain of creativity and is now attracting a lot of attention from researchers.

In this chapter, all the three—logical, system, and creative—approaches for problem solving are briefly described. Since there is usually very little emphasis in education and training on creativity, this book attempts to discuss it more elaborately.

What is a Problem?

We can define a problem as a perceived difference between what a situation is and what it should be. Such a definition means the following: (i) Such difference is perceived and, there-

problem
A perceived difference between what a situation is and what it should be.

problem solving
Closing the gap or reducing the difference between what a situation is and what it should be.

fore, a problem exists with respect to a person or a group; (ii) what the solution "should be" indicates a liking or preference; (iii) the reason for the problem is not known, and (iv) in a decision making situation there may be many ways of solving the problem, closing the gap, or reducing the difference, but the best one is obscure.

The first aspect implies that a problem solving process begins with the recognition of a problem. If the problem is not recognised or identified, no effort will be made by the individual or the group to solve it, and the problem continues. A problem may be identified wrongly and an irrelevant solution to the problem will be sought (see Type III error in Chapter 2) and the problem will continue.

The second aspect is that the gap is not acceptable to the decision maker who feels the need for closing it and is, therefore, motivated to make problem solving efforts. In any management problem, it will be necessary to clearly understand new viewpoints of the problem because the perceptions of individuals or groups related to the problem may be different and the individuals or groups may have different mechanisms for solving the problem. This leads to the concept of ownership of the problem. Thirdly, if the reasons for the problem are not known, then an investigation or enquiry will be needed to gain understanding of the problem, in other words, a research approach will be needed.

Even when the reasons for the gap are not known with any degree of certainty, several alternate methods of solution may be available to the problem solver [as in decision-making situations (Ackoff, 1981)]. Choosing the one that best closes this gap is a problem. In practice, however, the quality of problem solving by managers depends upon the quality of understanding of the problem, defining the alternatives, the quality of evaluating the alternatives, and of understanding what the alternatives will end in. Scientific methods will become important in such situations as replacements for purely judgmental methods of solutions. This is typified by the operations research (OR) approach.

In decision-making situations a problem can be solved so that it is satisfying (Ackoff, 1981), calls this resolving). It can be solved optimally or the system and its environment in which the problem is embedded can be changed, so that the problem ceases (in other words, it is "dissolved", as defined by Ackoff, 1981).

types of problems
Problems may be simple vs. complex, well-defined vs. ill-defined and tame vs. wicked. Simple problems are those whose components and their interrelationship are transparent; complex problems are those in which several simpler sub-systems interact; well-defined problems are those where the problem solver is sure what the problem is; ill-defined problems are those in which it is difficult to formulate a definition of the problem; tame problems are those where the description of the problem is definite; and wicked problems are those in which description of the problem is not definite and solutions are difficult, inaccurate and not appropriate.

Types of Problems

Problems can be classified in several ways. Hicks (1991) classifies them as (i) simple and complex; (ii) well-defined and ill-defined; and (iii) tame and wicked.

Simple and complex problems Simple problems are those whose components and their interrelationships are transparent or are easily understandable. Complex ones are those in which several simpler subsystems interact in ways that are difficult to comprehend. Further, complex problems in management are generally related to large systems where some mechanistic and some heuristic subsystems interact. Breaking down such problems into smaller ones and then trying to solve them may not yield appropriate solutions to the total system problem. In such cases, interactions across boundaries of the subsystems will have to be explicitly considered. OR approaches are supposed to concentrate on such problems. In OR, a symbolic model of the system is generally attempted. But restructuring of problems may encourage the modeller to use oversimplifying assumptions and to fit a specific model type to the problem and solve a wrong problem. This is considered, by many, as a weakness of the OR approach.

Well-defined and ill-defined problems When the problem solver is not sure of what the problem is, definition of the problem becomes difficult and it may have to be viewed from many perspectives. For example, when a firm has failed to convert a technology idea into a suitable product, it becomes necessary to look at it from the point of manufacturing, R&D, consumer requirements, marketing, and technical manpower. One may have to redefine the problem to arrive at a correct definition of the right problem.

Tame and wicked problems These are determined according to some scale on which the whole problem solving process may be rated. A wicked problem may be one in which the description of the problem cannot be definite, derivation of solutions is difficult, alternatives are too many, solutions cannot be accurate, and confidence in the appropriateness of the solution is low. The following is an example.

> Several technologies are available for power generation. Several technologies exist for enhancing efficient utilisation of fuel. The parameters involved in the selection and combination of these technologies involve the consideration of parameters such as life cycle costs, degradation of environment in their use, the rate of global depletion of the fuel, threatening exhaustion, and so on. The answer to such problems calls for several viewpoints of several organisations and an enormous cooperative effort.

Modern researchers in management meet with problems varying from simple to complex, ill-defined, and wicked ones.

problem solving approaches
There are three major approaches: logical approaches, soft-system approaches and creativity approaches.

Problem Solving Process

Hicks (1991) presented a model of the problem-solving process, which is a modified version of the Parnes model (1972) (see Fig. 3.1).

problem-solving process
It starts with identifying the problem and consists of collecting data, defining the problem, generating ideas for problems, evaluating ideas, obtaining solutions and implementation of the best solution.

1. The problem solving process starts with identifying a problem, which perplexes the problem solver and appears chaotic. It is termed a mess (Ackoff 1981), as many aspects of the problem are not clear.
2. In the next step of data gathering, both objective and subjective data are collected. Objective data are the facts regarding the problem, where it is located, how it arises, and so on. Subjective data includes feelings of people and their views and perceptions of the problem. In addition, constraints in the system are obtained.
3. A definition of the problem is made. This may include many redefinitions of the problem defined initially or as given by the decision maker. Redefinitions involve viewing the problem from many angles, which are those of the various entities in the system.
4. Ideas for the problem solution are generated using individual and group approaches creatively.
5. Ideas are evaluated and solutions using the most promising ideas are obtained.
6. The best solution is implemented.

It can be seen from the model that it is not different from the problem-solving process as defined in operations research or in work study. The reader is referred to (Bell 1999, Krick 1962). However, the real differences lie in the modus operandi at each stage of the process and

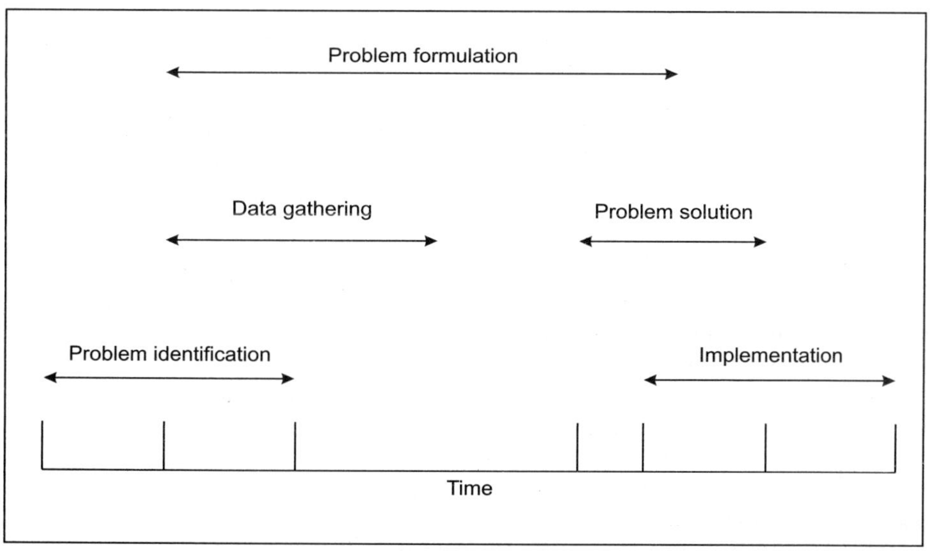

Fig. 3.1 General problem-solving process

what kind of approach is used. Hicks (1991) classified these approaches as: (1) logical approaches, (2) soft system methodology, and (3) creativity approaches.

While, in general, any of the approaches can be useful at any stage of a problem solving situation, due to certain inherent strengths of a particular approach, it is specially useful at certain stages (see Fig. 3.2). Logical approaches are very powerful in formulating and solving problems when the system is not dominated by human behaviour (for example, inventory systems and financial systems).

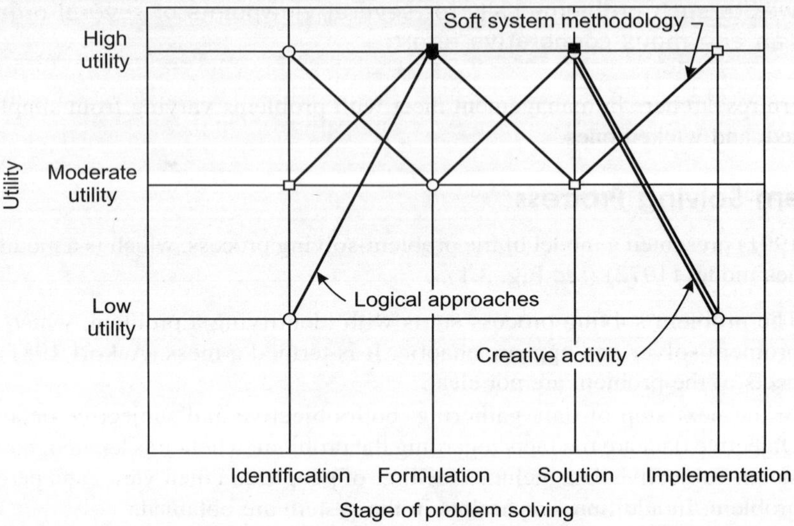

Fig. 3.2 Relative utilities of methodologies of problem solving

But they are not generally very efficient in problem identification and implementation phases. Creative methods are very useful in problem identification and generating alternate solutions. Soft system methodologies are very effective where complex problems are to be adequately formulated and implementation of the solutions has to be achieved because it can take total system consideration of the problem and facilitate actual use of its solution by using the concept of multiple owners of the problem. Further, it allows conflicting viewpoints to be integrated (see, for example, consensus methods in Gigch, 1987).

Let us now look at each of the three approaches.

LOGICAL APPROACH

logical approach In this approach a problem is abstracted and expressed mathematically or diagrammatically or descriptively.

This approach involves abstraction in which a problem is expressed mathematically, diagrammatically, or descriptively. Such an expression will only be an approximation to reality. Through a process of deductive reasoning one proceeds to define relationships. Breaking the problem into parts or sub problems can facilitate such an inferential process. Sometimes it is easier to solve a problem backwards from the final solution desired. This is possible when the objective is clear, but starting from the existing situation is not clear or easy. Each backward step leads to what is required at the beginning of the step in order to accomplish the condition. This process is continued until the present condition is reached.

One of the greatest advantages in using a logical approach is its ability to check whether an already established standardised solution method is useful in solving the problem. A classical example is a standardised OR technique like Linear Programming (LP), Dynamic Programming (DP), and inventory modeling.

In general, it is easier to solve special problems because of simplifying assumptions. From solving the special problem one can proceed to solving more general problems by relaxing the assumptions one by one. Solving general problems may be more complex. Sometimes transformation of the problem by changing its form to another, in some other area which has already been solved, is useful. [For example, see Krishnaswamy and Ganguly, (1987)].

A systematic and logical approach to search for new ideas is Morphological Analysis (MA) (Zwicky, 1969). Various attributes or features of the problem are listed. These are represented in the form of a grid. Various ways in which the combinations of these attributes can be provided are then generated. MA is widely used for exploring new opportunities or new ways of developing product ideas, manufacturing methods, markets, or new materials. In morphological analysis, a problem is broken down into parts, which can, to some extent, be treated independently. Several solution approaches to each part are obtained. An overall solution is obtained by considering one of the possible solutions for each part. The total number of solutions is equal to the number of combinations possible, taking one solution to each part. If, for example, a problem can be broken into three parts, such that there are two solutions to the first part, three for the second, and two for the third, then the total number of solutions is $(2 \times 3 \times 2) = 12$. The next step is to determine which of these 12 combinations are feasible (interaction between potential solutions may rule out certain combinations). Once the feasible solutions have been identified, the best overall solution can be chosen. The gaps in the grid are carefully analysed and evaluated for this purpose. MA can also be used for analysing problem situations to identify the structure of the problem.

morphological analysis
Morphological analysis is the systematic and logical approach to search for new ideas, used much in developing new product and new material ideas.

Illustration Automobile propulsion morphology.

Table 3.1 shows the different parts and solutions to the problem of designing an automobile propulsion system.

There are $(2\times 4\times 2\times 3\times 3\times 3\times 4) = 576$ possible combinations.

1. Let us take, for instance, combination $P_1^2\ P_2^2\ P_3^1\ P_4^2\ P_5^3\ P_6^4$
   This will be a four wheel automobile, solar power driven turbine two wheel drive with mechanically transmitted power and is feasible.
2. Take another combination $P_1^1\ P_2^2\ P_3^1\ P_4^2\ P_5^1\ P_6^3$
   This is a three wheeler with two wheels driven by an IC engine through mechanical transmission, but powered by third rail, which is clearly not feasible.

Similarly, feasible and not feasible combinations maybe identified and only feasible solutions considered.

Table 3.1 Automobile Propulsion

	Parts	Solution			
		1	2	3	4
P_1	Wheels (No)	3	4	—	—
P_2	Driven Wheels (No)	1	2	3	4
P_3	Engines (No)	1	2	—	—
P_4	Transmission	none	mechanical	fluid	—
P_5	Engine Type	IC Engine	Tuabnic	Electric motor	
P_6	Power drive	Hydrocarbon fuel	Secondary battery	Third rail	Solar power cell

Potential Problem Analysis (Kepner and Tregoe, 1981, p142-143) is also a systematic analysis using structured questions by an individual for disclosing and treating potential problems that are likely to occur in a system. It is considered to be a complete approach. The basic questions that are addressed in it are about what can go wrong, and what can be done about it. The four stages of the process are: (i) identification of the weak areas, (ii) identification of potential problems in these areas, (iii) identification of causes, and (iv) identification of needed activities. Further, individual motivation is an important aspect of potential problem analysis.

potential problem analysis
This is a systematic analysis using structured questionnaire for disclosing potential problems.

SOFT SYSTEM APPROACH

When mathematical modelling of a complex system is attempted, the structural modelling procedure is useful *ab initio* (Finley (1985), Geoffrion (1987)). In this procedure, an observation of the real world system is made and depending upon the researcher's experience and comprehension, a complete scenario is developed. The problem space is extracted for detailed modelling. The development of scenario and problem space can be achieved effectively by using the soft system methodology (SSM). This may aid the structural modelling advocated by Geoffrion. Alternatively, interpretive structural modelling (Warfield, 1974) can be used before the mathematical model is finally developed (see Chapter 4).

soft system methodology
In this method all complex details like opinions and reactions are obtained qualitatively, a clear differentiation is made between the clients, the problem solver and the problem owner. Roles of these are listed in a pictorial diagram, called Rich Picture. A conceptual model is developed using the human activity system.

Making a meticulous observation of the system all complex details are obtained in a qualitative and descriptive manner. Attitudes, reactions, and opinions of various parties (individual and organisational units) involved in the problem are gathered. In addition, factual or quantitative data and reactions to the interactions of existing problem solutions are also obtained. In the main, each of the human activity systems, connected with the problem situation is briefly described as a separate module. This will help in giving a good insight into the problem situation. For each of these systems a separate model is developed. A simple overview of the SSM is given in Fig. 3.3. (Hicks, 1991, pp.227). In this method, a clear identification is made among the client, the problem solver, and the problem owner (Checkland et al, 1990) and their roles are listed in a pictorial diagram (Rich picture). This is developed without imposing a structure on it. Its purpose is to convey a meaning to the problem solver and to provide ease of communication with others. From Fig. 3.3, a root definition (a descriptive statement of the activity system that is being modelled) is obtained. It is desirable to generate alternate root definitions so that a choice can be made after evaluation. Checkland suggests that a good root definition should include ownership, actions, customers, environmental situations, global view, and the transformation process.

Fig. 3.3 Soft system methodology (Source: Hicks 1991)

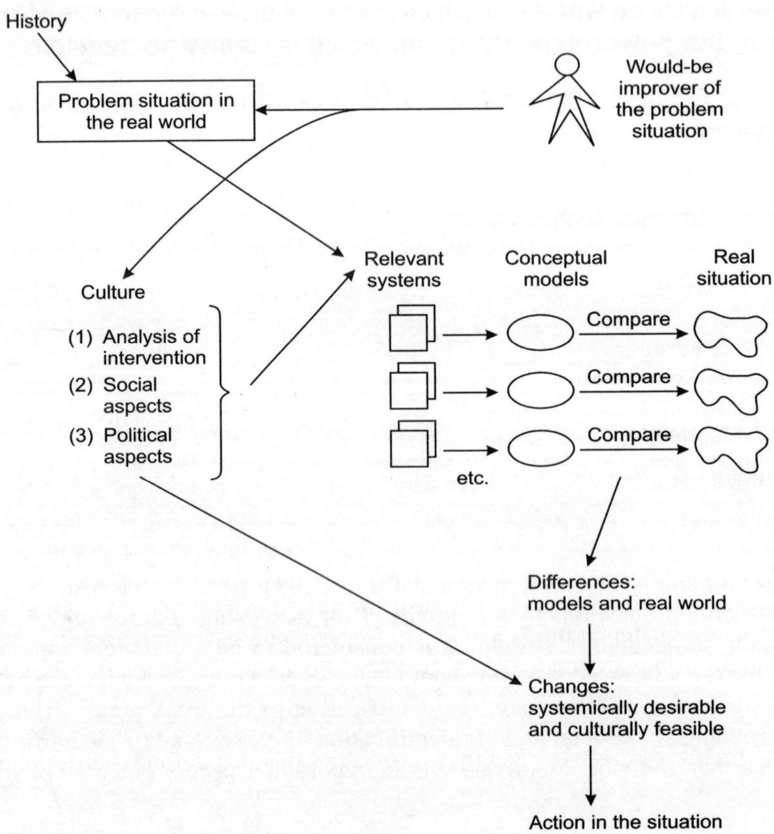

Finally, a conceptual model is developed using the activities of the human activity system and logically relating them through dependency relations (the activities are used as verbs). [Detailed treatment of SSM and logical methods are given by Checkland (1981) and Kepner and Tregoe (1981), respectively, and [Shekar (1999) gives application of SSM to foundry production planning and control]. An illustrative case of application of SSM is given in the annexure to this chapter.

CREATIVE APPROACH

In research, as in any other undertaking, one can learn its tools and techniques. One can become proficient in them and become a competent technician. But in order to enable one to make original contributions to one's field of research, one has to give oneself to it in a special way, that of creativity. This requires absence of mental regimentation, a strong motivation, and freedom of self-expression. Creative ability exists in every individual and exercise of experiments in creative work is probably the best way to develop it. This section deals with creative thinking, factors of creativity, and general approaches for its development in the context of the problem-solving process. Some autocatalytic procedures on creativity, suggested by researchers, are also discussed.

creative approaches
These require absence of mental regimentation, strong motivation and freedom of self-expression which leads to a thinking process conducive to solving a problem in a novel way.

Thinking Process

A thought is an interpretation of the relationship existing in the external universe. While there is a mechanism to generate thoughts, there is no mechanism in the brain to distinguish the correct thought from the incorrect one, that is, to distinguish the correct interpretation of the true relationships from the wrong interpretation. Creative thinking can be construed as the perception of a more correct interpretation of the true relationship in the world we live in, a discovery of what always existed. Scientific method, however, is valuable in testing new relationships, though it is of little use in generating it.

When an external signal (stimulus) impinges on the brain and the nerve cells connected in a complex network in it, a pattern of energy flow sets in. However, this pattern depends upon resistance at each synapse (connector of a cell). There is a mechanism in the brain, that varies the resistance at each synapse, depending upon the signal and its time of occurrence.

Generally, however, these resistances are lower when the pathways (synapses) are used frequently, and higher when they are in disuse. Further, the energy flow can go on in the network even when the external signal is no longer present. In the first case, thoughts (patterns of energy flow) are stimulated by an external signal and in the second, a self stimulated thinking process has been set up. This is possible because of closed loops, which exist in the network of nerve cells. Depending upon which group of cells is connected at any instant of time, a number of pathways are stimulated and a thought occurs. Association between two signals sets in when they occur simultaneously and there are pathways to handle them. In younger people, free association takes place as there are fewer pathways to block new information. In the older people, since strong associations are already formed due to experience, often incorrect ones, only limited understanding of the external universe is possible to them (Prince 1970, Csikszentmihaly, 1996).

Indirect associations are formed through any item of similarity. Different patterns of association, built up by different individuals due to their unique experiences, result in different thought patterns in these individuals as a response to the same sensory impressions received by them. Associations used in trying to grasp the relationships of the external world may be correct or incorrect depending on how these associations were formed. One of the most important relationships in understanding the world is cause-effect relationship. In cause-effect relationship, there is never a certainty of identifying all possible items, which are causes for a particular effect, and therefore, an error always exists in such relationships. Further, these cause-effect relationships may change overtime and this is a definite barrier to creative thinking.

thinking process
Many types of thinking processes are employed in problem solving. Terms used to indicate the thinking process are classified as logical or analytical (vertical thinking, critical thinking and strategic thinking) and creative or heuristic (lateral thinking, outcome thinking, and divergent thinking).

Thinking processes in problem solving There are many types of thinking that are employed in problem solving. Some of the terms used [De Porter, 1992] to indicate them are:

Logical thinking: In this type of thinking cause-effect relationship is the dominant preoccupation of the individual.

Vertical thinking: In this, the thinking process proceeds in a chosen line, step by step or stage by stage towards the problem solution in a manner similar to climbing a ladder. It elaborates on methods to overcome obstacles in the chosen line.

Critical thinking: This way of thinking is evaluative or judgmental. In it the problem solver checks the feasibility of an idea or solution to a problem.

Analytical thinking: In this type of thinking a problem or idea is broken down into parts. Each part is examined to understand how it functions and fits with other parts, like a puzzle, and explores how the parts are interrelated. It is also referred to as convergent thinking, that is, thinking towards a single solution.

Strategic thinking: Developing a specific overall route and direction to take for handling large scale problems, for example, large scale project planning. In this process, the problem will be looked at from all possible angles.

Lateral thinking: [de Bono 1971] This type of thinking looks at the problem from several angles and jumps from one ladder to another (of vertical thinking). It tends to shift radically from an initially chosen line of thinking and reformulates the problem.

Outcome thinking: In outcome thinking a problem is attacked/tackled from the perspective of the desired solution or result.

Creative thinking: In this mode of thinking existing factors of a problem are rearranged or reset to come up with a flash of a new concept. This involves lateral thinking.

Divergent thinking: It is a type of thinking in which one makes different associations with a problem and takes different lines of arguments to arrive at different solutions.

Heuristic thinking: In heuristic thinking one makes rules of thumb based on an experience, hunch, or insight in specific situations and applies them to similar situations.

Generally, a particular researcher may use any type of thinking at any stage of research. But, it is important to recognise that the predominant type of thinking switches from one to another during transition from phase to phase of the research process; for example, creative during identification, logical during definition, analytical during design, analytical and creative during solution, critical during literature review or observation, and judgmental and evaluative during inference and reporting.

The above thinking modes may be classified as logical and creative or analytical and heuristic (Ray and Myers, 1986).

Logical/Analytical	***Creative/Heuristic***
Vertical (convergent)	Lateral
Critical	Outcome
Strategic	Divergent

There is some evidence to consider the two categories as emerging from the two hemispheres of the brain (left hemisphere—logical/analytical, right hemisphere—heuristic/creative). However, it is now generally argued that a combination of both the modes of thinking makes problem-solving effort more effective.

Creative Thinking

Creative thinking is characterised by sensitivity to problems, fluency and flexibility of thinking, originality, ability to analyse and synthesise, and the ability to redefine things (Guilford 1959). Prince (1970) propounded a theory that there are six discrete operations of thinking in problem solving context. These are wishing, retrieving, imaging, comparing, transforming, and sorting. According to him, in creative thinking wishes may not be achievable; retrievals are approximate; transformations are at high level; comparisons lead to more wishes, transformations, and retrievals, and, therefore, a tendency in favour of thorough learning is strong.

creative thinking
Creative thinking is characterized by sensitivity to the problem, fluency and flexibility of thinking, originality, ability to analyse and synthesise to redefine things. The important factors in developing creative thinking are using systems and variables, identifying assumptions, finding probability, and deductive changing relationship.

Important factors in developing creative thinking according to Pacifico (1966) are (i) using systems and variables, (ii) identifying assumptions, (iii) finding probability, and (iv) detecting changing relationships. These factors are elaborated below.

Using systems and variables Any change in any item will affect all other items in the universe, which is a large system to a more or less degree. Since the universe is a very large system, its total analysis becomes impossible and over cumbersome. We, therefore, partition the universal system and simplify it in order to study it. This very act of simplifying is a source of error. But this error is generally recognised when simplified systems are analysed with existing tools.

In a system, some factors vary and some are constant. A factor that is constant with respect to one system may vary with respect to another since every factor in the universe belongs to more than one system. Creative thinking is the main tool for identifying factors influencing the system. It recognises that each system is unique. Many problems requiring creative solutions may arise in a system. A few of them, according to Pacifico, (1966) are: (i) changing the objectives, (ii) broadening the system, (iii) simplification, and (iv) considering variables and constants. These problems will have to be examined with the following in mind: (a) a system exists only in an instant of time, and (b) every variable must be considered significant until it is proved otherwise.

In creative problem solving, visualising relationships is useful. As the number of variables increases, such visualisation becomes more difficult (the simplification that takes place may be like linearisation). The important criterion of needing creativity is the difficulty in identifying the relationships.

In most cases where complex systems are involved, it would be desirable to set objectives for the creative effort in order to avoid wasteful and misdirected efforts. The objectives should preferably be a trifle too broad rather than too narrow to avoid pre-selecting a particular system and eliminating the relevant ones. From the point of view of management research, setting an objective may sometimes result in creatively seeking a solution to an imaginary problem (problem in the mind of the researcher rather than in the real management world). Desirably this should be avoided by carefully checking the real world for the relevance of the research objectives.

Identifying assumptions Any object belongs to several systems. When we study the change in an object, we may wrongly assume that a particular system, which is active, is causing it. For example, if a job shop has a considerable number of finished stock items in its inventory, we may conclude that the scheduling system is causing it, that is, producing earlier than needed. But the system that is causing it may be a particular group of consumers that is in financial difficulties and is reluctant to take it because it is unable to pay for it immediately.

However, it is impossible to isolate a system so that it contains only items that influence it. In dealing with assumptions it is important to note that while no amount of facts can substantiate an assumption, a single fact can refute it. A rich field for applying creative thinking is, thus, that of confirming or disproving the basis for the assumptions underlying the accepted system.

Handling probability This refers to the likelihood of a relationship being true. Probability refers not to the existence of relationship but to its correct identification. Probabilities indicate areas where the relationship has not been established.

Detecting changing relationships Relationships change with time but time is not involved in the change. Many natural relationships change as the degree of one's experience of it changes. In this context, experience must be viewed with caution. Ignorance helps in thinking creatively in relatively well known areas. The creative thinker should (a) constantly examine the relationship to be sure that it is not changing, (b) identify as sources of errors, the change in the composition of groups or collection of objects, or should notice the degree of change in one of the objects, or should notice that the same relationship is different in various systems, and (c) synthesise and put together relationships in a new combination. For example, in determining economic order quantities, the cost of transportation may not be included in the client organisation because delivery is free. If it becomes necessary for the client to bear the transportation costs (and these costs are related to the quantities ordered) then the derivation of economic order quantities should also include these costs in the model.

Creative Efforts in Research

Four of the situations in which creative efforts may have considerable impact on solutions to problems are given as illustrations. These only serve as a sample.

Situation A There are areas where no relationships have been established before, as in virgin fields. The tools of research are old, but the territory is new. Initial creative work is easy and more obvious relationships will be established quickly.

Illustration In the last decade, batch processor scheduling problems have attracted the attention of researchers, particularly in semiconductor industries [Mathirajan et al (2002)]. A batch processor (BP) is a processor that can operate on a batch of jobs (that can possibly be grouped upto the capacity of the machine) simultaneously, with common beginning and end times (unlike a discrete processor that which processes one job at a time). Once the process begins, the batch processor cannot be interrupted. Thus, no job in a batch can be released from the BP or added to the BP until the processing of the entire batch is complete.

Mathirajan (2001) studied the production planning and control of heat treatment furnace in the post-casting stage of the steel casting industry. A review of published literature revealed that this aspect had not so far been researched using analytical/heuristic procedures. Heat treatment operation is important because it determines the final properties that enable components to perform under demanding service conditions such as large mechanical load, high temperature, and anti-corrosive processing. Further, since the processing time at Heat Treatment Furnaces (HTF) is often much longer than at other operations in the steel foundry, it affects the scheduling and the overall flow time considerably. Effective management of heat treatment operations is hence key to maintaining a smooth flow through the HTF.

The problem in scheduling jobs on HTF is a batch processor scheduling problem, which is analogous to the problem of scheduling oxidation/diffusion furnaces [Devpura et al (2000); Kempf et al (1998) and others] in wafer manufacturing in semiconductor industries. This study successfully developed a few implementable fast heuristic algorithms for scheduling HTF.

Situation B The domain of knowledge is extended by replications of a successful research study in different setups, cultures, and societies. These are new areas on the fringes of known ones and may support or refute the original research results.

Illustration Shenoy (1975) investigated 35 profit-making industrial organisations in India for studying the organisational context, structure, and performance. He replicated the interdisciplinary study of the Aston group led by Pugh (1968). Attempts were made to determine the dimensions of organisational context and structure in the Indian environment and the relationships between contextual and structural variables.

The methodology and analysis procedures were similar to that of the Aston study. Slightly modified questionnaires were used for data collection in a descriptive study.

The results and conclusions indicated many findings similar to the ones in the Aston study, but the following conclusions were at variance with the Aston study.

1. The study established the need to consider a larger context than in the original study. It should include product situation in the market, governmental policy, and cultural factors.
2. The study established five structural factors and the first three of them only are operating in the Indian situation.
3. There is simultaneous contextual influence on the structure and performance.
4. There is a lack of relationship between structure and performance.

Situation C Modifications to and improvements in established relationships are needed. These involve incremental efforts and constitute a sizable proportion of the total creative effort at any given time.

Illustration A research study was conducted on the system of inventory and distribution for an engineering industry dealing with consumer durables and having a network of factories, godowns, and outlets. Transportation from factory to godowns and godowns to consumer outlets was by trucks only. Transportation cost depended on whether the quantity transported was less than half a truck load, equal to half a truck load, more than half a truck load or more than one truck load. Clubbing of different items was ruled out because the origins for different products were different. There were many studies dealing with inventory-transportation interactions while developing the economic order quantity, but none with this set of constraints which change transportation cost structure. A set of special models was developed to meet these requirements. (Krishnaswamy et al. 1995).

Situation D Conversion of established relationships is the objective of research. In the first place, the established relationships are shown to be wrong or inadequate.

Illustration Ramasastry (1974) developed a model of optimum leave reserve for a bank using simulation procedures. The model borrowed from the well known shrinkage allowance models form quality control. Like extra material has to be provided for shortages arising out of rejections in the manufacture of a product item, extra manpower (reserve manpower) needs to be kept for offsetting effects of absence due to leave for the employees. This model was inadequate for a manufacturing shop where worker absenteeism is combined with the breakdown of machines. The above model was modified incorporating the probabilistic machine breakdown by Krishnaswamy and Ganguly (1987).

Barriers to Creativity

The absence of pathways in the brain is a barrier to creative thinking. It can, however, be overcome by recognising the difficulty and by studying the subject deeply. Incorrect data, incorrect direct sensory impressions, and incorrect associations cause pathways as barriers. All human beings have incorrect thought patterns on broad subjects, and they try to study some limited aspects of the system and engage in generalisations within the system. Experience, the noblest school with heavy fees, may also be a block to creative thinking.

barriers to creativity
These are due to absence of pathways in the brain. Barriers can be overcome through discussion with others, using groups, trial and error method and changing areas which help in opening up new pathways in the brain.

New pathways in the brain overcome the above block and handle new relationships. Coming in touch with the primary data can considerably increase them. This is costly from the viewpoint of effort and, is also less efficient. Discussions with others broaden pathways. Using groups for problem solving enhances the limits of these pathways in an individual brain (for example, brain storming). Performing experiments whose by products enlighten some other problem situation, trial and error methods, changing areas, and contexts might also help in increasing creative outputs.

Creative Problem Solving Process

stages of creative process
There are four stages in a creative problem solving process: preparation, incubation, illumination, and verification.

Hutchinson (1949) presents four stages of a creative process as:

1. *Preparation:* The stage in which the problem is investigated in all directions with intense effort, which is given up in the later part of investigation.
2. *Incubation:* The stage, during which the individual is frustrated, exhausted, and is not constantly thinking about the problem, and is relaxed.
3. *Illumination:* The stage during which the idea occurs along with psychological factors like emotional release. Vividness of ideas and a feeling of insurgence immediately precede it and accompany its appearance.
4. *Verification:* The stage in which the validity of the idea is tested and evaluated. The idea is reduced to an exact form.

Hutchinson, after studying 250 most famous thinkers, differentiates between systematic thinking and insight (creative insight). According to him systematic thinking has the objective, problem, and method clearly defined. The method is slow and deliberate, logical and associative thinking is maximised, trial and error is minimised, and little emotion is felt during the process of thinking. It is widely used during formulation of plans where only a small number of variables and hypotheses are involved.

Insight is associated with baffling problems. An unpredicted feeling of frustration sets in, in the initial periods. In the final stages, effortless integration and feelings of exultation take place. From the point of view of emotions, the two types of thinking can be represented as follows:

Systematic thinking	Degree of	Insight
Low ←	Psychic frustration	→ High

Development of Creativity

development of creativity
There are two principles of creativity development: principle of deferred judgment and principle of extended effort in idea production. In addition, Saaty (1959) lays down following few thoughts for creativity development: experimentation with creative process, adequate motivation, competing in the world of ideas, patient and independent thinking, trial and error method, representation of familiar things, emotional involment and use of imagery in problem solving.

As we have said earlier, most people are creative to some extent and possess many of the traits (Guilford, 1967) that are given below, to a greater or lesser degree.

- Independence
- Curiosity
- Intuitiveness
- Unconcern for social norms
- Sensible risk taking
- Introversion
- Wide span of interests
- Cognitive flexibility
- Self acceptance

It is generally felt that an individual's creativity can be consciously developed by following certain principles. Some useful guidelines are available for an individual researcher to develop a higher level of creativity.

Parnes (1964) outlines the following principles on the development of creativity.

- *Principle of deferred judgment:* All problems that are implicit in a problem situation should be considered. Problem sensitivity has to be developed. To do this, evaluation should not take place while enumerating all problems.
- *Principle of extended effort in idea production:* Generally, in problem solving one gets an idea, sees it as a possible solution, and settles for it without further ado. The creative problem solver on the contrary persists with getting more ideas and different problem formulations until exhaustion results. It is found empirically that later portions of effort bring more productive ideas than the initial portions.

Saaty (1959) has outlined some of his thoughts on creativity and its development. These are useful for all researchers.

- The growth of mental potentialities through experimentation with the creative process broadens an individual's capability for original contribution.
- Severe regimentation stifles creative talent but balanced guidance could be given through goals and objectives
- The cause of creativity may be one of the following: adequate motivation, competing in the world of ideas, a challenging situation, excitement about a particular kind of work, compulsive desire for improvement, or self expression.
- Stimulation could be different and independent for each subject.
- Patient and independent thinking should be encouraged.
- Trial and error methods must be attempted.
- Extensive production of a large number of versions/solutions of a problem is desirable. (This results in superior and imaginative solutions.)
- Re-creation and re-presentation of already familiar things and ideas are useful in creative problem solving.
- Through serendipity one idea leads to others not sought for (mind wandering may take place) and an entirely new chain of ideas is formed. This is a useful tool in creativity.
- Comprehension is necessary but not sufficient for creativity.
- For gainfully using memory in creative thinking, the following techniques may be useful.
    - Close involvement of oneself with one's emotions and one's aesthetics feelings.
    - Learning things as a whole—relationship between parts are well set in the mind.
- Imagery is important in creativity.
- A problem is redesigned in as many number of ways as possible. Further, the concepts underlying the problem are investigated and not so much the problem itself. It is desirable to consciously abandon conventional thinking in solving problems.
- Groups are used for extending the creativity of the individual mind. Creative thinking can be improved by increasing the number of pathways available with a brain. These additional pathways exist at different levels of abstraction. Some of the methods for obtaining additional pathways are:
    - Reading or discussing how others have handled similar problems in the past.
    - Reading or discussion to obtain general knowledge relating to the subject.
    - Changing location to obtain entirely different pathways on methods that might lead to a solution.
    - Forming of groups of different backgrounds to work on the problem so that each may contribute new pathways to others.
    - Convening a number of people of different backgrounds under conditions in which new pathways may be built one upon another.
    - Direct experimental work.
    - Internal formation of new pathways by cutting off external signals temporarily.
    - Internal formation of new pathways by consciously combining data already present, in ways that seem to be related to the problem.

In an interesting article in Reader's Digest (1993) Epstein lists useful techniques of creativity.

techniques of creativity

Capture the fleeting ideas, daydream, seek challenges and expand your worlds. These are useful techniques for creativity development.

- Capture the fleeting idea.—You must be ready to capture it, that is, be poised, drop whatever you are doing to attend to the idea, enter it in a diary or jot it down.
- Daydream—Transitional state of mind is useful anywhere for idea generation. Be alone with your thoughts (loneliness helps this).
- Seek challenges—Recurrence of old behaviour in challenging situation is resurgence. More behaviours mean more possible interconnections. Put crazy things like toys on your table.
- Expand your world—Blend ideas from different worlds and different people.

Illustration A bar of sweet is to be cut by a mother of two children into two equal halves. Cutting the bar into two exact halves is difficult. Each child is obstinate about getting the bigger piece of the bar cut unequally.

Creative solution The mother asks one of the children to cut the bar subject to the condition that the other child will have the first choice between the cut pieces. Such an approach may be useful in settling disputes between two groups with conflicting interests.

Greiner (1977) proposed many interesting techniques of idea generation as a part of creative effort. Ray and Myers (1986) suggest some creativity developing approaches in the Stanford Research Institute course in creativity. Succinctly their recommendations are the following:

1. The creative task is heuristic rather than algorithmic.
2. The origin of creative ideas is the inner resource that they call 'essence', which is intuition driven by will—a compelling, unifying, and singular purpose.
3. When intense conscious effort fails to solve the problem one has to surrender (give up striving), that is, to give up mental striving, in other words, let go physically and mentally, sleep and dream about the problem and practice meditation.
4. A spirit of enquiry has to be maintained and dumb questions have to be asked.
5. Judgment has to be destroyed—both self judgment and judgment by others.
6. Intrinsic motivation is conducive to creativity but extrinsic motivation is detrimental.
7. Curiosity should be created.
8. What is easy, effortless, and enjoyable only should be done.

Students desirous of assistance in their search for approaches to creative thinking should refer to instant creativity—a checklist designed to help in creative thinking, given as an appendix to the book by Pacifico (1966). [Refer Appendix A3 for further information.]

GROUP PROBLEM SOLVING TECHNIQUES FOR IDEA GENERATION

Introduction

group problem solving techniques
In this a formalized group of people come together to identify a problem or to develop solution to a problem. Diverse viewpoints throw light on several aspects of the problem, interaction among group members makes idea generation efficient, a number of new ideas can be created. Brain storming and Delphi are two major examples.

During the formulation of a problem or generation of a hypothesis in developing a theory, the researcher may like to take the help of a group in order to generate problem ideas. This is a creative process, which can be formalised into a set of group problem solving techniques. There is probably no single set, which is assertable. For a detailed discussion of many of these techniques the reader is referred to Olsen (1982), Hicks (1991) Rawlinson (1994) and other references given at the end of the chapter. Brief and quick outlines of these techniques are presented in this section as a communication to the student of research and as a means of helping awareness.

As the problems become more complex and the environments of the problems become large in number and interconnected they require knowledge and information from many disciplines. A team of researchers or experts from diverse backgrounds, values, and perspectives can come together to assist in the identification of such problems and/or in developing solutions to them.

The reasons for the efficiency of groups in solving problems are many:

- Diverse viewpoints throw light on several aspects of the problem
- Interactions among people are found to be very efficient in generating viable ideas
- A total lack of knowledge in a particular field may also be very helpful in creating a new idea rather than in winning an argument in conventional committee interactions.

These methods are very popular among design teams. However, students of research can gainfully employ them.

The intense questioning attitude prevalent in many management oriented topics like work study, decision analysis, value analysis, and value engineering can also be used for problem solving. The intense and systematic questioning, though often very tiring, can yield rational solutions. Any amount of questioning by an individual is generally not considered as effective as the interactions of a group charged with the aim of creating new solutions. Rational solutions are generally not creative solutions. Decisions often are the result of a group problem solving effort, which are less efficient. On the other hand, some of the methods developed for the purpose of creative solutions will infuse the efficiency of creating new solutions. [For a good discussion of this aspect refer *Methods Engineering* (Chapter on 'development of alternatives') by Krick (1962)].

Two group solving approaches—brainstorming and Delphi—are outlined in the following sections. Other group solving approaches such as Issue Based Information Systems (IBIS), Nominal Group Technique (NGT), and Synectics are outlined in Appendix A4. Further, interpretive structural modelling is discussed in the fourth chapter on model formulation as an aid to structural modelling.

Brainstorming

Brainstorming is a group process in which members, usually from different backgrounds, respond to a central question/theme. The emphasis is placed on generating a large number of ideas while deferring criticism and evaluation. The method is especially useful for attacking new problems or for identifying new ways of looking at old problems. The originator was Osborne (1963). Brainstorming sessions usually take place in a free and uninhibited atmosphere. The central principle involved is deferment of judgment on the quality or viability of the ideas presented by any member of the group. A group consists of approximately six to ten people. Half of these are experienced core participants and the others are from as many disciplines as possible that will be able to understand and contribute to the solution of the problem. The operational procedure has a warm up session in which an introduction is made to the subject. Some interactive warming up takes place. The problem for focus of the particular session must be presented in a form that is terse, clear, and sharp, which will allow the formation of a range of ideas. The participants are advised to relax, just express whatever ideas come to them (free wheeling), improve other people's ideas, and not evaluate anyone's ideas, including their own.

brain storming
This is a group process in which 6 to 10 members from different backgrounds respond to a central question. The participants express whatever ideas come to them (free wheeling) without evaluating the ideas of others.

A checklist may be useful for the participants:

- Using who, what, when, how, and where type questions to study the problem;
- Expanding, contracting, combining, reversing, eliminating, and modifying the problem;
- Forcing relationships among items seemingly unrelated;
- Morphological analysis;
- Encouraging wild idea generation; and
- Reverse brain storming, where problems are anticipated.

A panel of experts will later evaluate the ideas obtained in the session. The prime protagonists of this method believe that the larger the number of ideas generated the better it is. A few or at least one may be exceptionally original.

Delphi Method

The Delphi method is a survey technique for achieving consensus among isolated anonymous participants with a controlled feedback of opinions. This method is the application of expert opinion to problem solution, problem identification, or the temporal location of a problem. The central principle underlined in the Delphi method is that a structured and interactive questionnaire, a kind of remote conferencing procedure, can serve as an effective means to draw an expert opinion in relation to certain kinds of problems or predictions. There are many purposes for the technique but the ones that are of definite interest to students of research are:

delphi method
This is a survey technique for achieving consensus among isolated anonymous participants. It is an application of expert opinion for problem identification or problem solution. Main features are anonymity, interaction, controlled feedback and statistical responses.

- To determine and develop a range of possible alternatives.
- To explore and expose underlying assumptions or information leading to different judgment.

The Delphi method has become an important tool in applied research in many areas of physical sciences, social sciences, business administration, and engineering; and is extensively used in technological forecasting.

Delphi's main features, which are anonymity, interaction, controlled feedback, and statistical responses, are intended to minimise the biasing effects of dominant individuals or irrelevant communications and of group pressures towards conformity. The Delphi method utilises a series of three or four polling, with questionnaires, the first of which is generally open ended. The objective of Delphi is to get significant and substantial group consensus on priorities among items or divergent opinions. It would appear that any use of Delphi for problem generation would involve a single poll rather than multiple ones since consensus and validation are not of prime importance at that stage.

SUMMARY

Many types of thinking can be applied to problem situations. The researcher usually switches between dominant types of thinking from stage to stage of research. Two broad categories, logical and creative thinking are presented. There are three approaches to problem solving, (i) hard logical procedures, (ii) soft system methods, and (iii) creative approaches. Logical procedures are considered suitable for problem solution. They heavily employ some system of questioning and focus on the cause-effect relationship in solving problems. Morphological analysis and potential problem analysis are two techniques presented to illustrate logical procedures. Soft system methods are qualitative in nature and provide 'a rich picture' of the problem situation. They are described as powerful tools for problem identification and implementation of solution. Creative approaches are considered original and new ways of looking at phenomena and arriving at the true relationships present in them. Creative thinking is considered a four-stage process consisting of preparation, incubation, illumination, and verification. It is construed as a metaphorical thinking involving much emotion and originality. Suggestions of some outstanding researchers on creativity for improving and developing creative problem-solving skills are presented. These include emotional involvement, grappling with the problem, broadening of interests, associations, extending the horizon of knowledge, experience of new situations, and group approaches. Several creative group problem solving procedures are available. Of these, the Delphi method, brainstorming, and interpretive structural modelling are of special interest to students of management research.

ANNEXURE 3.1

An Illustration of a Case of Application of SSM (Krishnaswamy 1998)

Machinery Manufacturing Company (MMC) is a textile machinery manufacturer. MMC, in keeping with its policy/mission of manufacturing and marketing textile machinery in India, decided to manufacture spinning frames. The spinning frame (SF) is the last operation machine in textile fibre manufacture. The manufacture of SFs at MMC started in 1970 at its unit in Madras. The first spinning frame manufactured was the DEEJEF, in collaboration with a European firm (EEIS). The DEEJEF was a 400 spindle SF. Initially, the help of the collaborator came in the form of technical details, specifications, drawings, and training of technical personnel. As in the case of all other textile machinery items manufactured in MMC, M/s Vidyut Limited markets the SFs. All other functions relating to sales, R&D, and pilot mill facility for testing are centralised in the parent unit in Kerala.

In 1980 MMC, based on its policy of manufacturing the latest (world class) textile machinery, considered going in for manufacture of a newer SF. In 1982 MMC went into a collaborative agreement with M/s EEIS in keeping with the top management policy of opting for an outstanding collaborator. Over a period of time, EEIS developed strong

Contd.

interactions with MMC, especially in production-related activities. It also sells the products developed by MMC in its brand name in the global market. This is testimony to the high quality of MMC's products. Over a period of time, these products were shelved from EEIS' manufacturing, leaving MMC the sole manufacturer. EEIS has a coordinator stationed at MMC to help and ensure that proper standards and specifications are attained in the manufacture of these products. The collaboration package was similar to one taken for DEEJEF. The model was called GIFFON, and had product features superior to DEEJEF in terms of automation, machine speed, increased production rate (1000 spindles), and better quality of yarn.

As the top management emphasised, the world class quality of its product, total incorporation of the design into the product was the primary aim of the production unit. The performance of this product was found to be excellent (in technical terms) and found acceptance in foreign markets. But there were problems in selling this version of the SF in domestic markets, though demand existed for SFS. This was due to the following reasons:

- MMC failed to give enough advance information to customers about the new product (about its sophistication, with respect to automation, and so on) in order to prepare them for its use or to enable them to give useful feedback for any modifications desired.
- Customer mills were not equipped to accommodate this longer and superior machine in terms of compatibility with other existing machines on the production floor and also in terms of the size of the factory.
- Technical personnel in the customer mills were not trained to cope with the sophistication of the machine.
- Since the top management of MMC stuck to the policy of selling its products through the agents, market research was not emphasised.
- The marketing department is generally not consulted while evaluating the suitability of technology at the time of drawing up collaboration agreements and valuable feedback from the customers is not available owing to the distance between the marketing department and customers. Thus the suitability, or otherwise, of the technology to Indian market came to light only during sales and it became evident that matching of technology to customers' needs had not been adequate at the planning stage.
- The R&D department is engaged in studying the inability in manufacturing newly collaborated products and new designs, and development will be carried out for the items subcontracted by the collaborator. Any product modification is done using the feedback from the sales (after sales).

These problems along with market resistance led to the design of a model with alterations to suit the existing mills in the country. The modified product was called GIFFON (M)—the 'M' standing for 'manual'.

This spinning frame was shorter in length, had a lower automation, had a smaller number of spindles (860), had reduced spindle diametre (to reduce power consumption), and had the original raw materials substituted due to non-availability in local markets and also in order to reduce costs (for example, using sheet metal in place of aluminum for the fan). MMC's policy of manufacturing the latest (world class) technology machine items for the textile manufacturing industry has some implications for the manufacturing of other machinery items with a similar policy.

The collaborated GIFFON design offer for SFs, replacing the older model DEEJEF, introduced features like automation, higher machine speeds, increased number of spindles, and higher quality yarn. MMC, after purchasing the technical documents for GIFFON, absorbed the technology and produced these frames to match international quality. The frames were introduced successfully in foreign markets through the collaborator. But the mission of the company to provide world class technology to indigenous manufacturers suffered an initial setback in this instance.

The frames were not found to be acceptable to textile manufacturers in India. SF is one of the many machines serially connected in a process industry. The existing level of technology of the production line of the Indian manufacturers was made up of machines belonging to older technology and GIFFON was incompatible with these lines. The output capacity was also not commensurate with the capacity of the line; GIFFON frames being much faster. Further, the operating personnel found it difficult to handle this technology. They had to be trained by MMC. These problems led to alterations to the original design of GIFFON to suit the existing manufacturing systems of the customers. This can easily be seen as a customised R&D effort. MMC invested in R&D and made the SFs with shorter length, lower automation, a smaller number of spindles, reduction of input energy, and with a provision for using local raw materials. The R&D department successfully adapted these machines and found acceptance in the indigenous market. This is a case where R&D efforts have been used to bring down the level of technology rather than bringing it up. While clearly the adaptation has taken place on the part of MMC, R&D has been used as a weapon to prune a technology.

Contd.

The choice of technology would, therefore, appear to be considerably influenced by the status of related technologies with which it has to enmesh. The mission of producing world class technology and to choose a technical collaboration to meet this may be self defeating if the indigenous technology development is not considered. This is particularly true of machinery and equipment items, which are parts of larger production and flow systems.

Application of SSM

Rich picture: The rich picture of MMC is shown in Exhibit 3.1. The rich picture gives patterns, arrangements, connections, and relationships among the activities in MMC. The vital links are shown in the figure. In the picture some of the subjective comments are included with restraint. No confidential information is divulged in the rich picture. The picture is not intended to be a complete representation of the problem situation of MMC, but to be a vivid and clear picture. It is felt that it has given sufficient information on the problem situation for us to identify what corrective actions need to be taken.

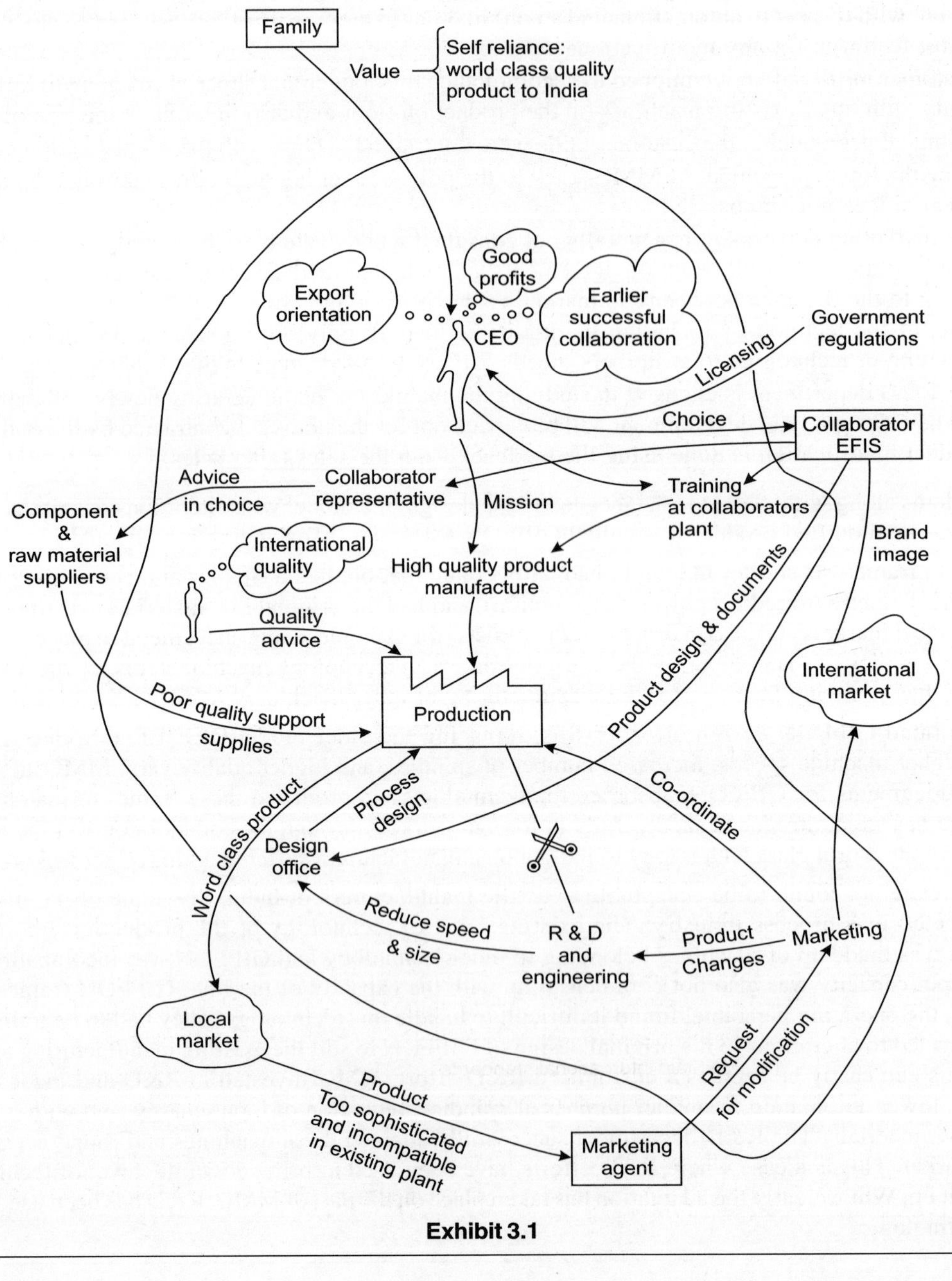

Exhibit 3.1

Contd.

System's primary tasks and issues of concern: These are presented in the Exhibit 3.2 and 3.3. Further, the major activities of MMC are given in Exhibit 3.4. The root definitions that were developed are not displayed.

The conceptual model: The conceptual model developed using the relevant systems (Exhibit 3.5) gives the interactions in an idealised system configuration and is in some ways prescriptive. It is shown in Exhibit 3.6.

Comparison of rich picture and conceptual model: An observation in this particular case is that the rich picture is not very different from the conceptual model developed and therefore the discussion will be limited to the differences.

1. The collaboration for a foreign technology is undertaken with the primary view of developing the export market for spinning frames. Choice of collaborator, training of manpower abroad, and understanding of the international market have been the primary concern of the organisation.
2. In building quality products, the motivation has been for the quality of the outgoing product. The collaborator also helps the organisation and serves its own the interest in maintaining high product quality, so that it can be effectively marketed globally.
3. The marketing department is directly concerned with export. A marketing agent, however, addresses the local market.

1. Produce world-class textile machinery for export
2. Make profits
3. Provide local employment
4. Indigenise all components and materials
5. Be self reliant as far as the manufacturing inputs are concerned
6. Modify SFs to suit Indian market

Exhibit 3.2 Primary tasks of MMC

1. Considerable scrap
2. Poor communication between R&D and production departments
3. Product unacceptability in local market
4. R&D used for clipping down product quality
5. Maintain international quality
6. Increase operational efficiency

Exhibit 3.3 Issues of MMC

1. Collaborate for design
2. Get government clearance
3. Obtain materials
4. Train people
5. Design process
6. Set up plant
7. Produce spinning frames
8. Sell abroad through collaborators
9. Sell through agents in India
10. Maintain international standards
11. Provide modifications through R&D
12. Administration

Exhibit 3.4 Major activities of MMC

Contd.

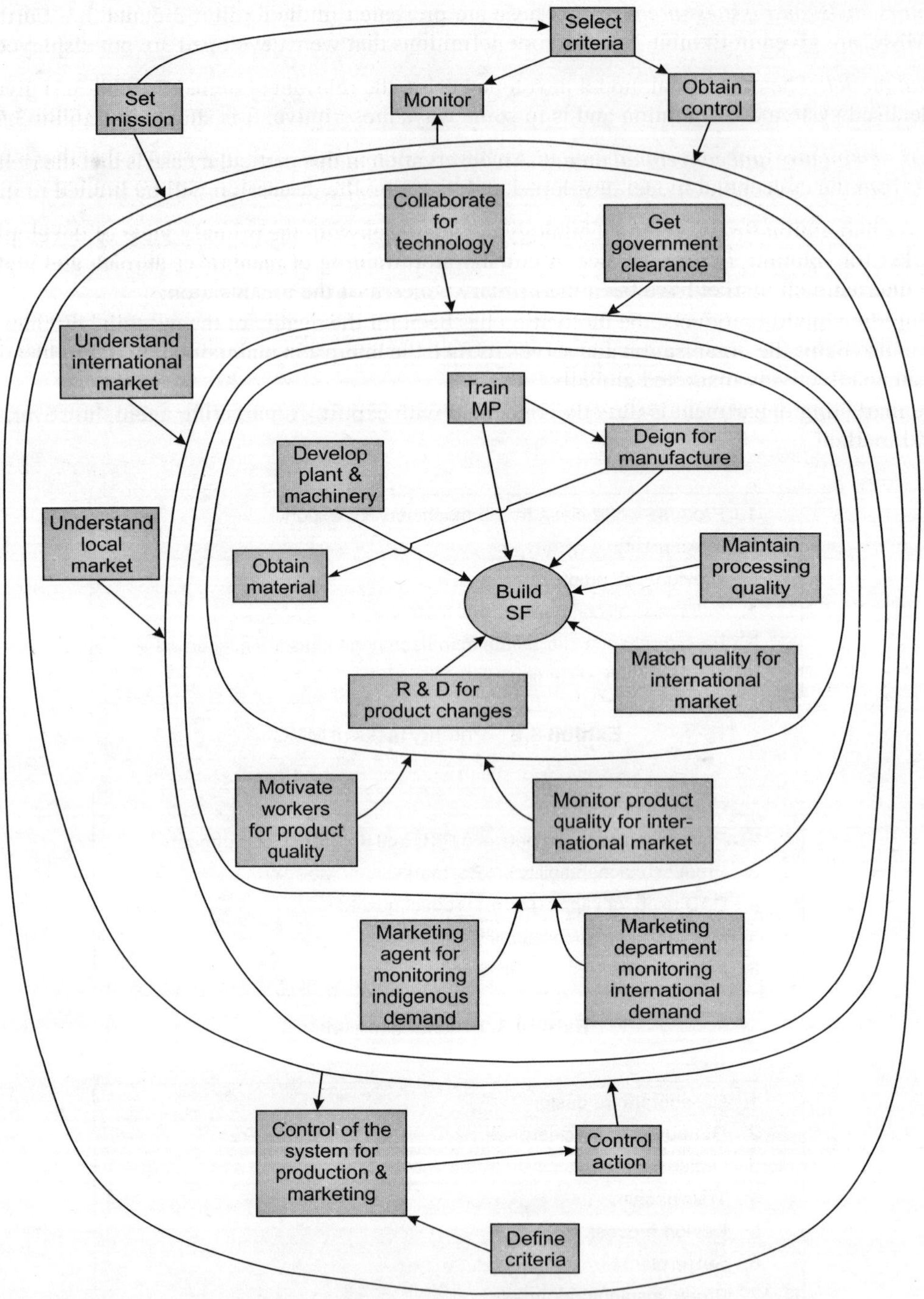

Exhibit 3.5 Conceptual model of MMC

4. Requirements of the local market at the time of selection of the technology have not been specially considered. This is an important consideration in the conceptual model.
5. The company, as compared with the conceptual model, has not specifically addressed quality of processes.
6. R&D is highly de-linked from manufacturing and is clubbed with engineering having little role during technology selection.

Contd.

1. Manufacturing system for producing SFs
2. Engineering and design system for manufacturing design
3. A R&D system for product upgradations and modifications
4. A supply system for obtaining quality components
5. A quality assurance system for maintaining international quality
6. A system for providing employment and training to local people
7. A marketing agency system for indigenous selling of SFs
8. A planning and monitoring system for operation
9. A planning and monitoring system for the business

Exhibit 3.6 Relevant systems of MMC

Based on these differences the following changes are considered desirable.

- The corporate marketing and R&D departments should be jointly entrusted with the responsibility of assessing the collaborated technology for suitability to Indian markets.
- R&D should be strengthened and linked strongly with manufacturing and marketing so that manufacturing design (process improvements) is geared for more efficient operation.

Suggested Readings

- Checkland, Peter B and J. Scholes (2000). *Soft System Methodology in Action*. Chichester: John Wiley.
- Hicks, Michael J. (1991). *Problem Solving in Business and Management: Hard, Soft and Creative Approaches*. London: Chapman and Hall.
- Kepner Charles H., and Benjamin B. Tregoe (1981). *The New Rational Manager*. London: John Martin Publishing.
- Ray, Michael and Rachel Myers (1986). *Creativity in Business*. New York: Doubleday.

QUESTIONS AND EXERCISES

1. What approaches would be used in getting new product ideas from
   (a) consumers
   (b) experts
   (c) sales representatives
   (d) R&D engineers
2. What is the essential characteristic of morphological analysis? Demonstrate with an example.
3. In what ways does brainstorming differ from synectics? Do you think these two techniques will be efficient for all stages of problems solving?
4. How does soft system methodology differ from (i) creative approaches and (ii) system methodology?
5. Which techniques of problem solving will be appropriate and efficient in the following problem situations? Explain your answer.
   (a) An industrial relations problem arises out of a worker's dismissal.
   (b) High rejections occur in a particular component manufacture while for all other components rejection is quite low in a manufacturing division.

(c) A new product is performing poorly in a test market, though the market research department feels that there is a large potential market for the product.
(d) A vendor's request for developmental support is under consideration of the General Manager in charge of manufacturing.
(e) There are a few suggestions to be considered for evaluating award for "innovation" in a suggestion scheme.
(f) A new computerised production control system is to be introduced in a manufacturing organisation.

6. (a) In what situation of forecasting Delphi method is most suitable? Least suitable? Why?
(b) What is attribute listing? Where is it useful?

7. Search research literature in your area of specialisation and locate an application of each of the following. From the application what can you say about the techniques?
(a) Synectics
(b) Brain storming
(c) IBIS
(d) Delphi
(e) Morphological analysis
(f) Kane simulation

8. What is the principal advantage of the NGT over other procedures? Do you think a research problem can be generated for academic research using the NGT? Elaborate by giving reasons.

9. In how many ways can the following be used? Try hard to get a list as long as possible. The longer the list, the better it is. Do it alone first. Then do it with a couple of fellow research students or friends. Compare them. Evaluate the useful one's after generating answers.
(a) A brick
(b) A metal rod of a yard length
(c) A coil of iron thick stainless steel wire
(d) A rubber ball
(e) A sheet of plastic

List as many possibilities as you can by yourself at first, and then as a group. Compare the two lists and evaluate them.

10. Solve the following puzzles.
(a) Arrange numbers 1 to 9 in the cells of the square below such that the numbers add up to 15 in all direction. After solving the problem, write down the thought processes adopted by you.
What methods did you use?

(b) Can you connect all the points using only four straight and continuously drawn lines? The lines may cross but retracing of lines is not permissible.

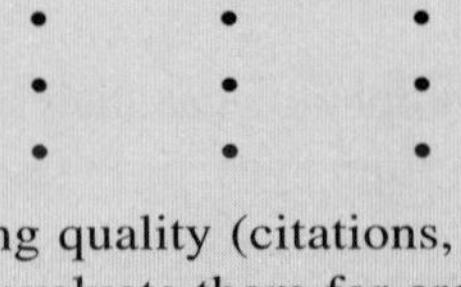

11. Select a few research papers of outstanding quality (citations, or guides or experts view may be taken, or reviewers may be used for selection) and evaluate them for creativity? If so try to support your answer by using the material presented in the book.

12. Select a few theses and scan them for:
1. Problem identification
2. Problem formulation/hypothesis generation
3. Model building
4. Data collection
5. Data analysis

13. A team trying to stem a drop in sales and increase sales views the challenge as a shoreline being eroded by stormy weather. They suggest using sand bags for temporary relief, building a jetty for an intermediate solution and calling in the Army Corps of Engineers to uncover a permanent solution.
Use metaphorical thinking or analogy. Work out an ideal project for the sales problem.

CHAPTER 4

Formulation of Research Problems

- Introduction
- Approaches to Management Research Problem
- Exploration for Problem Identification
- Hypothesis Generation
- Formulation of the Problem

Spotting the Culprit

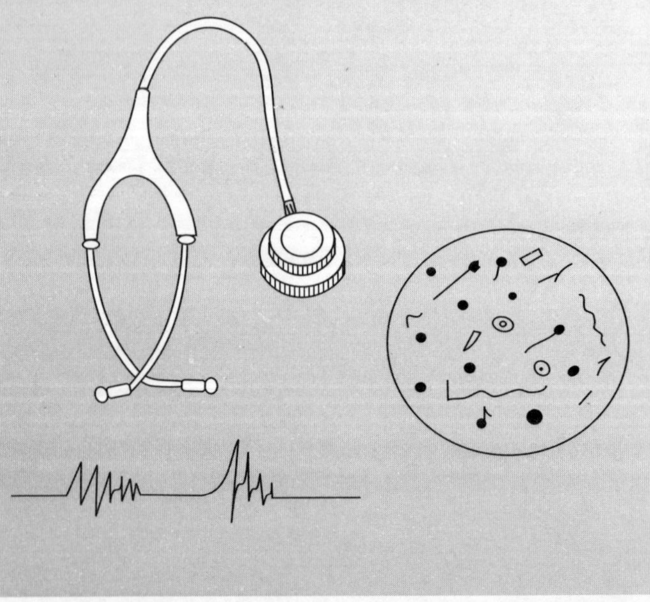

LEARNING OBJECTIVES

Upon completion of this chapter, you will be able to:

- ✓ Understand the systems concept and its importance in problem formulation
- ✓ Understand approaches to research problem
- ✓ Enumerate ways of exploring for problem formulation
- ✓ Find out how to search for literature relevant to the research problem and organise it succinctly using modern techniques
- ✓ Outline the role of variables in problem definition
- ✓ Understand how to convert management and research questions into hypotheses using a theoretical framework
- ✓ Understand deductive and qualitative methods in hypothesis generation
- ✓ Understand the use of system study in model formulation
- ✓ Appreciate concepts of structural modelling

INTRODUCTION

The emergence of research problems in the perception of a researcher is a complex process and some what ill-defined. This must have been evident while studying Chapter 3. In this chapter two major aspects of research problem—problem identification and problem definition—are discussed. Problem identification requires some sort of exploratory effort on the part of the researcher. These explorations may take many forms, many of them are mentioned, but only two of them are detailed in this chapter. One is research literature review, in which the problem is unearthed from knowledge, gained from previous research. The other is when the problem is eked out from a critical observation of the system of decision-making and its environment—a system study—as is done in all cases of manager presented problems. Of course, any exploration for problem identification may involve a combination of several methods. The treatment of problem definition is relatively more structured than the problem identification. It deals with the identification of variables (those from literature) and specification of the variables (reflecting the researcher's additional perception and efforts in system study). These will be used in developing propositions, hypotheses, and relationships as in pure research, based on the framework of theory that has already been developed in earlier research. In a manager originated problem, it may take the form of specific relationships or models stated in a verbal form.

It has already been stated earlier that when an interaction takes place between a manager and a researcher for investigating a decision problem, there is a need for the researcher to make a study of the total system in order to formulate effectively the research problem. The researcher has to keep in mind the symptoms detailed by the manager in such a study. Further, he has to clarify the significance and the importance of several aspects of the organisation which may, prima facie, seem unconnected with the problem.

In systems study, it is necessary for the investigator to look at problems from the perspectives of different organisational units and executives. Such an approach can be gained by the investigator through an understanding of the systems concept, which is outlined in Appendix A1 at the end of this book.

In this chapter, three modes of approaching the research problem are detailed. Exploration for the research problem is dealt with in two sections—literature survey and system study. Hypotheses generation and problem formulation in the modeling context are finally discussed.

APPROACHES TO MANAGEMENT RESEARCH PROBLEM

There are many approaches through which a researcher identifies and formulates the research problem. These approaches evolve from several contexts. The typical approaches are as follows: (i) A manager is in need of solving an organisational problem that he cannot solve by himself. (ii) A mature researcher is cognitively aware of research problems in his field of research and any signal through conversations, discussions, conferences, or reflection may trigger an idea for research. (iii) A fresh scholar of research is systematically introduced to the process of research through research training program courses and literature review in an area of interest to him. These approaches will be elaborated in the following sections. An overview of these three approaches are integrated and presented graphically in Fig. 4.1.

Management Problem is Posed to the Researcher

In this mode, a management problem is felt by the decision-maker who seeks a scientific solution through the help of a researcher. The researcher may be located either within the organisation or he may be from outside, for instance, an academician. The problem posed by the executive generally serves more as a symptom than as the research problem itself. The researcher needs to identify the real problem by means of his/her own analysis. The dialogue between the manager and the researcher will give information on the nature of the problem experienced, its consequences in the system and the general terrain of the problem.

A researcher is like a doctor. From this information, he has to develop the research questions or investigation in a manner similar to a diagnosis carried out by a doctor.

For example, a production manager of a plant, during a dialogue with a consultant, expresses that he is unable to meet the delivery schedule requirements of the many customers of the organisation. The researcher will have to convert this problem of the production manager into questions like: Is the load on the plant and its capacity well matched? Is the production control department using a scheduling rule? If 'yes', is the rule appropriate to the plant and the type of production handled? If 'no', what rule should be designed? The first question is a system evaluation question (needing a system study). The second question needs a technique/method for evaluation or investigation. The third becomes a development question, which will lead to a new alternative to decision making (the researcher has to develop, test, and demonstrate the usefulness of the new alternative).

The researcher may follow the classical two-stage approach to solve this problem. In the initial exploratory stage, the feasibility is assessed or a quick system study is carried out in which several people in the organisation will be interviewed and interacted with. An analysis will be made of the communication pattern in the organisation. A system view is taken towards the problem, in which the effects of a problem in one area or sub-system are not necessarily considered restricted only to the same area or sub-system. A problem in one sub-system may be viewed to be due to a malfunctioning or an inadequacy in some other sub-system of the organisation. Keeping this basic tenet in mind, the researcher will make a system study and correctly formulate the research problem. The formulation is generally a statistical or mathematical model, which is very common in operation research approaches.

If the researcher has inadequate knowledge with respect to certain aspects of the problem, as obtained from research literature, then he may formulate a hypothesis type of research. Then the domain of research will be acquisition of knowledge required to solve the problem. Further to this, a reference to and verification from literature may follow. If the method of solving the problem is available in literature, no scientific research of the basic type or of the applied type is called for. The method is straight away applied to the problem for obtaining a solution. If there is a method in literature which requires modifications to suit the existing system, then application oriented research will be carried out by the researcher and some creative effort will be required for this modification. The principles formulated by Ackoff for finding solutions to practical problems can be useful. In the evaluative research, the researcher will evaluate alternate methods for problem solving and the best method is chosen. If, however, the researcher finds that there is a need for developing a new alternative, then it becomes a sort of developmental research.

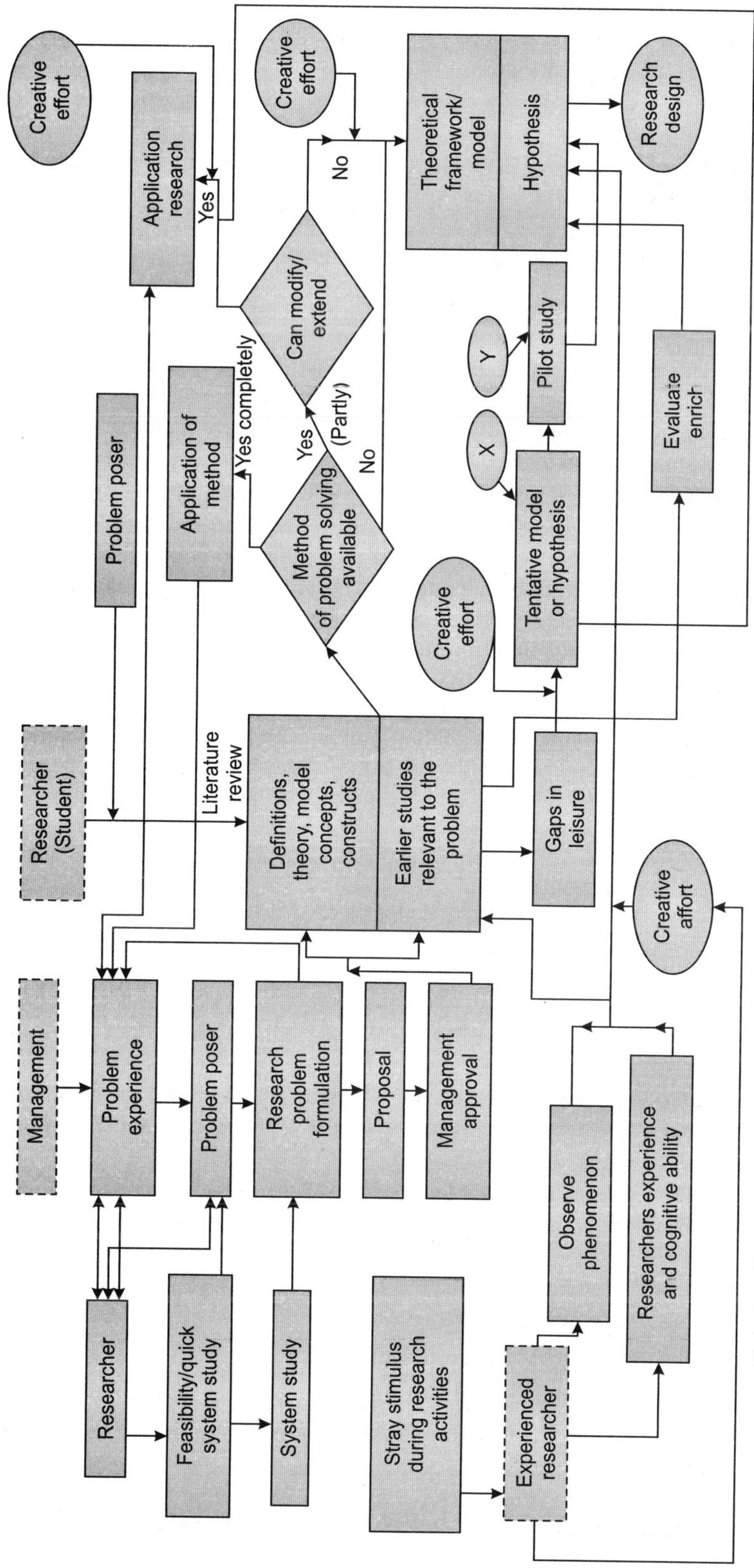

Note: See Fig. 4.3 for details of X & Y

Fig. 4.1 Approaches to research in management

Example The use of economic order quantity (EOQ) for items to be purchased is well known and has been used for decades. The simplest model of economic order quantities is the one that minimises the sum of ordering costs and inventory holding costs over a period of time.

The model equation is

$$TVC = \{(C_h \times Q)/2 + C_o \times (d/Q)\}$$

and the corresponding economic order quantity is

$$Q^* = SQRT\ ((2C_o{}^*d)/C_h)$$

Where C_o is the ordering cost/order,

d is the demand for the item in a period, and

C_h is the holding cost/unit/period.

This model is applicable in many situations in industry where the assumptions of the model hold good—costs involved are only holding cost and ordering cost, all in one supply, stock-outs are not permissible, demand is uniform, and the lead time for procurement is fixed. The model is shown to be quite useful even where some of these assumptions do not hold. With an adequate safety stock it performs quite well in practice.

Now, let us consider a number of godowns of a factory, which order a manufactured product on the factory warehouse and retail them to customers. Under normal circumstances the EOQ model should be adequate to represent the system. But let us consider the transportation cost from the factory to warehouse and from warehouse to godown as variables. Let us also consider a special situation in which the transportation is by trucks and the cost of transportation depends on the quantity transported (Q) every time an order is delivered. If the quantity Q is less than a truckload the total cost of transportation is for full load, that is, the transportation cost/unit is T_c/Q. If Q is smaller than a truck load, the transportation cost/unit goes on increasing and as Q approaches the truck load, transportation cost per unit goes on diminishing until a minimum is reached. If the order quantity is greater than an integral number of truck loads such that

$$(n \times QTF) < Q < (n \times QTF + Q_1)$$

Where QTF is one truckload quantity,

n is the number of truckloads, and

$Q1 = CTF/C1H$ beyond which quantity CTF will be incurred.

Here CTF is a cost of transporting with full truck load and $C1H$ is a cost of transporting one unit when $Q_1 < QTF$.

Under this condition, the model equation becomes (Krishnaswamy et al, 1995),

$$TVC = CH \times Q/2 + d/Q\ [C_0 + n \times CTF + (Q - n \times QTF)\ C1H]$$

And the new optimal quantity is shown to be

$$QN^* = SQRT\ (2d \times [C_0 + n \times CTF - n \times QTF \times C1H]/CH)$$

For all $(n \times QTF) < Q < (n \times QTF + Q_1)$,

Where QTF is one truckload quantity.

(*Note* Q^* is different from QN^*).

Such modifications and adjustments to basic models are noticed frequently in literature. This calls for the re-examination of assumptions and transformation of model equations to suit a particular application.

Investigation of an Idea by an Experienced Researcher

In the case of an experienced researcher, a stray stimulus, a critical review of connected research, or an unacceptable solution to a research problem may trigger a research idea or concept. Suggestions from earlier researchers or an analogy between an unconnected area of research and his own may lead to a research idea. The researcher will then reobserve the phenomena to which the problem is related and integrates his/her own research experience and cognitive abilities to identify a problem. He will build a theoretical framework and a hypothesis, which he will set about evaluating through search of exsisting literature. Then he will investigate it through a process of rigorous logical or statistical analysis after collecting pertinent data.

Initiation of a Novice/Student to Research

A research student in a university usually has multiple origins of research ideas. The research guide of the student may pose a tentative problem for investigation. In the absence of such a poser, the student may embark upon a literature review in the area of his interest/specialisation in order to identify gaps in research. Now, since the student is a novice in the area of research, he may consciously take the two-step process. He will make a tentative hypothesis or build a tentative model depending upon whether the research is basic or applied. He will then carry out a pilot study (initial exploration) in order to confirm that his hypothesis or model is meaningful, the variables that he has used in them, the measures that he has developed, and the instrument of data collection he has designed are all appropriate. In most cases, modifications to many or all of these may take place as a result of the pilot study. With the theoretical framework tentatively accepted by the student, he will proceed with the investigations to develop the research design (Fig. 4.2).

Illustration from Real Research

Marketing Programmes and Technological Developments Across Product Life Cycle (Mohan, 1995)

This exploratory study, in machine building sector of India, aimed at identifying variables of the marketing programme and of technological developments dominant in different phases of the product life cycle. Its objective was to explore the relationship between marketing programmes and technology developments, and to generate and test related hypotheses.

A tentative set of marketing programme and technology development variables were identified in research literature and in a preliminary study with a semistructured questionnaire and interviews with executives in the related areas. This was followed by a pilot study in two phases to finalise the variables, questionnaire, and the relationships to be sought.

Pilot study

This study required measures of both marketing programmes and technological developments. The measures of technological developments available from a previous work done in the Department of Management Studies, IISc, Bangalore, (Madan Mohan, 1991) were used to develop the portion of the questionnaire related to technological developments.

For measuring the marketing programmes at the different phases of the PLC, different variables have been prescribed by various authors. But most of these are prescriptions based on studies and experience by the authors in the American and European context. In the Indian context, however, there was one study that discussed differential marketing performance based on the product portfolio (Thakur and Das 1991). Thakur and Das discuss marketing and accounting measures in two phases, namely, growth and maturity phases of the life cycle. The relevant marketing programme elements for the other two phases of the PLC, the introduction and decline phases, were obtained on the basis of the suggestions received from the experts interviewed in the preliminary study.

Thus, the first phase of the pilot study was aimed at eliciting the specific elements of marketing programmes at the four phases of the product life cycle to verify and improve the relevance of the variables suggested by literature and the preliminary study.

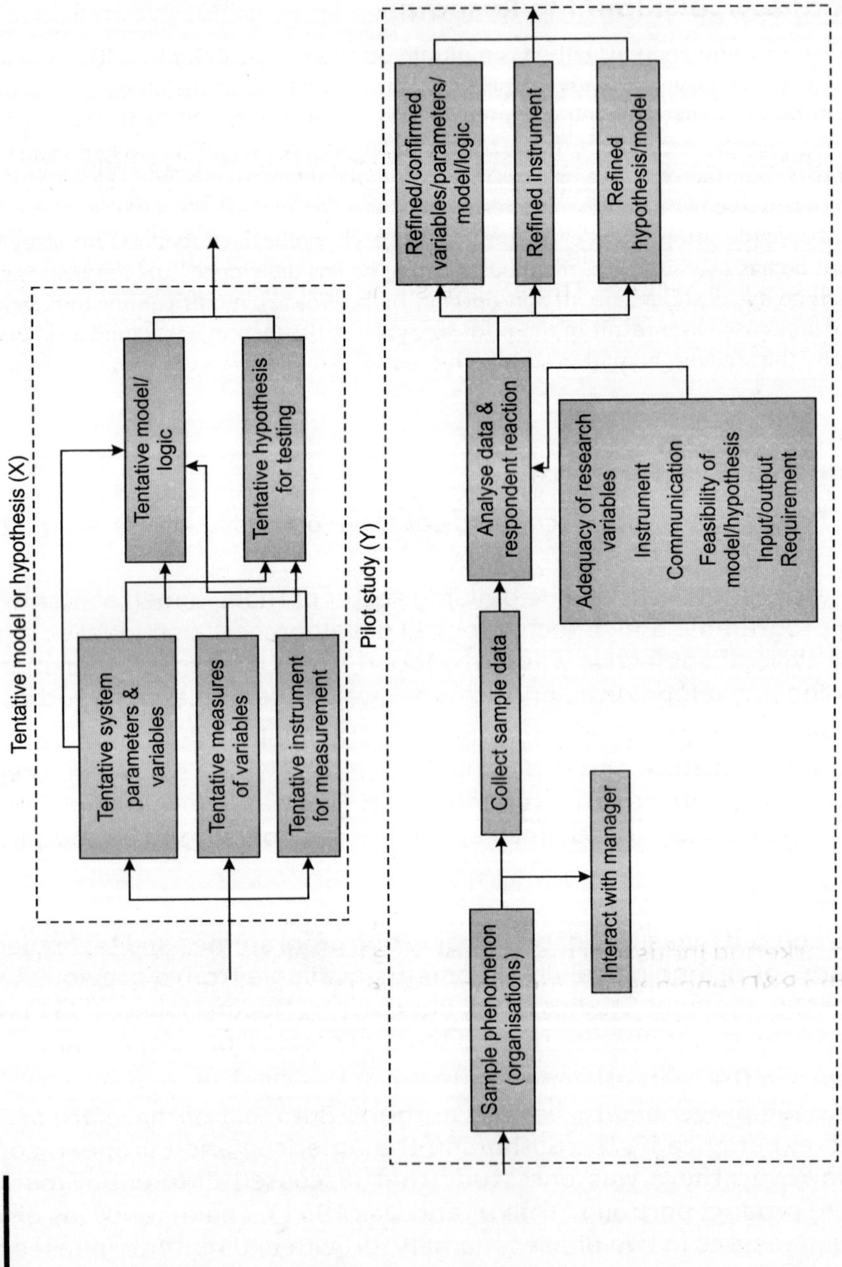

Fig. 4.2 Exploratory or Pilot Study

Pilot study—Phase I The portion of the semi-structured questionnaire with the thirty variables (which were elements of a marketing programme) and the three market performance measures for products in the four phases, namely, introduction, growth, maturity, and decline phases of the PLC, were used to elicit data from marketing managers in nine organisations that manufactured and marketed general purpose machinery and their components. A 'yes/no' scale was provided before each variable and if the answer was "yes" by the executive, the question posed was for the executives to indicate the extent to which the variables were considered important at different PLC phases, on a strongly disagree-strongly agree format for each variable.

The results of the study helped in eliminating two variables, which are (1) advertisement utilisation ratio, and (2) distribution outlets. According to the respondents, they are not relevant to the Indian context. The study also helped in obtaining the variables that were relevant to the different PLC phases. (The variables were selected based on mean scores and t values of the data collected from the questionnaire). Not only did practicing managers identify these variables, but the variables also find support in the studies of a number of researchers. In all 28 variables were elicited. There were some marketing variables common at the different phases, (5 between introduction and growth phases, 20 between growth and maturity phases, and 4 between maturity and decline phases) but their relative importance was different.

Pilot study—Phase II The focus of this phase of the pilot study was to see how technological developments and marketing programmes (the elements that were common) vary and to examine if any relationships exist between them at different phases of the PLC. It sought to validate (content validity) all the variables selected and, whenever necessary, to modify the scales intended to measure the variables. In addition it also sought to ascertain if the questionnaire developed was eliciting the responses as required and to incorporate any changes in the final instrument suggested by the respondents.

The questionnaire was in three parts. The first part of the questionnaire had questions regarding demographic details of the organisations, like number of employees, products manufactured, sales turnover, and date of incorporation. The second part contained questions related to the marketing programmes for products in the four phases of the PLC. Questions in the third portion of the questionnaire were related to the technological developments, with respect to products and processes done in-house. (Answers to all the questions were elicited using a five point Likert like scale given for terms in the questionnaire representing a variable).

The study was carried out in eleven organisations, in the city of Bangalore (India), manufacturing and marketing industrial machinery. The respondents were senior managers of the marketing and the R&D/engineering functions in the 11 organisations. The public relations officer or the personnel manager in each organisation was contacted and was made to understand the reason for the study. The officers helped in identifying the relevant executives to answer the questionnaire.

The results of the study indicated that marketing programmes and technological developments do vary depending on the phase of the PLC. The results also indicated that the relationship between the two were different at different PLC phases. The study also helped in making the necessary changes in the format of the questions to elicit the required responses. Two more marketing variables were added, which were found to be important by respondents given the changing conditions in the country (the process of liberalisation). The questionnaire was finalised.

EXPLORATION FOR PROBLEM IDENTIFICATION

exploration for problem identification
Such exploration includes surveying earlier literature, observing and studying the phenomenon (system), discussion with experts, attending conferences and seminars, and creatively reflecting on the problem area.

Rarely, if ever, is a research problem offered to a researcher for finding a solution. Initially, problems tend to be disclosed as difficulties for which a lack of clear understanding of a way out exists. Some unsupported hunches may exist in the mind of the individual experiencing the difficulty. These will be couched in a general language and expressed in a matter of fact manner and is typical of management originated problems. In scientific conferences/seminars/symposia problems may be stated in a more definitive language but they still tend to be opinions or broad and general statements. In every case the researcher has to subject such problem statements to rigorous questioning; check whether an earlier research has treated the problem partially or completely; has tackled problems that are not the same as the ones posed, but a slightly different ones. In the end, he must decide whether the problem that is posed is a new one or a modified version of an already treated one. Thus, there are many ways an exploration may be carried out for identifying a research problem, such as:

- **Scanning of earlier research literature**, which is very vital in all academic research. One looks at the knowledge already generated and gaps that exist in it.
- **Observing and studying the phenomena** as a researcher will do when investigating a decision problem faced by the manager for which a research solution is sought. This is typically a system study.
- **Discussions with experts** in the area/executives with considerable decision-making experience, with specific requests for advice. This will provide multiple insights. Interactions with experts are radically affected by the current surge of information technology. E-mail has reduced the time of the transactions and online computer interaction facilitates hastening of the process. Groups of interacting people scattered physically can be brought virtually into a small enclosure for fast interchange of ideas/research details through video teleconferencing.
- **Attending conferences and seminars** and scholarly lectures by eminent scientists and keeping one's mind open for suggestions and indications for research.
- **Brain storming sessions** with a select a group of people, aimed at generating problem ideas.
- **Creatively reflecting** on the problem area after intense questioning and critical enquiry.

In the next two sections, we will discuss in detail research literature survey and systems study as aids to problem exploration.

Literature Survey

literature survey
This is a critical informational analysis procedure and therefore a descriptive research. Literature survey consists of choice of literature, search for location or source, its study and its organization.

The process of literature survey or literature review is a critical informational analysis procedure. Listing of bibliography is not research. Critical evaluation and analysis of research material for purposes of interpretation and comparison requires reflective thinking and can, therefore, be considered descriptive research. In this sense, classical literature review would demand that the researcher provide a critical analysis and comparisons to be called a part of research.

In academic research, literature review holds a key place because any knowledge gained in the research is placed in a total perspective of the existing knowledge and integrated with it. *a priori* the problem is not formulated before the literature review. It is in a sense an outcome of the review. The role of literature review, related to research problems translated from the problems faced by the manager, is only to check whether a similar problem was researched earlier and solved, whether it is totally new, or whether a method in the literature needs a modification to solve the current research problem. Therefore, literature review is close to the problem formulated and is less emphasised and can be brief.

Literature review has four broad aspects: (i) choice of literature, (ii) search for location/source of literature, (iii) study of literature, and (iv) organisation of literature.

Choice of literature In academic research, a researcher gradually gains focus. An area of research is chosen by the student depending upon his interest and practical experience, if any. If he is not a scholar in his area of research, he has to study widely a number of books, journal articles, reports, reviews, and so on. The study can be extensive but not necessarily highly critical. Armed with this background knowledge, he will choose a topic of research of interest to him. He may get an indication of a problem area from his guide and start a more focused literature review, which needs to be selective. He will have to choose portions of books for intensive study, look for reviews of specific books, bibliographies in the problem area, and treatment of techniques and methods peculiar to the problem area or mostly used in it.

choice of literature
Choice of literature means identifying books, journal articles, reports and reviews in the area of research.

Search for location/Source of literature The institution/university where the scholar is carrying out research may have a good library but in most cases that would be inadequate for getting all the literature required for the problem area. However, it may help him to locate the source through indexes to periodicals, which list journal articles in alphabetical order; particularly indexes in special areas like business management, operations research, science and technology, and so on.

search for location
Search of the university library only would be inadequate. Sources, like index to periodicals and special areas, dissertation abstracts, e-libraries, and internet, have also to be searched.

In addition, the most important/widely read journals in the general research area and problem area also have to be located and relevant recent articles are to be obtained. While locating research information in the problem it is desirable to start with the most recent issues of the journals and go sequentially backwards for speedy location. It is very useful to write them down in suitable cards in the format required for the research report.

Dissertation Abstract International is another source for locating research work done in the problem area. Based on its usefulness, checked with the abstract of a particular thesis, a microfilm can be obtained. The theses themselves yield a wealth of information on relevant literature, on methodologies, and analysis types that are generally used.

In addition, computer search libraries are also available in many universities, each having its own search language/syntax. There are many virtual libraries in the World Wide Web that can be searched online. A guide to these are well provided in Cooper and Schindler (1998). Some of the sources of information are listed in the appendix.

Study of literature In recent times, the literature available in any research area is generally voluminous. Care must be taken to organise the material the researcher is studying. He can divide/partition the research literature into three broad categories. Firstly, general literature in the broad area of specialisation has to be browsed quickly, noting only the portion that may have a bearing on the problem area. Secondly, literature related to the problem area in which research is being carried out. This has to be studied intensely and a bibliography may be developed. Summaries of some of the designs adopted, measurements made, and analysis methods and findings may be generated. The gaps must be identified (if the problem is not already coarsely formulated). One of the gaps may be chosen as a problem with the help of the guide/supervisor. Then a very critical review is made of the journal articles, theses, and research reports close to the problem. Their methods, merits, shortcomings, difficulties should be elaborately detailed to be able to efficiently formulate the research problem and investigate it. Critiques may be summarised for each of these and kept in cards or on the computer for use while developing the thesis/report.

study of literature
Three categories of study are: browsing quickly the general literature in the area, intensely studying literature related to the problem, and critically reviewing journal articles, theses and research reports closely related to the problem.

Organisation of the literature The literature studied and noted in the above step should be organised and arranged (may be at a later date) in a meaningful and systematic way for presentation in the thesis or report. The following points are important.

- The sequencing of literature presentation should be from the general and broad to the specific and critical, leading to the problem statement.
- The general literature should occupy fewer pages in the review than the specific one. In general literature only the prominent ones or milestones need to be dwelt upon and others may be clubbed together in a summarised manner, for example, "A large number

of studies on technology developments are experiential ones [Levitt, 1965, Smallwood, 1973, Cliffort, 1977, Pessemier, 1977, Enis et al, 1977, and others]" (Gash, 2000)

- In the literature, close to the problem the details of each study should be specified, classified, and critically evaluated. Shortcomings should be discussed and shown how they are related to the research problem at hand. These features can be depicted in a taxonomy. For example, the problems of deterministic scheduling of batch processor (BP) production includes several features like the number of batch processors, job, processing time, and objectives. The utility of taxonomy is that it can help the researchers and practitioners to identify the type of problem that they are confronting. If the characteristics define a well known problem, then the existing algorithms can be applied with/without any additional features to solve the problem. On the other hand, if the problem has not received much research attention, then a new BP scheduling problem could be defined. For details see an illustrative example in Annexure 4.1.

organization of literature
The literature should be organized in a systematic way as follows: sequencing the literature from the general to the specific leading to the problem, indicating milestones in the general literature, detailing and critically evaluating the literature closely related to the problem using taxonomies wherever necessary.

meta analysis
This is a systematic and statistical examination of several research studies in an area to synthesize their findings.

Meta analysis* Meta analysis is a relatively recent development. It is a systematic and statistical examination of several previous research studies, in order to combine their findings or synthesise the researches. The statistical methods employed cover a wide range (examples are location of data collected, level of analysis, suitable size, types of sample, occupational subjects, number and the type of dependent variables, time frame, nature of verification, and validation of results). The statistical procedures used in meta analysis are essentially the same as those used for analysis of collected research data.

When a large body of research studies is available in an important topic or area of research, the research techniques used, measurement approaches, the type of units studied, the analysis procedures, and experimental designs may vary enormously. To assess what knowledge these studies have added is indeed a research effort in its own right. The task of integrating the research efforts by simple narration or description was once considered adequate; but the sheer volume and variability of current research efforts make it no longer tenable. Glass (1981) referred to the newer approach to such integration needing statistical analysis and sophisticated measurement techniques as meta analysis of research. Meta analysis is integrative in approach and is an analysis of analyses, which is distinct from primary research.

For example, many researchers studied the current practice of reviews of research and found them wanting in critical examination of methods and analysis, completeness of review (partial review), refined representation of findings, consideration of research design, result relationship, and disclosure of methods of review. Generally research integration does not employ unambiguous and explicit methods with which another scientist could replicate the findings. Meta analysis is supposed to overcome most of these shortcomings. Meta analysis is nothing more than the attitude of data analysis applied to quantitative summaries of identical experiments (researches). It is not a technique but a point of view. Meta analysis is the quantitative (using statistical methods) influence of a particular study on the findings in general. It is considered an approach based on empirical analysis not *a priori* on opinions or judgment.

In other words, it looks at the forest not the trees. Good generalisation ignoring insignificant differences is all that matters in meta analysis. In the process, research methods are applied to "characteristics and findings of research studies". A number of meta analysis cases are described by Glass et al (1981).

The process of searching for literature and finding relevant studies in the modern context is not one that particularly inspires confidence in the researcher and is in fact often beset with feelings of frustration. In reviewing a large body of literature, the researcher cannot ignore unpublished material. Glass, et al (1981) conclude from their empirical studies of publication bias that "failing to represent unpublished studies in a meta analysis may produce misleading generalisation". Meta analysis serves the purpose of not only measuring the research findings in an integrated way but also of describing, classifying and coding the research studies. Mea-

* This section may be skipped by non-research students.

suring study findings may involve (i) making use of statistical significance tests, statistics, and their associated probabilities (for example, significant and non-significant).

The chi-square method may be applied to a group of studies having different significance levels to yield a significance, or otherwise, of the group, a standardised mean difference, pooled estimates of standard deviation, and others. Of course, it is necessary to use different procedures for different kinds of studies (for example, experimental design and correlational studies).

The techniques of analysis used in meta analysis are, in general, multivariate data analysis procedure (see Chapters 17 and 18). Univariate analysis for the purpose of simple description of research studies is also useful in gaining insights into research literature. Multiple linear regression, analysis of variance, inferential methods of statistics, non parametric methods, and Monte Carlo simulation can also be used in meta analysis. An important point to note is that modifications to many estimates, coefficients, and scores are required to be carefully considered. For a detailed treatment of the subject the reader is referred to the book by Glass et al (1981). An example of meta analysis is shown in Annexure 4.2.

System Study*

System study is the counterpart of literature study, and surveys the phenomena of problem identification. The objectives of system study, in general, are, (a) to improve the system, (b) to determine general theories of how a system develops, and (c) to advance science [De Greene, 1970). Churchman et al (1957) and Checkland (2000)] discuss this problem in a classical way. The study of the system is directed towards four major aspects of the problem: (1) The decision system, (2) objectives of the system, (3) the environmental system, and (4) the options open to the executives for action. It follows from the above that system study is essentially one of understanding (i) the information flows and how these information flows are made use of by the decision maker, (ii) the transactions taking place between organisations and its environment, and (iii) the informational transfers taking place among the several functional components like production, marketing, R&D, and others.

system study
System study is the counterpart of literature survey and surveys the phenomenon for problem identification. Four major aspects of the problem—decision system, objective, environmental system, and the option open for the action—are to be studied. The steps in a system study are: a formal definition, detailing the system influences, breaking down the system into major sub-system, detailing sub-system activities, development of total informational flow.

Churchman et al (1957) propose human neural networks for an understanding of the way in which the researcher might develop the information networks in an organisation. Thus, system study is a basis for determining:

(a) An understanding of the problem, environment, and informational flows from the environment to the organisational system.
(b) The feasibility of a particular approach to problem solving.

The study of the system from the point of view of problem-solving and model-building would follow, more or less, the following steps.

1. *Formal definition of the system* General definitions are inadequate and root definitions have to be developed for the total system and sub-systems comprised by it. (Wilson 1984). Each system/sub-system is viewed from various angles (various people or organisational sub-units) and a world view of the system is developed. It is necessary in system study to identify the range of world views and select the most appropriate one from the point of view of the problem under investigation. [Checkland (2000), Kapsoi Agnes and Mayers Margaret (2001)].
2. *Detailing features of system influences* These influences are from higher systems of which the system under study is only a part. For example, for a manufacturing organisation the following influences may be relevant.
    1. Nature of the product
    2. Nature of demand
    3. Relationship with other manufacturing organisations in the industry

* Basics of systems concepts are briefed in Appendix A1.

4. Interactions with statutory constraints
5. Local customs
6. Competition

3. *Division of system into major sub-systems* This particular activity emphasises the need for an analytical approach in the initial stage of the study to be followed by a synthesis at the end. If a manufacturing organisation is being studied, the sub-systems that may be relevant are: (a) the procurement system, (b) the material control system, (c) the planning system, (d) the shop control system, and (e) the man-machine system in the shop. For further development of sub-systems, root definitions are used for each sub-system. A careful selection of root definition (which is nothing but the real objective of the sub-system with respect to the problem at hand) is very important at this stage.
4. *Detailing each activity of each sub-system* The level of detail depends upon the problem and the time available to the researcher. An ideal approach to this problem is to check whether each activity can be a good source of questioning the sub-system functioning and performance. Each activity is subjected to questioning so that the way it is performed, the resources it requires, who performs it, and how well it is performed can be obtained.
5. *Developing the total information flow system* Using the detailed information in the first four steps, the total information flow system is developed. These information flow systems cover procedures and information requirements for decision-making. Systems analysis techniques (Barish, 1957) are used for efficient representation of the information, as shown in Fig. 4.3.
6. Each of the activities is expanded to give greater detail of the information model, that is, each block in the block diagram is now exploded into greater detail.

   The above steps must be carried out keeping in mind the following points:

   (i) People involved in system/sub-system /activity should be communicated with.
   (ii) Resources needed for system/sub-system/activity should be noted.
   (iii) Controls provided by the organisation for monitoring the system/sub-system/activity should be detailed.
   (iv) The way performance is reported in respect of system/sub-system/activity should be obtained.
   (v) Management requirements of control and monitoring and performance of any system/sub-system/activity should be determined and defined.
   (vi) A seminar with the managers with the results of the system study is useful.
   (vii) Appreciation of the capabilities of the system/sub-system/activity through an experience matrix is desirable. This is a matrix developed using potential existing in sub-system areas of the organisation against task areas. The cells of the matrix have numbers ranging from 1 to 7, as shown below:

   1 = enhanced understanding
   2 = improved organisation of information
   3 = new organisation structure and/or process
   4 = improved level of service
   5 = better utilisation of resources
   6 = reduced operation costs
   7 = increased productivity

The system study detailed in this section will provide the framework for an information system in which the decisions are made and will facilitate the formulation of the research problem by studying the decision-making process. This will be further discussed in the Section on formulation of the problem in model building context (p 93).

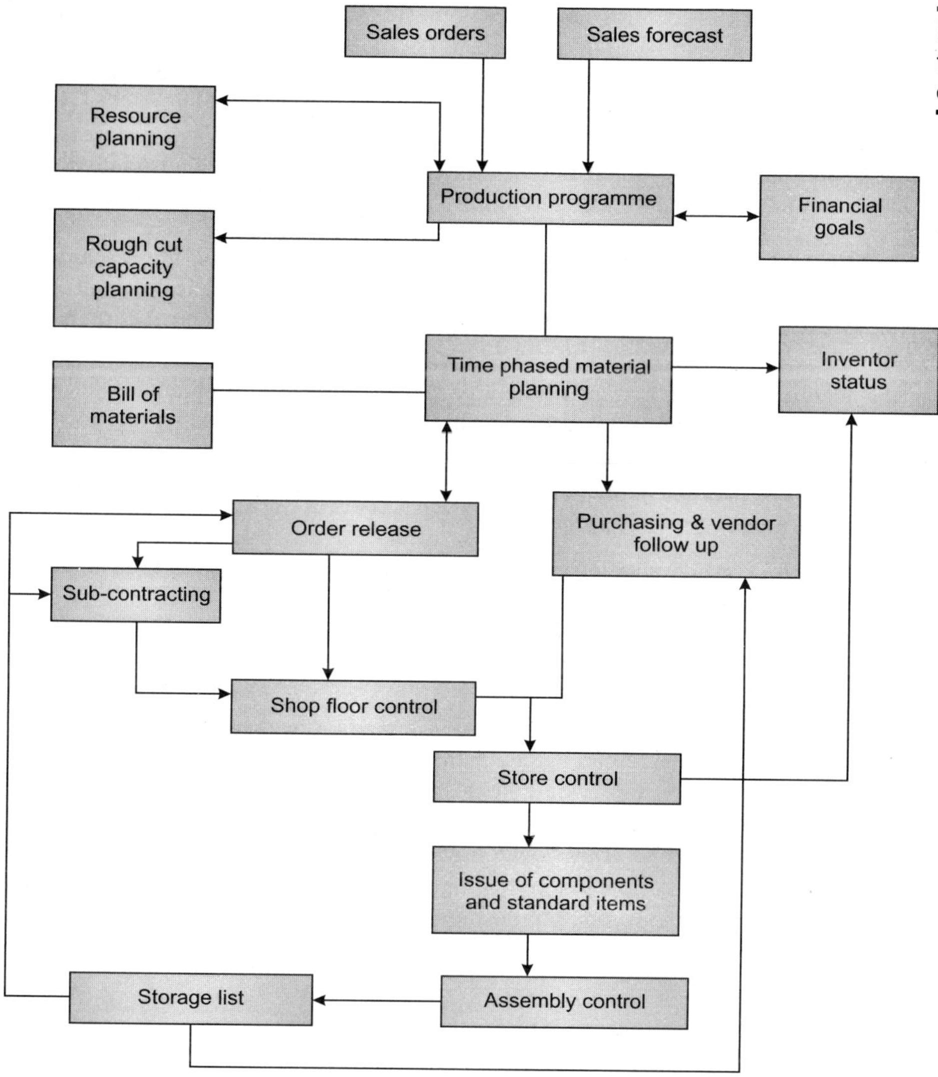

Fig. 4.3 Information flow system for production control

Errors of Problem Identification in Research

At the stage of problem identification, it is necessary for the researcher to be aware of some of the errors that may creep in. These errors are associated with the type of problem dealt with in research. Some of the problems may be environmentally generated. Others may appear as technical deficiencies in the organisation, such as inadequate control systems and ineffective leadership. Some other errors may be due to the self-aggrandising behaviour of the manager through which decisions tend to be made for the benefit of the individual (manager). An identification error relates to large resources being committed either to the solution of a wrong problem or to the pursuit of solving a problem that does not exist. These are termed Type III errors. Some methods of reducing Type III errors are discussed by Graham and others (1982). They detail three approaches, namely a reductionistic approach, a systems approach, and a dialectical approach.

HYPOTHESIS GENERATION

Introduction

The identification and formulation of the research problem is one of the most difficult phases of research faced by a student. The problems of management research may be classified into two major categories. The first centres around hypothesis testing or predicting, with or without statistical analysis, using empirical data to develop or extend theories. The second emphasises mathematical models in a decision-making environment. Though the broad steps for research appear to be the same, there are some distinctive features for each category. The purpose of this chapter is to delineate some of the differences. As theory develops progressively, the researcher tends to address problems in the higher rungs of the ladder of abstraction. It will be noted that with this development, the number of variables grow; and as variables grow the formulation of hypothesis tends to become more abstract and complex. The research design becomes more sophisticated and may tend to introduce constraints on the research process itself. The demand for development of newer research designs is increasingly felt. However, careful and detailed work is necessary at whatever level of abstraction one tries to theorise and set hypotheses.

theoretical framework

This is a precursor to hypothesis generation. Some of the features are identification of relevant variables, discussions of relationships among variables, indications of nature and direction of relationships, explanations of the expected relationship and development of a schematic diagram of the framework.

First the features of a theoretical framework are discussed as a precursor to generating hypothesis. Next, variables of different kinds will be discussed, followed by origins of hypotheses. The problem of generating hypothesis will be discussed next.

Sekharan (2000) sets down some of the common features of the theoretical framework that are necessary for evolving hypotheses.

1. The variables considered relevant to the study should be clearly identified and labelled in the discussions.
2. The discussions should state how two or more variables are related to each other. This should be done for the important relationships that are theorised to exist among the variables.
3. If the nature and direction of the relationships can be theorised on the basis of the findings from previous research, then there should be an indication in the discussions as to whether the relationships would be positive or negative.
4. There should be a clear explanation of why we would expect these relationships to exist. The arguments could be drawn from previous research findings.
5. A schematic diagram of the theoretical framework should be developed so that one can clearly visualise the theorised relationships. An illustrative example of theoretical framework is shown in Annexure 4.3.

Variables

variables

Variables relevant to problem definition are independent variables and dependent variables. These include moderator variables and intervening variables.

In generating variables or relationships, creative problem-solving methods can be gainfully used. One of the effective methods that can be used for this purpose is the Interpretive Structural Modeling (ISM) developed by Warfield (1972, 1973, 1973a, 1974).

There are several kinds of variables that are relevant to a problem definition and hypothesis formulation*. The following are among the most important of these.

- Independent Variable (IV) or predictor variable, which influences the Dependent Variable (DV) or criterion variable.
- The dependent variable or criterion variable is of primary importance for research.

There can be more than one independent/dependent variable in a problem situation. Two other kinds of variables—moderator variable and intervening variable—also need to be defined.

moderator variables

A moderator variable has contingent influence on the relationship between the independent and dependent variables.

Moderator variable (Modulating variable) The modulating variable (MV) has contingent influence on the relationships between the independent variable and the dependent variable. The following examples illustrate this.

Environment variables in an organisational study are independent variables and the performance variables of the organisation are dependent variables. An organisation's performance is

* The way in which these variables are named is slightly different for statistical modelling procedures as compared to those for operation research modelling procedures.

influenced by its environment. If the environment is placid, then the performance of the organisation may be very high in terms of market share and profits, but if the environment becomes more turbulent, the performance is going to be affected and profit and market shares may fall. But this relationship between performance and environment can be altered by the development of a suitable strategy by the company (Fig. 4.4) such that the profits and market shares do not fall with the increased competition as much as before. The role of a strategy is to alter the relationship between the environment and performance and, therefore, strategy is a moderator variable.

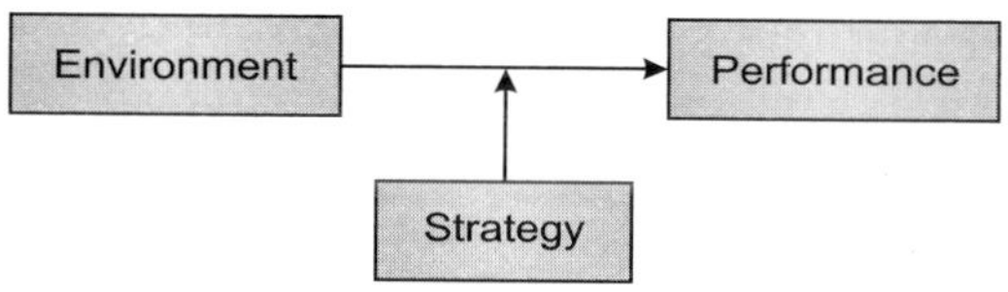

Fig. 4.4 Strategy as a moderator variable

Other examples could be organisational climate as an independent variable, job performance as a dependent variable, and job design as a moderator variable. Similarly, the influence of training (independent variable) on worker performance (dependent variable) can be modulated by willingness to work or motivation (modulating variable).

intervening variables

An intervening variable has temporal dimension not adding to the variance of the dependent variables as explained by the independent variables, but is necessary in the relationship.

Intervening variable Another kind of variable is recognised in most social psychology research. This is called intervening variable. The intervening variable has a temporal dimension. It does not add to the variance of the dependent variable as explained by the independent variable but it is a necessary variable, included in the relationship with the time dimension. Fig. 4.5 makes this point clear.

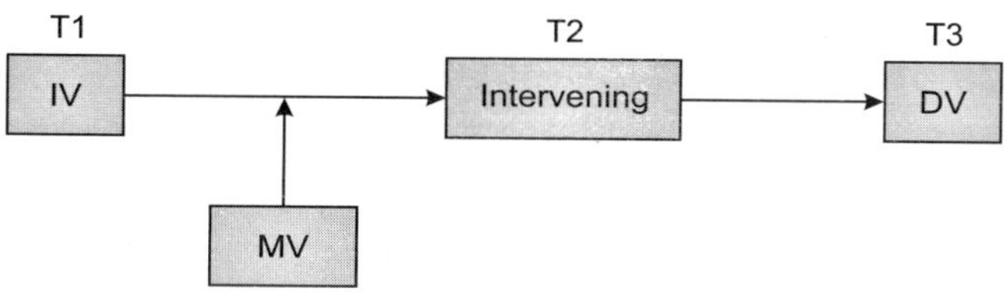

Fig. 4.5 Intervening variable

Illustration Ettlie and Bridges (1982) studied the impact of turbulence in the environment on the innovativeness of 54 organisations. Earlier studies concentrated on the measurement of environmental uncertainty. But the relationship between environmental uncertainty and adoption of innovation was not directly studied. The results of the earlier studies presented a controversial picture in that while one study proposed that environmental uncertainty is positively related to organisational innovation, the other study suggested that complexity of a firm's management (diversified skills) affects the firm's perception of the environment and reduces the perceived environmental uncertainty, thereby, affecting the firm's strategy.

Further, productive capabilities are enhanced. These contradictions were interpreted by the authors as a suggestion that environmental uncertainty influences organisational innovativeness through some aspect of the firm's strategy. They proposed this as the variable of technology policy. Several research questions are raised. The first is the direction of this relationship. Again, there is a controversy in research literature. One study suggests a direct relationship and another a reverse one. The second is whether the relationship is recursive or non-recursive. Does the causation flow from perceived environmental uncertainty or does innovativeness cause change in uncertainty? Is there any relationship between perceived uncertainty and the actual one. Taken together, these studies indicate that technology policy, in the long term, has a profound influence on the innovative behaviour of the firm and is treated as the intervening variable in the study and several propositions are made based on this premise.

The propositions set for testing were:

- The impact of perceived environmental uncertainty on organisational innovativeness operates through the intervening variable of organisational technology policy. The direction of this relationship is not specified.
- Actual (objective measures of) environmental uncertainty and perceived environmental uncertainty are likely to operate independently on a firm's innovativeness.
- Different patterns of new product development and adoption of major and minor process innovations will occur depending on the specific, dominant causes of a firm's environmental uncertainty (for example, suppliers versus competitors versus customers)
- An aggressive organisational technology policy will result in the existence of a special organisational group to evaluate new process technology, which, in turn, will increase the likelihood of the adoption of major, but not necessarily minor, process innovations.

Ettlie and Bridges first developed a definition of organisational technology policy and developed a 46 item measurement device for it. The information gathered from the 54 organisations was analysed using factor analyses and the causal model was developed using path analysis.

The results indicated that the global measure of environmental uncertainty has two components, active and passive. The active components act directly on the future innovativeness and the passive components act on the future innovativeness only through the organisation's strategic adjustments, that is, through the intervening variable of organisational technology policy.

Characteristics of a Good Hypothesis

good hypothesis
A good hypothesis must be conceptually clear, empirically based, must be specific in order to facilitate testing, and must be deduced from theory.

Since generation of hypothesis is typically a creative process, it is very likely that a large number of hypotheses will be generated at one time or the other by any researcher with respect to a research problem. Many hypotheses are entertained for a short duration but a good number of them are allowed to fizzle out. Gleaning good and useful hypotheses from a number of randomly generated ones is possible only by a rigorous mental standard for acceptance. Since acceptance of a hypothesis involves putting in a lot of effort through instrument design, data collection, and statistical analyses, it is necessary to be a hard evaluator of a hypothesis from the point of view of usefulness.

1. A hypothesis must be conceptually clear, meaningful, communicable, grounded in previous knowledge, and commonly acceptable by research workers in the field. In other words, a hypothesis should be compatible with the bulk of the existing scientific knowledge (Bunge, 1967, p229).
2. A hypothesis should be empirically based. If it is theoretically derived or obtained from value judgment, the researcher should seek measurable facts in the phenomenon relating to the problem, in order that it may be worded properly.
3. A hypothesis must be specific in order to facilitate its testing. The specificity can be evaluated by seeking whether it can be tested quantitatively using operational definitions. If necessary, a hypothesis can be split up into sub-hypotheses, which are more specific. This may need some sort of a conceptual analysis. For example, it may be hypothesised that educational standards are declining. This observation is very general and needs to be split up into levels (primary, secondary, higher secondary, and university), and to the location, whether in states or in institutions; operational definitions of standards must be obtained; and features of education have to be delineated before many sub-hypotheses can be formulated with more specific questions relating to teaching methods, vocational guidance, training of teachers, campus facilities, and motivation of teachers and others.

4. It is desirable that the hypotheses are formulated so that the existing testing techniques can be used. Many times the structure of the testing techniques help the formulation and wording of hypotheses. However, it is not necessary that a strongly felt hypotheses should be relinquished because a testing method is not available to the researcher or is not identified by him. Formulating a hypothesis itself is a game in scientific terms and can become a future work for related studies until testing procedures are developed (many examples, like Marxian socioeconomic hypotheses, exist; (refer Goode and Hatt, 1952). The best way to tackle this aspect is to refer to conventional hypothesis testing practices by other researchers in the relevant area.
5. Hypotheses should be deduced from theory (Kerlinger, 1986) in order to extend or enhance it. Hypotheses unconnected with theory are not desirable since relationships are tested in hypotheses. A precedence is always desirable, except possibly in a totally unexplored research territory.

Classification of hypothesis may be according to:

(i) Form (Syntactical)
(ii) Reference (Semantic)
(iii) Cognitive Status (Epistemological) (Bunge, 1967)

Statistical hypotheses are examples of syntactical grouping; local or global aspects covered in the hypothesis indicate precision of the hypothesis; References to experience or fact, or both, are semantic. In the epistemological classification, the emphasis is on inception, observation, and depth of hypothesis.

Origins of a Hypothesis

There are several origins for a hypothesis. Some of them are:

1. Hypotheses related to decision-making are products of managerial and organisational value systems in the culture. When research is carried out in decision-making in a different culture, the value systems change and a hypothesis relevant to one culture may not be relevant to another. Replications of research in one culture, carried out in another are still valid and are useful for extending theory across cultures or formulating different sets of hypotheses. Since different cultures emphasise different value systems, scientific questions have got to be relevant to the cultural settings. (Section on alternative perspectives on management research in Chapter 1)
2. Scientific theory gives direction to research on the basis of what is known. Juxtaposition of logical reasoning on these theories would yield further hypotheses.
3. Observation of nature or phenomenon in other disciplines for causal relationships could be a good source of hypothesis for management research. But such analogies have to be pursued carefully and with caution. Analogies are suggestive but beyond this they are hazardous and must be very carefully evaluated. Analogy may be substantive (similar in kind) or structural (similar systems).
4. Personal experiences or viewpoints, idiosyncrasies or 'bees in the bonnet' could also be sources of hypothesis.
5. A deviant case may provide a new hypothesis. It could refute a hypothesis that might or might not have been verified in an earlier testing.
6. Intuitively found hypotheses are those that spontaneously occur to the researcher. But this normally happens after a lot of logical reasoning, much observation, deliberate thinking, and extended pondering.
7. Hypothesis may be deductively obtained from stronger propositions as logical consequences or derivations.
8. A hypothesis may also be obtained using the Cuckoo technique. In this, a theory in a completely different field is used to derive a hypothesis (biological theories in organisation theory development; growth of a species in technology diffusion studies). Considerable use of probability theory is made in such hypothesis generation.

origins of a hypothesis
A hypothesis may originate from cultural differences, a juxtaposition of logical reasoning on theories, suggestive analogies (which may be substantive or structural), idiosyncrasies, a deviant case, spontaneous intuition, deduction from stronger hypotheses, and by using Cuckoo technique.

constructing hypothesis

In hypothetico-deductive method, initially a broad problem statement is made. Then theoretical framework is developed. A clear problem statement is made and broken into a set of hypotheses using critical analysis. In qualitative methods, theoretical framework is carefully avoided, propositions or untested hypotheses are continuously developed parallely during data collection using enquiry from within.

Process of Hypothesis Generation

It is not advisable to state a well-structured procedure for developing a hypothesis, primarily because it is a creative process. However, there are some general approaches that will be useful for the researcher to keep in mind while constructing hypotheses. The intention of this section is to present such general approaches with systematic procedures developed by various researchers in the field.

When a broad problem statement has to be made, a quick review of literature or a quick pilot study of the phenomenon relating to a particular area of interest of the researcher is usually undertaken. Preliminary interviews held with people in organisations, meetings with executives, and participation in conferences provide a broad knowledge base in the area of interest. The researcher may then attempt to make broad statements of several problems that are felt to be useful and worth investigating. The main purpose of such a search is to ensure that important aspects of the problem are not ignored and aggregate viewpoints and results, both in research and practice, are obtained. This will also help in clarifying the problem to a greater extent. It may also help in determining the relevance of the problem for investigation and may make the investigator more assured. This helps the researcher in appreciating two vital aspects:

1. Knowledge of the research area can be demonstrated by him, and by reflecting creatively upon the area he can generate a few broad problem statements.
2. Theoretical framework which he may intend to develop for his problem is built essentially on the theoretical work that has already been done. This will ensure that the problem and framework of the research are well grounded in theory as well as supported by empirical feedback.

The process is shown in Fig. 4.6 and will presumably end up with (a) definition of a problem as a gap, or (b) a problem as an unanswered or inadequately answered question. Once a problem is clearly stated, it must be converted into a set of hypotheses. In order to convert it into a set of hypotheses, it will be necessary to develop a set of variables that are relevant to the problem stated. Further, a theoretical framework is a conceptual model of the relationships among the set of variables. Such a framework must be built as a consequence of critically analysing the findings in literature in a systematic and classified manner.

Fig. 4.6 Process of obtaining problem statement

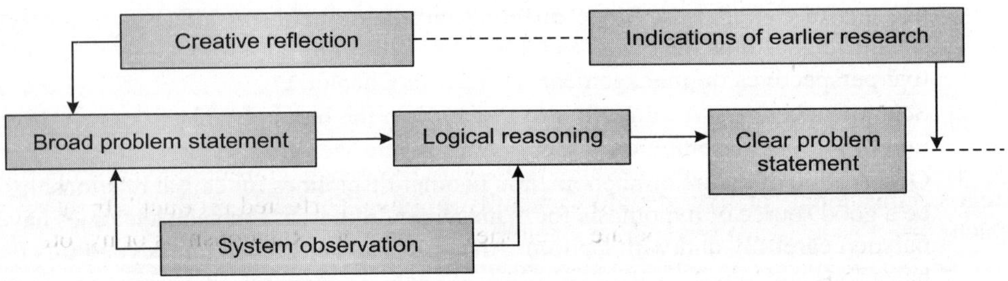

According to Goode and Hatt (1952), there are three main difficulties in generating hypotheses.

1. Absence of a theoretical framework
2. Absence of logical utilisation of theoretical framework
3. Lack of knowledge of research techniques available for phrasing the hypotheses

A suggested method for overcoming these problems is to select the area of study. Replication of earlier work can be attempted as a way of starting research. In management and social science research, this method is useful as cultural effects may influence the relevance of the intended hypothesis. If cultural effects do not have significant influence, such replication may add new knowledge. Sometimes a look at the data that is collected in this process may reveal the possibilities of developing hypotheses. But, generally, a more rational approach for a study would be to start with a broad theory, deduce a likely relationship from it, and formulate it as a hypothesis. Such a formulation of hypothesis tends to be general and ambiguous and not specific. It is good to have a working hypothesis and later on modify it suitably after the research programme. Assertions based on commonsense may be used for generating hypotheses after critically examining them. Commonsense is not integral to science, and as such commonsense observations are acceptable in investigations only as hypotheses to be tested. One thumb rule could be to grapple with commonsense statements in the problem area. Complex, ideal types of relationships (Goode & Hatt, 1952) can be used for investigation. These are logically derived relationships from existing theory and these relationships can be tested empirically to extend the theory (Fig. 4.7).

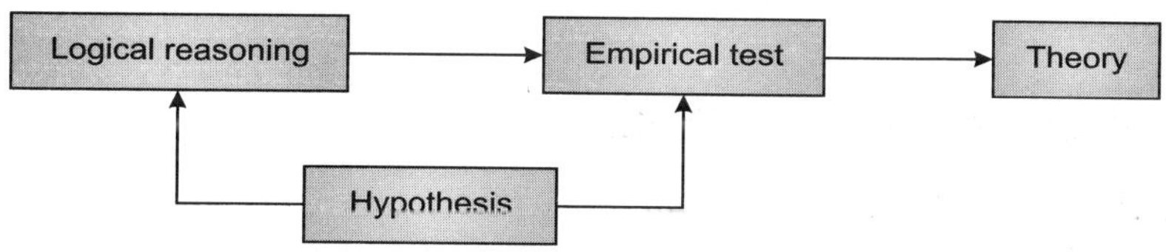

Fig. 4.7 Process of developing theory

These provide an opportunity for an analytically oriented investigator to generate hypotheses without looking at the empirical world. Examples are problems of inventory and production.

Two examples of hypothesis generation are given in Annexure 4.4.

Hypothesis Generation Using Qualitative Methods

Writers like Glaser and Strauss (1967), Patton (1980), Maanen et al (1982), Smith and Dainty (1991), and Gummesson (2000) have stressed the importance of qualitative methods in management research, particularly in organisational research. What was discussed earlier followed more, if not entirely, the natural science mode of research. Hypothesis generation, which is the main objective of most qualitative research methods, takes a stance that is different from the one taken by the scientist approaching the research using hypothetico-deductive methods.

Grounded theory (Glaser and Strauss, 1967), which is the discovery of theory from data, is considered a major task of the researcher. The theory derived from data is illustrated by characteristic examples. The theory, which is a set of propositions or untested hypotheses, is continuously developed during data collection. Collection and analysis of data are parallel activities. As more data is gathered, the theory goes on emerging or developing. The main difference between the quantitative and qualitative research is that in the former a theoretical framework is necessary to develop a hypothesis, whereas in the latter, a theoretical framework is carefully avoided so that there is no bias in the generation of hypotheses (theory). In sociology and organisational research, development of sound theories is considered very important. A theory is considered "an ever developing entity, not as a perfected product". In such an approach, theory is analysed to generate categories of concepts. Relationships or hypotheses are developed in an attempt to generalise the relationships among these categories. These are, of course, untested but they do get some support from the data, though not rigorously. As the work progresses with the phenomena under study, the data are collected, coded, and analysed, and the type and frequency of further data collection are decided upon. Thus, whatever sample is progressively covered, it is by theoretical sampling, for the purpose of hypothesis generation.

The qualitative method, as described above, leans heavily on 'enquiry from within' the community, organisation, or group. They use methods of unobtrusive observation, discussion, participant-observation (to be dealt with later), case studies, and rely on being immersed 'physically and psychologically' in the phenomenon. The decided advantage of this method, discussed by Gummesson (2000), is that it provides access to the facts, perception, and relationships in an organisation, which the researcher from outside (like an academic or a person who specialises in natural science) cannot obtain. Therefore, the hypotheses/theory generated from the data gathered from these methods tend to be important and useful from a practical point of viewpoint.

In these, the hypothesis is based on case examination and is inductive in nature. Bunge (1967) discusses two kinds of inductive generalisation:

1. First degree induction is one in which inference is made from the particular to the general.
2. Second degree induction is the generalisation of generalisation. Take for example, an inventory control decision. When order quantity, a decision variable, is increased, holding costs increase but order costs decrease. This is the first generalisation. If this is extended, stating that whenever any decision is made, with the increase in a decision variable one cost goes up and another cost goes down, it becomes a second degree induction.

FORMULATION OF THE PROBLEM

Model Building Context

Often, in empirical research, the concept of a problem is obtained from an observation of the phenomenon. The problem, as in many OR type modelling situations, is either posed by the practitioner to the researcher or is identified by the researcher on observing the system. However, the academic or theoretical researcher may study the models developed earlier and identify their lacunae or inadequacies. He may start researching into the models in order to improve them or to modify them to suit certain observed situations not so far treated in research. In such cases, he has to relax certain assumptions that earlier researchers had made, add to them, or modify the structure of the problem. However, in this section we will predominantly deal with a problem that is felt by the practicing manager. The problem will be expressed by the manager in terms of certain symptoms or even personal viewpoints, which are communicated to the researcher. The researcher observes the real world through a systematic study of the setting in which the symptoms are observed (This has already been dealt with in detail in the section on system study earlier in this chapter).

Here attention will be focused on those aspects of diagnosis or investigation directly involving the detailed formulation of the problem. The problem itself is split up into its components.

1. The decision maker and his objectives
2. The environment of the system
3. The alternative courses of action open to the decision maker

Such splitting of a problem into its components is necessary in order to ensure that the solution obtained by the researcher has a higher chance of implementation and that any significant aspect of the problem is not overlooked or a superfluous aspect is unduly considered (a protection against Type I/Type II errors).

The main considerations in problem formulation are the following:

1. Appreciation of particular aspects of the system, which the manager desires to maximise or minimise.
2. Understanding of constraints that hamper the manager's freedom in choosing the resources the way he would like to, in achieving his objective as in (1) above.
3. Delineation of the boundary conditions of the system that influence his decisions.
4. Alternative courses of action that the manager/researcher is cognisant of.

decision-making structure

Decision-making structure gives information on who sets policies and objectives, on how they are set, on procedures for their approval, evaluation and execution.

For each one of the above considerations, either a new mathematical representation or a modification to an existing one is needed. The components of the problems are discussed in detail in the following sections.

Decision Maker and His Objectives

A study of the decision-making structure will give information regarding who sets policies in the organisation and how it is set. Procedures for approval of expenditure, procedures for executing a decision, procedures for evaluating the outcome of a decision and the information that is generated by discussion with the decision-makers in the organisation are not directly relevant for formulating the problem; but they provide a guiding (therefore constraining) framework for problem formulation.

objectives
Objectives can be classified as maintenance objectives in which the managers keep up the past performance and accomplishment objectives in which a strategy for growth and enhanced performance are dynamically chalked out.

Objectives The objectives can be classified as maintenance objectives and accomplishment objectives. The maintenance objectives, in which the managers would like to keep up the past performance of the organisation, are based on antecedents. In the second case, the decision maker is more dynamic and chalks out a strategy for growth and enhanced performance. The objectives of the decision-maker alone will not wholly reflect those of the organisation. There may be others, whose objectives sometimes become critical to the performance of the organisation. It may appear that getting at an objective is an easy process, but it never is usually an easy one. When diverse sets of objectives are given by various managers in the organisation, it becomes necessary to edit them. While editing the objectives the researcher should look for (a) independence of several objectives. If objective A implies objective B, then B is eliminated. For example, when Rate of Internal Return (ROI) is given as an objective, profit as an objective may be eliminated, as getting maximum ROI implies getting maximum profits. Another objective may be that maximising sales promotion may include advertising. When similar or essentially same objectives are identified, they should be combined.

Environment

The study of the environment of the organization is, in fact, key to proper problem formulation. Aspects like, kind of competition, governmental policies, and statutory regulations have to be clearly understood before recommending a particular course of action to the manager. For example, when competition is based on quality, for a high cost consumer item like the automobile, cost reduction approaches may get little consideration as a course of action. This is because the market may not be sensitive to changes in prices of automobiles. Then environmental aspects like plant capacity, availability of sub-contractors, availability of technology, and budgets to various functional groups also influence the course of action. For example, even though sufficient plant capacity exists for most production plans, certain kinds of machine capacities may have to be sub-contracted because of shortage of those specific machine capacities. It may then be necessary to optimise the plan considering the extra cost of sub-contracting against the cost of machine idle time.

These environmental aspects will help the researcher introduce constraints on internal and external availability of resources into his model.

Alternative Courses of Action

The courses of action available to the decision-maker include those that already exist or those that he cognitively comprehends. It also includes those that the researcher might develop during the course of an investigation. The researcher will have to evaluate the existing alternatives for their capabilities of accomplishing the edited objectives. If he finds that they are not efficient, he may develop new alternatives that are not originally cognitively available to the decision-maker. In either case, the choice of an alternative has to be related to its efficiency in achieving the objectives (see Section on the formulation of effectiveness function later in the chapter).

As in the case of objectives, it is necessary to edit the alternatives obtained. It may be done by any one of the following means:

1. Eliminate previously tried alternatives which were found unsuitable.
2. Eliminate those that demand time and funds beyond what the management can provide.
3. Consider whether the short-term objectives or long term ones are emphasised. For example, in an inventory control procedure, if short-term benefits are to be obtained, the more costly items can be controlled using individual inventory models. If, however, policies have to be developed for long term control of the overall inventory, policy models will have to be developed and aggregate control becomes more important.

Scenarios and Structural Modelling

structural modelling
In structural modelling the scenarios of management structure and interrelationships are developed for identifying the patterns of the mess or the problem. It narrows down the problem-space to be subsequently modelled by transforming the communicated perceptions of the managers into a systematic presentation.

The conceptual framework, emphasised in fundamental research, is very relevant to mathematical modelling for decisional research. As far as gaps in the theory or research are the origins of the research problem, a theoretical or conceptual framework arises necessarily out of a critical review of research literature. However, when the research problem emerges from the empirical world of management, where problems are experienced, model development has to be well-grounded in the system that is observed. The framework for the model can be obtained by generating the scenario, the major elements of a management structure, and the inter-relationships among them for identifying the broad patterns of the mess or the problem. This is accomplished by structural modelling (Finlay, 1985 and Geoffrion, 1987), which will selectively provide a narrowed down problem-space to be subsequently modelled. Structural modelling helps in transforming the perceptions of the manager about his problems and context, into a systematic presentation of the scenario, problem-space, and the portion of the problem-space that needs to be modelled in mathematical terms. This transformation can take a soft system approach, as described in Chapter 3. The emphasis is on systems thinking and defining specific goals of the system. Structural modelling, distinct from the detailed mathematical modelling, as highlighted by Finlay (1985), is shown in the Fig. 4.8.

Fig. 4.8 The link between structural and detailed modelling (Source: Finlay, 1985)

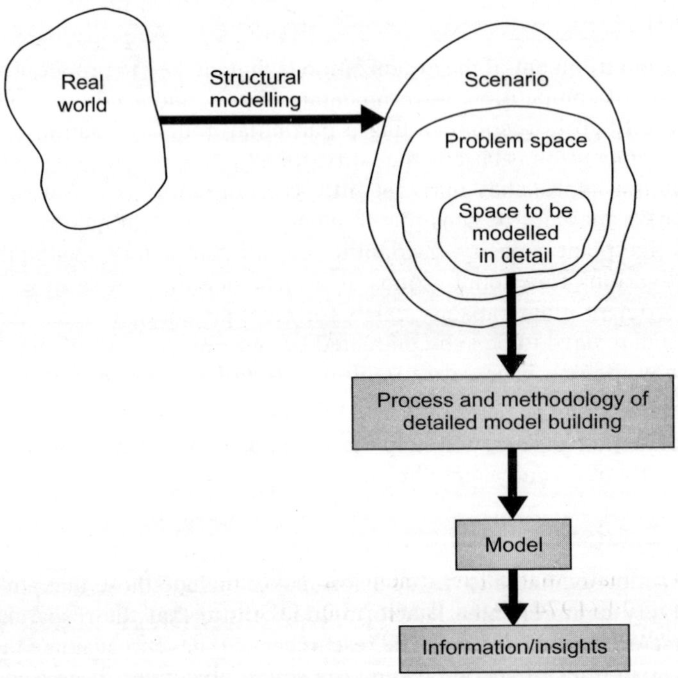

The environment and the system are two parts of the overall system in which the problem is experienced or embedded. The environment itself is further divided into local environment and external environment. The local environment significantly influences the managers' decisions and is in turn influenced by his decisions, for example, other parts of the organisation. The external environment is comparatively immune to his decisions but has effects on his decisions (Fig. 4.9). Key variables are defined for each of these sub-systems. The interaction of the local environment, external environment, and the system are then studied using well-defined variables.

A list of such variables will be useful in the structural modelling process. The constraints in the system are limitations on the range of values that these variables can take. This applies to both the system and its environment.

Finally, the relationships and constraints are expressed verbally in a language that is suitable for developing the detailed model. An illustrative example of system study and problem formulation is shown in Annexure 4.5.

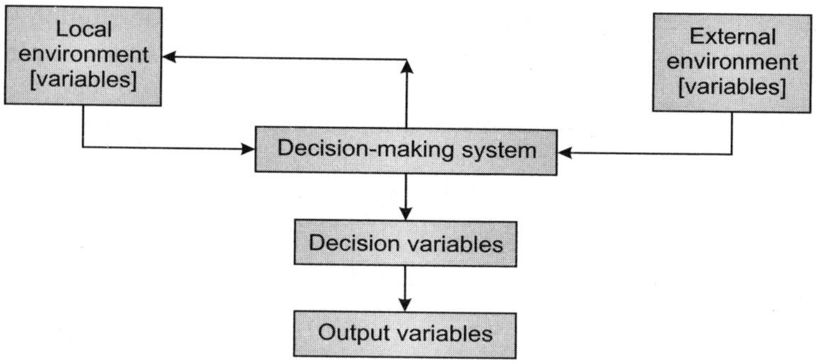

Fig. 4.9 Influence of local and external environments on the decision-making system

Interpretive Structural Modelling (ISM)

This is a systematic procedure of affiliation of the principle of graph theory to efficiently construct a directed graph or network representation of the complex patterns of contextual relationships among a set of elements (Malone, 1975). This is a computer-assisted interactive learning process whereby structural models are produced. Learning is through graph interaction. The vehicle for learning is accumulation of information in the interaction to construct an ISM of Map(s) through group discussion, ISM software is available. The main benefit is in learning to structure complex systems or themes in order to improve them. It can be used for various purposes like management of learning of disabled workers, priority setting in urban systems management, social learning, and city and regional planning (Baldwin, 1975).

interpretive structure modeling (ISM)
This is a systematic computerized procedure of graph theory to construct a directed graph or network representation of a complex pattern of contextual relationships among the relevant set of elements and variables. Important elements of the system or problem are identified and listed using relationships of dependence, influence and consultation and then structured into a graph.

Normally in modelling relationships, the human mind can tackle only a small number of elements as there is restriction on the short-term memory. But socioeconomic problems are often complex and involve a very large number of elements. ISM can help us to tackle them in a systematic way.

In ISM, the important elements of a problem or system are identified and listed, and using interrelationships like dependence, influence, and consultation (one or more), they are structured. The process of developing the structure depends upon asking questions such as 'does A contribute to B?', 'does A influence B?', 'is A prerequisite to B?', 'does A take less time than B?' and so on, depending upon the objective of modelling. The process, though dealing with a large number of elements, proceeds only in pairs of elements. The relationships are stored in a matrix and using some logic, the matrix is connected into a meaningful structure in the form of a graph.

In practice, the group discusses only relationships between two elements at a time and is, therefore, highly controlled and focused. ISM helps the group in learning a lot about the problem at hand. The mathematical treatment can be found in Harary, Norman and Cartwright (1965) and Warfield (1974). As a group problem solving process, ISM can be described in terms of three components (Warfield, 1974):

1. People: a broker, a facilitator, technician, participants, and observers;
2. Equipment: mainly a computer and class room features; and
3. Substantive content: (the information and dealing with it) this may be a theme, issue, or problem element, and contextual relationships, votes, relation maps, and interpretations.

The output of the process are the MAPS (ISM models) of relationships. These are linear hierarchical relationships. The important aspect of ISM is that a large variety of relationships can be represented. ISM can develop structure of intent, priority, attribute, enhancement process, or mathematical dependency. The relationships that can be handled are comparative, definitive (common logical), influential (causal), spatial (direction) and temporal (time sequences/independent).

Example Interpretive Structural Modeling—Research as a Social Process

Research can be understood as a social process. Research output is greatly influenced by the researcher and his or her experience. Research perspective, a theoretical underpinning of the research methodology, is formed by researchers in which the research institution (university) and the research questions play a part. The previous experiences of the institution in which the researcher carries out research, similar experience of these researchers, their research perspective, and the experience of the use of research methodology and its output in earlier research affect the researcher. The researcher is also influenced by his family, education, sex, age, personality, and culture. Research output is, thus, the result of a complex combination of influence of this social process. Develop a structural model for the influence type.

Solution: The elements of the structure can be stated as:

(i) Researcher
(ii) Previous research experience
(iii) Research perspective
(iv) Research methodology
(v) Research institutes
(vi) Research output
(vii) Research question
(viii) Family
(ix) Education
(x) Sex
(xi) Age
(xii) Personality
(xiii) Culture

The development of the structural model in steps is shown in Exhibits 4.7a to 4.7e in Annexure 4.6. The arrows in the diagram indicate the influence directions. The diagrams are self explanatory.

The matrix of influences is displayed at the end of Annexure 4.6 in Exhibit 4.8.

Formulation of Effectiveness Function

effectiveness function
When comparing alternative courses of action to choose the optimal one, an effectiveness function is used. This function gives the aggregated effectiveness of each alternative against a set of objectives.

Using the edited objectives and alternatives, the effectiveness of each alternative against each objective has to be determined. The determination of optimal choice of the alternative course of action would naturally require the determination of the effectiveness of each alternative against all objectives. This is called the effectiveness function. The effectiveness function is given by the following.

$$E_{fi} = \sum_{j=1}^{m} eij \qquad (1)$$

Objectives 1, 2, ...*j* ... *m*

There are, however, certain aspects to be considered.

1. The efficiency e_{ij} (efficiency of ith alternative with respect to objective *j*) has to be first determined. This may not be a deterministic function. There may be a range of *e* values available from past behaviour. For example, given probability *p* of sales increase per unit of advertising expenditure e_k, in which case, the expected value of e_k is obtained as follows.

$$\bar{e} = \sum_{k=1}^{n} p_k e_k \qquad (2)$$

where $\bar{e}$ is the expected value (and efficiency *e* is per cent sales Rs 1000 expenditure)

2. The values of *es* against various objectives, like O1, O2, ..., and so on, have to be obtained. O1 let us say gives the market share in percentage, O2 gives profit in monetary value, and O3 gives rank in leadership. When these have to be aggregated as given by equation (1), it will be necessary to convert these efficiency figures into a common measure. Usually, in management situations, all of them will be converted into monetary value. This brings in a problem of finding a balance between the various efficiency values and a monetary value. For example, Fig. 4.10 below shows the conversion of market share into profit.

   The graph of Fig. 4.10 is called a transformation curve, which gives inter-relationship between a particular variable and a monetary objective. Such inter-relationships have to be developed before an aggregate effectiveness function can be developed. If, for some

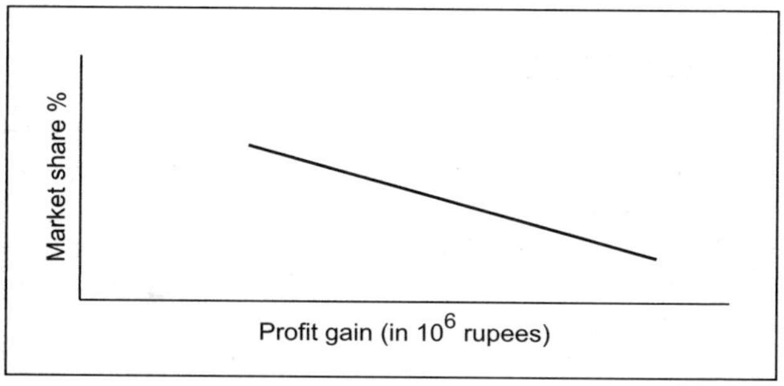

Fig. 4.10 Transformation curve between market share and profit

reason, such a transformation is not possible, then the particular combination has to be eliminated from the analysis. This is a limitation of the quantitative modelling approach.

3. The third aspect which is of importance in deriving the effectiveness function is to obtain the relative weights attached to each objective. When multiple objectives exist, it is necessary to know their relative importance. This is obtained by weighing the objectives as follows:

$$E_i = \sum_{j=1}^{m} e_{if} W_j \tag{3}$$

Where, W_j = Weight of jth objective.
The assumption in the equation (3) is that the total efficiency is a linear combination of individual efficiencies and is therefore a simplification (This is given to demonstrate the thinking behind a general procedure of model building rather than a strictly rigorous expression for an effectiveness function).

The weight w_j has to be carefully obtained. Usually competent groups (k) will rate the relative weights of the objectives. In a practical situation, the importance given to a group k rating the weights I_k, composite weight W_j of jth objective is given by,

$$W_j = \sum_{k=1}^{1} I_k W_{jk} \tag{4}$$

Where W_{jk} = Weight given to the jth objective by k^{th} group.

An example of application of such weighting procedure is job evaluation. After obtaining weights w_j, they will be standardised. There are many procedures that are used for obtaining w_{jk}'s. These are discussed in Churchman (1957). Thus, we can state that the effectiveness function for i^{th} alternative is obtained as follows:

1. Develop measures of efficiency for each alternative against each objective (e_{ij}), using probability distributions.
2. When the objectives are in different units, make a transformation to a standard value (that is, v_j).
3. Obtain the relative importance of each objective (w_j) through weighting by group procedures.
4. Obtain the efficiency of attaining each objective through each alternative, e_{ij} using (a), (b), and (c) above.
5. For each alternative, sum these efficiencies to obtain the effectiveness of the alternative course of actions.

$$E_i = \sum_{j=1}^{k} e_{ij} w_j V_j \tag{5}$$

Once the efficiency function and effectiveness function have been developed, the problem is stated as—Find the ith alternative for which E_i is maximum subject to the constraints in the systems.

In addition to the above, readers may refer to the detailed modelling of a decision problem outlined in Chapter 7.

SUMMARY

Review of research literature will enable the researcher to identify gaps as a prelude to research problem identification and generation of theoretical framework in the context of hypothesis formulation. The recent development of meta analysis helps in this effort. The primary research tasks are defining variables and discussing their relationships. In particular, the intervening variables—so important in social science research—are considered carefully. There are many types of hypotheses. There are many major origins of hypothesis like theoretical framework, analogy, negative case, and experience. The characteristics of good hypothesis are clarity, specificity, empirical basis, and comparability with existing analysis techniques. In qualitative research, hypothesis is generated as data accumulates and the meaning of data goes on unfolding.

Looking at decisional problems as belonging to total systems is central to the approach of mathematical model building in decisional research. System approach, particularly open systems approach, is relevant to management research. There are four types of systems: natural, human activity, social and cultural systems. All these use concepts of directive correlation, feedback and back reference period. Soft system analysis procedures are relevant to system study in which the components of a management system, namely, the decision maker, objectives, alternatives, and courses of action are successively described. These will lead to detailed model formulation in which each course of action in achieving the objectives is stated mathematically and the best course is chosen.

ANNEXURE 4.1

An Example of Taxonomy

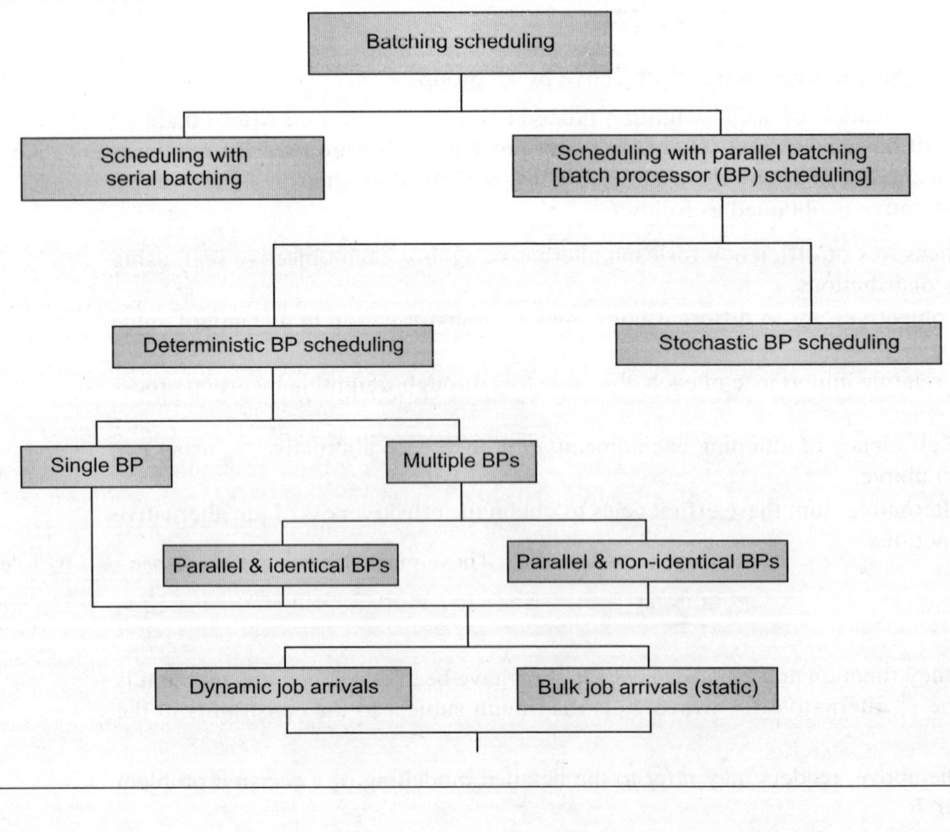

Contd.

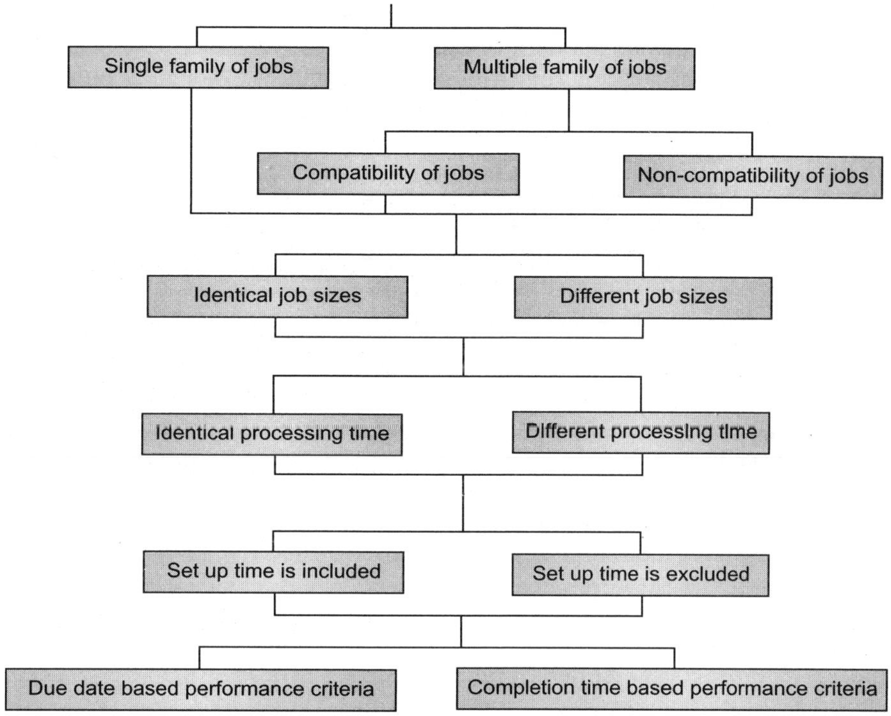

Exhibit 4.1 A Taxonomy for Deterministic Batch Processor scheduling

ANNEXURE 4.2

An Example for Meta Analysis

Assmus et al (1984), reported a meta analytic study. The authors of this paper have attempted to give a generalised result of how advertising affects sales, using a set of published studies on this topic. Various econometric models that estimate the short run and long run advertising effects on sales are examined. Each estimate is used as a data point in the analysis.

Here various studies are considered imperfect replications of an overall unplanned experiment, which is a form of meta analysis called 'replication analysis'. It configures parameter estimates in a natural experimental design where variances can be easily analysed and systematic variations of particular study characteristics are assessed. These are adjusted to give generalisations about common elements in the studies. The analysis proceeds in four steps—the description of studies used, development of hypotheses about the effect of different model specification, measurement procedures, estimation methods, and research environments. It reports the analysis of variance results and finally discusses the implications of the study, offering suggestions for further research.

The data contains 128 models reported in 22 studies published before 1981. These studies were identified from earlier reviews of articles reporting sufficient details. They are taken from both econometric and marketing literature equally, but the procedure used is neither a random selection nor an exhaustive one. It is not a complete work. It is just a starting point for attempting generalisation. This is because of the publication bias present and the exclusion of implausible estimates and unpublished industrial studies. These may otherwise make sense in a broader context.

The common measures used for comparison here are (1) short term advertising effect, (2) goodness of fit (measured by R, multiple correlation coefficient), and (3) advertising carry over. These three are always analysed separately, since sample sizes differ and carry over and coefficient of determination are always not specified. Elasticities are used to show the short term advertising effects. Coefficients are used in the case of multiplicative models. The product of regression coefficient and the ratio of means of the dependent variable and the advertising measure are used in linear models.

Contd.

Equilibrium short term elasticities and lagged dependent variable coefficients all lie within the range of zero and one. The distribution of the estimated parameters can be taken as plausible. Anyway, the means of all the three measures differ systematically because of large inter-study differences. Though econometric studies readily offer comparable set of results as compared to consumer decision process models, they do not provide as good an environment as the Fishbein models. Problems arise due to variations in studies on model structure, measurement, and the research environment. Unlike in Fishbein models, econometric model variables are not structurally identical. Meta analysis implicitly assumes that a true model specification is not totally idiosyncratic to each situation. Also, measures are not at all comparable because of differences in variable definition. Some models are built on brands and some on products. Even research contexts differ in many aspects such as location, products, estimation methods, variables definition, and time frame. Though this kind of contextual variability is required for meta analysis, if the variables are in large numbers, for all practical purposes there will exist no exact replication.

Development of hypotheses is divided into two parts. The first is related to model specification, measurement, and estimation. The second is related to the research environment.

Model specification usually differs in terms of variables included, the assumed timing of the advertising effect, and the functional form of the equation used. Besides, multi-colinearity, omitted variables also create problems leading to specification bias. Exclusion of exogenous variables like macroeconomic measures and socio-demographics also gives upward biased results whereas measures like seasonality have a neutral effect on the estimates. Anyway, excluded variables with high correlation with model variables should fit well. It was earlier established that omission of the carryover effect constitutes wrong specification. Choice of model and variable definition are also expected to make some difference in advertising estimates, but not in carryover estimates. Advertising elasticities estimated using Ordinary Least Squares (OLS), in contrast to the simultaneous equation method, gives a bias in the positive direction though the compensatory mechanism implies a negative relationship between market share and current advertising appropriations. Anyway, OLS should fit better, *ceteris paribus*, since it minimises squared errors.

Qualitative features of the market environment also affect results. For example, for goods that are purchased frequently, experience is the main source of information and its advertising elasticity may be relatively lower than for search goods like durables. Elasticities of high risk goods also should be relatively higher and timings of advertisement exposure and purchase also matter. Elasticities should be higher during the early phase of growth rather than its maturity phase because of the information gathered by customers. Advertising elasticity differs among geographic markets and its level. Problems arise in matching the time frame of advertising measurement and advertising effect on sales. Time series elasticity should be smaller than the cross-sectional one and aggregate measurements combine media of different effectiveness and averages the effect.

The studies are classified according to model specification and research environment factors, and all categories are considered design variables in a quasi-experiment. This, however, lacks a prior research plan configuration. The empirical design is highly unbalanced but takes only those variables with at least 10 observations. Univariate t-tests were performed to compare mean values of estimates with a given characteristic estimate. Non-orthogonal factors present add to the problem of 'shared variance' and the design matrix of the consumer behaviour models is singular, which requires some reduction in it to make ANOVA feasible. It also gives rise to co-linearity problems.

Some less frequent variables are grouped together under other classes and inversion of the matrix is made possible. The carryover coefficients and transformed goodness-of-fit measurements indicate severe problems and a degree of shared variance in the resulting ANOVAs. These make the assessment of the effect of specific factors difficult. Replication is required to estimate these ANOVA parameters, but the number of available observations are considerably smaller than the data needed for analysis. In meta analysis, calibration of shared variance is a product rather than a deficiency.

With regard to the substantive results and their implication, the grand mean in short term elasticity ANOVA was significantly greater than zero and other mean elasticities unadjusted by ANOVA for other factors. This implies that advertising may be more effective in the short run than average estimated elasticities. Short term elasticities in models that incorporate carryover effects are significantly smaller, but not much from average estimates, implying that elasticity captures carryover effects even if it is not specified. Cross-sectional data produce higher short term elasticities than time series data, indicating that cross-sectional disaggregation of time series should be done whenever possible. Elasticities differ among products and settings, being higher for food products and higher in Europe than in the US. It implies that Europe under advertises because of media restrictions on companies or that in the US organisations over-advertise for some unspecified reason. Short term elasticities vary systematically with data interval, suggesting that high level current research results are needed for better assessment. Within the study, variation on the data interval would be very useful. Elasticities are significantly higher in additive models than in multiplicative specification due to asymmetrical averaging down of linear models. Advertising has a minor impact on product class sales. The OLS method produce better fits than other methods, as hypothesised.

Regarding methodological implications, the mean values of the studies provide good initial estimates and the test of hypotheses in future models should use null values for elasticities and lag effects. Meta analysis can provide predictions for specific situations that have not been studied in actual combination, but have been assessed individually. This can be made by using ANOVA coefficients related to them.

The major implications for future research is that programmed research, if used, can eliminate the defects of the 'natural' experimental design. Several factors related to significant differences are suggested by univariate tests and new data in this line are needed to expand the available combinations of research environment characteristics. Also alternative specifications and estimation methods can be tried out and experimented. Further studies are required for alternate modelling and estimation procedures. The framework of meta analysis would facilitate systematic assessment of the impact of the various available modelling options on the results. Also, unpublished industrial and academic studies are useful for expanding the available database.

ANNEXURE 4.3

An Illustrative Example of Theoretical Framework

Exploring the Relationship between Marketing Programmes and Technological Developments Across the (PLC) Product Life Cycle (Mohan 1995).

Theoretical framework and research questions This thesis deals with marketing programmes and technological developments and their inter-relationships for products across PLC phases. The study is carried out in a sample of Indian organisations manufacturing general purpose machinery.

From the discussion and analysis of the related research literature it has emerged clearly that business strategy and marketing programmes influence technological developments. But the exact nature and dimensions of the influence are relatively undefined. More particularly, there are no empirical studies on the relationship between marketing programmes and technological developments, once a product is launched and goes through different PLC phases.

Further, from various discussions and from research literature it is understood that PLCs do not occur naturally and automatically. They are an outcome of controllable variables (endogenous to the firm) like marketing and technology development efforts and uncontrollable variables (exogenous to the firm) like government policy, market structure (customer concentration, supplier concentration, and so on). Therefore, to enable an organisation to control the growth of its products through their life cycle, each phase of the PLC calls for different patterns of management, particularly of marketing and technology management involving appropriate changes in the marketing mix and in the efforts towards technological developments.

Thus, marketing programmes, and technological developments, and the interrelationships between them are expected to vary from phase to phase in the PLC phases (Exhibit 4.2).

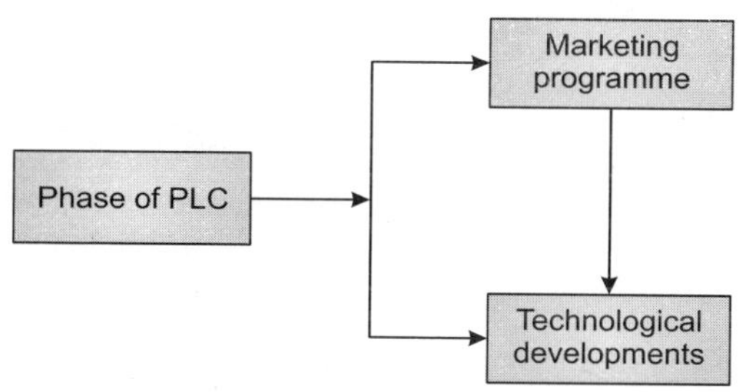

Exhibit 4.2 Marketing programme, technological developments, and their interrelationships in a PLC phase

Exhibit 4.2 shows three relationships:

- The influence of PLC phase on the marketing programme
- The influence of PLC phase on technology developments
- The influence of marketing programmes on technology developments

Though the arrows indicate the direction of influences strongly indicated by earlier researchers, since this study is exploratory, only correlational relationships will be attempted. This study is directed towards answering the following research questions:

Contd.

- Which variables of marketing programmes and technological developments are relevant in different phases of the product life cycle?
- Which variables of marketing programmes and technological developments distinguish between the different phases of the PLC?
- Are the levels of variables that are dominant in distinguishing between the successive phases of the PLC different or the same in different phases?
- Which marketing programme variables are associated with the different dimensions of technological developments in the different phases of the PLC?

ANNEXURE 4.4

Examples of Hypothesis Generation

Example 1 The effects of anonymity of evaluators and the evaluative tone on idea generation were studied by Connoly et al (1990).

(a) Previous research provides a framework that indicates that the group interactions are consequences of (i) the properties of group members, (ii) their patterned relationships, (iii) the task situation, and (iv) the broad environment in which they are working. Each of these factors is influenced by the interaction process.

(b) The researchers propose that an evaluative tone is an important property of the group members and their anonymity is a critical aspect of patterning their relationships.

(c) Based on the framework at (a) above, the authors postulate that each member of the group working alone is capable of generating some ideas (as the group task is of interest to him). Embedding these individual ideas in group interactions could enhance or reduce contributions depending upon whether the group encourages (positive force) or inhibits (negative force) a contributor. The group's overall effectiveness in generating ideas depends upon the balance it achieves between positive and negative forces (Exhibit 4.3).

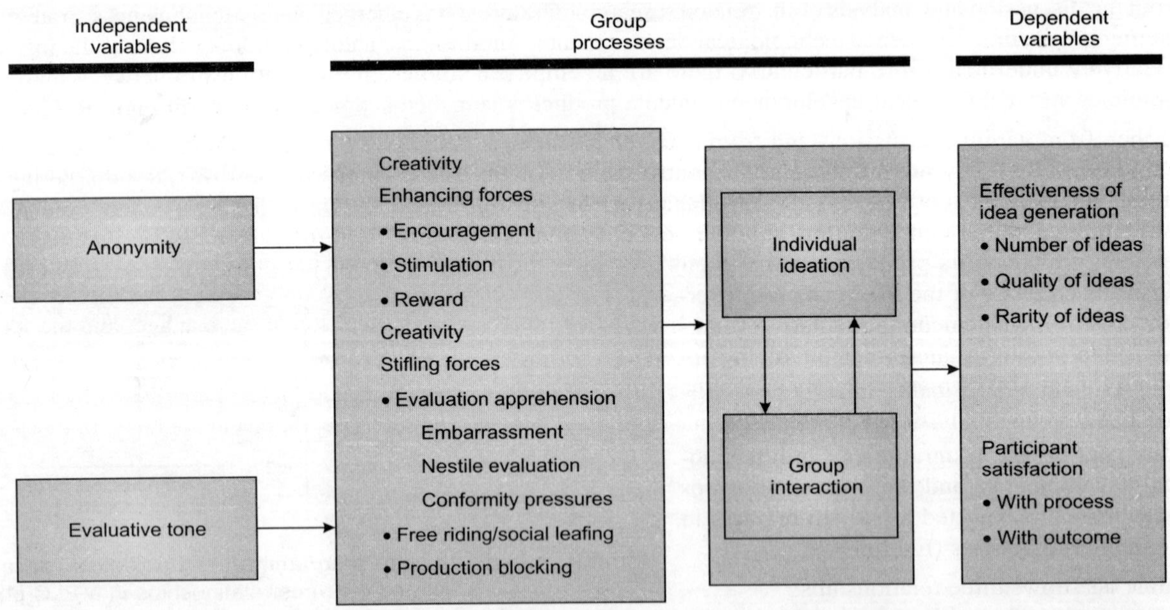

Exhibit 4.3 Anonymity and evaluative tone in idea generation (Source: Connolley, Jessup and Valacich, 1990)

(d) The balance of force analysis enables one to predict the effect of the evaluative tone on the effectiveness of idea generation. Groups in which ideas are criticised would be less effective than those in which ideas are encouraged and supported. Thus, the following hypothesis is proposed:

Contd.

H_1: Groups with a supportive evaluative tone will be more effective in idea generation than those with a critical evaluative tone.

(e) The balance of the force model does not clearly indicate the predictability of the effects of anonymity on idea generation. Previous research work indicates that anonymity can induce socially undesirable behaviour. On the other hand, loosening of social bonds by anonymity is valueable to the individual in a group process by encouraging full participation and expression of unpopular, novel, or heretical opinions. The authors assume that anonymity, though tending to weaken socially facilitative forces (which are weak anyway), clearly weaken inhibitive forces like production blocking, hostility of evaluation, group pressure, and fears. On the basis of this, the authors propose the second hypothesis as follows:

H_2: Anonymous groups will be more effective at generating ideas than identified groups.

(f) Earlier research indicates that the satisfaction of the group with processes and outcomes is important for effective idea generation, hence the following hypotheses:

H_3: Members of the supportive groups will be more satisfied with the group process and outcome than members of critical groups.

H_4: Satisfaction differences between supportive and critical groups will be larger when group members are identified rather than when they are anonymous.

Thus, the propositions indicate that the effectiveness of an idea generating group is determined by a subtle balance between facilitative and inhibitive forces.

A 2 × 2 factorial design experiment was used on 72 upper division business students for verifying the hypotheses. Hypothesis 1 was rejected but hypothesis 2 clearly gained support and while hypothesis 3 was strongly supported, hypothesis 4 received no support. Thus, the theory was only partly supported and needed further research.

Sometimes these complex relationships may be represented at a higher level of abstraction. Changes in one variable are then related to changes in another.

Example 2 In order to describe quality management practice in an organisation, the authors (Benson et al, 1991) use organisation theory. They use the system-structural view of quality management to explain it. The system-structural view holds that the manager tunes his organisation to the exigencies of the environment and brings about changes in it to 'adapt' to the shifting environment. The manager perceives the organisational context of quality. Based on his perception, he determines the need for changes in the organisation as a means of response to the changing context. The organisational context consists of outside quality demands, past performance in quality, resources available for quality improvement, and top management support for it. This model is integrated with the problem-solving approach. In the problem-solving approach, the problem is identified as the gap between the ideal quality performance and the actual quality performance. This mixed model approach is highlighted in Exhibit 4.4 and used as the conceptual/analytical basis for hypothesis generation. Ideal quality management and actual quality management are two variables defined in the study. The first is a belief and aspiration of the manager and the second is a perception.

The ideal and actual quality management are measured in terms of eight critical factors established by the same authors in an earlier study, developing a valid and reliable instrument for measuring them and are listed in List A and List B.

List A

1. Divisional top management leadership for quality
2. The role of the quality department
3. Training
4. Product/Service design
5. Supplier quality management
6. Process management (design and control)
7. Quality data and reporting
8. Employee relations

In addition to management knowledge and corporate support for quality, there are five product/process contextual variables, identified in earlier studies. Past quality performance variables and market context variables as well as

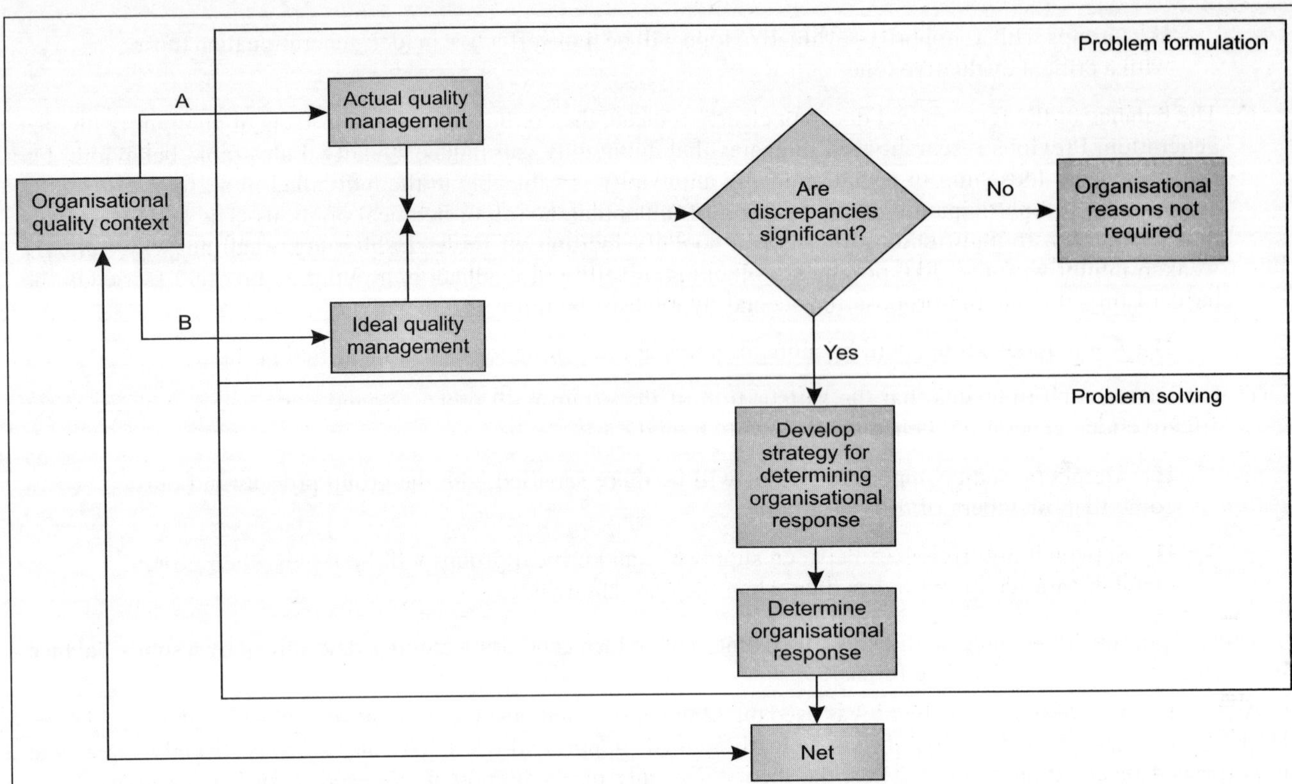

Exhibit 4.4 Mixed model of quality management (Source: Benson, Saraph and Schroeder, 1991)

company related variables (in all 16 variables) are also used. A special instrument is designed in the study to measure these variables. The list of extracted (after factor analysis) contextual variables is given in List B.

List B

1. Management knowledge
2. Corporate support for quality
3. Rate of product/process change
4. Proportion of products/processes purchased from outside
5. Degree of manufacturing content
6. Extent of batch versus continuous process
7. Product complexity
8. External quality requirements
9. Barriers to entry into industry
10. Degree of competition
11. Past quality performance
12. Manager type QM/GM
13. Company size (large/medium/small)
14. Company type (manufacturing/service)

The main focus of the paper is to investigate the relationship between the organisational context and quality management. Research literature suggested that ideal quality management concept is unaffected by the organisational context and only actual quality management is affected. The model depicted in Fig. 4.11, on the contrary, suggests that both are affected by organisational context. However, the authors investigated this through two hypotheses.

> $\mathbf{H_1}$: A manager's perceptions of actual quality management are influenced by organisational context variables.
>
> $\mathbf{H_2}$: A manager's perceptions of ideal quality management are not affected by organisational context variables.

Using factor analysis and canonical correlation analysis on the relevant data collected, the authors found support for the first hypothesis but the second hypothesis was refuted. These results supported the model that was developed.

Annexure 4.5

System Study and Problem Formulation – Allocation of Assembly Manpower (Karthikeyan 1986)

This study was carried out in the assembly department (for a class of products) of a large electronic equipment manufacturing organisation (hereafter referred to as EEMO). This organisation manufactures several classes of electronic items, from small single items to large complex assemblies. It has a large number of individual production units centrally controlled and monitored in the plant. A detailed description of the assembly department is given in the following sections.

Description of the assembly department of EEMO The manufacturing division produces twenty types of a class of assembled products. The process flow chart for this class of products is shown in Exhibit 4.5. A process type of layout exists in the assembly department of the manufacturing division. The production facilities are arranged according to process types required for a variety of sub-assembly operations to be performed. The various types of sub-assemblies and assemblies moves through the process groups. The end use of these products are in Defence, Post and Telegraphs, and consumer goods.

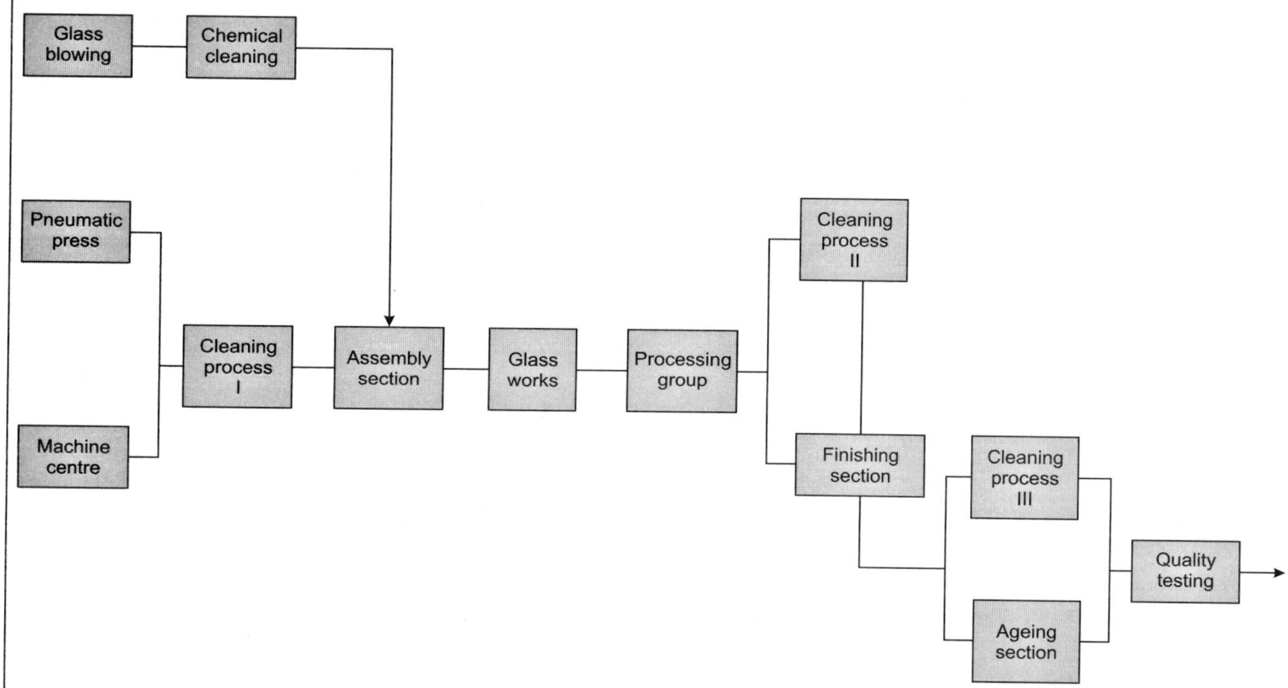

Exhibit 4.5 Manufacturing process flow diagram

Skillmix in manpower The assembly shop performs not only assembly operations but also fabrication activities for intricate parts that go into the final assemblies. The workers in the shop are grouped according to their skills and certain groups of workers are engaged in assembling particular types of assemblies. A few among these workers are highly versatile and can perform a wide variety of assembly operations. Certain sub-assembly operations need more skilled workers than others. However, there are some cases where a certain worker cannot be assigned to a particular sub-assembly operation. The reason for this may be lack of ability, deficiency in technical knowledge, lack of training, inadequate experience, and so on.

The problem The present practice of assigning/allocating workers to jobs is mainly on a hunch or the judgment of the supervisors in the shop. The difficulty in doing this mainly arises due to differences in the capabilities of the workers. It is very frequently possible that the production plan for a few products can be met completely, and it can be completely ignored for a few. Sometimes assemblies can also be produced in excess of the demand. On the other

Contd.

hand, for certain assemblies the production plan cannot be met due to shortage of a particular skill even though some manpower is available in the shop in other skills. The supervisors in the assembly shop find it impossible to strike an optimum balance between utilisation of worker hours (man hours) and maximum realisation of the production plan. At present in the assembly department of EEMO, the overall demand for manpower is marginally higher than the available capacity to produce. The department receives rush orders at short notice and these constitute about twenty per cent of the regular orders accepted for undertaking assembly work. The particular problem facing the manager of the shop is to allocate workers to various sub-assembly operations for normal orders, based on the production plan and simultaneously handle these rush orders during each planning period.

Assembly operation details The assembly department is multiproduct in nature. Exhibit 4.6 displays a sample of details of the assemblies produced, sub-assembly operations involved, operators (workers-coded in numerals) performing them, quantity of sub-assemblies required per assembly, production rates for each sub-assembly is depicted as output/day. There are in all 20 assemblies, 62 sub-assemblies, and 26 assembly workers.

In general, a sub set of workers can perform an operation and a worker can perform a subset of different operations. However, a few workers are very versatile and can perform a very wide variety of these operations. Further, certain operations can be performed by only one worker, though every worker can perform more than one operation. This obviously makes some activities more critical than the others.

Manpower for rush orders The clients and the products of EEMO are such that urgent or rush orders cannot be avoided and are a normal feature of the demands further more, they occur randomly. To allow for this situation, EEMO has a policy that such special rush orders are accepted and completed on priority. To this end, it requires that the assembly department notionally keeps an unscheduled twenty five per cent of manpower, of versatile workers, for each period to attend to these rush orders. Seventy five per cent manpower is allocated for the various sub-assembly operations for meeting the assembly demand as per the production plan for that week.

Non-inventoriable nature of sub-assemblies: The assembly shop at EEMO is not permitted to produce sub-assemblies in excess of the requirements so that they can be inventoried and used later. The technical reasons for this are two-fold.

1. If the production of sub-assemblies is greater than that needed to produce the required number of assemblies there would be an excess of inventory, which would need a costly rework operation if not consumed immediately after production.
2. Storing of sub-assemblies only, over a period of time makes it unsafe.

It has been widely recognised that one of the major fire hazards in industries is due to storage of inflammable materials. Storage of such inflammable articles like gaseous containers, highly volatile liquid tanks, and so on have proved to be increasingly difficult for EEMO. Hence, following the guidelines set by various industrial safety agencies, EEMO requires that sub-assemblies should not be kept as inventory. Stocks in an uncompleted stage or in excess of requirement would be cause for major concern. Therefore, all sub-assemblies produced should be used up immediately. If it is not possible to utilise it immediately, the assembly shop management are required to alert and initiate steps such that all items go through the full rework process from the start.

It follows, therefore, that all relevant sub-assemblies produced should be exactly equal in number to those required to meet a specific number of assemblies.

Further, certain categories of manpower available may be, in general, greater than the requirement and in certain other categories, may be less than the requirement of the forecast. This double imbalance causes considerable problems while assignments are made.

To summarise, the situation under consideration, each worker should be allotted the required time to complete the individual sub-assembly operations. The different sub-assemblies that go into the making of the final assembly can be made in integer amounts. There would be no uncompleted or excess items. If this is not possible, particularly in some cases due to non-availability of allotable man hours with a particular worker, other compatible workers might be selected. In the event of all these considerations failing, any other different judicious ratio of time can be allotted to the worker. Subsequently, the production plan for that week, for that particular assembly item has to be reduced.

Statement of the problem It is required to evolve an optimal procedure for allocating skilled man hours in the department to various sub-assembly operations, to meet the production plan (demand) to the maximum extent possible, subject to the constraints and requirements given below. Hereafter this would be referred to as the MPA problem.

Contd.

Since notionally there are two categories of skilled workers (a) versatile and (b) non-versatile, a small portion (say 25 per cent) of the man hours available from versatile workers should be kept free to attend to rush orders. The manpower allocations should be for the sub-assemblies so that the shop supervisors can make appropriate assignment of operators

(a) No build up of sub-assembly inventory is allowed since any unfinished sub-assembly in inventory entails costly rework.
(b) Whether or not the forecast is met, the produced sub-assemblies should be in the exact quantities required to make the assembly.
(c) Production beyond the quantity on the plan for any assembly is not permitted.
(d) The possibility of allocating several workers in part to a sub-assembly and several sub-assemblies in part to a worker should be considered.

Assumptions:

- The allocation procedure considers the weekly production plan (demand) on the shop and allocates workers for normal production.
- A minimum percentage of time available with skilled workers is reserved for special orders. This time is not taken into consideration during allocation.
- Set up time between any two sub-assembly operations is assumed to be negligible.
- All workers who can perform an operation are considered to have the same efficiency, in other words, the same rate of production per day.

Assembly code	Sub-Assembly operation	Workers code	Quantity per assembly	Normal output per day	Demand
01	Tube assembly	9, 10, 12, 13, 14, 19, 15, 7	1	30	360
	Anode assembly	Anybody	1	250	225
02	Tube assembly	9, 10, 12, 13, 14, 15, 3, 4	1	30	225
	276 Shield	Anybody	1	480	
03	Tube assembly	10, 13,14,11	1	15	40
	Anode assembly	Anybody	4	250	
04	Tube assembly	10, 13, 14	1	15	48
	281 Shield	Anybody	8	480	
	282 Shield	Anybody	1	480	
05	Tube assembly	10, 13	1	10	15
	Anode arc welding	5, 6	1	96	
	126 Anode assembly	4	1	200	
06	Tube assembly	4	1	5	20
	134 Shield	4, 10	1	48	
07	Tube assembly	10	1	6	15
	186 Shield	4, 10	2	48	
	Mount 1	1, 2, 5, 6, 8	1	96	
08	Tube assembly	9, 10, 12	1	5	48
	Filament FC-25	16	1	60	
	Anchor	24, 26	2	48	
09	Tube assembly	4, 5, 6	1	5	48
	Anode assembly	19	1	200	
10	Tube assembly	7, 8	1	6	39
	Filament	12, 14, 16	1	25	
	Gride 1	10	1	30	
	Gride 2	11, 15	1	40	
11	Tube assembly	9, 11	1	6	38
	Filament	9, 16	2	60	
	Grid	9, 10, 15	1	40	
	Anchor	14, 16	4	192	
	Sealing Met 1 L Cup assembly	8, 9, 10, 11, 16	1	800	
	Anode assembly	19	1	24	

Exhibit 4.6 Details of Assembly shop (sample only) **** Not referred in the text

Contd.

Objectives of the study To formalise a method of allocating workers to sub-assembly operations, such that:

1. The production plan for the assemblies are met to the maximum extent possible.
2. To maximise (optimise) the utilisation of skilled manpower in the shop.
3. To honour orders at short notice, and hence to obtain goodwill of customers.
4. To evolve an easy, communicable, and reliable procedure for management to use in manpower allocation procedure. The simplified procedure, even if not optimal, should be a good practical procedure.

Scope of the study The study attempts to investigate whether any optimisation procedure could be applied for maximising the manpower allocation. In doing so, it might be necessary to try to model the problem in a variety of standard models and solution methodologies for applicability in the present situation. The management of EEMO requires that a procedure for optimising manpower allocation be evolved for them. But they further mention that, if a procedure that needs little time and sophistication is built, it would be welcomed by shop managers. From these discussions the following conclusion emerges:

- Man hours required by a ith worker to perform the a $k_j{}^{th}$ sub-assembly operation belonging to an jth assembly will be the decision variables.
- Man hours available with any particular worker i will be the resource constraint.
- Demand for any assembly j expressed in terms of assembly operation man hours will be the manpower demand for the product.
- The parameter r $(r_j k_j)$ is the ratio of a sub-assembly operation (k_j) man hours to its assembly (j^{th}) operation man hours. This value is fixed and is a fraction. This ratio should always be maintained in any solution in order that there is no inventory of sub-assembly.

Note: Using these variables the problem was formulated as a linear programming problem as well as a heuristic programme. (For details refer Karthikeyan and Krishnaswamy, 1990).

ANNEXURE 4.6

Development of Structural Model

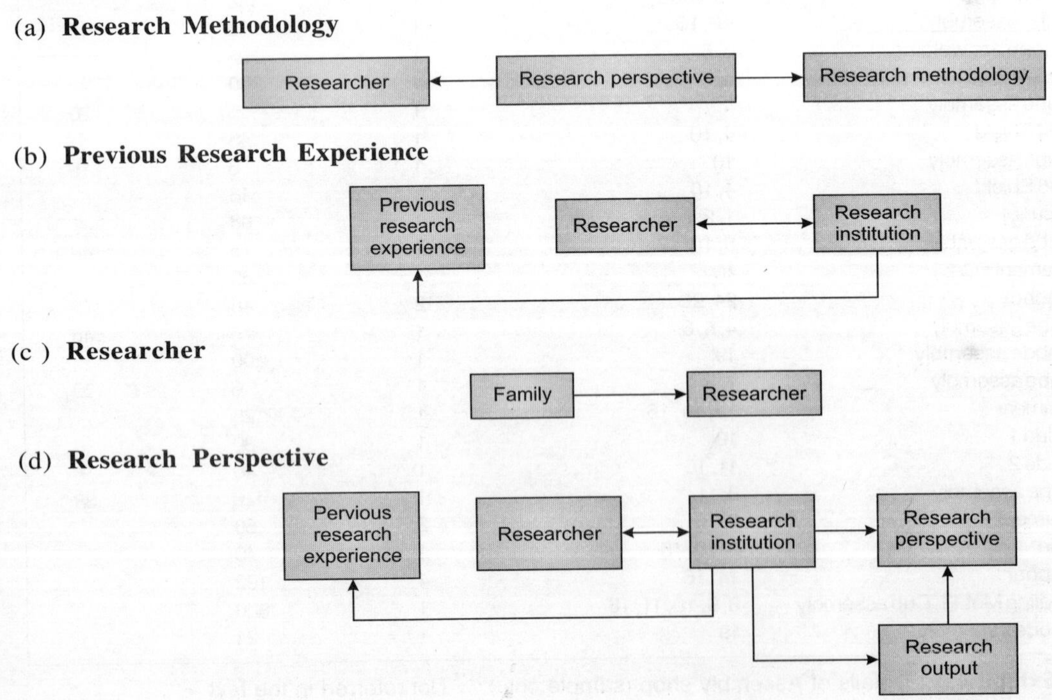

Contd.

(e) **Research Output**

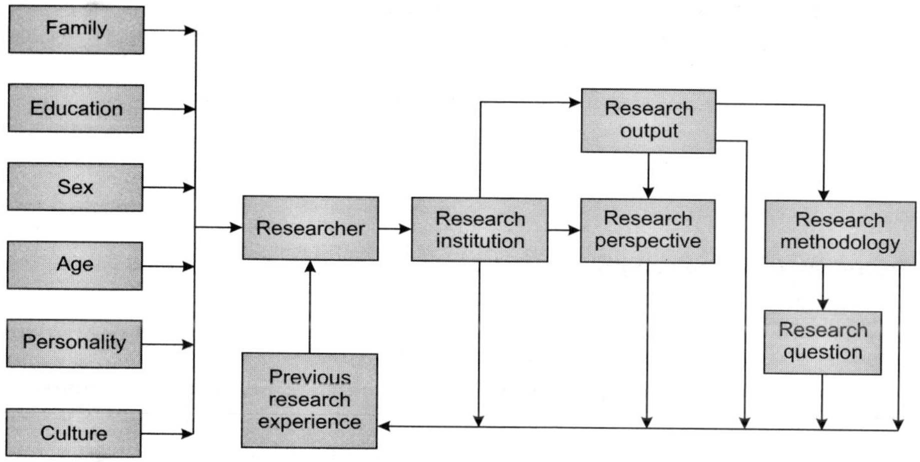

Exhibit 4.7 Interpretive structure models of research

	Research	*Previous Research Experience*	*Research Perspective*	*Research Methodology*	*Research Institution*	*Research Question*	*Research Output*	*Family*	*Education*	*Sex*	*Age*	*Personality*	*Culture*	*Total*
Researcher	0	0	1	0	1	1	0	0	0	0	0	0	0	3
Previous Research Experience	1	0	0	0	0	0	0	0	0	0	0	0	0	1
Research Perspective	0	1	0	1	0	0	0	0	0	0	0	0	0	2
Research Methodology	0	1	0	0	0	0	1	0	0	0	0	0	0	2
Research Institution	1	1	1	1	0	1	0	0	0	0	0	0	0	4
Research Question	0	0	1	1	0	0	0	0	0	0	0	0	0	2
Research Output	0	1	0	0	0	0	0	0	0	0	0	0	0	2
Family	1	0	0	0	0	0	0	0	0	0	0	0	0	1
Education	1	0	0	0	0	0	0	0	0	0	0	0	0	1
Sex	1	0	0	0	0	0	0	0	0	0	0	0	0	1
Age	1	0	0	0	0	0	0	0	0	0	0	0	0	1
Personality	1	0	0	0	0	0	0	0	0	0	0	0	0	1
Culture	1	0	0	0	0	0	0	0	0	0	0	0	0	1

Note: 0 indicates 'no influence' and 1 indicates 'influence'

Exhibit 4.8 The Matrix of Influence

Suggested Readings

- Adams, J. L. (1979). *Conceptual Block Bursting—A Guide to Better Idea*, 2nd ed. CA: Stanford Alumni Association.
- Churchman, C. West, R. L. Ackoff and E. L. Arnoff (1957). *Introdcution to Operations Research*. New Delhi: John Wiley & Sons.

- Gash, S. (2000). *Effective Literature Searching*. Aldershot: Gower.
- Kaposi, Agnes and Margaret Myers (2000). *Systems For All*. London: Imperial College Press.
- Lundberg, C. C. (1976). "Hypothesis Creation in Organisational Behaviour Research", *Academy off Management Review*, Vol. 1, pp. 5–12.
- Wilson, B. (1984). *Systems Concepts Methodologies and Applications*. New York: John Wiley.

QUESTIONS AND EXERCISES

1. What is system approach? How is it useful in research?
2. Differentiate between planning, controlling, and organising, as given by system approach and as treated as managerial functions.
3. What are the dominant characteristics of biological systems that are useful for research in management? Give examples.
4. What is the difference between natural relationships and synthetic relationships in a system?
5. Draw a schematic diagram of a Ph. D. student as a component of several systems.
6. Why is simplification necessary while representing a system?
7. What is of central importance while segregating a smaller system from a larger one? Give examples.
8. Represent research work in any general area of research, which is of interest to you, as a system. Trace how you are going to research into various components of this system. Use schematic diagrams to illustrate your points.
9. Is a system imaginary? Give reasons to justify your answer.
10. What is the difference between a model and a hypothesis? Support your discussion giving one example for each.
11. What is a composite hypothesis?
12. Choose five research papers not in the area of your research interest. After going through the papers in depth, develop three hypotheses to partially bridge the gap given by the five papers as literature.
13. Is it possible to develop and test a hypothesis without using statistical measures? If your answer is 'yes' give an example. If 'no' give your arguments.
14. If a case study confirms a theory or a hypothesis, could we construe that the hypothesis is acceptable? If, however, the case study refutes the hypothesis should we reject the hypothesis? Give your arguments.
15. It is stated that a single exception to the hypothesis disproves it. In view of this what is the importance of sampling for hypothesis testing?
16. A manager feels that by working certain operations in a single shift and certain others in two shifts, will lead to an improvement in productivity. Develop suitable hypotheses to reflect the feelings of the manager and indicate how they could be practically tested.
17. Choose a thesis, study it. Make a proposal to your would be guide as if you are carrying out the research. Give all details.
18. Suppose you are in the faculty of a management department of a university and the research project undertaken by another faculty member is terminated half way before data collection and closed incomplete, make a re-proposal to the funding agency for completing the project. *Hint:* Make necessary assumptions or take a project and consider only a partly completed problem.
19. In what way, if any, do you think, should a public limited funding agency solicit research proposals?
20. When a manager approaches you as a researcher with a problem of his, what do you do to solve his problems? Give the sequence of steps followed by you.
21. Study the proposal of a research study that has been successfully completed. Carefully evaluate the proposal from the point of view of the material given in this chapter and in the references. What weaknesses and strengths do you find? How can you improve it?

22. The manufacturing department of a large firm manufacturing (a) household equipments, (b) electronic items, or (c) chemicals approaches you as a research consultant to study its manufacturing planning and control system to suggest the introduction of a model based computer system. Make a feasibility research study proposal.
23. Nothing is mentioned in the text about training research assistants in larger projects. Why do you need to train research assistants? In what areas would you impart training, and how?
24. In formulating problems for the mathematical modelling of a decision situation, it is generally necessary to make assumptions. Why? What purpose do the assumptions serve in the formulation of a model?
25. Choose any suitable model from literature in OR, which you fully comprehend. Now, convert this model into a set of hypotheses and indicate the research methods of testing them. Which approach do you think is better? Make a presentation.
26. Hard and sincere work by an individual may open up opportunities for better work. It is equally likely that better opportunities may motivate the worker to put in greater effort. How would you hypothesise these relationships? Givc points to support your answcr.
27. There are a number of variables that affect the degree to which manpower planning is practiced in an organisation. In particular, the management philosophy of the organisation influences the manpower planning function. Five variables are identified as management attitude towards manpower planning, goal orientation of the organisation, strategies used for acquiring manpower, attention to an individual's aspiration, and personnel policies. The five systems of manpower planning are identified as the rudimentary system, fragmentary system, integration seeking system, integrated mechanistic system, and the enlightened human resource system and the firms can be rated against these five systems. Given this framework develop at least five hypotheses and state the theoretical framework. If, in addition, an environmental system is defined with variable labour-supply condition, manpower market, and national manpower policy, how would the framework change? Formulate additional hypotheses.
28. What is an intervening variable? How is it useful in research? Give an example from literature to support your answer.

Note: Questions 17–19, 21 and 23 may be answered after studying Chapter 5.

CHAPTER 5

Research Proposal

- Research Proposal
- Purpose of a Research Proposal
- Types of Research Proposals
- Development of the Proposals
- Requirements of the Sponsoring Agent
- Evaluation of Research Proposals
- Some Implicit Considerations

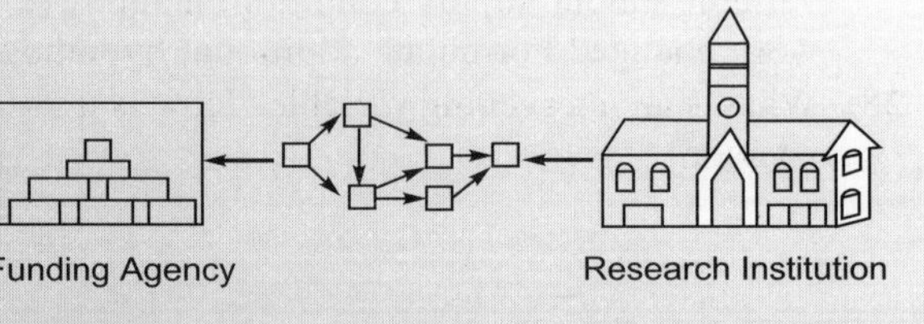

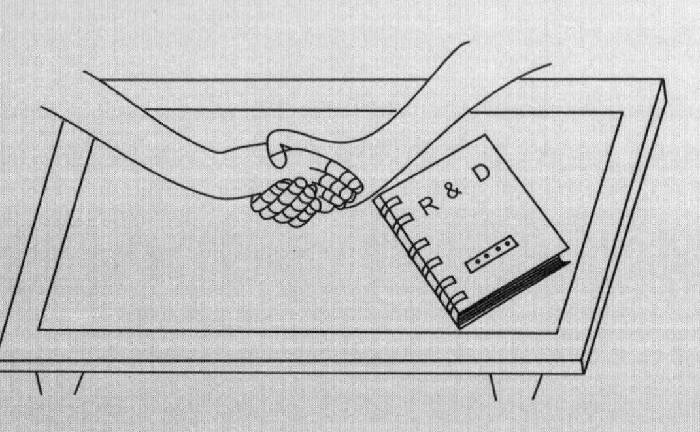

LEARNING OBJECTIVES

Upon completion of this chapter, you will be able to:

- ✓ Understand the importance of the research proposal in the overall research flow
- ✓ List the objectives and types of research proposals
- ✓ Write a research proposal
- ✓ Evaluate a research proposal
- ✓ Understand the legal and ethical aspects of research

RESEARCH PROPOSAL

When a researcher needs approval and/or financial support for an intended research, he prepares a formal proposal and submits it to an appropriate approving/sponsoring authority. It is a bid for undertaking research. The proposal is the form of a research design, which is the blueprint for conducting and controlling research. It can also be considered a research plan or a research project.

Making a research proposal and getting it approved and supported may appear to be an administrative activity rather than a step in the process of research, but it is not so. Therefore, it is necessary to define research proposal as an integral part of the general research flow. Figure 5.1 details the process of research in three stages: (i) The preliminary investigation stage in the first step, at the end of which a research problem is defined with a great degree of confidence. It may also be derived from the study of the actual problem of a manager or from a feasibility or an exploratory study carried out on the scientist's perceptual formulation of the research problem. (ii) When the problem becomes clear, the next step of the process is research planning, comprising research design (the technical planning of the details of the research process) and the managerial portion of planning to obtain resources, in terms of outside help, equipment, scientific manpower, time and funds. Every research requires resources, the allocation of which must be planned in advance. (iii) After obtaining approval of research proposal and resources, research activities can be initiated and executed as per the design and within the framework of control by the funding agency. The form and content of the research proposals vary depending upon the researcher and his organisation, the client's organisations, and the supporting agency. The research proposal serves as a means of communication between the researcher and the research supporter, and must necessarily be drawn up with care and clarity.

research proposal
A research proposal is a blueprint for conducting and controlling research. It is considered as a research plan to serve as a means of communication between the researchers and the research supporters.

In this section, the purpose, content, types, and format of research proposals will be presented. Needless to say, the details for a typical proposal will be presented with qualifications wherever necessary and illustrations will be provided.

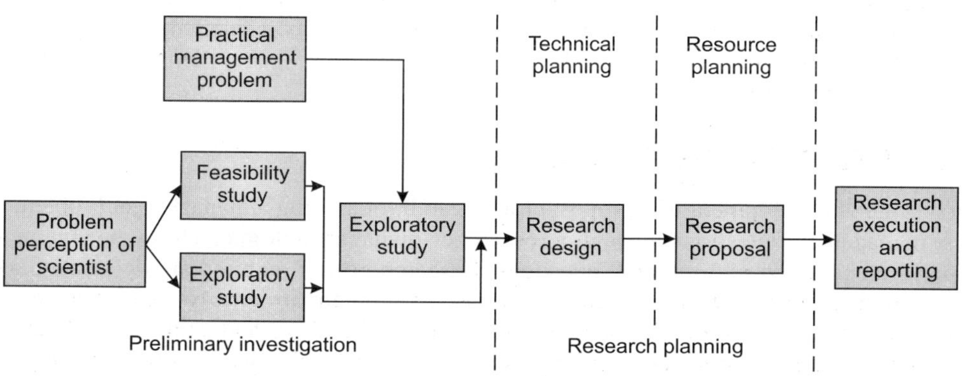

Fig. 5.1 Research proposal in research flow

purpose of research proposal

The purpose is to communicate clearly the need of the research, the benefits and the beneficiaries, the kind of data and types of analysis, the duration, the usefulness to other organization and the credentials of the proposers.

PURPOSE OF A RESEARCH PROPOSAL

The purpose of a research proposal is to clearly communicate the following to the sponsor:

1. Need of the particular research
2. Benefits of the research
3. Beneficiaries of the research
4. Kind of data to be collected and the means
5. Type of analysis that will be done
6. Whether help of other organisations will be needed
7. Duration, facilities, and funds required to carry out the research
8. Credentials of the proposers

A research proposal is critical, for it makes the researcher think of the possible roadblocks on the way and alternate bypasses to be taken in such cases. Another very important use of a research proposal is that it helps the decision maker and the researcher to arrive at agreements on the problem with regard to objectives, information required, and the methods of analysis.

TYPES OF RESEARCH PROPOSALS

types of research proposals

The types of proposals: (a) academic research proposal for conferments, (b) proposals internally generated and funded, and (c) proposal internally generated and externally funded either by a public or private funding agency.

The type of proposal depends on the type of project it deals with. It may range from a simple pilot study to a large complex project. It may originate from corporations (firms), research students (graduates), faculty in a university, or research organisations, both private and public, or research consultants. One way of classifying research proposals is to consider them as internal proposals or external proposals.

Internal proposals These are proposals generated within an organisation or agency and submitted to its management for approval or funding. They are responses to specific management needs of problem solving or product or process development, and are funded internally. The emphasis is on solving the immediate problem or developing new product/process or modifying old ones. They do not emphasise literature reviews. An executive summary is required in these proposals for quick management appreciation. Schedule of funds and time frame for completion should also be included. Project plans like Program Evaluation and Review Technique/Critical Path Method charts are not generally required.

External proposals A proposal generated within an organisation and directed to an outside customer, organisation, or funding agency, is an external proposal. This may be against an advertisement or solicitation from the customer. Then the proposal becomes a competing bid. It may also be unsolicited, in which case the proposing scientist or organisation makes the proposal based on a perceived general/natural need after a preliminary/feasibility study. Usually, the external proposal is larger in scope because it aims at winning funding for research, as in research institutes/universities, or winning contracts to generate profits, as in industry.

In external proposals, objectives, detailed research design, credentials of the research scientist/team, and the budget become vital. In complex and large projects, a detailed project plan like PERT charts may be required but specifications of the funding agency must be met in this regard (Krathwohl, 1988).

development of research proposal

Management questions are stated and converted into research questions. Objectives, data required, instruments of data collection, methods of analysis, the timetable of activities and costs are detailed.

DEVELOPMENT OF THE PROPOSALS

The first stage of development of a proposal for research for solving a management problem is to elicit management questions through a researcher-manager dialogue. These management questions are converted into research questions. Research efforts required are delineated and described to the manager. Data required for solving the problem are clearly communicated to the manager and his cooperation is ensured. The methods of analysis and a timetable of activities are mutually agreed upon. The credentials of the research scientist/team for carrying out the research are depicted.

Considerable amount of time and expenditure must be spent on the effort of developing a project proposal. Preliminary literature review, some feasibility or preliminary study to firm up the scope, objectives, data requirements and analysis methods may have to be conducted at the expense of the scientist or his organization. Where the project is large and complex, building up a team of expert scientists will be an arduous coordinating and planning task. Whether to bid or not to bid in a particular situation must take into account many questions relating to the stiffness of competition, technical suitability of the team, the capability to compete within the time and cost stipulated, previous experience with the soliciting organization etc.

Formatting the Research Proposal

Formats of the research proposal vary considerably depending upon whether the research is (i) academic, (ii) internally generated and funded; (iii) internally generated and externally funded and monitored, (iv) the funding agency is public or private; and (v) the research project is small or large. This has been well discussed in modules by Cooper and Schindler (2000). The essential items for all proposals are problem statement, research objectives, research design, and schedule (an example of a typical format is shown in Table 5.1 (also see Annexure 5.1 for the format of a real project proposal).

Table 5.1 **Format of a Typical Research Proposal**

Item No.	*Typical Section of a Research Proposal*
1	Project title
2	Broad subject
3	Subject area
4	Duration
5	Total cost
6	Principal investigator's details
7	Co-investigator's details
8	Project summary
9	Origin of the proposal
10	Objectives
11	Review of status of R&D in the subject
12	Importance of the project in the context of reviewed status
13	Review of expertise available with the team
14	Methodology
15	Work elements
16	Time schedule
17	Utilisation of research results
18	Budget details
19	Current research projects with the investigators.

Contents of the Research Proposal

contents of a proposal
These are the objectives, the research design, schedule of work, and budget of the research project. Credential of the researcher and a brief literature review are also included.

Research objective This item states the purpose of the investigation. It could be to test a hypothesis, as in a causal study, or answer a research question, as in descriptive areas, or obtain a solution to a problem. This should emerge naturally from the problem statement and constitute achievable goals of the research. The remaining items of the proposal should be consistent with the research objective, for example, data obtained, its analysis, and conclusions.

Research design This is the technical portion of the proposal indicating the phases/steps of the research action to be taken. Such tasks as sample size determination, sample selection, data sources, and method of data collection are stated. Also, the design of the instrument, procedures for data collection, giving possible reasons for rejecting alternate approaches, whenever they do exist, are also given. For example, in a causal study, why a descriptive field study was used instead of experimentation will be elucidated.

Schedule of work Time table of the major phases of the research should be included in this, for example, literature review, pilot study, finalisation of questionnaire, (main study) data collection, data preparation, report generation where the project is large and complex, a summary CPM/PERT network showing the interrelationship of the phases, and project duration may have to be provided, particularly when the sponsoring organisation demands it.

There are a few items required only by industry or sponsoring agents but not required in academic research like master's thesis/doctoral thesis. These are generally the credentials of the researcher, the budget, details of project management, and an executive summary.

Credentials of the researchers These include the academic qualifications, positions held, industrial/managerial/research experience, areas of expertise, papers published in reputed journals, by the team members and the consultations offered, memberships of technical/managerial/research institutions/associations held by them, and honours/medals awarded to them. This will give an indication as to the competence and technical capabilities of the team to carry out the research study proposed.

Budget In all cases of internal and external proposals, except very short ones, a maximum estimated cost of the research in some form of budget is a must. A typical "Budget Sample" format is shown in Table 5.2.

Table 5.2 Budget Sample

Item		*(Indian rupees in 000s)* *Year 1*	*Year 2*	*Year 3*
A Recurring				
1. Salaries/Honorarium				
a. Consultant		100	100	35
b. Project assistants		275	275	70
2. Consumables				
a. Computer and printer		100	—	—
b. Postage and communication		20	20	10
c. Stationery & printing		50	50	75
d. Books/Periodicals		75	25	—
3. Travel		200	200	10
4. Other costs				
(meetings, workshop, conference participation)		20	20	30
	Total	840	690	230
Overheads (organisation) 20%		168	138	46
	Grand Total (A + B)	1008	828	276

Other items which are part of any management research in the industry literature review, facilities and other resources, bibliography and glossary are provided in the case of academic research and very large projects involving large funding.

Literature review A review of literature should concentrate on recent research studies or developments, company data, or computerised data banks. From a quick comprehensive review in the general area of the research, it should delve critically and elaborately into the problem area, clearly bringing out the research premises on which the research methods and approaches have been developed in the proposal. Short comings, lacunae, and gaps in current research should be brought out. At the end of the review, a short summary pointing to the need of the research should be included. Whenever a literature review is mandatory, a bibliography is a must and it must follow one of the standards suggested by research manuals (see Turabian, 1971). A few other details like special equipment, glossary of special terms specific to a research area, and instrument details also have to be provided.

REQUIREMENTS OF THE SPONSORING AGENT

There may be other requirements of the sponsoring agents (SA), such as the following:

1. The project proposals should clearly focus on any of the areas listed by it.
2. Every project should have local project advisory committee of experts constituted by the research team in consultation with the SA.
3. The organisation carrying out research must take the responsibility for administering the project.
4. Proposals will be reviewed by experts in the field. The principal investigator has to make a presentation to the experts who may require the investigators to modify the proposals.
5. Periodic expenditure statements have to be submitted by the research organisation to the sponsoring organisation, with respect to funds received for the project.
6. A percentage of overheads will have to be earmarked for the institution in the budget proposal.
7. The report should be prepared as per the guidelines shown in Table 5.3

Table 5.3 Guidelines for Preparation of Project Completion Report

1. Format of cover page:
   (a) Title of the project
   (b) Name of the sponsoring organisation with project reference number
   (c) Address of the implementing institution with year of completion of the project
2. Report should be typed neatly in double space on A-4 size white paper
3. Fifteen copies of the final project report should be submitted
4. If the report contains data collection from other sources, these should be duly acknowledged
5. Wherever possible, pictorial presentation of data should be provided
6. The report should cover broadly the following:
   (a) Preface
   (b) Summary
   (c) Recommendations
   (d) Acknowledgements
   (e) Contents
   (f) Introduction
   (g) Methodology
   (h) Detailed analysis of the data
   (i) References
   (j) Annexure, including a copy of introduction letter, blank questionnaire, and other items.

EVALUATION OF RESEARCH PROPOSALS

An evaluation of the research proposal by the proposing research team/organisation can also be very useful before a proposal is finalised. Sometimes, using the draft proposal, a pilot study is conducted and every aspect of the project is rehearsed, so to say, in order to derive insights into the loop holes, flaws, inadequacies, and possible improvements in the proposal. The proposal is modified, particularly the sample, instruments, and sometimes even the scope of the study before submitting it to the SA.

In unsolicited proposals of single bidders, the SA may evaluate the proposal and suggest modifications as per the suggestions of the experts reviewing the proposal. In the case of competitive bidding, test of criteria for evaluation are developed and the bidders will be rated against them. Weightage factors may be provided for each criterion. Scores are obtained by multiplying the ratings and their weightage factors and summing them up. Whichever organisation scores the highest is chosen for funding. An independent expert panel may be used for this purpose.

Implicit considerations in proposed research

Ethical aspects, training aspects, cooperation of other organization and legal aspects are of great importance in executing the research study proposed.

ethical aspects of proposals

Safety, confidentiality and anonymity are three important ethical aspects of the proposed research.

SOME IMPLICIT CONSIDERATIONS

A few important considerations not specifically dealt with in the research proposal are discussed in this section. However, they are extremely critical in the execution of research study in a professional manner:

Ethical aspects Whenever human subjects are involved in the research—experiment, interviews, observation, and response to a self administered questionnaire—three aspects have to be carefully kept in mind. They are safety, confidentiality, and anonymity.

- *Safety:* This aspect is particularly important in experiments. No subject should undergo any harm, physical or psychological, while (and after) participating in an experiment. If there are risks involved, they should be clearly explained to the subject and a written consent should be obtained. Secret observation of an individual (if involved in the experiment or study) should not result in anyway in jeopardising the professional career of the individual or tarnishing his/her personal image
- *Confidentiality:* Any information obtained from the individual, group, or organisation should be kept strictly confidential and be merged in the aggregated disclosed information. If such individual information is necessary to be disclosed in the research, it should be disclosed only with the written consent of the individual unit. Personal data should be revealed only with prior written consent.
- *Anonymity:* Any sensitive information disclosed in a research study should not lead to the identity of the individual/group/organisation. Anonymity of these units should be strictly maintained.

Training aspects Qualified personnel hired/employed as project assistants should be adequately trained to make the execution of the project successful. The training may consist of (i) orientation and (ii) rehearsals.

- *Orientation:* The objectives of the study, the kind of data collection to be carried out, and the type of data preparation and analysis to be carried out should be explained to the assistants. It may be useful to them to study some relevant literature. What they should do and how they should do it, the exact nature of work and its details should be spelt out to them. Likely problems, difficulties, and restrictions in their work should be discussed. The importance of a good approach and human relations must be stressed.

- *Rehearsals:* Some mock up situations should be used so that the assistants (a) carry out interviews (among themselves or with the investigators), (b) get questionnaires filled up, (c) extract data from records, (d) make scientific observations, and (e) analyse fictitious data.

Cooperation Any research project involves the participation, in some way, of co-investigators, managers, and other employees and administration of an organisation, and the project assistants. Cooperation of all these people is vital to the success of a research study. Openness about the research study, data needed, assured confidentiality, and sincerity are essential to secure this cooperation. One of the most important factors to secure cooperation is to minimise the manager's work in the project and make it easy and clear. At each stage, human relations is a dominant factor. A *sine qua non* for securing cooperation is to make a written request for their participation and obtain consent as a regular procedure.

Legal aspects One of the best ways to get the approval for the project is to get it whetted by the University Research Committee, which has the responsibility of protecting the safety and confidentiality of the subjects, or use public procedures laid down by the national committees on safety and confidentiality of research. The core of the whole legal aspect is to obtain the consent of the individual unit after revealing the details of the project and the implications to the individual unit (for details with respect to this subsection please refer to the appropriate sources in the bibliography).

SUMMARY

Once the problem is formulated and the research design is clear, the researcher is ready to present a case for support and will be in a position to develop a research proposal. The research proposal is a means of communication between the researcher and the research supporter. Research proposal development is a part of the research process and enables the researcher to get funds for his research and execute it. The proposal should be prepared with care and in a suitable format. It should succinctly give the statement of the problem, objectives, usefulness of the result, the kind of data to be collected, and the methods of analysis proposed, in addition to communicating to the evaluating agency, the resources and time required for research. It also includes the credentials and competence of the researcher(s) who will carry out the research.

ANNEXURE 5.1

Sample (Real) Research Proposal (Krishnaswamy et al, 1997)

Development of Decision Support Systems (DSS) for Efficient Routing and Scheduling in Transport Systems

Project summary One area of transport planning where there is a vast scope for improving efficiency in operations is the routing and scheduling of transport fleets in various spheres of activities. Apart from the efficient distribution of foodgrains, cement, fertilisers, petroleum, and such other products, there is another dimension to efficiency in the routing of transport fleet. Specifically, a large number of organisations, both in the public and private sectors, provide buses for pickup and dropping of their employees. The magnitude of investments, the operational costs related to the daily running of these buses, and the associated fuel costs are phenomenal. Planning, routing, and scheduling of the fleet in these organisations is generally based on subjective judgements and intution. However, the efficiency achievable by scientific methods of operations research and the availability of present day microcomputers could be effectively used to meet the transport requirements at the minimum possible costs. The potential for savings in terms of reduction in fuel costs in this area alone would be of the order of several crores of rupees across the country. Similarly, in the collection and distribution of milk, food, and civil supplies from warehouses/central facility to various distributing outlets calls for optimal routing networks.

A recent study at the Indian Institute of Science has led to the development of a heuristic algorithm for better routing and scheduling of transport vehicles. The use of this algorithm in routing of employee pickup buses in a large public sector organisation in Bangalore shows scope for saving several lakhs of rupees every year in fuel costs alone. It is proposed to develop improved algorithms and a user friendly software in the form of a Decision Support System (DSS) as part of the proposed project. The objective is to ensure that these are implementable at the operational level in the various organisations involved in this type of transport operations across the country. A second DSS for efficient routing for the distribution of goods and services is also contemplated.

Origin of proposal The sponsoring agency has identified transportation as a thrust area under engineering sciences in its "identified areas of research". In recent years, following the energy crisis, which worsened after the Gulf War, there has been an urgent need to conserve diesel oil by efficient planning in the day to day usage of transport fleets in various sectors of the economy. In this regard, the investigators were associated with a number of real world studies related to the efficient routing and scheduling of vehicles in a few transport systems so as to minimise the unnecessary running of buses as well as the associated fuel consumption while simultaneously catering to the required demand. Some of these are briefly described below.

1. One study related to the efficient routing of vehicles for a public sector organisation in Bangalore involving the transportation of about 12,000 employees across four shifts from 410 pickup points in and around Bangalore by a fleet of about 100 buses. A practical heuristic method developed for the specific situation resulted in the reduction of the total mileage covered from 14,000 kilometres per day to 12,600 kilometres per day without affecting the timely transportation of employees. In terms of fuel consumption alone, this implies a 10 percent savings. The scope for potential savings for this organisation alone was of the order of several lakhs of rupees

Contd.

per annum. Additional advantages included lesser number of buses and drivers lower fuel consumption, higher seat utilisation factors and, on an average, lesser journey time for the employees. A similar study in another organisation involved the development of a heuristic method based on coordinate geometry and sweep algorithms, but was not implementable.

2. One student project involved the scheduling of buses across routes and scheduling of drivers across shifts to effectively manage peak load problems in another public sector organisation in Bangalore having a fleet of 250 buses to cater to the pickup and dropping of nearly 20,000 employees every day. The objective was to meet the varying demand during the day with minimum fleet size and crew size by effectively scheduling the fleet.
3. Another study related to the efficient allocation of buses to depots for the Bangalore Transport Service that had a fleet of 1200 buses on 8 depots at the time of the study. Use of simple integer linear programming methods to minimise dead mileage subject to depot capacity constraints indicated a savings of Rs 20 lakh in the form of operational costs.

Apart from these, investigators have considerable interest in several real world problems in the area of least cost distribution of milk, optimal distribution planning of foodgrains and rationed articles, efficient garbage disposal systems by city municipal corporations, and several other studies related to transport system efficiency. The networking of these on a computer system and optimisation of routing offers tremendous scope for improvement.

Definition of the problem Specifically, two types of problems related to transport planning would be addressed in this project. The first one of these relates to the pickup and dropping of employees of large scale organisations, both in public and private sectors. For example, in Bangalore city alone there are dozens of such organisations collectively having a fleet strength of more than 2000 buses, as per statistics obtained from the Motor Vehicles Department of the Government of Karnataka. In particular, four large scale public sector organisations, namely, Hindustan Aeronautics Limited (HAL), Indian Telephone Industries (ITI), Hindustan Machine Tools (HMT), and Bharat Electronics Limited (BEL) together transport nearly 60,000 people every day by a fleet of about 1,000 buses, covering 80,000 kilometre and consuming about 20,000 litres of diesel per day. The amount of fuel consumed is directly dependent on how efficiently the routes are designed across various pickup points and the fleets allocated across the various shifts. There is an urgent need to develop an efficient planning mechanism to use the transport fleets effectively, using the power of microcomputers.

A second problem of similar nature is related to the distribution of goods and services in many public systems. For example, the collection and distribution of milk, mail, and foodgrains would also need a similar scientific approach for achieving efficiency in transport operations. The characteristics of this decision problem varies greatly from the employee pickup problem. For example, the routing of a milk delivery van can be circuitous whereas that of an employee pickup bus should be almost unidirectional. It is planned to develop optimisation algorithms and associated computer software for this type of planning problems as part of the project. If successful, perhaps, these could be extended to the macro level for both statewide and nationwide transport operations.

Objectives The overall objective is to bring efficiency to transport operational planning through the optimisation power of scientific methods such as operations research and the computational capabilities of micro computers. The following objectives are envisaged:

1. To develop an efficient algorithm for routing and scheduling of transport fleets for employee pickup and dropping, so as to minimise fuel consumption, unnecessary mileage, and maximise fleet utilisation.
2. To develop a user friendly Decision Support System (DSS) for incorporating the algorithm in (1).
3. To test this algorithm and the DSS in a real environment through one or two case studies.
4. To develop an algorithm, and a DSS for transport fleet associated with the collection and distribution of milk and other goods and services at the urban and district level operations.

Review of status of research and development in the subject In western countries, realising the impact of transport planning on the state of the economy, tremendous emphasis is being placed in recent years on research in transport planning, which would lead to implementable methods and algorithms. In particular, considerable research effort is being made in the field of vehicle routing and scheduling. This reflects the widespread impact of microcomputers on computerised vehicle routing for commercial users. The availability of PC-based routing software has resulted in a drastic reduction in transport expenses. Some of the major contributions in this direction could be listed as follows:

- Fisher et al (1982) developed a system for Du Pont for the distribution of clinical equipment and supplies and helped reduce costs by 15 per cent (50 routes, 1500 customers, 1000 cities, 2 plants, and 5 depots).

Contd.

- Bell et al (1983) developed a routing system for Air Products and Chemicals Inc. for the distribution of industrial gases nationwide, which resulted in savings of 6 per cent to10 per cent (340 vehicles, 3500 customers, and 23 depots).
- Belardo et al (1985) developed an interactive system on an IBM PC/XT for Southern Corporation to construct routes for supplying a chain of departmental stores, which resulted in savings of $1,000 per day (7,000 stores).
- Evans et al (1985) developed routing system based on computer graphics for Kraft Inc. involving food service delivery vehicles, which resulted in variable costs savings of 10 per cent (13-18 vehicles, 15-\0-250 customers/day, and a single depot).
- Brown et al (1987) developed a system for Chevron for dispatching petroleum tank trucks, which helped reduce transportation costs by 13 per cent (430 vehicles, 50,000 orders/month, and 120 bulk terminals).
- Yano et al (1997) developed a system involving the delivery of goods to retail stores with backhaul option, which resulted in savings of $450,000 in 1996 (11 trucks, 40 stores, and a single depot).

In conclusion, it could be pointed out that considerable research work on the efficient routing of other modes of transportation problems is still going on in western countries. In recent years, both the US Government and the private sector have funded several projects and implementation research related to the routing and scheduling of different transport fleets.

To the best of our knowledge, there is very little work done in the area of transportation planning in India with specific focus on efficient routing and scheduling. One or two sporadic investigations in the past have attempted to indirectly address this planning problem in a local framework. The work mostly relates to theoretical exercises, with virtually no emphasis on implementability. Perhaps a major reason for this in the past was the non-availability of microcomputers at the user organisations. However, the advent of powerful microcomputers and their widespread adaptation in many spheres of organisational decision-making has now made it possible to implement such efficiency oriented algorithms through decision support systems in real life.

The need for fuel conservation at the national level needs no further emphasis as a large amount of foreign exchange is spent every year in importing fuel.

Methodology When formulated as a mathematical programming model, the vehicle routing and scheduling problem become a combination optimisation problem, involving millions of (0-1) integer variables. It is well known that these are complex mathematical problems that are difficult to solve for exact optimal solutions, even with the latest available computational capabilities of computers. Several types of heuristic approaches have been attempted in western countries, each being appropriate in a specific environment. However, the routing problems associated with employees' pickup and dropping, which has certain special constraints, have not been addressed earlier. It is only recently that this problem has been modelled by the researcher of this project and an exploratory heuristic algorithm was subsequently developed.

It is proposed to study and develop new heuristic approaches, including the possible modified/improved adaptation of the recently developed algorithm in the first phase. The efficiency of these would be compared on the optimal results obtainable from mathematical programming (combinatorial) methods on small scale test problems. Extensive tests would be conducted using linear and integer programming software. The best suited heuristic method would be coded as a software in an appropriate computer language so that it is usable in a PC/XT or PC/AT environment. The next step is to provide mechanisms in the form of development of a DSS. Specifically, the input structure in the form of demand at pickup points and distance matrix across various pickup points would be established along with flexibilities to inquire, update, and process information. These would be done in close interaction with the transport departments of one or two large public sector organisations in Bangalore, such as ITI, BEL, HAL, or HMT. Two workshops are contemplated to be held in this connection. The first one, in the early stages of the project, would be towards appraisal and identification of all the problem parameters associated in this type of vehicle routing problem. The second one, planned to be held towards the end of the project, will consist of the demonstration, training, and actual use of the DSS developed in the project.

As regards the routing of a transport fleet for the movement of goods and services, modelling and algorithm development would be attempted at an exploratory level only at this stage, keeping the routing problems within an urban framework. Traditional multiple travelling salesman problem type algorithms would be attempted to develop appropriate heuristic methods. A distance matrix of various nodes in Bangalore city is to be developed as part of the input data structure of the DSS for demonstration purposes. One or two case studies related to efficient routing and distribution would be taken up. No workshop is contemplated for this part of the routing problem in this project.

Contd.

Work elements The overall work in the project could be broken down to the following work elements. This includes both technical and administrative activities related to the project. The anticipated duration for each activity and the starting and ending months, from the project initiation date, are also given in brackets.

1. State of the art survey consisting of the current routing practices in a few organisations in Bangalore and an update of research literature (2 months; 0-2).
2. Recruitment of staff and project appraisal/orientation (3 months; 0-3).
3. Procurement of benchmark optimisation, transport networking, and routing software such as LINDO, TRNET 88, TPRO 88, and so on (6 months; 1-7).
4. Development of a mathematical model and appropriate heuristic algorithm-1 for routing and scheduling of employee pickup fleet (9 months; 3-12).
5. Development of Decision Support System (DSS) on a PC/XT or PC/AT environment incorporating the heuristic algorithm developed in (4) above for the routing and scheduling of employee pickup buses (6 months; 12-18).
6. Interaction meetings with likely user groups involving problem identification, delineation, and initiation (2 months; 6-8).
7. Case study analysis; extensive problem analysis, data gathering from one or two user organisations (such as HAL, HMT, BEL, or ITI), including test data on shiftwise and pickup-pointwise demand, distances across pickup points, nodal dropping centre, and so on (4 months; 15-19).
8. Testing the heuristic algorithm and DSS in the wake of case study data (2 months; 18-20).
9. Interaction meeting and/or workshop with likely user organisations on the use of the algorithm and DSS developed (2 months; 20-22).
10. Development of mathematical model and heuristic algorithm – 2 for distribution of goods and services (6 months; 12-18).
11. Development of a distance matrix mechanism in an urban environment, through the example distance matrix for Bangalore city (2 months; 16-18).
12. Development of a DSS for routing of transport fleet involved in distribution of goods and services (6 months; 18-24).
13. Case study and test data from one or two Bangalore-based user organisations involved in the distribution of goods (4 months; 23-27).
14. Extensive testing of the algorithm for efficiency and the DSS for effectiveness (3 months; 25-28).
15. Report preparation and submission (2 months; 28-30).

Time schedule The absolute time required for each work element or activity as well as the likely starting time and ending time, in months, are given under 232: Work Elements. However, since some of these activities could be carried out parallelly, the overall duration is much less than the cumulative absolute time. Details of the activitywise durations in relation to the starting time of the project are also given in the form of a bar chart under 410: Time schedule bar chart, from which it is estimated that the project would require a total of 30 months.

The important milestones and the anticipated times at which these are expected to be achieved are as follows:

1. Development of an algorithm to solve the efficient routing and scheduling of transport fleet for employee pickup and dropping (12 months from the start of the project).
2. Development of a DSS for (1) above (18 months from the start of the project).
3. Development of a practical algorithm for routing of transport fleet for goods and services in a micro or urban environment (18 months from the start of the project).
4. User friendly DSS for (3) above (24 months from the start of the project).
5. Implementation and usage (30 months from the start of the project.

Utilisation of research results Since this project is aimed at the development of implementable algorithms and decision-support systems, its ultimate goal is in its effective utilisation. In this context, two workshops are contemplated. The first one, in the early stages, is oriented towards identification and delineation of problem areas and would be confined to organisations involved in employee transportation in the Bangalore region. The second workshop, to be held at the end of the project duration after the successful development of the algorithm and the DSS for efficient routing and scheduling of transport fleet for employees pickup, would be at the national level. In this workshop, extensive orientation and training of the participants in the use of the DSS would be provided.

In addition to these workshops, wider dissemination is contemplated in the form of presentation of papers and demonstration of software in national and international seminars, forums of professional associations, and publica-

Contd.

tion in the form of papers and articles in journals and industry magazines. When successful, it is anticipated that the results would be of universal value to many developing countries, in addition to India.

Budget estimates

Item		*Budget (In Indian Rupees '000s)*			
		I Year	*II Year*	*III Year*	*Total*
A Recurring					
1. Salaries		51	107	117	275
2. Consumable		15	25	40	80
3. Travel		10	25	35	60
4. Other costs		37	44	94	175
B Permanent equipment		75	—	—	75
	Total (A+B)	188	201	276	665
Plus Institute Overhead (@ 10%)		18	20	37	66
Of which total FEC		(75)	—	—	(75)
	Grand Total	206	221	304	732

Note: Since the financial year is deemed to be from April to March, it is presumed that the work would be taken up only in October of the current year and, therefore, a total of six months only is considered for the first year. The project duration is 30 months (two, and a-half years) and, therefore, the remaining two years would have full duration of 12 months each.

Suggested Readings

- Krathwohl, David R. (1988). *How to Prepare a Research Proposal*, 2nd ed. New York: Syracuse University Book Store.
- Lefferts, Robert (1990). *How to Write Successful Grant Proposals*. Englewod Cliffs Prentice Hall.
- Locke, Lawerence F., Warren Wynck Spiduso and Stephen J. Silverman (2000). *Proposals That Work: A Guide to Planning Dissertations and Grant Proposals*, 5th ed. Thousands Oaks: Sage.

QUESTIONS AND EXERCISES

1. Why is the research proposal considered as a technical part of research?

2. Why is it necessary to carry out a feasibility study of a research before submitting the proposal for approval?

3. What need does a research proposal serve

(i) when soliciting funds? (ii) when submitting it for academic purpose to a university authority?

4. When the research design is not clear to the researcher can a research proposal be made? If yes, how? If no, why?

5. What are the ways of evaluating a research proposal?

(i) For seeking funds (ii) For acceptance towards a university degree

6. Study a research proposal (i) for doctoral research, (ii) for funding by the Department of Science and Technology.

Comment on the adequacy and various items of the proposal.

7. Study a Ph. D. thesis in a restricted way, as follows:

(i) The background of the problem and relevant literature (ii) The problem statement in a broad way (iii) The research design outlined in the initial chapters

Now write a research proposal using the above information.

8. Study the research report of an externally funded research project in a restricted way, as follows:

(i) The background of the problem and relevant literature (ii) The problem statement in a broad way (iii) The research design outlined in the initial chapters

Now using the above information, write a research proposal (compare with the original proposal if available).

Part C

Research Design—Types of Research

CHAPTER 6

Experimental Research

- Experimental Research
- Principles of Experiment
- Laboratory Experiments
- Experimental Designs
- Quasi-experimental Designs
- Action Research
- Validity and Reliability of Experiments and Quasi Experiments
- Sources of Invalidity of Experiments and Quasi-experiments
- Choice of Experimental Design
- Analysis Procedures Used in Experimental Design

Ronald Fisher

To call in the statistician after the experiment is done may be no more than asking him to perform a postmortem examination; he may be able to say what the experiment died of.
~ Indian Statistical Congress, Sankhya, ca 1938

LEARNING OBJECTIVES

Upon completion of this chapter, you will be able to:

- ✓ Understand experimental research
- ✓ Learn inductive reasoning as the basis of experimental design
- ✓ Enumerate steps in experimental design in order to make it efficient
- ✓ Familiarise with experimental designs in common use and their features
- ✓ Appreciate the difference between field experiments and laboratory experiments
- ✓ Study action research as a qualitative research experimentation
- ✓ Understand potential errors in experiments which invalidate them
- ✓ List means of validating experiments to assess that they do what they are intended to
- ✓ Identify reliability concepts to understand accuracy and bias in experiments
- ✓ Learn how to choose an experiment for a research situation

EXPERIMENTAL RESEARCH

In this chapter causal research designs using experimentation are dealt with. In an ideal experiment dealing with two variables, the independent variable I (supposed to be casual) and the dependent variable D (supposed to be affected) are studied in a controlled manner in a completely artificial environment. Changes are induced experimentally in I and changes in D are noted. No other variable is allowed to interfere (all other variables are kept constant) in the experiment. The researcher then concludes I is causal to D if every change in I induces a change in D. Such experiments are bound by certain principles and concepts, which will be dealt with. Just by using these principles any set of Is and Ds can be included and studied but the details of the experiments need to be planned or designed. This is the subject matter of experimental design. Only the most frequently used designs are dealt with. When the degree of control in certain experiments cannot be high due to practical reasons, quasi experiments, that is, field experiments are used. This chapter studies laboratory and field experiments in some detail. The relative strengths and weakness, the errors that creep into them in actual practice, and the ways of reducing them will also be dealt with. The validity and reliability of experiments will be discussed. Design and analysis of experiments is a subject in its own right in statistics. The treatment here, in general, is to provide a framework for the understanding of experiments, choosing them properly, being aware of the limitations and difficulties, and exercising caution about errors met with in experimental research. The statistical treatment of experimental, data for some simple statistical designs is presented in Chapter 16.

causal research design

Experimentation in which a researcher systematically changes the values of one or more independent variables to measure their influence on one or more dependent variables.

PRINCIPLES OF EXPERIMENT

The majority of managerial decisions are made on the basis of observations of relationships among variables. For example, a manufacturing manager may observe that people high on aptitude tests usually obtain high merit rating scores after one or two years' service in the firm. Such inferences on relationships show only associative relationships. No cause-effect relationship is implied. Sometimes the manager wants to make an inference on the relationship like whether a special programme of training a specific grade of workers will increase the productivity of the workers. In such cases he will have to base his inference on theoretical foundations based on experimentation. Causal inference is based on the following logic. If variable P causes variable Q then:

- Changes in P will cause changes in Q
- P will always occur before Q
- To infer that P causes Q, other possible causes must not exist.

In view of the above, statistical tests commonly used in the analysis of experimental data are analysis of variance techniques. The third condition mentioned above entails that P should be varied and the resulting variation in Q should be observed, keeping all other variables, which can cause changes in Q, constant by some degree of control over the change process. This is the basis of experimentation. An experiment is the setting up of a situation in which a researcher systematically changes the values of one or more independent variable(s) to measure the influence of these changes on one or more dependent variable(s). Experimental research is considered the ideal method of research because of its power in testing hypotheses (Hicks 1982).

Experiments have been conducted in such management areas as marketing (evaluating new products and selecting advertisement themes), production (use of production control systems, alternate inventory policies, effect of uncertainty in lead times on the MRP system, and influence of job design changes on worker productivity), personnel (training methods, organizational structures), finance (portfolio selection, investment decisions), and R & D (project control). There are a variety of methods available for experimentation. They are:

method for experimentation
Various methods of experimentation are: laboratory experiments, natural experiments, ex post fact experiments, trial-and-error experiments, controlled observationS and field experiments.

1. Laboratory experiment
2. Uncontrolled experiment/ natural experiment
3. *Ex post facto* experiment in which the cause is traced back from effect after an incident that has already occurred in the natural setting
4. Trial and error experiments used by lay men
5. Controlled observation study
6. Field experiments like action research, evaluative research, and simulation experiments.*

An experiment is an ideal tool for purposes of causal analysis. It induces great confidence in the researcher about assertions regarding causal relationships. Whenever field research or descriptive research is carried out, any declarations regarding causal relationships are always done in guarded and diffident expressions, because such research lacks the control present in an experiment.

Experimental research requires both manipulation and measurement of variables. In this sense, it tends to become a true experiment when a single variable is used for purposes of control. As against this, in a survey or a field study, the researcher would like to include as many variables as possible to make the setting more natural.

Basic terms used in experimental research There are a few basic terms which one must be familiar with in order to understand experiments, the experimental unit, factor, and treatment.

Experiment An experiment is a set of one or more runs of a system under specified conditions.

experimental unit
This is the study object from which the data are collected in the experiment.

Experimental unit An experimental unit is the study object from which data are collected in the experiment. If study objects are people (as in OB research, psychological research, marketing research or research in ergonomics/human engineering), they will be referred to as 'subjects' or else as 'tests units' as in engineering research.

factor
A factor is an independent variable which is either qualitative (nominally or ordinally scaled) or quantitative (intervally or ratio-scaled).

Factor A factor is an independent variable. Factors may be qualitative (nominally scaled or ordinally scaled) and are generally attributes/characteristics. Factors can be quantative when they are measurable on interval or ratio scales. They can be manipulative (whose values can be changed, like price in marketing or purchase quantity in inventory control) or can be classificatory (whose values cannot be changed but can be used for classification (brand of a product, "A" items in inventory control). Blocking factor is the name of an independent variable that is extraneous. It vitiates an experiment and does not serve the purpose of the experimentor. Factor level is the value of a factor.

*Simulation experiments are dealt with in Chapter 9 on modelling.

Nuisance variable A **nuisance variable** is a quantity (measurable) that cannot be controlled but which affects the dependent variable (one or more).

Treatment It is a specific experimental condition and denotes a combination of treatment-factor levels. Experimental units subjected to a particular treatment are called treatment group or experimental group.

treatment
This is a specific experimental condition.

Experimental design This is the research design of the experiment and typically consists of the layout of the experiment specifying all the details of data, data collection, sample size, and analysis involved in the experiment. A **design frame** is the specification of (i) which in dependent variable will be held constant, (ii) which in dependent variables are design factors, and (iii) which system outputs will be measured.

experimental design
This is the research design of the experiment consisting of layout, specific details of data, sample size and analysis.

In an experiment, the research question is directed to the experimental variables that can be controlled. The subjects (items experimented upon) carry with them their own individual variables and these are called subject variables/organismic variables. Two approaches can be used for making a true experiment.

1. Variables of little interest to the researcher, called the extraneous variables, will be held constant through careful sampling.
2. Subjects are assigned randomly to experimental conditions. Randomness is the essence of a true experiment. Randomness also controls all the extraneous variables and equates the two groups, one subject to experiment, and the other not subject to experiment, except insofar as the control variables are concerned.

Random assignments Random assignments are different from random sampling. Random sampling is used to make a sample of subjects, used in experiment, representative of the population from which it is drawn. Random assignment takes place from the random sample. The subjects in the random sample are randomly assigned to **experimental groups** and **non-experimental (control) groups**. Random sampling, thus, selects the representative subjects but random assignment allocates the subjects without bias to treatments. The experimental and control groups can also be different by chance. The chance of one group being different from the other is small when random assignment is used but the difference does exist. Usually the random assignment is checked for a significance of $p < 0.05$ or 0.01.

random assignment
The subjects in a random sample are randomly assigned to the experimental group and the control group.

LABORATORY EXPERIMENTS

Experiments create exact conditions required in which some variables are controlled and some are manipulated and observations are made on the dependent variables. This is a simple definition. The specialties of experiments are exact situations and precise control. In all research on experimentation, refinement of the manipulation process is the hall mark of progress. The laboratory is not meant for duplicating a real life situation; on the contrary it depicts pure situations.

Hypotheses, hunches and insights arise in real life setting but the definitive result and explanation can be derived only in laboratory experiments. The artificial conditions in the laboratory enables the researcher to verify and elaborate our knowledge obtained from observation or field studies.

Difficulties of Performing Laboratory Experiments

Major difficulties are encountered during laboratory experiments in management research. These are:

1. The strength (force) of variables is weak in laboratory experiments. One danger is weakness may result in no measurable change in the dependent variable or different conditions.
2. Manipulations of several variables simultaneously is difficult, particularly if the manipulation is through verbal instructions, as is generally the case.

3. Variables may be irrelevant, that is, no relationship is found (or else, the manipulations are not strong enough to evoke response in both the control group and the experimental group). The researcher is seldom sure of this in the present state of knowledge.

Design of Laboratory Experiments

laboratory experiments These experiments create exact conditions required for controlling the variables. Some are manipulated and others are precisely controlled. In the laboratory experiments, in general, the strength of the variables is weak, the manipulation of several variables simultaneously becomes very difficult, and some variables may be irrelevant.

The first step in the experimental design is to state the problem in experimental terms, specifically and clearly, keeping the following points in mind (Festinger and Katz, 1953).

- With *a priori* knowledge, the design must be drawn carefully in a deliberate manner, giving details of data, data collection method, sample size, and any analysis required.
- The measurement device required, like a reliable questionnaire or a test, must be developed.
- Any deficiency in the experimental design is rectified progressively with a few interactions in the same conditions or (as often is the case) in trial experiments.

Execution of Laboratory Experiments

There are several considerations in the execution of a laboratory experiment (Festinger and Katz, 1953) such as;

- Selection of subjects
- Size of the group
- Cognitive aspects of the subjects
- Choice of activities of the group
- Orientation of the subjects
- Control and manipulation of variable
- Measurement

These are discussed below in brief.

The kind of subjects that may be used in the lab experiment for decision situations are people, groups of people, operations, money, equipment, decisions, procedures, structure of organizations, and many others. Among these the selection of people as subjects is probably the most difficult. Uncontrolled conditions in subjects may arise depending upon the purpose of experiment, (i) they are friends/strangers, (ii) they belong to the same religious affiliations/different religious affiliations, and (iii) they are organised/unorganised. Repeated meetings of the groups may change these situations. Contacts outside the experiment and duration for which the group is formed may also change these. So checks will have to be made for these aspects while selecting the subjects, in order to keep the conditions equivalent for both experimental and control groups.

Manipulation of variables may take place sometimes at the time of selecting the subjects or during the experiment, through specific instructions. The attraction of the subject to the group interests in the group activity or the dislike of the group activity will be assessed and the subject will be allocated to the group accordingly.

It is generally preferable to have the same size of group for different treatments and different experiments, but it would appear that variable size groups are practically desirable as people may not participate after promising to do so, may not come in time for experimentation in the group, or may drop out at the last minute, causing a lot of problems in conducting the experiment. To keep the size constant, considerable operational planning and thoroughness is called for.

How the subjects perceive the experimental situation is an important aspect of experimentation. The subjects may completely believe that the experimental situation is the real one or at the other extreme the subject may know that it is an experimental situation. Their attitude to experimentation changes considerably with the perceptions of 'real' or 'experimental'.

When the subjects cognitively feel they are in an experiment, it would be very difficult to bring out powerful forces when variables are manipulated. On the other hand, with the feeling that it is 'real' the manipulation brings about more powerful changes, which is in the best interest of the experiment. The researcher may use subterfuges in order to make the experiment real to the subjects (Festinger and Katz, 1953, discuss several examples).

Activities of the group in the experiment are chosen on the basis of how the activities reflect the variables. The activities, like discussions, may be so arranged to give the subjects a feeling that the situation is real. The type of activities that are generally used are:

(i) Discussions in which the participatory and the communicative aspects are studied,
(ii) Problem solving,
(iii) Simple plays are used for experiments and sophisticated computer games for more mature subjects who may be drawn from the executive group of a company.
(iv) Work situations, when the variables like status and hierarchy may be important in the experiment.

The purpose of the experiment should be communicated to the subjects prior to the experimentation. If this is not done, there is a risk of the subjects in the groups making guesses and assumptions in the absence of informed purposes. These would introduce different conditions, upsetting the equivalence of the groups as well as post- and pre-experiment comparisons.

manipulating variables
This involves pre-experiment instruction, differential instrument, use of false reporting, paid participants and restrictions of behavior of participants.

Methods of manipulating variables Following are several methods of manipulating variables.

1. Pre-experiment instructions are given to the subjects by the experimenter. These instructions should be kept simple, as otherwise misinterpretations and variability of interpretation may introduce undesirable conditions. This method is, however, suitable for one variable manipulation.
2. Differential instructions may be employed with advantage for purposes of treatments, for example, one group may be made competitive, another cooperative by giving different types of instructions to these groups.
3. False reporting is used sometimes, but if it has to be successful, it has to be plausible. The false reporting procedure is not very successful (Festinger and Katz), probably due to the fact subjects generally come to know about the falsification of the report and react to it adversely.
4. Paid participants are a powerful technique for manipulating and controlling variables, but are expensive. These are generally accepted as regular subjects in the experiment and they act and behave in a manner decided by the experimenter so that certain conditions are brought about in the groups.
5. The behaviour of participants can be restricted- The activities of the group are characterised in some restricted way so that certain variables are manipulated or controlled. An example is insistence on making written notes in place of oral communication between any two subjects of the group. In this case, not only is the content and type of communication available, but its direction too is obtained by a series of such notes. Generally, to make sure that manipulations are actually working in the experimental situations it may be necessary to carry out preliminary experimentation.

Measurements can be made at all stages of the experiment. The main measurements are made during the recruitment and selection of the subjects, during the assembly at the laboratory experimentation stage, during experimentation, and at the end of experimentation. At the time of selection, and after the experiment, results will show the change in the variables before and after pre-experimental and post-experimental situations. Measurements made at the beginning of experiment may be used for checking the equivalence of the control group and the experimental group. Measurements during the experiment are the most important ones. The relationship between these measurements may be obtained through correlations or covariances. Measurement during the experiment takes many forms depending upon the variables. These are observations of the product of the experimental group activity, write-ups and notes kept by the experimental subjects, responses to questionnaires, voting procedures, interviews, and the administration of standardised tests.

Strength and Weakness of Experiments

Experiments do not ensure complete surety of results but the results can be stated more confidently than with other methods because internal validity is high. The disadvantages are:

1. Poor representation of natural process, which is sometimes called artificial testing of hypothesis or analogs of nature.
2. In practice, the representativeness of the sample is extremely difficult to be accomplished, even for the segments.

Errors in Experiments

errors of experiments
There are 10 potential errors in experiments. They adversely affect the validity of the experiment.

There are a number of potential errors that may creep into the results of experiments. These are caused by extraneous factors. Much of the variations in experimental designs are to ensure that these errors are minimised. Some of them are briefly discussed here (Tull and Hawkins, 1987).

1. ***History*** This does not refer to events before the experiment. It pertains to the extraneous variables (other than those manipulated) that occur between pre- and post-measures and affect the value of the dependent variable. For example, rejection in operations. Quality control of an operation affected by variables in input material quality.
2. ***Premeasurement*** This is a change in the dependent variable, which is solely the effect of initial measurement. If a measurement affects a subsequent measurement, then this error occurs.
3. ***Maturation*** Maturation is a psychological, organisational, or physical process that varies systematically over time (independent of any context) and affects the measurement of the dependent variable. Examples are press tool wear in quality control measurement and aging of respondents in a time series experiment.
4. ***Selection*** When the control group and experimental group are unequal, with respect to the dependent variable, this error occurs. Random assignment/blocking can minimise this error. Statistical regression is an example of this error. When certain subjects are preferred in experimental groups, this error occurs.
5. ***Interaction error*** This is a change in the effect of an independent variable because a pre-measure changes the respondents sensitivity or responsiveness. (attitudes, opinions, or awareness). This is the joint effect of premeasurement and an independent variable.
6. ***Instrumentation error*** This is due to a change in measuring instruments over time (efficacy of observation and interviews may change due to fatigue, loss of interest, or involvement).
7. ***Reactivity error*** This error may occur in case of human subjects because of the artificiality of the experimental condition or experimenter and cannot be controlled in laboratory experiments.
8. ***Mortality*** This problem arises, when a subject or respondent is lost during an experiment from the group due to various reasons, like death, and this loss may be different for different groups.
9. ***Timing errors*** Those errors arise out of inappropriate timing of measurements (both pre and post). They can be minimised by making measurements over a period of time (compare with measurements on stabilised values in simulation experiments).
10. ***Surrogate situation*** When the environment of treatments and/or the population sampled are different from those in an actual situation or the real world (that is, are surrogates) this error occurs. (for example, MBA students in place of business executives as subjects of experiments).

The above errors adversely affect the validity of experiments—both internal and external validity. How they affect the validity are discussed in the subsequent sections. First, the concept of validity and reliability will be discussed and the validity of experiments will be presented and finally the sources of invalidity are summarised for both experiments and quasi experiments. With this background, the choice of experimental design to eliminate them is presented finally.

EXPERIMENTAL DESIGNS

There are three measures of the amount of information generated in an experiment. They are variance, confounding, and bias. Variance indicates the precision with which the information is generated (for example, β_0, β_1 on the regression line). Confounding is a measure of the confidence with which the values of β may be asserted and bias is indicated by the degree to which the estimated values of β_0, β_1 measure their values. Various experimental designs are tools to reduce these measures. For example, factorial designs (to be dealt in this section) reduce variance, confounding, and bias, which are large in one-at-a time experimental designs.

The design of experiments generally has five steps (Barton 1999):

1. Definition of the goals of the experiment.
2. Identification and classification of variables (dependent, independent, intermediate, and extraneous) or factors.
3. Development of a model of relationship between independent and dependent variable (linear regression, hypothesis testing, ANOVA, ANCOVA, and so forth).
4. Choice of an appropriate experimental design, run conditions, choice of a standard design, computer program generated, graphically generated, and so on).
5. Ensuring the validation of the design.

The designs of an experiment can be classified as (i) basic designs, where the number of independent variables dealt with is one, and (ii) statistical designs where the number of independent variables dealt with are more than one, and will generally involve statistical considerations in design as well as in the analysis of results.

Basis of Experimental Design

Modern experimental designs are based on the principles/canons propounded by Mill on inductive logic. They are reproduced below (Mill, 1990):

Method of agreement If two or more instances of the phenomenon under investigation have only one circumstance in common, the circumstance in which alone all the instances agree is the cause (or effect) of the given phenomenon (Fig. 6.1).

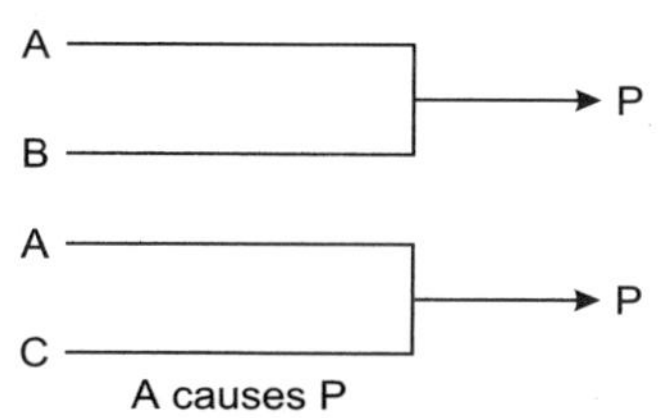

Fig. 6.1 Method of agreement

Mills cannons on induction

Modern experimentation is based on these cannons: method of agreement, method of difference, joint method of agreement and difference, and method of concomitant variations.

Method of difference If an instance in which the phenomenon under investigation occurs and an instance in which it does not occur have every circumstance save one in common, the one occurring only in the former, the circumstance in which alone the two instances differ is the effect, cause, or a necessary part of the cause of the phenomenon (Fig. 6.2).

Joint method of agreement and difference If two or more instances in which the phenomenon occurs have only one circumstance in common, while two or more instances in which it does not occur have nothing in common save the absence of that circumstance in which alone the two sets of instances differ is the effect, cause, or a necessary part of the cause, of the phenomenon (Fig. 6.3).

Method of residues In any phenomenon such part as is known by previous inductions to be the effect of certain antecedents, the residue of the phenomenon is the effect of the remaining antecedents.

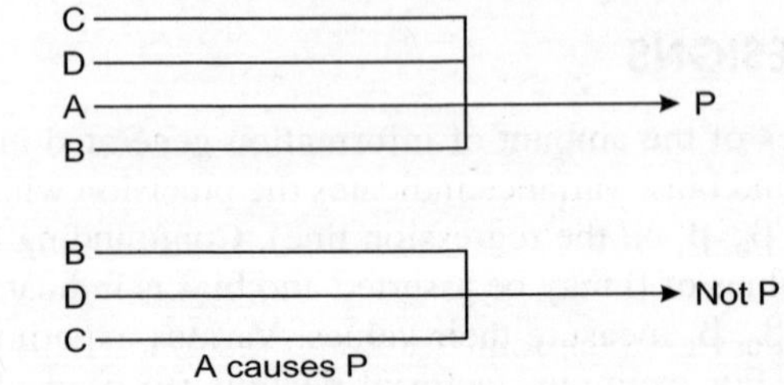

Fig. 6.2 Method of difference

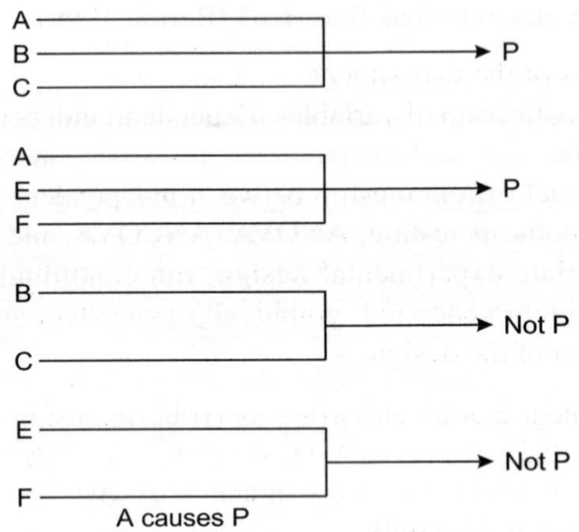

Fig. 6.3 Method of agreement and difference

Method of concomitant variations Whatever phenomenon varies in any manner whenever another phenomenon varies, in some particular manner, is either a cause or an effect of the second phenomenon, or is connected with it through some fact of causation.

An example of a laboratory experiment is given in Annexure 6.1.

Basic Designs

basic designs

There are three basic designs: randomized two group design, before-after two group design, and Solomon four-group design. These are based on Mill's cannons for logical induction.

The three basic experimental designs are: (i) Randomised two group design (after-only with control group design), (ii) Before-after two group design, and (iii) Solomon four group design (Four group six-study design). These are used with single variable manipulations. They are sometimes used with modifications and further developments. These experimental designs are based essentially on the Five Cannons of Mill for logical induction. The following notations are used in representing the experimental designs.

T = Treatment

O = Observation, outcome, dependent variable or effect, as the case may be

R = Random assignment

Design 1—Randomised two group design This is the simplest basic design (Fig. 6.4). Subjects are randomly assigned, both to the experimental group (to which experimental treatment is given) and to the comparison group (the control group to which no treatment is given). The difference between observations 01 and 02 would clearly be due to the treatment if the two groups are equivalent groups from the point of view of the threatening alternate explanations. Generally, bias elements as well as the maturation effects, which are time dependent, are also eliminated by observing the groups at the same time(s). There is, however, a need to check the subjects (subjects are individuals or groups as is mostly the case in social science research and management research) for historical events prior to the experiment or events influencing them during the experiment. If both groups are observed in similar conditions or circumstances, then the biasing events during the experiment will be largely eliminated. It is necessary to make a critical check for historical events. Instrumentation errors are also eliminated by keeping the

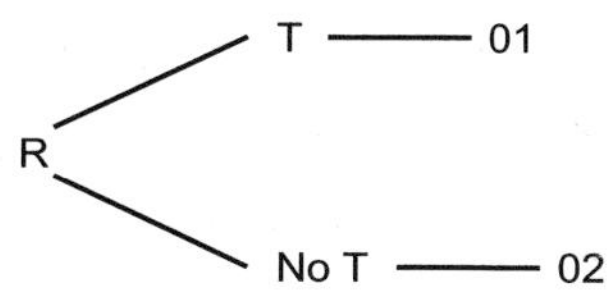

Fig. 6.4 Randomised two group design

conditions during the observation the same for both the groups. This design is the simplest and the safest from the point of view of predicting causal relationships. However, selection and mortality errors are not controllable in this design. An example of a randomised two group experiment is given in Annexure 6.2.

Design 2—Before-after two group design This design is the same as the pre-test post-test design. Pre-tests are carried out on both groups before the treatment is given to the experimental group to ensure that the groups are equivalent. This is a check on random assignment (Fig. 6.5).

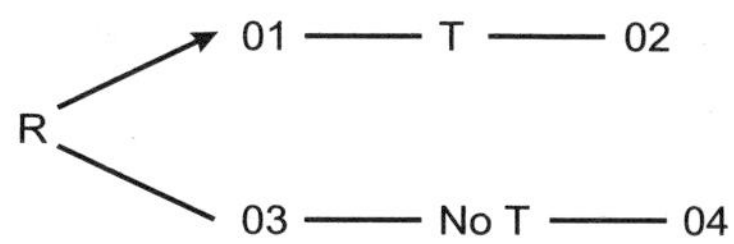

Fig. 6.5 Before-after two group design

Each subject is observed before and after the treatment for the experimental group. At the same times and under the same circumstances, observations are made of the subjects in the control group also.

Instead of observing the difference between 02 and 04, the difference between 01 and 02 and 03 and 04 are made and used for causal analysis purposes {(01–02) – (03–04)}. This is much more powerful than the first design as intra-individual comparisons are possible, are more precise, and the measure of the treatment effect also tends to be more precise. However, there is a weakness in the design. If the pretest affects the 2 groups differently, then the post-test difference between the two groups would be confounded by this fact, that is, one cannot say that the difference between 02 and 04 is due to treatment only. The design would not provide a solution to this. (See Annexure 6.1 for an example experiment by Shalley).

Design 3—Simulated before-after design This design deals primarily with attitudes and knowledge of human subjects. This controls the premeasurement and interaction errors using separate groups for pre- and post-measurements. However, the history effects may still remain (Fig. 6.6). This design is used extensively in advertising management/research.

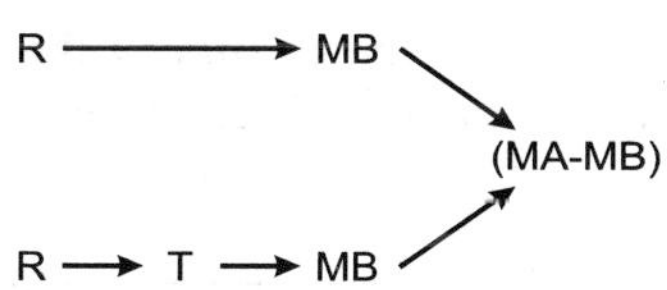

Fig. 6.6 Simulated before-after design

Design 4—Solomon four group design (Four Group Six-Study Design): This is a combination of design 1 and design 2 (Fig. 6.7).

Solomon design
When interaction of two separate effects is examined, this design is used.

There will now be greater number of groups for a single variable experiment. There will be two groups for each design (that is, 1 & 2). Pre-test and non-pre-test groups are included and for each an experimental and a control group are required. When one wants to examine the combination of separate effects, this design is used. The combination of pre-testing and treatments produces effects that are called interaction effects.

Fig. 6.7 Solomon four-group design

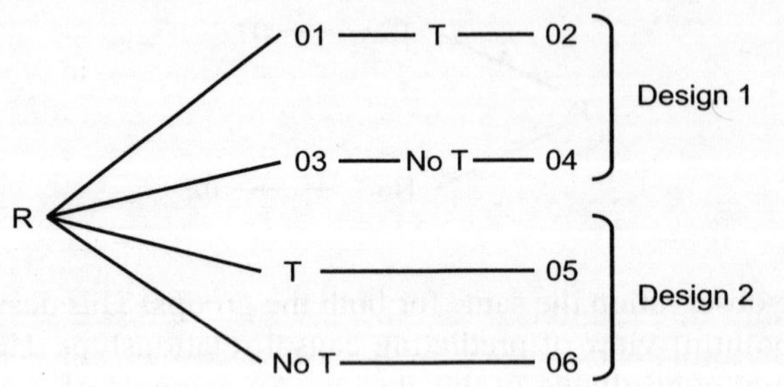

The results of the Solomon experiment can be used as follows:

Experimental Group 1	:	02 – 01 = E + U + I
Control Group 1	:	04 – 02 = U
Experimental Group II	:	05 – (01 + 03)/2 = E + U
Control Group II	:	06 – (01 + 03)/2 = U

Where E - Experiment effect,
I - Interaction effect,
and U - Uncontrolled variance.

An illustrative example of Solomon four group designs is given in Annexure 6.3.

Statistical Designs (Campbell & Stanley 1979)

statistical designs
These designs are used when dealing with the effects of more than one variables in an experiment. More commonly used statistical designs are factorial design, within subject design, randomized block design, Latin-square design and cross-over design.

These are designs in which there are two or more treatments. They can deal with the effects of more than one variable in experimentation. The principle features of the designs are:

1. Experimental layouts to assign treatment levels to subjects, and
2. The statistical techniques employed to analyse the data from experiments.

The more commonly used design layouts are (i) Factorial design, (ii) Within subjects design or repeated measures design, (iii) Randomised block design, (iv) Latin squares design, and (v) Cross-over design.

Factorial design When it is necessary to experiment with concomitant variations of two or more independent variables, this design is to be used and is, therefore, very common in social science and management experiments.

The design consists of experiments with every possible combination of two independent variables V1 and V2. (These are called factors for the purpose of experimental design.) Now it can be seen that the number of experiments required rapidly increases with additional independent variables (Fig. 6.8).

A 2 × 2 design (two variables) has four experiments; if there are 3 variables there are 8 experiments (2×2×2), and if there are *n* variables, 2^n experiments are required.

Fig. 6.8 Factorial design

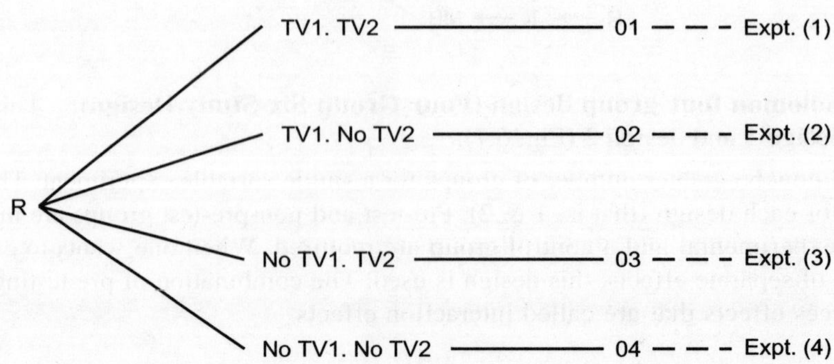

In a factorial experiment, equal number of observations are made of all combinations (involving at least two variables). The experiment makes it possible to study the interactions among the desired variables. In a factorial experiment test is done for main effects and when replication is done, the interaction effects can also be obtained. The aim of the experiment is to obtain the best combination of variables in order that some outcome (pay off as measure of effectiveness) is achieved. An illustrative example of factorial design is given in Annexure 6.4.

Within subjects design or repeated measures design In this design, the same subject is exposed to different treatments as against one treatment to each subject in the earlier design. The performance/outcome is measured (after each treatment) repeatedly. Variations caused over the repetitions in the outcome of a single subject are noted. These will correspond to the manipulated variables under the control of the experimenter. The design is more efficient, fewer subjects are required because the total number of experiments get reduced, the measures are more subject sensitive and, therefore, the comparisons are more accurate. The limitation is that the subject variables cannot be used with repeated measures design.

In interactions, say, of a combination of two variables, varying each of the two variables separately may not have any effect on the outcome/observation of experiments; but by varying both concomitantly may have a significant effect on the outcome. In general, individual effects may be totally different from the combination effect.

When the number of combinations or cells is large, the number of factorial experiments increases very rapidly. Usually, a minimum of five subjects are chosen for each experiment. The number of two factor interactions ($2n$), number of three, four, and five factor interactions will add up to an unwieldy, large number of interactions in factorial design. In such situations, repeated measures design is employed (say, 10 subjects are required for a 2×2 factor design for within subject experimentation, whereas 20 (5×4) would be required for between subject design).

Randomised block design These are experimental frameworks for cases of multivariate classifications. They are used when the researcher is interested in eliminating uncontrolled variation from the error term. So that large errors do not mask the effects due to treatment, these errors are blocked. An illustrative example of randomised block design is give in Annexure 6.5.

Latin square design These are multivariate designs in which interaction effects among variables is assumed to be negligible. The number of experiments can, therefore, be reduced and all the main effects can be estimated.

Latin square designs

These are multivariate designs in which the interaction effects among variables is assumed to be negligible.

In a full factorial experiment (4×4×4), with one replication (variables V1,V2 & V3), using the Latin square design, only 16 observations need to be made (see table below).

V2\V1	V11	V12	V13	V14
V21	V31	V32	V33	V34
V22	V34	V31	V32	V33
V23	V33	V34	V31	V32
V24	V32	V33	V34	V31

To illustrate the procedures for randomisation of a latin-square design, assume that we have four treatments. Also assume that we have the following four 4 × 4 latin-square design:

(a)	(b)	(c)	(d)
A B C D	A B C D	A B C D	A B C D
B A D C	B C D A	B D A C	B A D C
C D B A	C D A B	C A D B	C D A B
D C A B	D A B C	D C B A	D C B A

In general, the procedure involves selecting, at random, one of the 4 × 4, randomising the rows and columns of the square, and assigning the treatments at random to the letters A-D.

Assume we have randomly selected square (a). Using a table of random numbers, we can write down three random permutations of the numbers 1–4:

(1) 1,3,4,2
(2) 4,1,2,3
(3) 2,4,3,1

Using permutation (1), we rearrange the rows of square (a), which gives us:

1 A B C D
3 C D B A
4 D C A B
2 B A D C

We now rearrange the columns of this square in accordance with permutation (2) above:

4 1 2 3

D A B C
A C D B
B D C A
C B A D

Finally, if the treatments have been numbered 1–4, we arrange them in accordance with (3). This results in:

Permutation 2 4 3 1
Treatment A B C D

Thus, treatment 2 is assigned to A, 4 to B, and so on, in the latin square.

Cross-over design This is a design in which different treatments are applied to the same test unit during different time periods. One of the problems of this design is that the successive observations may not be independent, that is, they may have carryover effects from the previous observation. If there is no carry over effect, a latin square design can be used. This design reduces the effect of variation among test units. The following is an example of a randomised block latin square design (see table below) with no carry-over effect.

Test Unit	***Test Period***		
	1	2	3
I	A	B	C
II	B	C	A
III	C	A	B

When carry-over effect is there it could be assumed that an effect in a particular test unit, in a particular period is the sum of the test unit-period effect, the effect due to treatment in the period and the effect due to treatment of the previous period. An experiment is designed as follows (see table below).

Notice that B follows A twice and A follows B twice. This design is known as a double change over design and consists of reversing the sequence of treatments in two orthogonal latin squares.

Test Unit	***Test Period***		
	1	2	3
I	A	B	C
II	B	C	A
III	C	A	B
IV	C	B	A
V	A	C	B
VI	B	A	C

Panels in experimental designs This is very often used in marketing experiments. The before-after design with a control group or Solomon's design is employed in such cases. Problems of selection and testing constitute their limitation. (see Green et al, 1988, pp 224 & 229)

FIELD EXPERIMENTS

One of the features of a field experiment, distinguishing it from a laboratory experiment, is that it takes place in a realistic situation. Therefore, considerations of strong effects of variables are more easily exploited. There is not really much difference between laboratory experiments and field experiments. The difference is primarily in the degree of control. Some control is always possible in field experiment but is limited by the situation, whereas this limitation doesn't exist in a laboratory experiment. However, a field experiment is ideally suited for social science subjects like education, social psychology, organisational behaviour, and management studies.

The manipulation of independent variables and randomisation of both treatments and assignments of individuals to treatments is possible. But this should be achieved after obtaining the consent and cooperation of the participants in the experiments. Such cooperation can be elicited if the purpose of the experiment is clearly explained. Further, it is possible, by ingenuity and persistence, to make the field conditions close to laboratory conditions by a suitable choice of the situation. This may entail several alternatives to be examined/discussed before the final choice is made. Since the situation is realistic, the effects of the variables will be strong. The more realistic the situation, the stronger the effect of the variables. The realistic environment of field experiment gives it a strong external validity, which may not be directly possible in a laboratory experiment.

One of the biggest advantages of field experiments is that very complex social and management situations can be studied. This would not be possible in laboratory experiments. This method can be used for both, testing theory and problem solving, as in a laboratory experiment. However, field experiments are weak in precision. Measurement problems are generally complex. A high level of noise will be present in the experimental situations. Therefore, it will be necessary to maximise the variance of the manipulated variable and any other variable that is included in the experiment. This will tend to increase the variability of the dependent variable, which needs to be measured very precisely. Under these conditions, a laboratory experiment will be highly successful. But unfortunately in social science, researchers have very often found that dependent variables are sluggish and are not very sensitive to even large variances in independent variables *(refer to the field experiment example given in Annexure 6.2)*.

The purpose of the field experiment is to find the causal relationship in the natural setting. It is different from a field study. In a field study, correlations among measured existing conditions (variables) are determined. In a field experiment, the conditions are, to a greater or lesser degree, manipulated by the researcher. Crucial to the field experiment is the design of ways and means of manipulating the conditions. The researcher studies ongoing changes in the phenomena and their effects in an experimental design. This is a natural experiment. Only if some changes have occurred this experiment is possible. Crude, *ex post facto* experiments may also be conducted as natural experiments.

On the other hand, in a field experiment, changes of independent variables are contrived, at least in part. The purpose of field experiments may vary widely between development of theory, on the one hand, and complete practical application, on the other. Both these extremes may be present in action research, thereby serving a dual purpose. However, research preponders towards practical applications, for example, evaluation of two advertising appeals. Like any other experiment, a field experiment generally assumes easy availability of theory. Another important consideration is that subjects behave differently in the laboratory and in the field. Subjects in laboratory experiments may be constrained by the rules and procedures not found in real life situations (a classical example is the Hawthrone study). Artificial social aspects may creep into field experiments. Artificiality, therefore, varies in its extent, and not variety, in field experiments and lab experiments. Therefore, a simple creation of experimental design for field experiment is not possible, that is, one may not be able to lay down the experimental design in the initial stages of observation and experimentation. The design shapes itself slowly and opportunistically.

Problems that are very large or very complex cannot generally be handled satisfactorily in a laboratory experiment. In such cases, field experiments are preferred and only the influence of major independent variables are studied (just as major variables may be used in model building in OR/Simulation). It is desirable to note that field experiments may result from field studies with confounding hypotheses, (for example, the direction of causal relationship in a field study is not clear). The power of control of the researcher over the extraneous variables is usually limited because of difficulties in obtaining certain kinds of data. The field experiment tends to be more valid when the researcher has freedom of access to organisational data. [For further details of planning and conducting field experiments refer to Katz in Festinger & Katz (1953) and Cook (1983)].

Refer to the illustrative example of field experiment using randomised block design in Annexure 6.5 of this chapter.

QUASI-EXPERIMENTAL DESIGNS

quasi-experimental designs
Quasi-experimental deigns are used when true experiments are not possible. These are designed to study phenomenon naturally and in natural settings, involving no random assignment of subjects to treatment.

When true experimental designs are not possible, for various reasons, one may choose quasi-experiments. They provide designs to study phenomenon naturally and in natural settings. They are a compromise between poor experiments and true experiments; and they have found use throughout the history of social science research as a viable research method for social treatments.

In quasi-experiments random assignment of subjects to treatments is not made. Comparison groups may not exist in many cases. In quasi-experiments comparisons are made between (a) treatment and no treatment on non-equivalent groups, and (b) between prior and post treatment for the same group (without having a comparison group). Causal relations can be studied and verified, but certain threats exist in all quasi-experiments and should be constantly eliminated by data assignments and arguments by the researcher.

Quasi-Experimental Designs

Some of the quasi-experiments will be discussed with respect to poor experimental design.

Design 1—Interrupted time series design The related poor experimental design is pre experiment. Pre-experiment is a one shot case study (Fig. 6.9).

T ⟶ O

Fig. 6.9 After only experiment

This is a very weak design. There is no pretest data or information. The rival threats may be selection, history, and mortality. In selection, the sample experimented may have changed before treatment. In mortality, if there is sufficient time lag for O to occur after T, some Y's may vanish in O.

Illustration Smoking causes cancer. If no pretest is done on the sample, some of the subjects may have cancer even before starting smoking (selecting history) and in an observation of this sample at a point of time, some subjects might have died for other reasons, thus confounding the results. Since the lags are of considerable duration of time at the point O, cancer might have developed because of the influence of other variables not measured in the experiment, like air pollutants. It may have also developed because of the interaction of smoking with an unknown variable (not considered in the experiment).

In order to make a pre-experiment viable as an experiment, the interrupted-time series design has been developed. In this design the same group is studied repeatedly. A series of observations on samples are made in the pre-experiment (one shot). This eliminates the threat of the rival statement. This is a longitudinal design (Fig. 6.10).

1. 01 02 03 .... 06 T 07 08.....
2. 01 02 03 T 04 T 05 T .... T = Testing (Treatment)

This can have two types of designs in which a T is given only once in the series as in 1 or repeatedly as in 2 above. The arguments are the same for both. Random assignment and maturation testing can be eliminated, if there is a difference between say, 06 and 07. The difference is due to either treatment or maturation. If successive differences between 01 & 02, 02 and 03 and so on, show a trend, not a marked difference, then it can be attributed to treatment alone.

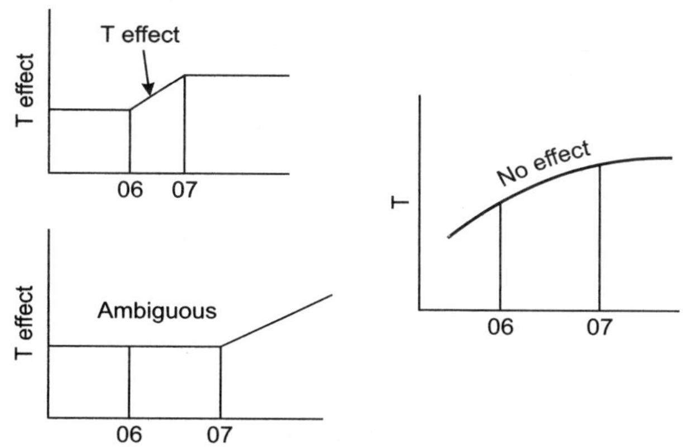

Fig. 6.10 Longitudinal quasi-experimental design

Maturation, if it is not a cyclic phenomenon, may coincide with a treatment effect. Situations like these have to be carefully checked before accepting the treatment effect.

Repeated treatment will produce similar differences. Trends in data, before and after treatment should be carefully studied before drawing conclusions about causal relationships. In this design, more than one group may be included in the series in which case it is called multiple interrupted time series design. It will be necessary to test the threat of history, which may not be revealed in the successive treatments because all series may be affected the same way. This is ideally suited for quasi-experimenting with actual data subjected to this experiment.

Design 2—Regression discontinuity design The pure experimental design from which this design has been developed is the Static Group Comparison. Two groups are considered in this design as follows.

Group 1 .... T 01

Group 2 .... T 02

The groups are naturally selected with an assignment which follows some method that is not random. The main method of treatment is interviewing.

SMOKING ⟶ CANCER .... Causal relationship

Rival explanations that will be relevant for the experimental design are the following.

1. Selection as a major threat.
2. Mortality or dropouts for other reasons.
3. Selection history interaction, that is, exposure to some earlier event may not change relationship and, therefore, reduce internal validity.

Illustration The field survey data on several companies in India show that the productivity of many companies has gone down after the introduction of wage incentives. This apparently paradoxical relationship can be explained using the concept of rival explanations and, in this particular case, of history. The stimulants for higher productivity are many, like good work design, sound time standards, proper environmental conditions, good union-management relationships, and adequate training of workers. If some, or all of these, are lacking in a company, the lowering of productivity continues even after wage incentives are introduced. Earlier, the declining trend of productivity prior to the introduction of wage incentives (T) would not have been seriously noticed because measurements of productivity have started after the introduction of wage incentives. The decline continued, indicating no effect of the treatment. But the decline was wrongly attributed to T.

The static comparison groups essentially use correlation analysis. Negative/positive relationships and strong/weak relationships are elicited from the data.

In the regression discontinuity design, two groups (or more than two groups) will be studied at the same time in a cross sectional manner (Fig. 6.11).

G1 G2 G3 G4 .... G6 ....

01 02 03 T 04 T 05 T 06 ......

In this design the threats of rival statements are similar to those of the interrupted time series design. But the results of the design give greater confidence because a number of groups reinforce the causal relationship.

Fig. 6.11 Regression discontinuity design

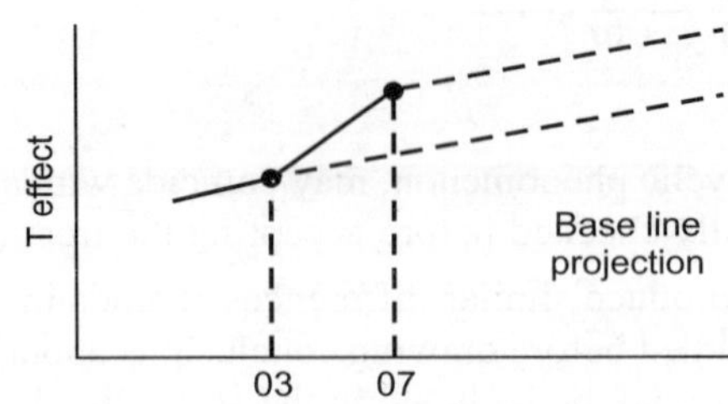

Design 3—Pre-test and post-test non-equivalent design This is a combination of one group pretest-post test design and a pre-experimental design.

Group 1 .... 01 T 03
——————————— .... Non-equivalent groups.
Group 2 .... 02 04

The results are more interpretable than either pre-experiment or the static group comparisons. Group 1 and Group 2 above are pre-existing and pre-selected groups. No random assignment is made to the groups. Group 2, the control group, is similar to Group 1, the experimental group, but not equivalent. This design enables the experimenter to eliminate certain kinds of threats, but maturation interaction may be present, confounding the results.

It is necessary in this design that a pre-test difference exists between the groups. From the Fig. 6.12 (a) and (b), maturation interaction may be present in (a) but, clearly, it is not present in (b).

01 is higher than 02 in (a), indicating this marginal higher value may be due to maturation in Group 1 for raising a variable value (positive slope), whereas in (b), 01 has a lower value of the variable than 02, which would not be the case for an increasing 03. However, underestimating reduces the variable by itself and increases it in interaction with the T. Then we can say that there is no maturation at intersection point in (b). For the variable under treatment in the group

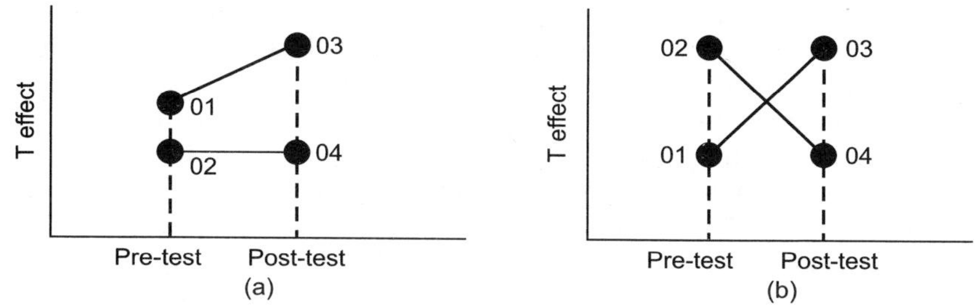

Fig. 6.12 Pre-test, post-test non-equivalent design

1 in (b), the values are crossing and maturation is not observed in Group 1 at the time of experiment, and is, therefore, ruled out.

A Comparison of the Two Quasi-Experimental Designs

In this section, a comparison is made between non-equivalent design and interrupted time series design and two case studies are discussed for the above two types of designs. One case study is on job enlargement and the other is on change in technology from batch to mass production.

1. One of the major advantages of a time series design over other forms of quasi-experimental design is that we can assess the maturational trend prior to intervention.
2. Time series are subject to many influences of a cyclical nature, including seasonal variations in performance, attitudes, or communication patterns; and these influences can be inadvertently interpreted as treatment effects. Since controlling of cyclical change obviously requires estimating the cyclical pattern along the time series, it is necessary to test this particular threat.
3. Time series design is useful when it is combined with a non-equivalent comparison group.
4. In a time series design, a pattern over time, before and after the change, could be examined. Also, adjustment over time, after the change has been introduced, is possible.
5. One observation before the change and one after change is made in non-equivalent design, whereas many observations are made in time series design, both before and after the change, and is, therefore, more reliable.
6. The cost of conducting the time series experiment will be more than the cost required for conducting the non-equivalent control group design. However, all situations cannot be studied with the non-equivalent group design, in which case time series design is the only alternative.

Use of Quasi-Experimental Designs

Quasi-experiment is undertaken when causal statements are to be made in cases of evaluation research related to social interactions, and studies like social programmes/management programmes for organisational development and training.

Quasi-experiment is best suited to the following:

1. Actual data is used in interrupted time series or over longer periods of time.
2. Social or management programme evaluation uses discontinuity regression design because wider data will be available and a cross-sectional study is desirable.
3. In doctoral research, generally the student uses his/her own data collection in pretest-post test non-equivalent design. This would not only make it cross-sectional but also reduce the width of data range.

Validity Quasi-experimental designs are attempts to compromise between maximising internal validity (true experiment) and maximising external validity (field study). It is better than field experiments or laboratory experiments, because subjects are not randomly assigned and the biases of naturally occurring selection are present. Truer field conditions, which give them higher external validity, are present. An important aspect of validation is the tackling of rival explanations, particularly selection. In many cases (like psychotherapy and certain training programs) subjects choose treatments by themselves, that is, self selection, which may be more appropriate in such situations, takes place (Kidder, 1981). This has to be carefully investigated. If the subjects are randomly assigned to treatments, there is a danger of their feeling of being made guinea pigs and a feeling of being part of a lottery among the subjects. This takes away much of the external validity. If the subjects are not randomly assigned, self selection bias occurs and internal validity gets lowered. The art and science of quasi-experiment is to strike a good compromise between the two.

ACTION RESEARCH

Defining Action Research

action research

Action research is a field experiment to solve practical problems involving the researcher and practitioners in the experiment. It is aimed at discovering facts and altering certain unsatisfactory conditions experienced by the organization by changing the process of the system itself. Action research is a quasi-experiment using generally the interrupted-time series design. Extraneous variance is high, internal validity is low and external validity is high for action research.

Action research may be thought of as a field experiment to solve practical problems. In action research, the researcher and practitioners work together. However, some confusion exists in the literature regarding the precise nature of action research. Different researchers emphasise different aspects or dimensions of the same construct.

Curle (1949) states that action research aims not only at discovering facts, but also at altering certain unsatisfactory conditions experienced by the community/organisation. Rapoport (1970) addresses the ethical issues involved and, therefore, defines action research as a type of applied social research differing from other varieties in the immediacy of the researcher's involvement in the action process. He explains that action research aims at contributing both to the practical concerns of people in an immediate problematic situation and to the goals of social science by joint collaboration within a mutually acceptable ethical framework. Forster (1972) adopts the definition of Rapoport with an extension that emphasises the specification of the linkage between researchers and the creation of an organisational change. He, therefore, defines action research as a type of applied social research differing from other varieties in the immediacy of the researcher's involvement in the action research process and the intention of the parties, who with different roles, are involved in the change process of the system itself.

French and Bell (1978) give a definition of action research, which emphasises the collaborative nature of action research as, "the collaboration of researcher and practitioner in the diagnosis and evaluation of problems existing in the practical setting."

Action research is the result of the integration of the following four different streams of development (Rapoport, 1970).

1. The Tavistock stream of experience that brought together psychologists and social anthropologists with psychiatrists.
2. One stream of operational research that joined social science.
3. The Group dynamics stream that emerged from the work of Kurt Lewin and his followers.
4. The applied anthropology stream, emphasising the need to approach problems such as the ones concerning industrial relations in cultural and sub-cultural terms.

Thus, action research is a multi-disciplinary problem-solving and theory development tool.

According to Clarke (1972), the distinctive features of action research are based on three dimensions—researcher's problem orientation, dominant diffusion channel, and audience. Action research is oriented to solving practical problems. Its results are channelised to the sponsoring enterprises and practioners are its audiences. An action research case is detailed in Annexure 6.6.

Process of Action Research

The processes of a design for action research, as outlined by French and Bell (1978), are:

1. The identification of a problem area about which an individual or a group is sufficiently concerned to (want to) take some action.
2. The selection of a specific problem and the formulation of a hypothesis or prediction that implies a goal and a procedure for reaching it. This specific goal must be viewed in relation to the total situation.
3. The careful recording of actions taken and the accumulation of evidence to determine the degree to which the goal has been achieved.
4. The inference from this evidence of generalisations regarding the relation between the actions and the desired goal.
5. The continuous re-testing of these generalisations in action situations.

Susman and Evered (1978) suggest a slightly different approach for an action research programme which is represented as a block diagram in Fig. 6.13. A comparison between the two approaches indicates that although there are minor variations in the 'steps' the overall philosophy of the approach is the same. It is to be noted that these are general guidelines and in an actual action research plan there may be overlaps and differences. The design depends on the setting and context of the organisation in which the research is carried out.

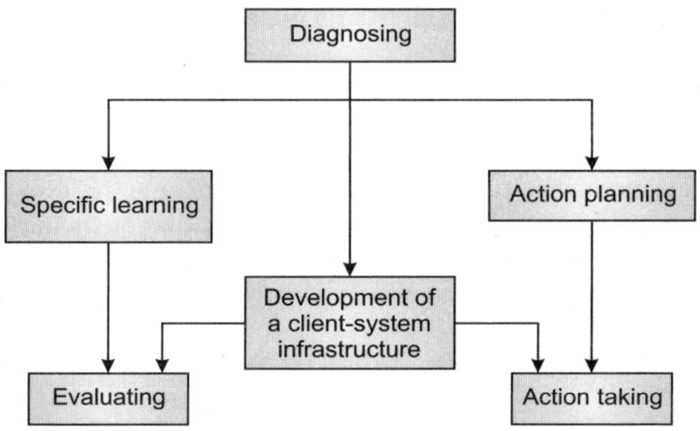

(*Source:* Susman and Evered, 1978)

Fig. 6.13 After-only experiment

Action research may be thought of as a field experiment induced by researcher-client combination in the beginning and an evaluation research later to assess how well the goals of the experiment are obtained in practice. With this thinking in the background, it is compared with experiment and evaluation research.

Comparison of Action Research with Experiments

Action research, by its very nature and setting, is a quasi-experiment. There are several quasi-experimental designs, and the design that best categorises an action research is the interrupted time-series design. In the action research intervention, itself is treatment; increasing or decreasing of organisational performance variables reflects the treatment effect. For an experiment to have internal validity it is important to have a high systematic variance and a low extraneous variance. The following observations are relevant in comparing action research as an experimental design.

1. Systematic variance is moderately high for action research. This is evident from the fact that an action research programme results in specific and clearly defined actions being taken. This aspect must be interpreted with caution. While the systematic variance for the programme on the whole is high, the systematic variance for the individual actions that make up the programme is very low.
2. In theory, it is possible to set up experiments in an action research programme so that the systematic variance is strong for each of the actions by: (i) segregating groups, (ii)

implementing different actions for different groups, and (iii) assigning a control group where no treatment is provided. But the researcher would need to satisfy himself with regard to the following issues.

(i) Delay in solving of the problem, and the responsibility towards clients.
(ii) Generation of needed knowledge to solve the problem, and responsibility to scientific community.
(iii) Generation of needed knowledge useful to solve problems being faced by other organisations, and responsibility to the community.

Action researchers face similar ethical issues at every stage of the action research process (Rapoport, 1970), and such issues place additional constraints on the design of experiments.

1. **Extraneous variance** This aspect is high in action research. It is evident from the fact that the establishment of trust between the client and researcher is a crucial factor in any action research programme. The outcome of an action research programme is, as considered by many researchers, largely attributable to the personality of the researcher. Therefore, the personality of the researcher is one major extraneous variables influencing the outcome, over and above the other extraneous variables that would be present. This increases extraneous variance.
2. **Internal validity** This internal validity of the experiment is low, like for all quasi-experiments.
3. **External validity** This external validity of action research results is high. The same feature that promotes internal validity can jeopardise external validity (Kidder, 1981). In action research the internal validity is sacrificed for external validity. External validity requires that the conclusions be true not only across people but also across conditions. Since the first part of action research is a thorough diagnosis and because the data generated is highly reliable and valid, the conditions surrounding the problem are very clearly identified, leading to a theory that is generalisable.

Comparison with evaluation research Action research is similar to formative evaluative research. And yet it is something more than formative evaluation. This is because of the fact that action research does not stop with asking the question 'does it work?'. It not only asks the questions 'what is it?' and 'how does it work?' but goes beyond this aspect towards finding a solution by asking 'what needs to be done to make it work?'.

Clarke (1972) identifies key differences between action research and summative evaluation research. The former has a tentative purpose as against a clear one in the latter. The former evolves the future from the present as against considering the present in the context of future. The former handles a much wider range of factors than the latter. In an action research programme, the employees themselves are involved in the data collection, and even in the design of the questionnaire, making the data that is collected a closer representation of truth. Traditional research methods cannot be used to study organizational problems that are caused by the structure itself and in such situations only action research methods can provide valid data. Further, action research is in addition to being evaluative.

Scientific Merits of Action Research

A critical evaluation of the merits of action research reveals that action research compromises scientific methods in order to be more practically useful. Susman and Evered (1978) argue that when action research is value driven, it does not meet the critical requirement of being value free as per scientific canons. The phases leading to action in the classical model are considered as a linear model:

1. Pure research
2. Applied research
3. Development
4. Application/Action

This is inappropriate for social sciences. Cherns (1972) cites a more appropriate model proposed by the Tavistock Institute of Human Relations in which the action research process is described as follows.

"On the whole, the social scientist has to reach his fundamental data (people, institutions) in their natural state and his problem is how to reach them in that state. His means of gaining access is through a professional relationship, which gives him privileged conditions. The professional relationship is a first analogue of the laboratory for the social sciences. Unless he wins conditions privileged in this way, the social scientist cannot find out anything which the layman cannot find out equally well, and he can only earn these privileges by proving his competence in providing some kind of service. In a sense, therefore, the social scientist begins to practice, however imperfect scientifically, and works back to theory and the more systematic research which may test this and then back again to improved practice."

Cherns (1972) describes this as the spiral model, which he quite rightly claims is a distinct improvement on the linear model. This 'spiral' or 'oscillatory' model versus the 'linear' model distinction is evident because two philosophical and pragmatic values underlie action research, as given below.

1. Action plans and programmes designed to solve real problems should be based on validated public data generated collaboratively by clients and consultants. This thinking calls for actions to be based on diagnostic research, which is similar in nature to the classical model.
2. Action in the real world should be followed by research on that action so that one can build up a cumulative body of knowledge and theory of the effects of various actions directed to solving real world problems—this helps to build better social science theories. It is this value that is absent in the classical model.

Action research can base its legitimacy as a science in philosophical traditions that are different from positivist science. Action research constitutes a different kind of science with a different epistemology, which produces a different kind of knowledge (Susman and Evered, 1978)—a knowledge that is not just restricted to the laboratory scientists but a knowledge that is created in the minds of every member of the organisation, a knowledge that develops the capacity of members to solve their own problems, and is thus an 'enabling' science.

VALIDITY AND RELIABILITY OF EXPERIMENTS AND QUASI-EXPERIMENTS

Concept of Validity and Reliability

In management research, establishing validity is complex, especially where behavioural and psychological properties are measured. In physical sciences, measurements are generally direct and the problems of validation are not difficult. Whereas in management sciences, the measurements are indirect, for example, managerial efficiency may be measured indirectly through such diverse aspects as profits earned by the company, industrial relations, worker satisfaction, organisational climate, and productivity. The measurement of many of these may be indirect or complex. In such cases, the measurements may be of doubtful validity and reliability. Therefore, validation assumes great importance.

Validity is relevant to any aspect of measurement—the instrument, the process of measurement, and the product of the measurement. We speak of validity of questionnaires (instrument), of observation and experiment (process), and of data (product). The types of validity discussed in the following sections are essentially the same for all, but the procedures and techniques may vary.

The concepts of validity and reliability are first examined. Next, various techniques of validation and ensuring reliability are discussed. Finally, the specific aspects of validity and reliability in experiments and quasi-experiments are dealt with.

Validity The commonest definition of validity is epitomised by the question "Are we measuring what we think we are measuring?" The emphasis in the question is what is being measured. (Kerlinger, 1986). This is a simple definition but the term "what" needs to be elaborated.

validity

Validity is epitomized by the question "are we measuring what we think we are measuring"? This question refers to contents of an instrument and its ability to predict behaviour. Validity means the measurement must be unbiased and free from systematic errors.

- In some situations the "what" would indicate the contents of the instruments (a questionnaire). Are they such that they can measure the "what"?
- In some cases "what" connotes the use to which the instrument is put, say prediction of behaviour. Content is of no concern in validation if the behaviour or a performance is predicted correctly.

In certain situations in management and behavioral research, the "what" refers to the theoretical construct or relationship in a hypothesis.

In research, generally, the last mentioned validity is the most important one. From the point of view of errors, validity means that the measurement must be unbiased, that is, free from systematic errors. The source of systematic error may be the instrument itself, the subject or the environment in which the measurement is carried out.

reliability

Reliability is the ratio of true-variance to the total variance yielded by the measuring instrument. It indicates stability and also the internal consistency of a test.

Reliability Another criterion by which a particular measurement can be accepted in research is its reliability. Reliability is related to the variable error of measurement. It means the extent to which measurement results are free from variable or experimental errors. Reliability can be defined in three ways. If the same set of objects are measured again and again with the same or comparable measuring instrument and the results obtained are the same or similar, then the measuring instrument is said to be reliable. This definition implies that reliability is stability, dependability, and predictability. If the measures obtained from a measuring instrument are true measures of the property measured, then the measuring instrument is said to be reliable. This is an accuracy definition. If the errors of measures are less, then the measuring instrument is said to be more reliable; and the reliability is the accuracy or precision of a measuring instrument. Any set of measures has a total variance. The total variance includes true and error variances. Thus:

$$V_t = V + Ve$$

Where V_t = total variance,

V = true variance, and

Ve = error variance

If there were no errors of measurement, then

$$V_t = V$$

But there are always errors of measurement. Thus, reliability of an instrument is more if the error is less. This gives rise to two equivalent definitions of reliability. There are:

- Reliability is the 'true' variance to the total obtained variance yielded by a measuring instrument.
- Reliability is the proportion of error variance to the total obtained variance yielded by a measuring instrument subtracted from 1.00, the index 1.00 indicating perfect reliability.

The definitions can be put in the equation form as follows

$$r_{tt} = V/V_t$$

$$r_{tt} = 1 - Ve/V_t$$

$$r_{tt} = (V_t - Ve)/V_t$$

where r_{tt} is the reliability coefficient.

Interpretation of reliability coefficient The square of the simple coefficient of correlation r is the coefficient of determination, which gives the proportion or percentage of the variance shared by two variables. The reliability coefficient is also a coefficient of determination. Theoretically, it measures how much variance of the total variance of a measured variable is 'true' variance. Reliability coefficient can be obtained by correlating the true scores with the scores of the measured variable and by squaring the resulting coefficient of correlation.

$$r_{tt} = r_t^2$$

Although it is not possible to calculate r_{tt} directly, it is helpful to understand the rationale of reliability coefficient.

There is a theoretical interpretation of reliability. Let $x_t s$ (test scores) be derived from administering the test to a set of individuals x a large number of times, other things being equal. Let them be ranked. The first administration yields a certain rank order of the set of individuals. If the second, third, and other measurings all tend to yield approximately the same rank orders, then the test is reliable. This is a stability or test-retest interpretation of reliability.

Another interpretation is that reliability is the internal consistency of a test if the test items are homogeneous. Take any random sample of items from the test and any other different random sample of items from the same test. Treat each sample as a separate subtest. Each individual will then have two scores: one xt_1 for one sample and another xt_2 for another sub-sample. Correlate the two test scores, continuing the process indefinitely. The average inter-correlation of the two sub-samples shows the test's internal consistency.

Improvement of reliability Some of the procedures to improve the reliability are as follows:

- Write the items of measuring instruments unambiguously. An ambiguous event can be interpreted in more than one way and it permits error variance to creep in. Such interpretations tend to be random, hence, increase error variance and decrease reliability.
- If an instrument is not reliable enough, add more items of equal kind and quality. This will increase reliability by a predictable amount.
- Clear and standard instructions tend to reduce errors of measurement. Great care must be taken in writing the instructions and in stating them clearly.
- Reliability should be valued and appreciated. To be interpretable, a test must be reliable, unless one can depend upon the results of the measurement of one's variable, one cannot, with any confidence, determine the relationship between variables. The objective of research is to discover relations among variables. The discovery of these relations becomes a difficult and tenuous process if a high degree of reliability is not achieved.

Validity in Experimentation and Quasi-Experimentation

There could be many types of validity when trying to develop a framework in which to understand experiments in complex field settings. Campbell and Stanely (1979) invoked two, which they called 'internal' and 'external' validity. Internal validity refers to the approximate validity with which we infer that a relationship between two variables is causal or that the absence of a relationship implies the absence of cause. External validity refers to the approximate validity with which we can infer that the presumed causal relationship can be generalised to and across alternate measures of the cause and effect and across different types of persons, settings, and times.

types of validity
The two types of validity are internal validity and external validity. Internal validity refers to the confidence with which a causal relationship can be stated from the measurement. External validity refers to the extent of generalizability of the results.

Internal validity Internal validity addresses the question, "To what extent does the research design permit us to say that a change in the independent variable A causes a change in the dependent variable B?" As Kidder and Judd (1986) note, in research with high internal validity we are relatively more able to argue that the relationship is causal, whereas in studies with low internal validity, causality cannot be inferred at all. In lab experiments where cause — effect relationships are substantiated, internal validity can be said to be high (Sekaran, 2000).

Even the best designed lab studies could be influenced by different factors that might affect the internal validity of the lab experiment. That is, some confounding factors might still be present, which could offer rival explanations as to what is causing the dependent variable. These possible confounding factors pose a threat to internal validity. There are several major threats to internal validity. These were earlier discussed in the section on errors in experiment.

External validity External validity refers to the extent results can be generalised. Field experiments have more external validity (that is, the results may be more easily generalised to other similar organisational settings); but they have less internal validity (that is, we cannot be certain of the extent to which variable X alone caused variable Y). But in the lab experiment, the reverse is true. The internal validity is high but the external validity is rather low. There is, thus, a trade off between internal and external validity. If we want high internal validity, we should be willing to settle for lower external validity and vice versa. To ensure both types of validity, researchers usually try to first test the causal relationships in a tightly controlled artificial or lab setting, and once the relationship has been established, they try to test the causal relationship in a field experiment (Sekaran, 2000).

Validity of Quasi-Experimentation

There could be many types of validity, depending on situations. For convenience, they subdivide the two validity types, namely, internal and external, into statistical conclusion validity, internal validity, construct validity of putative causes and effects, and external validity. The discussion given below on different types of validity has support from Cook and Campbell (1979).

Statistical conclusion validity In evaluating any experiment, three decisions have to be made about covariation with the sample data on hand: (i) Is the study sensitive enough to permit reasonable statements about co-variation? (ii) If it is sensitive enough, is there any reasonable evidence from which to infer that the presumed cause and effect co-vary? (iii) If there is such evidence, how strongly do the two variables co-vary?

The first of these issues concerns statistical power. It is vital in reporting and planning experiments to analyse how much power one has to detect the effect of a given magnitude with the variances and sample sizes on hand. In planning studies, the power analysis usually consists of discovering the sample size required for detecting an effect of the desired magnitude. In research probing causal hypothesis, statistical analyses are primarily used for deciding whether a presumed cause and effect co-vary. In many studies, a decision about covariation is made by comparing the degree of covariation and random error observed in the sample data to an *a priori* specified risk of being wrong in concluding that there is covariation.

Statistical conclusion validity refers to inferences about whether it is reasonable to presume covariation given a specified alpha level and the obtained variances. As such, statistical conclusion validity seems more closely related to tests of statistical significance than to the magnitude of estimates. Here the stress is on statistical significance because decisions about whether a presumed cause and effect co-vary logically precede decisions about how strongly they co-vary. Moreover, in most reports where magnitude estimates are given without corresponding statistical significance tests, it is usually presumed that the estimates of, say, the difference between two means, are statistically significant.

Some of the major threats to statistical conclusion validity are low statistical power, violated assumptions of statistical tests, fishing and error rate problem, low reliability of measures, low reliability of treatment implementation, random irrelevancies in the experimental setting, and random heterogeneity of respondents.

Internal validity Once it has been established that two variables co-vary, the problem is to decide whether there is any causal relationship between the two and, if there is, to decide whether the direction of causality is from the measured or manipulated A to the measured B, or vice versa. The task of ascertaining the direction of causality usually depends on the knowledge of a time sequence. Such knowledge is usually available for experiments, as opposed to most passive correlational studies. In view of this, in quasi-experiments, most of which require both pre-test and post-test measurement, the researcher can relate some measure of pre-test and post-test change to differences in treatments.

It is possible for more than one internal validity threat to operate in a given situation. The net bias that the threat cause depends on whether they are similar or different in the direction of bias and on the magnitude of any bias they cause independently. Clearly, false causal inferences are more likely when there are more numerous and powerful validity threats and when the direction of their effects is more homogeneous.

Some of the specific threats to internal validity are (in addition to those given under true experiments) ambiguity about the direction of causal influence, diffusion or imitation of treatments, compensatory equalisation treatments, compensatory rivalry by respondents receiving less desirable treatments and resentful demoralisation of respondents receiving less desirable treatments.

Estimating the internal validity of a relationship is a deductive process in which the investigator has to systematically think through how each of the internal validity threats may have influenced the data. Then, the investigator has to examine the data to test which relevant threats can be ruled out. In all of this process, the researcher has to be his or her own best critic, trenchantly examining all of the threats he or she can imagine. When all of the threats can plausibly be eliminated, it is possible to make confident conclusions about whether a relationship is probably causal. In randomised experiments, randomisation takes care of many threats to internal validity.

With quasi-experimental groups, the situation is quite different. In the absence of randomisation, the investigator has to make all the threats explicit and rule them out one by one. (The principal reason for choosing to conduct randomised experiments over other types of research design is that they make causal inference easier.)

Construct validity of putative causes and effects Construct validity is what experimental psychologists are concerned with when they worry about confounding. This refers to the possibility that the operations, which are meant to represent a particular cause or effect construct, can be construed in terms of more than one construct, each of which is stated at the same level of reduction. Confounding means that, whatever one investigator interprets as a causal relationship between theoretical constructs labeled A and B, may be interpreted by another investigator as a causal relationship between constructs A and Y or between X and B or even between X and Y. The reference to the level of reduction in the definition of confounding is important because it is always possible to translate sociological terms into psychological ones, or psychological terms into biological ones.

construct validity
This refers to the interpretation of a construct and to the confounding in an experiment or causal inference. Construct validity is assessed by testing for a convergence across different measures and testing for divergence between measures related to conceptually distinct "things". It has connotation of both internal and external validities.

Concerns about construct validity begin to surface at the planning and pilot testing stages of an experiment, when attempts are made to fit the anticipated cause and effect operations to their referent constructs, whether or not these are derived from formal social science theory or from policy considerations. Such fitting of interest to the construct is best achieved (i) by the careful pre-experimental explication of constructs so that definitions are clear and in conformity with public understanding of the words being used, and (ii) by data analyses directed at some of the four following points, but preferably all of them. Assessing construct validity depends on two processes: first, testing for a convergence across different measures or manipulations of the same thing and, second, testing for a divergence between measures and manipulations of related but conceptually distinct things.

For details of threats to construct validity of putative causes the reader is referred to Campbell and Stanley (1963).

External validity External validity refers to the extent the results of a causal study can be generalised to other people, events, or settings. Bracht and Glass (1968) have succinctly explicated external validity, pointing out that a two-stage process is involved: a target population of persons, settings, or times has to be first defined and then samples are drawn to represent these populations. Very occasionally, the samples are drawn from the populations with known probabilities, thereby maximising the final representativeness discussed in textbooks on sampling theory (for example, Kish, 1965). But usually samples cannot be drawn so systematically and are drawn instead because they are convenient and give an intuitive impression of representativeness, even if it is only the representativeness entailed by class membership. Accidental sampling, as it is technically labelled, does not guarantee that the achieved population is representative of the target population of which they are members.

Generalising to well-explicated target populations should be clearly distinguished from generalising across populations. Each is relevant to external validity—the former is crucial for ascertaining whether any research goals of those specified populations have been met, and the latter is crucial for ascertaining which different populations (or sub-populations) have been affected by a treatment, that is, for assessing how far one can generalise. The distinction between generalising to target populations and across multiple populations or sub-populations is also useful because critics of external validity have often implicitly stressed one over the other.

The threats to external validity are the interaction of selection and treatment, interaction of setting and treatment, and the interaction of history and treatment. Some of the models that could be used to increase the external validity are: (i) random sampling for representativeness model, (ii) model of deliberate sampling for heterogeneity, and (iii) impressionistic modal instance model.

SOURCES OF INVALIDITY OF EXPERIMENTS AND QUASI-EXPERIMENTS

The sources of invalidity of experiments are the various errors that creep into experiments. The errors in different experimental designs are different. None of the errors is present in all the designs. The sources of these errors are summarised in Table 6.1.

CHOICE OF EXPERIMENTAL DESIGN

The experimental designs are attempts to streamline procedures and layouts of experiments in order to eliminate or minimise these errors so that the accuracy of the causal relationships is achieved to a greater extent (for greater details refer to Campbell and Stanley, 1979).

In order to facilitate the choice of experimental layout for a given situation, a guide in the form of a flow chart is developed by Tull and Hawkins, (1987) which is reproduced in Fig. 6.14.

Fig. 6.14 Choice of experimental design

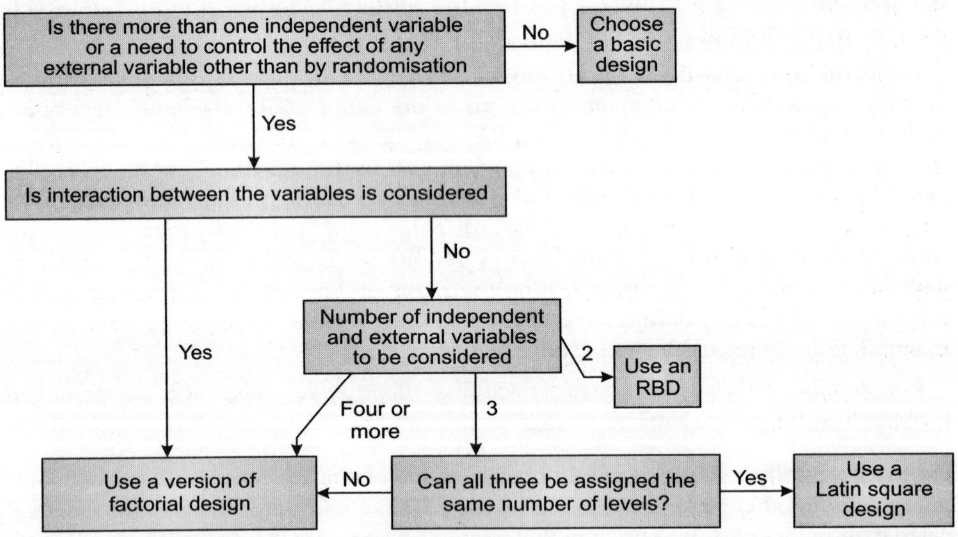

ANALYSIS PROCEDURES USED IN EXPERIMENTAL DESIGN

- The analysis of data from true experiments is most often done using analysis of variance and covariance techniques (Chapter 16) and testing hypotheses. As an alternative to this, path analysis or structural equation modelling can be used to determine the causal relationships between several independent and dependent variables. Path analysis is discussed in Chapter 17.

Table 6.1 Sources of Invalidity and Selected Experimental Designs

	Sources of Invalidity										
	Internal								External		
	History	*Maturation*	*Testing*	*Instrumentation*	*Regression*	*Selection*	*Morality*	*Interaction of selection and maturation, etc.*	*Interaction of testing and X*	*Interaction of selection and X*	*Reactive arrangement*
One-Shot Case Study X 0	-	-				-	-			-	
One-Group pretest-Posttest Design 0 X 0	-	-	-	-	?	+	+	-	-	-	-
Time Series 0 0 0 0000 0 0	+	+	-	+	+	+	+	+	-	?	?
Multiple Time Series 0 0 0 0000 0 0 0 0 0 0 0 0	+	+	+	+	+	+	+	+	-	-	?
Static-Group Comparison X 0 0	+	?	+	+	+	-	-	-		-	
Non-equivalent control Group Design 0 X 0 0 0	+	+	+	+	?	+	+	-	-	?	?
Posttest-only control Group Design R X 0 0 0	+	+	+	+	+	+	+	+	+	?	?
Separate sample Pretest posttest design R 0 (X) R X 0	-	-	+	?	+	+	-	-	+	+	+

- In quasi-experiments, cross-lagged panel correlation may be used when causality and deduction between two variables is measured at two or more points of time (Campbell and Stanley, 1979).

Some simple illustrative examples of analysis of experimental data are given in Chapter 16. However, detailed discussion of these are beyond the scope of this book.

SUMMARY

Experiments are ideal tools for purposes of causal analysis. In an experiment, independent variables are manipulated and the influence of these manipulations on dependent variables is obtained. Usually, a small number of variables are controlled in an experiment. But in any experiment there are extraneous variables that confound the results and introduce errors. The design of experiments addresses the all important aspect of minimising these errors. For this purpose, subjects are randomly assigned to the experimental group (in which manipulation takes place) and to the control group. Such a procedure enhances the internal validity of an experiment. Experimental designs are based on Mills cannons of inductive logic. Three basic designs are used when there is only one independent variable in the experiment. The statistical designs experiments are used in cases where two or more independent variables are committantly controlled. True experiments carried out in laboratories suffer from two main drawbacks. Firstly, the number of variables that can realistically be handled is small. Secondly, their external validity is low as the variable manipulations are handled in an artificial environment.

To allow for both these aspects, Quasi-experiments in which subjects are not randomly assigned and field experiments that are carried out in real world environments are conducted. Both of them are less rigorous but more practical. The two quasi-experimental designs, interrupted time series and regression discontinuity designs are the most frequently used ones. Quasi-experiments suffer from a large number of errors like self-selection, mortality, and maturation. Field experiments have an advantage over laboratory experiments in that, large and complex situations can be studied. However, they are considerably less precise.

Action research is an experimental research in which the experimenter participates through intervention in the changes of social interactions in an organisation. It uses principles of group dynamics and is aimed at solving a specific organisational problem in addition to developing theories relevant to organisational change.

There are a number of errors in experimental research, which are eliminated or reduced through the use of appropriate designs for specific situations. The major analysis procedures used in statistical designs are analysis of variance, hypothesis testing, and path analysis.

ANNEXURE 6.1

A Laboratory Experiment

A study by Shalley (1991), reports the results of a laboratory experiment conducted as part of a doctoral dissertation at the University of Illinois. The purpose of the experiment was to examine the effects of contextual factors on creative performance.

The contextual factors chosen for the study were: (i) presence of productivity goal, (ii) presence of creativity goal, and (iii) personal discretion. A 'three factors between subjects' design was used to investigate the effects of these factors on two performance measures, namely, creativity and productivity.

A total of 270 twenty-one-year-old undergraduates were the subjects in the study. Each of them was assigned an in-basket exercise. The exercise involved responding to 22 memos in the role of a managing director of a company. The exercise and memos were designed, based on two pilot studies, to yield a high integrated reliability for the

Contd.

performance measure of creativity. The 270 subjects were randomly divided into 18 groups of 15 members each. The exercise was the same, including the order in which the 22 memos were presented for all the 18 groups. However, the control variables, namely, production goal, creativity goal, and personal discretion, were introduced through appropriate changes in an otherwise standard instruction.

One of the three levels of production goals was assigned to every subject. A difficult production goal (complete 14 memos), do your best production goal (generate a solution for as many as possible), and a no production goal (work at your own speed) were the three levels of production goals. Similarly, one of the three levels of creativity goals was assigned to every subject. The subjects also had an instruction, which provided one of two levels of personal discretion. Thus, there were 3×3×2 different combinations of goals and personal discretion. So, each of the 18 groups had one specific combination.

After the exercise was administered, the responses were rated by 3 experts on a 7 point scale for each solution, using the consensual assessment technique—a technique successfully adopted by an earlier researcher for assessing creative performance. Cronbach's alpha was calculated for each memo, which established integrated reliability of the exercise and memos. The rating for each subject yielded a performance measure of creativity. The performance measure for productivity was simply the number of memos to which a solution was generated.

A structured questionnaire was also administered to the subjects after the task was completed and this confirmed that the communication of the presence of the appropriate level of goals and personal discretion had been complete. The data obtained was analysed by a three way ANOVA and one way between groups ANOVA.

The significant result of the analysis was that the goal could be used to effectively enhance the performance in a specific direction. Persons assigned difficult goals performed significantly better than those assigned 'do your best' goal. Goal-setting can be used effectively to enhance creativity when the creativity goal is assigned. In general, individual performances were higher when goals were set than when no goals were set.

ANNEXURE 6.2

A Randomised Two-Group Experiment

A major experiment by Fishburer et al (1988) to compare approval voting with regular plurality voting took place during the annual TIMS meeting in 1985. Most of the voters filled out an experimental approval ballet along with an official plurality ballet, thereby permitting a detailed side-by-side examination of the two methods. The experiment involved 1800 voters in 3 multi-candidate elections. Approval voting differs from plural voting in that it allows each voter to vote for any number of candidates. Each vote is a full vote so that if n people are to be elected, n candidates with most votes win. Plural voting is similar, except that each voter votes for utmost n candidates with more than two candidates for a position. The results would be different. In multi-candidate elections having two or more candidates beyond the number of positions to be filled, the two methods may produce different outcomes. Approval voting may be viewed as an extension of plural voting, which allows voters to express their preferences more fully in multi-candidate elections and then providing a more complete measurement of the support for each candidate. A number of studies were made prior to this experiment with respect to approval voting. Many studies suggested approval voting as superior and demonstrated that many majority candidates might well lose in the elections.

The questions addressed in the TIMS experiment were:

(i) Does approval voting make a difference?
(ii) What causes this difference?
(iii) Is it feasible?
(iv) Will voters behave effectively?

The TIMS experiment consisted of 3 elections: E1, E2 and E3. The candidates and voters were agreeable to the experiment.

Results

In E1, candidates A, B, C are contenders. C wins officially on plural voting by a mere 0.4 per cent, but B would have won on an approval voting by 6.1 per cent. C has a loyal following that is greater than B's. Among A's followers more approve of B than of C. It was concluded that there is no clear majority of candidates, but an approval voting picks a clear winner. A broader acceptance of a candidate and greater information regarding the support to the candidate can be obtained by plural voting. Similar results were obtained for the other two votings.

Contd.

ANNEXURE 6.3

Solomon Four-Group Design

An experiment was conducted by Mizerski et al (1980) as a corrective adjustment for eliminating undesirable effects of inaccurate or misleading information from a prior advertising. A corrective adjustment eliminates the undesirable effects on target beliefs, but does not influence non-target beliefs. However, earlier studies showed that corrective advertisement has very little effect on target beliefs, but significantly affected non-target beliefs. The limitations of earlier studies were that in experimental settings, a commercial medium was not used. Single exposure to corrective treatment was given as against multiple exposures, as injuncted by the court. The subject's sensitisation due to the possible knowledge the subject had of the experimental hypothesis.

The experiments related to Listerine antiseptic. Seven hypotheses were proposed.

H1: Subjects repeatedly exposed to the corrective advertising treatment will have a weaker belief that Listerine "fights colds and sore throats" (target belief) when their pre-test and post-test beliefs are compared and when their post-test belief is compared with a control group's belief on those attributes.

H2: Subjects repeatedly exposed to the corrective advertising treatment will not have different beliefs about the non-target attributes of Listerine when their pre-test as well as post-test belief is compared with a control group's belief on those attributes.

H3: Subjects repeatedly exposed to the corrective advertising treatment will not have a different belief about the perceived honesty of Listerine's manufacturers in comparison with a control group's perception of honesty.

H4: Subjects repeatedly exposed to the corrective advertising treatment will not have a different saliency for the target belief in comparison with a control group's saliency for the target belief.

H5: Subjects repeatedly exposed to the corrective advertising treatment will not have different saliencies for non-target beliefs in comparison with a control group's saliencies for the same non-target beliefs.

H6: Subjects repeatedly exposed to the corrective advertisement treatment will not have a different effect toward Listerine in comparison with a control group's effect toward Listerine.

H7: Subjects repeatedly exposed to the corrective advertisement will not have different intentions to purchase Listerine in comparison with a control group's intention to purchase Listerine.

To collect data in a natural setting, an on-campus radio station was chosen in a large university. The transmission was not a public transmission but specific to the university. The generalisability of results was restricted by the fact that the sample was only from the student community of the university. A systematic random sample was used to make initial contact with the students. The knowledge of the subject under investigation was completely camouflaged by letting the students know that the survey was intended to improve campus programmes that were to be broadcast. Potential subjects having a separate radio in their dormitory were taken as experimental group. Those who did not have it constituted the control group. Four half-an-hour listening periods were allotted for experimental transmission.

The participants were given some financial incentive and also a prize in a lottery. Forty-nine experimental subjects provided data for the experiment. The control group also received the same incentives.

A Solomon four-group experimental design was used because it allowed for direct measurement of change over time in, both the control and the experimental groups. As a pre-test, one experimental group and one control group filled up a questionnaire on the radio station. The questions were scaled on a 7 point horizontal scale—unlikely to likely (belief statements). Listerine was included among many other items like beer, local audio items, books, and soap.

The experimental group listened to the radio programme in the four allotted periods in a week. The students were instructed to behave normally as if they were listening to a general radio programme. The corrective advertisement was a professionally prepared adoption of their current Listerine advertisement. The corrective message was placed non-predominantly in the middle of the transmission. The subjects were asked to go to the radio station and fill up a questionnaire about their feelings and attitudes towards listening experiments. After a period of 11 to 13 days of the last experiment exposure, the experimental subjects were administered a final questionnaire.

The areas of questioning being demographic data, opinions and attitudes perceived honesty of listerine and beliefs about the product on a 7 point horizontal scale (likely -- unlikely, like -- dislike, important -- unimportant). The gap of 11 to 13 days was intended to reduce the sensitivity of the subjects. The subjects were interviewed after filling the

Contd.

questionnaire. The control group also received the questionnaire and was interviewed after a total of 18 to 20 days. The analysis of results using F-test, ANOVA, and MANOVA supported all the hypotheses. The author concluded that multiple exposures did have actual corrective effect on lowering the subject's target beliefs and there were no significant changes in the damping of the subjects' non target beliefs.

ANNEXURE 6.4

Factorial Design

A laboratory experiment by Sawyer et al (1979) tested three managerially controllable elements—marketing mix, price-product grade, and point of purchase information. The research question was 'what price levels are acceptable to consumers?' This is important from the point of view of distributors. Though the production costs prevented any profitable price decrease it was speculated that demand might be sufficiently inelastic to make it profitable to increase price.

Producers were interviewed in addition to obtaining consumer reaction to product grade distributions due to colour. Product information was included in the experiment to ascertain if the information about low percentage of pure syrup (maple syrup) and presence of artificial additives would result in fewer purchases. Three hundred female subjects from three cities were selected. It was ensured that these subjects had used maple syrup for the past 3 months and were desirous of continuing to use the product. The experiment used the previous three factors mentioned above and these factors were used on a 'between subjects' basis. The design was a 5×3×2 factorial with five price levels, three grades, and two levels of consumer information. The 300 subjects were randomly assigned to one of the 30 experiments for a total of 10 subjects/cell. Each subject was interviewed in an interviewing room and was asked about the past usage of various brands of syrup. They were shown 12 ounce bottles of syrup to several brands. The first three brands were commercial. Each bottle had a price tag in the front (current retail price).

The price and grade for the pure syrup was varied according to experimental conditions to which subjects were assigned; and the 'grades of pure syrup were indicated on the label. (fancy - grade A - grade B). The syrup color was varied with the grade. An information card was placed on the back of all the four bottles. The cards contained factual information about the contents. The subject, after seeing the four bottles, was asked to rate them on a six point semantic differential scale in the following five dimensions. Unfamiliar -- familiar, artificial -- natural, low quality -- high quality, poor value -- excellent value, and so forth. These dimensions were chosen based on past results. A sum of money marginally greater than the price of the costliest bottle was offered to each subject who was asked to purchase the brand of syrup using that money. Any change remaining would be retained by the subject. Finally, the subject was asked to give reasons explaining why they chose the brand that they did.

The following three hypotheses were formulated.

(i) Price would be inversely related to the choice.
(ii) Choice of pure syrup would be increased with the consumer information condition.
(iii) The fancy grade would be selected more often than grade A, which, in turn, would be more often selected than grade B.

The results obtained are:

- Price was, as hypothesised, inversely related to whether the pure syrup was chosen, and this was statistically significant.
- Neither consumer information nor the differences in colour were important determinants of choice.
- All the interaction effects of price grade and information were very small and statistically insignificant.

ANNEXURE 6.5

Randomised Block Design

A field experiment by Mizerski et al (1980) was carried out to determine the impact of physically attractive models on the subject perception of the advertisers by specifically examining the effects attributable to physical attractiveness. The study included both male and female models. The following hypotheses were tested.

Contd.

H1: Female will rate an advertisement higher than males on all dimensions, when a male model is present in the advertisement. Whereas, males will rate higher than females on all dimensions when a female is present in the advertisement.

H2: Both males and females will rate an advertisement higher on all dimensions when the advertisement contains a model who is physically more attractive than the others, regardless of the sex of the model.

H3: Physically attractive female models have a stronger positive impact on advertising ratings provided by males rather than those provided by females. Physically attractive male models will have a stronger positive impact on advertising ratings by females rather than those provided by males.

H4: Physically attractive male and female models will have a stronger positive impact on ratings by both males and females when the advertising product has romantic overtones than when the advertising product does not have such overtones.

These hypotheses were tested in a 2×2 random block design.

An experimental design was used for research for several reasons. The causal nature of physical attractiveness has been well demonstrated in social science research. This research has shown that physical attractiveness can be manipulated by use of photographs, without jeopardising internal and external validities.

The factorial design used allows testing of interactions among variables. It also allows the purpose of the research to be disguised.

The two independent variables manipulated in this study were physical attractiveness (attractiveness verses unattractiveness) and type of product advertised. (coffee/perfume/cologne/after shave lotions). The sex of the subjects, male or female, served as a blocking variable. Two different advertisements were developed, one for use with a male model and the other with a female model. Each subject was shown an advertisement with a male model and an advertisement with a female model.

The physical attractiveness of the model was manipulated by use of color photographs either for attractive or unattractive model. The pre-test consisted of having university students look at each of the 10 photographs and indicate on a 7-point semantic differential scale (1-unattractive …, 7-attractive) the physical attractiveness of the person in the photograph. The male and female models with the highest and lowest mean scores were selected as the stimulus persons for the experiment. The production type manipulation was implemented on both types of advertisements by using a few key words. By exchanging only four key words in the male advertisement and three key words in female advertisement, two distinct products could be advertised through the same advertisement copy.

In writing the copy, care was taken to choose words that would not create unique connotations that depend on the product.

Several item statements were used to measure the effectiveness of the advertisements. The items covered were cognitive, affective, and conative. In all 10 items were judged to provide reasonable of the three components.

Potential subjects from the total student community were chosen on the basis of their agreement to participate in the research. A written description of the experiment was given to the students. Any question by the student was discussed and answered. A data collection sheet was given to the subject to fill up for the 10 items on a semantic differential scale, and the ratings were obtained.

The results were generally, though not completely, consistent with the initial hypotheses. H1 and H2 were supported. H4 was supported only for the female model. These findings suggest that the sex and physical attractiveness of an advertisement model influence people's evaluation of the aesthetic qualities of advertisements.

ANNEXURE 6.6

An Action Research Case

This study by Pasmore and Friedlander (1982) describes a classic action research intervention that solved an organisational problem in an electronic industry located in a rural area. Most of the foremen and workers in this

Contd.

industry were residents of the surrounding area, while the managers were drawn from all over the country. Most jobs were fairly simple, although fine hand-eye coordination was required to perform the tasks. Ninety per cent of the production workers were females, while all supervisors were males. There were no unusually harsh working conditions and the traditional style of management was common throughout the corporation.

This plant was afflicted by unique, work-related injuries (not accident related). The injuries were increasing year by year for five years before an action research intervention was decided upon. The injuries involved damage to muscles in the wrist, forearm, and shoulder.

For the three years previous to the action research intervention, the plant manager had employed medical and technical experts to find the cause of the problem in the plant. All studies were conducted using accepted traditional research procedures. No cause could be identified but the injury rate continued to steadily increase.

These early studies generated a host of data. For example, it was found that age was correlated with injury, but, at the same time, newer employees were more often affected. Black females were more prone to injury than white females. Drinkers and widows were more susceptible than others while prescription drug users were less prone. A clear finding was that the injuries tended to occur in runs within one shift of workers while workers using the same equipment on other shifts were not affected. Variables not related to injuries included sex, blood pressure, smoking habits, weight, height, and hours of overtime work.

One reason for the consultants to resort to action research was the belief that the employees had data vitally important to understanding the problem. As a general rule, the authors believed that traditional research methods cannot be used to study problems in organisations, which are caused by the structure itself and in such situations only action research methods can provide data necessary for effective change.

The first action in the research was to bring together a representative group (five in number) of employees. These five, two foremen, the manager of employee relations, and the research consultants (the authors of the paper) made up the entire team, which was named as the Studies and Communication Group. The group members were indoctrinated to the action research philosophy and underwent training in data collection methods such as participant observation and conducting interviews. The group also developed and administered a survey questionnaire with 134 questions. An atmosphere of openness and trust was created.

A rigorous analysis of the data collected through interviews, questionnaires, and participant observations indicated that in the minds of the plant employees the injuries were due to both direct and indirect causes. The direct causes were identified as repetitive motion, improper equipment, and inadequate training. But the pattern of data revealed that the direct causes did not fully explain the injuries. The indirect causes identified were less tangible, such as stress, frustration, individual inability to handle anxiety and the like. The direct and indirect causes, as identified by the employees, helped finally diagnose the problem as being composite in nature, made up of two problems. It proved to be a case of medical tenosynovitis acting together with mass psychogenic reactions.

While providing feedback on the findings, much defensiveness was displayed by the managers and they vigorously attacked the group's conclusions as the data pointed towards problems traceable to the style of management in the plant. However, after the managers were convinced, and the findings were shared with the employees, the following actions were jointly drawn and initiated.

1. Biomechanical adjustment of equipment.
2. Continuation of the studies and communications group as a sounding board for managements plans.
3. Formulation of a methods-rearrangement group to experiment with work arrangements.
4. An institution for training foreman.

On implementation of these plans, the injury problem showed definite signs of improvement and in three years time, it was completely eliminated.

This study, apart from validating several theories, further contributes to theory development of stress-related problems of groups of a different nature. This group of employees were loyal to the organisation and always felt grateful to the organisation for having employed them, so much so that the employees had refused to be unionised out of a sense of loyalty. Further, the group of females had implicitly accepted male superiority as a way of life.

Suggested Readings

- Anderson, Mark J. and Patrick J. Whitcomb (2000). *DOE Simplified—Practical Tools for Effective Experimentation*. New York: Productivity Inc.
- Barton, Russel R. (1999). *Graphical Methods for the Design of Experiments*, Lecture notes. Shelton, CT: Springer Verlag.
- Hicks C. R. (1982). *Fundamental Concepts in the Design of Experiments*, 3d ed. New York: Holt, Rinehart and Winston.
- McNamara, Gerry and Jack Whitehead (2002). *Action Research: Principle and Practice*, 2d ed. London: Routledge.

QUESTIONS AND EXERCISES

1. Are *ex post facto* studies experiments? Discuss.
2. Give an example for each of the ten types of errors in experiments.
3. Is pre-measure error same as interaction error? Explain.
4. There are six basic designs discussed in the text. Compare any two of the designs and list the items of comparison.
5. Is the purpose of randomisation the same as matching in experimental designs? Explain your answer.
6. Why are simulated before and after designs popular in field experiments?
7. How does one determine which experimental design to use?
8. Which of the following questions can be tested experimentally and which cannot? Where a test is possible, briefly suggest an approach. Where a test is not possible, explain why.
   (a) Do children from urban areas drink more coffee and less milk than those from suburban areas?
   (b) Would frequent shoppers' reaction to a retailer changing his store layout differ from those of infrequent shoppers?
   (c) How will purchase behaviour change if a manufacturer of greeting cards changes the package?
   (d) Why do clothing fashions change?
   (e) Should a gasoline company add a covering over the gasoline pump at its retail outlets?
9. Can you suggest an experimental design to test whether worker satisfaction has been affected by the introduction of CNC machines in a plant? Give details.
10. Are field experiments more suitable for management research than lab experiments? Discuss your answer, considering the behavioural and situational dimensions of decision-making.
11. Choose a journal article of interest to you in your area of research, which involves experiments or quasi-experiments. After studying the paper carefully, develop an alternate method of experimentation and compare your method with the one in the original paper. Discuss with others.
12. Choose three outstanding experimental research studies reported in research journals. Cite and analyse the experiments in terms of Mill's Cannons.
13. What is experimental optimisation? How is it different from a true experiment?
14. Distinguish between internal and external validity.
15. What is blocking? Why is it done?
16. What characteristics differentiate a true experiment from the others?
17. Describe the conditions and situations in which a Latin-square design is used. Discuss an example from research literature.
18. Which is more appropriate, an experiment or a simulation, for the following situations?
    (a) Influence of wage incentives on the direct labour cost/unit of output.
    (b) A policy of promoting 50 per cent of the supervisors to managerial cadres and recruiting the other 50 per cent directly from outside. The influences of such a policy on the promotion opportunities of the supervisors.

(c) The effect of a new scheduling system on meeting of the due dates of preferred customers.
(d) Influence of training with computerised management games of middle level managers on their decision-making behaviour.

19. Should all research be conducted strictly to attain the criterion of generalisability? Give reasons to support your answer.
20. What do applications of research have to do with generalisability?
21. What is confounded relationship? Why and when does it occur?
22. What is the tradeoff between internal and external validity? In management research to which do you preponderate in general? Why ?
23. Co-variance control is the essence of experimentation. Discuss.
24. Take an example of application of action research from research literature. Discuss the experimental errors that might have crept into it. Do these errors influence the outcome of the action research?
25. How are accuracy and reliability related?
26. Take two research publications, one each on laboratory experiment and field (quasi experiment) experiment. Compare their validity and reliability issues. Are they same or different? If they are same, what do you conclude? If they are different how do you explain it?
27. Explain the following concepts:
    (a) Confounding
    (b) Construct validity
    (c) Noise in experiments
    (d) Natural experiments
    (e) Blocking
    (f) *Ex post facto* experiments
    (g) Action research
    (h) Surrogate error

CHAPTER 7

Ex Post Facto Research

- Introduction
- *Ex Post Facto* Research by Objective
- *Ex Post Facto* Resrach by Nature of Study
- Qualitative Research Methods
- Evaluation Research
- Outcome Evaluation

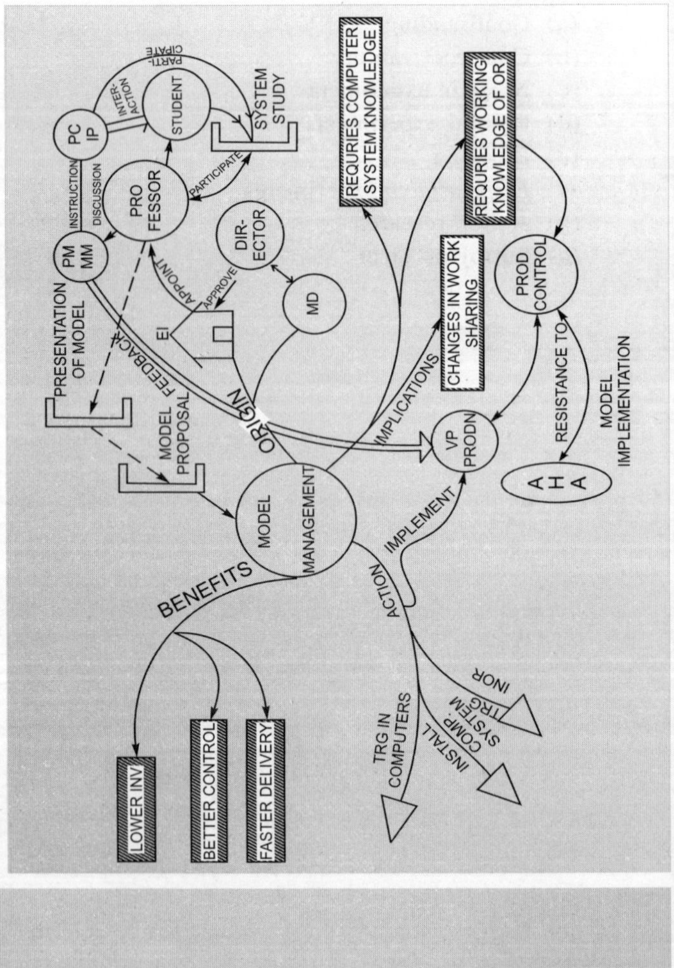

LEARNING OBJECTIVES

Upon completion of this chapter, you will be able to:

- ✓ Appreciate the similarities and differences in various kinds of *ex post facto* research
- ✓ Study special features of explorative, descriptive, evaluative and historic researches
- ✓ Understand survey research—how a design is made
- ✓ Find out how to design a field study
- ✓ Compare field study and survey research
- ✓ Understand the importance of participant observation in qualitative research
- ✓ Learn to use ethnography to study social aspects of organisation and management
- ✓ Learn to use case studies for developing 'thick' information
- ✓ Study qualitative research as a means of hypothesis generation
- ✓ Learn to appreciate the use of repertory grid technique for exploring the cognitive world of the decision-maker
- ✓ Learn to use critical incident technique as a tool for intensive observation of human behaviour in organisations
- ✓ Find out how to do research for development program evaluation

INTRODUCTION

Ex post facto research is concerned with non-manipulated variables of a phenomenon. Much of what is generally emphasised is descriptive research in which hypotheses are formulated and/or tested while studying the phenomena in their own settings (in the field). *Ex post facto* research can be classified into three broad categories (see Section 2.5 and Fig. 2.3).

ex post facto research
This research is conducted with regard to event or influences in a phenomenon after they have occurred or as they are occurring. It is concerned with non-manipulated variables of a phenomenon and has common fallacy (post hoc fallacy) in general.

1. Exploratory research
2. Historic research, which describes what occurred
3. Descriptive research, which describes that which exists

Exploratory research is not considered as a separate category as our view is that some exploratory component always exists in any kind of research, *ex post facto* or experimental; and is a precursor to it. However, we shall study it separately as it has some unique features.

As the name itself implies, *ex post facto* research is conducted with regard to events or influences in a phenomenon after they have occurred or as they are occurring. One of the principal features of *ex post facto* research is that the researcher does not have direct control over the independent variables and does not intervene in the phenomenon. All field studies in which data is collected using questionnaires and/or interviews/records either at a point of time or over a period fall under this category. In this context, the researcher has to face the following:

- Whenever the research interest is a causal relationship, like if X then Y, the extraneous independent variables (Zs), which are not of interest to the researcher, exists in the phenomena and there is no way of eliminating the effects of Z on Y. Y has occurred in the phenomena due to the combined effects of X and Zs. Attributing the variation of Y to the variation of X would only be the common fallacy (post hoc fallacy) in *ex post facto* research. However, in experimental research, X is measured and controlled and Zs are not changed in the experimental environment with the changes in X; and, therefore, the researcher will be able to answer if X then Y with a greater amount of confidence. In this sense, *ex post facto* research is a weak design of research.

- Even if, to a certain extent, the Zs in the phenomena are kept within reasonable limits of variation by a suitable choice of samples and individual subjects, it would still cause problems. In experimentation, extraneous influences, which may not have been completely covered in experimental environment, are eliminated through a process of randomly assigning subjects to treatments or treatments to subjects. This is clearly not possible in *ex post facto* research. However carefully the sample is selected, the treatment-subject assignments are not within the control of the researcher; and, therefore, a considerable amount of confounding will result.

- Another important consideration is sampling. In *ex post facto* study subjects are self selected. Now this self selection to a particular category/group to a particular treatment takes place because of attributes of subjects beyond the purview of the researcher. The following example will clarify this point.

Let us say that the influence of organisational climate on worker performance is being studied. Categorising workers into good performers and poor performers is to be done to facilitate testing a relevant hypothesis. Some of the workers may be categorised as poor performers because there is a lack of fit between job design and the worker. This may put the worker, straight away, under a low performance category and any variation in organisational climate may not influence this particular subject. He has self categorised himself as a poor performer because of an extraneous variable, namely, job design, which is not considered in the study. As can be seen, the above may happen either in an experimental study or an *ex post facto* study. But this aspect becomes crucial in *ex post facto* because already inherent weaknesses exist in the design.

In this context, one of the important aspects of *ex post facto* research is the need for testing multiple hypotheses or alternate hypotheses. Testing of alternate hypothesis may include alternate dependent variable or alternate independent variable. An acceptance/rejection of a null hypothesis would be facilitated by the rejection/acceptance of alternate hypotheses with different variables. This will be discussed later in greater detail under testing of hypothesis.

Illustration 1—*Ex post facto* research A comparative study of suggestion system and socio-technical system concepts in Japan and the United States of America was made by Hull et al (1988). The aim of the research was to test whether American factories generated as many improvements as a result of employee suggestions as Japanese factories did. The researchers contended that several systematic differences existed between Japanese and American firms with respect to several characteristics such as marketing, material inputs, m/c automation, and production methods. One major reason for better performance could be attributed to a high rate of suggestions by employees in Japan. So this study was directed to investigate into the causes and consequences of suggestion rates on factory improvements. This was carried out in both the countries. The basis for comparison were product type and size. The data pertained to 1982–83. Many measurement problems were faced by the researchers, since there was a considerable difference in the number of suggestions per employee between the two countries.

An earlier version of the questionnaire was used after shortening it, which resulted in uneven rates of completion and comparison factors. A host of factors of socio-technical design was responsible for improvements in organisations. Only the impact of suggestion rates was considered.

The questionnaires were followed by interviews. Finally, 85 factories in United States of America and 110 factories in Japan were included in the study. Two groups, one in each country, carried out the data collection work.

Correlation was carried out using five-point scale scores, indicating the level of intensity for dependent variables and independent variables. Factor analysis was performed first and subsequently multiple regression was carried out. The results showed that quality control was probably an intervening variable. Subsequently, a longitudinal study using a quasi-experimental design was conducted to prove this.

Ex Post Facto Research by Objective

Exploratory Research

The most important objective of an exploratory study is the identification of researchable problems. It also helps in achieving greater precision in the formulation of problems and development of new courses of action. It can be used as a preliminary part of a large study, (as in a two-stage research process).

exploratory study Some form of an exploration always exists in any kind of research and is a precursor for it. The research design is flexible and adaptive and changes as the research area becomes more clear. Its objective is problem identification.

There is no fixed design of exploratory studies. The design is flexible and adaptive and changes as the research area begins to become more clear to the researcher. After gaining insights into the phenomena, specific research questions may be raised.

Pure unstructured researches are not possible. But, generally, in exploratory studies some broad framework must be available. In this sense, they are definite because most of the current studies are constrained by resources and time. Factor analysis is usually used in the exploratory part for extracting natural variables and defining constructs. Factor analysis is a powerful tool but is rather demanding and exacting from the point of view of data control. The measurements have to be reasonably accurate in order that the measures are defensible. The samples have to be adequate and in field studies the interview should be well structured rather than open ended. Standard coding practices have to be used. This is the most important aspect of exploratory studies using factor analytic approaches.

Exploratory studies are not carried out without some hypotheses. Mostly such hypotheses are in the mind of researcher and are not spelt out. Operational definitions might not be given, but some measures are available in such cases; the problem size and scope have to be limited. That is, the problem should be looked at in a limited way. This causes elimination of many causal variables which may be left out from the study and, therefore, weak confirmations or rejections of propositions may result.

The following stages may be identified in most exploratory studies (Green et al, 1988).

- *Search of secondary source of information:* Sources of secondary information are published research journals, conference proceedings, report of studies in universities, government agency reports, company records, and company special study reports.
- *Obtaining information from knowledgeable persons:* An experience survey can be conducted. This survey is unstructured and looks for competent persons with experience in the research area, who are willing to talk and discuss. The knowledge and contacts of one respondent may be used to suggest other experts. Samples are obtained by snowball sampling or convenience sampling. A focus group interview technique may be used for data collection (see Chapter 11).
- *Examination of analogous situation:* This consists of case heuristic simulations in which a few cases with similar situations are analysed for obtaining common information on relationships.

In an exploratory study, discovering of factors, isolation of variables, specification of a system or even the measurement methodology may be addressed.

Example 1—Explorative Research Ravi Rammurthy (1987) investigated into the performance evaluation of state-owned enterprises (SOEs). The research problem was to explore the goal orientation of SOEs in India. The objective was to develop a behavioural theory of SOEs because of their importance to Third World countries in looking after public interest, rather than in the maximisation of profits. The spread of SOEs within the nations has raised stakes for governments that are anxious to manage them better and improve their performance. Their spread in international markets has raised stakes for private firms. Therefore, policy-makers in these countries are generally anxious to assess their impact on free markets. Thus, the goal orientation of SOEs, focusing on their actual behaviour, is important and concerns both owners and competitors of SOEs.

The research design consisted of searching for patterns in the subjective evaluations of a set of Indian SOEs by critical environmental factors. The study attempted to get the espoused theory of each respondent for performance evaluation against original goals as well as for practice (theory in use) as compared to the prescriptions of welfare economics. Five models of performance evaluation varying in criteria and weighing schemes were considered. A total of 104 firms were sampled and the response rate was 33 per cent, warranting great caution in interpreting the results. Only manufacturing firms (SOEs) having more than 1000 employees were considered, resulting in only 35 organisations for analysis. These accounted for 76 per cent of the total sales of SOEs in India during 1982–83. The population of external key controllers were in all 7 to 10 ministers, 30 to 40 senior bureaucrats, 20 to 30 members of media, 10 to 20 union leaders, and a few parliamentarians conversant in depth with the workings of SOEs. Ministers and union leaders were excluded from the study because they were unlikely to evaluate SOEs publicly. The data was collected through questionnaires.

Correlation analysis was done on the data and R was determined. Further, a multiple regression was also carried out.

The correlation between bureaucrats' response to statements A and B is – 0.85 ($p < 0.001$), which suggests that bureaucrats see a logical connection between goals and performance criteria. The average weightage for other criteria were: employment creation (10.5 per cent), exports (6.1 per cent), sales growth rate (10.3 per cent), import substitution (10.0 per cent), quality of industrial relations (9.3 per cent), technological capabilities (12.3 per cent), and others (13.9 per cent).

In the inter-correlation matrix among performance measures, only six inter-correlations were significant at $p < 0.05$. The random assignment model is rejected for all bureaucrats, that is, subjective assessments of bureaucrats are systematically related to objective performance data even though the number of SOEs included in the questionnaire is large. For bureaucrats as a group, over 70 per cent of the variation in evaluation can be explained by commercial profitability alone. The results of regressing respondents' scores against objective data on the seven performance measures are as follows.

- All coefficients in the multiple regression analysis had signs as expected, except, most notably, employment creation, which was negative in all the three cases in which the coefficient was significant.
- Technological independence had the opposite sign to that expected in only one out of the four cases where it was significant.
- In the group model for bureaucrats, multiple regression produced profitability as the only significant criterion.
- Commercial profitability assumes far greater importance as a criterion for performance evaluation, according to the revealed preference of bureaucrats, than one would expect from either their espoused preferences or official statements of SOE goals.
- A second example of exploratory research is given in Annexure 7.1.

Historical Research

historical research

This is different from most of the other kinds of research because of heavy dependence on logical analysis based on others' experiences and opinions. It may concentrate on a historical problem in management or historical view of a current management problem.

This kind of research is, in a way, different from most kinds of research conducted by social scientists, economists, and management researchers. It is useful in many disciplines (for examples in educational research; see Best and Kahn [1986]). The research may be one that concentrates on a historical problem in management or one that takes a historical view of a current management problem. In the former, a particular problem of the past, its description, and explanation will be the primary concern. In the latter, a mere look at the current status of the phenomenon or the relationships of its variables, as in a cross-sectional study, may not be adequate to explain the relationships. In such cases, the researcher collects data of the past events and occurrences, which historically lead to the present problem or condition. This is a longitudinal study over a period of time. In these instances, case studies may be used as tools of research in which the historical development of an organisation or a function, like training, is considered. Literature review of research developments to identify gaps or important areas of current investigation is a historical research of the latter type.

There are three steps of historical research related to management (Bennet, 1991).

1. Data collection.
2. Critical analyses of data to establish its authenticity or worth.
3. Validation and orderly presentation of data.

The sources of data for historical studies are:

- Primary data from oral account of eyewitnesses either as observers or participant observers. This is feasible only in researches of recent history and may truly be primary data. The others like documents, reports, newspapers, magazine accounts, advertisements, books, journals, articles, and personal communications and remains or relics as in some areas like archaeology, are in a true sense secondary data.
- The secondary data is reports of non-observing or non-participant reporter. It must be noted that the same source may be primary or secondary depending upon the context of the research.

As in educational research, the researcher may try to make a historical generalisation or use a hypothesis to find why or how a particular critical event in history took place, for example, the influence of English education on the Indian education system during a particular period of history. Such a hypothesis may not, however, be explicitly stated by historic researchers.

The greatest obstacles to scientific historical research are:

- Difficulty in stating the problem specifically and precisely.
- Heavy dependence on logical analysis of data derived from other's experience/opinion, rather than on direct observation.
- Difficulties in primary sources of data.

Some examples of typical historical research are:

- Growth of trade unions in India.
- Evolution of alternate exchange rate regimes.
- Trends in the silk cocoon production growth in Karnataka during1930–1995.

Descriptive Research

descriptive research
Descriptive research is defined as fact finding with adequate interpretation. It uses simple analysis of data, develops thinking and elaboration of patterns and obtains tentative generalizations as hypotheses. It falls into two categories: cross sectional and longitudinal.

Descriptive research is defined as fact finding with adequate interpretations. Fact finding would involve just data gathering. In descriptive research more is involved in the form of reflective thinking. Reflective thinking relates the facts gathered to the objectives and the assumptions of the study. It, therefore, means that the descriptive research entails an objective and assumptions behind that objective. Simple analysis of data gathered, like central tendency, standard deviations, or correlation coefficients, may be used. But their use in research will not make the study a descriptive research. These statistically obtained parameters must be discussed and interpreted. In many so called research projects, the material collected as data is put into classificatory schemes. By itself this cannot be research, at least not university research. Otherwise, many of the tabulated figures published on various demographic, economic, and political activities would be called research. Data gathering for the sake of data gathering is not research. In any research effort, the data that is gathered should lead to developments of thinking, elaborations of the patterns indicated by the data, and refinements of principles underlying the data. At the least, tentative generalisations are necessary. Generalisations are at once a test and stimulus for further research. In a descriptive study, it would be philosophically appropriate for the researcher to continue generating hypothesis along with data gathering.

A descriptive research study may be guided by a hypothesis. It is typically concerned with the frequency of an occurence or with some general predictions. These studies require the what, where, when, who, why, and how of the research (Churchill, 1987). Data collection is usually delayed until how the data is to be analysed is decided upon. For this purpose, a dummy table may be designed to give all aspects of the data to be recorded, except the data itself (proforma). Variables are specified, categorisation decided, and ranges of values spelt out for purposes of classification. This will also help in phrasing questions for data collection.

In our scheme of classification of *ex post facto* research into historical and descriptive, descriptive research embodies all research activities conducted in the current time (or immediate past) of the phenomena. Thus, it includes both the hypotheses generation and the hypotheses testing types of research. Only the degree of knowledge or the definiteness of data relating to the variables differs in them. In hypothesis generation, greater emphasis may be placed on theory based reflective qualitative thinking and intensive data collection, as in case studies or field studies. But greater emphasis will be placed on statistical thinking and extensive data collection in surveys or case collections. Descriptive studies are generally concerned with univariate questions or hypotheses relating to the state, size, form, distribution, or existence of a variable. Sometimes correlational analysis of the bivariate/multivariate type may also be used.

Descriptive studies can be further classified into cross-sectional or longitudinal categories. The former is the most common and familiar and cuts across a large number of elements (large sample). In the latter, panels are employed over several periods for related measurement and the sample elements are fixed. The cross-sectional study can be a field study or a field survey at a point of time. The distinction between these two is mainly that in a field study the depth of study is greater and the sample may be very small; on the contrary, in a field survey there is greater coverage of population and greater scope due to larger samples and summary statistics being the major discussion. The first is more useful in understanding complex phenomena and the second in generalisations.

Criteria for descriptive research* A number of criteria are important and should be kept in mind in order to make a true descriptive research and not a mere fact-finding exercise. These are (Churchill 1987):

- Problem solving/problem determination through cross-sectional study.
- Obtaining well-refined research objectives and research hypotheses.
- Making predictions based on observable trends in data, as in longitudinal studies.
- Classifying data from case studies or generalisation.
- Use of spread and distribution rather than means for purposes of interpretation.
- Making tentative conclusions about causal relationships based on the values of 'R'.
- Identifying concomitant variables.
- Checking for reliability of data.
- Developing valid standards of comparisons or plans related to problems.
- Making tentative generalisations and adequate interpretations.

Note: *An example of Descriptive Research is given in Annexure 7.2.

EX POST FACTO RESEARCH BY NATURE OF STUDY

Field Studies

field study
This is an ex post facto study aimed at hypothesis testing or determination of relationship in real world organizational groups and individuals. No manipulation of independent variable is undertaken. It has greater depth of information but less generalization capability.

A field study is an *ex post facto* study aimed at hypothesis testing or relationship determination in real world situations, for example, studies of organisations, groups, classrooms, and so on. The distinguishing feature of a field study is that inspite of its having hypothesis testing as the main objective, no manipulation of independent variables is undertaken. A field study, for example, can be carried out on the relative efficiency of conference methods. Even though the researcher might sit in a conference, observe, and even talk, he is not intervening in the process of the conference. Through this study, he can test a hypothesis as to when one type of conference is more efficient than another.

Hypothesis testing research in field studies usually has the problem of validation. Variations are large, situations are real, and, therefore, the field study is ideally suited for finding out correlates. Great care must be exercised when causal relationships are derived from these studies. Field studies versus experiments is like heuristics versus analytical procedures in/or terminology. They are good for practical problem-solving but their strength in developing scientific theories always remains questionable. Problems of precision abound in field studies, which are therefore generally scientifically weak.

Field studies in general have two effects on research in social sciences and management. Experiments have been brought to field through direct observation of the phenomenon. This has enriched knowledge and motivated experimentation. Field studies, though they are classified as *ex post facto* research, some times through the use of participant observation, are not strictly *ex post facto*, but are concurrent with the facts/events of a phenomenon.

Field studies share much in common with sample surveys but there are significant differences. The most important of these differences is the greater depth of field studies as against the greater representativeness of sample surveys, with respect to the population. In field studies, representativeness may or may not be evident. The typicality of findings is essential to sample surveys, but the detailed and thorough account of the process under consideration is of greater concern in field studies. Typicality may not be sought in a field study. Sample surveys serve larger interests, like an economy, a country, a region, or a large community, and in this sense they are macro studies. Field studies, on the other hand, tend to become micro in their nature by detailed study of a single group. In sample survey, any understanding or inference of the ongoing processes (for example, decision-making pertaining to an economy or an organisation) is inferred through the end effects, which are measured or obtained statistically. In field study, ongoing processes are directly observed and measured and are, therefore, capable of giving greater insight into relational matters; for example, reciprocal relationships and labour-management relations. It should not be construed that the sample survey and field study are competing candidates for any research design.

In most scientific field investigations, they are best considered as supplementing one another. In other words, in the sample problem area, the micro and macro aspects can be well fitted to gain a better understanding of the population. Field study can sharpen variables in view of their deeper study of the relations and these sharpened variables could then be used in a survey to get a better understanding of the population.

Types of field studies Typicality of field studies is, by and large, a matter of differences in degree of measurement of the variables and relations. There are two major types.

1. The first type is a descriptive field study with large generalisation, which throws up hypotheses.
2. The second type, which is common in sociology, anthropology, and educational research, is the participant observation. It is a dominant tool for data gathering, which may be supplemented by conducting interviews and referring records, diaries, newspapers, and other documents. The only scientific game in such a study is the interpretation of data, which may be, as in all earlier studies, purely reflective in nature; or as in most recent studies, statistically treated ones. If the measures are difficult to obtain, two methods may be used for obtaining them.
   (i) *Objective method* In this, the measures are given by a panel of judges who are well versed with social or managerial settings and their problems.
   (ii) *Subjective method* In this, the measures are given by individuals themselves. They may be corroborated by the objective measures obtained as in (i) above. However, many field studies may leave the measurement problem to other field studies and may indicate only the importance of the measures. This is particularly so where the measures involve highly difficult and complex aspects. For example, a study attempted the measurement of technological development in terms of technological upgradations, but a comprehensive measure of either technological change or level was not available for the study. The researcher defined a set of management, organisational, and environmental variables to denote the technological level of an organisation and using these surrogate measures, compared a few organisations (Madan Mohan, 1991).

When actual data collection is carried out by investigators, the following salient points may be kept in mind.

- Contact should be broad (at least one individual from each group).
- Informants having wide contacts should be preferred.

- Both formal and informal leaders in the organisation should be included for interviews.
- Differences found in the information from the interviews of various groups should form the basis of further exploration, rather than discouraging the field worker. Information should be assessed in relation to the informant's position or role in the organisation or community.
- Both personal beliefs and social climate must be sought.
- Rigorous note-taking is important.
- Initial impressions and global judgments both should be duly considered.
- Participant observation is an ideal tool for field studies.
- Records and secondary sources of information should also be studied.

In hypothesis testing type of field study, the degree of elaborateness and the specificity of predictions are both important.

Design of field studies It is better to develop the design of a field study along with scouting (pilot study) and not to treat it as a separate activity, that is, overlap the pilot study and the development of the design, as desirable. Katz (in Festinger and Katz, 1953) describes several steps in developing a field study design. He recommends preliminary planning, developing scope, and general objectives of the field study, followed by the classical two-step process consisting of a scouting expedition (that is, pilot study), as an exploratory part, and the main study. Important forces in the situation, design of the general kind of instrument used for data collection, a broad theoretical framework, and a set of working (tentative) hypotheses are the major inputs to exploratory scouting. Katz gives a list of variables that would be of significance in most studies.

In exploratory research, netting information to formulate possible relationships and hypotheses to be tested later are important. For hypothesis testing, well defined measures are essential. Both these aspects are present in most current field studies. Sometimes, however, definite hypotheses exist and the researcher is interested in adding additional hypotheses. In such cases of exploration for a new hypothesis, the study will combine testing of already existing hypotheses with the generation of new ones. Such composite designs considerably reduce the time period and cost of research, which are often major constraints on research.

Further, an important aspect of exploratory field study is pre-testing of research instruments like form, behaviour scales, questions in terms of wording of items, schedules and administration. Pretesting includes:

- Testing of wording in each question, for communication purposes.
- Comparability and appropriateness of questions with respect to variables.
- Analysis of maturation, which generally consists of data recombination, comparisons of sub-group correlation analysis, and specific treatment of the conditions with which the relationships will be analysed, as the field study is generally susceptible to cluster effects.

Field studies are not without some aspect of experimentation, though the term field experiment or lab experiment may not be applicable to it (Emery & Trist, 1960). Festinger and Katz (1953) describe a field study of war prisoners. Rehabilitation of war prisoners is a natural experiment. There is no control group but manipulation of variables is powerful. Design difficulties are great, but detailed analysis of independent variables can manifest in the group. In such natural experiments, control groups should be used.

The degree of elaborateness and specificity of problem are important as are also the advantage of such kind of hypothesis testing studies. The hypothesis itself may be elaborated through a set of independent propositions.

In order to analyse field study data, at the design stage itself a set of tables may be set up to clarify the problems of hypothesis testing and other statistical analysis.

The timing of certain variables can be obtained in field studies where causal hypothesis may have to be tested. This is not possible in *ex post facto* studies. In this sense, a survey is different from a field study, though generally field studies are included as *ex post facto* studies. This is because, the current social relationships are directly observed.

Illustration—1 Field Research Organisational innovativeness was studied by Norman (1971) in large Swedish companies from various industries. The motivation for research was that earlier studies in the field of organisational innovations had been mostly inconclusive. It was desired in the study to gain an understanding of how structure influenced innovativeness in product development, and also to validate the existing theories regarding structure and innovativeness. thirteen case studies were developed in product development from 12 large companies, the small sample size entailing in poor generalisability. This was because the study aimed at depth of understanding. An important aspect of field studies was pre-testing of research instruments. Pre-testing was aimed at depth of understanding. Data was collected from documents and through long unstructured interviews with connected personnel. The design was essentially through empirical deductions from case studies.

The analysis procedure was one of classification of information to various categories, after re-orientation, into (i) systematic (ii) idiosyncratic and (iii) managerial. Open systems logic (using the product moment correlations between the environment and organisation) was used for further analysis.

All interviews were taped and details were typewritten. Content analysis was carried out on the material from documents. An initial theoretical postulate was made using this qualitative data.

The results, showing treating variations and reorientation as two different types of innovations, do explain some of the contradictions in previous research. The results confirm that March and Simon's (1958) and Lawrence and Lorch's (1967) theories of organic and mechanistic structures are valid for reorientation innovations.

A second example of field research is presented in Annexure 7.3.

Survey Research

Surveys usually cover large heterogeneous populations. Classically they have been used for demographic studies, consumer finance, occupational classifications, and so on. Many organisations conduct these surveys, for example, Times of India Foundation systematically carries out surveys in specific areas like urban areas and regional sectors, and in aspects like R&D and education.

Some characteristics of survey research There are two basic approaches to gather primary data. One is to observe behaviour, events, people, or processes and the other is to communicate with people about them (Cooper and Schindler 2000, p.78). The survey method uses the latter. The survey method is very popular in management research because it is versatile. Attitudes and opinions can be elicited only by questioning either directly or through well designed questions. Information about past events, opinions about current events, and thinking about future events or possibilities of events can be captured. It is more economical than observations, which are expensive in terms of time and effort to get the same information.

However, questionnaires (questioning approach) have weaknesses. Respondents should be willing to cooperate in truthfully and accurately providing the information. Lack of clear perception of the purpose of the study, lack of personal value in participation, or sensitiveness of the elicited information may lead to distortions in the information provided. Further, there may be lack of knowledge on the part of the respondents in giving suitable answers. Poor understanding of questions also leads to poor information. Worst of all, the respondent may provide misleading information.

- Information on age, qualification, income, and product details will be generally accurate.
- Information on events with which the respondent is not directly experienced (second-hand information) is unreliable.
- Information on beliefs, expectations, or attitudes can be accurate provided the questions are direct or indirect, appropriate to the information sought. They may generally produce meaningful data.

- Questioning can be carried out through personal interviews, telephone interviews, mailing questionnaires, computer polling, or a combination of these.

Choice of the survey method Some of the criteria for selecting a particular survey method are outlined below:

1. *Personal interviewing*
   (i) Yields deep and rich information.
   (ii) Researcher has more control over the quality and quantity of information.
   (iii) Expensive but intercept interviews in central/strategic places can reduce cost.
   (iv) Probing is possible.
   (v) Interview schedules can be used.

   Where representativeness of the sample is crucial to the study and the richness of information is beyond what is implied in the questions planned is desirable, this method is best suited, even with higher cost.
2. *Telephone interviews* These are useful in arranging personal interviews and screening large populations of unusual respondents, and is a unique mode of communicating with respondents. Computer assisted telephone interviews (CATI) are used in research organisations [for details see Cooper and Schindler, 2000, page 301-303].
3. *Self administered survey* The most popular and widely used are mail surveys. These have become universal and used almost in every information gathering area. The questionnaires may be sent by post, faxing, e-mail, or through internet services of a computer. The cost of this approach is low and coverage can be very large. Unlike in interviews, the respondent has time to think out the answers. Complex questions can be addressed and reaching the respondent is surer.

On the other hand, the response rate may be poor (it can be improved to some extent by reminding/repeat posting of questionnaire). Probing and correction to misdirected responses are not possible as in the case of an interview through intervention. When time and costs are a major consideration and richness of information is not of great importance, mail survey is the ideal choice.

Improvement of response rate The returns of self administered mail surveys are generally poor and one of the preoccupations of the researcher in this regard is to find ways and means of improving the returns in research literature. Some suggestions are given (Mangione, 1995).

- Well timed multiple follow up reminders are sent.
- Previous notification (before sending the questionnaire) is given.
- The length of the questionnaire is minimised.
- The research sponsorship details are communicated.
- Addressed return envelopes are enclosed with the questionnaire.
- An appeal for cooperation is made in a covering letter.

Generally the above efforts improve the response rates.

research survey

This is used primarily for a research study in order to assess the current status of various research issues of management and organization like use of management techniques and methods. It uses designs such as un-weighted cross section, weighted cross section, contrasting samples, and successive cross sections.

Research survey A research survey is an organised effort to analyse, interpret, and report the present (current) status of managerial or social institutions, organisational groups, or management areas. It deals with a cross-section of the population at the current time. The research survey may be used for classification, generalisation, and interpretation. It may also be used for the evaluation of a practice, for the development of methods in an organisation, or for improvement of existing systems (for example, industrial engineering practice and vendor development). The development of methods would include an assessment of the status, use of several methods reported in literature, and thereafter, observing the reasons for some methods not being used and suggesting ways and means of using them.

A research survey may be employed both in applied research as well as pure research and is a basic tool for management research.

For academic research, however, research survey is of special interest in studying specialised aspects of large population. For example, factors affecting the mobility of people. (Ref. Katona and Morgan, 1952).

In research survey, often, a screening survey is done initially to identify population to be surveyed. This method is known as the double sampling method in survey language. A sample within a sample, is also a method often adopted for specialised surveys. For example, getting reactions to a particular social or managerial issue from well informed people, would be of particular interest. On the other hand a sample survey is carried out for the general population. A double sampling approach or a sample within a sample approach can be used to get the population of well informed people, whose opinions are of greater importance to the researcher than the opinions of comparatively less well informed. An example of research survey is given in Annexure 7.4.

Survey research design There are several survey designs and some of them are discussed briefly below (Campbell and Katona, 1953).

1. *Unweighted cross-section* This is the simplest design and is primarily aimed at the classification of the population at a point of time in a cross-sectional study. The averages and the distributions of the variables are obtained. The averages of several classes (sub groups) are generally compared. Correlation analysis of important variables is also performed.
2. *Weighted cross-section* This is a variation of unweighted cross-section design. In this design some sub-groups of special importance are over sampled (particularly when the relevant subgroups are a relatively small percentage of the total population). The sample design is thus unbalanced but allows the researcher to obtain greater confidence of the results for the special group in which he is particularly interested; examples are income groups, age groups, and level of education groups. In an industrial setting, a researcher might want to determine the features and aspects of new entrants (or employees with more than a stated number of years of service). This design can be effectively used in such a situation.
3. *Contrasting samples* In this design, sub-groups having high and low values of a particular variable are chosen. Correlations between desired variables are performed within each group and then these relationships are compared. It is important to note that there is no assumption of linearity between these sub-groups.
4. *Successive cross-sections* These designs are used to study changes in two different ways.
   (i) **Before-after-design** The changes that occur in a group as a whole due to a change of event of stimulus event is studied in this. The stimulus or change will be in between the two interviews, and hence the name.
   (ii) **Trends** A series of interviews (generally more than two) are carried out over a period of time. There is no deliberate attempt to study any particular stimulus or change. Changes and stimuli may occur naturally in the course of events. It is not necessary in this design that the same people should be interviewed in the re-interviews. The basis for comparison or measurement of change is the parameter of the group as a whole, that is, mean, proportion, variance, and so on.

When the same individuals are interviewed in a series of interviews, the design is known as a panel interview design.

Analyses in the context of surveys Analyses of survey data usually consist of the following:

- Comparisons of parts of the sample.
- Linking behaviour and attitude of groups. (For example, it may be required to determine the behaviour of high productive and low productive employees and their attitudes in career analysis, slow movers and fast movers in the organisation could be studied from the point of view of behaviour and attitude.)
- Study of factors contributing to certain decisions in an organisation using causal relationships.

cross classification analysis
This is used for analysing survey data in order to establish categories occurring together and to determine relative frequencies of joint categories.

- Prediction or forecasting using causal relationships.
- Cross-classification analysis to establish simultaneously occurring categories, to determine relative frequencies of joint phenomena in properly spaced surveys.
- Cohort analysis, which can be used for, say, age-based consumption patterns in marketing analysis (Renty et al, 1983).

Reliability and validity of surveys One of the important ways of estimating reliability and validity of data gathered in surveys is to retest the data using one of the following methods.

- The related questions may be asked in different forms.
- The same question may be repeated differently in turns.
- Another important way of improving the reliability of responses would be to minimise the period of recall on the part of the respondent, particularly when eliciting opinions, rather than facts.

In validating the individual response, the direct responses may be compared for each individual but this is not usually very popular. What is generally attempted is the determination of the consistency of mean and distribution of the aggregate responses in different interviews rather than validating individual scores.

Another method of validation is to compare the demographic aspects of the sample (means and distribution) with the census data. This, at best, can be a sort of partial validation.

longitudinal study
This descriptive study is carried over a period of up to ten years and can be used for tracing evolutionary or developmental nature of many aspects of management. It depends on panel data and panel method.

Continuity description/longitudinal studies This is also a descriptive research carried over a fairly long period of time. When the periods are long enough they could be called longitudinal studies. The evolutionary or developmental nature of many aspects of organisation and management can be studied in this manner. For example, to know how certain specialised functions have developed in organisations over time, one has to make a number of cross-sectional studies at different points of time and obtain the development as a time series of changes or statuses. Sometimes controlled data may be gathered. For example, responses to specific questions over periods of time up to 10 years are obtained and frequent checks of facts of change are obtained. These studies are much stronger than cross-sectional studies, which are weak in reporting development aspects. Sometimes exploratory surveys are also undertaken to throw light upon certain practices that may not be reflected in research literature.

Longitudinal research depends upon panel data and panel methods. A panel is a fixed sample of subjects that is studied repeatedly. The variables measured remain the same in all measurements in conventional panel studies. In more recent research, the Omnibus panel is used. In this, the sample of elements is maintained but the kind of data collected may vary. At one time, attitudes may be measured and at another time preferences towards specific things may be collected. Turn over tables can be generated (which are similar to transition tables) and can be analysed in a number of ways (for details see Churchill, 1987, p.81-95).

QUALITATIVE RESEARCH METHODS

qualitative research methods
In qualitative methods the truth is captured using qualitative reasoning. These methods rely heavily on interviewing in depth to obtain participant perception and respondent's view of the phenomenon. Qualitative methods aim at describing and translating the meaning of naturally occurring phenomenon in social contexts.

Qualitative research methods, in general, and case studies, in particular, have long been used in social sciences and management research. A good deal of theoretical and empirical advancement has come from these approaches since the days of the Frederick Taylor and Hawthrone studies. Of late, there is a resurgence of qualitative methods in basic and applied research in management disciplines with quantitative methods not coming up too well. Counting and classifying have limitations. Meaning and interpretation are required to complete their usefulness in applied research. Neither of the approaches, quantitative nor qualitative, can capture the truth and should play complementary roles. The outline of treatment of the following qualitative methods will be of interest and use to researchers, managers, and consultants alike [Gummesson 2000; Foreword by John Van Maanen].

Qualitative methods rely very heavily on interviewing in depth, in which the participants' perceptions can be obtained and also how the respondents' view of the phenomena can be elicited. All qualitative methods aim at describing and translating the meaning of naturally occurring phenomena in a social context (Van Mannen, 1983).

First, several methods of qualitative research are succinctly discussed. These are case study, participant observation, the ethnographic method, critical incidence technique, repertory grid technique, projective techniques, protocol analysis, cognitive mapping, and the diary method. Triangulation, a method adopted, particularly in qualitative research, to improve confidence in the findings, is discussed in the end.* Subsequently, the methods of analysis of qualitative data obtained in the above research (data collection) methods is discussed briefly.

Case Study Research

Case study is a complete analysis and report of an individual subject with respect to specific phases of its totality. The case group investigations are particularly useful when generalisation can be made, which would otherwise be impossible from a single case. While a case study details the facts of an organisation or management situation, there is a need for qualitative reasoning to get generalisation and interpretations. This requires considerable skill on the part of the researcher. The case, however, will not validate any of the conceptual models and hypotheses that the researcher may proffer. In this sense, a case study is a good exploratory study; but the exploration is for a hypothesis or a conceptual model. A case study as a qualitative method cannot be used strongly as a hypotheses verifier but can be used as a hypotheses rejecter. This is known as 'Negative Case Analysis'. A systems study or analysis prior to the development of an OR model, described in Chapter 4, is an excellent example of a case study. Case study is qualitative in nature and has the advantage of being an in-depth study. Observation, reference to documents, interviews, content analysis, messages, and questionnaires may all be used in collecting data. It is a non-statistical approach and according to Goode and Hatt (1953), a way of organising data, so that the totality of a social unit like an individual, group, or an organisation can be obtained. It may include information regarding development of a unit over time, or its cultural aspects.

case study
This is a complete analysis and report of an individual entity with respect to different aspects of its totality. Qualitative reasoning is used to generalize and interpret data. It can be used as a rejector of hypothesis but cannot be strongly used as a hypothesis verifier. It can depict development over time or cultural aspects of an organization.

One of the primary problems of case studies is the determination of what data to collect. There is an intrinsic limit to the data to be collected (wholeness is not limited). Considerable degree of problem arises in controlling the type and amount of data to be collected. A case study is not unique. If it is unique it is not generalisable, but if it has to be generalised to some extent, the case study must be related to a scientific investigation.

In a case study, large amounts of broadly ranging data are usually generated. It enables the researcher to grasp the information pattern in the unit, that is relevant to the problem area. It also gives information on many other facets of the unit, like its economic, technical, procedural, managerial, and organisational facets. One of the important approaches that the researcher has to take in this situation is to obtain the typicality of the information or a classification of the information. The first task, after collecting data, is to write a case record. The case record extracts and organises data into an understandable database. It includes all information required for case analysis. Information is edited, redundants are sorted out, parts are fitted together and organised for ready access, chronologically and topically. The technique of qualitative coding is employed as a classification procedure. Indicators relevant to the variables of the hypothesis are identified and data is gathered with respect to these indicators. A critical appraisal is made to asses a desired from the data, thus classified. (The data may relate to processes, motives, predispositions, structures, functions, or intensity). One of the great advantages of a case study is that changes in the unit over a time period can also be conveniently documented, as in the case of longitudinal research.

The case study method has many problems and limitations.

- Only a narrow experience is depicted in it, thus making it unsuitable to generalisation.
- The relative importance of vital facts may be drowned in the large volume of data. There may be a general tendency for failure while testing the reliability of data.

**Note:* Projective techniques, depth interviews, and group and focus interviews are discussed in Chapter 10 as part of data collection procedures. Content analysis is discussed in Chapter 13 as a part of general preliminary analysis of data.

However, there are many excellent advantages of case analysis. These are as follows:

- It can be used gainfully when a hypothesis is to be formulated or a doubtful hypothesis needs to be modified.
- It can be used prior to the design of a questionnaire.
- Deviant cases are very helpful in fine tuning or sharpening a hypotheses.
- A wider range of information is provided, which may be relevant to the hypothesis or problem and which may be recognised as important post hoc.

An example of case study research is shown as 7.5.

Participant Observation

participant observation

This is a qualitative research method which uses mainly inductive approaches for generation and modification of hypothesis. The formulation of a research is essentially one of checking exceptions by studying a series of relevant incidents, occurrences or cases.

Participant observation is a qualitative research method. It is an inductive form of research and generally very helpful in the generation and modification of hypotheses. In deduction, hypotheses or experimental results will be accepted or rejected based on tests. Participant observation is used while formulating hypotheses and collecting data to check for exceptions. For example, when a researcher formulates a hypothesis from previous research work, before formally designing a research method for testing the hypothesis, he may like to ensure that the form of hypothesis is really adequate and that it reflects the facts of the particular phenomenon from which he collects data for refining the hypothesis (for example, the testing of management hypotheses in different cultures).

The starting point for participant observation and its objectives, will be hypotheses. During observation, the researcher will study a series of incidents, occurrences, or cases related to the hypotheses. If the cases (more generally) support the hypotheses, then not much research value is gained; but if a particular case is contravening the hypothesis then the researcher has a chance to enrich the hypotheses.

The participant observation method is particularly suitable to the socialisation process, career analysis of managers, and roles played by both individuals and groups in organisations. In the model building context, when a system study is carried out, if time permits, the participant observation method may yield various aspects of a problem, which would add to or modify the problem the manager posed initially. This is particularly true with respect to aspects that are not easily quantifiable or for which some scale or trade off has to be generated by the model builder.

The participant may either be a fully participant member of the group in the phenomenon or he may be a rigorously participating member. The data generated is usually in the form of field notes based on interviews/discussions and observations. Participant observation data tends to be subjective, but it is noticed that the biases entering in the process are smaller than those that can creep into survey researches and experiments, because of the researcher's aloofness. This higher freedom from bias, contrary to expectations, might be accomplished by the lack of anonymity of the participant.

The sample of observations or cases is of no real concern in participant observation. The identification of a negative case is all that matters. Analyses are useful in understanding the phenomenon in familiar terms (Goode and Hatt, 1953).

Ethnographic Methods

ethnographic method

Research using ethnographic method strives to grasp the individual's point of view and his relation to the organizational life. It gives an insider picture of the research situation under study.

Ethnography is the process of studying and describing a culture. It is "a field of study that is primarily concerned with the description and analysis of culture" (Saville, 1982). The central aim of ethnography, as Malinowski (1972) puts it, is to "grasp the native's point of view, his relation to life and to realise his vision of his world". In other words, ethnography attempts to provide an "insider's picture" of the community under study.

Ethnography is the systematic, organised, and detailed description of a particular culture and it also includes the process through which such information is collected. In other words, the term "ethnography" refers to both the research process and the descriptive results, and thus encompasses both the means and the end.

The origins of ethnography can be traced to cultural anthropology from which it derives its conceptual and methodological bearings. Cultural anthropology is the study of the patterns of thought, behaviour, and artifacts of a given culture.

Initially, ethnography was limited to the studies of 'primitive' small scale societies. However, this shortcoming is being rapidly overcome by the increasing number of ethnographic studies of modern western social groupings of varied nature. Education (Thapan, 1986), family units, science laboratories (Latour and Woolgar, 1979), organisational settings (Allen, 1977 and Dubinskas, 1988) are just a few of the areas of application of ethnography.

Hymes (1978) classifies ethnography into three types.

1. Comprehensive ethnography in which the ethnographer seeks to document a total way of life by covering most areas (under study) of a community.
2. Topic oriented ethnography in which the ethnographer focuses on one or more aspects of a community.
3. Hypothesis oriented ethnography in which the ethnographer seeks to generate specific hypotheses about a community.

Data collection is 'field work' in ethnographic parlance. Field work generally makes use of two tools, namely, participant observation and ethnographic interviews. Participant observation refers to "research characterised by a period of intense social interaction between the researcher and the subjects in the milieu of the latter" (Bogdan and Taylor, 1975). The aim of participant observation is to enable the researcher to engage in activities appropriate to the situation and to observe the activities, people, and physical aspects of the situation. Participant observers keep a record of both 'objective' observations and subjective feelings. Participation may be active or moderate or passive, depending on the type of study. The highest level of involvement for ethnographers probably comes when they study a situation in which they are already participants, that is, when a member of a community becomes an ethnographer and makes a formal study of his/her community.

Ethnographic interviews are open-ended and unstructured, the topics for which are determined by the context. The advantages of these flexible ethnographic interviews are that they not only reveal more information that may also enable the researcher to capture the discrepancies between 'ideal' and 'real' values, beliefs, and perceptions that a community holds.

Apart from these two tools, ethnographers also utilise questionnaires, document analyses, frame-elicitation techniques, and time keeping studies, depending on the nature of the study.

Strengths and weaknesses of ethnography The greatest value of ethnographic data are the rich insights they provide in understanding social situations without trying to reduce them to a few simple categories. They also provide processual data, that is, data that take place over a period of time. They are also useful in action research. The main weakness of ethnographies is that they are time consuming and that the analysis of voluminous data can be problematic.

Survey research and ethnographic research Ethnographies differ from surveys in terms of the goals of research, research perspectives, research design, methodology, the relationship between the researcher and the community studied, and the nature and the use of findings obtained. These are discussed in detail in Spradley (1979), Mouly and Ramani (1990) and others.

Illustration—Ethnographic case study In the Indian context, an R&D setting was studied using ethnographic research methodology over a period of eighteen months (Mouly, 1990). The aim of this study was to describe the day-to-day functioning of R&D team during its project life. Using participant observation, ethnographic interviews and a communication study questionnaire, Mouly found out the members' perceptions of their lives in their organisation, the major problems they faced at work, and their recommendations for resolving the same.

The central thesis of her ethnography was that centralised administration, excessive bureaucracy, authoritarianism at various levels in the hierarchy, along with professional mediocrity and an apathetic superior, could very adversely affect the quality of life and work of an R&D team. This influence could manifest in severely strained interpersonal relationships, distinct lack of identity as a group, poor self-images of team members, apathetic attitudes towards work, and low quality of research output.

Using these findings as a base, a comparative study was carried out by Mouly (1990) on a private sector R&D team. The main difference between this and the previous study was that it was conducted over a much shorter duration, and was initiated with the hypotheses raised from the initial study. Hence, this study could be termed as a hypothesis oriented ethnography. Both studies revealed the processual richness of R&D life, seen from the insider's point of view, which would not have been possible to obtain through surveys or one-off interviews.

Critical Incident Technique

critical incident technique
This is a set of procedures for making direct observations of human behaviour that are complete enough to enable the researcher to make inferences and prediction regarding the person making it.

Critical incident technique is a set of procedures for collecting direct observations of human behaviour. It is intended for collecting incidents having special significance to the analysis of a problem. Further the procedures should meet certain well specified criteria. Its origin is in studies on aviation psychology programmes in the United States of America. Main contributions to its development were in the Pittsburgh University [Flanagan, (1954); Woolsey (1986); and Hockey and Westerman (1994)].

An incident is defined as any observable human activity, which is complete enough to enable one to make inferences and predictions regarding the person performing it. The situation of the incident must be known to the observer and the objective and intentions of the performer and their effects must be understood clearly. Keen observers are using some form of the technique all the time. Critical incident technique is a refinement of these through a set of procedural steps. There are five steps included in the technique (Flanagan, 1954). The two basic principles on which critical incident technique is based are: (i) facts of behaviour are more important than their interpretation or estimates by the observer, and (ii) only those aspects of behaviour which significantly contribute to the activity should be reported. A competent observer should distinguish between 'vital few' and 'trivial many' in this context. The technique has several steps, as follows:

- Finding out the general aim of the activity in the incident—this is done by obtaining a consensus of authorities in the field of the problem.
- Designing plans and specifications for collecting data regarding the activity/incidents—this should help in classifying and analysing behaviour by the observer.
- Collecting data about the incident—this may involve interviews or written statements by the observer. The data must be objective, recorded statement of factual aspects and should be devoid of opinions, hunches, and impressions of the observer. Critical incidents provide only raw data in this sense and do not provide any answers or solutions to the problem at hand.
- Analysis of data—efficient summary of this data must be obtained so that it can be used in application. To a certain extent this may tend to be subjective.
- Interpretation and derivation of the activity requirements.

Any possible errors or limitations of each step performed has to be clearly mentioned.

Critical incident technique is flexible and, therefore, highly versatile in applicability. The applications include: (i) measurement of performance, (ii) training, (iii) selection and classification, (iv) determination of failure and success, (v) leadership, (vi) motivation, (vii) counselling, and (viii) operating procedures [Flanagan, (1954) and Hockey and Westerman (1994)].

The set of critical behaviours are obtained with the help of determining activity requirement and interpretation in terms of aptitude, training, and context. The technique is useful in many areas of management research, like organisational effectiveness, organisational climate, and training.

Repertory Grid Technique (RGT)

repertory grid technique (RGT)
The theory of RGT is that the people are engaged in making sense of their world by evaluating incoming social data and translating them into decisions. It helps in understanding the cognitive structure of the responses of a decision maker in a research situation.

This technique was proposed by Kelly (1955). The theory underlying the technique is that people engage in making sense of their world by evaluating incoming social data and translating it into decisions. They tend to formulate hypotheses to test them against the experience and to renew them.

The RGT is used in several disciplines. The technique is simple to apply and computer analysis is possible with it. It has many possibilities of application in management research. The theory is concerned with understanding cognitive structure, but is loose. What the researcher should bear in mind is that the meanings of the respondents in a research situation are far more important than his/her own meanings. For example, how the manager views his associates and his environments while making a decision is more important than the researcher's construct about the decision-maker's environment. The RGT is structured but content-free and will help in drawing up an individual's mental map.

The three basic areas of RGT construction are: (i) elements, (ii) constructs, and (iii) methods of linking them.

Elements These can be products, different roles, situations, or people. (It is essential not to mix-up people with things while developing RGT, because the cognitive and behavioural aspects are not the same for things and people.)

Constructs Qualities that are evaluatory attributes of elements are called constructs. The method of triad is applied in developing constructs. Elements are written on cards (the smaller the number of elements, the better it is and usually it is not greater than 12). Three cards are chosen at random to elicit the construct. These cards (elements) are offered to respondents who are asked which two elements are most alike and least like the third. Then the respondent is asked to state the reason for the two cards that are alike and the reason for the third being dissimilar. Both the reasons should be written down. The steps are repeated with different sets of cards until the respondent cannot generate additional constructs. The constructs generated using such a procedure will be bipolar.

The last step in the grid generation is to get the respondent to scale or grade each element with respect to the construct. This could be either by ranking or scaling. (Refer to Exhibit 7.1 and 7.2, and Table 7.1.)

In this particular case, the respondent is rating his colleagues whose roles are perceived by the respondent. The RGT generates concepts and clear linkages between constructs and elements. Some computer packages are available for constructing RGT. (See Smith and Dainty, 1991, p.166).

The analysis of the grid yields:

To what extent an individual is cognitive complex

- In how many dimensions he views other people or issues .
- How individuals perceive others as similar or dissimilar.
- The pattern of association of constructs that are similar or dissimilar.
- The RGT gives in management research, how the manager or the individual decision-maker construes his interpersonal world at work (liked or disliked individuals). Clusters can be formed and identified in such situations to help understand the cognitive structure of the decision-maker. Discussions with respondents would be very useful in verifying this; which, may be extremely difficult.

In field research, the RGT can be very helpful in getting the evaluation of a wide range of topics and issues important to the decision-maker. The RGT is different from other research methods like interviewing, questionnaire, participant observation, and case study methods in that it is a special form of communication depending on the trust and goodwill of the respondent. It demands privacy and neutrality of the researcher and confidentiality and may take about an hour's time for the researcher to identify/disclose the research purpose to the respondent. For greater details refer to Smith and Dainty (1991).

1	Myself at work
2	The person I report to (my manager)
3	The person my manager reports to
4	Least liked subordinate
5	Favourite subordinate
6	My best friend at work
7	Favourite colleague
8	Least liked colleague
9	An unsuccessful colleague
10	A successful colleague

Source: Smith and Dainty (1991)

Exhibit 7.1 Role sheet

Honest	Not straight
Uncaring	Professional
Easy going	Capable
Street wise	Intellectual
Good communicator	Poor communicator
Poor leader	Good with people
Naive	Political
Tough minded	Tender minded
Hard working	Not hard working

Source: Smith and Dainty (1991)

Exhibit 7.2 Sample constructs

Table 7.1 Example Repertory Grid

	Constructs	*Elements*	*Myself at work*	*Margaret*	*Fred*	*Ron*	*John L*	*John R*	*Bob*	*Ivan*	*Kavin*	*Brain*		
	1 2 3 4	*5 6 7*												
			1	2	3	4	5	6	7	8	9	10	11	12
1	Honest	Not straight	1	4	7	6	4	1	1	1	1	1		
2	Uncaring	Professional	5	5	5	1	4	1	4	1	5	6		
3	Easygoing	Capable	7	7	6	1	7	7	4	1	5	7		
4	Street wise	Intellectual	3	1	2	4	5	5	4	3	5	2		
5	Good Communicator	Poor communicator	3	1	7	3	4	4	4	5	4	7		
6	Poor leader	Good with people	6	7	7	2	4	4	5	2	4	6		
7	Naïve	Political	5	7	7	6	4	5	5	5	2	5		
8	Tough minded	Tender minded	3	1	2	4	4	4	3	3	5	3		
9	Hard working	Not hard working	4	7	5	7	4	4	4	7	4	4		
10														
11														
12														
	1 2 3 4	5 6 7												

Some Additional Qualitative Research Methods

A few other methods often used in qualitative research are now briefly discussed. They are diary methods, protocol analysis, cognitive mapping, and projective techniques.

Diary methods Diaries have been used in social research for a long time. Diaries can be qualitative or quantitative. Diaries are kept as records of events in organisations. They are personal journals of the research process for time management, for recording personal reflection and perspectives on what went on, on attitudes, and on motives, providing a rich picture of the situations being studied. The main use of the diary method is that employee perspectives can be obtained. Comparison of diaries written by several writers can provide variable information. Interaction and questioning are not allowed but many diaries can be used as extensions to the researchers effort of data collection. One basic requirement is that the diary writer must be capable of expressing well in writing. Secondly, the researcher must provide some focus for the diary writer in the form of a list (classification) of specific aspects of the work to be recorded. The diary should be required to be written away from the place of work to reduce aberration in writing due to workplace emotions/conflicts (Easterby-Smith et al, 2002).

Protocol analysis This is a way of analysing episodes unique to an individual immediately after the episode has occurred. It seems to help in unearthing the logic behind the way people think. In managerial research, a decision-maker is asked to comment on what is going on as the event happens (or immediately after the event has happened using a recording of the event). Both the individual's analysis of the episode and the researcher's can be obtained in protocol analysis. It is often used in marketing decisions, buying behaviour of consumers, and managers' action and learning. This technique can be used along with many other techniques (employing discussions) in which the manager is made to talk freely after securing his trust and cooperation.

protocol analysis
This is a method of qualitative analysis which analyses episodes unique to an individual manager immediately after the episode occurs. The data is secured freely under trust and cooperation of the respondent manager.

Cognitive mapping The complexity of a problem situation, as perceived by an individual, is represented as cognitive maps. These are simple to understand and analyse. This technique is developed from group interviews by the researcher. It is the picture, as a model, of the perceptions of the decision-maker or participants about a problem. The perceptual data are presented in a hierarchical or ladder like diagram in which values are placed at the top, consequences in the middle, and component attributes at the bottom. The perceptions are all numbered. The linkages, as perceived, are drawn as lines joining the particular perceptions. The links represent relations. The perception into which the links merge at the top will have the highest value number. The values of attributes will be the lowest. When a particular perception or node has a large number of links it is considered vital to the problem. (An example of a cognitive map is given as Exhibit 7.3)

cognitive mapping
The complexity of a problem situation as perceived by an individual is represented as a cognitive map developed from group interview by the researcher. It is a model of the perception of decision maker or participants of the problem and offers holistic picture using qualitative information.

The maps offer a holistic picture of problem perception and give a very rich picture of qualitative information (cf rich picture in soft system methodology). These are very useful in developing various strategies for an organisation, through a process of interactions, using the maps between key personnel/individual clients, and top managers. This will make the exercise more client oriented. It is also particularly suitable for action research programmes in which organisational development is the main outcome. For greater details and examples of cognitive mapping the reader is referred to Eden et al (1983), Baker (1996) and Clark and Mackaness (2001).

Triangulation

Many researchers have discussed complementing survey with field work to arrive at better results. "The combination of methodologies in the study of the same phenomenon" (Denzin, 1978, pp.291) in order to arrive at a better understanding of a given setting or community without spending too much time in any one setting is called triangulation. The assumption underlying triangulation is that when a researcher uses two methods, the weaknesses of each method can be overcome by the other. While quantitative methods contribute to greater confidence in the generalisability of results obtained by qualitative methods, qualitative data illuminating the context-specific, site-specific and situation-specific details can be especially useful when suggesting conclusions about a specific setting. Surveys become more meaningful when interpreted in the light of critical qualitative information. Many researchers suggest specific ways in which triangulation can be obtained. They generally agree that it is beneficial to start studying a setting in-depth through qualitative research tools and then use that understanding to study more settings using surveys that are time saving.

triangulation
Triangulation is used to combine several methodologies for solving a problem. The underlying assumption is the weakness of the different methods can be overcome in the combination and the greater generalizability of the results can be obtained.

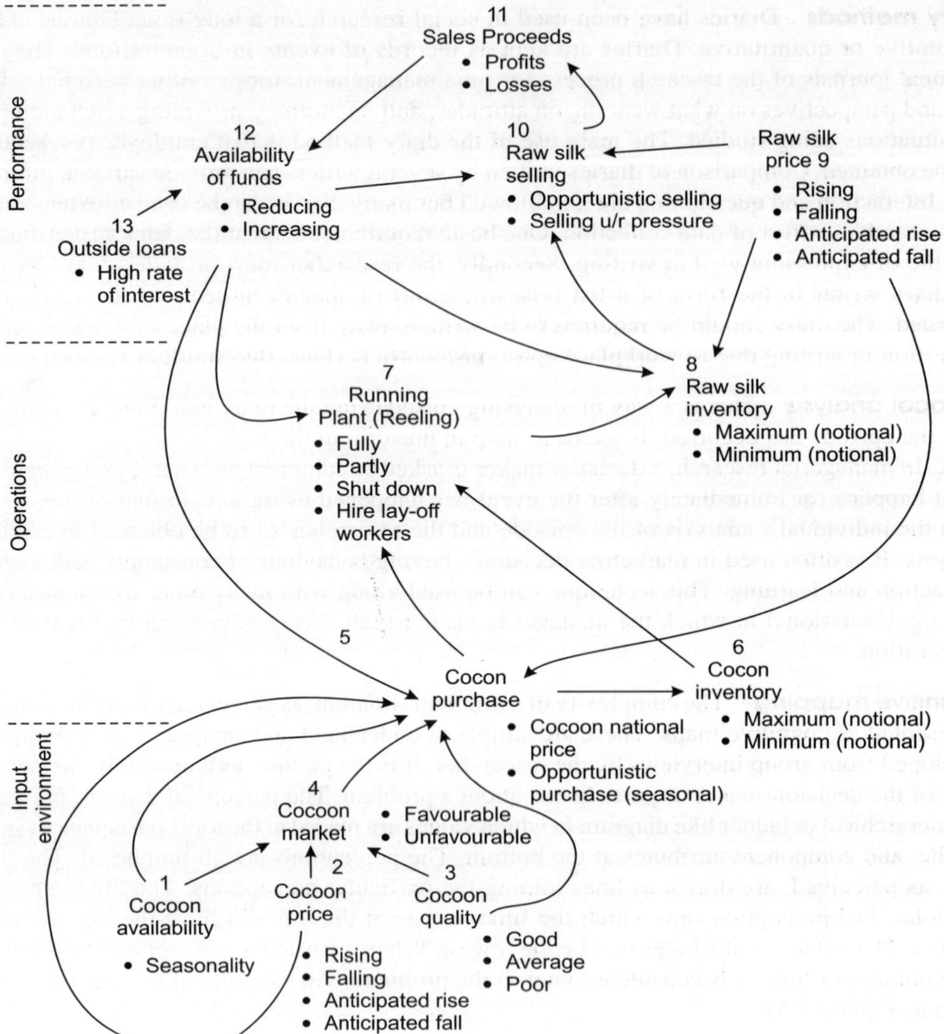

Exhibit 7.3 Cognitive map of several reelers

Analysis Procedures for Qualitative Data

Qualitative data collected using the methods detailed in section 7.4.6 tend to be voluminous, complex, situation specific, and in differing forms and structures. The real problem of analysing qualitative data is in condensing it into a form that presents a narration or story that is convincing to the reader or evaluator. This involves a good balance between description of situations and events on the one hand, and interpretation and explanation on the other. Obviously all data is not displayed but samples and quotes need to be given so that the reader can make his own explanation and form his own conclusions. The researcher may take a more positive approach, giving more emphasis to frequencies (to convert into numeric statements) and hypothesis testing or the researcher may take a social constructionist approach of philosophical approach along with data interpretation to generate hypotheses or state problems, objectives, or concerns. Based on this promise, two broad approaches of data analysis can be considered useful in analysing qualitative data. They are (i) content analysis, which is deductive and numerically oriented, and (ii) grounded analysis, which is holistic, inductive, and subjective.*

* Content analysis is discussed in Chapter 13 as a means of preliminary analysis of data.

Grounded analysis This is basically derived from the grounded theory approach in which the structure of the problem situation is obtained from data rather than imposing on it an external structure determined *a priori.* Themes, patterns, and categories are extracted from the data and the research is, therefore, well grounded in the phenomena (Glaser and Strauss, 1967). Over the last 30 years grounded analysis procedures have undergone considerable changes and development and there are many analysis procedures that can be used. (Charmaz, 1983 and Karen Locke, 2001) grounded analysis can be characterised as follows: (i) data collection and analysis are simultaneous; (ii) the process of analysis and the findings are formed from the data and not *on a logically deduced* theoretical framework, as used in positivist ie approaches; (iii) checks are not made on the categories obtained; and (iv) theory as a process and understanding and interpreting the phenomena itself is a process and not a finished product. The analysis of qualitative data obtained in interviews can consist of the following steps (Easterby Smith et al, 2002).

grounded analysis
This analysis is derived from grounded theory in which the structure of the problem emerges from the data. Themes, patters, and categories are extracted.

1. *Formalisation* The transcripts of data are studied, in order to note (i) information recorded, (ii) relationship between research and respondents, (iii) attitude of the respondents, and confidence in the data obtained.
2. *Reflection* (i) on missing out on crucial issues, (ii) on data evaluation in the light of the previous research, (iii) on supporting or challenging earlier research, and (iv) on differences from other research.
3. *Conceptualisation* It is understanding the concepts expressed by respondents while examining the construct. They may be expressed as explanatory variables.
4. *Cataloguing Concepts* The concepts expressed by respondents are suitably recorded in a database in cards or by computer labelling in the researcher's own language, detailing their links for future ready reference.
5. *Recoding* Checking, by back tracking to data, that each concept was interpreted in the same way by different individuals. For example, the concept of creativity might have been interpreted as technical creativity by a few, as organizational creativity by some, as procedural creativity by others, and so on. In that case, the concepts are recoded suitably.
6. *Linking* With the emergence of concepts and patterns, the analytical framework becomes more clear. Now they can be integrated into a more holistic theory. This is done by repeated movements between literature and data. Respondents, colleagues and peers can be asked to collaborate in order to scrutinise the draft findings.
7. *Re-evaluation* Depending upon the outcome of scrutiny at 6 above, the drafts are rewritten incorporating (i) additional work if needed, (ii) reconsideration of issues, and (iii) elimination of contradictions. A four-step analysis of qualitative data is suggested. (Glaser and Strauss, 1967 and Strauss and Corbin, 1998)

Step 1—Comparing incidents applicable to each category. First categories are conceptualised using data notes and are then compared.

Step 2—The categories are integrated for getting a meaningful whole.

Step 3—The theory is delimited. This is achieved with respect to, both categories and the whole.

Step 4—The theory is written.

Initially, the emergence of theory was considered to be a process almost without researchers' aid but, later (Strauss and Corbin, 1998) increased prescription and elaboration have been included. In this approach, the sampling of data and analysis are concurrent. Further, the sampling used is theoretical sampling (open sampling), which provides the best opportunity of obtaining relevant data related to categories (related sampling) and data that relates categories (discriminate sampling).

Use of computers in analysing qualitative data Use of computers in qualitative data analysis can be at two levels.

1. The transcripts of interviews and other data can be stored using standard word processing packages. This can be used for searching for concepts.
2. Many qualitative analysis packages like (Quasps) can be used to identify patterns, themes, categories, and so on. (Seale 2000). Websites (http://www.qst.com.au and http://www.atlasti.de) can be searched for details of sophisticated computer packages for qualitative data analysis. (Easterby-Smith et al. 2002).

EVALUATION RESEARCH

evaluation research This research is used for evaluating developmental programs in management and social contexts. The research may evaluate the outcome of the program as to whether the program is a success or a failure or it can evaluate the quality of the implementation of the program.

Generally, evaluation research is directed towards the evaluation of original programmes on social developmental work, like rural development programmes and training programmes. It can be directed to programmes of change, of introducing new procedures or new techniques/ models in an organisation/area. Evaluation research is different from other kinds of research, more in objective than in methodology. However, it has some distinctive features as it is an applied research and because the results of research are required in a short term, causing time pressures on the researchers.

The emphasis on measurement in any research is generally on a single aspect. However, in evaluation research the emphasis on measurement has a dual purpose. First is the measurement of impact of a programme on the community or organisation in the form of broad changes. Second is the measurement of the objectives of the programme. This includes achievement, attitudes, interests, ideals, ways of thinking, work habits, and social adaptability.

There are two types of evaluation research.

1. Evaluation research directed to the determination of the outcome of the programme, to evaluate whether it is a success or a failure. This is called summative evaluation or outcome evaluation research.
2. Evaluation research directed to the evaluation of the process of implementation of the programme and deals mainly with the quality of implementation. This is called formation/ process evaluation research.

Outcome Evaluation

Outcome evaluation comes at the end or about the end of the implementation process, as shown in Fig. 7.1. The questions that are asked in outcome evaluation are about whether it worked and whether it should be continued. The first question relates to the success or failure, the second question is whether the programme should be used in the long run with additional funding, that is, a repetitive use of the programme to cover wider sectors of society.

Outcome evaluation usually involves the collection of quantitative data, use of statistical analysis, (causal analysis) experiments, and quasi-experiments.

Example Kidder (1981) discusses an experimental programme for rehabilitating delinquent children. The experiment used a sample of 500 children out of which 250 were subjected to the rehabilitation programme and other 250 were the control group. The experimental group was visited twice a month during the programme to ensure that the programme is adequately carried out, with respect to these children. The experimentation is in the form of following up of both groups after 30 years, through records in courtrooms of criminal activities, alchoholic centres; through finding them and interviewing them.

One of the major problems of outcome evaluation, as in the example quoted above, is that very often it takes a long time to identify the influence of the programme on the individuals. Administration is not generally willing to wait that long. It would like to have a quick evaluation. Therefore, experiments and quasi-experiments don't find favour among practising programme administrators.

Evaluation research is characterised by the following aspects:

- *Conflicts* These arise between the evaluation researcher and administration. The researcher tends to evaluate the people implementing the programme rather than the

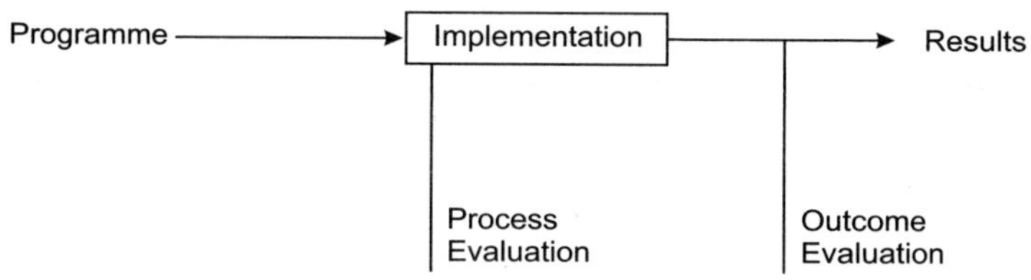

Fig. 7.1 Evaluation research

programme itself. Fig. 7.2 indicates the kind of conflict that generally arises in outcome evaluation research because the careers of the implementors are involved and the administration will always counter the adverse evaluation of the performance of the implementing team.

- *Pressure of time* This arises because the evaluation result is required by the administration in a very short period of time for making the primary decision on whether to continue the programme. At that point of time the initial programme is likely to be completed. So the tools of analysis used get truncated. Experiments and quasi-experiments become relatively useless and only causal analysis has to be carried out on what is probably hastily collected data.
- *Funding decisions* These decisions may be a result of the vested interests of politicians, administrators and the government.
- *Ambiguous and contradictory results* The results of the programme may be successful in some aspects and a failure in some others. Policy decisions regarding continuation of the programme becomes more a matter of judgment and group pressure in which contradictions and ambiguity may be present.
- *Delayed effects of the programme on society* In most rehabilitation programmes that involve education and economic and social reforms, the results always take a considerable amount of time. In a given administrative set up the decision-makers may not be inclined to wait.
- *Alternative experimentation* If the administration has an alternative experimentation in programme implementation and evaluation becomes easier and continuance of the programme becomes a comparatively simpler decision.
- *Definition of success and failure* In any large programme publicly funded departments and agents are involved in the implementation. The concept of success and failure should become equivocal in spite of different view points. This is made clear by the following case.

	Researcher Evaluation	**Administrator evaluation**
Program successful	Good programme Good (people's) performance	Good programme Good (people's) performance
Program failure	Good programme Poor (people's) performance	Poor programme Good (people's) performance

Fig. 7.2 Evaluation by researchers and administrators

Illustration—Evaluation research Case of Astra ole (Suresh Babu, 1990) During 1984, the Government of Karnataka, India, took up a massive programme for diffusing Astra ole (wood stove) developed at the ASTRA centre, at the Indian Institute of Science, Bangalore, India. A well defined organisational structure was set up to manage the large scale diffusion programme. Using information from earlier diffusion studies, the activities required for dissemination were clearly identified and executed. A large number of stove builders were trained initially. An evaluatory study was conducted by the Karnataka State Council for Science and Technology (KSCST) after about 4 lakh stoves had been diffused in various rural districts of Karnataka. The evaluation information was obtained through a mailed questionnaire survey to all Astra ole users. The questionnaire consisted of information regarding the type of astra ole, type of home in which it is used, occupation of the owner, family size, cost, subsidy details, various technical details of the stove, condition of its working, its use, satisfaction with the stove, fuel used, the type of food items cooked, and problems experienced in the use of the stove.

Subsequently, the information obtained from the survey was analysed. The data was analysed using regression equation, chi-square test, and tests of significance for proportions and correlation coefficients. The results of the study indicated the proportion of users and general patterns of use. It was found that all varieties were used in approximately 60 per cent of the cases. There were significant differences in the proportions of use for the various kinds of food items, like the design meant for cooking other food items compared to that used for cooking rice. There was a significant difference in use among various zones in the state. With regard to occupations, the percentage of use was found to be maximum among agricultural labourers and poor farmers (75 per cent to 80 per cent); and in the salaried classes, the percentage was significantly lower (50 per cent to 55 per cent).

To derive the relationship between design parameters and the performance of the stove in use, correlation analysis was performed. From this it was found that different parameters affected the performance of different models differently.

The three performance variables used were—fuel consumed, time taken for cooking, and amount of smoke emission. It was found that all the three affected the continued use of the Astra ole, the time for cooking being the most critical variable. Two important policies were generated for monitoring the use of the Astra stove in the field. Three pan stoves were considered suitable only for cooking rice. Projects for developing different designs should be funded. Educating and training of both builders and users was found to be critical in the success of diffusion.

Formative Evaluation Research

Formative evaluation research enjoys a far more conducive environment than outcome evaluation, due to the very nature of the research. It helps administration in the early part of the programme, which gives the program administration substantial leverage in making changes and improvements. It is a qualitative procedure as against the highly quantitative one in outcome evaluation. It is a continuous process and somewhat like inspection/social audit, so that the facts from the field are used as feedback by the policy makers. It has a connotation of guidance and controlling of all concerned in the programme.

Generally, it is done by people who are embedded in the programme, either fully or partly. This is the method of participant observation. Personal interviews, surveys, and field experiments can also be used for this evaluation.

SUMMARY

Ex post facto research consists of exploratory, historic, and descriptive types of research and deals with events and influences that have already occurred or are occurring. Field studies in which data is collected using observation, questionnaires, and interviews fall under this category. Ex *post facto* research is weak from the point of view of establishing causal relationships.

In exploratory research, problems are sought, and the design is, therefore, flexible and emerges as the study progresses. Exploratory study consists of getting information from research literature, secondary sources, and from knowledgeable persons.

Historical research concerns a historical problem or historical view of a current management problem. Cross-sectional studies are generally adequate.

Descriptive studies are fact finding with adequate interpretations. In these studies, simple analysis of extensive data using central tendency or correlation coefficients are employed. Both hypothesis generation and testing may be carried out. The cross-sectional descriptive studies are field studies and sample research surveys. In the former, in-depth analysis, yield rich and particular information. In the latter, global and thin information, which is capable of greater generalisation, is obtained. These two types of research are complementary to each other. The former is characterised by case studies and ethnographic studies, and the latter uses multivariate statistical analysis to determine relationships of a large number of variables in the phenomenon. Factor analysis is employed for the parsimonious description of a phenomenon. In research survey, information from well informed people is gathered, the status of managerial institutions is obtained, or evaluation of a practice is made. Continuity description is a descriptive research carried out over a fairly long period of time using panel design and panel data. Case method is a nomothetic method, in which extensive and detailed data on interactions in organisations and groups is collected in a particular unit. A negative case is a potential method to modify or streamline hypothesis generated by survey research.

There are many qualitative methods used in descriptive research. Participant observation is one in which inductive methods for generating and modifying hypothesis are extensively used. This method is particularly suitable for studying social and organisational processes. Content analysis is another in which documents, publications, reports, and letters are studied and the content of their communication is obtained. Ethnographic methods are qualitative descriptive studies, primarily concerned with culture trying to unearth an insider's picture of the community or organisation under study. Critical incidence technique, another qualitative research tool helps in studying human behaviour through a collection of incidents, which are observable human activities. Other qualitative research methods, like diary methods, protocol analysis, and cognitive mapping are briefly presented. Grounded analysis for analysing qualitative data is presented in detail. In the use of qualitative research methods, an important approach is triangulation or corroboration of results of two or more methods to gain greater confidence in the results.

Evaluation research, unlike other kinds of research, is aimed at evaluating a social programme, like a rural development programme, but uses the tools and methods employed in any research.

Repertory grid technique is concerned with the understanding cognitive structure of managers in an organisation and probing how their views affect their decision-making.

ANNEXURE 7.1

An Example of Explorative Research

Although it has been realised long ago that market orientation will increase market performance, business practitioners have had no specific guidance as to what precisely a market orientation is and what its actual effect on business performance is. The authors (Narver and Slater, 1990) have attempted to validate relationship between market-orientation and market performance via an exploratory study.

They discussed the concept of market orientation, examined the behavioral characteristics and management policies of market-oriented business, and inferred that market orientation consists of five components, three behavioural components of equal importance, long term focus, and profitability. The authors hypothesised that market orientation is a one-dimension construct consisting of the above five components and that they can be measured reliably with a multi-item scale. They also described the tests employed to establish the face validity of the construct.

Contd.

The sampling units in the study consisted of a member of top management in each of 140 single business units (SBUs), of both commodity and non-commodity businesses. A questionnaire was the chief instrument. It had questions relating to (i) the competitive prices, (ii) strategies, competitive environment, and (iii) performance of an SBU in its principally served market.

The data obtained was subjected to tests for assessing reliability and validity of the instrument. The authors report evidence of convergent validity, discriminant validity, and concurrent validity of the three-component model of market orientation. As regards the relationship of the three component market orientation to business performance, the authors hypothesised that the greater a business's market orientation, the greater the business's profitability will be, other things being equal.

The authors identified eight situational variables that may affect the profitability of a business. These eight variables are buyer power, supplier power, seller concentration, case of entry of new competitors, rate of market growth, rate of technology, change, and the size of business in relation to that of its largest competitors. The authors advanced that these must be controlled in analysing the effect of market orientation on profitability.

Ordinary least squares regression analysis was used to test the hypothesis that market orientation and performance are associated positively. The findings support their hypothesis. For both commodity and non-commodity businesses, relative costs reported as an important determinant of profitability, and so also is market growth. They observed in their study that the business having the highest degree of market orientation was associated with the highest profitability but added that none of these businesses had attained the maximum possible market-orientation score.

Because of the precedence that internal validity considerations took over external validity, the authors were apprehensive about the generalisability of the findings. They have also made suggestions that future research might address.

ANNEXURE 7.2

An Example of Descriptive Research

The study is based on 904 accidents involving buses in three bus transport corporations in India, which operated 1652 buses with 4000 drivers in 1984 (Vasudevan and Victor, 1987). Ten major factors were considered. The factors are listed below:

1. Geometric features of road
2. Type of area of accident occurrence
3. Age of bus driver
4. Driving experience
5. General educational level of bus driver
6. Primary cause of bus-related accidents
7. Collision patterns
8. Age of bus
9. Damages to bus due to accidents
10. Hourwise, daywise and monthwise distribution of accidents

The influence of these factors on the occurrence of accidents was studied in detail based on the data obtained from the three corporations. The major findings of the study are briefly given below:

- Nearly 71 per cent of the total accidents occurred on straight stretches of roads, whereas curves and intersections accounted for only 18 per cent of the accidents. Greater caution among drivers and better observance of traffic rules by all road users are necessary to reduce these accidents.
- Residential areas and bus stands accounted for nearly 37 per cent of total accidents.
- With increase in age and driving experience, bus drivers tend to be involved in fewer number of accidents. Empirical relations connecting the above factors are presented.
- The data of the study seems to suggest that there is no marked correlation between the general educational level of bus drivers and their involvement in accidents. This finding is contrary to the popular belief that drivers with

Contd.

better education may be expected to be safer on the road. However, transport operators would do well to recruit drivers with at least high school studies and give placement training.

- Nearly 39% of the bus-related accidents were attributed to the fault of the bus driver. There is a strong case for the transport corporations arranging for periodic training of drivers, particularly in defensive driving.
- The fact that mechanical defects contributed to only 1 per cent of the total accidents testifies to the high level of periodical preventive maintenance practiced in the three transport corporations considered.
- There is no significant relation between the age of the bus and accident involvement up to the bus age of 7 years.
- Nearly 78 per cent of the total accidents occurred during day time (06 to 18 hours).

The authors suggest that though the findings of the study are based on data from three transport corporations in one state, it is likely that the findings may be broadly applicable to other corporations in India, operating in non-hilly terrain. Since any traffic accident is generally due to more than one cause and since human error is the predominant cause for accidents, the importance of driver training and road user education in ensuring safer travel on the road cannot be over emphasised.

ANNEXURE 7.3

An Example of Field Research

A field study was conducted in Hospital emergency units in order to explore the relationships among variables "input uncertainty", " means of coordination" and "criteria of organisational effectiveness" in them (Linda Argote, 1982). Three hypotheses were formed to specify the expected relationships. They were:

- The higher the input uncertainty, the less programmed means will be used for the organisational coordination.
- The higher the input uncertainty, the more non-programmed means will be used.
- Programmed means of coordination will make greater contribution to organisational effectiveness than non-programmed one.

The measures of input uncertainties, coordination and organisational effectiveness were described. The reliability and validity of data were also tested.

A 10 per cent stratified random sample of 30 hospitals out of 44 participants were drawn. Data was collected from hospital administrators, physicians, registered nurses and licensed practical nurses working in the emergency units. Interviews were conducted (Response rate 95 per cent) and questionnaires were mailed (response rate 86 per cent). Hospital records, and census reports were also used. Relationships between "input uncertainties" and "organisational effectiveness" were tested through Pearson product moment correlation. Relationships between "means of coordination" and "organisational effectiveness" were analysed using modulated regression. The results suggest that the use of programmed means of coordination is most appropriate in emergency units experiencing low uncertainty, while the non-programmed means of co-ordination is most appropriate in emergency units experiencing high uncertainty. The criteria of appropriateness used is the efficiency with which the patients are processed, the quality of nursing and medication received.

There is little evidence that the actual method used to coordinate units depends on input uncertainty indicating that emergency units are not using the appropriate method of co-ordination. Uncertainty plays a key role in the effectiveness of hospital emergency units.

ANNEXURE 7.4

An Example for Survey Research

Krishnaswamy (1985) studied exploratively the manpower planning (MPP) practices in Indian manufacturing organisations in order to build models of manpower planning. The objectives of the study were (a) to identify the general nature of specific characteristics of manpower planning activities to gain an appreciation of the status of the function and (b) to highlight connected issues and problems.

Contd.

The methodology used was a combination of specially designed questionnaire and in-depth interviews with personal managers, industrial engineers and heads of manufacturing divisions. Two hundred companies from top 300 companies in India, in electrical power equipment, electronics and telecommunication, textiles, chemical, drugs and dyes, metals, automobile and automobile accessories, agro-based, machine tool, general engineering and heavy engineering industries were sampled. The details were sought for (1) corporate planning support (2) manpower forecasting methods (3) manpower inventory (4) manpower audit (5) involvement of line and staff functions in MPP activities (6) recruitment (7) career planning (8) availability of job information (9) reasons for employee turnover (10) size of the organization and (11) prevalent objectives and scope of MPP. Only 49 organisations responded out of which 45 were ultimately suitable for analysis. From the analysis of the data collected, the following observations were made by the author:

- Only one-third of the companies having more than 2000 employees had corporate manpower planning activities but 60 per cent had some formal cell or group to look after the MPP function.
- 60 per cent of the companies had one of the following objectives of MPP: recruiting highly talented/skilled/qualified employees, fitting worker to right job, anticipating changes in quality and quantity of manpower and developing employees.
- Only 25 per cent in the sample had personal function represented on the board of directors.
- It was found that requests made by the divisions was the most common basis for forecasting (80per cent companies). Manning equipment, productivity index, and plant capacity were used in multiple approaches to MPP in many organisations.
- Manpower inventory was maintained according to department, length of service and category in two-thirds of the companies. Inventory by qualifications, skills and age, on the contrary, were maintained only in 25 per cent of the companies. These were not maintained continuously but were obtained in special studies directed by the top management.
- Manpower audit was not very strong in the sample companies. Only 20 per cent did it sporadically. However, manpower reviews were made in about 50 per cent of the companies when the level of activity in the company changed or nature of activity was changed or organisational changes were made.
- Work force adjustments were very marginal. Companies preferred reecruitment of casual workers during fluctuations and over time when increased activity was needed.
- Recruitment efforts were more often ad hoc and not based on planned manpower inputs. Recruitment against 'vacancies sanctioned' was the most common basis.
- Career planning was only an emerging function; 28 per cent of the companies have started giving serious consideration to it.
- Use of age profiles and exit interviews as an input to MPP was found only in 15 out of 49 companies.
- Job descriptions were maintained in 90 per cent of the companies for the worker category. For others like technical and clerical categories, only 45 to 50 per cent of the companies were using them.

The main conclusions were that there was not much difference between large public sector and private sector companies as far as MPP was concerned. Smaller sized public sector companies seem to have better developed MPP systems. MPP is generally highly decentralised function, the top managements showed greater interest in MPP forecasting than in the analysis of internal manpower market. There is, generally, a lack of forward looking, to succession of key managers and lack of enthusiasm in development of people for managerial and supervisory positions.

ANNEXURE 7.5

An Example for Case Study Research

An institute of higher learning through its engineering and research capabilities developed the technical know-how for the manufacture of a specialised camera (referred to as SC from here onwards) for scientific use. This camera can be used to take x-ray diffraction photographs of single crystal samples. It can also be used to take photographs of powder, and oscillation and rotation photographs of biclinic and monoclinic crystals.

Contd.

Mr Mohan who was doing his MS in an engineering department in the same institute, came to know that technology for a specialised camera had been developed and was available for transfer. He was planning to start a manufacturing unit and be self-employed. So he approached the concerned scientist in the institute and requested him for the technical know-how. It was offered to him free of cost. He was given only the drawings but no prototype. Mr Mohan undertook development of the technology and set up a unit, Southern Electronics, to manufacture the SC.

While manufacturing he found that the design catered to components of very high precision which was not required for its normal functioning. This resulted in higher costs of the product. Moreover, it was realised that the designers had used mixed standards for the components. This happened because the original instrument was developed in the Institute with available components imported from various countries and with different specifications. Mr Mohan felt that problems in a laboratory model can easily be solved since it is one shot affair and for better results and precision, imported components were used. On the other hand, the problems that are faced in a product for commercialisation are difficult to handle since preferably indigenous materials to local specifications, which are readily available in the market, must be used. The problems of using imported materials with the procedures and long lead time involved, are well known. Therefore, a number of changes had to be made by Southern Electronics (SE) in the technology before the product could be launched for commercialisation.

The model developed in the laboratory was not subjected to tests like vibration tests etc. which a commercial model undergoes. In general the SCs would be transported to user's place and a good working model would not function well if it gets slightly damaged in transportation. The designers at the institute did not anticipate this trouble and, therefore, carried out no special tests. However, they made claims that the product they had developed was a marketable one and ready for production. According to Mohan, the designers were over enthusiastic and made certain technical claims which SC did not possess.

The donor, however, helped Mr Mohan in market survey, locating potential customers for SCs, locating and contacting subcontractors to undertake the manufacture of the components of SC. Last but not the least, the donor made available the testing facilities to M/s. SE to test the commercial models.

The proprietor, an engineer himself, was solely responsible for further technical development of SC. Also he was the only person in the organisation who had good technical and engineering background. He feels that export potential is there for SCs, but he proposed to export only after the equipment underwent considerable field tests and customer audits in the country.

Mr Mohan was unhappy that in this technology transfer, if a working prototype had been given to him he would have avoided many problems in manufacturing commercial models. Since only drawings were provided, he faced very many technical and economic problems before he commercialised the product.

He also felt that there is a need for scientists to understand the problems of commercialisation. One of the problems he faced was use of mixed standards. Because of this and also use of imported components in the laboratory model, he was unable to get indigenous substitutes for the same. Also he found that designers did not mention the specifications for some of the components. Because of this he could not get, for example, the equivalent bearing specified in the drawings and the equivalent indigenous bearings did not match with it causing some engineering problems. Another problem about commercialisation was cost. The laboratory model had very high precision components which were not normally required. This affected the quality of the product. He felt that development design must try to use, as far as possible, simple specifications and indigenous materials to keep the cost of the product low. In other words, design developers must be cost conscious while developing the product.

He also felt that designers could have informed or mentioned the possible technical problems and defects in the designed model. Also they could have pointed out some key components which are critical ones. Eventually Mr Mohan agreed that it was partially because of his inexperience, he did not ask the designers about the technical problems associated with the manufacture of SCs and blindly jumped into the project. In addition, he felt that the donor himself was new to transferring technology. This might partly be the reason for the difficulties.

Mr Mohan, though somewhat unhappy with the initial material given to him during technology transfer, was satisfied with the generous help from the donors in many aspects. He said that he learnt a lot from the donor while commercialising SCs successfully. Therefore, he had no hesitation to go to the same donor once again for some other new products. M/S. Southern Electronics had not recruited any other technical person for the manufacture of SCs and he felt that he was quite competent for the job and did not regret his decisions to take technology from this institution of higher education. This could be considered one of the successful technology transfer cases.

Contd.

Regarding some other aspects in technology transfer, Mr Mohan strongly felt that technology transfer must be on an "exclusive basis". If the same technology is offered to a new entrepreneur, the problems of the first entrepreneur must be resolved successfully or they must be taken into consideration before giving it to a new entrepreneur. As for paying royalty to the donor, he felt that if at all a royalty had to be paid by small industries, it would be convenient for such units to pay it in a deferred way with a small amount as initial payment.

Talking about one of his non-technological problems, Mr Mohan said that banks cannot understand the problems faced by small industries manufacturing complex equipment. Generally, all the customers tested the equipments for the given specification and accuracy and once they were satisfied about the same they make the payments. Therefore, buyers do not agree to take possession of equipment through banks and banks are ready to give credits to such units. Because of limited finance, non-payment of buyers as soon as they receive the equipment and non-availability of credits from banks, technology-based small units face special problems in working capital management.

The study yielded good insight into the problems of technology transfer from institutes of higher learning and research. The study indicated the following propositions to be researched further as hypotheses.

- "When only the design of a new product is transferred to a manufacturer by an Education and Research Institute (ERI) the transfer in a larger proposition of cases will be successful when there is assistance by the ERIs to the manufacturer than when there is no such assistance."
- Technology transfer from research institutions to a small scale manufacturer will be more successful when the recipient is a technocrat than when he is not.

These could be tested in a separate study as hypotheses.

The main weakness of case study research, that of inability to generalise the findings is attempted to be partly redressed by the use of the logic of the survey method, in case cluster method (for details see Meclintock et al, 1979) where a cluster of case studies of similar situations is statistically analysed to develop Heuristics and in multiple case analysis (for details see Madan Mohan, 1999) where simple aggregations of specific experiences and correlation analysis of data on variables are performed to obtain some degree of greater generalisation and streamlining the hypotheses for rigorous investigations.

ANNEXURE 7.6

Example of Cognitive Mapping

Silk reeling operations in the Sericulture industry in Karnataka were studied. An attempt was made to model the reeling operations using a heuristic model since analytical modelling was not feasible. In order to understand the perceptions of the reelers in general, several reelers were interviewed and a cognitive map was developed. It is displayed in Exhibit 7.3. Three hierarchical levels were identified as input environment, operations and performance in the output environment. It is seen from the cognitive map that the chain 'cocoon purchase decision', 'Running the reeling plant' and 'availability of funds' is the most important one in the perception of the reelers, for economic performance of the reeling operation and its management.

Suggested Readings

- Carol A. Bailey (1995). *A Guide to Field Research*. Thousand Oaks, California: Pine Forge Press.
- Gomm, Roger and Peter Foster (2000). *The Case Study Method*. Hammersley.
- Gummeson, Evert (2000). *Qualitative Methods in Management Research*. New Delhi: Sage Publications.
- Roger, Sapford (1999). *Survey Research*. New Delhi: Sage Publications.

QUESTIONS AND EXERCISES

1. Distinguish between (a) case studies and statistical surveys (b) *ex post facto* research and experimental research.
2. What are the limitations of a field survey as a method of causal research?
3. Can an exploratory study be longitudinal and ex post facto? If not, why not? If yes, explain giving a hypothetical example.
4. Explain the concepts (a) *ex post* fallacy, (b) causal comparison, (c) scouting, (iv) cohort analysis, (d) continuity description, (e) negative case, (f) ethnography, (g) triangulation, (h) formative evaluation, and (i) critical incident.
5. In most organisations, many of the specialised functions are evolutionary in nature. How would you study this, say, for a staff function like OR (Operations Research) applications in production control? Give details of the research design.
6. Why is pilot study necessary in many field researches?
7. What are the basic problems of validating qualitative research like case studies?
8. Distinguish between assessment study of an evaluation research and a descriptive research process. Illustrate with examples.
9. Could survey type of research study be helpful in arriving at solutions to the crime problems in large cities? Give details of your arguments.
10. Select a thesis of *ex post facto* research and give details of the research design and the hypotheses. Can you suggest an experimental method for these research questions and hypotheses? If you cannot what are the reasons?
11. Explain the meaning and significance of research design with reference to an *ex post-facto* study.
12. Choose five publications using field study from research journals which are closely related to a particular area and topic of interest. Using the material of these five papers as literature, develop a hypothesis and design a field study to test this hypothesis. Give an outline of the research design.
13. Surveys can provide sound information on what peoples action in the future will be, and this is the major reason for using it in management research. Do you agree or disagree with this statement? Defend your answer.
14. Many researchers feel that qualitative research is mainly for generating the hypothesis rather than for testing it. Give your critical comments on this.
15. Where is observation more effective— in subjective survey research or objective survey research? Give your reasons for the answer.
16. A management researcher decides to test the hypothesis that intelligence and motivation are the principle determinants of managerial performance in the organisation. Will his research be experimental or *ex post facto*? Why?
17. Choose any research publication having a couple of hypotheses. Without studying the paper, develop research design for the hypothesis considered in the paper, compare it with what the author has designed. Make critical comparative comments.

CHAPTER 8

Modelling Research I—Mathematical Modelling

- Introduction
- Mathematical Models
- Composite Modelling Methods

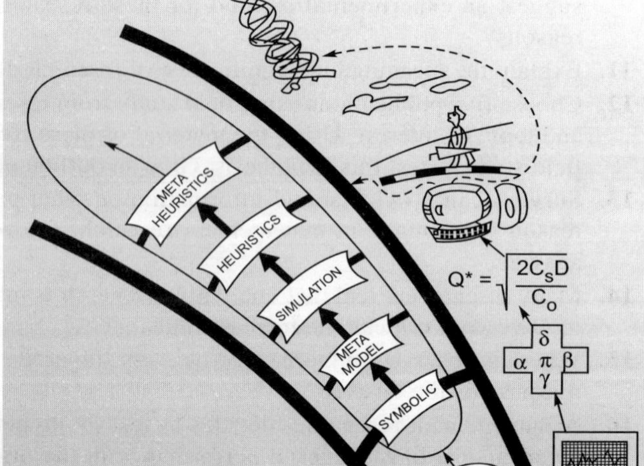

Abstraction Ladder for Modelling

LEARNING OBJECTIVES

Upon completion of this chapter, you will be able to:

- ✓ Understand models as only representations of phenomena in order to understand and study the behaviour of phenomena
- ✓ Appreciate modelling as a process of conceptualisation, verbalisation, symbolisation, and manipulation
- ✓ Get familiar with some basic principles of modelling research
- ✓ Understand model building in the context of theories
- ✓ Study modelling as a process of problem structuring, symbolic representation and solution derivation
- ✓ Understand the importance of analogy in creative modelling
- ✓ Understand approximations as part of modelling research
- ✓ Compare model testing and hypothesis testing
- ✓ Understand the need for composite modelling methods in many actual research situations

INTRODUCTION

Rational procedures of decision-making depend upon a well founded scientific method, based on logic as well as on empiricism. Phenomenological research emphasises more on statistical approaches using empirical data whereas decision models use both statistical and mathematical models dealing with comparatively more highly controlled situations in an organisation. Moreover, they are prescriptive in nature, as against descriptive models (which are based on empiricism) of phenomenological research. They tend to prescribe what should be done by the manager, what alternative to choose when there are a number of alternatives to choose from, for example, what quantities to order for a particular item, what route a vehicle should take to minimise transport costs in a physical distribution system, or what scheduling rule should be used so that customer requirements are met. In many disciplines of management like inventory control, logistics and production, scheduling, plant management etc., well developed theories are available from which causal models can be developed with greater confidence. In these disciplines there is less of intervention of human behaviour and, therefore, they are more amenable to modelling treatment. The decision models are typically causal models and are logically structured. However, some of these problems are analytically very complex and computationally very intractable. With the advent of high speed computers in recent times, these problems are dealt with by modelling procedures that have moved from purely logical processes, as found in the earlier management science (MS) models to simple heuristics to meta-heuristics, simulation, and artificial intelligence approaches, like expert systems. In these approaches, mathematical models based on human ingenuity are utilised. In this section, some of the basic aspects of models, the processes involved in developing models, and some precautions to be observed while applying them will be examined. Some of the procedures in which multiple models are used in an interconnected way will also be outlined.

decision models
These are statistical or mathematical models dealing with controlled situations in an organization. They are generally prescriptive models, intended for indicating the best way of solving a decision problem.

MATHEMATICAL MODELS

What is a Model?

A model is a way of representing a phenomenon. A model can be a verbal model or an iconic model, or an analog model or a symbolic model.

A **verbal model** is a representation of a phenomenon or a decision-making situation using sentences in which well-defined terms are employed. It is meant for communication purposes and may be the first step in other modelling procedures.

model
A model is a way of representing phenomenon. The behaviour of the phenomenon can be studied by studying the behaviour of the model under different conditions.

The **iconic model** is a replica of the physical system, usually 'scaled down' in dimensions, for example, construction models. It also can be scaled up, as in the case of models of molecules of hydrocarbons. These models are widely used in engineering and technology.

A **schematic model** is one in which relationships are shown in a diagrammatic manner, for example, network, flow chart, and so on.

An **analogue model** is a representation in which an analogy is made use of, for example, a map.

symbolic model
These are generally mathematical models. They require a high degree of abstraction, are capable of high degree of manipulation and require a high degree of analysis.

A typical **symbolic model** is a mathematical representation of a decision-making situation as is widely used in management science, for example, an inventory model. The above classification is based on the degree of generality of the model (Fig. 8.1).

Symbolic models can be further classified based on the planning horizon, nature of variables, purpose of application, and methods used for deriving solutions. Static planning horizon refers to single period models and dynamic models are those that take into consideration period-to-period interactions in a multi-period study of a phenomenon. The uncontrollable variables used in the model may be deterministic or probabilistic. In decision-making situations usually the researcher will be interested in normative results. That is, what action/decision is prescribed to the manager to obtain the best result in a given situation. But in relatively unexplained situations in which the researcher is interested in understanding the behaviour of the system, a descriptive

Fig. 8.1 Classification of models

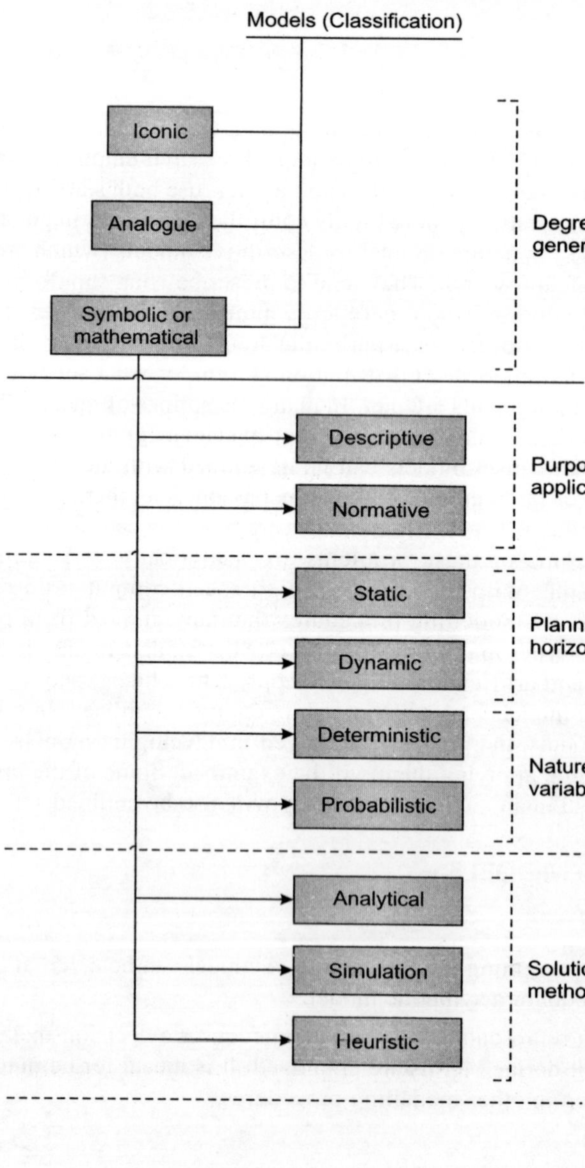

model will be developed. When the problem is amenable to deriving a solution directly by exact mathematical methods, analytical solutions are obtained. When analytical solutions are not possible or are computationally intractable, heuristic procedures using rules of thumb may be used to derive solutions for special problems [Miller-Merbach (1981) and Zanakis and Evans (1981)]. When a system becomes too complex to solve by analytical methods, simulation methods are generally used. These will be discussed in detail in the next chapter.

The behaviour of the phenomenon under dynamic conditions can be understood by studying the behaviour of the models representing them under simulated conditions. The degree to which such representations can be made depends on the type of model one is using. Models as representations are typically simpler than the reality or phenomenon and are only approximations. They can be used for demonstrating the understanding of relationships within a phenomenon or several aspects of the phenomenon and most importantly for predicting the future performance of the phenomenon. Models related to decision-making can also be used for the purpose of controlling a situation.

As the modeller gains understanding of the phenomenon or the system for which the decision is to be made, the model tends to improve and to become closer to reality in subsequent attempts. Thus, model building follows a procedure of successive approximations. Further, models serve an important purpose in research, because:

1. They improve our understanding of the key features of a system.
2. They help in predicting the behaviour of a system and in controlling it.

Development of Models

The extent to which models can be developed and used depends upon the type of model. In this context, three aspects of model building will be of special interest to research students.

1. Degree of abstraction
2. Capability of manipulation
3. Degree of analysis required for developing models

The first of these gives an idea of the degree of difference between the phenomenon and the model in its general physiognomy (Fig. 8.2). The second reflects the degree to which the modeller will be able to apply experimental procedures in order to understand changes in phenomenon. The third indicates the amount of research or scientific effort that is required to be put in to develop the model. Table 8.1 indicates how these three aspects vary over the basic kinds of modelling.

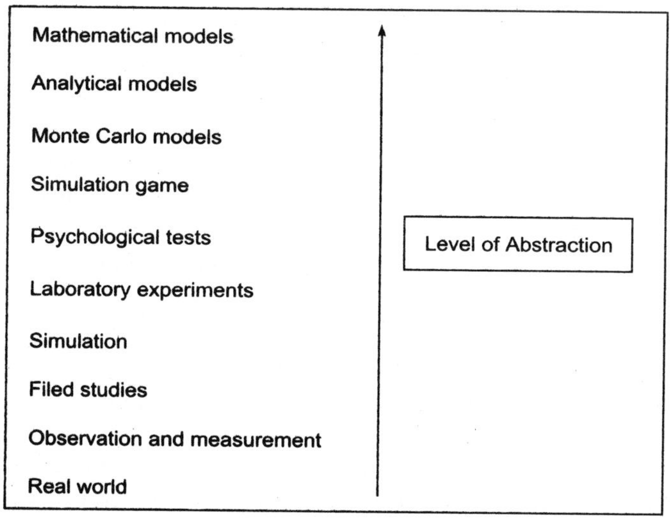

Fig. 8.2 Level of abstraction

Table 8.1 Comparison of Different Types of Modelling

Type of modelling	*Degree of abstraction*	*Capability of manipulation*	*Degree of analysis required*
Iconic	None to low	Low	Low
Analogue	Moderate	Moderate to high	Moderate
Symbolic	High	High	High

It is seen from Table 8.1 that symbolic models have greater benefits from the point of view of representing, understanding, and predicting the behaviour of any phenomenon or system.

art of symbolic modelling
This consists of correct assumptions, identifying key variables and measuring them and mathematically representing the relationships among them. The symbolic models must be robust and capable of enrichment.

The main art of symbolic modelling is in:

1. Correct assumptions.
2. Selection of the key variables.
3. Obtaining a satisfactory means of measuring variables.
4. Representing relationships of the variables.

The process of model building begins with a discussion with managers, careful observation of the system behaviour, and collection of data, as follows. Firstly, the description of the system is obtained. This includes: (i) objectives, activities, resources, environment, and management; (ii) helpful simplifications; (iii) a conceptual model that gives an insight into the system structure and operation; and (iv) flows of information and materials that are helpful in obtaining the first approximation and tentative rough conceptual representation. In the next step a mathematical model is derived from the conceptual model. Finally, the model is tested or experimented with, using collected data to predict system behaviour. The second and third steps are repeated if necessary.

It is desirable that the model so developed has the following characteristics (Morris, 1967):

1. Relatedness to other well developed and tested models.
2. Transparency with respect to interpretation of the result.
3. Robustness under varying assumptions.
4. Ease of enrichment for varied and more complex applications.

A symbolic model can be represented as:

$$V = S(xi, yj)$$

Where *xi* are decision variables, under control of the manager,

yj are exogenous variables not under control of the manager, and

V is some performance measure of a decision typically cost or profit. An overview of some standard operations research models is given in Rivett, 1994.

Stages in model building The structured modelling phase of problem formulation, discussed in the Section on scenarios and structural modelling in Chapter 4 provides a set of broad-based statements about the system to be modelled and its environments. These statements will be comprehensive. The detailed statements, in algebraic or mathematical form, will form the content of the model.

According to Finlay (1985), the stages in mathematical model building are:

1. *Conceptualisation* The modeller translates the manager's problem into his own view of the problem by suppressing the richness of information, introducing rigour, and emphasising precision. The problem may have to be redefined using a backward look from the manager down to the problem, a sideward look into the standard methods of operations research available, and a look at how the model may be used by the manager:
2. *Verbalisation* The logical model produced in (1) above, leads to the next stage, that of verbal specifications of relationships between variables and parameters (see the model building example shown in Fig. 8.3). Variables and parameters are precisely defined. From this verbal stage, the model builder may describe the relationships among aspects

Fig. 8.3 Simulation model for reserve manpower

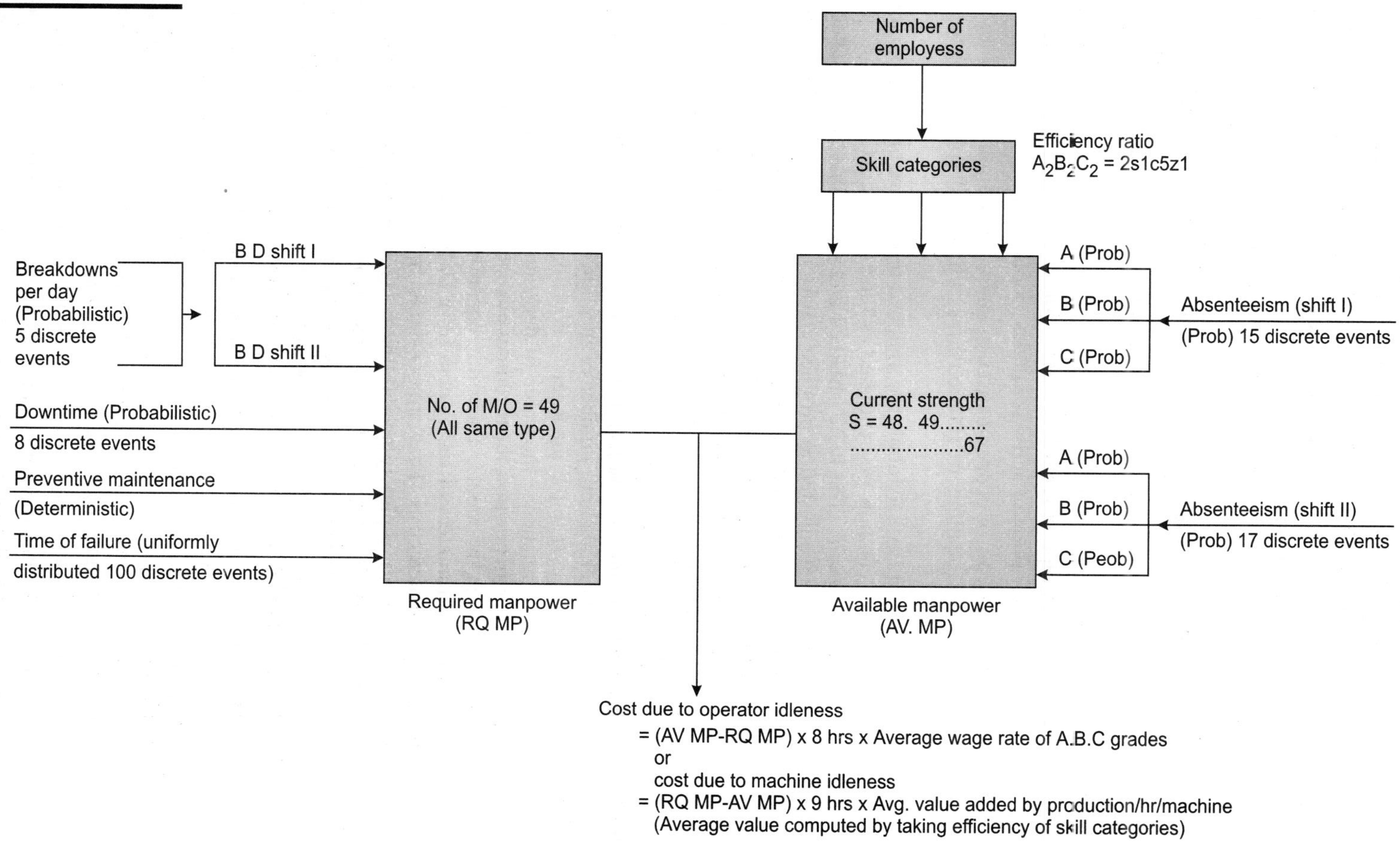

and variables of the problem in a qualitative way. Typical of such qualitative procedures is a schematic diagram or a schema. A crude and simplified version of relationships is indicated here so that the problem is crystallised and clarified to a greater extent and then each linkage shown in the schema is attempted to be converted to a mathematical relationship. An example of this is given in Fig. 8.3. (Krishnaswamy and Ganguly, 1987).

Wilson (1984) gives several illustrations of such conceptual models and suggests that the structure and logic of the model are illustrated using cause-effect relationships. Industrial dynamics models are replete with such diagrams using the states and flow of a system (Forrester, 1961).

Such a qualitative representation of the relationship is, in reality, a conceptual model, which would precede mathematical modelling procedures. These would clarify certain aspects of the problem, which include:

- Boundary of the problem being modelled.
- Assumption regarding interactions.
- Description of activities in the problem area.

A few cycles of conceptualisation and verbalisation may finally lead the researcher to firm specifications of relationships, which will enable him to develop the symbolic model.

3. *Symbolisation* Symbols are assigned to the variables and parameters so that the relationships can now be expressed as functions, equations, or inequalities.
4. *Manipulation* The logic obtained and symbolised variables/equations are now rearranged or readjusted to produce clarity in the model and ease in handling them while solving it. This completes the logical model of the system.
5. *Data definition* The kind of data required to test the model are specified at this stage; the bounds of data over which the model would be valid are clearly stated. This will indicate the final form, content, precision, and accuracy of the data. The end result of this stage is the data model.

decision variables
Resources like manpower or capital or machines are typically the decision variables and they are subject to constraints.

Decision variables are subject to constraints. Typically, the decision variables are resources, such as manpower, capital, number of machines, tools, inventory, and production quantities, which are of interest to the manager in decision-making. In a decision-making situation, the manager has to so choose the value of decision variables so that this system performs optimally. However, in practice, the resources available to the manager are limited and these have to be represented in the model. Therefore, equations representing the constraints are developed. In addition, parameters of the system have to be considered. These parameters are, in OR, typically estimated costs. They are constants, but are subject to errors of estimation. The cost parameters are not typically accounting costs, but have to be extracted from an accounting framework and, therefore, tend to become error prone. Since the parameters affect the values of the results of optimisation, it will be necessary in modelling to clearly understand the influence of these errors on the model outcome. A conscious effort has to be made to find such influences through what is known as sensitivity analysis.

Management problems are system problems that arise as a result of inadequate interaction of several organisational/functional sub-units. Therefore, in the real world of management, rarely, if ever, is a single problem item addressed in a decision process. This makes the modelling somewhat more complex. In such cases, models tend to become large combination models that contain several models of individual problems. These are discussed in detail in on composite modelling at the end of this chapter.

One of the classic examples of such models is the case of production planning and scheduling problems. In a marketing situation, production planning tends to optimise the profit of the company. If several products are produced, an optimal mix of the products has to be obtained and this problem can be addressed by standard linear programming (LP) techniques. The products may be manufactured either on different lines of production or on shared lines of production. Two products p_1 and p_2 are produced on line 1 and line 2. Line 1 and line 2 produce only special components of the products (Fig. 8.4). The common components of the products are produced on line 3. The sequencing of components on lines 1 and 2 are independent of the relative quantities of products p_1 (Q_1) and p_2 (Q_2). The production line 3 and, therefore, its scheduling will be influenced by the ratio of Q_1 to Q_2. For different ratios of Q_1 to Q_2 (for each planning horizon the solution of LP may give a different ratio of Q_1 to Q_2) the sequencing of components of p_1 and p_2 will be different.

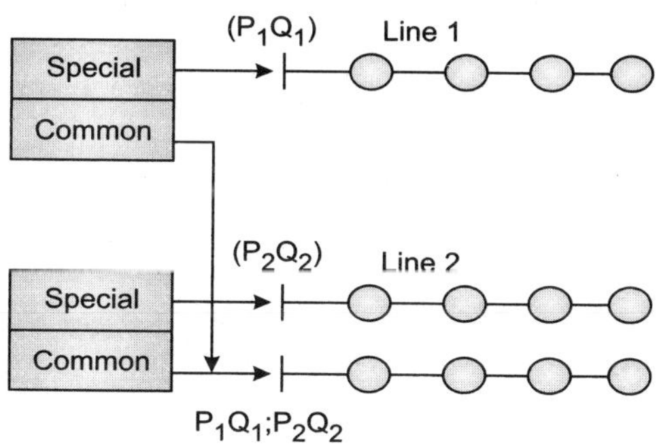

Fig. 8.4 Production scheduling of two products

It can easily be seen that for multi-period production planning this problem becomes more complex. Therefore, a researcher, when modelling the system, may include a single model of control, which combines the sequencing model of line 3 and the product mix linear programming model. Two illustrations of detailed modelling are given in Annexure 8.1 to this chapter.

Principles of Modelling

Morris (1967) gives several principles, which will provide useful guidelines of modelling. The more important ones are discussed below.

principles of modelling
There are many principles of modelling. Some of the important principles are: models should be validated before use; a model cannot be better than the data that goes into it; and models cannot replace decision makers.

1. A complicated model should not be built when a simple one is sufficient.
2. The problem should not be moulded to suit a technique.
3. The deduction phase of the modelling should be conducted rigorously.
4. Models should be validated prior to use.
5. Models should never be taken too literally.
6. A model shouldn't be expected to do anything for which it was not intended.
7. Primary benefits of modelling are those of developing it.
8. A model cannot be better than the information/data that goes into it.
9. Models cannot replace decision makers.
10. When the model tends to be complex, the underlying complex relationships should be broken down into groups of simpler ones.

The first principle is directed towards a graded approach to model building. Simple models should be tried initially for representing a system, with a considerable number of assumptions being made to simplify the structure. Subsequently, the assumptions can be relaxed one after another in order of ascending difficulties in treatment. Thus, successive approximations to reality can be obtained.

The second principle is in the nature of a warning to the researcher that while a problem is being modelled, the problem is much more important than the modelling technique. Specialisation in techniques tends to make the researcher blind to certain aspects of the problem in his eagerness to apply a particular technique, which may appear *prima facie*, the correct modelling technique.

The third principle emphasises the deduction phase, which is the heart of modelling. While the identification of the problem involves judgement, creative effort, and inductive reasoning, the development of the model has to be deductively rigorous in order to make it an efficient tool for decision making.

The fourth principle is very important from the point of view of scientific research. Just as a hypothesis is to be verified before acceptance, a model has to be validated before application. The fifth principle warns that after a phenomenon has been modelled, the researcher runs the risk of looking at the phenomenon through the model and any result of the model may tend to be interpreted as reality.

In principle eight, the cardinal importance of the quality, reliability, and accuracy of data that is used for constructing the model is emphasised. The ninth principle places mathematical models in the correct perspective with respect to real world decision-making. They can be, at best, strong decision supports. The tenth principle emphasises the synthesis of simpler models of the parts of a complete system. This is further elaborated in composite modelling at the end of the chapter.

In addition to the above, the following aspects of models are important and must be borne in mind.

- Models are invented and theories are discovered.
- The extent to which a phenomenon is understood is generally inversely proportional to the number of variables required to explain it. There is a drive among social scientists to achieve parsimony in explaining phenomena through methods like cluster and factor analyses. These will be discussed in a later chapter. There is, thus, a trade off between the degree of understanding and the ease of handling variables.
- Modelling follows a cyclic process. A model is constructed, data from phenomenon are used as inputs to the model, the performance of the model is compared with the actual behaviour of the system; typically a statistical test (any other test may be employed) of the significance of difference between the two is made, and if the difference is significant, the process of modifying or rebuilding the model is started all over again.

Patterns of Model Building

Ackoff (1963) discusses five patterns of modelling based on the degree to which the structure of the problem under study is clear or transparent. In the first two patterns, the structure is transparent and in the remaining three patterns it is not transparent. In the first, the causal structure is clear and no effort needs to be made by the researcher to unearth it. In the second, the structure of the problem is relatively transparent, but representing it symbolically is difficult and a comparative analysis with other systems will help to represent the problem symbolically. In the third pattern, an insight cannot be obtained into the problem unless some data is extracted from the phenomenon. In an initial cursory analysis of this data, the structure emerges. The fourth pattern is used where the theory itself is not developed substantially to support a model building effort. Efforts made during initial data analysis are not adequate to reveal the structure of the problem. In pattern five, additional experimentation has to be made in order to clarify problem situations. Ackoff discusses a two way experiment, as shown in Fig. 8.5. His discussions are only relevant for the complete development of a theory, based on which decision models can be developed. However, the important point is that in the decision-making area the researcher may meet with a problem situation in which substantial theoretical research support

Fig. 8.5 Schematic diagram of model-construction pattern 5

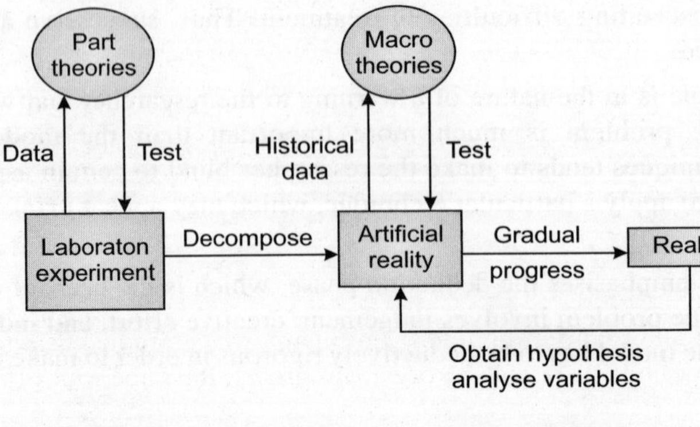

is lacking. In that case he/she is inexorably drawn to research in these areas (refer to illustration given in the section 'the research process' in Chapter 2). A more comprehensive scheme of pattern development with models is given in Fig. 8.6.

The modelling process is divided into three phases for convenience and they are—identification of problem structures (PS), symbolic representation (SR) or development of model, and deriving solutions (DS). Much of Ackoff's discussion deals with interactions between the PS and SR phases in the model-building effort, but there are also many interesting aspects in deriving the solution. Once the PS is made transparent, the researcher will develop the model SR. This process may either be easy or extremely difficult. An analogy in many cases will help the researcher make the symbolic representation. It will also help at the stage of deriving a solution. If, however, the researcher fails to do that, an alternate modelling research will be undertaken or a mathematical breakthrough has to be accomplished in order to solve the model.

phases of modelling process

There are three phases: identification of problem structure, symbolic representation and deriving solution.

Deriving analytical solutions from mathematical models in many cases may not be possible. When it is possible, a further problem is one of whether the solution can be obtained through computational procedures that are not tedious. When deriving analytical solutions is not possible, a researcher may decide to get approximate solutions, imposing certain simplifying conditions on the equations or reducing the range of solution capability. If, however, approximate models are not tenable/acceptable then theoretical research in mathematical disciplines will become a necessity.

However, approximate methods that are available to the manager are not merely mathematical methods but judgmental ones. Also available are heuristics, which are amalgamations of hunches, experience, judgement and simple mathematical and/or, logical thinking. These are very powerful methods for solving ill-structured problems.

Further, for problems, which can be solved optimally when computational time is very large as in the case of many computationally intractable combinatorial problems, the researcher may choose non-optimal solutions through application of heuristics. The primary aim of such heuristics is the reduction of computer time (more aptly the reduction of search for solution).

Another method employed in management research is computer simulation. In this, one may split the complex system of equations into simpler modules/sub systems. They are then linked up in simple ways to yield the representation of the total system. The total system model is then simulated on a computer, particularly when stochastic elements are present in the model. In such cases, it will be necessary to check the heuristics against the optimum solutions in at least small size problems to establish the validity of the heuristics. If, however, a non-optimal solution is not acceptable, the problem leads to further research on the theoretical aspects of the model.

Use of Analogy in Modelling

When the problem is transparent but its symbolic representation becomes extremely difficult, the use of the analogy may be attempted in order to develop the model. These analogies relate a particular kind of problem structure in one knowledge domain to a problem in another domain. For example, in the study of social systems, substantial inspiration has been drawn from biological research. The development of systems theory grew out of biological theories. The use of an analogy with birds and insects in the design of aircrafts is well known. We will examine a few cases of modelling in the area of management research where the cross-fertilisation of ideas across different disciplines has taken place through analogy.

analogy in modelling

When a problem, though transparent, is extremely difficult to represent symbolically analogy may be useful. The analogy may be from one problem domain to another.

[A] Biological models are used in manpower planning. The growth of manpower of a company is modelled on the lines of growth of population using an exponential relationship.

[The equation of the growth curve is $N = \dfrac{KR^t}{R^t + C}$ where $C = \dfrac{K}{N_0} - 1$] (Fig. 8.7) (Krishnaswamy, 1983).

[B] The growth of an organisation in terms of manpower is studied using an analogy to the growth of an organism. When the organism grows, the cube root of its size or volume

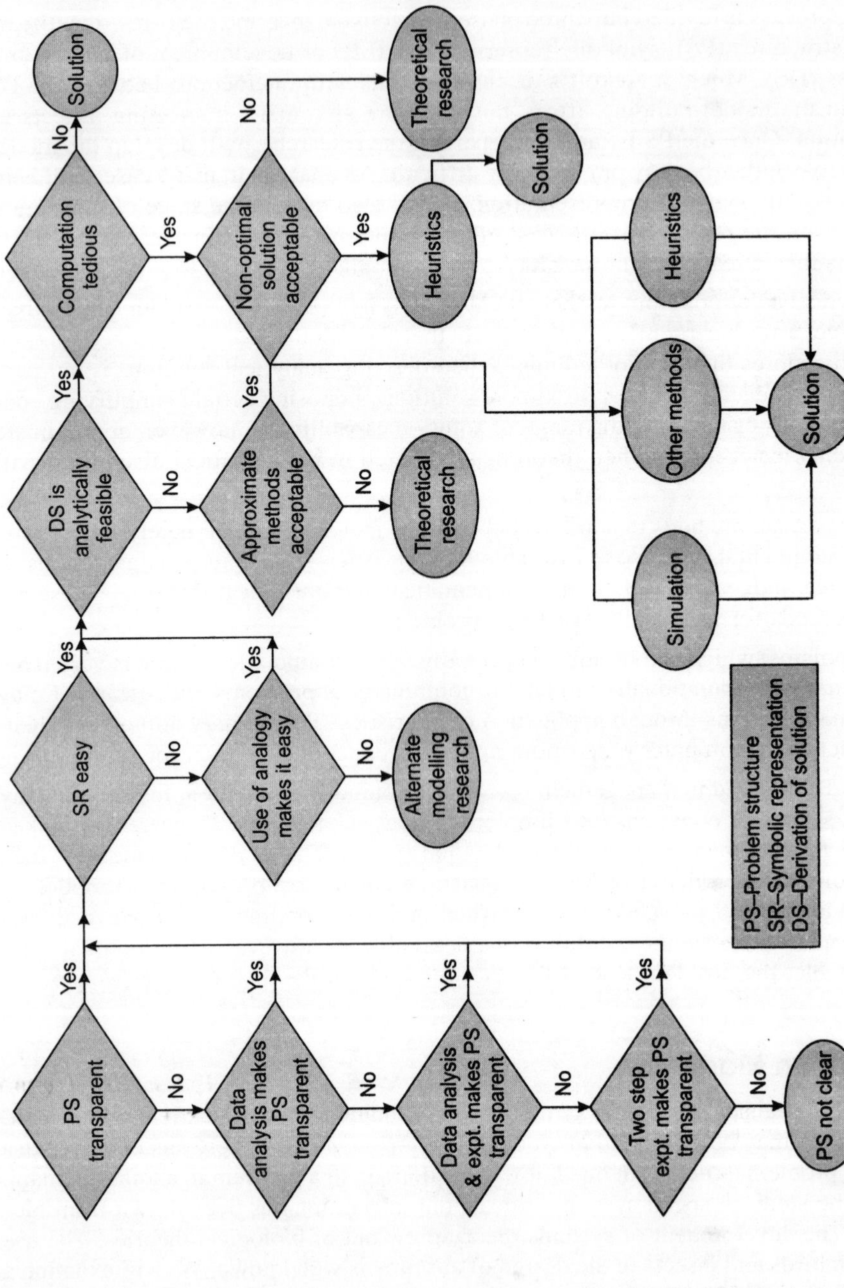

Fig. 8.6 Patterns of modelling

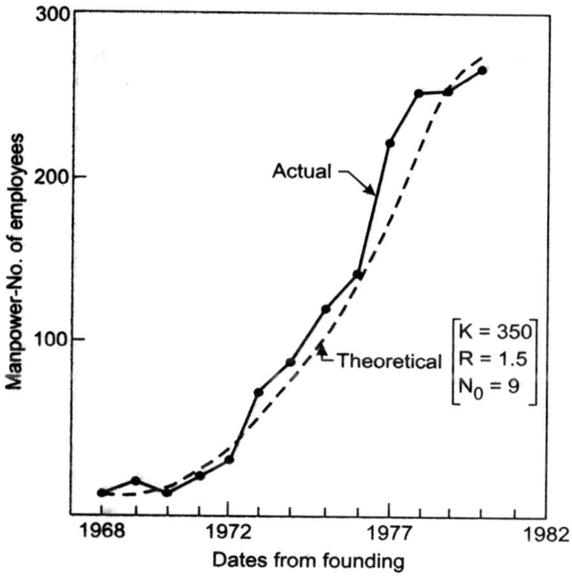

Fig. 8.7 Growth of an organisation

is linearly related to the square root of the surface area. This is compared to the growth of two different departments of an organisation. The internal manpower is analogous to the size of the organisation and external manpower is analogous to the surface area. When the two are plotted by regression equations, a significant regression is noted. Using this model, the mix of people who perform activities related to the boundary of the departments can be predicted as the organisation grows as shown in Fig. 8.8 (Krishnaswamy, 1983).

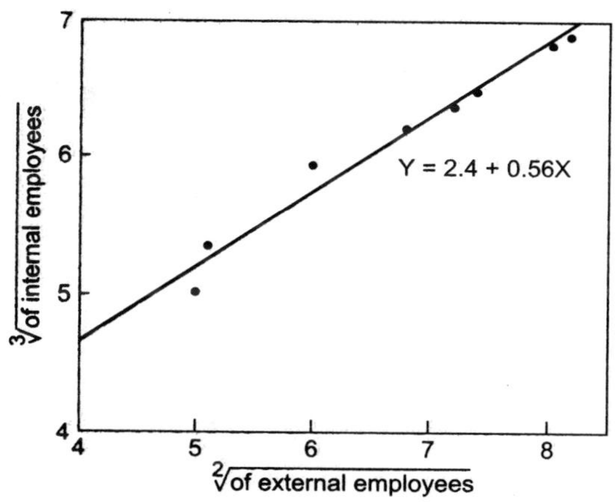

Fig. 8.8 Relationship between internal manpower and external manpower

[C] A quality control model structure is used in manpower planning. Every organisation experiences a certain degree of absenteeism of its employees. Absenteeism is a stochastic variable having properties of seasonality. In order to stave off the ill effects of absenteeism, a manager keeps extra operatives in order that the loss of production due to absenteeism is minimised. If too few reserve operators are maintained, the cost of production loss tends to be high. On the other hand, if too many are employed, the cost of excess spare manpower is high. So the problem is one of determining the optimal reserve manpower. This problem is analogous to what is known as the shrinkage allowance problem in quality control.

This is illustrated in Fig. 8.9 below. If an initial 100 items of the product are produced on machines 1, 2, and 3, at each stage, there is a loss (2, 3, and 2 numbers) and finally,

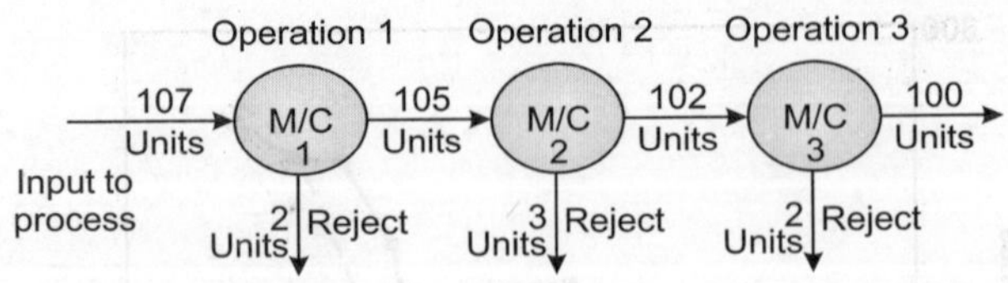

Fig. 8.9 Shrinkage allowance

a quantity of 93 units is produced. To avoid this shrinkage from 100 to 93, the process will be started with extra units, say, 107, to get an output of 100.

The cost equation for the model is given as:

$$VCi = [\ C_1(R - ai) + C_2\,(ai - R)\ ] \text{ .... (1)}$$

Where VCi = Variable cost of the system on day i
C_1 = Cost of idle worker/day when R > ai
C_2 = Cost of production loss/day per idle machine occurs when $V_i > a$
ai = absenteeism on the ith day in number of workers
R = number of reserve workers

Since the ai's are distributed in a general distribution and are seasonally varying, optimising VC/year would be mathematically intractable.

$$VC/\text{year} = \Sigma\, C_1\,(R - a_i) + \Sigma\, C_2\,(a_i - R) \text{ .... (2)}$$

Hence, the model is simulated over a year and for various values of R, the total costs of the system are obtained. The plot of the total cost verses R will yield the minimum or optimal R. (Krishnaswamy and Ganguly, 1987).

[D] Inventory control models are in a sense analogous to hydraulic systems, where a tank is replenished by a valve (continuous supply) or by a container (all in one supply). The demand is represented as a valve emptying the reservoir continuously. The levels in the reservoir are plotted and these will be similar to those of inventory models. Such analogies will facilitate the symbolic representation of inventory problems (Fig. 8.10).

[E] The inventory model represented above can be used for designing capacity of dust bins used in solid waste management. Dust/garbage is collected daily in the dustbins from nearby households, and the level of garbage in the bin gradually increases. In a collecting system, a truck will visit this bin periodically and remove all that is collected in the bins in one shot. The levels of garbage in the bin are shown in the diagram, which is similar to the inventory diagram in Fig. 8.10 (Shekdhar et al, 1986). Another interesting analogy for the use of the inventory model structure is in vault-cash management (Rama Sastry, 1974).

Models as Approximations

Much of the material in this section is based on Ackoff's (1963) discussion. Models, as a rule, are simpler than the reality they represent. Such simplicity may be accomplished because of two reasons.

1. The reality is too complex for accurately modelling it.
2. If the model is a complete representation of reality, the derivation of solution may be extremely difficult or impossible.

need for approximation

When reality is too complex for accurate modelling, approximations are used to simplify representation through assumptions. Successive approximations are used to move closer to representing reality accurately.

Obviously, in any modelling effort there is a trade off between accuracy of representation and mathematical tractability. The degree to which the model approximates the reality, however, is an important consideration in modelling. It depends upon the stage of development of a particular category of models.

With a need for approximation, it becomes necessary for the model builder to make all assumptions of the model very explicit so that model falsification is avoided and the range of situations in which the model is applicable is clear. The trade offs in the approximations discussed above involve two types of costs.

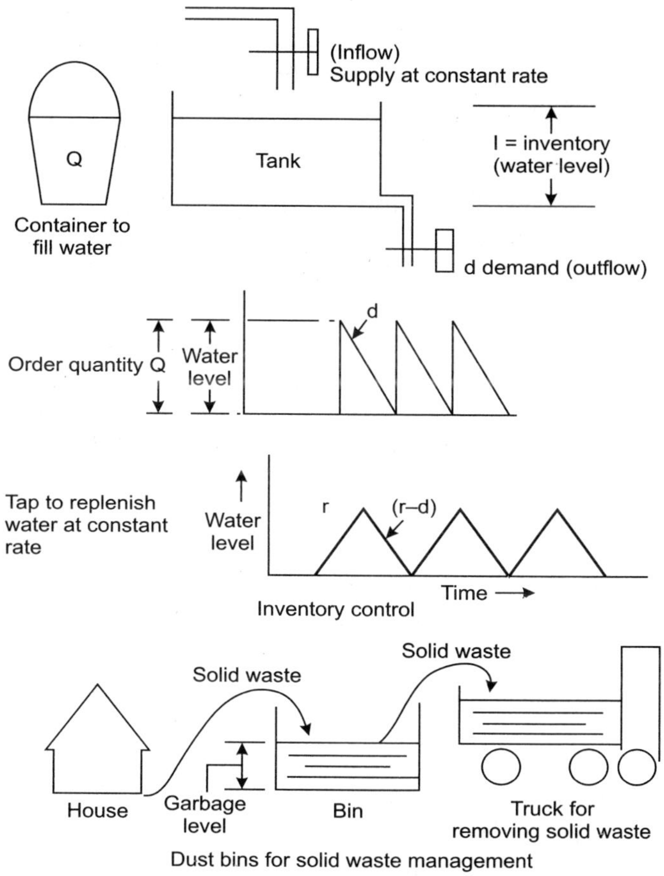

Fig. 8.10 Schematic representation of inventory problems

1. Cost of processing with the model when it is accurate.
2. Cost of reduced model performance with an approximate model (reduced model performance in a OR model would mean increase in cost, calculated as a per cent of optimal cost by using the approximate model).

Such costs obviously may be nominal in most cases. However, in general, the model building process uses successive approximation procedures, (i) up from simple representation to complex ones, or (ii) when complex modelling is to be accomplished, it can be down from complex to simple. The objective in the former approximation will be the achievement of closeness of the model to reality. In the latter, practical use of simple models in situations, which would give acceptable and good solutions. (In the latter case, both types of costs are more easily obtainable; for example, heuristic programmes and large integer programming models.) These approximations can be accomplished by several procedures, as follows:

successive approximations

These are accomplished by omitting a decision variable of little consequence, by omitting an uncontrollable variable of little importance, by changing nature of variables, modifying relationships and changing constraints.

Omitting decision variable This variable is of little consequence as far as performance is concerned (or can, with simple applications, be shown to be so).

Omitting uncontrollable variable This variable too has little consequence on the performance of the model. For example, when inventory control models are developed, cost of transportation, though an important consideration for the supplier, may not greatly influence the optimal quantity as far as the buyer is concerned. In this case, transportation costs can be omitted from economic order quantity calculations. Sometimes the uncontrollable variables can be reduced, for example, in scheduling different families of products from a single variable is used for each family. The above two procedures can be seen as the application of the first principle of modelling, as contained in section on principles of modelling earlier in this chapter.

Changing nature of variables The common practice is to change variables from continuous to discrete, or stochastic to deterministic, or sometimes from a variable to a constant. Changing from a continuous to a discrete variable is usually possible as a sequel to the problem of measurement. For example, time may be measured in minutes, hours, shifts, days, and so on. The change from stochastic to deterministic is by and large a simplification and the analytical burden connected with model formulations will be considerably reduced. An EOQ model is a classical example of this. But in subsequent approximations, the stochastic nature may be restored, that is, change of a variable to a constant is generally undertaken when the variations of the variable are very small, or in case where the variations are inconsequential to the outcome of the model. However, a certain value of the variable is indispensable for the model.

Modifying the equation Models are usually represented as equations and the approximations may come as changes of the equations, typically simplifying them. In management research literature, one finds the use of linearisation very frequently. Typically, a cost curve of a project activity is seldom really proportional to its duration but is often assumed to be so for convenience; alternatively, a series of piecewise linear segments might more closely approximate the curve.

Changing constraints In the initial stages of modelling, one may include all possible constraints, and working even with partial data one can notice that certain constraints are not significant from the point of view of the problem at hand. Such constraints may then be removed. Constraints, however, may be added to move towards a closer approximation. A classical example is that of the constrained optimisation problem, like Lagrangian multipliers (first models are developed ignoring the constraints, then constraints are introduced to modify the model).

The above discussed procedures will have to be applied using judgement; sometimes in a trial and error process, but, in every case, with the acquisition of greater knowledge on the part of researcher about the phenomenon being investigated.

Data Consideration in Modelling

inadequacy of data
Unavailable details of data required for model building, doubtful accuracy of data and sensitiveness of certain kinds of data cause inadequacy of data which makes model implementable in one organization, unimplementable in another.

In practice, there is a strong influence of the availability of data on the construction and structure of a model. The type of data envisaged by the researcher at the time of model building may not be adequately obtainable during collection of data. The inadequacy of data may be due to one of the following reasons:

- Records might have aggregated data for accounting purposes and the model builder would require the details. For example, when collecting absenteeism figures, daily records may not be available after some time but monthly totals and averages may be available. If daily data are required for the model, some method, such as the Monte Carlo method, should be used to generate partially pseudo data. If seasonality has to be very accurately estimated, it may not be possible to accomplish it with monthly figures.
- The accuracy of the data is doubtful. For example, when scaled quantitative data pertaining to past states or activities is obtained in interviews, they may be affected by the errors of recall of the respondents.
- Sometimes the amount of data is inadequate. This problem is typically met with in cases where statistical distributions of variables/parameters have to be obtained. If time and energy permit, these data can be generated over extended periods of time and then subsequently used in the model.
- The data required may be sensitive from the point of view of the organisation and is, therefore, deliberately distorted, for example, tax and financial data.
- While checking the accuracy of data, for example, by correlation methods, two different sets of data are preferred and it is very difficult to make a reasonable choice between different data sets.

From this, it can be seen (principle 8 in Section on principles of modelling) that a model that is adequate and implementable in one situation or organisation may not be capable of being applied in another due to differences in the quality of data.

Models as Heuristic Instruments

In decision-making situations, which are discussed in most models, the alternatives are known *a priori* and the modelling procedures take these alternatives into consideration to give the optimal course of action. From the point of view of management research, there is a powerful use of models, as instruments for generating additional courses of action. In this sense, the model is used creatively for purposes of discovery. Some cases are discussed in Ackoff (1963).

models as heuristic instruments
A powerful use of models is as an instrument in discovering/generating additional courses of action.

Solutions of Models

In models used for decision-making, the most important advantage is in evaluating alternate courses of action or alternate policies. The solution procedures involved in such evaluations using models would fall under three categories:

1. The direct analytical procedure, using classical methods of calculus and algebra; for example, a simple EOQ model.
2. Numerical procedures using iterative techniques; for example, linear programming (LP) solutions.
3. When neither the analytical procedure nor numerical procedures using iteration can yield solutions, the Monte Carlo or model sampling techniques of simulation may be used for deriving solutions.

Testing of Models

In model testing, all errors in the model will have to be dealt with and minimised. The objective of model testing is similar to that of determination of Type I and Type II errors in hypothesis testing. A model may include variables, that are not relevant (which is Type I error) or it may fail to include relevant variables (which is Type II error), which significantly affect the models effectiveness. Further, the model may represent a wrong relationship—a relationship that is different from the true one. This is analogous to the Type III error (reference Chapter 4), which is characterised by wrong identification of the problem. Even when all these three errors are under control, the model may not give good results because of poor estimates of the parameters.

objective of model testing
The objective is to minimize all errors in the model. Errors are: inclusion of variables not relevant (Type I error), exclusion of relevant variable (Type II error) and representation of a wrong relationship (Type III error).

In testing models, all these aspects will have to be dealt with consciously by the researcher, and for this the model has to be tested concurrently. However, in most cases, model testing follows the process shown in Fig. 8.11.

The above aspects will be examined in the box which indicates adjustments of the models. This is similar to the validation of statistical and simulation models.

While collecting data for testing the model, the following aspects are important:

1. Identification of the operational definition of variables, which may be enumerative and metric. Generally, in modelling they are metric quantitative measures.
2. In measuring a variable, sampling procedures must ensure that the sample chosen represents the entire population in the system may have to be used. Sometimes, instead of random samples, typical samples (judgemental) may be used. The data obtained through sampling must be transformed to a form, which is directly used for testing the models. This is called 'data reduction'.

The testing of a model will conclude with a testing of its solution. The simple heuristics that can be used for this purpose are:

1. The model gives a solution that is an improvement over the solution obtained in current practice when dealing with decision models.
2. The model gives a solution that is close to the solution obtained in the current practice when dealing with descriptive models.

Fig. 8.11 Model testing

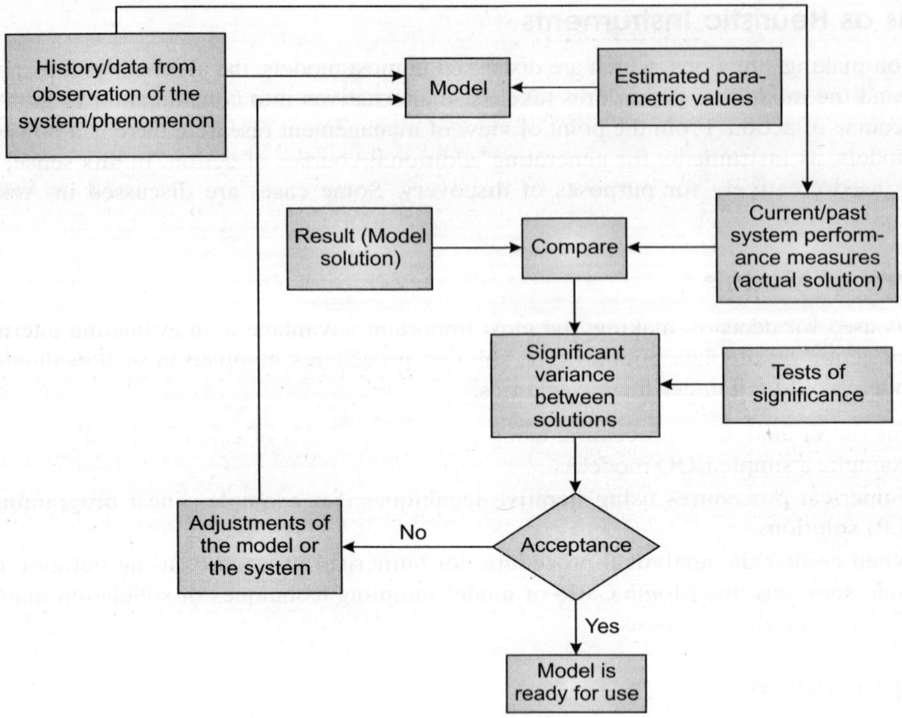

Other tests that may have to be used are as follows:

1. The variability of the model results will be obtained by repeated use on different sets of data and a test is made to check whether these variances are due to the variability of the parameters or they are chance variations.
2. Varying only one parameter and observing the variability in the model results make a sensitivity analysis. The joint variabilities of parameters could also be tested similarly. The important thing is that while such tests are being made the entire population of the system cannot be handled adequately and, therefore, sampling has to be resorted to.

sensitivity analysis Varying only one parameter and observing the variability in model results on a sample is sensitivity analysis.

These procedures will ensure that the external validity of the model is high and the internal consistency and sensitivity to parameters is acceptable. (The reader is referred to an excellent treatment of this in the chapter on Model testing in Churchman et al, 1957.)

COMPOSITE MODELLING METHODS

composite models When large complex systems are modelled the total system is broken down into simpler parts which are modelled separately. These models will be integrated into composite models to represent the total system.

When parts of a larger system are modelled, models may tend to become single models of the types of individual OR models like linear programming, queuing theory application or replacement models, or statistical models like regression or factor analysis, which will be discussed later. However, when dealing with total complex systems a single model may not fully represent the system. Usually, in such a situation, the problem structure is broken down into parts and a different type of model is used for each part. In order that a satisfactory solution is derived to the total problem, these individual models have to be integrated into a composite model. Generally, individual models will be tested for internal consistency and the integrated model will be tested against total performance of the system. Two examples are drawn from research literature and briefly presented in Annexure 8.2. The main aim of the presentation in Annexure 8.2 is to bring out the composite nature of the modelling process rather than the intricacies of modelling and testing. A schematic diagram accompanies each simplified presentation to communicate the integration process.

SUMMARY

A model is a way of representing a phenomenon. Mathematical models of decision-making situations are widely used in management research. Models can be classified according to the degree of generality, purpose of application, nature of variables and solution methods. By studying the behavior of well-constructed model of a system, the systems behavior can be understood, analysed or predicted.

The art of modelling consists of making correct assumptions, selecting key variables, developing satisfactory measures of the variables and symbolically presenting the relationships among the variables. Model building process consists of several stages. The conceptualisation stage is marked by the conversion of manager's problem into a research problem. In verbalisation stage, schematic and verbal pictures of the relationships are developed. Symbols are assigned to variables and equations are developed in the next stage and manipulated such that a practical model is obtained which could be solved. Accurate data is collected for testing the model in the final stage. Typically, a mathematical model, for aiding decision-making, consists of an objective function, for the system under consideration, which is maximised or minimised under a set of system constraints. There are a number of principles related to simplicity, rigor, deduction, validity, and accuracy of data and limitations of models, which help build good models.

Model building follows several patterns, depending upon the transparency of the problem structure, difficulty of symbolic representation and method of deriving solution. Analogy can help in unearthing a complex problem structure and making symbolic representation. Heuristics and computer simulation are useful in deriving solutions to complex models. The models have to be tested prior to employing preferably empirical data in order to validate them and to minimise errors and sensitivity to parametric estimates.

When complex system modelling is attempted the system is broken down into simpler sub-systems which are modeled individually, tested and integrated suitably into a composite model of the total system. Finally, the composite models are validated and tested for performance.

ANNEXURE 8.1(a)

Illustration of Modelling — A

Illustration*— A An efficient distribution policy for an electronics home products manufacturer (ELHOP) is to be modelled (Krishnaswamy and Raghavendra, 1992). The firm has a number of factories, godowns, and retail locations located all over India. The simple diagram illustrated below could describe the conceptual background for the model. The numbers in the square brackets indicate the existing number of factories, godowns and retail locations, respectively.

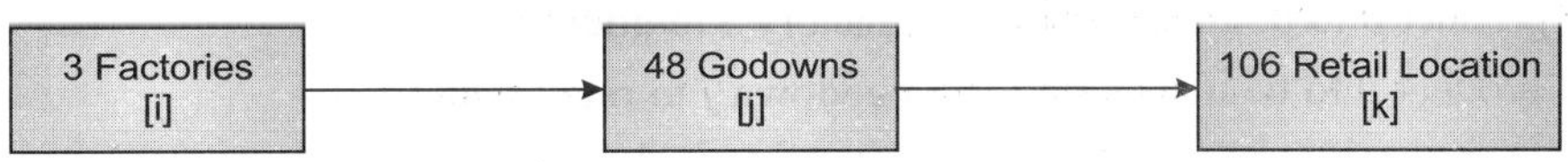

The decision variables of the problem are:

1. The quantities of each product to be transported from each factory to various godowns.
2. The quantities of each product to be moved from each godown to various locations.

The objective of the model is to find the best values of the decision variables (quantity of products to be moved), which would minimise the overall cost of transportation, sales tax, octroi, and any other associated costs. The time horizon of the model is one year but can be converted to shorter durations such as quarters or months.

Contd.

* May be skipped by the less mathematically-oriented researcher/reader

The operating limitations (or constraints) considered in the model are:

1. The demand at each one of the location for various products.
2. The capacities, if any, at the factories for each product. (Currently, these were not explicitly considered as they were not the limiting factors as of now. However, they could be included in the model at a later date).
3. The inventory-holding capacity at any godown during a particular period, if necessary.
4. Flow balance at the godowns (each godown can supply its retail locations only as much quantity of each product that it receives and no more).

The information required for using this model basically falls into three categories:

1. The productwise unit cost of transporting from each factory to each godown (this also reflects separately the sales tax and octroi, as applicable to various places).
2. The productwise unit cost of transporting from each godown to its retail location.
3. The demand for each product at each one of the retail locations.

The above problem can be formulated as a standard linear programming model. The linear programming model that developed, along with the definition of variables, the objective function and the operating limitations (constraints) is described in the next section.

The Model

Parameters

$$i = 1, 2, 3 \text{ (factories)}$$
$$j = 1, 2, 3, \ldots 48 \text{ (godowns)}$$
$$k = 1, 2, 3, \ldots 106 \text{ (locations)}$$
$$p = 1, 2 \text{ (products)}$$

Cijp = Unit cost of transporting one unit of product p from factory i to godown j (this is the sum of the basic transportation cost from factory to godown plus sales tax plus octroi).

Cjkp = Unit cost of transporting one unit of product p from godown j to retail location k (this is the sum of the basic transportation cost from godown to location plus sales tax plus octroi).

Uncontrolled Variable

Dkp = Demand of product p at retail outlet k (in numbers).

System Variable

Sip = Capacity at factory i for product p (in numbers). At present no limit is enforced on the production capacity at factories since whatever is required is being produced. However, if this becomes a serious limitation at a later date, it can be easily incorporated in the model.

Decision Variables

Xijp = quantity of product p to be transported from factory i to godown j

Xjkp = quantity of product p to be transported from godown j to retail outlet k

Assumptions

Each, *Cijp* and *Cjkp*, are constants, indicating a linear relationship between the cost of transporting and quantity transported.

Xijp and *Xjkp* are either zero or positive.

Therefore:

Cijp Xijp = Cost of moving quantity *Xijp* of product p from i^{th} factory to j^{th} godown

Cjkp Xjkp = Cost of moving quantity X_{jkp} of product p from j^{th} godown to k^{th} retail location

Contd.

The LP Model

Objective Function

$$\text{Minimise} \sum_{ijp} C_{ijp} X_{ijp} + \sum_{jkp} C_{jkp} X_{jkp}$$

Subject to (constraints)

(i) *Demand (annual) at location*

$$\sum_{j} X_{jkp} \geq D_{kp} \text{ for each } k \text{ and } p \quad (1)$$

Equation (1) ensures that the demand for the products are met at each location. That is, adequate quantities, as represented by demand forecasts, are shipped to the locations.

(ii) *Warehouse-Flow Balance*

$$\sum_{i} X_{ijp} - \sum_{j} X_{jkp} = 0 \text{ for each } j \text{ and } p \quad (2)$$

Equation (2) ensures that there is adequate supply to each godown from the various factories so that the godown, in turn, can supply the products to associated retail locations.

(iii) *Capacities at factories*

$$\sum_{i} X_{ijp} \leq S_{ip} \text{ for each } i \text{ and } p \quad (3)$$

Equation (3) indicates the annual manufacturing and/or supply capacities of each factory for the concerned product.

(iv) *Non-negativity*

$$X_{ijp}, X_{jkp} \geq 0 \text{ for each } i, j, k, \text{ and } p \quad (4)$$

This is a linear programming model for the product distribution policy for ELHOP, which can be solved by using a standard linear programming software like Linear Interactive Discrete Optimiser (LINDO).

ANNEXURE 8.1(b)

Illustration of Modelling — B

Illustration* B Raghavendra and Mathirajan (1992) formulated media planning models using dynamic programming methods. With the growth in advertising avenues available via multimedia exposures, decision-making in the Indian advertising context has become a complex task. Advertisers are constantly faced with questions regarding the choice of media, the specific media vehicle (publication in the press medium or programme slots in television or radio), the number of insertions, as well as the intensity with which advertising campaigns are to be undertaken in the wake of increasing competition. The complexity is confounded by the fact that advertisements in the mass communication media in India could be made in more than 15 Indian languages in addition to English. The geographic and demographic spread of the population being very vast, the coverage and appeal obtained by each media vehicle appears to be substantial and, therefore, cannot be ignored. Even for small budgets and regional markets, there are millions of combinations of media schedules that could be chosen. The job of a media planner is to select an ideal media plan, which achieves the desired objective(s) at minimum cost. Optimisation models could play a prominent role in assisting media planners in this task.

Contd.

*May be skipped by the less mathematically-oriented researcher/reader

Advertising performance measures Perhaps the best measure of advertising effectiveness is the resulting sales of a product or service, provided that it is measurable as a direct consequence of advertising. However, it is well known that the sales of a product or service depends on several factors, such as the quality, price, the extent of competition, and such other factors, and it is extremely difficult to measure the specific marginal effect of advertisement. Therefore, advertisers traditionally choose surrogate objectives that focus on advertisement exposures on the target audience. In India, the planned performance of an advertisement campaign is normally measured by one or few of the following criteria:

Reach This is the number of distinct individuals exposed to the advertisement, at least once. Traditionally used in new product ad campaigns.

Average opportunities-to-see (OTS) Also known as the average frequency of exposure, this is defined as the average number of times the persons reached are exposed to the advertisement. Generally used for advertisements of consumer products, which are characterised by competition and a repeated cycle of buying.

Gross OTS This is equivalent to the cumulative number of exposures to individuals; this is, counting individuals as many times as they are exposed to the advertisements. Being the product of reach and average OTS, this criteria is used when continued awareness is the objective.

Minimum cost per person reached (CPPR) This is the ratio of the total media cost to the number of persons reached. Generally used with prior minimum limits on reach and in situations where the budget is a prime limiting factor.

There are other concepts such as Gross reach, CPPR, cost per OTS, and so on, which are used occasionally by a few advertisers. Reach is also used with various modifications such as average reach, percentage target reach, and net percentage reach achieved. Some advertisers interchange the use of gross reach and gross OTS. At times, minimum total cost is specified as an objective of an advertising campaign when limits on reach are specified. However, this is not considered an advertising objective, but is rather a limiting parameter influencing media decisions.

Evaluation models Since the number of readers is not the same as the circulation of a publication and since not all the readers pay attention to all the advertisement insertions in a publication, probability concepts are used in evaluating exposures. The basic objective of evaluation models is to provide a theoretical basis for OTS distribution, which gives the probability distribution of the number of people exposed to the advertisement once, twice, thrice, and so on. Additionally, it provides a mechanism to compute various performance measures.

Notations:

i, j = 1,2,..M (Media vehicles ranked in the order of target readership)

N_i = Target group readership of vehicle i

p_i = Probability of exposure in vehicle i

X_i = Number of insertions in vehicle i

C_i = Cost per insertion in vehicle i

$Z_r(X_i)$ = Probability of r OTS if X_i insertions are made in vehicle i

$Dr(X_i)$ = Number of readers exposed to exactly r insertions if X_i insertions are made in vehicle i (r=0,1,2,....X_i)

$G(X_i)$ = Gross OTS from vehicle i if X_i insertions are made in it

$R(X_i)$ = Reach from vehicle i if X_i insertions are made in it

$A(X_i)$ = Average OTS from vehicle i if X_i insertions are made in it

$C(X_i)$ = Cost per person reached by vehicle i if X_i insertions are made in it

The probability of a reader exposed to exactly r insertions out of X_i insertions in vehicle i is given by the binomial law:

$$Z_r(X_i) = \sum_{r}^{X_i} (p_i)^r \times (1 - p_i)(X_{i-r}) \text{ for } r = 0,1,2,\ldots.. X_i$$

Contd.

The distribution of the number of readers being exposed to exactly r insertions of the advertisement out of X_i insertions is given by

$$D_r(X_i) = N_i \times Z_r(X_i)$$

The Gross OTS from vehicle i if X_i insertions are made in it is obtained by

$$G(X_i) = \sum_{r=1}^{X_i} (p_i)^r \times D_r(X_i)$$

The reach from vehicle i if X_i insertions are made in it is given by:

$$R(X_i) = \sum_{r=1}^{X_i} N_i x Z_r (X_i) = [1 - Z_0 (X_i)] x N_i$$

The average OTS obtainable from vehicle i if X_i insertions are made in it is expressed by:

$$A(X_i) = G(X_i)/R(X_i)$$

The CPPR from vehicle i if X_i insertions are made in that vehicle is:

$$C(X_i) = C_i \times X_i/R(X_i)$$

Occasionally, some publications give quantity linked price discounts based on the number of ad insertions placed within a certain period. In such situations, the numerator of the right hand side of equation (6) could be modified appropriately.

Media selection models and optimization

While the evaluation models provide a background for developing exposure distributions and methods of computing performance measures, they are not capable of assisting the media planner in developing an ideal media plan to suit a given objective. This drawback could be overcome with the development of optimisation and heuristic methods for media planning. The techniques of dynamic programming (DP), integer programming (IP) and heuristic methods are being used in the Indian environment. The DP model for the media planning is given below.

Dynamic programming In this section, two DP models, which aim to prescribe the best possible media plan for maximisation of reach and maximisation of Gross OTS, are described. In both these cases, the evaluation criteria defined in the earlier section is used for deriving performance measures. The following notations are used in DP.

n = Stage in dynamic programming model; stage n indicates the first n vehicles considered together in the ranked order (vehicles (1,2,......, n –1) and n at stage n).

s = State of the dynamic programming model; represents cumulative number of insertions in all the media vehicles considered upto that stage.

$TC_n(s)$ = Total cost at stage n for state s

$R_n(s)$ = Reach at stage n for state s

$G_n(s)$ = Gross OTS at stage n for state s

$A_n(s)$ = Average OTS at stage n for state s

$C_n(s)$ = Cost per person reached at stage n for state s

$R^*_n(s)$, $G^*_n(s)$, $A^*_n(s)$ and $C^*_n(s)$ would indicate the optimal values of the respective measures at stage n for state s.

Maximising reach The 'stages' of the dynamic programming procedure are the media vehicles taken cumulatively with a publication added at each stage.

At stage n, the first n vehicles in the rank order are considered cumulatively; that is, vehicles (1,2,.., and n). The 'states' of the DP model are s, the cumulative number of insertions in all the vehicles considered upto that stage. The decision variables are Xi, the number of insertions in vehicle i.

To start with, the reach obtainable for each possible number of insertions in the first vehicle is considered. Subsequently, the maximum possible reach, $R^*_n(s)$ is obtained for s insertions at stage n using:

Contd.

$$R_n^*(s) = \text{Max } \{ R(X_n) + R_{n-1}^*(s - X_n) \} \text{ for } 0 < X_n < s \text{ and } R_0^*(s) = 0 \quad X_n$$

While computing the reach for the nth vehicle, care is taken to ensure that the duplication of readership of this vehicle with respect to the previously included vehicle(s) is eliminated. Further, for each possible value of s, the specific value of Xn namely, X^*n, which gives this maximum value of reach is recorded. That is,

$$[R(X_n^*) + R_{n-1}^*(s - X_n^*)] > R(X_n) + R_{n-1}^*(s - X_n)$$

Proceeding in this way, starting from vehicle 1 and continuing till all the M vehicles are considered, the maximum value of $R_M^*(s)$ would give the maximum possible reach obtainable from the m vehicles. Using the traditional dynamic programming approach, one can read the solution backwards through all the stages in terms of the number of insertions in each vehicle that would give the corresponding maximum reach. When the procedure is computerised, a variety of additional information can be generated. For example, in addition to the maximum possible reach, the corresponding value of gross OTS, average OTS, total cost and CPPR can also be computed.

Maximising gross OTS This is similar to the procedure used for maximisation of reach. The criteria of optimisation is based on the maximum value of $G_n(s)$ and the recursive relation is given by:

$$G_n^*(s) = \text{Max } \{ G(X_n) + G_{n-1}^*(s - X_n) \} \text{ ...(9) with } 0 < X_n < s \text{ and } G_0^*(s) = 0 \; X_n$$

In the last stage, the maximum possible value of $G_M^*(s)$ would give the maximum attainable gross OTS and the corresponding media plan could be read backwards from the last stage of dynamic programming to the first stage, across all the intermediary stages.

ANNEXURE 8.2

Illustration for Composite Methodology — A

Rao, Raghavendra, and Krishnaswamy (1993) considered a major problem faced by the operating managers in a large fertiliser complex (FC), that of maintenance of uninterrupted operation of the production system. The reliability of large scale process industries like FC is often affected due to design considerations aimed at thermal economy, which results in increased degree of complexity and interdependence in the plant. Keeping standbys for equipment or additional streams to the plant itself in a bid to decrease downtime and improve plant utilisation can increase the reliability of a plant.

The above problem was formulated into two parts. The first part deals with constructing a model for analysing the effects of configurational changes on the performance of individual plants within the industrial processing complex (IPC); this is called the microanalysis of the process plant. The second part deals with building a model for analysing production interruptions in the entire IPC, which is called the macro analysis. Finally, a generalised composite methodology linking both the micro and macro models has been formulated.

Micro analysis

In an IPC comprising n plants interconnected in such a way that output of plant 1 is an input to the plant 2, the output of plant 2 is an input to the plant 3, and so on, ultimately the final product is output of the plant n. Assume that each plant is a combination of k streams arranged through parallel and serial connections.

The output of a plant is a function of its state and time. Now, how does an addition of one or more streams to the existing k parallel streams in one of the plants, affect the performance of the total plant? In an attempt to answer this question, modelling of the system with k processes and k+1 processes are carried out.

An analytical model for a (continuous processing plant) with k parallel streams is developed by assuming transitions of the system from one state to the other to be a stationary Markov process with all possible states as random variables negative-exponentially distributed.

Using the Markov property, the steady state probability of operating the system is obtained. The system output as a function of three factors (r, m and s) is derived.

Contd.

A Markov simulation model for the system with the k+1 process is developed as systems using k+1 streams are not physically available. All possible configurations of the system with k+1 processes is compared with that of the system with k processes for the purpose of decision-making.

Macro analysis

For an IPC comprising plants 1 to n, interruption due to failure of equipments and other reasons like mechanical, electrical, instrumentation, and process failures caused in each plant will have varying contributions to the total production loss. If the probability distribution of the arrival of interruptions, duration and probability of their occurrence in a plant i of type j are known, then the whole process of interruptions to the production can be structured as an interruption tree. The plants of IPC are shown as intermediate nodes in the interruption tree, indicating them as the areas of interruptions in the overall production.

Using the interruption tree, based on the relevant probabilities derived from the past data of the IPC, a simulation model (for estimating system performance) is used in order to obtain an estimate of system availability and system productivity.

The expected system availability (ESA) is calculated as a percentage of the effective system hours available for operation to the total hours.

$$\text{ESA} = \frac{\text{Hours of system availability for production in a period}}{\text{Total hours of system time for the same period}}$$

To avoid a state of interruption in the existing system, the system requires either investments in spare capacities or implementation of a better maintenance policy. Each basic node of the interruption tree contributes, to a different degree, to the total system availability and is therefore differently critical to the system performance. Thus, the sequencing of selecting the schemes to avoid the states of interruption become important, particularly when funds available for investment are limited and may not cover the entire range. In such a case, an optimal sequence can be identified by the weightage factors of the nodes to enable improving system performance in an optimal number of steps.

Then,

$$\begin{aligned} W_{ij} &= \text{Weightage factor of a basic node } j \text{ under the intermediate node } i \\ &= p_i \, p_{ij} \, L_{ij} \\ W_i &= \text{Weightage factor of an intermediate node } i \\ &= \sum_{j=1}^{M_i} p_i \, p_{ij} \, L_{ij} \end{aligned}$$

Estimated expected proportion of production loss in the entire system is equal to

$$= \sum_{i=1}^{n} W_i$$

This model was simulated on a computer to estimate the performance of the production system in terms of ESA, quantity of production, and operational productivity of inputs, given alternate policies of investments, which select different schemes to avoid interruption states.

Composite methodology

A generalised composite methodology linking both micro and macro models was formulated.

The sequence of steps to be followed in such a methodology is presented in Exhibit 8.1. It connects a micro block consisting of models to evaluate the configurations of a plant (sub-system) and a macro block with models to evaluate the entire system across plants (sub-systems). Using the Markovian approach at the micro level, the effects of proposed changes to the configurations of the process plants of the FC on the overall system performance were identified. By developing an ITM of the FC, macro analysis was carried out to identify suitable policies to reduce interruptions in the fertiliser complex.

Contd.

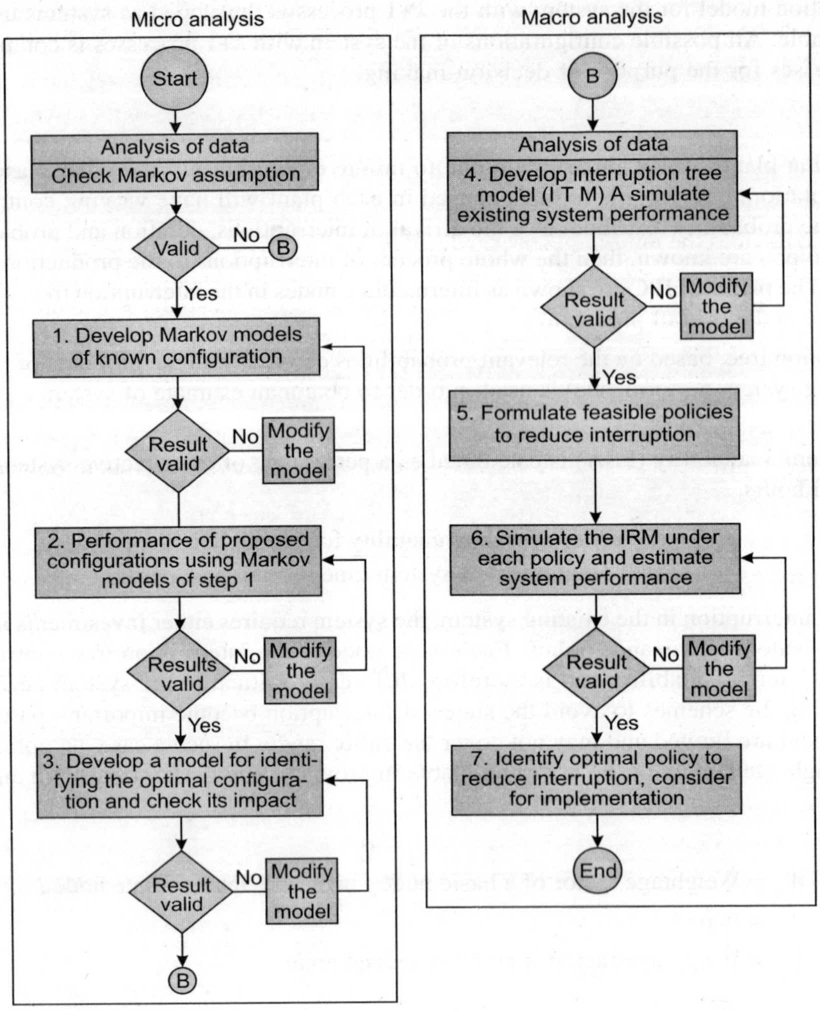

Exhibit 8.1 Flow chart for composite methodology—Illustration A

ANNEXURE 8.2

Illustration of Composite Methodology — B

This study (Patel, 1979) brings out the experience with the application of operations research techniques in regional planning (planning new roads and social services centres) for Dharampur area in Gujarat, India.

The specific objective of the study was to produce an integrated plan for rural development, aimed at the rural poor in the region. The taluka has a population of 194,000 (of whom 92.5 per cent are tribals) and has land area of 800 sq. miles. It has hilly and flat areas, and a majority of people lived in abject poverty.

An important part of the developmental plan was to set up 'service centres' in locations dispersed over the taluka to provide minimal infrastructure, health, and education facilities. These centres would provide agricultural extension, primary schools, cooperative service societies, fair price shops, and post offices. It had been observed that the functionaries were not located near the villages where they were to work and their work places were scattered amongst several villages. These factors resulted in poor availability of functionaries to their client groups and it was difficult for the population to avail their services.

To meet the objectives of the service centres, an analysis was made to choose suitable locations. Many considerations like whether some of the required facilities were already existent, population, growth potential, proximity to

Contd.

highways, and the natural heritage of adjoining areas were taken into account. The analysis led to selection of 44 out of the 237 villages in the taluka for location of service centres. The estimated cost was Rs 5.5 million.

The rough estimate provided was that the cost would be about Rs 90 million, covering a length of 400 miles of all-weather roads. The total amount available from the tribal sub-plan of the government of Gujarat for the Five-Year Plan was no more than Rs 130 million. It seemed that the road programme would hamper the programmes for irrigation, soil conservation, agriculture, forestry, and other projects. This was the stage at which an attempt at applying operations research was made.

The problem was to devices the minimum cost road network to connect the 44 service centres to the existing main highways. A simple modification of minimal spanning tree algorithm Kruskal's was employed. The shortest algorithm provided the minimum cost solution of Rs 19 million, which is substantially less than the original estimate of Rs 90 million.

The next problem was to locate service centres. It was found that Rs 5.5 million, required for the construction of service centres would not be available in the five-year period, as suggested in the plan. The amount that would have been available to the planners for the next five years was estimated at around Rs 1.3 to 1.4 million. Thus, part of the objective of the service centres programme — namely, the number of service centres to be constructed in the next five years — had to be within the available budget.

Discussions were held with leaders, voluntary workers, and officials on this issue. Ultimately, the planners decided that they should establish an objective criterion for the choice of service centres, which would lead to a balanced level of services to the entire region. The criterion chosen was to minimise the total cost as a linear integer-programming problem. Interestingly, the problem had the special structure of the set-covering problem of integer programming. The problem was solved by parametrising the maximum distance of a village from one of the chosen service centres (service level). An optimum solution was obtained for different values of service level, the results of which are given in Exhibit 8.2.

Service Travel	*Number of Service centres*	*Budget (Rs Millions)*
4.5	16	not possible
5	13	2.33
5.5	11	1.65
6	8	1.39
6.5	8	0.99
7	8	0.86
8	5	0.65
9	4	0.58
10	5	0.48

Exhibit 8.2 Optimal solutions for different service levels

Once the choice of the service centres for the five-year plan period was determined, the next problem was to solve the phasing of the construction of the centres over the five-year period. The specific problem was balancing expenditure over time as well as balancing service levels over the years. The criterion chosen was to provide the best time-averaged service level, subject to the constraint that the expenditure in each year is within 10 per cent of the average annual expenditure (Rs 277, 000).

Dynamic programming technique was used to solve this problem. An 11 dimensional Boolean vector defined states, where 1 in the ith element meant that the ith service centre was already built, and a 0 meant that it had not yet been selected. A dynamic programming routine was used to compute the optimal solution. The optimal solution had a total service level of 51.8 miles and an average annual service level of 10.36 miles. The results are given in Exhibit 8.3.

	Year				
	1	2	3	4	5
Centres to build	11, 15, 27	5, 31	30, 40	1, 18	21, 31
Service level	17.5	12.5	8.6	7.0	6.0
Cost (Rs 000's)	275	255	285	285	285

Exhibit 8.3 Optimal solutions for phasing the construction of the 11 service centres

The study shows how several operations research models can be used sequentially, very effectively, used as tools in infrastructure planning for regional development. This experience reveals that there is potential for operations research models to be used to provide an objective rationale for administrative decisions, making them less vulnerable to the arbitrary push and pull of power politics. The flow chart for the study is given in Exhibit 8.4.

Contd.

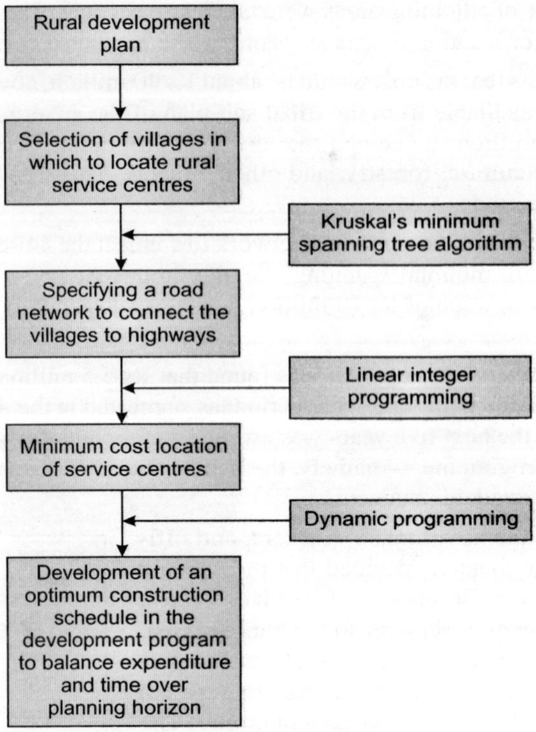

Exhibit 8.4 Flow chart of study

Suggested Readings

- Finlay, Paul. N. (1985). *Mathematical Modelling in Business Decision Making*. London: Croom Helm.
- Morris, W. T. (1967). 'On the Art of Modelling'. *Management Science: 707–711*.
- Rivett, Patrick (1994). *The Craft of Decision Modelling*. Chichester: John Wiley.

QUESTIONS AND EXERCISES

1. Take one case each in the following as an example from literature especially from a journal like the *Journal of Operations Research Society* or *Management Science* and identify in what way the reality has been simplified in the model.
   (a) A linear programming application
   (b) A queuing application
   (c) A simulation model
   (d) An inventory problem
   (e) A distribution problem
   (f) A scheduling model
2. From literature (journals or web sources) choose some OR models (publications) and classify the pattern of modelling adopted in each of them.

3. Why is consideration of data adequacy important in modelling? Discuss with an example.
4. Discuss each of the cases used in questions (1) and (2) above. Which of the principles of modelling that you learnt, have been implicitly present?
5. What is structural approach to model building? Illustrate it in the case of any model you have come across. Can you develop an ISM for the same (as in Chapter 4)?
6. Select a few composite model research studies from the literature. Develop flow charts like the one illustrated in the text. Are the individual models strictly connected? Discuss.
7. Search for models, which use analogy from different disciplines or problems areas. Is the analogy of form or of content? Discuss. Could you have formulated the model with the use of a different analogy? Discuss.
8. When is it hard to test the efficiency of a heuristic algorithm? When is it easy? Are there situations in which heuristics cannot be tested for efficiency? Give examples. What is the situation?
9. Give examples for the following from models derived from literature (models you are familiar with).
   (a) Omitting decision variables
   (b) Omitting uncontrollable variables
   (c) Changing the value of variables
   (d) Hanging on to equations
   (e) Changing the constraints
14. What is the narrowing technique in model building?
15. Does the concept of analogy relate to the form of a problem or its contents?
16. How is the measurement of utility important in model building and its application to management research?
17. Consider a familiar process like commuters waiting at the terminus of a city bus. Discuss how an iconic, analogy, or symbolic model of the operation can be constructed.
18. Examine a few research papers in journals like *Operations Research, Management Science, Operations Research Quarterly*, and so on, and determine the pattern of model construction, the type of solution, the influence of data reliability, and the simplification of reality.
19. Write detailed comments on the interaction between models in a research paper where combination methods are used.
20. What is the relationship between structural modelling and detailed mathematical modelling?
21. What kind of error is mostly likely to creep in if the structural modelling phase is overlooked? Why?

CHAPTER 9

Modelling Research II–Heuristics and Simulation

- Heuristic Optimisation
- Simulation Modelling

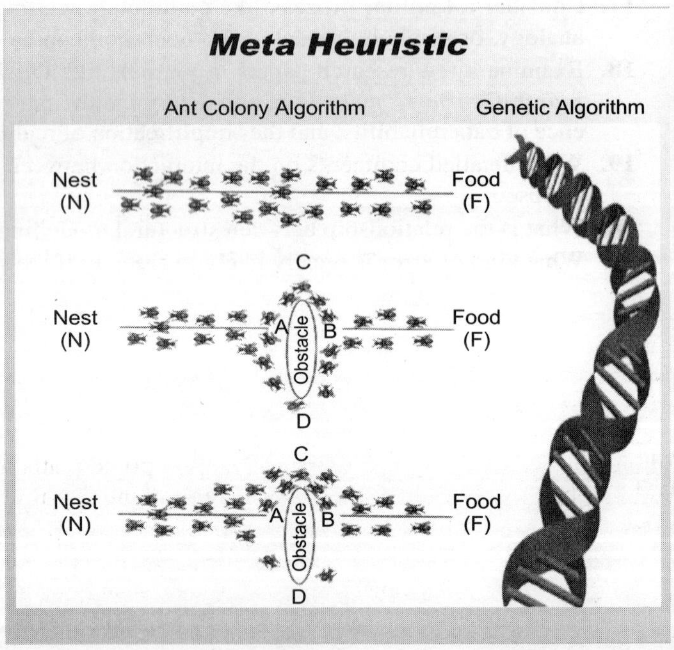

Learning Objectives

Upon completion of this chapter, you will be able to:

- ✓ Understand the concept of heuristic
- ✓ Become familiar with different kinds of heuristic methods
- ✓ Get to know about computational experiment on heuristic performance
- ✓ Learn advantages and limitations of heuristic methods
- ✓ Understand the basics of heuristic optimisation
- ✓ Appreciate meta heuristics
- ✓ Understand the meaning of simulation and in what ways it can be applied to research in management areas
- ✓ Learn the basics of Monte Carlo Simulation
- ✓ Become aware of different kinds of simulation model
- ✓ Get insights into simulation as an experimental arm of modelling to study dynamic behavior of systems
- ✓ Get the feel for the process of simulation experiments

This chapter deals with the application of heuristics, for problem-solving and simulation, to research in management. Both of these can handle ill-structured problems, either from the point of view of formulation or from that of deriving solutions better than mathematical modelling, and are being increasingly used in management research.

Our objectives in this chapter are two fold. First, we wish to provide an introduction to heuristic methods and simulation for researchers, decision analysts, and managers who have some familiarity with the basic techniques of operational research. Our intention is not to give a general recipe for constructing heuristic methods and/or simulation, nor do we intend to make comparisons of the many existing heuristic methods and/or simulation and their performances in various problem domains. However, our second objective is to identify important issues related to the use of heuristic methods and simulation and research in heuristic methods and simulation, on which additional research is required.

Heuristic Optimisation

Admittedly, in assuming that we have an appropriate mathematical representation of the real world problem, one could argue that we are ignoring the most difficult aspect of an operations research (OR) study, namely, the development of the mathematical model itself. In this connection, White (1975) provided an interesting account of the so called secondary decisions in an OR study, namley, what objectives to consider, what constraints to include, and what alternatives to test. However, it is important to recognise that—particularly as we address more complicated decision problems—realistic formulations are likely to lead to mathematical problems that are very difficult, if not impossible, to solve exactly (this is, to a considerable extent, due to the combinatorial nature of many practical problems). That is, computing optimal solution, is computationally intractable for many combinatorial optimisation problems—for example, those known as NP-Hard—and in practice, users are usually satisfied with 'good' solutions, which are obtained by simple heuristic/meta-heuristic algorithms. Thus, we believe that the topic of heuristic solution procedures for well defined mathematical problems is of increasing importance to decision analysts. Furthermore, for unstructured problems, the only possible solution procedure is the heuristic method.

heuristics

The word is derived from Greek and means 'serve to discover or stimulate investigation'. In problem solving situations heuristics are 'rules of thumb' that allow one to factor the complex perceived world into simple components and help in reduction of search in the problem-solving activities. Generally, heuristics are based on experience, analogy or creative reflection of the analyst. It is generally an iterative algorithm converging towards a feasible and good solution.

Definition of Heuristics

The concept of heuristics is not new. The word 'heuristic' was initially coined by the Greeks; its original form was *heuriskein*, which meant "to discover". Heuristic, as an adjective, means, "serving to discover or stimulate investigation". In heuristics, one endeavours to understand the process of solving problems, especially the mental operation of a human problem-solver, which is most useful in this process.

There clearly appears to be two streams of thinking in heuristics or heuristic research, the first one highlighted by works of Moustakas (1992) and the other emerging from the work of Simon and Newell (1958).

Moustakas takes a totally creative process approach to heuristic research and enunciates the heuristic research as described in Chapter 3. The approach is dominated by qualitative data and analysis, and the applications discussed are subjects related to culture, self confidence, experience of love, family relationships, poetry, and so on of socio psychological relevance. On the other hand, works emerging from Simon's pathbreaking research are aimed at problem solving, where established mathematical methods flounder in getting solutions. The implications are the same—that of using creative approaches—but the former tends toward qualitative approaches and the latter to quantitative ones. We take the latter approach for discussions but reiterating that the essence of heuristic research is creativity, individual experience, and intuition.

According to Simon and Newell (1958) heuristics are, "rules of thumb, that allow us to factor, approximately the complex perceived world into highly simple components and to find, approximately and reasonably reliably, the correspondences that allow us to act on that world predictably".

Tonge (1961) defines heuristics as, "principles or devices that contribute, on the average, to the reduction of search in problem-solving activity". According to Merbach (1981) heuristics is usually understood as "an iterative algorithm, which converges toward the solution of a problem". Thierauf et al, (1975) gave a simplified definition of heuristic programming in the computerised analysis as "heuristic programming utilizes rules of thumb or intuitive rules and guidelines and is generally under computer control to explore the most likely paths and to make educated guesses in arriving at a problem's solution rather than going through all of the possible alternatives to obtain an optimum one". Eglese (1986) defines heuristics as "a procedure for solving problems by an intuitive approach in which the structure of the problem can be interpreted and exploited intelligently to obtain a reasonable solution".

The foregoing definitions are representative rather than exhaustive. Differences in the scope of these definitions can be explained by the fact that the statements were tailored to the specific application of heuristics under consideration by their respective authors. The first emphasises the usefulness of heuristics in mathematics. On the other hand, Simon (1958) and Tonge (1961) stressed the importance of computers in duplicating rules of thumb employed by human decision makers. Merbach (1981) has emphasised reduction of computational time in intractable combinatorial problems. Eglese (1986) pointed out that heuristics are very problem dependent.

Today, the term is used almost exclusively in operations research (OR), computer science, and management to describe algorithms that are effective at solving complex problems quickly, but yield less than optimal solutions because of the accompanying speed improvement. For example, the Traveling Salesman Problem (TSP) is a classic enigma in OR for which OR analysts have devised many heuristic solutions.

Applications of heuristics (Zanakis et al., 1989) Most management-oriented heuristic programmes apply to what may be characterised as combinatorial problems because of the extremely large number of ways in which a series of decisions can be made. Heuristic programmes have been applied in management areas even as far back as in 1966 (Weist, 1966), with varying degrees of success, to a wide range of problems such as:

- Assembly line balancing
- Facility layout
- Portfolio selection

- Job shop scheduling
- Warehouse location
- Vehicle routing and scheduling
- Inventory control
- Resource allocation to large projects

Why Use Heuristics?

There are several reasons for using heuristic methods for solving problems. These, according to Silver, et al (1980) are as follows:

1. The mathematical problem is such that an analytic (closed form) or iterative solution procedure is unknown.
2. Although an exact analytic or iterative solution procedure may exist, it may be computationally prohibitive to use or it may be unrealistic in its data requirements. This is particularly true of enumerative methods, which, in theory, are often applicable where analytic and iterative procedures cannot be found.
3. The heuristic method is simpler for the decision maker to understand, hence, it markedly increases the chances of implementation.
4. For a well-defined problem that can be solved optimally, a heuristic method can be used for learning purposes, for example, to develop an intuitive feeling as to what variables are important (this closely parallels one of the primary reasons for using simulation methods in operations research).
5. In implicit enumeration approaches, a good starting solution can give a bound that drastically reduces the computational effort. Heuristics can be used to give such "good" starting solutions.
6. Heuristics may be used as part of an iterative procedure that guarantees the finding of an optimal solution. Two distinct possibilities exist:
    - To easily obtain an initial feasible solution, for example, the so called Northwest Corner Rule for obtaining an initial solution to the Transportation Problem.
    - To make a decision at an intermediate step of an exact solution procedure, for example, the rule for selecting the variable to be entered into the basis in the Simplex Method is heuristic in that it does not necessarily minimise the number of steps needed to reach the optimal solution.

Heuristic Methods

For purposes of our discussion it is useful to think of heuristic methods as a master set containing three subsets: (i) heuristic problem solving, (ii) artificial intelligence, and (iii) simulation of human thought (Fig. 9.1):

heuristic methods
Heuristic method consists of three overlapping subsets: artificial intelligence (AI), simulation of human thought and heuristic problem solving.

Artificial intelligence This is when the use of computer-oriented heuristics in programmes that may accomplish one or more of the following:

- *Search*—the systematic investigation of the solution space.
- *Pattern recognition*—the acceptance of certain groupings of elementary units as identifiable entities.
- *Organisation planning*—the breaking down of a complex problem into sub-problems, the sequencing of analysis according to priorities and recombination into a solution of the higher-level problem.
- *Learning*—programme modification resulting from experience.
- *Inductive inference*—generalisation for the purpose of prediction and decision-making.

The orientation is towards efficient use of the computer to obtain an apparently intelligent method of solution rather than to attempt to reproduce the step-by-step thought process of a human decision-maker.

Fig. 9.1 The subsets of heuristic methods

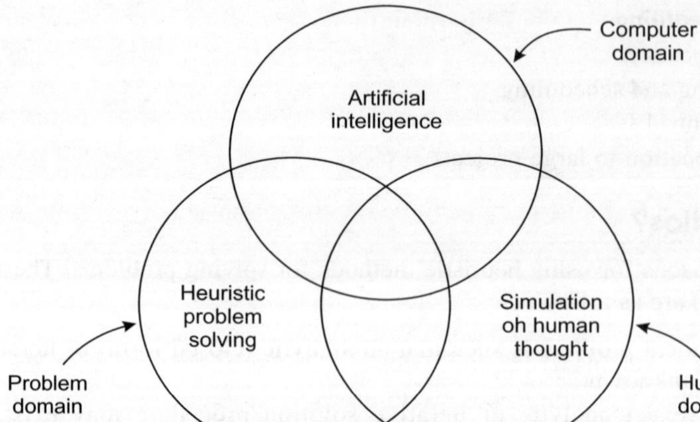

Simulation of human thought In this method, heuristic computer programme is used to replicate the thought process of a human decision-maker.

heuristic problem solving
In this a heuristic is used to achieve reduction of search and computational effort in the attainment of a satisfactory solution in problem-oriented situation. Either a simple rule or a combination of several rules in the form of an algorithm can be used in problem solving.

Heuristic problem solving This method involves the problem-oriented use of heuristics to achieve a reduction of search in the attainment of a satisfactory solution (Foulds, 1983). Drawing from knowledge and experience, we devise simple rules of thumb (heuristics) to help us face the countless problem-solving situations that confront us each day, which free us from the task of solving the same or similar problems over and over again.

For example, consider the rule, "When the sky is cloudy, take an umbrella to work." The problem at hand is how to defend oneself against the potential discomforts of the weather. This simple heuristic avoids more complicated problem-solving procedures such as reading the weather report, calling the weather bureau, analysing barometer readings, and so forth. For many problems of this kind, we lack the time or inclination to employ more throught for problem solving procedures. A simple (if not infallible) rule serves us well in such situations.

Businessmen frequently develop and follow various heuristics in their operations, some of which are given below:

- *Stock market investing*—"Buy when prices move rapidly in one direction with heavy volume," or, "Sell when the good news is out".
- *Inventory control*—"When the stock gets down to ten, that is the time to buy some more", (Such heuristics are called 'trigger-level' rules).
- *Accounting*—"Value at cost or market, whichever is lower" or, "First in, first out".
- *Job scheduling*—"First come, first served", or, "schedule jobs with shortest operation time first".

All of the above heuristics could be improved by further elaboration to take into account exceptional circumstances or additional information. Thus, the inventory control rule might also take into consideration recent trends in usage rates and expectations of future demand for a stocked item. Instead of a simple rule of thumb, a combination of rules might be better. This leads to the heuristic programme.

Heuristics Problem-Solving Approaches

We now turn to a categorisation of heuristic problem-solving approaches (generally termed as heuristic methods). There are a large number of "proven" approaches, which are discussed below [Ball, et al, (1981); Silver, et al, (1980); and Weiner, (1975); Zanakis et al (1989)].

Decomposition methods Here the problem under consideration is broken into smaller parts that are solved separately, but taking account, at least in a crude way, of possible interactions among the parts. Decomposition is prevalent in the traditional separation of problems into the functional areas of an organisation. A second common type of decomposition is the separation of system design from system operation. Commonly the operational effects are ignored in the design phase and then the operational rules are developed based on the design having been chosen. An important virtue of such decomposition is that it is consistent with how most organisations actually function.

Inductive methods The idea here is to generalise from smaller (or somewhat simpler) versions of the same problem. For example, in a problem involving the location of several facilities (such as plants and warehouses) to satisfy customer demand, the solution may be relatively easy to obtain for the case of a few facilities. Properties of solutions for such simpler cases may be profitably used to develop a heuristic for more general cases with several facilities (Bilde and Vidal, 1973). In addition, sometimes the situation where a particular parameter becomes very large is particularly easy to analyse, again providing insights for a more difficult case of an intermediate (not too large or not too small) value of the parameter. An example is in the general area of renewal processes where the aggregate effect of a large number of processes display Poisson behaviour.

Feature extraction (or reduction) methods The general approach here is to first obtain the optimal solutions to several numerical cases under consideration. Common features of these solutions are extracted and are assumed to hold in general. Examples might include that a particular variable always takes on the value 0, or that certain control variables are highly correlated, or that a particular constraint never appears to be binding. A more extreme version of reduction is to assume (by analysis of simpler versions of the problem or simply by "gut" feel) that good solutions must satisfy certain properties, where these properties substantially simplify the analysis. Then, once the solution is obtained one verifies that, indeed, the properties are met (White, 1969). A good example of this approach is the use of the assumption that in any reasonable inventory control strategy, the frequency of stockout occasions will be quite low. Another example is provided by Hitchings and Cottam (1976) in the context of a facilities layout problem. They recognised that, if certain facilities were judiciously fixed in location or certain pairs were constrained to be adjacent to one another, this reduces the dimensionality of the problem, thus permitting each potential solution to be evaluated much more quickly.

Methods involving model manipulation The idea here is to change the nature of the model in some way so as to facilitate the solution and then use the solution of the revised model as representative of the solution of the original mathematical problem. In a more general sense, this is what one does when using a mathematical model of a real world problem and then interpreting the solution of the model as being the solution for the original problem. Examples of model manipulation include:

- Modification of the objective function; for example, linearisation of a non-linear function.
- Relaxation of certain constraints, some of which may be flexible in any event, (for example, a budget constraint need not necessarily be rigid).
- Change nature of probability distributions; for example, the assumption of normality instead of a more complex distribution.
- Aggregation of variables, the idea being to reduce the number of decision variables (however, eventually the value of the aggregate variable has to be apportioned among the original disaggregated variables).

Constructive methods The basic idea of a constructive method is to literally build up to (that is, construct) a single feasible solution, often in a deterministic, sequential fashion. An example is the so called nearest neighbour rule for solving the travelling salesman problem. To establish a single circuit that passes exactly once through each city, one starts with a particular city (*say*

greedy algorithm
There are many heuristic problem-solving approaches. One of them is called greedy algorithm which does the best in each single step and which is constructive in nature. It suffers from a myopic viewpoint of considering only the next decision point.

look-ahead heuristics
Look-ahead heuristics are rules based on bound calculation which reduces the myopic viewpoint of the greedy algorithm.

i) and first goes to the nearest city (*call it j*) from *i*. From *j* one next goes to city *k*, the nearest city to *j* that has not yet been visited, and so forth. This is an example of a so-called 'greedy' algorithm; greedy in the sense that it does the best it can in each single step. For certain classes of problems (not the case of the travelling salesman) a greedy heuristic leads to very good solutions [Cornuejols et al (1997), Jenkyns (1976) and Lawler (1976)]. However, the nearest neighbour rule generally provides a poor solution to the travelling salesman problem; it suffers from its myopic viewpoint of only considering the nearest node. This is in contrast with heuristic methods that use so called 'look-ahead' rules (see Muller–Merbach, 1975); an example for the travelling salesman problem is given by Muller–Merbach (1974), where the look ahead rule is based on bound calculations.

Local improvement methods In contrast with the constructive procedures, here we start with a feasible solution and improve upon it iteratively. The work centre location problem can be solved in this fashion (for example, refer Hitchings and Cottam [1976]). The initial feasible solution may be the existing layout in the manufacturing plant or it may be the solution of a constructive procedure. One method of local improvement is to attempt to switch pairs of centres; when an attractive switch is found, it is made and the process is continued until no further improvement can be achieved by any single switch. A relevant question is whether or not to continue searching when the number of possible switches remaining is extremely large; in other words, what is an appropriate stopping rule? Similarly, if repeated trials are made with a constructive method, one would like to have a reasonable rule for when to stop generating solutions. Randolph et al (1973) have examined the use of Bayesian (subjective probability) approaches to constructing such rules. Even when an exact enumeration method (for example, branch and bound) is used, one is often faced with the same type of stopping problem in that considerable further computation may lead to an insignificant improvement in the solution. Heuristic reasoning can be useful in the development of stopping rules.

Further details on local improvement methods and neighbourhood search can be found in Morton and Pentico (1993). Lin and Kernighan (1973) use a local improvement approach in their method for solving the travelling salesman problem.

It should be emphasised that the categories are not meant to be mutually exclusive. Indeed, it often makes sense to blend two or more of the types in the solution of a particular class of problems. In addition, one should not overlook the possibility of using two distinct heuristic methods parallel by which to solve the same problem, choosing the better of the two solutions, that is, do not necessarily bank on the good performance of a single method. Finally, where possible, one who develops a heuristic method is well advised to first have a sound understanding of the theoretical work that has been done on the particular problem under consideration; often such theory will suggest specific lines of attack that are likely to be fruitful in developing an effective heuristic procedure. At present, however, the design of heuristics is very much a trial and experiment art, guided only by the past experience, judgement, and ingenuity of the designer.

It is generally accepted that human interaction is especially useful in situations where objectives or constraints are difficult to characterise with precision. For example, it may be desirable to design a heuristic procedure, which ignores certain constraints, and then to allow a human to select a final solution from a set of candidate solutions produced by the heuristic procedure. In other situations, it may be possible for a human being to interactively guide a heuristic search. Here, the relevant tradeoffs are among the elapsed (that is human) time required to obtain a solution, the machine time utilised, and the quality of the solution.

Until the 1980s, heuristics was essential because of the limited computing power available at that time. It was only by taking very careful account of the problem structure that good solutions could be produced in the time available. However, with the increase of computing power came the use of more general approaches, which could be successfully applied to a wide variety of problems. Such approaches came to be known as meta-heuristics.

Meta-Heuristics

Nowadays, heuristic techniques have gone beyond their traditional definition as simple rules of thumb. They are inspired by nature, biology, statistical mechanics, physics, and neuroscience, to name but a few. Heuristic techniques, such as evolutionary and genetic algorithms, simulated annealing, and Tabu search, proofed themselves in solving many problems where traditional problem-solving methods failed. Modern heuristic techniques, such as ant colonies, immune, memetic, and scatter search, are taking firm steps as robust problem-solving mechanisms. These types of heuristics are generally termed as meta-heuristics.

meta-heuristic
Meta-heuristic is another heuristic problem-solving approach, which starts with a feasible solution and improves upon it iteratively taking into account the problem structure. Simulated annealing, tabu search, genetic algorithms, ant colony algorithm are generally termed as meta-heuristic algorithms. These algorithms are inspired by natural phenomena like biology, statistical mechanics, physics, and neuroscience.

Osman and Kelly (1996) define meta-heuristics as, "an iterative generation process which guides a subordinate heuristic by combining intelligently different concepts for exploring and exploiting the search space using learning strategies to structure information in order to find efficient near optimal solutions". This definition may be rather more precise and restrictive than some would consider necessary, but it does encapsulate the general principles involved in all well known meta-heuristics developed to date.

Conceptually, a meta-heuristic refers to a master strategy that guides and alters other heuristics to produce solutions beyond those that are normally generated in a search for local optimal solutions. The meta heuristic may be a higher-level procedure or may embody procedures to describe available moves for converting one solution into another, along with a related evaluation rule. Heuristics are generally regarded as rules of thumb or iterative procedures that terminate when there is no improvement, in iteration, over the solution of the previous one. Such heuristics use descent methods, ascent methods, or local search methods. Meta-heuristics embody these heuristics in a master design. Generally, meta-heuristics are classified according to these basic design choices: (i) use of adaptive memory, (ii) the type of neighborhood search adopted, and (iii) the number of solutions carried across two successive iterations. In this section, a few of the more important ones are presented in a very simple way for creating awareness in research students.

simulated annealing (SA)
SA is based on the analogy between annealing of a solid and optimization of a system. SA can avoid local minimum in search for a global one by allowing uphill moves in the case of a minimization problem and downhill moves in the case of a maximization problem.

Simulated Annealing (SA) SA is a method for obtaining good solutions to difficult optimisation problems. Kirkpatrick et al (1983) first introduced SA to solve difficult combinatorial optimisation problems. SA is based on the analogy between annealing of a solid and optimisation of a system with many independent variables. A typical SA procedure is as follows:

Starting from an initial solution, SA generates a new solution in the neighbourhood of the initial solution. Then the change in the objective function value (denoted as ΔC) is obtained. In minimisation problems, if $\Delta C<0$, transition to the new solution is accepted (this transition is called a downhill move). If $\Delta C>=0$, then transition to the new solution is accepted (this transition is called an uphill move) with a specified probability, which is generally obtained using the function $e^{-(\Delta C/T)}$, where T is a control parameter called the temperature. By allowing uphill moves like this, SA can escape from a local minimum in its search for the global minimum. SA repeats this process L times a temperature, where L is a control parameter called epoch length. The parameter T is gradually decreased by a cooling function as SA progresses, until a given stopping condition is satisfied. A simple constructive heuristic and SA are demonstrated using a simple numerical example, and the same is presented in Annexure 9.1.

tabu search
Tabu (derived from the word taboo) search is concerned with imposing restrictions to guide a search process to negotiate otherwise difficult regions. The guidance includes search of alternatives classed as forbidden (or taboo). That is, tabu search has flexible memory structure to maintain the knowledge of selective history of the solutions already encountered in the search process in order to discourage their selection in further search.

Annealing is the process of finding out the different energy states of a solid by initially melting the metal and then lowering the temperature slowly, spending a long time at temperatures close to the freezing point. In analogy, the different states of substance correspond to different feasible solutions to the combinatorial optimisation problem. The determination of the initial temperature, the rate at which the cooling takes place (temperature is reduced), the number of iterations at each temperature and the criterion used for stopping, all have a bearing on the performance of the algorithm. A permutation method is used for iterations of the algorithm and a stopping criterion is used for stopping the search for the best solution.

Tabu search Tabu search is a metaheuristic method developed by Glover (1989, 1990a, 1990b) for solving combinatorial optimisation problems. Webster's dictionary defines tabu or taboo as "set apart as charged with a dangerous supernatural power and forbidden to profane use or contact...", or, "banned on grounds of morality or taste or as constituting a rick ...". Tabu search scarcely involves reference to supernatural or moral considerations, but instead is concerned with imposing restrictions to guide a search process to negotiate otherwise difficult regions. These restrictions operate in several forms, both by direct exclusion of search alternatives classed as 'forbidder' and also by translation into modified evaluation and probabilities of selection.

Tabu search uses flexible memory structures to maintain knowledge about a selective history of the solutions encountered during the search. By giving recently or frequently (or infrequently) visited solutions a tabu status, so as to discourage their selection in the search process, it guides other searching methods to move away from local optimal solutions. Tabu search has three major components, a short term memory process, an intermediate memory process, and a long term memory process (Glover 1990c, Glover et al, 1993).

The short term memory process is based on a set of tabu conditions and aspiration criteria. Through recency or frequency-based memories, tabu search characterises a subset of potential moves as tabu, or forbidden, to avoid repletion or reversal of previously visited solutions. The intermediate memory process is implemented by restricting the search within a set of potentially prosperous solutions to intensify the search. The long term memory process is invoked periodically to lead the search to new regions that might have not been explored as it diversifies the search.

Working mechanism of tabu search Tabu search methods operate under the assumption that a neighbourhood is constructed to identify adjacent solutions that can be reached from a current solution. Pairwise exchanges (swaps) are generally used to define neighbourhoods in permutation problems, identifying moves that lead from one solution to the next. Corresponding to each swap is a move value, which represents the change of the objective function value. A chief mechanism for using memory in tabu search is classifying a subset of moves in a neighbourhood as forbidden (tabu). The classification depends on the history of the search, as given by the recency or frequency of a certain move or solution and components called attributes, which have been involved in generating past solutions. However, tabu restrictions are not inviolable under all circumstances. When a tabu move results in improvement, the restriction is overridden. Such a condition is called an aspiration criterion. An independent evaluation sub-routine provides information on the move values and identifies the best move. The best move is selected and a new current solution is obtained. This is repeated. The tabu search consists of: (i) initialisation in which the initialisation module generates a starting solution; (ii) move evaluation in which the neighbourhood moves are evaluated using tabu restrictions and the objective function value is also evaluated; (iii) the best (swapping) move is executed; (iv) the objective function is updated.

For more details on tabu search, including many successful applications of tabu search, interested readers can refer Glover (1990a, b) and Glover and Laguna (1997).

genetic algorithm
Genetic algorithms are stochastic search methods that mimic the process of natural selection and mechanism of population genetics. Its starts with creation of a set of solutions referred to as a population. Then a new generation of solution is formed by applying genetic operators similar to one from natural evolution: crossover, mutation, selection and reproduction. Each solution is evaluated using an objective function. This process is repeated until a convergence is obtained.

Genetic Algorithm (GA) Genetic algorithms are stochastic search methods that mimic the process of natural selection and the mechanism of population genetics. They were first introduced by Holland (1975) and later developed further and popularised by Goldberg (1989). Genetic algorithms are used in a number of different application areas ranging from function optimisation to solving large combinatorial optimisation problems. The GA is an algorithmic model of Darwinian evolution that begins with the creation of a set of solutions referred to as a population of individuals. Each individual in a population consists of a set of parameter values that completely describes a solution. A solution is encoded in a string called a chromosome, which consists of genes that can take a number of values. Initially, the collection of solutions (population) is generated randomly and at each iteration (also called generation), a new generation of solutions is formed by applying genetic operators analogous to ones from natural evolution (crossover, mutation, selection, reproduction). Each solution is evaluated using an objective function (called a fitness function), and this process is repeated until some form of convergence in fitness is achieved. The goal of the optimisation process is to minimise or maximise the fitness. The following pseudo code shows how a GA works:

```
BEGIN/*genetic algorithm*/
        Generate initial population;
        Compute fitness of each individual;
        WHILE NOT finished DO LOOP
                BEGIN
                        Select individuals from old generations for mating;
                        Create offspring by applying recombination and/or mutation
                        to the selected individuals;
                        Compute fitness of the new individuals;
                        Kill old individuals to make room for new chromosomes,
                        and insert offspring in the new generation;
                        IF population has converged THEN finishes : = TRUE ;
                END
END
```

Genetic algorithm again raises a couple of important features. First, it is a stochastic algorithm; randomness has an essential role in genetic algorithms. Both selection and reproduction need random procedures. A second very important point is that genetic algorithms always consider a population of solutions. Retaining more than a single solution in memory at each iteration offers a lot of advantages. The algorithm can recombine different solutions to get better ones so that it can use the benefits of assortment. The robustness of the algorithm should also be mentioned as something essential for the algorithm's success. Robustness refers to the ability to perform consistently well on a broad range of problem types. This is not a particular requirement on the problem before using GA, so that it can be applied to resolve any problem. All these features make GA a really powerful optimisation tool.

Ant colony (ACO) algorithm Real ants are capable of finding the shortest path from a food source to the nest without using visual cues. Also, they are capable of adapting to changes in the environment, for example, finding a new shortest path once the old one is no longer feasible due to a new obstacle (Beckers et al, 1992). Consider that ants are moving on a straight line that connects a food source to their nest. It is well known that the primary means for ants to form and maintain the line is a pheromone trail. Ants deposit a certain amount of pheromone while walking, and each ant probabilistically prefers to follow a direction rich in pheromone.

ant colony (ACO) algorithm

Ants can find the shortest path which reconnects the broken line after sudden appearance of an unexpected obstacle has interrupted the initial path. This behavior of ants has inspired the development of ACO algorithm to solve many optimization problems such as travelling salesman problem, vehicle routing problem, job-shop scheduling, etc.

This elementary behaviour of real ants can be used to explain how they can find the shortest path that reconnects a broken line after the sudden appearance of an unexpected obstacle has interrupted the initial path. In fact, once the obstacle has appeared, the ants that were just in front of the obstacle cannot continue to follow the pheromone trail and, therefore, have to choose between turning right or left. In this situation we can expect half the ants to choose to turn right and the other half to turn left. A very similar situation can be found on the other side of the obstacle. It is interesting to note that the ants that choose, by chance, the shorter path around the obstacle will more rapidly reconstitute the interrupted pheromone trail compared to those who choose the longer path. Thus, the shorter path will receive a greater amount of pheromone per time unit and in turn a larger number of ants will choose the shorter path. Due to this positive feedback (autocatalytic) process, all the ants will rapidly choose the shorter path. The most interesting aspect of this autocatalytic process is that finding the shortest path around the obstacle seems to be an emergent property of the interaction between the obstacle shape and ants' distributed behaviour: although all ants move at approximately the same speed and deposit a pheromone trail at approximately the same speed and rate, it is a fact that it takes longer to contour obstacles on the longer side than on the shorter side, which makes the pheromone trail accumulate quicker on the shorter side. It is the ants' preference for higher pheromone trail levels that makes this accumulation even quicker on the shorter path. Many researchers showed how a similar process can be put to work in a simulated world inhabited by artificial ants that try to solve the travelling salesman problem, vehicle routing problem, job-shop rescheduling problem, and so forth.

Choice of Heuristic Methods

Some factors that significantly affect the choice of a particular heuristic method are (Silver, et al, 1980):

- Strategic (system design) versus tactical (system operation) problem—strategic decisions (for example, capital investment in plant facilities) are one time major decisions for which a rather elaborate analysis is justified, in contrast with tactical decisions (for example, quality control, production scheduling, and so on), which is more minor and repetitive in nature. In addition, in tactical decisions there are opportunities for adapting to compensate for errors made in earlier decisions.
- Frequency of the decision—the researcher has to find out if the problem being dealt with is a one-off or a repeated decision problem. A criterion of good average performance makes more sense with repetitive decisions and use of heuristics is appropriate.
- Amount of computational effort permitted—generally, the selection of a heuristic method is dependent upon the desired solution time.
- Number of decision (controllable) variables—the number of such variables affects the need for a heuristic in the first place and should influence the choice of approach.
- Number of uncontrollable variables—this factor is particularly important in terms of testing heuristic methods. The larger the number of uncontrollable variables, the less likely that a probabilistic analysis is possible.
- Size of the problem—as an example, consider the travelling salesman problem. One heuristic method may be best for a case with 30 cities, whereas another heuristic may be better for a different case having 100 cities.
- Discrete versus continuous variables—most of the general literature on heuristic methods has been concerned with combinatorial problems involving integer variables. Perhaps, different approaches are more appropriate when variables are continuous.
- Deterministic versus probabilistic variables—most of the research literature has been concerned with large scale deterministic methods.

Perhaps, it makes sense to devise very different heuristic procedures for probabilistic problems, which also usually involve a limited number of variables.

Evaluation of Heuristics

From the foregoing discussions of heuristics and meta-heuristics, it is seen that heuristics are based on experience, analogy, or the creative reflection of the analyst. As in the case of mathematical models, no internal validation can be established for heuristics algorithms. As in statistical modes (to be dealt with in later chapters), the statistical significance (validation) of the results is also not directly relevant. Therefore, one should rigorously validate the results in an external comparison (external validation) to establish acceptability of heuristic methods, like it is done in simulation models whose internal logical accuracy cannot be established. There are special problems of evaluating (testing and validating) heuristics. This section deals with them, first presenting the criteria for evaluation and then discussing various methods available for evaluating of heuristics.

criteria for evaluating heuristics

Quality of solution, running time, difficulty of implementation, flexibility, robustness, simplicity, analysability, and interactive computing are the criteria for evaluating heuristics.

Criteria for evaluating heuristics Ball and Magazine (1980) presented the following seven heuristic evaluation criteria:

1. ***Quality of solution*** Quality in this case is measured in two ways: (i) the proximity of the objective function value to the optimal value, to the estimated optimal value, or to the known standard algorithm's solution to the practiced solution, and (ii) the ability of the algorithm to generate a feasible solution whenever one exists. There are various tech-

niques for measuring the quality of heuristic solution and these are discussed in the next section.

2. ***Running time and storage*** Again, a variety of techniques was mentioned, including worst case, probabilistic, and empirical analyses. This category was not discussed in detail since it applies to all algorithms, not just heuristics.
3. ***Difficulty of implementation*** Two principal "difficulties" were mentioned: the intricacy of the coding and the extent of the data requirements. However, it was admitted that it is difficult to measure these characteristics.
4. ***Flexibility*** Since heuristics are typically involved in the solution of real world problems it is important that they be flexible. In particular, they should easily handle changes in the model, constraints, and objective function.
5. ***Robustness*** The group placed a number of desirable algorithmic characteristics in this class. Included were the ability to perform sensitivity analysis and the ability to generate bounds on the solution obtained. An extension of the generation of a bound is the generation of a good characterisation. That is, along with the solution, a set of information, such as a dual solution, would be generated. A good characterisation would enable a user to use this information to prove the solution was optimal or to prove the solution was within a percentage of the optimal solution. In many cases, an algorithm does not generate a feasible solution. In these cases, it would be very desirable for the algorithm to generate information that would enable the user to determine why a feasible solution was not generated.
6. ***Simplicity and Analysability*** It was generally agreed that there is significant appeal to algorithms, whcih can be simply stated and which more readily lend themselves to analysis. Extremely complex algorithms are much less likely to be analysed in terms of flexibility, quality of solution, and so on, than a simple algorithm.
7. ***Interactive computing*** The idea of using man-machine interaction within an algorithm came up on numerous occasions. It was generally accepted that little was known about this class of algorithms and that other criteria should be developed to evaluate interactive algorithms.

Methods for evaluating heuristics When a new heuristic method is proposed for the solution of any research problem, its solution quality should be evaluated scientifically and reported in an objective manner. Recently, a considerable amount of detailed research has been carried out to evaluate heuristics [Barr et al (1995); Rardin and Uzsoy (2001)]. There are three methods suggested in the literature for evaluating the quality of the solution being obtained using heuristics. These methods are: (1) Performance evaluation, (2) Probabilistic analysis, and (3) Empirical analysis.

methods for evaluating heuristics

These are: performance evaluation, probabilistic analysis and empirical analysis.

1. ***Performance evaluation*** This method is subdivided in two parts dealing with: (1) worst-case performance, providing a bound on the error or time [Fisher (1980)], and (2) average performance, by calculating measurements like mean error or time, mean square difference or mean absolute deviation, from a sample of heuristic solutions to simulated or literature benchmark problems [Petersen (1974) and Zanakis (1974)].
2. ***Probabilistic analysis*** This method includes: (i) investigation of statistical properties of heuristics, assuming a simple probability distribution of the data input, and (ii) point/interval estimation of true optimum based on statistical distribution of heuristic solutions obtained (Zanakis and Evans, 1981).
3. ***Empirical analysis*** Generally, practitioners found that the worst case bounds were too loose to be useful in justifying solutions, and probabilistic analyses tended to assume unrealistic probability spaces. However, algorithm designers did find the analyses useful in providing a better understanding of the problem and the heuristic. Thus, it appears that the most trusted form of analysis appears to be empirical analysis (Ball and Magazine, 1980). This is due to the fact that this approach does solve problems, similar to those that researchers are interested in. Furthermore, performance of meta-heuristics is usually investigated empirically, since normally no useful worst-case guarantees can

empirical analysis

This is the most trusted method for evaluating heuristics. In this method the performance of the heuristics is compared with optimal solution or bounding or estimated optimal solution or best known result.

be given. Furthermore, in practice, meta-heuristics are powerful in terms of solution-quality, and are easy to implement. This has resulted in the fact that for checking the quality of the heuristic solution, in empirical analysis, heuristics are compared to the optimal solution, the estimated optimal solution, or to the known standard algorithm's solution to the practice for a number of problems.

Evaluation of Heuristics in Empirical Analysis

Comparison with the optimum solution One would like to be able to compare the heuristic solution with the best possible solution over a large number of problem instances. Usually this is not possible, in that, as discussed earlier, a major reason for using a heuristic procedure in the first place is that it may be impossible or prohibitive to obtain the optimal solution from a computational standpoint. One may have to resort to simulation to estimate the value of the best solution (in a case where the objective function is only indirectly expressed in terms of the controllable and uncontrollable variables). Also, it may be necessary to concentrate on small scale problems (of smaller size than at least some of the instances of interest) to reduce the computational effort to a reasonable level.

Even when the optimum solution can be found there remains the question of what problem instances to use for testing purposes, that is, what set of values to assign to the uncontrollable variables. This is clearly a question of experimental design, to be used to generate test instances. Insight (partly from an understanding of the related theory) and an investigation of the results of preliminary experiments can suggest which variables are likely to be important.

Problem relaxation—Bounding When the optimum solution cannot be found (often the case when a heuristic is used), an alternative approach is to relax the problem so that a solution that is at least as good as the optimum solution can be evaluated, hence, providing a bound on the value of the optimum solution, that is, the value of the optimum solution cannot be better than the bound. The relaxed solution itself need not be obtained; all one needs is its value or, even less, a bound on its value. Then we check how close the heuristic solution is to this bound. This is really only a one-way test. We know that the value of the optimal solution must lie between the value of the heuristic solution and the bound. Thus, if the value of the heuristic is very close to the bound, it must be very close to the value of the optimum solution. On the other hand, a large gap between the value of the heuristic solution and the bound may be caused by the heuristic being poor, the bound being too loose or both. Note that the heuristic method itself gives a bound of the opposite type, that is, the value of the optimum solution cannot be worse than the value of the heuristic solution.

The most common way of relaxing a problem is to ignore one or more constraints. We present two illustrations:

- In an integer linear programming, a bound can be obtained by ignoring the integer constraints and solving the much simpler, continuous variable problem.
- In a travelling salesman problem, difficulty is caused by the constraint that every city must be visited precisely once in a single tour. Removing the single tour constraint leads directly to a bound on the original problem.

Extreme value statistical methods Combinatorial optimisation problems usually have an enormous number of feasible solutions. The idea of statistical estimation techniques for optimal values is to use a sample solution to predict where the true optimum may lie. Under such circumstances, the value of each generated solution can be considered as a random variable. Then we are interested in the extremes of many of these (not necessarily independent) random variables. The theory of extreme value statistics can be used to develop estimates of the value of the optimal solution of the problem at hand. Intuitively, it seems reasonable to assume that the distribution of heuristic solutions could be Weibull (Golden, 1977). There are many procedures available in research literature for estimating optimal value for combinatorial optimisation problems (Zanakis, 1979). Recently, Rardin and Uzsoy (2001) have presented a very simple procedure to estimate optimal solution using Weibull distribution. This procedure was used to estimate optimal utilisation of batch processors by Mathirajan et al (2004).

Other comparisons For discussion purposes we shall assume that we are dealing with a problem in which we wish to maximise some objective function. Thus, any bound obtained by relaxing the model would be an upper bound. Where such a bound cannot be easily obtained or is suspected to be poor, one can resort to comparisons of the heuristic solution with other types of solutions, where the latter produce lower bounds on the value of the optimum solution. Possibilities include:

- *Enumerative method* This method requires much more computational effort, which is terminated after a large amount of computation, but likely without having found the optimal solution. An example would be a branch-and-bound procedure (see Wagner, 1975), for a description of such procedures), stopped after a certain large number of branches were generated. Such a "truncated" branch-and-bound procedure would also give us an upper bound (in a maximisation problem) on the value of the optimal solution.
- *Performance of decision-maker* There are compelling arguments in faour of comparison either during an earlier time frame or directly in parallel. Identification of signifi cant improvement over existing procedures is probably much more important for encouraging implementation than any proof of optimality, or nearness to optimality.
- *Other heuristic procedures* Where other heuristic solution methods have been proposed and/or used, one certainly can compare 'our' heuristic against the others. The danger is that the other heuristics may be particularly bad, in which case, even though 'our' heuristic's performance was judged the best, it may still be a poor solution method.
- *'Random' decision rule* An extreme type of heuristic is where one makes a decision completely at random. Conway's (1965) illustration shows hour in looking at heuristics for sequencing jobs at work centres in a job shop context, researchers used the decision rule of choosing the next job to process at a work centre, by a random selection among the jobs waiting at the centre for a baseline comparison. In general, a 'random' rule should produce a rather poor bound on the value of the optimum solution, hence can be useful for quickly rejecting a poor heuristic method.

As more ill-structured problems are investigated, empirical research using heuristics becomes unavoidable. However, it is noted that there is still a lack of uniformity and there are no widely accepted guidelines for empirical studies. In particular, there is a definite need for a standard set of easily obtainable test problems. In selecting test problems, one important goal is to create problem instances that are representative of the general problem class. Hall and Posner (1996) refer to this property as correspondence. The trap to avoid is the inadvertent creation of 'easy' problem instances that do not really require the ingenuity of a solution procedure.

problem instances
Problem instances area required to conduct computational experiments in evaluating heuristics empirically. The data from real-life application would be ideal ones. In the absence of these, the researcher can randomly generate pseudo-problem instances based on observation of a real-life situation. Published and/or online problem instances of well-known research is another source.

Sources of Problem Instances

One of the greatest practical challenges in conducting any computational experiment is getting the required problem instances. No matter how carefully we structure the experimental design, it cannot be implemented without sufficient quantities of realistic and appropriate test instances that have the size and variety to span all problem characteristics that are of interest (Rardin and Uzsoy, 2001). The various possibilities of problem instances are:

- ***Real world data sets*** The best instances are probably those taken from real application. The advantage of having this type of problem instance is that a host of hidden patterns and relationship between the details of the instances are automatically represented. But, unfortunately, mostly it is very difficult to obtain more than a few real data sets for any computational experiment. This is (mostly) due to the proprietary considerations of the industry. Finally, collecting a real data set is a time consuming and tedious effort that take longer than experiments can wait.
- ***Random variants of real data sets*** Keeping the macro structure of the actual application, one can develop an appropriate experimental design by defining all the important problem factors and their level of variability. Using the experimental design, it is possible to randomly generate (pseudo-real) data sets.

- ***Published and online libraries (bench marking data)*** As any research problem passes through a life cycle, there is a possibility of having bench mark data, openly available for any researcher working on a particular topic. For example, there are libraries of data for the travelling salesmen problem, vehicle routing problem, job-shop scheduling problem, and so on.
- ***Randomly generated instances*** When none of the other sources mentioned above provide an adequate supply of test instances, or even when they do yield enough data sets but we wonder about hidden biases, the remaining alternative is pure random generation. Instances are synthesised entirely artificially, although their properties may be controlled by broad parameters and their general form inspired by applications. Random generation is certainly the quickest and easiest way to obtain a rich supply of test instances, but it is also the most controversial. For example, (a) are the problems, generated suitably difficult or representative, or is there some hidden structure that makes them especially easy (or hard) for specific heuristic algorithms? and (b) given that a heuristic procedure performs well on the experimental data sets, how likely is it to perform well in another environment? However, Rardin and Uzsoy (2001) highlighted many conveniences in randomly generating instances for computational testing of heuristics.

Performance Measures/Measure of Effectiveness

performance measures

Quality of the solution and computational time in CPU seconds are two basic measures for comparing the performance of heuristic procedures. Quality of the solution can be measured by taking the ratio of heuristic solution to the known best solution or relative deviation of heuristic solution to the known best solution. In either case, if the known best solution tends to become zero, a suitable factor is used in its place.

The performance measures used in evaluating the experimental results for comparing heuristic procedures are the solution quality and the run times in CPU seconds. In research literature, the relative differences among the solutions from the various algorithms are calculated in many ways. According to Baker (1999) the most intuitive choice of a performance measure for comparing heuristic procedures is the ratio:

$$V_0 = L / L^*$$

Where L denotes the value of L_{max} produced by a given heuristic,

L^* denotes the optimal value (or a bound or an estimated optimal value or a standard/known solution being obtained from the best procedure available at that time), and

V_0 measures the performance of the heuristic.

In an experimental approach, values of V_0 would be averaged over a set of randomly generated test problems in order to summarise the effectiveness of a particular procedure. Unfortunately, there is an implicit premise in this choice: a notion that average values of V_0 near one indicate good performance. However, it is possible to have L^* turn out negative, or even zero. In such cases, the value of V_0 tells us more about the optimal value of *Lmax* than about the sub-optimality in the heuristic procedure.

One way to alter the summary measure is to use the difference between the heuristic and optimal value [or estimated optimal value or known standard solution (= practical solution or solution being obtained from the best known procedure at that time)] in the numerator:

$$V_1 = (L - L^*) / L^*$$

Although the numerator will always be non-negative, V_1 still approaches infinity when the optimal solution is near zero. In such cases, V_1 still tells us little about sub-optimality. We could force the denominator to be non-zero by shifting the due dates sufficiently, but there is another problem. A shift in all the due dates by a constant leaves the numerator unchanged but alters the denominator. Thus, even for a problem instance where L^* is positive, V_1 decreases when all the due dates are shifted upward, even though the shift does not change the essential problem to be solved. In an attempt to avoid this type of instability, many researchers used the following alternative:

$$V = (L - L^*)/p$$

Where, p denotes the average processing time in a schedule.

The metric V measures the amount of sub-optimality in proportion to the average processing time. The value $V = 0$ occurs when a heuristic produces an optimal solution, and, obviously, small values of V are desirable. The value $V = 1$ may also represent a useful target, indicating that no job is later than the average run time. Compared to V_1 this measure may be a little less intuitive, but V is not unstable for L^* values near zero, nor does it change when all due dates are shifted by a constant.

Furthermore, the relative differences among the solutions from the various algorithms are calculated in two ways.

The first deviation measure, denoted by d_1, is the relative percentage deviation of the heuristic solution value from the minimum obtained. It is calculated as:

$$d_1 = (h - min)*100/min$$

Where h is the solution value delivered by a given heuristic and

Min is the minimum of all solution values obtained.

The second deviation measure, d_2, is the relative deviation of a solution value from the minimum, scaled by the range of all solution values. It is calculated as:

$$d_2 = (h-min)/(max-min),$$

Where *max* is the maximum of all solution values; consequently, the results are normalised between 0 and 1, 0 corresponding to the best solution.

Examples of Heuristic Optimisation

In order to highlight the heuristic research process, we have presented an illustration of heuristics and the main issue of 'empirical analysis of heuristics' in Annexure 9.2 to Annexure 9.3, respectively.

Advantages and Limitations of Heuristic Methods

Some advantages of using heuristics are (Turban, 1990) that they:

- Are simple to understand and, therefore, easier to implement.
- Help in training people to be creative and come up with heuristics for other problems.
- Save formulation time.
- Save programming and storage requirements on the computers.
- Save computer-running time (speed).
- Produce multiple solutions.

However, there are problems in using heuristics in that:

- Heuristics that consider all possible combinations can seldom be achieved in practical problems.
- Sequential decision choices can fail to anticipate future consequences of each choice.
- "Local improvement" can short-circuit the best solution because heuristics lacks a global perspective.
- Interdependencies of parts of a system are ignored by the heuristics. This can sometimes have a profound influence on solution to the problem in the total system.

simulation
A simulation is the imitation of the operation of a real-world process or system over time. A simulation model is a descriptive model which represent a dynamic phenomenon, a set of decision alternatives, cause-effect relationship, etc. It involves the generation of an artificial history of the system in order to draw inferences about the real system. It is also known as the experimental arm of operations research.

SIMULATION MODELLING

There are several meanings attached to simulation. It can be the subject of replicating a mathematical model over time to study the behaviour of the system it represents. It will be used as an integrating sense by breaking a large complex system into smaller parts and then synthesising them using approximate relations among the parts. The synthesised system is then run on a computer over a period in order to fit well with reality. In this sense it is an experiment. It can be used as a numerical method to derive solutions to models and test them. The simple Moute Carlo system and simulation experiments are detailed along with illustrations.

Meaning of Simulation

Simulation has different meanings for different people and in different contexts. Its applications range from physical to biological systems, aerospace to military systems and political systems, health care to industrial systems. Computer simulation modelling has had an impact on studying complex social phenomena. Mathematical, simulation and artificial intelligence models are being applied to research in social and behavioural sciences (Liebrand et al, 1998). For the purpose of research methodology in management, our interest will be in application simulation for problem solving in a decision making context. Problems formulated for simulation are symbolically modelled. Their solutions are derived either analytically or numerically. Analytical solutions are derived using calculus, algebra, or probability theory. When the solutions cannot be derived or are extremely tedious to derive, numerical methods are employed. In these methods, numerical test values of variables and parametres are arranged over a range iteratively and a set of solutions are obtained. The best solution is chosen. Simulation is one of the procedures undertaken in numerical methods of solutions to models.

A simulation is the imitation of the operation of a real-world process or system over a period of time. Whether done by hand or on a computer, simulation involves the generation of an artificial history of a system, and the observation of that artificial history to draw inferences concerning the operating characteristics of the real system.

The dynamic behaviour of a system, over a period of time is studied by developing a simulation model. This model usually takes the form of a set of assumptions concerning the operation of the system. These assumptions are expressed in mathematical, logical, and symbolic relationships between the entities, or objects of interest, of the system. Once developed and validated, a model can be used to investigate a wide variety of 'what if' questions about the real-world system. Potential changes to the system can first be simulated in order to predict their impact on system performance. Simulation can also be used to study the behaviour of physical systems in the design stage, before such systems are built. Thus, simulation modelling can be used as an analysis tool for predicting the effect of changes in existing systems, and as a design tool to predict the performance of new systems under varying sets of circumstances. As Ackoff (1963) puts it "models represent phenomena, but simulation imitates it".

What is Simulation?

Simulation is, in one sense, a mathematical model that describes a system behaviour over time. A simulation model is a descriptive model, which may collectively represent a dynamic phenomenon, a set of decision alternatives, cause-effect relationships, and so forth. Simulation involves manipulation of the model so that it yields a representation of reality.

In another sense, simulation is a sort of experimentation, made on paper and/or on a computer, based on a symbolic or mathematical model and involves the underlying cause-effect relationships of the system or phenomenon being studied. It is also known as the experimental arm of operations research.

In a broader sense, simulation is a methodology for conducting experiments using a model of the real system. In the simplest form, any make-believe model of a real-life situation can be described as a simulated environment. For example, a toy train set is a simulated version of a real train; a programmable model car simulates a real life automobile; a planetarium shows a simulated version of space; a game simulation, a war simulation, and so on. But, instead of an explicit analytical solution, the simulated model uses several test values of the variables and derives the corresponding solutions. Thus, simulation models can be more general than mathematical models.

Simulation should not be regarded as a panacea for problem solving. A simulation model includes uncertain events. Hence, the answers it provides should be regarded as approximations subject to statistical error. Simulation only compares alternatives instead of generating an optimal solution. Since it is a numerical experimental procedure, a large number of simulation runs may become necessary. This makes a simulation experiment a fairly costly proposition, especially when studying a complex system. Management simulation models are computer models since it is virtually impossible to perform a practically useful simulation experiment manually in any reasonable period of time.

Applications of simulation models As a research method, simulation models may be built when:

1. Past data is not available on the possible cause-effect relationships of policy decisions.
2. Optimisation models are not possible due to lack of data and/or functional relationships.
3. The results or outputs or the behaviour of the system is dependent on random or uncontrollable factors.
4. Analytic models are unable to provide solutions. For example, transient (time-dependent) solutions for complex queuing models are not possible by analytical methods but are readily obtained by simulation methods.
5. Analytical techniques exist but are too complex to utilise and simulation can provide a simpler alternative.
6. The use of alternate decision models has to be tested and the choice of a more appropriate model has to be examined.
7. Experimentation with prototype models can be carried out for the purposes of studying system behaviour or when modifications during the model development process are to be examined.
8. Model parameters are to be estimated from available data on variables and system outputs.
9. Alternative courses of action, not included in model formulation, are to be tested.
10. The boundary of a problem that is changing over time has to be studied.

Classification of Simulation Models

discrete vs. continuous simulation

In discrete systems simulation, the simulated time changes in a step-wise discrete fashion while in continuous simulation time changes occur smoothly.

Digital simulation can be classified into two types, namely, discrete and continuous simulation. This classification is based on the consideration that whenever a system is simulated it will be observed either continuously over time or at specific points of time, depending on the type of system being simulated. In discrete system simulation, the simulated time changes in a stepwise discrete fashion, (that is, observation at points of time) while in continuous simulation, time changes occur smoothly (that is, observation is continuous). If the clock representing the simulated time is updated at regular time intervals, then the discrete simulation is said to be time oriented. If, on the other hand, the clock is updated whenever the next event occurs, then the discrete simulation is said to be event oriented. In a time-oriented simulation, the simulated time is increased by a fixed amount L for each transaction. Thus,

$$t = t + L$$

Where t represents the current simulated time.

In an event-oriented simulation, the simulation time is updated when input or output or specific change of the system takes place.

Typically, time-oriented simulation is deterministic (this can be probabilistic also, for example, stock market simulation on a daily basis, and pre-scheduled inventory reorder process), whereas an event-oriented simulation is probabilistic. The probability distribution of the events can be uniform or non-uniform. (For detailed treatment refer to Deo, 1979.)

A third type of simulation is called hybrid simulation, in which the system being simulated is a combination of the discrete and continuous types, where one subsystem is subjected to discrete simulation and the other to the continuous simulation.

Such a hybrid simulation model must contain appropriate links to integrate the outcomes from the two component simulations.

The Process of Simulation

There are, as mentioned earlier, many kinds of simulation. Let us consider simulation of mathematical models of systems whose variables are subject to random variations. The simulation process follows the procedure given below (Fig. 9.2).

(a) The model of the system to be simulated is formulated.
(b) The method of generating input data for the model is selected.
(c) The model is programmed on a digital computer.
(d) The simulation model is validated.
(e) The simulation model is replicated according to an experimental design.
(f) The outputs of the simulation experiment are subjected to statistical analysis to determine confidence and accuracy.
(g) The results are interpreted.

Fig. 9.2 Process of simulation experiment

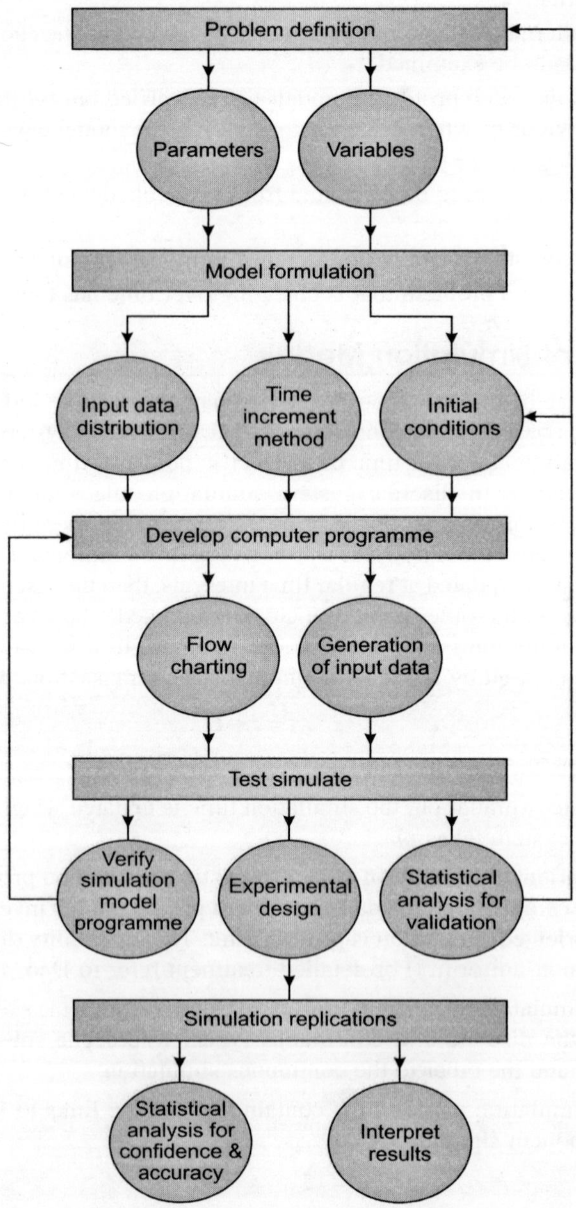

Generation of output data for the model There are three methods of generating output data for the simulation model:

1. Actual past data on the variables of the system is collected and used for comparing different models available for the system.
2. The past data on the variables of the system are converted into cumulative distributions, which are randomly sampled for feeding into the model during replication. The random sampling is known as the Monte Carlo technique.
3. When past data on variables is not available, the distribution of the variables is assumed to follow a standard distribution from which data will be sampled for feeding into the model during replication. This also uses the Monte Carlo method.

Monte Carlo method The heart of Monte Carlo simulation is to generate the values of the variables of a model in a random sequence. The steps followed in Monte Carlo simulation are depicted in the flow chart (Fig. 9.3), which is self-explanatory.

Monte Carlo simulation

In this simulation, the values of the variables are generated in a random sequence. It is a method of sampling values of the variables which can be used in any simulation model.

Fig. 9.3 Monte Carlo simulation steps

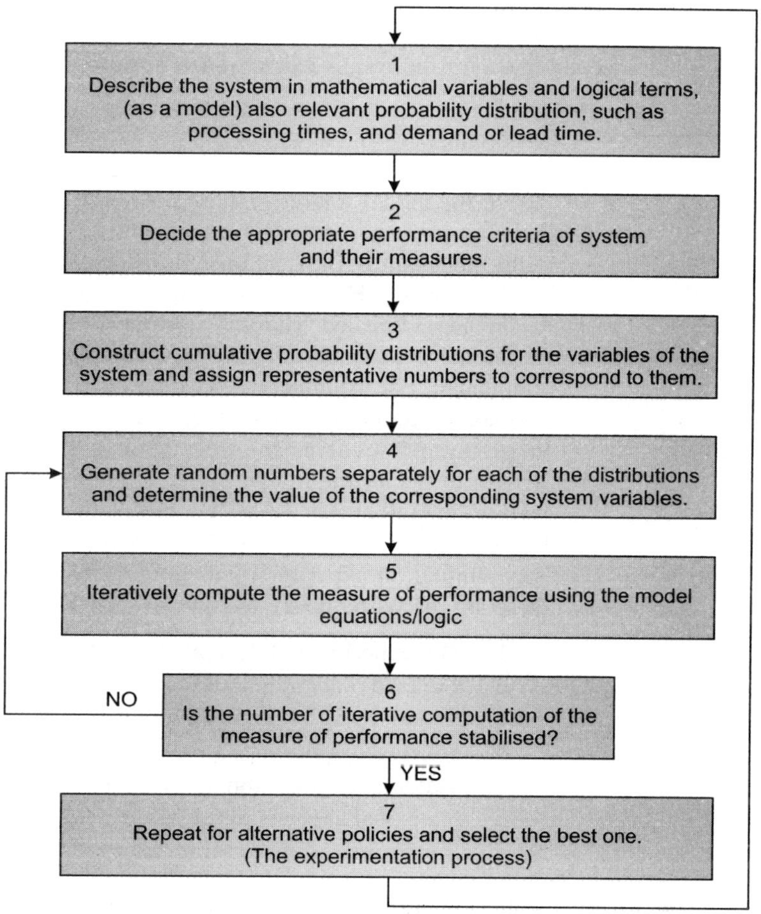

The key points to note in this flow chart are:

1. A different set of random numbers is generated for each variable.
2. Each random number is equated to the cumulative probability value, and the corresponding value of the relevant (random variate) variable is obtained from cumulative probability distribution.
3. This value, along with similarly generated values of the variables, is used to get the model output in the iteration.

4. A number of such iterations are made and the aggregate measures of the model results (performance) are obtained for evaluation or testing.
5. The number of iterations are established simultaneously taking into account whether the results are stabilised. The confidence and accuracy with which the result can be stated and its variance are established.

Strictly speaking, Monte Carlo method refers to use of sampling methods to estimate values of deterministic variables. An illustrative example of Monte Carlo simulation is given in Annexure 9.4.

Key Steps in Simulation Experiments

Three basic steps are involved in all computer simulation experiments, as follows:

1. Formulation of the mathematical model of the system to be simulated.
2. Programming, which involves choice of the programming languages and design of the programme.
3. Design of the experiment, in which treatments of research interest are given to the model, which will be replicated an adequate number of times in each treatment so that a comparison of the results can be made in support of a hypothesis or a proposition.

- The formulation of the model follows the procedures described in the section on development of models in chapter 8. Usually, in simulation some form of a mathematical model is used. An important aspect of simulation modelling is the validation of the model. The overall performance of model of a complex system is validated against the actual performance of the system, which is being modelled. Initially, the details of the relationships used in the model are considered as a block box for this purpose. However, the validity of the components of the overall model has also to be established. The principle question examined is whether the behaviour of the model component closely approximates the actual behaviour of the system component. For example, if lead-time distribution in the model is considered to be normal, a sample of the actual lead times should show the normal property.
- Programming involves the development of appropriate computer programmes written to depict the model logic. These programmes incorporate all the design features in FORTRAN, PASCAL, or 'C', or make use of readily available packages like DYNOMO, SIMULA, GPSS, SIMSCRIPT, SLAM, and others.
- Any simulation experiment has the following features and the details of each of these are discussed briefly below:
    1. The experimental design
    2. Time advance methods
    3. Variance reduction techniques
    4. Starting conditions
    5. Validation of the simulation model
    6. Statistical analysis of output
    7. Random number Generation

1. Experimental design The means and variances of output variables are compared under different system conditions. The effect of different variables is studied analytically based on responses from the experiments. Optimal conditions are tried to be estimated from these responses. The effect of different variables on the model output can be studied based on responses to the various treatments in the experiment. When sufficient range of treatments is taken care of, it will be easy to identify the optimal conditions by plotting the outcome over the range and finding out the point of inflection. (Ref. Krishnaswamy and Ganguly, 1987)

When the simulation model is run on the computer within the framework of accepted experimental designs, the inferences made from the results regarding model behaviour can be correct. In many simulation studies, the problem and the courses of action are transparent and strict experimental designs are not needed (as in deterministic cases). But, in cases where it is not so (as in stochastic models), careful choice of experimental design is important to enable the researcher to interpret the result. Various methods of experimental design are discussed in Chapter 6.

2. Time advance methods A time advance method requires a method of marking time or advancing the clock during simulation. If the models are time dependent, this becomes overtly important. Generally, time advancing is carried out by fixed times or the advance may be obtained by the variable time increment method in which only the next event time is marked. Since in most cases the simulation deals with stochastic variations of system variables, a random number is generated for sample events of the model, using appropriate probability distributions; or simply, uniformly distributed random numbers may be generated.

3. Variance reduction techniques In any hypothesis testing or experimentation like simulation, it is necessary to reduce the variance of the output. Indeed, the whole of experimental research is directed to this end because the predictions of the system can be made more accurately and with greater confidence if the variance is reduced. The following approaches are used to reduce the variance of the output.

variance reduction
This is one of the statistical analyses of the simulation output data. The purpose of this is to reduce the variance of the simulation output in order to test any hypothesis. The whole experimental research is directed to this end to make the prediction more accurately and with greater confidence.

- Increase of sample size/number of runs.
- Instead of simple random numbers for estimating for stochastic variable, stratified random numbers are used. This gives more samples in groups/clusters, which contain larger amounts of information.
- Antithetic variables are used. This procedure attempts to generate pairs of random variables having a high negative inter-correlation, so that the biases are evened out.

Since the outputs are random variables or combinations thereof, it is necessary to obtain desirable statistical precision while estimating the output values. One way of obtaining precision is to make use of a large sample. Another is to use a run length to satisfy the desired level of statistical error and confidence, which are specified *a priori*, like + 2 per cent error with 95 per cent confidence.

4. Starting conditions The main idea of determining the starting condition of a simulation run is to assume that measurement of system results are not made during transient conditions. The starting conditions must be such that the system attains steady-state condition quickly. In most experiments, however, an initial run may be made of the system until a steady-state condition is reached and the simulation is continued for the purposes of evaluation or experimentation, for a sufficient number of runs. Therefore, starting conditions are important because they affect the length and period of the transient condition and, therefore, the length of run. It is necessary to use good starting conditions to control one or the other. (see Conway and Maxwell, 1959 and Fisherman, 1971)

5. Statistical analysis of output Some of the standard types of analysis are as follows:

(i) Independent replication use different sets of random numbers.
(ii) A time series analysis is made to check for auto correlations in the data.
(iii) The results are classified into separate batches or groups and the performance of each batch or group is compared with the other. The basis of comparison is the estimate of variance. In this kind of analysis, no re-initialisation of the experiment is required.

6. Random number generation There are many methods of generating random numbers. Only three of the preferred ones are discussed for a basic understanding of the problem of making random numbers really random.

(i) *Ordinary random numbers* These are generated from uniformly distributed random numbers where each random number has equi-probability of being selected. Modulo-arithmetic concepts are used for this purpose. For example, Middle Square Method.

(ii) *Congruential method* X and Y are congruent modulo m if (X – Y) is an integral multiple of m.

X (Modulo m) = Y – Derived random number.

Y is the integer reminder when X is divided by m: The resulting values of Y would have equal probability of (1/m) in selected range. [Y = 0, 1, 2, (m-1)] or (Y = 1, 2,). Example: 857 (modulo 10) = 7

(iii) *Multiple congruential method* Any random number obtained by the above process in the selected range will have equi-probability of being selected, but in any useful application of simulation, the general value of the random variate would follow either its actual cumulative probability distributions (pdf) or a hypothetical cumulative distribution.

An example of simulation from actual research carried out is given in Annexure 9.5.

Validation of Simulation Models/Experiments

Validation of the simulation models can be done using several methods like checks for consistency of logic, comparison of real data with simulated results, validation by parts, multi stage validation, experimental judgment, or by changing the random number sequences.

The main question addressed in validation is, how do we know that the model we have used is an accurate representation of the system being simulated? The goal of the validation is two fold:

- To produce a model that represents true system behaviour closely enough for the model to be used as a substitute for the actual system, for the purpose of experimenting with the system; and
- To increase the credibility of the model to an acceptable level, so that the model will be used by managers and other decision-makers.

The above goals of validation ensure that the model is a valid representation of reality so that conclusions and inferences from experiments on the model can be applied to real life situation.

Some general perspectives on validation Before going into the details of methods of validation of simulation models, we should consider some general perspectives on validation. The following perspectives should not be thought of as definitive recommendations on how to validate a simulation model, but as somewhat philosophical considerations to be kept in mind when attempting to validate a model of a real-world system.

- Experimentation with a simulation model is a surrogate for actually experimenting with an existing or proposed system. Thus, a reasonable goal in validation is to ensure that a model is developed with a decision-maker can actually use to make the same decision that would be made, if it were feasible and cost effective, to experiment with the system. Although this statement is hard to disagree with in theory, knowing how to effect it in practice is a different story. Naylor and Finger (1967) shed some light on this matter and discuss a three-step approach to validation.
- A simulation model of a complex, real world system is always only an approximation to the actual system, regardless of how much effort is put into developing the model. Thus, one should not speak of the absolute validity or invalidity of a model, but rather of the degree to which the model agrees with the system. The more time (and hence money) that is spent on validation, the closer the agreement of the model with the system should be. However, the most "valid" model will not necessary be the most cost-effective. One should always keep in mind the overall objective of the simulation study, which is often to save money by determining an efficient system study.
- A simulation model should always be developed for a particular purpose. Indeed, a model valid for one purpose may not be valid for another (since simulation models often evolve over time and are used for different purposes, every simulation study should include a thorough documentation, not only of the computer programme but also of the assumptions underlying the model itself).

- A simulation model should be validated relative to a specified set of criteria, namely, criteria that will actually be used in decision-making.
- Validation is not something to be attempted after a simulation model has already been developed and only if there is time and money still remaining. Instead, model development and validation should be done hand in hand throughout the course of the simulation study.
- The use of formal statistical procedures is only part of the validation process; at present most of the 'validation' done in practice seems to be of the subjective variety. One reason for this is that most classical statistical techniques cannot be directly applied in the context of simulation-model validation.

SUMMARY

Heuristics and computer simulations are useful in deriving solutions to complex models. They are used in modelling a wide variety of management problems, indicating a shift from purely analytical approaches based on numerical procedures and on human ingenuity in problem-solving. Heuristics give good practical solutions, which may not be optimal, by considerably reducing the computational time of large computationally intractable problems, and makes possible solutions to problems, that cannot currently be solved by optimisation methods.

There is a large variety of heuristics. They range from simple rules made between 1960–1980, to more complex ones in recent times. The latter may combine many heuristics and/or draw analogy from diverse fields like annealing in metallurgy to biological evolution and genetics, they are called meta-heuristics. Simulated annealing, tabu search, and genetic algorithm are outlined in a simple way for a general appreciation. The evaluation of heuristic methods is elaborately dealt with. Some illustrations of heuristic applications are also presented.

Computer simulation imitates the operation of a real world process, develops pseudo system operation from the historic data of the system, to draw inferences concerning the description, operation, and behaviour of the system. Digital simulation, the most generally used simulation procedure, involves the development of a model of the system, generating input data using the Monte Carlo procedure and running the system repeatedly so that a steady-state condition is reached. It is validated for internal consistency and external appropriateness. It is considered as the experimental arm of operations research. Simulation experiments have to be designed using the principles of experimental design. A couple of examples are detailed.

ANNEXURE 9.1

Demonstration of Constructive Heuristics and SA

Numerical example There are 10 jobs available at time = zero. Data on each job's (a) required processing time; (b) size, in terms of number of boards required; and (c) priority is given in the table below. Priority is often a function of one or more of the following: (i) job's size (high, low), (ii) job's value (high, low), and (iii) Customer (export, import). When there is only one burn-in oven with capacity = 10 [boards], how do we construct batches and when do we schedule the constructed batches in the given burn-in oven to minimise C_{max} (= completion time of the last batch).

Job Cost (JC)	J1	J2	J3	J4	J5	J6	J7	J8	J9	J10
Processing Time (PT)	5	6	4	8	7	6	5	3	9	8
Job Size (JS)	4	6	5	7	4	3	5	4	3	6
Priority (P)	2	1	2	3	1	2	3	1	2	3

Contd.

The outline of the SA approach (Mathirajan et al, 2004) for scheduling a burn-in oven and its demonstration using the above numerical example are presented here.

Outline of the SA approach—Greedy heuristic and SA

Step 1: Set T=500; r = 0.9

Step 2: Generate initial solution

Step 2.1: Sort all jobs (i) based on 'job's priority' in ascending order, and (ii) within the priority based on 'job's size' in descending order.

Step 2.2: Combine jobs while progressing sequentially, taking into account the machine capacity.

Step 2.3: Determine the objective for the initial solution. Let current solution (C_{max}) = initial solution.

Step 3: Set n = 0

Step 4: Generate neighbouring solution: Starting with b = 1. If $p_j < p_k$ (where j is a job in batch b' and k is the longest processing time job in batch b) then exchange j and k when the machine capacity is not violated. Repeat this step for b = 1, 2, 3, … B, where B is the number of batches.

Step 5: Calculate the objective of the neighbouring solution (C'_{max}).

Step 6: If $C'_{max} < C_{max}$, current solution =neighbouring solution and $C_{max} = C'_{max}$. Else, if uniform [0,1] < exp $\{(C_{max} - C'_{max})/T\}$, current solution = neighbouring solution.

Step 7: $n = n+1$;

Step 8: $T' = r*T$; $T = T'$

Step 9: Repeat steps 3–8 until stopping criteria is true.

Demonstration of Greedy/Constructive Heuristic

JC	J1	J2	J3	J4	J5	J6	J7	J8	J9	J10
PT	5	6	4	8	7	6	5	3	9	8
JS	4	6	5	7	4	3	5	4	3	6
P	2	1	2	3	1	2	3	1	2	3

↓

Heuristic: List the jobs in 'priority order'

↓

JC	J2	J5	J8	J1	J3	J6	J9	J4	J7	J10
PT	6	7	3	5	4	6	9	8	5	8
JS	6	4	4	4	5	3	3	7	5	6
P	1	1	1	2	2	2	2	3	3	3

↓

Heuristic: Short the jobs within each 'priority order' by SPT order

↓

JC	J8	J2	J5	J3	J1	J6	J9	J7	J4	J10
PT	3	6	7	4	5	6	9	5	8	8
JS	4	6	4	5	4	3	3	5	7	6
P	1	1	1	2	2	2	2	3	3	3

↓

Contd.

Heuristic: Select a set of feasible jobs from the top of a sorted-list until the burn-in oven capacity is utilised to the maximum extent and repeat this heuristic until all jobs have been scheduled.

↓

JC	J8	J2	J5	J3	J1	J6	J9	J7	J4	J10
PT	3	6	7	4	5	6	9	5	8	8
JS	4	6	4	5	4	3	3	5	7	6
P	1	1	1	2	2	2	2	3	3	3
BP	6/10		7/9		9/10			5/5	8/7	8/6

↑

Reached the final solution as per the heuristic

Note: BP – Batch processor

Demonstration of Simulated Annealing

Initial solution [using Greedy Heuristic Algorithm]

↓

JC	J8	J2	J5	J3	J1	J6	J9	J7	J4	J10
PT	3	6	7	4	5	6	9	5	8	8
JS	4	6	4	5	4	3	3	5	7	6
P	1	1	1	2	2	2	2	3	3	3
BP	6/10		7/9		9/10			5/5	8/7	8/6

$C_{max} = 43$

↓

Repeat steps 3–8 (refer the outline of the SA procedure) until stopping criteria is true.

Iteration 1:

JC	J8	J3	J5	J2	J1	J6	J9	J7	J4	J10
PT	3	4	7	6	5	6	9	5	8	8
JS	4	5	4	6	4	3	3	5	7	6
P	1	2	1	1	2	2	2	3	3	3
BP	4/10		7/9		9/10			5/5	8/7	8/6

$C'_{max} = 41$

↓

Iteration 2:

JC	J8	J3	J1	J2	J5	J6	J9	J7	J4	J10
PT	3	4	5	6	7	6	9	5	8	8
JS	4	5	4	6	4	3	3	5	7	6
P	1	2	2	1	1	2	2	3	3	3
BP	4/10		6/9		9/10			5/5	8/7	8/6

$C'_{max} = 40$

↓

SA terminates with this C_{max}.

Contd.

ANNEXURE 9.2

Illustration of Heuristics

Illustration Mathirajan (1995) developed a heuristic model for employee pick-up vehicle routing for urban organisations, both in public and private sectors in India. In Bangalore city, for example, there are several such organisations collectively having a fleet of more than 2000 buses, as per the statistics obtained from the Motor Vehicles Department of the Government of Karnataka. In particular, four large scale public sector organisations, namely, Hindustan Aeronautics Limited (HAL), Indian Telephone Industries (ITI), Hindustan Machine Tools (HMT), and Bharat Electronics Limited (BEL) together transport nearly 45,000 employees every day by a fleet of about 800 buses (both ways for pick-up and dropping), covering an estimated 80,000 km. The amount of fuel consumed is directly dependent on how efficiently the routes are designed across various pick-up points and how effectively the fleet is allocated across the various shifts. The magnitude of investments, the operational costs related to the daily running of these buses and the associated fuel costs are phenomenal.

The routing and scheduling of the transport fleet in these organisations is generally based on subjective judgments, intuition, and experience. However, the efficiency achievable by scientific methods of operations research (OR) and the computing power of microcomputers could be effectively used to meet the transport requirements at maximum efficiency and minimum possible costs. It is estimated that the potential for savings in terms of the reduction in the annual fuel costs in this area alone would be of the order of several crores of rupees across the country. The employee pick-up problem can be viewed as a particular case of vehicle routing problem (VRP). The simplest version of EPVRP can be defined as follows:

A number of employees (demand) at known locations (pick-up points) are to be picked up or dropped off by vehicles that are serviced from a single depot (factory/organisation). The number of pick-up points is fixed and the distances between all pairs of pick-up points are known. The demand at each pick-up point is assumed to be deterministic and also the vehicle capacity is fixed and is known. Further, there could be limitations on the maximum distance allowed for each vehicle or route. The objective, generally, is to develop a set of routes so as to minimise the total travel distance (or running cost or journey time) of all vehicles.

Optimisation approaches are not feasible. Waters (1988)* reported an investigation for the feasibility of using the SCICONIC software, which is a commercially available package and which uses the branch-and-bound technique for solving integer-programming problems for exact solutions, in solving some small scale VRPs (maximum of 9 pick-up points). Sutcliffe and Board (1990) estimated that a simple extrapolation of Waters' (1988) approach using the SCICONIC software might take nearly 1,20,000 years of CPU time on a VAX 8600 machine to solve a VRP with 38 pick-up points Further, it was observed that the linear interactive discrete optimiser (LINDO) software took approximately 28 hours on a PC/AT–486 to solve a 10 pick-up point employee pick-up routing problem. Since a real VRP might have hundreds of pick-up points, the exact approaches are as yet not feasible.

As a result, heuristic methods are to be used in practical situations. This is evident in almost all the practical applications of VRP models in which attempts have been made to obtain reasonably good solutions, although they may not be the optimum solutions. This is true for EPVRP also.

Heuristics for employee pick-up vehicle routing problem In an employee pick-up problem, an employee, while being picked up for work, would prefer to travel 'inwards' only (that is, towards the work spot), rather than 'outwards', (that is, away from the work spot). Similarly, while being dropped off from work, the employee would prefer the shortest route and does not prefer routes that involve even a partial 'inward' journey,. The above mentioned requirements can be embedded in routing algorithms using the approaches based on the 'nearest neighbour rule'. This approach is considered and computerised for solving the EPVRP.

Nearest neighbour rule The general principle of the nearest neighbor rule for routing of vehicles is as follows. Initially, a route consists of the single depot only. At each iteration, an unvisited pick-up point, which is closest to the current 'end point' of the route, is selected and added to the route and this becomes the route's new end point. The selection is restricted to those pick-up points whose addition is feasible with respect to constraints on capacity of the vehicle and distance, if any. A new route is started any time the capacity is full and/or the search fails, unless there are no more employees to schedule.

Nearest neighbor with tie-breaking (NNTB) heuristic In this method, the basic idea of the nearest neighbor rule is used in addition to the following two heuristic rules.

Contd.

1. Every route that starts from the depot, first links the farthest pick-up point, with respect to the factory from the uncovered set of pick-up points'.
2. Further, while finding the closest feasible pick-up point using the nearest neighbour rule, if more than one such feasible pick-up point exists then the tie can be broken with some 'myopic' criteria based on distance or demand. This tie-breaking logic should also be incorporated into the basic nearest neighbour rule.

The step-by-step procedure of this method is as follows:

Step 0: Assign a separate route for the pick-up points whose demand is greater than their vehicle capacity. Update the demand in these pick-up points.

Step 1: Initialise the route by starting from the depot and linking the farthest pick-up point from among the non-visited pick-up points.

Step 2: Find the pick-up point closest to the last pick-up point, added to the route subject to the EPVRP constraints on vehicle capacity and distance being satisfied.

Step 3: Check for 'tie' for adding the feasible pick-up point identified in step 2, break it with the help of any one of the following 'myopic criteria'. Add the best feasible pick-up point to the last pick-up point in the route, which has:

(a) Minimum distance to the depot or starting point

(b) Minimum distance to the next feasible pick-up point

(c) Maximum demand

(d) Minimum distance per person

Step 4: Repeat Step 2 to Step 3 until the capacity of the vehicle is filled to get a complete route.

Step 5: Repeat Step 1 to Step 4 until all pick-up points on the routes are covered.

The above heuristic method was coded into a computer programme using the TURBO C language and the same was used on a PC/AT-486 (at the rate 33 MHz) machine to solve four routing problems associated with the four shifts of the organisation referred to in an earlier work (Raghavendra et al [1992])* on EPVRP at the Indian Telephone Industries (ITI) Limited. The results for these four real world routing problems are given in the Exhibit 9.1.

Procedures	Shift 1 distance (km)	Shift 2 distance (km)	Shift 3 distance (km)	Shift 4 distance (km)	Total distance (km)	Savings (in %)
Existing (Manual)	1977.0 (322)*	2163.0 (294)*	1808.3 (270)*	1056.7 (241)*	7005.0	—
Proposed Method: (NNTB)	1817.7	2040.8	1740.7	858.9	6458.1	7.81

Note: Cell value indicates Distance in km for pick-up only
* Represents number of pick-up points

Procedures	Shift 1 trips	Shift 2 trips	Shift 3 trips	Shift 4 trips trips	Total trips	Reduction in (%)
Existing (Manual)	64	66	53	30	213	—
NNTB	57	63	51	23	194	8.92

Note: Cell value indicates number of routes for pick-up only

Procedures	Shift 1 vehicle utilisation	Shift 2 vehicle utilisation	Shift 3 vehicle utilisation	Shift 4 vehicle utilisation	Average utilisation in 4 shifts	Increase in seat utilisation (%)
Existing (Manual)	89.00	84.00	90.00	54.00	79.25	
NNTB	97.21	96.34	92.55	72.98	89.77	13.27

Note: Cell value indicates number of pick-ups only.

Exhibit 9.1 Comparison of the results of heuristic method versus existing system

Contd.

The results for the four problems are quite promising from several angles. Firstly, they demonstrate that PC-based software is feasible for handling even large size employee pick-up problems. Secondly, it is expected that heuristic method(s) could be used to solve very large VRPs.

ANNEXURE 9.3

Illustration for Empirical Evaluation of Greedy Heuristics*

The transportation problem constitutes an important problem area of logistics management. There are many applications apart from shipment of commodities that may be formulated as transportation problems, such as an urban transport undertaking, to minimising dead kilometres, approximating certain linear programming problems, and so on.

Various methods are available to solve the transportation problem for devising an optimal solution. All the basic solution algorithms for solving transportation problems need an initial basic feasible solution to obtain the optimal solution. There are various heuristic methods available to get an initial basic feasible solution, such as North West Corner rule, Best Cell Method, Vogel's Approximation Method (VAM), and others. Further, Kirca and Satir (1990) developed a heuristic called total Opportunity-cost Method (TOM) for obtaining an initial basic feasible solution for the transportation problem. In this study, the basic idea of Kirca and Satir (1990) is extended using the VAM procedure.

Variants of vogel's approximation method (VAM) The TOM is an effective application of the 'best cell method' along with some tie-breaking features a total opportunity cost (TOC) matrix. The TOC matrix is obtained by adding row opportunity cost matrix (for each row, the smallest cost of that row is subtracted from each element of the same row) and column opportunity cost matrix (for each column of the original transportation cost matrix the smallest cost of that column is subtracted from each element of the same column). When we apply the best cell method (lease cost method) on a TOC matrix, if more than one TOC cell is competing for allocation, the following tie-breakers are used in the order given:

(i) Make the allocation to **the cell** with the smallest cost.
(ii) In the case of a tie in (i), make allocation to **the cell** with the largest possible allocation.
(iii) In the case of a tie in (ii), make allocation to **the cell** with first occurrence.

As VAM usually yields a better initial solution than other initial basic feasible solution methods, the reasoning behind the TOM and Goyals (1991) note motivated us to couple VAM principles and the basis of the TOM to derive two variants of VAM. These variants are (1) VAM, applied on total opportunity cost matrix [VAM-TOC] and (2) VAM with tiebreakers, applied on total opportunity cost matrix [VAMT-TOC]. These along with the basic version of VAM and VAM with tie breakers, applied on the original transportation cost matrix [VAM-TC and VAMT-TC, respectively] are also included along with TOM in the computational analysis. Further, it is sufficient to note that the algorithms follow the steps of Krica and Satir (1990), except that allocations are done using VAM instead of the best cell method on the TOC matrix.

Computational experiments carried out to evaluate the VAM, variants of VAM and TOM, with their results, are described in the next section.

Experimental evaluation of the heuristics proposed The main goal of the experiments was to evaluate the quality of the solutions obtained by VAM and its variants and TOM by comparing them with optimal solutions. An experimental approach of this sort relies on two elements: a measure of effectiveness and a set of test problems. Performances of the proposed heuristic algorithms are compared using the following measures:

1. *Average Relative Percentage Deviation (ARPD)* The ARPD, which indicates the average performance of the variants of VAM and TOM with respect to optimal solution over the number of problem instances, is computed using the following equations:

$$ARPD\ (H) \equiv \sum_{i=1}^{N} RPD\ (H, i)$$

Contd.

* This experimental analysis relates to the heuristic derivation of initial basic feasible solution to a transportation problem [Mathirajan and Meenakshi (2004)]

$$PD\ (H,\ i) \equiv \{(U_H - U_1)/U_1\} \times 100$$

Where $ARPD\ (H)$ = $ARPD$ of heuristic 'H'

$RPD\ (H,\ i)$ = Relative percentage deviation of the heuristic 'H' with respect to the optimal solution for the instance 'i'

U_H – Total transportation cost yielded by the heuristic 'H'

U_1 = Optimal transportation cost, and

N = Number of problem instances

2. *Number of Best Solutions (NBS)* This a frequency that indicates the number of times the VAM and its variants and TOM yielded the solution corresponding to the 0 percent – 3 percent loss of optimality over the number of runs (problem instances).

Experimental design In 640 problem instances, the performance of the VAM and its variants and TOM are compared. The problems are randomly generated based on the experimental design framework presented in Kirca and Satir (1990), but restricted to 'full dense' transportation problem (The transportation problem is fully dense, if there exists a route from each origin to each destination). The details of the experimental design used are as follows:

- Cost Structure (C_{ij}): Problems with four cost ranges (R) are tested.

  R = (20, 100, 500, 1000); mean = 500

  For each range, costs are randomly generated from the following uniform distribution:

  U [(C_{ij} : (Mean Cost – R/2 , Mean Cost + R/2)]

- Supply and demand structure (S_i and D_j): The mean supply is expressed as

  Mean Supply = K [(n * Mean Demand)/m]; Present mean demand =100

  Where K indicates the degree of imbalance between total supply and total demand.

  Mean supply values are generated for four values of K = (1, 2, 5, 10)

  S_i and D_j are then generated, respectively, from the uniform distributions of

  U (S_i : [0.75 * Mean Supply , 1.25 * Mean Supply])
  U (D_j : [75 , 125])

- Problem size (m × n) : The sizes (m × n) of the problems experimented with are (10 × 20), (10 × 40), (10 × 60) and (10 × 100).

The experimental design for generating test problems using the above three parameters is summarised in Exhibit 9.2. The experimental design adopted in this paper is implemented in C++. For each combination of values for [(m × n), K, R] 10 problem instances are randomly generated, yielding a total of 640 [= 10 × (4 × 4 × 4)] problem instances. All 640 problem instances are unbalanced and 76 problem instances have total demand greater than total supply and 564 problem instances have the total supply greater than the total demand.

Evaluation of VAM and its variants and TOM against Optimal Solution For deriving an optimal solution for transportation problems, the LINDO package is used. VAM and each of its variants and TOM were implemented using Turbo C++. For each problem instance, the heuristic solutions were obtained using VAM and each of its variants and TOM. The performance of the VAM and its variants and TOM in comparison with the optimal solution is presented below.

Evaluation based on Average Relative Percentage Deviation (ARPD) First, for each problem instance, the value of the 'relative percentage deviation (RPD)' of each variant of VAM and TOM, with respect to the optimal solution was computed. Secondly, for each level [(m × n), K, R] the values average RPD (ARPD) was computed over 10 problem instances. Further, for each level [(m × n), K], the average RPD was computed over 40 problem instances

Contd.

No.	Problem Factor	Levels	# Levels
1	Problem size (m×n)	{ 10×20; 10×40; 10×60, 10×100}	4
2	Degree of imbalance (K)	{ 1, 2, 5, 10 }	4
3	Cost structure - Range (R)	{ 20, 100, 500, 1000 }	4
Number of problem configurations			4×4×4 = 64
Problem instances per configuration			10
Total problem instances			64×10 = 640

Cost Structure (C_{ij}): U [C_{ij}: (Mean Cost–R/2, Mean Cost+R/2)]
Where Mean Cost = 500
Supply (S_i): U [S_i: (0.75 x Mean Supply, 1.25 x Mean Supply)]
Where Mean Supply = [(k x n x Mean Demand)/m] and Mean Demand = 100
Demand (D_j) : U (D_j: [75, 125])

Exhibit 9.2 Summary of experimental design

(that is, over the number of cost range "R" and 10 problem instances within each cost range "R") and presented in Exhibit 9.3.

Problem Factor			Average {ARPD} over "R"				
			Basic Variants of VAM		Proposed variants of VAM		Kirca and Sattir
Size (m x n)	Degree of Imbalance (K)	Cost Structure - Range (R)	VAM-TC	VAMT-TC	VAM-TOC	VAMT-TOC	TOM
10 x 20	1	{20,100,500,1000}	4.41*	4.42	3.74	3.74	6.44
	2	{20,100,500,1000}	10.70	10.70	1.53	1.53	41.06
	5	{20,100,500,1000}	12.04	12.04	2.10	2.10	55.07
	10	{20,100,500,1000}	18.09	18.09	1.35	1.35	118.10
	Overall Average		**11.31**	**11.31**	**2.18**	**2.18**	**55.17**
10 x 40	1	{20,100,500,1000}	2.73	2.72	2.40	2.40	8.62
	2	{20,100,500,1000}	3.78	3.81	0.13	0.13	48.32
	5	{20,100,500,1000}	10.13	10.15	0.16	0.16	86.10
	10	{20,100,500,1000}	14.81	15.45	0.40	0.40	142.90
	Overall Average		**7.86**	**8.03**	**0.77**	**0.77**	**71.49**
10 x 60	1	{20,100,500,1000}	4.71	7.51	4.01	4.01	8.46
	2	{20,100,500,1000}	2.77	18.22	0.35	0.35	31.66
	5	{20,100,500,1000}	1.71	31.19	0.12	0.12	81.43
	10	{20,100,500,1000}	1.73	8.88	0.18	0.18	95.79
	Overall Average		**2.73**	**16.45**	**1.17**	**1.17**	**54.33**
10 x 100	1	{20,100,500,1000}	2.67	7.26	2.18	2.19	8.22
	2	{20,100,500,1000}	2.09	20.65	0.16	0.16	29.10
	5	{20,100,500,1000}	2.44	29.39	0.23	0.23	71.87
	10	{20,100,500,1000}	3.62	15.16	0.29	0.30	109.59
	Overall Average		**2.70**	**18.12**	**0.72**	**0.72**	**54.69**

Note: * Each 'cell' value indicates the average of ARPD in the 40 problem instances, that is, 10 problem instances for each "R".

Exhibit 9.3 Average performance of the variants of VAM and TOM

It is clear from Exhibit 9.3 that for each variant of VAM and TOM, the values of average (RPD) significantly vary and irrespective of the problem parameters considered in this study, on an average, the variants VAM-TOC and VAMT-TOC yielded better results compared with VAM-TC, VAMT-TC, and TOM. This indicates that coupling

Contd.

TOC with VAM consistently will yield better starting solution in comparison with either basic version of VAM or TOM. Also, the 'tie-breakers' used in this study do not have any influence in the solution yielded by VAM coupled with TOC.

Evaluation based on Number of Best Solutions (NBS) From the detailed results obtained, the number of times the VAM and its variants and TOM yielded 0 per cent, 0.5 per cent, 1 per cent, 2 per cent, and 3 per cent loss of optimality were observed over the 640 problem instances. From the analysis, the performance measure NBS provides indicates that VAM-TOC and VAMT-TOC are better options for obtaining initial basic feasible solution for the transportation problem. Further, the variants VAM-TOC and VAMT-TOC, yielded the optimal solution 20 percent of the times and very efficient solutions with 0.5 percent loss of optimality about 80 percent of the of total problem instances. Further, from the analysis, the basic version of the VAM appears to be better than TOM in all cases of 0 per cent to 3 per cent loss of optimality.

Conclusions Two variants of Vogel's approximation method were proposed in this paper by coupling the basic idea of Kirca and Satir (1990) with VAM. It is concluded that VAM (TOC) is a better choice than TOM and other variants of VAM considered in this study.

ANNEXURE 9.4

Illustration for Monte Carlo Simulation

A product is stocked to cater to uncertain demand. In the past, the demand per week followed the distribution pattern shown in Exhibit 9.3. The lead-time for replenishment was also a stochastic variable whose distribution is given in Exhibit 9.4. The company follows a policy of ordering 15 units of the products when the inventory level is less than or equal to 2 units. Examine the adequacy of the policy of stocking not more than 1 in 20. The steps followed in the process of simulation are shown Fig. 9.3.

1. The important variables are inventory levels and frequency of stockouts. These will have to be tracked in the simulation. Frequency of stock out will be the measure of performance of the system.
2. Probabilities, cumulative probabilities, and random number ranges are shown in Exhibits 9.4 and 9.5. Two digit random number ranges represent the cumulative probabilities have been assigned (since the random numbers are uniformly distributed, each digit has equal probability of being chosen). For example, in Exhibit 9.5, any digit from 00 to 99 has a probability of 1/100 in a possible range of 00 – 99. If more precise probabilities are required (as in the distribution), a higher digit random number (RN) can be chosen. The random numbers used in the simulation are obtained from the random number table or when computerisation is employed, pseudo random numbers are generated. RN series should be selected for each variable at different points on the table, proceeding in the manner of ordinary reading or writing. In computer simulation, different seeds have to be used for different sets of random numbers.

No. of units demanded (d)	P(d)	Cumulative p(d)	Random Number Range (RNR)
0	0.10	0.10	00–09
1	0.40	0.50	10–49
2	0.30	0.80	50–79
3	0.20	1.00	80–99

Exhibit 9.4 Weekly demand, probability, cumulative probability, and random number

Lead time from order holder	P(LT)	Cumulative p(LT)	(RNR)
0	0.20	0.20	00–19
1	0.50	0.70	20–69
2	0.30	1.00	70–99

Exhibit 9.5 Probability distribution for lead time

3. The random number for demand is successively applied to Exhibit 9.4 to generate the series of simulated demand/wK. For example, if the first RN is 39, it is entered in the table at RN 10–49 and the demand of 1 unit is obtained. Similarly, for lead time (LT), RN of 76 gives a lead time of 2Wks.
4. The simulation proceeds as shown in Exhibit 9.6. Demands generated for every week are initially subtracted from the beginning inventory of the week to obtain ending inventory. For this purpose, an initial inventory of

Contd.

15 is assumed (starting conditions are important in simulation). Ending inventory for week (WK) 1 is (15–1) = 14. This process is continued until week 8, when the ending inventory is 1 unit (< 2) and an order is placed (RN=76, LT=2WKS). Since the demand during the 9th week is one unit, inventory falls to 0. There is a stockout in the 10th week, as the demand of 1 unit in it cannot be met. In this way, simulated system performance is obtained. The table shows average ending inventories and stockouts for 20 simulation runs. Note that the time is incremented through 1 week.

(1) WEEK NO.	(2) RECEIPTS	(3) BEGINNING INVENTORY	(4) RANDOM NO., RN	(5) DEMAND	(6) ENDING INVENTORY	(7) STOCKOUTS	(8) ORDER PLACED	(9) RN	(10) WEEKS TO ARRIVE	(11) AVERAGE OF (6)	(12) AVERAGE OF (7)
0					15						
1	0	15	39	1	14					14.0	0
2	0	14	73	2	12					13.0	0
3	0	12	72	2	10					12.0	0
4	0	10	75	2	8					11.0	0
5	0	8	37	1	7					10.2	0
6	0	7	2	0	7					9.7	0
7	0	7	87	3	4					8.6	0
8	0	4	98	3	1		15	76	2	7.9	0
9	0	1	10	1	0					7.0	0
10	0	0	47	1	0	1				6.3	.100
11		15	15	93	3	12				6.8	.091
12	0	12	21	1	11					7.2	.083
13	0	11	95	3	8					7.2	.077
14	0	8	97	3	5					7.1	.071
15	0	5	69	2	3					6.8	.066
16	0	3	41	1	2		15	23	1	6.5	.063
17	0	2	91	3	0	1				6.1	.118
18	15	15	81	3	12					6.4	.111
19	0	12	67	2	10					6.6	.105
20	0	10	59	2	8					6.7	.100

Exhibit 9.6 Simulation details for a run length of 20

5. From Exhibit 9.6, it is seen there are 2 stockouts in 20 periods or 10 per cent, that is, higher than 1 in 20, and therefore, the system performance is poor and the policy has to be revised.
6. However, in general, the stabilisation of the performance shown in Fig. 9.12 should be tested statistically and the simulation has to be continued until the performance has stabilised.
7. The same experiment can be repeated with the same economic order quantity and different minimum inventory levels of, say 3 units, 4 units, and 5 units. The stockout probabilities in each case is determined and the best policy can then be chosen.

ANNEXURE 9.5

Illustration for Simulation from Actual Research

*Rao, et al (1993) studied the performance of the proposed configuration of a complex process plant using a computer simulation model.

The production system chosen is large fertiliser complex. Following thc total system study, the issue selected for the investigation was to determine the effects of changes in the configuration of process plants on overall system

Contd.

performance in order to evaluate a proposal for an additional facility to the existing complex. To achieve this objective, the following method was envisaged: (a) formulation of the production system as a Markov process, and (b) determination of optimal production system configuration using Markov simulation.

Analysis of a process plant using Markov simulation Consider an industrial processing complex (IPC) comprising n plants interconnected in such a way that the output of plant 1 is an input to plant 2, output of plant 2 is an input to plant 3 and so on, and ultimately the final product is the output of plant n. Assuming each plant as a combination of K streams arranged through parallel and serial connections, the state of a plant can be represented by S_{rms}, where $(r + m + s) = K$. The number of running streams in a plant is represented by r, streams under maintenance by m, and idle streams by s. Output of a plant is a function of its state and time. A model of the processing system with the above description is presented in Exhibit 9.7.

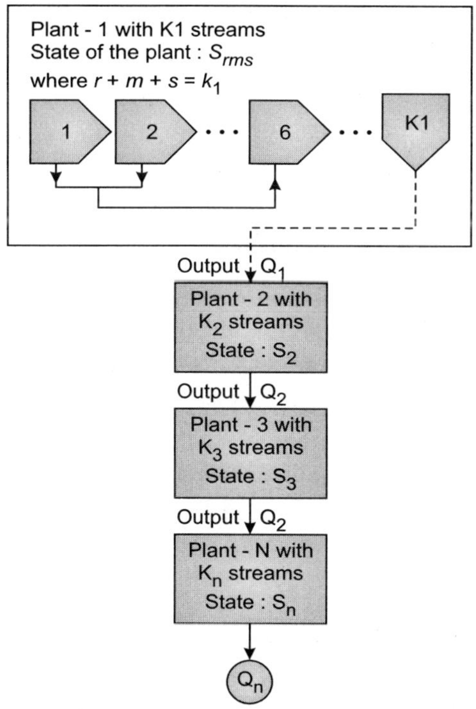

Exhibit 9.7 Schematic diagram of model representing an industrial processing complex

It is now desired to add one more stream to the existing K parallel streams in one of the plants. How does such an addition affect the performance of the total plant? In an attempt to answer this question, modelling of the system with K processes and K+1 processes is discussed below.

System with K processes—an analytical model Consider a continuous processing plant with K parallel systems. The transitions of the system from one state to another are assumed to be a Markov process with all possible states as random variables. Unless there are any changes in the configuration of the plant, the transition probabilities will remain stationary. It is assumed that the times between events are negative-exponentially distributed, satisfying the conditions for Markov and stationary probabilities.

The maximum number of states N the system can occupy is given by:

$$N = (K+1) + K + (K-1) + ...1 = (K+1)(K+2)/2 \tag{1}$$

The Transition Probability Matrix (TPM) P, of size N × N, along with its transition diagram, represents the Markov model of the system.

$$P = [p_{ij}],$$

Where

p_{ij} - probability of transition of the system from state i to j during the next time interval.

Then,

$$\sum_{j=1}^{N} p_{ij} = 1, 0 < p_{ij} < 1 \tag{2}$$

The long run performance/conditions of the system can be estimated by three steady-state probabilities given by Π_1, Π_2,.... Π_n, obtained from

$$\Pi = \Pi \text{ x } p \tag{3}$$

and

$$\sum_{i=1}^{N} \Pi_i = 1 \tag{4}$$

Contd.

Where

:

Π is the row vector with components Π_i, the vector of steady-state probabilities.

Using this Markov property, the steady-state probability of operating the system $p_r(k)$ is obtained. The system output as a function of three factors is given by

$$\text{System output} = F(p_r(k), r_i, t) \quad (5)$$

Where

r_i - the production rate while the system is in state I

t is the time period.

If the function F is analytically known then the output of the system can be determined analytically. If not, the system has to be simulated.

System with K + 1 processes—a simulation model It is assumed that the operational behaviour of the proposed (K+1)th stream will be identical to that of the existing K streams. The maximum number of states of the system with (K+1) stream is given by (as per equation [1]).

$$N_{K+1} = (K+2)(K+3)/2 \quad (6)$$

Because, developing a TPM with N_{K+1} states is not feasible as (K+1) streams are not physically available, it is necessary to simulate the Markov model with (K+1) streams having N_{K+1} state. For this Markov simulation, cumulative TPM of K streams and cumulative TPM of the $(K+1)^{Th}$ stream are the inputs.

It should be noted that, for the solution to the K stream problem, analytical solutions are possible or alternatively the system may be simulated. It will be seen subsequently that both solutions have been used, although with different objectives.

The simulated output contains relative frequencies representing the steady-state probabilities of NK+1 states. Using this approach, all possible configurations of the system can be evaluated. The steps discussed above are presented in Exhibit 9.8.

In the simulation model, the system output for (K+1) streams is obtained by using equation (5). The output of the system with (K+1) processes is compared with that of the system with K processes for the purposes of decision making. The above model was applied to a process plant in a fertiliser complex. The details are presented in the following sections.

Application of the model to a fertiliser complex The fertiliser complex that was studied produces urea using coal as raw material and consists of four plants: coal gasification, ammonia synthesis, stream generation, and urea synthesis. The number of parallel streams in operation in each plant is also indicated in the figure.

The designed capacity of the fertiliser complex is 900 tonnes per day of ammonia for an ultimate production of 1500 tonnes of urea fertiliser per day.

During the commissioning and subsequent operation of the plants, a number of shortcomings surfaced. Erosion and corrosion problems were faced in the coal gasification and ammonia plants. Materials of fabrication selected earlier turned out to be inappropriate to meet the service conditions. The consequent production interruptions due to equipment failures in many plants of the fertiliser complex resulted in capacity utilisation as low as 21 per cent to 49 per cent over the years. A detailed technical study by a consulting firm recommended addition of a fourth stream of coal gasification to improve the performance of the fertiliser complex. In order to evaluate proposal by estimating the improvement of overall productivity in terms of plant utilisation and urea production, the Markov simulation model proposed earlier was used.

Varying configurations of the coal gasification plant Currently, the coal gasification plant consists of three identical gasifier streams connected parallelly, each with a designed capacity of 32,333 normal cubic metres of raw gas with combined contents of carbon monoxide and about 84 per cent hydrogen. The raw gas generated in the gasifier is quenched with water before entering the waste heat boiler (WHB), in which a major portion of the sensible heat from the gas is utilised for generation of saturated high-pressure steam. The waste heat recovery system over each gasifier consists of a WHB mounted on top, which is capable of producing 18 tonnes per hour of saturated

Contd.

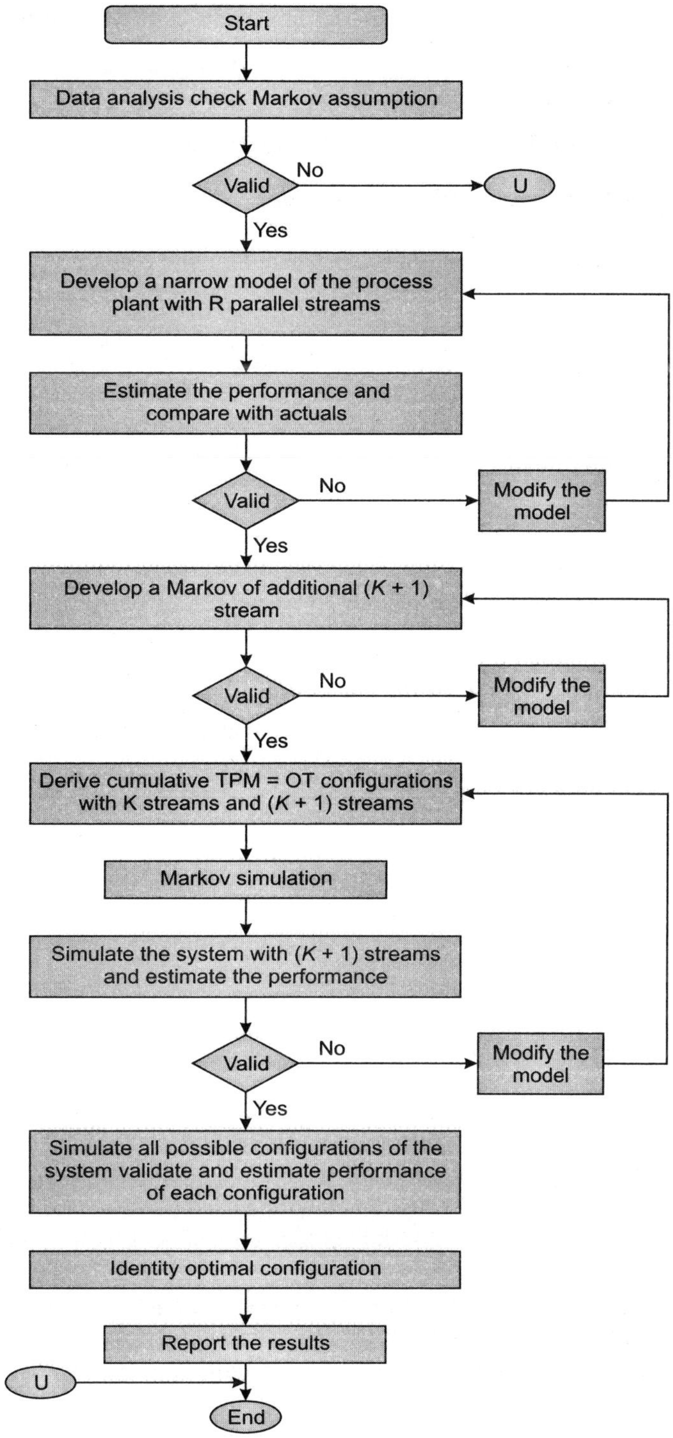

Exhibit 9.8 Macro analysis of process plant through Markovian approach

steam. It was observed that about 45 per cent of production interruptions in the gasification plant were due to failures of the WHBs. These were, therefore, studied using the model.

The configuration of the gasification plant is referred to by two parameters (g, w), where g stands for the total number of gasifiers, and w for the number of gasifiers having WHBs. The history of the plant running under different configurations is represented in the table below.

Contd.

Period	System configuration
November 1980 to March 1983	(3,3) Original design of WHB
December 1983 to April 1985	(3,0) All WHBs bypassed
April 1985 to April 1987	(3,2) Improved design of WHB

Markov model of the gasification system with three gasifier Out of three gasifiers, a set or subset of them may be in running condition (*r*), under maintenance (*m*), or in idle condition (*s*) due to non-availability of upstream/downstream plants. The state of the gasification plant represented by a variable S_{rms} can occupy any one of the 10 possible states, as shown below.

300	201	102	111
030	210	120	
003	021	012	

The 10 × 10 transition probability matrix *P*, along with its transition diagram, represents a Markov model of the system under study.

The transition of the gasification system states was studied with the help of data collected from the plant's logbooks, which contained a continuous record of all the events that have taken place with reference to each gasifier. From this basic information, the gasification system state S_{rms} and its time of occurrence were recorded for the period 1982–87, covering all the prevailing configurations: (3,3), (3,2), and (3,0). From this data, the changes in the system states were observed to be random, exhibiting a memory less property.

Further, the distributions of inter-arrival times of transitions across states of the system were developed. The transitions (presented in Exhibit 9……) were found to be negative-exponential. This was tested using the Kolmogorov-Smirnov test at a level of significance, a = 0.01.

The exponential distribution functions for the configurations are:

For configuration (3,3),

$$F_1(t) = 1 - \exp(-0.03285t) \tag{7}$$

For configuration (3,0)

$$F_2(t) = 1 - \exp^{(-0.03912t)} \tag{8}$$

For configuration (3,2)

$$F_3(t) = 1 - \exp^{(-0.02537t)} \tag{9}$$

Where

t represents the mean inter-arrival time of transitions across the system states.

Steady-state probabilities From the matrix of transitions, corresponding TPM was derived for each configuration of a fixed time interval of eight hours. The long run conditions and performance of the system, as estimated by the steady-state probabilities obtained from the Markov model for each configuration, are summarised in Exhibit 9.9.

To compare the system performance under the three configurations on a common basis, the factors $Sr(3)$, $S_m(3)$, and $S_s(3)$ were computed, representing the weighted average of steady-state probabilities of the system with three gasifiers in running condition, under maintenance, and in idle condition, respectively. These are shown in Exhibit 9.9.

Gasifier run hours per month were computed from the above probabilities using the relation

$$H = \sum_{i=1}^{N} f_i r_i K \tag{10}$$

Where

f_i is the relative frequency of state *i*

r_i is the number of running gasifiers in state *i*

Contd.

K is the average number of working hours per month

N is the number of system states

H is the gasifier run hours per month

State of the System	Configuration: three gasifiers		
	Three WHBs Old (3,3)	Zero WHBs (3,0)	Two WHBs New (3,2)
S003	0.039	0.031	0.059
S012	0.016	0.036	0.019
S021	0.013	0.007	0.007
S030	0.157	0.068	0.026
S102	0.0	0.002	0.019
S111	0.002	0.010	0.024
S120	0.282	0.068	0.139
S201	0.010	0.048	0.058
S210	0.439	0.442	0.478
S300	0.042	0.288	0.171
Sr(3)	0.436	0.641	0.589
Sm(3)	0.506	0.281	0.297
Sx(3)	0.058	0.078	0.114

Exhibit 9.9 Steady-state probabilities for the three-gasifiers system

Urea production per month was computed from *H*, using the relation between these two variables developed through regression analysis of past data. The relationship is given by the equation

$$U = -6304.956 + 20.964H \tag{11}$$

Where

U-the production of urea in tonnes per month.

The limits observed for *H* from past data were $960<H<1615$. The correlation coefficient was found to be 0.962. The appropriateness of the equation was tested through chi-square goodness-of-fit test.

The urea production estimated for the three configurations using equations (10) and (11) are presented in Exhibit 9.10.

Configuration —>	(3,3)	(3,0)	(3,2)
Gasifier run hours per month	954.84	1403.79	1289.91
Urea production per month (tonnes)	13712.00	23124.00	20736.00

Exhibit 9.10 Estimates of run hours and production from probabilities

From Exhibit 9.9, it is seen that the WHBs that are meant for thermal economy have reduced the system's availability for operation. From Exhibit 9.10 we can infer that the production of urea is higher for the system without WHB.

Markov simulation model of the proposed system with four gasifiers The proposal for addition of one more gasification stream is evaluated with the assumption that the operational behaviour of the additional stream will be similar to those of the existing three. It is assumed that breakdown of one will have no impact on the state of the other gasifiers. The maximum number of states the system can occupy with four streams is 15. Out of the 15 states, one state, S400, representing all four gasifiers in running condition simultaneously, is not physically feasible due to

Contd.

upstream/downstream design limitations. This results in a total of 14 possible states for the Markov model. As no data are available for 14 states, we simulate the Markov model with four streams having 14 states.

Simulation experiment The Markov model of a proposed four gasifiers system is simulated with cumulative transition probability matrices representing (a) a system of three gasifiers, and (b) a fourth gasifier, as inputs.

All the possible configurations of the system with four gasifiers were simulated to yield steady-state probabilities of the above 14 states in terms of relative frequencies. These were converted to equivalent production of urea fertiliser using equations (10) and (11). The results are presented in Exhibit 9.11.

System configuration	*Mean production of urea per month (tonnes)*
With three gasifiers:	
(3,3) with old WHBs	13,821
(3,2) with new WHBs	20,807
(3,0) all WHBs bypassed	23,126
With four gasifiers:	
(4,3)	27,752
(4,2)	28,721
(4,1)	29,757
(4,0)	30,593

Exhibit 9.11 Simulated performance of the gasification

From the above results, it is evident that by-passing of WHBs would improve production. It is also evident from the results that four gasifiers would improve the system availability and production of urea. However, the simulation experiments have to be validated. This is detailed in the next section.

Validation of the Simulation Model: The Markov simulation model has been validated using the historical experience of the gasification plant with three gasifiers between the years 1980–88. In addition to the external validation, the model was internally validated with reference to the distribution of the stochastic variable.

The model used to simulate the system of four gasifiers can also be used to simulate the system of three gasifiers. Performance of a three-gasifiers system under different configurations was simulated, taking the corresponding cumulative TPM as input. Simulations of three-gasifier configurations were carried out to compare the results against analytical values for further external validation of the model.

It was observed that the actual values lay within 95 per cent confidence intervals of the simulated ones for the configurations (3,3), 3,0), and (3,2). These results are shown in Exhibit 9.12. From this we can conclude that the model is internally consistent, externally valid, and closely represents the real system. The same model was extended for simulating the configurations of the four-gasifier system. External validation of the four-gasifier system is not directly possible because it is a hypothetical configuration. It is reasonable to assume that the model is a valid one for a four-gasifiers system also based on the above arguments.

Configuration	*Simulated mean gasifier run (hours per month)*	*Standard deviation*	*95% confidence interval for mean GRHPM*	*Actual GRHPM from past data*
(3,3)	960	55.68	948–972	972
(3,2)	1293	58.83	1281–1305	1280
(3,0)	1403	62.50	1390–1416	1392

Exhibit 9.12 Results of validation of Markov simulation model

The simulation model used the method of fixed time advance with the basic unit of time as eight hours, keeping the length of each run as one month, and a sample size of 100 runs. To keep the variance of sample mean to the minimum, reducing the basic unit of time from eight hours to 30 minutes increased the length of each run. It was observed that with a sample of 100 runs, each run to a length of one month and each observation at a fixed time interval of 30 minutes, the simulated mean reached about 95 per cent of the steady-state value.

Sample size estimates were made from the formula

$$n = [S^2 (Z_a/2)^2]/d^2 \tag{12}$$

Where

n = the sample size estimate,

S^2 = the sample variance,

Contd.

$Z_a/2$ = the normal vitiate equivalent to 1.96 for 95 per cent confidence level, and

d = the difference between sample mean and true mean.

The sample sizes used in the simulation runs were higher than the sample size estimates obtained from equation (12). Thus, the simulation model was completely validated.

Suggested Readings

- Severance, Frank L. (2002). *System Modelling and Simulation*. New York: John Wiley
- Law, A. M. and D. W. Kelton (1991). *Simulation Modelling and Analysis*. New York: McGraw-Hill.
- Rardin, R.L. and R. Uzsoy (2001). "Experimental Evaluation of Heuristic Optimization Algorithms: A Tutorial." *Journal of Heuristics*, 7 no 3: 261–304.
- Zanakis S. H., J. R. Evans and A. A. Vazacopoulos (1989). "Heuristic Methods and Applications: A Categorized Survey. *European Journal of Operational Research*, 43: 88–110.
- Glover, F. and M. Laguna (1997). *Tabu Search*. Hingham, MA: Kluwer Academic.
- Golden, B.L. and A. Assad (1988). *Vehicle Routing: Methods and Studies*. B.V. North-Holland: Elsevier Science Publishers.
- Morton, T.E. and D.W. Pentico (1993). *Heuristic Scheduling System: With Applications to Production Systems and Project Management*. New York: John Wiley.
- Goldberg, D.E. (2000). *Genetic Algorithms in Search, Optimisation and Machine Learning*. Singapore: Pearson Education.

QUESTIONS AND EXERCISES

1. Define heuristics and briefly explain when heuristics are used?
2. Compare artificial intelligence, heuristic problem solving, and simulation of human thoughts.
3. Briefly write about the desirable characteristics in the design of heuristic methods.
4. What is meta-heuristics?
5. How do we measure the quality of the heuristic solution?
6. Explain the merits and demerits of heuristic method.
7. One floor of a building has six office areas, which are all the same size. The current layout is shown here. The company feels that a lot of unnecessary movements are made between areas and would like to reduce this by at least 25 percent. During a random period records were kept of the number of movements between areas, which is shown in the following table. Use your own heuristic and show an improvement in the new layout proposed by your heuristic.

4	5	2
1	3	6

Original arrangement of office areas

		TO					
		1	**2**	**3**	**4**	**5**	**6**
	1	—	160	120	100	0	0
FROM	**2**	40	—	0	200	80	0
	3	60	0	—	0	80	10
	4	20	240	0	—	100	0
	5	0	0	100	0	—	120
	6	20	40	10	20	140	—

8. The aggregate, monthly demand for a family of products is shown below. If this is the only information available, suggest a monthly production schedule for the products using your own heuristics.

	January	February	March	April	May	June	July
Aggregate Demand	80	70	60	120	180	150	110

9. The minimum number of operators needed each day is as follows. What is the minimum number of operators should be employed, and how are they scheduled?

	Mon	Tue	Wed	Thu	Fri	Sat	Sun
Operators	1	2	3	3	4	4	0

10. Develop a simulation model to estimate the optimum number of coffee serving points needed to ensure that the probability of students waiting beyond a stated time is limited to a given probability. What data do you need for the model?

11. What is model sampling? In what simulation is it useful? Give some examples.

12. In simulation models, how do you ensure that the system is being modelled?

13. Select a few heuristic models from the literature used. Determine the type of heuristic developed.

14. How would you design an experiment to determine the relative effectiveness of various optimisation procedures? Give an example and demonstrate your answer.

15. Take the instances of the following familiar problems in the Indian urban context. Consider which scientific discipline or approaches can contribute to their solution. State how.

(a) Shortage of buses on certain routes in an urban transport system
(b) Planning of trees to aid abatement of air pollution in cities
(c) Location of dustbins in cities for solid waste disposal.
(d) Construction of subways/overbridges over roads for facilitating people crossing roads.
(e) Sequencing of power shout down in cities

16. Would you recommend experimental design or simulation for each of the following? Give reasons for your answer and suggest in some detail how you would make your design.

(a) Evaluation of alternate methods of line balancing
(b) A choice from several proposals of wage incentives
(c) Effect of levels of advertising and price reduction on a specific consumer product.
(d) Best design among the alternate designs of a workplace.
(e) Estimation of the level of acceptance of a new production control system by the organisation.

Part D

Research Design for Data Acquisition

CHAPTER 10

Measurement Design

- Introduction
- Primary Types of Measurement Scales
- Errors in Measurement
- Validity and Reliability in Measurement
- Types of Scaling (Scale Classification)
- Scale Construction Techniques

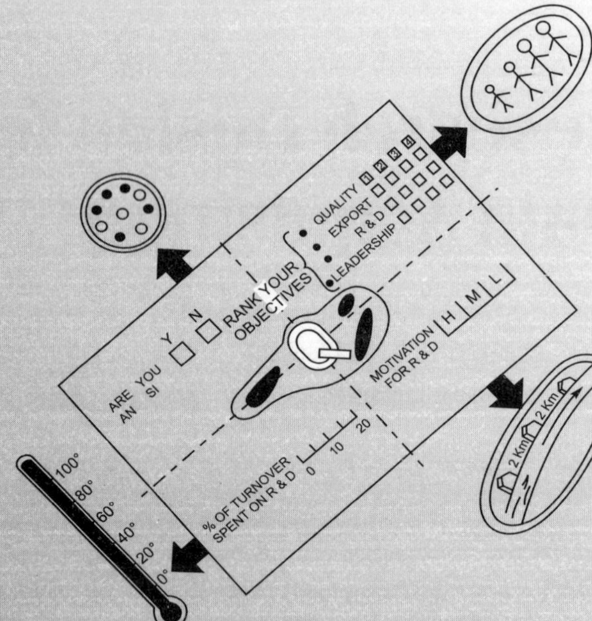

LEARNING OBJECTIVES

Upon completion of this chapter, you will be able to:

- ✓ Define measurement and scaling
- ✓ Study the different types of scales
- ✓ Learn about the errors of measurement
- ✓ Understand how to validate measurements
- ✓ Understand the concept of reliability of measurement
- ✓ Learn different ways of scaling research questions
- ✓ Become Familiar with unidimensional scale construction
- ✓ Appreciate multidimensional scaling

INTRODUCTION

In any research, hypotheses and theories are tested using empirical data already available or specially collected. In situations where data are collected specifically, the researcher exerts good control over the process of data collection to ensure good quality data. A research is as good as the data that is used in it. Data, when used for some quantitative analysis, as in hypothesis testing, is as good as the measurement done on it. It would not be an exaggeration to say, therefore, that a research is as good as the measurements made in it. Measurement is, thus, the most vital part of any research study.

Measuring physical entities used in physical sciences is comparatively easier and less prone to errors and approximations than the conceptual entities so much used in management theories. Measurement in respect of length, weight, inventory, number of rejections, and so on are easier than measuring concepts like attitude, morale, job satisfaction, perceived product quality and so forth. The second aspect related to measurement in management research is that many of the above mentioned constructs and concepts are multidimensional in nature, whereas physical entities (products, brands, and consumers) are unidimensional. Thus, in management research measurement becomes more involved and complex. Measurement is inalienably bound to scaling, which can be thought of as the continuum on which measurements are made and measured entity is located. There are three major ways of obtaining measured data. They are: (i) administering a standard instrument already developed, tested, and validated by others; (ii) administering an instrument that is specially developed by the researcher, (to be tested and validated); and (iii) record already measured data (such as inventory balances, absenteeism, numbers sold, and so on). Development of measurements and scales require scientific skills, considerable time, and effort. In this chapter, we will discuss some of the more important requirements. Definitions, the type of data required, scale construction, measurement errors, and validity and reliability of measurement will be discussed, in that order.

measured data
Measured data for a management research are obtained in three ways: administrating a standard instrument already developed, administering a specially designed instrument and extracting already measured data from records.

PRIMARY TYPES OF MEASUREMENT SCALES

Measurement has been defined as "the matching of an aspect of one domain to an aspect of another" (Stevens, 1968). Kerlinger (1973) has defined measurement as "the assignment of numbers to objects to represent amounts or degrees of a property possessed by all of the objects". In a simple way, measurement can be defined as the assignment of numbers (symbols) indicative of quantity to properties, characteristics, or behaviour of persons, objects, events, or states. The numbers (symbols) have the same relevant relationship to each other as do the things represented. Three important characteristics of numbers (symbols) are: (i) order—numbers are ordered, (ii) distance—difference between numbers are ordered; and (iii) origin—the series has a unique origin, which is indicated by number zero. The result of this is a scale of measurement.

scaling
Scaling is a procedure for attempting to determine quantitative measures of subjective abstract concepts.

In social sciences the term 'scaling' is applied to procedures attempting to determine quantitative measures of subjective abstract concepts. Scaling is defined as a "procedure for the assignment of numbers (or other symbols) to a property of objects in order to impart some of the characteristics of numbers to the properties in question" (Edwards, 1957).

Nominal Scales

nominal scale
This is a measurement procedure to classify objects, events and individuals into categories.

The lowest level of measurement is classification measurement, which consists simply of classifying objects, events, and individuals into categories. Each category is given a name or assigned a number; the numbers are used only as labels or type numbers without any relation like, order, distance, or origin between the numbered categories. This classification scheme is referred to as a nominal scale. Nominal scales are least restrictive and are widely used in social sciences and business research. Examples are telephone numbers or departmental accounting codes. There is one to one relation to each number and what it represents. Statistical calculations are not meaningful. Many researchers feel that this is not a scale at all (nominal means "in name only").

Examples

(i) Where do you live ______ ______ ______
City Town Village

(ii) Do you own a car Yes/No

Ordinal Scales

ordinal scale
This scale is used to measure data having transitivity property. It includes the characteristic of nominal scale in addition to indicating order.

These scales are used for measuring characteristics of data having transitivity property (that is, if $x > y$ and $y > z$, then $x > z$). They include the characteristics of the nominal scale plus an indicator of order. The task of ordering, or ranking, results in an ordinal scale, which defines the relative position of objects or individuals according to some single attribute or property. There is no determination of distance between positions on the scale. Therefore, the investigator is limited to determination of 'greater than', 'equal to', or 'less than' without being able to explain how much greater or less (the difference). Some of the examples of ordinal scales are costs of brands of a product and ordering of objectives according to their importance. Statistical positional measures such as median and quartile and ranking indexes can be obtained.

Examples

(i) Please rank the following objectives of the manufacturing department of your organisation according to their importance.

Objectives	**Rank**
Quality	______
Cost	______
Flexibility	______
Dependability	______

(ii) Please indicate your preference in the following pairs of objectives of R&D management.

Objective		Preference
1	2	(Sample Answer)
New product	New process	1
New product	Quality	1
New product	Cost	1
New process	Quality	2
New process	Cost	1
Quality	Cost	1

Derived Ranks		
Objective	No. of times ranked first	Derived rank
New Product	3	1
Quality	2	2
New process	1	3
Cost	0	4

Interval Scales

The interval scale has all the characteristics of the nominal and ordinal scales and, in addition, the units of measure (or intervals between successive positions) are equal. This type of scale is of a form that is truly 'quantitative', in the ordinary and usual meaning of the word. Almost all the usual statistical measures are applicable to interval measurement unless a measure implies knowing what the true zero point is. A simple example is a scale of temperature. Interval scales can be changed from one to another by linear transformation (for example, centigrade to fahrenheit degrees in temperature measurement).

interval scales
Interval scale possesses all the characteristic of nominal and ordinal scales. In addition, the units of measure (intervals between successive positions) are equal.

Example The link between the R&D and marketing departments in your organisation is:

Very strong	Strong	Moderate	Weak	Very weak
1	2	3	4	5

Ratio Scales

In essence, a ratio scale is an interval scale with a natural origin (that is, 'true' zero point). Thus, the ratio scale is the only type possessing all characteristics of the number system. Such a scale is possible only when empirical operations exist for determining all four relations: equality, rank-order, equality of intervals, and equality of ratios. Once a ratio scale has been established, its values can be transformed only by multiplying each value by a constant. Ratio scales are found more commonly in the physical sciences than in the social sciences. Measures of weight, length, time intervals, area, velocity, and so on, all conform to ratio scales. In the social sciences, we do find properties of concern that can be ratio scaled: money, age, years of education, and so forth. However, successful ratio scaling of behavioural attributes are rare. All types of statistical analyses can be used with ratio scaled variables.

ratio scale
A ratio scale is an interval scale with a natural origin (a true zero point) possessing all the characteristic of the number system.

Example What percentage of R&D expenditures is directed to new product development?

1	2	3	4	5
1–20	21–40	41–60	61–80	81–100

ERRORS IN MEASUREMENT

Precise and unambiguous measurement of variables is the ideal condition for research. In practice, however, errors creep into the measurement process in various ways and at various stages of measurement. The researcher must be aware of these potential error sources and make a conscious effort to eliminate them and minimise the errors. This is of primary importance in measurements using instruments specially designed by the researcher.

measurement errors
Major of these are: errors due to interviewer, errors due to instrument and respondent errors.

Variation of measurement consists of variations among different scales and errors of measurement. Sources of variation in measurement scales are presented in Table 10.1 (Lehmann and Hulbert, 1975).

Table 10.1 A Classification of Errors

Origin	*Type of Error*
1. Researcher	wrong question
	Inappropriate analysis
	Misinterpretation
	Experimenter expectation
	Communication
2. Sample	wrong target
	wrong method
	wrong people
3. Interviewer	Interviewer bias
	Interpretation
	Carelessness
4. Instrument	
(a) Scale	Rounding off
	Cutting off
(b) Questionnaire	Positional
	Ambiguity
	Evoked Set
	Construct-Question Incongrence
5. Respondent	Consistency/Inconsistency
	Ego/Humility
	Fatigue
	Lack of commitment
	Random

The major errors of concern are:

1. *Errors due to Interviewer bias* Bias on the part of the interviewer may distort responses. Rewording and abridging responses may introduce errors. Encouraging or discouraging certain viewpoints of the respondent, incorrect wording, or faulty calculation during preparation of data may also introduce errors.
2. *Errors due to the instrument* An improperly designed (questionnaire) instrument may introduce errors because of ambiguity, using words and language beyond the understanding of the respondent, and non-coverage of essential aspects of the problem or variable. Poor sampling will introduce errors in the measurement; whether the measurement is made at home or on site also may affect the measure.
3. *Respondent error* These may arise out of influences due to health problem, fatigue, hunger, or undesirable emotional state of the respondent. The respondent may not be committed to the study and may become tentative and careless. There may be genuine errors due to lack of attention or care while replying, that is, ticking a 'yes' when 'no' was meant. Further, errors may occur during coding, punching, tabulating, and interpreting the measures.

VALIDITY AND RELIABILITY IN MEASUREMENT

Knowing that errors will creep into measurements in practice, it is necessary to evaluate the accuracy and dependability of the measuring instrument. The criteria for such evaluation are validity, reliability, and practicality. The basic discussion on validity and reliability was presented in section on validity and reliability of experiments and quasi experiments of Chapter 6. In the following sections, they will be discussed with reference to measurements and measuring instruments (Judd and Mclleland 1998).

Validity refers to the extent to which a test/instrument measures what we actually wish to measure. Reliability has to do with the accuracy and precision of a measurement procedure.

Practicality is concerned with a wide range of factors of economy, convenience, and interpretability.

In any research, there are always measurement errors and non-sampling errors. There has been no accepted body of theory that may be used to predict either the direction or magnitude of these errors. One may ignore, estimate, or attempt to measure them. The measurement accuracy and measurement error can be defined as:

Measurement accuracy = r/t, and Measurement error = $(1 - r/t)$

Where r is the recorded sample value and

t is the true value

The attempt to measure t and compare it to r is concerned with the validity of the measurement. The measure of the variability in r is the reliability of the measurement. The works of Emory (1976), Tull and Albaum (1973), Nunnally (1967), and Sekaran (2000) discuss validity and reliability of measurement scales extensively.

Validity of Measurement

After a model has been chosen for the construction of a measuring instrument and the instrument has been constructed, the next step is to find out whether or not the instrument is useful. This step is usually spoken of as determining the validity of the instrument (Nunnally, 1967). A scale or a measuring instrument is said to possess validity to the extent to which differences in measured values reflect true differences in the characteristic or property being measured. Two forms of validity are mentioned in research literature. The external validity of research findings is their generalisability to " ... populations, settings, treatment variables, and measurement variables ..." (Tull and Hawkins, 1987). The **internal validity** of a research instrument is its ability to measure what it aims to measure.

Internal validity This is the extent to which differences found with a measuring tool reflect true differences among those being tested. The widely accepted classification of validity consists of three major forms: content, criterion-related, and construct.

Content validity Content validity of a measuring instrument is the extent to which it provides adequate coverage of the topic under study. Content validity has been defined as the representativeness of the content of a measuring instrument. If the instrument contains a representative sample of the universe of the subject matter of interest, then content validity is good. To evaluate the content validity of an instrument, one must first agree on what elements constitute adequate coverage of the problem, then determine what forms of these opinions constitute relevant positions on these topics. If the questionnaire adequately covers the topics that have been defined as the relevant dimensions, it is possible to conclude that the instrument has good content validity.

content validity
Content validity is the extent to which the instrument provides adequate coverage of the topic under study. This is judgmental in nature and requires, generally, a panel of judges and accurate definitions of the topic. Face validity is a minimum index of content validity.

The determination of content validity is judgmental and can be approached in several ways. First, the designer may himself determine the validity through a careful definition of the topic of concern, the items to be scaled, and the scales to be used. This logical process is somewhat intuitive and is unique to each research designer. A second way to determine content validity is to use a panel of persons to judge how well the instrument meets the standards. An example is provided in the Annexure 10.1.

Face validity This is a basic and the minimum index of content validity. Face validity indicates that the items that are supposed to measure a concept, on the face of it, do look like they are measuring the concepts. The commonly used other names of the content validity are intrinsic validity, circular validity, relevance, and representativeness.

criterion related validity
Is an external validity which reflects the success of measures used for some empirical estimating purpose.

Criterion-related validity This form of validity reflects the success of measures used for some empirical estimating purpose. One may want to predict some outcome or estimate the existence of some current behaviour or condition. These cases involve predictive and concurrent validity, respectively. They differ only in a time perspective. An opinionaire or opinion questionnaire that correctly forecasts the outcome of a union election has predictive validity. An observational method that correctly categorises families by current income class has concurrent validity. While these examples appear to have rather simple and unambiguous validity criteria, there are difficulties in estimating validity.

It is a must to assure that the validity criterion used itself is 'valid'. Thorndike and Hagen (1969) suggest that any criterion must be judged in terms of four qualities: relevance, freedom from bias, reliability, and availability.

Other authors have called predictive validity as empirical validity or statistical validity. An example of this is provided in Annexure 10.2.

Construct validity Construct validity testifies to how well the results obtained from the use of the measure fits the theory around which the test is designed. It is concerned with knowing more than just that a measuring instrument works. It is involved with the factors that lie behind the measurement scores obtained; with what factors or characteristics (that is, constructs) account for or explain the variance in measurement scores. One may also wish to measure or infer the presence of abstract characteristics for which no empirical validation seems possible. Attitude scales and aptitude and personality tests generally concern concepts that fall in this category. Even though this validation situation is much more difficult, it is necessary to have some assurance that the measurement has an acceptable degree of validity. In attempting to determine construct validity, one associates a set of other propositions with the results derived from using the measurement tool. If measurements on the devised scale correlate in a predicted way with these other propositions, it is easy to conclude that there is some construct validity.

multi trait – multi method
This method uses a matrix of correlations among the scores of the same trait or quality and the measurement methods. The largest correlation coefficient establishes the construct validity.

Construct validity is assessed through convergent validity and discriminant validity. Convergent validity is established when the scores obtained by two different instruments measuring the same concept are highly correlated. Discriminant validity is established when, based on theory, two variables are predicted to be uncorrelated, and the scores obtained by measuring them are indeed empirically found to be so.

One of the widely used methods of simultaneously establishing convergent and discriminant validity (construct validity) is the multi-trait multi-method matrix (MTMM), (Campbell and Fiske, 1959). The basic concept of multi trait-multi method matrix is that correlation among the scores of the same trait should be the largest correlations in the matrix (Refer Table 10.2).

Table 10.2 Multi-trait Multi-method Matrix

Construct (trait)	*Measurement method*	*Measure*	*Correlation Matrix*			
			M1	*M2*	*M3*	*M4*
C1	MM1	M1	1.00	0.92	0.30	0.28
C1	MM2	M2		1.00	0.50	0.22
C2	MM3	M3			1.00	0.83
C2	MM4	M4				1.00

The correlation between a measure of one trait (construct) and a measure of another construct should be smaller than the correlations between two measures of the same trait (construct). This would establish both convergent and discriminant validities.

Because of the common measurement effect, M2 is more highly correlated with M3 than those between M1-M3, M1-M4 and M2-M4 but will be lower than that between M1-M2 and M3-M4.

A single study doesn't establish construct validity. It is construed as an extending process of investigation; even tentative acceptance of construct validity demands some amount of aggregation of results of reliability and validity studies in a series. In any case it is not a certification of a measure (Peter, 1981). In literature, construct validity has been referred with different names such as trait validity and factorial validity. An example is provided in Annexure 10.3.

Reliability in Measurement

The reliability of a measure indicates the stability and consistency with which the instrument measures the concept and helps to assess the 'goodness' of a measure. A measure is reliable to the degree that it supplies consistent results. Reliability is a partial contributor to validity. A reliable instrument need not be valid, but a valid instrument is reliable. Reliability is not as valuable as validity, but is easier to assess. Reliable instruments can at least be used with confidence that a number of transient and situational factors are not interfering. They are robust instruments in that they work well under different conditions and at different times. This distinction of time and condition is the basis for identification of two aspects of reliability—stability and equivalence.

Stability The ability of a measure to maintain stability over time, despite uncontrollable testing conditions and the state of the respondents themselves, is indicative of its stability and low vulnerability to changes in the situation. With a stable measure we can secure consistent results with repeated measurements of the same person with the same instrument. It is often a simple matter to secure a number of repeat readings in observational studies but not so with questionnaires. Two tests of stability are test-retest reliability and parallel-form reliability.

Test-retest reliability The reliability coefficient obtained by the repetition of an identical measure on a second occasion is called test-retest reliability. Test-retest interviews are typically the only possible way to repeat measurements. When a questionnaire containing some items that are supposed to measure a concept is administered to a set of respondents now, and again to the same group, say, several weeks to few months later, then the correlation between the scores obtained at the different times from the same set of respondents is called the test-retest coefficient. The higher it is, the better the test-retest reliability, and hence the stability of the measure across time. But this test also has three measurement problems. If the time between measurements is short, the respondent may merely recall and repeat his earlier answers. The retest may also cause differences in transient factors (for example, the respondent may feel less on the second exposure to a question). The first measurement may also cause him to revise his opinions at the time of retesting. The reduction of these test-retest problems can be done in two ways. One is extension of the time interval between measurements so that the respondent will be less likely to remember his first answers. The second way is to divide respondents into two groups on a random basis, and then measure group A before the publicity and group B afterwards. The degree of stability can be determined by comparing results of repeated measurements. Along with repeated observations, we use statistical measures of dispersion, such as standard deviation or ranges of percentages.

test – retest reliability
This is a reliability coefficient obtained by repeating an identical measure on a second occasion. It is the correlation coefficient of measures obtained in the test and the retest.

Parallel-form reliability When responses on two comparable sets of measures tapping the same construct are highly correlated, there will be parallel-form reliability. Both forms have similar items and the same response format with only the wordings and the ordering of questions changed. This helps in establishing the error variability resulting from wording and ordering of the questions. If two such comparable forms are highly correlated, it is easy to conclude that the measures are reasonably reliable, with minimal error variance caused by wording, ordering, or other factors.

parallel-form reliability
When the responses on two comparable set of measures of the construct are highly correlated there will exist parallel form of reliability of the instrument.

Equivalence A second aspect of reliability considers how much error may be introduced by different investigators or different samples of the items being studied. Thus, while stability is concerned with personal and situational fluctuations from one time to another, equivalence is concerned with variations at one point in time among investigators and sample of items or with the internal consistency. A good way to test for the equivalence of measurements by two investigators is to compare their observations of the same events. We can give a similar type of test to interviewers by setting up an experimental comparison between them using test-retest situations.

equivalence
This is a kind of reliability which considers how much error is incurred when different investigators measure the same attribute in different conditions.

We test for item sample equivalence by using alternative sets of questions with the same person at the same time. The results of the two tests are then correlated. A second method, the

Split-Half Reliability technique, can be used when the measuring tool has a number of similar questions or statements in response to which the subject can express himself. The instrument is administered to the subject, and then the results are separated item wise into two randomly selected halves. The Spearman-Brown formula is applied:

$$R = n\ r/[1+(n-1)r]$$

Where

R = estimated reliability of the entire instrument

r = correlation coefficient between measurements

n = ratio of the number of items in the changed instrument to the number in the instrument

When $n = 2$, split-half reliability, $R' = [2r/(1+r)]$

These are then compared; if the results are similar, the instrument is said to have reliability in an equivalence sense. An example is provided in the Annexure 10.4 to highlight the reliability in measurement.

Inter-item consistency reliability is a test of the consistency of respondents' responses to all the items in a measure. To the degree that items are independent measures of the same concept they will be correlated with one another. The most popular test of inter-item consistency reliability is Cronbach's coefficient or Cronbach's alpha (Cronbach, 1951), which is used for multipoint scaled items, and the Kuder Richardson formulas (Kuder & Richardson, 1937) used for dichotomous items (Sekaran, 2000).

A series of two random subsets are chosen from the items. For each pair of subsets so chosen, the Spearman-Brown coefficient is calculated. The average of the series of coefficients generated gives the Cronbach alpha, which is a better indicator of reliability than the Spearman-Brown coefficient. A computer statistical package like SPSS calculates Cronbach alpha for a set of scaled homogeneous items.

Sometimes, we can combine our efforts to secure stability and equivalence in a single set of operations. One way is by giving alternative parallel tests at different times. Correlations of the results provides a combined index of reliability, which will be lower than either the separate stability or equivalence measures because it takes more sources of variation into account. A comparison of techniques of reliability is discussed by Peter (1979).

Practicality The scientific requirements of a project call for the measurement process to be reliable and valid, while the operational requirements call for it to be practical. Thorndike and Hagen (1969) define practicality in terms of economy, convenience, and interpretability.

TYPES OF SCALING (SCALE CLASSIFICATION)

There is no fixed way of classifying scales. From the point of view of management research, scales can be classified based on six different aspects of scaling.

- *Subject orientation* In this type of scaling, variations across respondents are examined. In this, the stimulus is (held constant) the same and difference in responses across respondents is studied. The stimulus-centered approach studies variations across different stimuli and their effect on the same individual.
- *Response form* Here the variation across both stimulus and subject is investigated. This is the most generally used type of scaling in data collection methods for research.
- *Degree of subjectivity* This reflects the fact that judgment and opinions play an important part in responses.
- *Scale properties* The scale could be nominal, ordinal, interval or ratio type.
- *Number of dimensions* This reflects whether different attributes or dimensions of the subject area are being scaled.
- *Scale construction technique* This indicates the technique of deriving scales—ad hoc, group consensus, single item, or a group of items, and whether statistical methods were employed or not.

Some of the more generally used scaling methods* are discussed below (McIver and Carminer, 1981).

Response Methods

Response methods/variability methods include rating techniques, ranking methods, paired comparison, and rank order scaling approach.

Rating scales A rating scale is a measuring instrument that requires the person doing the rating or observing to assign the person or object being rated directly to some point along a continuum, or in one of an ordered set of categories. Rating scales are used to judge properties of objects without reference to other similar objects. These ratings may be in such forms as 'like-dislike', 'approve-indifferent-disapprove', or other classifications using even more categories. There are many types of rating scales that are used in practice, differing in the fineness of the distinction they allow and in the procedures involved in the actual process of rating. The classification of rating scales, as given by Selltiz et al (1959), are graphic, itemised, and comparative. A graphic rating scale is one in which lines or bars are used in conjunction with descriptive phrases and is a common and simple form of scale. There are many varieties of graphic rating scales, namely, vertical segmented lines, continuous lines, unmarked lines, horizontal lines marked to create equal intervals, and so on. Other rating scale variants are three-point scales, four-point scales, five-point scales and longer scales. A second form, the itemised scale, presents a series of statements from which a respondent selects one as best reflecting his evaluation. These judgments are ordered progressively in terms of, more or less, some property. It is typical to use 5 to 7 categories, with each being defined or illustrated in words. Itemised rating scales are also referred to as category scales or numerical scales. The third type of rating scale is comparative scale where the ratings clearly imply relative judgment between positions. The positions on the scale are especially defined in terms of a given population or in terms of people of known characteristics.

rating scales
A rating scale is a measuring instrument that requires the person doing the rating to assign the person or object being rated to some point along the continuum or in one of the ordered set of categories.

Ranking scales In ranking scales, the respondent directly compares two or more objects and makes choices among them. Widely encountered is the situation where the respondent is asked to select one as the 'best' or the 'preferred'. When dealing with only two choices, this approach is satisfactory, but it may often result in the 'vote splitting' phenomenon when the respondent is asked to select the most preferred among three or more choices. This ambiguity can be avoided through the use of paired comparisons or rank ordering techniques.

ranking scales
A respondent directly compares two or more objects and makes choices among them. When large number of objects are involved choice becomes ambiguous. The ambiguity can be voided by using paired comparisons.

Method of paired comparisons With this technique, the respondent can express his attitudes in an unambiguous manner by making a choice between two objects. Typical of such a situation would be a product testing study where a new flavour of soft drink is tested against an established brand. In the general situation there are often many more than two stimuli to judge, resulting in a potentially tedious task for the respondents (there will be $n(n-1)/2$ judgments, where n is the number of stimuli). Using of these $n(n-1)/2$ judgements simultaneous evaluation of all stimuli objects is not possible in a simple manner. Thurstone developed an analytical procedure called 'law of comparative judgements' to derive quasi-intervally scaled paired comparison data (see Torgenson W.S. [1958] for details of this procedure).

Method of rank order Another comparative scaling approach is to ask respondents to rank their choices (if 5 items are chosen out of 10, only 5 need be ranked). This method is faster than paired comparisons and is usually easier and more motivating to the respondent. On the negative side, there is some doubt regarding how many stimuli may be handled by this method. Less than five objects can usually be ranked easily, but respondents may grow quite careless in ranking, say, ten or more items. In addition, the rank ordering is still an ordinal scale with all of its limitations.

---

* Some authors use the term "Monadic scaling techniques for interval and ratio scaling techniques and comparative scaling techniques for ordinal scaling techniques (also as non-metric scaling).

Example Following are the R&D objectives a firm generally meets with. Please indicate the objectives relevant to your R&D by ticking and rank them.

Objectives	Rank
1. New product development (NPTD)	——
2. New process development (NPSD)	——
3. Modification of existing product (MEPT)	——
4. Modification of existing process (MEPS)	——

A total of 200 respondents rank the four items of objectives as shown in the table below:

	First	Second	Third	Fourth
NPTD	96	52	20	32
MEPT	48	64	46	42
NPSD	42	46	34	78
MEPS	14	38	100	48

Is derived by weighting the number with the rank numbers assigned and summing up giving preference scores, for example,

NPTD – $(1 \times 96 + 2 \times 52 + 3 \times 20 + 4 \times 32) = 388$. Further, the following table (b) is formed.

Objective	Preference Score	Preference Rank order
NPTD	388	1
MEPT	482	2
NPSD	528	3
MEPS	582	4

New product development followed by modifying existing products are the top two preferences for the R&D objective.

Method of successive intervals Neither the paired-comparison nor the rank order method is particularly attractive when there are a large number of items to choose. Under these circumstances, the method of successive intervals is sometimes used. In this method, the subject is asked to sort the items into piles or groups representing a succession of values. An interval scale can be developed from these sortings.

Quantitative Judgment Methods

These include direct judgment methods, fractionation, and constant sum methods.

Direct judgment method The respondent is required to give a numerical rating to each stimulus, with respect to some designated characteristic. In the unlimited type, the respondent may choose his or her own number in graphical method to position the rating on a line, as shown.

|--|　　　| 1 | | | | | | 10 |

Unlimited response (graphical)　　　Limited response (graphical)

In limited type, the respondent has limited choice, as given by the researcher.

Fractionation methods In fractionation, a number denoting the ratio between two stimuli, with respect to some characteristic, is estimated.

Constant sum methods Constant sum methods are used to standardise the scale across respondents by requiring them to allocate a given total score (say 100) among the stimuli (total adds upto a constant and, hence, the name).

SCALE CONSTRUCTION TECHNIQUES

Scale construction techniques refer to the construction of sets of rating scales (questionnaire) that are carefully designed to measure one or more aspects of a person's attitude or belief towards some object. An individual's rating of a particular item in questionnaire is not of much concern. The individual's responses to the various item scales are summed up to get a single score for the individual.

scale construction techniques
These refer to construction of sets of rating scales (questionnaire) which are carefully designed to measure one or more aspects a persons' beliefs or attitudes. Scale construction methods are judgement scaling, factor scales and multi dimensional scaling.

In any data collection method using variability methods, raw data responses are obtained. The data are ordinal-scaled and a model or a technique of scaling for transforming this into scale values that are interval-scaled will be required. Thurstone's Case V scaling is relevant in this case. Raw data obtained from judgment methods can be scaled using the semantic differential method of Osgood, et al (1957).

Judgment Methods

Arbitrary scales It is possible to design arbitrary scales by collecting a number of items that are unambiguous and appropriate to a given topic. Arbitrary scales are easy to develop and can be designed to be highly specific to the particular case and content. They can provide much useful information, and can be quite adequate if developed by one who is skilled in scale design.

Consensus scaling In this approach, the selection of items is made by a panel of judges who evaluate proposed scale items and determine: (i) whether the item belongs in the topic area, (ii) its ambiguity, and (iii) the level of attitude that the scale item represents. The most widely known form of this approach is the Thurstone differential scale. Differential scales approach, known as the Method of Equal Appearing Intervals, was an effort to develop an interval scaling method for attitude measurement (Judd and Mclelland, 1998).

Thurstone differential scale
This scale is constructed using consensus of a panel of judges with equal intervals appearing on the scale. Is widely used for attitude measurement.

Item analysis In this procedure, a particular item is evaluated on the basis of how well it discriminates between persons whose total score is low. The most popular type of scale using this approach is the summated scale.

Summated scale This consists of a number of statements that express either a favourable or unfavourable attitude towards the object of interest. The respondent is asked to agree or disagree with each statement. Each response category is assigned a numerical score to reflect its degree of attitude favourablity, and the scores are summed algebraically to measure the respondent's attitude. The most frequently used form of scale is patterned after the one devised by Likert (Kerlinger, 1973).

Example of Likert Scale:

The objectives of the R&D department of your organisation are clearly set.

Strongly Disagree	Disagree	Neutral	Agree	Strongly Agree
1	2	3	4	5

Likert scale
This mostly used scale is based on judgement method using an agree-disagree format. Each category is assigned a numerical score. The scores on the scale are summed (summated scaling) up to get the total score for an individual.

Cumulative scales These scales are constructed as a set of items with which the respondent indicates agreement or disagreement. Total scores on cumulative scales have the same meaning. Given a person's total score it is possible to estimate which items were answered positively and which negatively. The major scale in category is the Guttman scalogram. Scalogram analysis is a procedure for determining whether a set of items forms a unidimensional scale, as defined by Guttman (1950). A scale is said to be unidimensional if the responses fall into a pattern in which endorsement of the item reflecting the extreme position results also in endorsing all items that are less extreme.

Case-V scaling Here the scaling uses a model of comparative judgment. If all of a group of subjects prefer A to B and only 60 percent prefer B to C, then Thurstone's model can help develop an interval scale from these stimulus-comparison proportions (Figure 10.1).

If R_j and R_k are mean values of the two judgment processes, then interval $R_j - R_k = Z_{jk}$ (Edwards, 1957).

Factor Scales

The term factor scales is used here to identify a variety of techniques that have been developed to deal with two problems that have been glossed over so far. They are (i) how to deal more adequately with the universe of content that is multidimensional, and (ii) how to uncover underlying dimensions that have not been identified. The different techniques used are latent structure analysis, factor analysis, cluster analysis, and metric and non-metric multidimensional scaling.

The Q-Sort technique This is similar to the summated scale. The task required of responder is to sort a number of statements into a predetermined number of categories.

Example (seven items on the scale):

Item*	Subject			
	A	B	C	D
1	+1	+1	−1	−1
2	0	0	0	0
3	+1	0	0	-1
4	−1	−1	+1	+1
5	0	0	0	0
6	−1	−1	+1	+1
7	0	+1	−1	−1

* Most agreed—1, 2 (two items); Neutral—3, 4, 5 (three items); Least agreed—6, 7 (two items)

Responses of the subjects A, B, C, and D are given in the table above. It can be noted that pair A and B and pair C and D seem 'most alike'. A subject's scores are correlated with every other subject and factor or cluster analysis is performed to get the groupings (Kerlinger, 1973).

Semantic differential (SD) This is a type of quantitative judgment method that results in assumed interval scales. This scale is obtained on factor analysis of these assumed scale values and can be used rather easily and usefully in decisional survey research employing multivariate

Fig. 10.1 Thurstone scale V

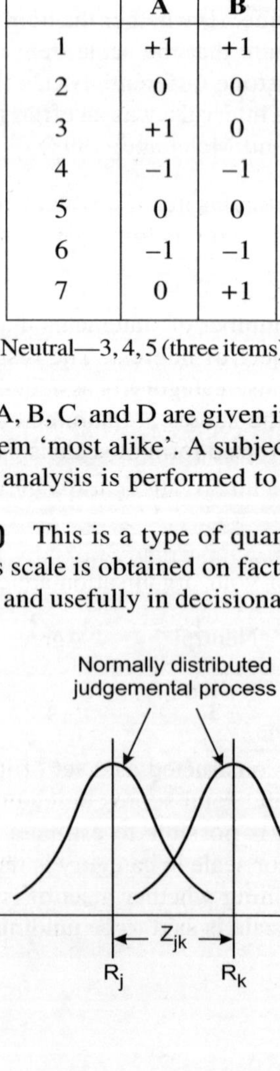

statistics. This scaling method, developed by Osgood and his associates (Osgood et al, 1957), is an attempt to measure the psychological meaning of an object to an individual. It is based on the proposition that an object can have several dimensions of connotative meanings, which can be located in multidimensional property space, in this case called semantic space, for example, both direction and intensity. One of the ways this is done is requiring the respondent to rate assuming equal intervals on a set of bipolar adjectives (like extremely clear —- extremely ambiguous; extremely strong — extremely weak, and so forth) and then arranging integer values to these intervals. Averages of these scores for two groups can be compared to get a semantic differential profile. Some of the major uses have been to compare company 'images' and brands, determine attitudinal characteristics of consumers, and analyse the effectiveness of promotional activities.

semantic differential (SD)
This is a quantitative judgement method that results in assumed interval scales. Uses bipolar adjectives like 'extremely clear' and 'extremely ambiguous'. Measures images, effectiveness, attitudes, etc.

Example Do you like the taste of apples?

Like extremely	Like	Neutral	Dislike	Dislike extremely
5	4	3	2	1

Stapel scale This is a modified version of semantic differential. It is an even numbered non-verbal rating scale using single adjectives instead of bipolar opposites. Both intensities are measured concurrently. Neither the equality of intervals nor the additivity of ratings of a respondent is assumed (Crespi, 1961). A format is shown below.

```
Reliable        |----------|----|----|------------------|
               +5         +1   −1                     −5
```

Multidimensional scaling Multidimensional scaling (MDS) is a powerful mathematical procedure that can systematise data by representing the similarities of objects spatially as in a map (Schiffman, 1981). In multidimensional scaling models, the existence of an underlying multidimensional space is assumed. This term describes a set of techniques that deal with property space in a more general way than does the semantic differential. With multidimensional scaling it is possible to scale objects, individuals, or both, with a minimum of information. A detailed discussion on MDS is presented in Section on MDS in Chapter 18.

Standardised instruments As in many instances of research, an available, standardised instrument may be selected to collect data instead of developing one. These standard instruments are developed and tested by experts and the results of using them may be compared with the results of other studies : A large number of standardised instruments are available for testing a variety of topics like personality, achievement, performance, intelligence, general aptitudes, and projective tests (sub-topics are also covered by them). Proper selection of instrument is important for its use in a specific research. For this purpose, specifications; conditions for use; details regarding validity, reliability, and objectivity; directions for administration; scaling; and interpreting should be considered carefully (for greater details about this refer to Conoley & Kramer 1989, Keyser and Sweetland 1986, Mitchell 1983).

SUMMARY

Measurement is the assignment of numbers to objects or is the amount of property possessed by objects. Since highly abstract and imprecisely defined constructs and properties are present in social science and management, measurement problems are specially difficult in research. The primary type of measurement scales used are nominal scales, which simply categorise objects; ordinal scales, which rank objects or attributes; interval scales, which are truly quantitative, enabling the use of statistical methods on data; and ratio scales, which are interval scales with natural origin.

In management and social sciences, the variables and constructs are highly abstract and their measurements tend to be indirect. Therefore, validity and reliability assume great importance. Validity means freedom from systematic errors or bias in measurement. It indicates the appropriateness of a measuring instrument. Reliability means freedom from variable errors or errors in repetitive use of the measure. It is the accuracy or precision of a measuring instrument.

A scale or instrument is said to possess validity when the extent of differences in measured values reflect true differences in the characteristics measured. There are two forms of validity—content validity, which is the extent of coverage of the topic being measured; and criterion related validity, which reflects the success of measures used for an empirical estimating purpose. By far, the most important form of validity is construct validity, which testifies how well the result obtained from the use of the measure fits the theory, which it is supposed to support. A valid instrument is reliable but a reliable instrument is not necessarily valid.

Reliability in measurement means stability of measurement under different conditions and at different times. Two tests of stability are: (i) test-retest reliability and (ii) parallel-form reliability. When different sets of items or two investigators measure a construct, how closely they agree gives the equivalence. A measure of the equivalence is obtained using the Spearman-Brown formula on the two measures. Cronbach alpha, based on the above formula, is a more popularly used measure of reliability.

There are several types of scaling methods; response methods, which includes direct rating, comparison, and ranking methods. Scale construction techniques refer to the construction of sets of rating scales (as in questionnaires). These are carefully designed and most often standardised for general use in research. These consist of: (i) consensus scales, which a panel of experts devise; (ii) summated scales where item analysis is used (and of which Likert scale is an example); and (iii) factor scales that are used to develop measures of dimensions of complex constructs using multivariate statistical techniques. Q-sort, semantic differential, and stapel scales are examples of factor scales. Multidimensional scaling techniques are used when measuring multidimensional complex constructs and they use proximity or similarity data. They reveal the dimensions relevant to the subjects.

ANNEXURE 10.1

Illustrative Example—Content Validity

An instrument for classification of decision-making styles of manufacturing executives was designed and tested* (Vijaya Kumar, et al, 1990). The instrument was intended primarily to classify executives as analytic and heuristic. These styles were defined based on the research of several authors on what constitutes analytic and heuristic. An integrated definition was evolved. A total of 54 questions embodying the indicators were offered to over 100 executives to judge them as analytic or heuristic in their opinion. The results were statistically analysed and 18 questions per style were extracted. In a second voting, these were condensed to 20 in all (10 per each style). Three situational factors were included to test these questions. The content validity was thus established on the basis of the judgment of the executives and the earlier theories and constructs related to decision-making style. The statistical procedure was used only to refine the judgments of the executives. The following simple example indicates the analysis followed in establishing content validity.

A statement of the questionnaire gets the following response.

Number responding	= 100
Analytical	= 89
Heuristic	= 10
Undecided	= 1
Analytical	= 89/99 = 89.9 %

Contd.

Heuristic = 10/99 = 10.1 %
= 100/((0.899*0.101)/99) = 3.03 %

For 99 per cent confidence level, the true estimate of proportion for the population will fall within 89.9 per cent + 2.58 × 3.03 (Maximum 97.71 per cent and Minimum 82.09 per cent) for analytical and within 10.1 per cent + 2.58 × 3.03 (Maximum 17.91 per cent and Minimum 2.29 per cent) for heuristic. That is, at least 82.09 per cent of the population would have rated the status analytical with a probability of 99 per cent. From the results obtained, only those items which scored more than 70 per cent were taken as the initial set of elements.

ANNEXURE 10.2

Illustrative Example—Concurrent and External Validity

For the instrument discussed as an example under content validity, the concurrent and external validities were established as follows. A 'decision profile form' was designed with a view to obtaining a self rating score, and also the superior's rating score of the respondent.

- The definitions of two styles were offered as 'P' type decision-making and not as analytical and heuristic.
- Using these definitions, ratings were obtained in the following format on a ten-point scale.

Type 'P'

Never 1 2 3 4 5 6 7 8 9 10 Always

Type 'Q'

Never 1 2 3 4 5 6 7 8 9 10 Always

These ratings were obtained both by the respondent for himself (which is a self rating score), and by his superior for the respondent (which is the superior's rating score). The questionnaire was also filled in by the respondents. They were scored simply as the total number of items generally agreed (GY), separately for analytic items and heuristic items. These are termed individual score for decisions for one's self and individual score for decisions for superior. The concurrent validity of the instrument was determined by finding the correlations between the individual's scores for decisions for self and self rating scores; and the correlation between the individual scores for decision for the superior and the superior's rating scores of the individual. Significant high correlations for the above two sets of scores indicate the desired validity.

Further, total scores of 'analytic' items, and total scores of 'heuristic' items were checked for correlation. If the two types of items are orthogonal and independent, we expect an insignificant correlation coefficient close to zero, and if they are significantly negatively correlated, then our contention that they belong to the same continuum would be borne out empirically. The decision profile form and the questionnaire were administered to a random sample of respondents from a group of production executives. Their responses were collected on a ten-point scale, as explained above.

The 'analytic' and 'heuristic' scores obtained for decisions made for one's self were correlated with the self rating scores of the individual respondents for the purpose of validation. Significant high correlation would indicate the validity of this questionnaire.

Simultaneously, yet another 'decision profile form' was given to the immediate superior of the above mentioned production executives who responded to the questionnaire. The decision profile form, on completion by the immediate superior, would indicate the level of his subordinates' decision-making capability, again on a ten-point scale. Such rating by the superior concerned was obtained without the knowledge of the subordinates. As part of the validation process, the questionnaire was administered to 100 executives, and their superiors were administered the rating forms. Similarly, the questionnaire, and later, a self rating form were administered to 100 other executives. Only 29 of the former, and 49 of the latter responded.

Results For a sample of 49, the correlation coefficient between the self scores and self rating scores for the analytic style was 0.60682, significant at 0.10 level (correlation coefficients would be 0.288 at 0.05 level and 0.372

Contd.

at 0.01 level, respectively). This validates the second portion concerning the analytical decisions for superiors. For the same sample, the correlation coefficient between scores of decision for superiors, and scores of superior's rating for heuristic style is 0.27153. This marginally fails to be significant at 0.05 level. However, the reliability of the instrument is sometimes taken as a measure of its validity and in view of the high reliability of the instrument, this failure is not considered serious.

ANNEXURE 10.3

Illustrative Example—Construct Validity

John and Reve (1982) developed an instrument (questionnaire with scaling) for assessing dyadic relationships in marketing channels. Multiple items were developed for each variable. The scales and the response formats were finalised using a pilot study. The core of the study was the assessment of construct validity of the measures developed for the inter-organisational dyadic structure and sentiment variables. Three dimensions of construct validity were considered and they are: (i) internal consistency as validity, (ii) convergent validity, and (iii) discriminant validity.

Reliability and internal consistency were assessed in two separate procedures. To assess internal consistency, the researcher analysed the pool of scale items developed for each variable by using item-total correlations and common factor analysis. Cronbach's alpha was estimated for the unidimensional scales that were extracted. The convergent validity was assessed by analysing multi-trait multi-method matrices of correlations where different structural and sentimental variables constituted the traits and the instruments from the wholesalers and retailers constituted the methods. The criterion of maximally different method was met. The discriminant validity was simultaneously assessed with convergent validity by using the analysis of covariance. The results showed that the scale items having higher scale reliability were distinctly different for wholesalers than for retailers. The convergent and discriminant validity results showed that validity was accomplished. However, the MTMM matrix of sentimental variables showed very low correlations, indicating a lack of ability to discriminate in cross-construct correlations. The same was tested in the structural equation analysis used in the study.

ANNEXURE 10.4

Illustrative Example—Reliability in Measurement

The equivalence reliability for the instrument discussed earlier was established under validation as follows:

To establish reliability, the split-half technique was chosen in order to check the internal consistency of the measuring instrument. A correlation analysis was made between the split-halves on a predominant sample of 150 executives. It was found that all the reliability coefficients using split-half method were significant at 0.01 level. Thus, we can conclude that the instrument is valid and reliable.

The formula used to arrive at the reliability coefficient is the 'Spearman Brown' formula (Anastasi, 1966):

$$r = 2\,r'/(1 + r')$$

Where

r = reliability coefficient of the whole test and

r' = reliability of the half-test, found experimentally.

When the reliability coefficient of the half-test (r') is 0.50, for example, the reliability coefficient of the whole test r by the above formula is: (2x0.5)/(1+0.5) or 0.667.

The whole test reliability coefficients are shown in Exhibit 10.1 (these are significant at 0.01 level). Thus, the instrument is considered to measure the true style reliably.

Contd.

Sample	For One's Self		For Subordinates		For Supervisors	
N = 150 #	Heuristic 0,7998	Analytic 0.7204	Heuristic 0.5130	Analytic 0.5070	Heuristic 0.5360	Analytic 0.6550

Note: # All values are significant at 0.01 level

Exhibit 10.1 Reliability coefficient for test

Suggested Readings

- Cox, T. F. and M. A. Cox (2001). *Multidimensional Scaling*, 2d ed. London: Chapman and Hall.
- Judd, C. M. and G.H. Mclleland (1998). "Measurement", in D.T. Gilbert, S T Fiske and G Lindzey (eds). *Handbook Social Psychology*, 4th ed. pp. 180–232 McGraw Hill.
- McIver, J. P. and E. G. Carmines (1981). *Unidimensional Scaling*. New Delhi: Sage Publications.
- De Vellis, Robert F. (2002). *Scale Development—Theory and Applications*. New Delhi: Sage Publications.

QUESTIONS AND EXERCISES

1. For what type of problem and under what circumstances would you find the following data gathering techniques most appropriate?
   (a) Likert scale
   (b) Questionnaire
   (c) Interview
   (d) Observation
   (e) Q-Sort
2. Construct a questionnaire that could be administered to a group of supervisors for the following topics.
   (a) Reasons for workers leaving the organisation.
   (b) What could be done to improve the quality on the shop floor?
   (c) Assessment of non-work interests of the workers.
   (d) Manager's interests in the welfare of workers.
3. Construct suitable scales for the following measurement situations.
   (a) Evaluation of worker performance and supervisor performance.
   (b) Assessing the organisational climate in an organisation.
   (c) The level of technology in production operations.
   (d) The degree of integration of production, R & D, and marketing.
4. When collecting facts, which one would you prefer to use—free answer, answer to a multiple choice question, or answer to a dichotomous question?
5. Evaluate the following questions.
   (a) What was the total sales of all products in your organisation last year?
   (b) Do you think your organisation encourages innovative behaviour? Evaluate on a scale. Very Strongly – ranging from not at all.
   (c) When did you last disagree with your boss?
   (d) As a manager of production, what decision would do you take with respect to inventories?

(e) How many meetings, on an average, do you attend every month?
(f) How do you rate your supervisor X? Evaluate on a scale of outstanding –satisfactory –poor.
(g) Have you changed your jobs often? YES/NO
(h) Please indicate performance of the water pump supplied to you, on a scale ranging from excellent to poor
(i) What improvements do you think should be made in the pumps?

6. Explain the concepts: (a) Scaling, (b) Operational definition, (c) Stimulus, (d) Proximity, (e) Configuration, (f) Latent structure, and (g) Trait validity.
7. Which of the definitions is relevant for measurement purposes? Why?
   (a) Ostensive definition.
   (b) Verbal definition.
   (c) Descriptive definition.
   (d) Operational definition.
   (e) Conceptual definition.
8. What are the situational characteristics of a measurement? Give examples.
9. Give a conceptual and two or more operational definitions for each of the following concepts.
   (a) Satisfied customer
   (b) Not meeting customer demands
   (c) Direct overheads
   (d) Financial implications
   (e) Worker participation
   (f) Manufacturing excellence
10. Develop scales for the operational definitions in Question 9.
11. Develop four different scales for measuring brand loyalty—one nominal, one ordinal, one interval, and one ratio.
12. Examine management literature (in the area of your interest where the measurement problems are tricky. Search and note down the definitions used by the authors and the scales used). Can you find an alternate operational definition and an alternate scaling procedure?
13. When is multi-dimensional scaling useful in measurement?
14. Give an example to illustrate the use of the following 10 scales. Develop the scale.
   (a) Non-comparative graphic rating scales
   (b) Non-comparative itemised rating scale
   (c) Comparative graphic rating scales
   (d) Comparative itemised rating scale
   (e) Paired comparisons
   (f) Rank order scales
   (g) Constant sum scales
   (h) Semantic differential scales
   (i) Stapel scales
   (j) Likert scales
15. Choose a hypothesis with the help of your guide or one that is available in literature, suitable for verification using a field survey with a questionnaire. Develop a questionnaire indicating scales and the variables. Discuss your questionnaire.
16. Construct a short rating scale to be used for the evaluation of the teaching performance of a new professor.
17. Construct a Likert type questionnaire for the following problems:
   (a) The members of the faculty of an institution of advanced learning taking up consultancy work.
   (b) Religious activities in an industrial organisation.
   (c) R&D to be directed to new product development.
   (d) Inadequate top management support to self development of employee in an organisation.
18. What statistical techniques can be used with a nominal scale?
19. Give examples of situational characteristics as components of measurement.

20. What kind of scale is appropriate for the following? Discuss how you arrived at your answer.
   (a) Determining the percentage of men in a town who require vitamin supplements.
   (b) Determining kind of top management support desired by employees for creative contribution to the organisation
   (c) Determining the average proportion of spare time scientists in R&D of an organisation require
   (d) Determining whether the company adopt flexible working hours for its employees

21. Develop different scales or measuring corporate dependency on universities for R&D. One nominal, one ordinal, one interval, and one ratio.

22. Search for published papers in good journals to give you atleast two examples of nominal, ordinal, interval, and ratio scales and describe them.

23. Develop sound measurements for the following.
   (a) Product leadership
   (b) Customer satisfaction
   (c) Top management support
   (d) Linkage between two departments
   (e) Effectiveness of models in decision making
   (f) Technology upgradation

24. How is internal comparison reliability different from split-half reliability ?

25. Can you group the following nine validity terms into two major categories? If not, explain why? If yes, categorise them giving reasons.
   (a) Content validity
   (b) Face validity
   (c) Criterion validity
   (d) Concurrent validity
   (e) Predictive validity
   (f) Construct validity
   (g) Convergent validity
   (h) Discriminant validity

26. What are the indicators of accuracy in measurement?

27. What are the problems of external validation? Discuss with examples.

28. How is construct validity achieved by achieving convergent and discriminant validities?

29. Which is more important in measurement related to decisional research, reliability or validity? Give reasons for your answer.

30. Select two research papers dealing with multi-trait multi-method matrix used in establishing validity. Compare them. Present them to a group, giving differences and similarities.

31. Select two recent research papers describing the development of a measuring instrument. Compare their validation procedures. Are there differences? If yes, explain why.

CHAPTER 11

Sample Design

- Introduction
- Non-probability Sampling
- Probability Sampling
- Determination of Sample Size
- Illustrative Examples of Sample Size Determination

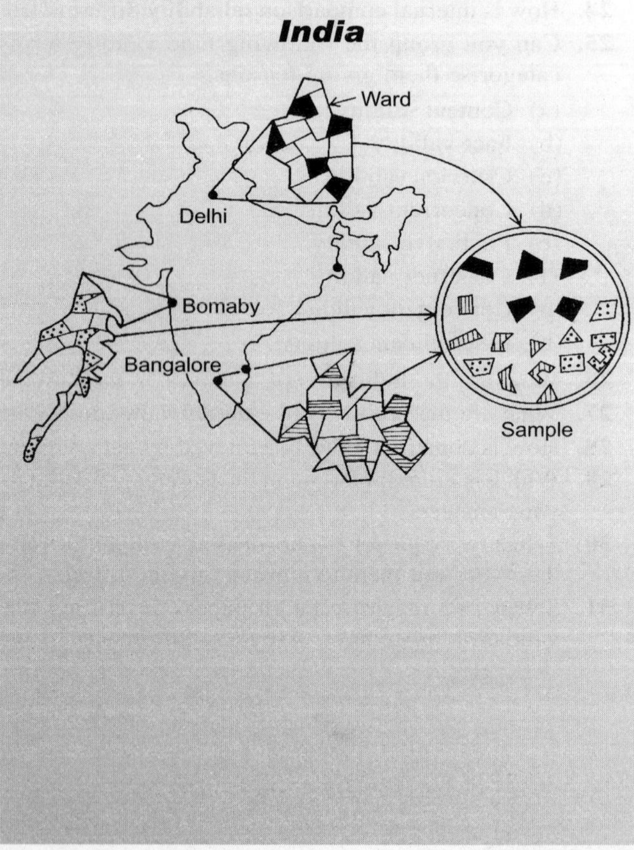

LEARNING OBJECTIVES

Upon completion of this chapter, you will be able to:

- ✓ Appreciate the significance of sampling in the overall research process
- ✓ Understand that sampling involves judgement for sampling design and statistics for sample size
- ✓ Identify errors associated with sampling and how to minimise them
- ✓ Enumerate steps in the sampling process
- ✓ Study the broad features of the more common types of sampling
- ✓ Learn to match the data collection situation with appropriate sample design
- ✓ Understand that design needs to meet several objectives in practical research sampling
- ✓ Compute sample size under several types of sampling

INTRODUCTION

A sample is used when it is not possible or practical to make all possible observations of a phenomenon that is being studied. Measurements are made on the sample characteristics and are used to estimate the characteristics of the larger group. Thus, samples enable parsimony of data collection effort. Collectively, the entire group of study objects is called the population. These may be people, geographic areas, organisations, products, services, and so on. If the entire group of study objects are investigated, then it is census. A sample may be one object (smallest sample) or one less than the population (largest sample).

The population may be of any size and may cover any geographic area. Therefore, the largest population, which is the ideal population regarding which the researcher would like to generalise his findings, rarely exists. Available population (which is accessible) is the practical population with which the researcher has to deal with. Therefore, he seeks a representative sample from a restricted portion of a population and tries to spell out details so that the relevance of the results to other portions of the population can be checked.

The terms 'population' and 'sample' are relative. The aggregate of elements that constitute a population for one purpose may be a sample for another. Consider, for example, average investments in R&D in small scale industries in Karnataka are obtained by considering all SSI units in it as population and a sample is taken from it for estimation purposes. If, however, we take all SSI units in Karnataka and compute the average investments in R&D for the entire country then that would be sample in the second instance. Further, populations are usually finite, that is, possible to count. In research, when the population is very large, it is practically considered infinite population.

The problem of sampling is to ensure that the sample is in some sense a fair representation of the underlying population. Ideally, selection procedures should be such that every individual in the population has an equal chance of being chosen. The population may consist of sub-populations of varying sizes, or the purpose of sampling may be to select special individuals in the population leading to different conditions of sampling. A sampling method has to be chosen to meet these conditions. Two questions that are to be answered in the use of a sampling method are:

sampling method
This answers two questions: How many observations should be made or subjects should be selected (size)? Which subjects should be selected (design)? There are two classifications of methods: non-probability methods and probability methods.

1. How many observations should be made or how many individuals should be chosen? This is a question related to sampling size.
2. Which sub-set of elements or environments should be selected? This is a question related to sampling design.

Samples serve to quickly and economically estimate certain properties of the population. However, estimates of the population parameters (means and variances), based on the mea-

sample size
Sample size may be determined based on judgement or statistically on the requirements of error and confidence.

surements of statistics of the sample are always associated with errors. The larger the sample size, the greater the confidence with which the estimates of the population can be obtained. Therefore, it is necessary, in any research using sampling methods, to make specific statements on the error (precision) and the confidence with which one can say this error is within stated limits. Precision is measured in terms of standard error of estimate—the smaller the standard error of an estimate, the higher the precision of the estimate. The sample size is determined based on the requirements of error and confidence.

Another type of error in sampling is bias. Bias indicates a consistently higher or lower value of estimated means as compared to the true population mean. A truly representative sample reduces the bias. Thus, the second requirement of sampling is to ensure this by careful selection of the sub-set.

sampling design
In sampling design elements are selected individually (unrestricted) or in a controlled way (restricted) from a list (sampling frame) of all objects in the population.

There are two aspects in sampling design. The first is the selection of elements from the population and the second is the basis on which representativeness of the sample is obtained.

The selection of the elements individually from large populations is called unrestricted sampling. When the element selection is controlled, the sampling is restricted sampling.

Often, in sampling design, the researcher uses a sampling frame (target, population), that is, a list of all objects in the population (for example, industrial directory for organisational selection, telephone directory for consumer surveys, and so forth). Generally, the sampling frame is smaller than the population.

Sampling Process

In Chapter 2 we outlined a six-step sampling process. Some details of the steps are provided in the following, with the illustration of an example.

Step 1—Definition of population A population is defined in terms of (1) elements, (2) sampling units, (3) extent, and (4) time.

In a survey of manufacturing organisations, the population was defined as:

Element—manufacturing, planning and control activity

Sampling unit—batch manufacturing organisation in engineering industries

extent—have been manufacturing engineering goods

time—the past two years

Step 2—Specification of sampling frame For probability sampling one has to have a sampling frame. Errors may occur when the researcher fails to access the elements through telephone or from industrial directories. In non-probability sampling, convenience or referrals may suffice to specify the sample; the researcher always utilises his/her own sense of judgment.

Example Government publication on industries, listing of batch manufacturing engineering firms in the Bombay Stock Exchange Directory, and the Maheswari Industrial Directory of India.

Step 3—Specification of the Sampling unit It is the basic unit containing the elements of the population.

Example Heads of manufacturing divisions like Directors, Vice Presidents, or General Managers were the sampling units directly approached in the selected organisations.

Step 4—Selection of sampling method Sampling method is the way in which the sample units are selected.

Example Use of check sampling method in an exploratory study. The method includes the selection criteria or just availability, if the number in the population is not large.

Step 5—Determination of the sample size The number to be sampled can be decided on statistical analysis when the sample size is large. It can be modified by considerations of availability, cost, and accessibility.

Example Size of the sample is based on availability.

Steps 4 and 5 are discussed in detail in the following section.

Sampling methods Sampling methods can be broadly classified into non-probability sampling and probability sampling, as given below:

Non-probability sampling	Probability sampling
(a) Quota sampling	(a) Simple random sampling
(b) Convenience sampling	(b) Stratified random sampling (proportionate)
(c) Judgement sampling	(c) Stratified random sampling (disproportionate)
(d) Purposive sampling	(d) Cluster sampling (systematic)
	(e) Cluster sampling (area)

NON-PROBABILITY SAMPLING

Non-probability sampling methods have a judgemental element somewhere in the procedure. Samples obtained by them are not representative of the population. However, they may yield good parameter estimates; objective estimates of precision and confidence cannot be obtained.

non-probability sampling
This is a judgement based procedure. It can be representative but precision and confidence cannot be obtained.

Quota sampling This is the most commonly used non-probability sampling method. Rough proportions of sub-classes (strata) in the population are estimated from an outside source (say, census). The number to be sampled in each sub-class is in exact proportion of sample size as the sub-class population is in the total population. The individual units in each strata/sub-class are chosen by the researcher based on judgement. Therefore, selection bias will be present in this type of sampling.

Example The overall work force n of a firm may be classified into two or three skill categories or grades n_g. If a number of individuals from any grade s_g are selected by judgement, then the sampling is quota sampling if

$$\frac{n_g}{n} = \frac{s_g}{S}$$

where S is the total number sampled.

Judgment sampling In this sampling procedure, a sample is obtained on the basis of sound judgment or experience on the part of the sampler who adopts a particular data collection strategy. The intention is that typical or representative subjects should be chosen. However, there is no way to check this (Selltiz, Wrightman and Cook, 1981). Gross dependence on expertise is good for small samples only. Errors increase with the sample size.

snow ball sampling
This is a non-probability sampling based on sampler's judgement and experience for studying special characteristics of a population. Initial sample is based on judgement subsequent samples are obtained by referrals by subjects in the initial sample.

Snow ball sampling This is a judgement sampling procedure used for studying special characteristics of a population. It is also called multiplicative sampling or mixed probability sampling. Initial subjects with desired characteristics are randomly selected (selection may also be judgmental). The additional respondents in the sample are obtained by referral or information provided by the initial subjects. This type of sampling is used to estimate characteristics that are rare in the population. The procedure increases the probability of finding the individual with the desired characteristics at a lower cost. (For details refer Darden et al, 1983 and Goodman, 1961).

Example In a study of Bangalore-based software companies servicing multinationals, an initial sample of experts in the field (company employees) is obtained. In discussions with these experts, their competitors and other possible units are further obtained.

purposive sampling
This also is a non-probability sampling which serves an objective or purpose.

Purposive sampling This is similar to judgement sampling, except that the sample is chosen so that a particular research purpose or objective is served and is adequate for it. The sample is typical rather than representative.

Example In a study of informal technology transfer from large public sector undertakings to small scale units, the sample of small scale units is chosen mostly by judgements based on scanning the products produced and by some referrals to large companies.

Convenience sampling These sampling procedures are ad hoc procedures. They are also called accidental sampling. Whatever is easily accessible, subjects who are cooperative, or subjects who can articulate are chosen. There is no way of knowing whether the sample size is small or large. These are not representative and are not recommended for research.

PROBABILITY SAMPLING

probability sampling
In this method random sampling is employed. Objective assessment of reliability of the sample is possible, but representativeness may not be assured.

In this procedure, one can calculate the likelihood of any population element being included in the sample. Since the process is objective, an objective assessment of the reliability of sample results is possible. This aspect has nothing to do with the representativeness of the sample. A non-probability sample may be more representative than an equivalent probability sample. But the sampling error can be computed in the latter and, in that sense, the adequacy can be established. This is not possible with non-probability samples. Different types of probability sampling are displayed in Fig. 11.1.

Simple Random Sampling

In this procedure, each population element has an equal chance of being selected. Any n units can be as likely a sample as any other n elements. Population is depicted in terms of parameters μ, σ^2 and p. The sample statistics are computed and used to estimate the population parameters with a stated confidence and precision. When this method of sampling is used, the following are to be noted:

1. The mean of all possible samples, the grand sample mean, is the mean of population.
2. The variance of sampling mean, in the case of finite population, is related to the population mean as follows:

$$\sigma_x^2 = [\sigma^2/\{n\ ^*((N-n)/(N-1))\}] \quad \sigma_x = \text{Sample standard deviation}$$

3. The distribution of sample means μ_x is normal and its standard deviation is known as standard error of sampling and is equal to $\sigma/\sqrt{n}$ when sampling from infinite population.
4. When a confidence interval is specified, the error of not including the population mean in the estimated interval can be calculated.

When the sample variance is not known, an unbiased sample variance is calculated and used as population variance in computing the error. This is acceptable for all practical purposes since variance changes slower than the level of a variable.

One way of selecting study objects in this method is to use random numbers, either from tables available or by generating them on a computer.

Example Suppose there are 300 potential study objects in a sampling frame and the desired sample size is 5, let us say we have obtained a sequence of ten 3-digit random numbers, which are:

268, 310 (out of range), 619 (out of range), 073, 735 (out of range) 183, 425 (out of range), 092, 661 (out of range), 035

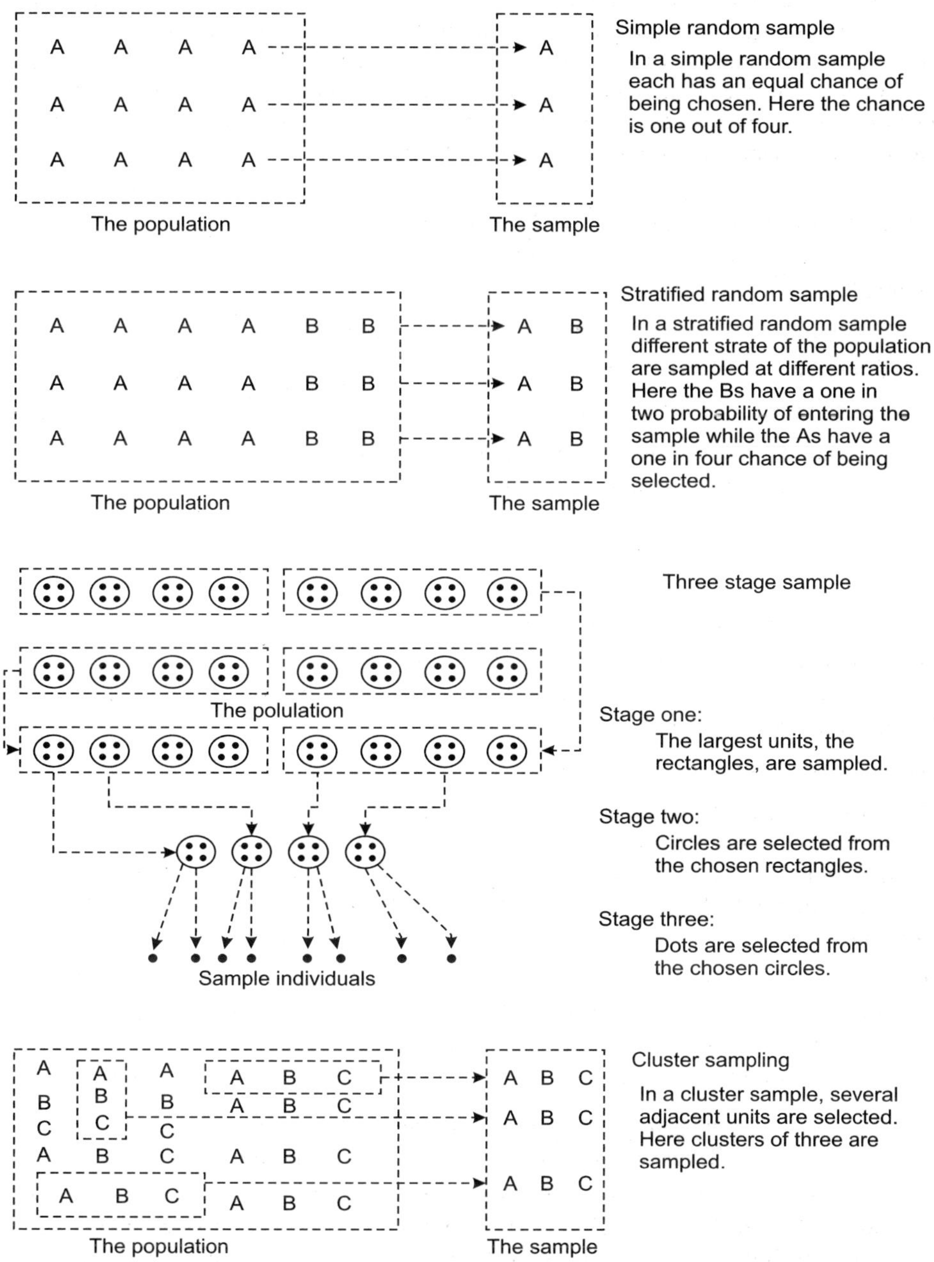

Fig. 11.1 Types of probability sampling

Then, 268, 73, 183, 92, 35 would constitute the serial numbers of the selected objects. For this we enter the table randomly and then systematically select the object number in the sequence of random numbers (in this case 3 digits) eliminating out of range values.

Stratified Random Sampling

Two basic steps are involved in stratified random sampling.

Step 1 Parent population is divided into mutually exclusive exhaustive subsets or groups/ classifications.

stratified random sampling
This is a probability sampling method. In this the population is stratified (partitioned) based on different features / characteristics of the population. A random sample is drawn from each stratum. In this sampling error is considerably reduced.

Step 2 A simple random sample is independently drawn for each stratum. Any element belongs to one stratum only. Since the number of possible samples in each stratum is reduced, (as the number in the population of the stratum would be smaller than the total population), the possible number of samples that can be drawn in stratified sampling as against simple random sampling is considerably reduced. It is, therefore, more restrictive and more precise. Two important statistics mean and variance are given below:

1. Mean of a stratified sample = $\overline{X}_s = \sum_{g=1}^{L} N_g / N \times \overline{g}$

   Where,

   N_g = number of elements in the population stratum 'g',
   N = total size of population,
   $\overline{x}_g$ = sample mean of stratum g.
   $\overline{x}_s$ = sample mean of the total stratified sample, and
2. Variance of stratified sample is $S_{xs}{}^2$ is given by:

$$S_{xs}{}^2 = \sum_{g=1}^{n} (N_g/N)^2 * S_{xg}^2$$

   Where $S_{xg}{}^2$ is the variance of the stratum g.

One strong reason for using stratified sampling very often in research is that its sampling error is reduced or, in other words, its precision is greater. Variability between strata does not affect the standard error of sampling.

The basis of stratification is as follows.

1. Two or more characteristics of interest (like educational levels, income levels, age, and so on) that significantly affect the population should be present.
2. Each stratum should be as homogeneous as possible. The standard error with respect to each stratum will be less but across strata will be large. There are two kinds of stratified random sampling.

   (i) *Proportionate stratified random sampling* The proportion of the sample size in each stratum, with respect to total sample size, is equal to the proportion of the population in the corresponding strata to the total population. The population proportion in each stratum must be known a *priori*, at least approximately.

$$\frac{\text{Sample size in stratum } g}{\text{Total sample size}} = \frac{\text{Population in stratum } g}{\text{Total population}}$$

   (ii) *Disproportionate stratified random sampling* This method of sampling is adopted when the researcher desires to balance the stratum size against stratum variance. If the sample size is proportional to the relative sample variability, this will be achieved.

$$\frac{\text{Sample size in stratum } g}{\text{Total sample size}} = \frac{\text{Variance of population in stratum } g}{\text{Variance of the total population}}$$

The argument here is if the stratum variance is, say, equal to zero, one item in it will give the correct estimate. This sampling is more efficient than proportionate stratified random sampling for purposes of estimation.

cluster sampling
This is similar to stratified sampling. In this population is divided into sub-groups, which are small scale populations. Random sample is selected from each sub-group.

Cluster Sampling

The steps involved in cluster sampling are:

1. Parent population is divided into mutually exclusive/exhaustive sub-sets.
2. Random sampling of the sub-sets is made.

(i) *One Stage Cluster Sampling* Aggregation of individual samples is done before selecting the random sample.

(ii) *Two-Stage cluster sampling* A random selection of the subsets is made and subjects from each sub-set is selected randomly.

Cluster sampling is similar to stratified sampling, but the criteria used for stratified sampling are different. The most important distinction is that in stratified sampling a random sample is selected from each group/stratum. In cluster sampling, the sub-groups are sampled. The sub-groups should be very nearly small scale populations, that is, as heterogeneous as possible.

Example Two-stage cluster sampling

Workers in different grades in different departments.

(a) DA	DB	DC			
SGA	SGB	SGC - - - -	$\sum_{(I = A, B, C)} SGI$	- - - - - RSC (Cluster Sample)	
RS1A	RS1B	RS1C - - - -	$\sum_{(I = A, B, C)} RS1I$	- - - - RS1	Random Sample
RS2A	RS2B	RS2C - - - -	$\sum_{(I = A, B, C)} RS2I$	- - - - RS2	
RS3A	RS3B	RS3C - - - -	$\sum_{(I = A, B, C)} RS3I$	- - - - RS3	

D:Department; SG:Subgroup (A,B,C); RS:Random sample; S:Strata or Grade; 1,2,3

From the point of view of statistical efficiency, cluster samples are not preferred to either simple random sampling or stratified random sampling; but cluster sampling is much more economically efficient than the other sampling methods. This is preferred for practical research by companies as it is more economical and, for a given sampling budget, allows a larger number of observations. Sampling plans can be compared on the basis of the notion of statistical efficiency. Statistical efficiency is measured by the standard error of estimate for a given sample size. If one sampling plan produces less error than others, for the same sample size, then it is more efficient.

Systematic Random Sampling

In systematic random sampling, a random beginning (first term choice) is made and every L^{th} item starting from the first item is selected. It is equivalent to single cluster sampling. It is an easy sampling procedure and often can be more representative, since it cuts across the population. Periodicity in the population listed may cause serious errors in estimation.

Example Slama and Taschchian (1985) selected socio-economic and demographic characteristic association in purchasing environment.

Area Sampling

This pertains to the primary sampling of geographic areas, like districts, towns, regions, or factories. If only one level of sampling takes place (say sampling of blocks) then the elements or sample from it is a single stage area sample. If one or more successive samples are taken within a larger area then it becomes a multi-stage area sample.

area sampling
The sampling area is divided into sub areas at different levels (eg. states-districts-cities-wards-houses) level wise successive random samples are chosen.

Example

(i) Multi-stage sample

Stage 1—Random sample of location (nationwise)

Stage 2—Random sample of blocks ...(locationwise)
Stage 3—Random sample of households (blocks/segmentwise)

(ii) One-stage sample

(a) Random sample of blocks
(b) Random sample of households in each block

DETERMINATION OF SAMPLE SIZE

sample size determination
There are many methods for this purpose but most often used ones are: All you can afford, required for a cell size and statistical models.

There are several methods of determining sample size (Tull & Hawkins, 1987).

1. Unaided judgement
2. All you can afford
3. Average for samples of similar studies
4. Required size for cell
5. Use of statistical models
6. Use of Bayesian statistical model

The last three methods (4 to 6 above) only will be discussed.

required cell size
In this method cells are formed using cross tabulation (eg. strata vs. characteristic). Minimum number for each cell is determined based on the type of analysis desired. This minimum number is not violated in any cell.

Required Size/Cell

Cells are formed using sample characteristics. Expected cross tabulation of data for analysis are determined. For each of the cells in two cross tabulations a minimum size of sample is obtained based on the kind of analysis desired (frequency distribution, regression, factor analysis). Total sample size obtained is distributed to these cells so that at least a minimum number is maintained for each cell. It is desirable to have 20 to 50 in each cell/(Applied Sampling, Sudman, 1976). This method is suitable for quota sampling and stratified random sampling.

Use of statistical models
This requires an estimate of population variance, allowable sampling error for research purpose and the desired level of confidence that this error is lower than a specified one.

Use of Statistical Models

There are three pre-requisites for the use of statistical models in sample size determination.

1. An estimate of the variance of the population has to be obtained.
2. The allowable sampling error from the point of view of the research problem should be specified.
3. The desired level of confidence that this error is lower than the specified sampling error should also be specified.

The steps involved in determining the sample size for single classification populations are as follows:

- Determine the number of standard errors (z) associated with the confidence level.
- Estimate the standard deviation of the population (or the population proportion, as the case may be).
- Calculate the size using the formula for the standard error of mean (or proportion, as the case may be).

(i) for means (normal distribution is assumed):

$$\sigma_x = e/Z;\ n\ \frac{\sigma^2 z^2}{e^2} \text{ (for infinite population)}$$

$$n = \frac{N^2 z^2}{Ne^2 + \sigma^2 z^2} \text{ (for a finite population of } N)$$

Where

e is the specified error and
σ is the standard deviation of the population

(ii) for proportions (binomial model):

$$\sigma_p = e/z = SQRT\ \{[\bar{p}(1 - \bar{p})/n]\}$$

$$n = [z^2 \bar{p}(1 - \bar{p})/e^2] \text{ (for infinite population)}$$

$$n = [N\bar{p}\ (1 - \bar{p})z^2]/[Ne^2 + \bar{p}(1 - \bar{p})z^2] \text{ (for finite population of N)}$$

Where

e is the specified error,
$\bar{p}$ is the mean proportion, and
n is the sample size.

Sample size for multinomial population When each of the elements of a population can be classified into more than two categories the population is called a multinomial population (multiple choice questions result in a multinomial population). The procedure, as given by Tull and Hawkins (1987), is as follows.

- Estimate the sample size for considering the population as a binomial population for the proportion of each item.
- Multiply the largest sample obtained (among the items) by a conversion factor, as given in Table 11.1 (Tortora, 1978).

Table 11.1 Factors for Converting Binomial Sample Size into Multinomial Sample Size

Confidence Coefficient	*Sample Size*					
	3	4	5	10	15	20
95%	1.53	1.66	1.73	2.05	2.37	2.53
90%	1.71	1.84	2.04	2.44	2.76	2.91

Hypothesis testing approach This sample size determining method makes use of type I error α and type II error β of H_0 while formulating hypothesis. Steps involved in calculating the sample size are as follows.

1. Specify p_o and p_1 for H_o (null) and $H1$ (alternative)(p_o and p_1 are proportions).
2. Specify α_o and β_1 of type I and type II errors.
3. Determine the number of standard errors associated with each of α and β (Z_α and Z_β).
4. Calculate n, which meets the requirement of both errors in 3 above.

(i) for means:

$\mu_o + Z_\alpha(\sigma/n) = \text{Critical value} = \mu_1 - Z_\beta(r/n)$

Therefore, $n = (Z_\alpha + Z_\beta)^2\ \sigma^2/(\mu_1 - \mu_o)^2$

(ii) for proportions;

$n = [\{Z_\alpha \surd\{p_o(1-p_o)\} + Z_\beta \surd\{p_1(1-p_1)\}/(p_o+p_1)]^2$

Where Z_α & Z_β are standard errors associated with α and β, respectively

The principal and general procedures used for other sample designs is the same as above, but the formulae are different [for details see Applied Sampling by Sudman (1976), Survey Sampling by Kish (1965) and Sampling Techniques by Cochran (1977)].

Whenever a sample size has to be determined so as to simultaneously meet several objectives of the sampler, the largest of sample sizes required for these objectives, individually, is chosen as the sample size.

Cluster sampling

M = Cluster size if constant

M_i = size of ith cluster, if cluster size is variable

$\overline{M}$ = Average cluster size

k = number of clusters, therefore, $kM = N$ or $k\overline{M} = N$, depending on constant or variable cluster size

μ_i = i^{th} cluster mean

σ_w^2 = variance between clusters assuming constant cluster size

μ = mean for clusters and σ_w^2 = within cluster variance

$$\text{When } \sigma_b^2 = \frac{\sum_{i=1}^{k} (\mu_1 - \mu) 2}{(k-1)}$$

σ_w^2 = within cluster variance

$$= M \frac{\sum_{i=1}^{k} (x_{ij} - \mu) 2}{k(M-1)}$$

Where x_{ij} is the measure of the jth element in the ith cluster

From Anova $\sigma^2 = \{\sigma_b^2 + (M-1)\ \sigma_w^2\}/M$

$$\text{Intra cluster correlation coefficient} = \frac{\sum (x_{ij} - \mu)(x_{ik} - \mu)}{\sum (x_{ij} - \mu)^2}$$

(Any standard text on Sampling theory will give a complete and detailed explanation of the cluster sampling method.)

Bayesian Method for Determination of Sample Size

Bayesian procedures (Green et al, 1988) are based on the principle that the best sample is that which results in the largest positive difference between the expected pay off of the sample information and the cost of sampling (this is known as expected 'net gain').

The procedure for sample size determination is as follows:

(a) Find the expected value of sample information for a given sample size.
(b) Estimate sampling cost.
(c) Find expected net gain with sample size.
(d) Repeat steps a, b, and c for other sample sizes, and select that which gives maximum expected 'net gain'.

The procedure and the underlining principle of this method are sound, but difficult to implement in practice. They are rarely used in literature [for details see Sudman (1976) and Kish (1965)]. Other methods of optimisation of sample size are discussed by Ackoff (1962).

ILLUSTRATIVE EXAMPLES OF SAMPLE SIZE DETERMINATION

Simple random sample It is desired to estimate the hourly wage rate of skilled workers in an industrial suburb within +0.05 precision at 95 per cent confidence level. An approximate estimate of the population standard deviation σ= Rs 0.835/-. How large should the sample size be?

Now, $n = [N\ \sigma^2/(N-1)\ D + \sigma^2]$

Where $D = e^2/z^2$, σ^2 = population variance,

N = number in the population,

e = error, z_σ = standard normal variate corresponding to confidence coefficient.

(a) When N is very large, $n = \sigma^2 z_\sigma^2/e^2$

$$n = \frac{(1.96)^2 * (0.835)^2}{(0.05)^2}$$

$$n = 1071.38 \text{ (say, 1072)}$$

(b) If $N = 20{,}000$,

$$n = \frac{2000 * (0.835)^2}{19999 * (0.05)^2/(1.96)^2 + (0.835)^2} = 1017$$

Stratified random sampling There are 4200 members in an association, 2800 of whom live in the locality and the others in far away places. The secretary of the association wants to take a stratified random sample according to residence, to estimate the total donations. Find the number of members to be contacted if the error is + Rs 10,000/-. How should this be divided between two strata? Standard deviations on donations from local and foreign members are Rs 30 and Rs 20, respectively.

$$n = \frac{N_1\sigma^2}{\left[(Ne^2/Z^2) + (1/N)\sum_{i=1}^{L}(N_1\sigma^2)\right]}$$

when estimating the mean. Now $\sigma_1^2 = 30^2 = 900$

$\sigma_2^2 = 20^2 = 400$

we are finding the sample total variance.

$$\sum_{i=1}^{L} N_1\sigma^2 = 2800*900 + 1400*400 = 3{,}080{,}000,$$

error on the total = $(e^2/Z_\alpha^2 n^2) = (10{,}000)^2/(1.96)^2*(1200)^2 = 1.476$

n = [3,080,000/(4200*1.476+(3080000/4200))]=444.28 = 445 (say)

$n1 = (nN1/N) = 445 * 2800/4200 = 296.67 = 297$

$n2 = (nN2/N) = 445 * 1400/4200 = 148.33 = 148$

The secretary should sample 297 from the locality and 148 from the foreign locations. (*Note*: When N is very large, $n = N/N * e^2 + 1$)

Cluster sampling A company engaged in assembling of an engineering product requires part p in lots of 5000. The parts are packed 10 to a box. The sampling plan calls for a sample of 120 with the diameter y (as the important variable). Twelve boxes of 10 were sampled at random. Measures were taken and data kept for cluster sampling. What is the equivalent random sample?

If $M = 10$, find $\sigma_{\bar{y}cl}$ and compare with $\sigma_{\bar{y}ran}$

Sample statistics obtained

$\bar{y} = 2.035$ mm

$S_b^2 = 0.0025$, $S_w^2 = 0.00080$

Solution: The following are calculated

(i) $\sigma 2$ = approximate sample variance $= \dfrac{S_b^2 + (M-1)S_w^2}{M}$

$$= \frac{0.0025 + 9x0.00080}{10} = .0097$$

given $M = 10$ $\sigma 2 = 0.00097 = S^2$

(ii) $\text{Rho} = \dfrac{S_b^2 - S^2}{(M-1)S^2} = \dfrac{0.0025 - 0.00097}{(10-1)\,0.00097} = 0.18$

(iii) $S_{ycL} = \dfrac{S^2}{n} = \dfrac{0.0025}{120} = 0.0000208$

$\sigma_{ycL} = \surd\,(0.0000208) = 0.0046$ mm

Note: If $\rho = 0$: then the clusters are independent and $\sigma_{ycL} = \surd(\sigma^2/n)$. We can compute variance of Y_{ran} (random sampling) is obtained to assess the precision

$$S_{yran} = \frac{\sigma^2}{n} = \frac{0.00097}{120} = 0.0000081$$

$$\sigma_{yran} = \text{SQRT}(0.0000081) = 0.0028.$$

A random sample of 44 (i.e. n = 44) would yield the same precision as the cluster sample of 120.

$$\text{estimated variance of sample mean} = \frac{\sigma^2}{n} = \frac{0.00097}{120} = 0.0000208$$

Solving for n this variance yields a sample size of 44.

If intra cluster correlation (ρ) is assumed to be zero, the answer would be based on 0.0028 and not on 0.0046 which would be erroneous.

Simple random sample (estimation of population proportions) A manufacturing organisation is considering discounting, by 20 per cent, the price of a particular item to buyers who double their monthly order. A randomly selection of 100 out of 860 buyers were contacted; 30 of them indicated that they would accept the offer to double their order. Estimate the proportion p of all 860 who would like to take advantage and also find the error of estimate.

$$\bar{p} = \frac{30}{100} = 0.3;$$

$$\sigma_p = \frac{p(1-p)(N-n)}{(n-1)N}$$

$$= \frac{0.3*0.7}{(100-1)}\,\frac{(860-100)}{860} = 0.00188$$

The estimate of $p = \bar{p} + 1.96\,\sigma_P$

$= 0.30 + 1.96\,\surd(0.00188)$

$= 0.30 + 0.085$

$= 0.385$

Error of estimate is 0.085

Stratified random sample for proportion For a production organisation having a strata of employees, managers, technicians, and workers; total population N_h; population proportion Π_h, and strata weightages ($w_h = N_h/N$) are given below. If the total sample size is 300, find their optimal allocation.

	N_h	W_h	Π_h
Managers	900	0.125	0.5
Technicians	1800	0.250	0.8
Workers	4500	0.625	0.1
	7200	1.000	

	N_h	W_h	Π_h	$W_h\Pi_h$	$\Pi_h\theta_h$	$W_h\Pi_h\theta_h$	$\sqrt{\Pi_h\theta_h}$	$W_h\sqrt{\Pi_h\theta_h}$
Managers	900	0.125	0.5	0.0625	0.25	0.3125	0.50	0.0625
Technicians	1800	0.250	0.8	0.2	0.16	0.0400	0.4	0.1000
Workers	4500	0.625	0.1	0.0625	0.09	0.05625	0.30	0.1875

$n = \Sigma W_h\Pi_h = 0.0625 + 0.2 + 0.0625 = 0.325$

$\Sigma Wh\sqrt{\Pi_h\theta_h} = 0.0625 + 0.1 + 0.1825 = 0.35$

$\sigma_p = \sqrt{((/n ((1 - f)}$

f = proportion sampled for simple random sample

EMBED Equation.3 for optimal allocation

$n1 = 300 * 0.0625/ 0.3500 = 53$

$n2 = 300 * 0.100/ 0.3500 = 87$

$n3 = 300 * 0.1875/ 0.3500 = 160$

SUMMARY

Samples serve to gain parsimony of data collection effort. Since the population characteristics are estimated based on the measurement of sample characteristics, the sample should be representative of the population and should be of adequate size. The sampling method is so chosen as to meet these two requirements of the sample. Sample size is determined on the basis of requirements of error and confidence level. A random sample is usually preferred as it enables the researcher to gain knowledge of the error of sampling.

There are two basic sampling procedures—non-probability sampling, which has a strong element of judgment and probability sampling, in which the sample error and reliability can be estimated objectively. In either case, the researcher has to make efforts to make the sample representative by giving consideration to such aspects as sub-classes in population, purpose for which the sample is taken, and the expertise in sampling available to the researcher. Among non-probability sampling procedures, quota sampling, snowball sampling and convenience sampling are widely used. Among probability sampling methods, the more important ones are simple random sampling, stratified random sampling, and cluster sampling.

Suggested Readings

- Cochran, W.G. (1977). *Sampling Techniques*. New York: John Wiley.

- Freund, Rudolph J. and William J. Wilson (1997). *Statistical Methods*, 2nd ed. San Diego: Academic Press.
- Sudman, S. (1976). *Applied Sampling*. New York: Academic Press.
- Tull and Hawkins (1987). *Marketing Research: Measurement and Method*, 4th ed. New York: Macmillan.
- Williams, F. (1968). *Reasoning with Statistics*. Austin, Texas: Holt, Rinehart and Winston.

QUESTIONS AND EXERCISES

1. What are the considerations in determining sample size?
2. How would you select a sample of 50 supervisors in an organisation having 400 supervisors for a morale study? What are the issues involved?
3. Why should you have to state the degree of precision and the degree of confidence in determining sample size?
4. If the population variance is not known, how does one determine the sample size with a stated degree of precision and confidence? After the sample size is determined, how is a desired confidence interval obtained?
5. How does one proceed to determine sample size when the research study involves multiple objectives?
6. What is snow ball sampling? When do you use it? Discuss an example from literature.
7. In which sampling procedure are estimates more precise, simple random sampling or stratified random sampling? Why?
8. How do you select a cluster sample? In what way is it different from a stratified sample? Explain with two examples.
9. What is statistical efficiency of a sampling procedure?
10. Describe a two-stage area sample. Why would you sample in two stages? Explain with an example.
11. For the following situations, identify the appropriate target population and sampling frame.
    (a) A children's health foundation wants to test the effectiveness of an advertisement—In a city in India "8-reasons for administering Triple Antigen to your child".
    (b) A wholesaler wants to evaluate dealer reaction to a price cut on Nirlep Cooking utensils.
    (c) A vacuum cleaner manufacturer wants to assess the adequacy of inventories held in wholesale godowns across the country.
    (d) A production manager wants to test a new press tool design among the manufacturing divisions.
    (e) The manufacturer of an efficient wood stove wants to test market in rural areas.
12. Distinguish between independent random sampling and dependent random sampling.
13. The production scheduler of a large manufacturer wants to determine the accuracy of time estimates of an operation set by the industrial engineering department. He randomly selects time and day to observe the operation. A sample time record of 115 operation times gave a mean of 4.35 meters and standard deviation of 1.42 meters.
    (a) Find 97 per cent confidence interval estimate of the average operation time per component for all components.
    (b) Find estimated operation time required in hours to produce 2480 components. What is 97 per cent confidence interval of the estimate?
14. A researcher wants to test the hypothesis Ho: $u = 3$ against $H1$:$u \neq 3$ for a normally distributed population with a variance of 1.44. If the statistician wants the test to have a power of 0.80 and the sample mean is 3.5, what sample size should be used, given $p = 0.10$?
15. A company wants to find budget for the maintenance of 170 company cars operated by company personnel. How many company employees should be contacted if the company wishes to estimate maintenance budget with a bound of Rs. 500 on the error of the estimate? Assume, based on past evidence, annual maintenance cost of about Rs 100 per car.

16. Explain the following concepts:
(a) Sampling error
(b) Sampling frame
(c) Sample statistics
(d) Probability sampling
(e) Cluster sampling
(f) Area sampling
(g) Double sampling

Part E

Acquisition and Preparation and Research Data

CHAPTER 12

Data Collection Procedures

- Introduction
- Sources of Secondary Data
- Primary Data Collection Methods
- Non-sampling Errors

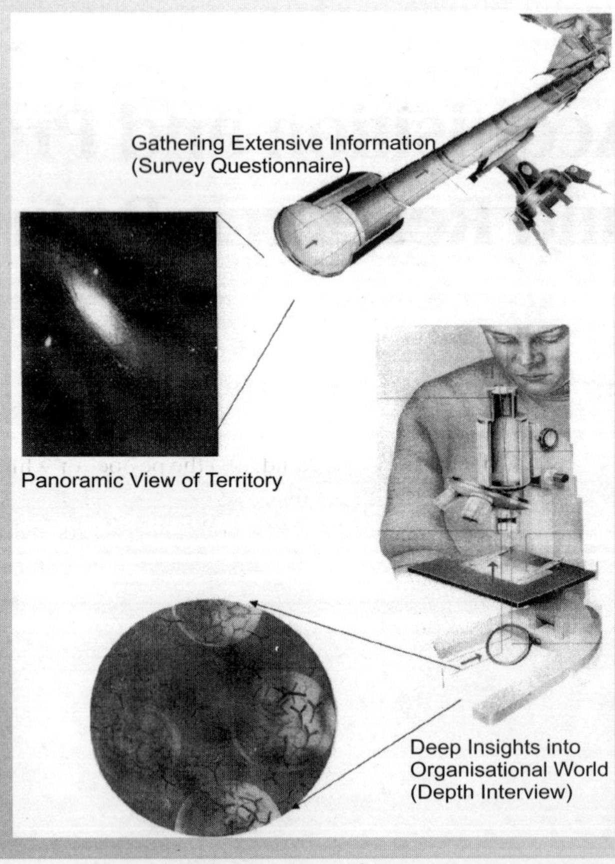

LEARNING OBJECTIVES

Upon completion of this chapter, you will be able to:

- ✓ Study the two data sources, primary and secondary, for research
- ✓ Learn to search for secondary data through computer systems
- ✓ Know about computer search through the WWW
- ✓ Understand that mixing primary and secondary data is tricky and that care must be exercised
- ✓ Learn the principles of scientific observation
- ✓ Learn to design questionnaires
- ✓ Understand how to conduct interviews
- ✓ Familiarise yourself with method and kinds of questions that are asked in research
- ✓ Understand the errors that occur in data collection
- ✓ Learn to validate the various methods of data collection

INTRODUCTION

Data required for management research can be classified into primary data and secondary data. Primary data is the data specially collected in a research by the researcher and his agents. These are the products of experiments, surveys, interviews, or observations conducted in the research. Secondary data is data collected by other researchers for their own use and which is of use to another research project. Primary data is generated and collected through specific tools of data collection, like questionnaires, by the researcher. Secondary data is searched for and obtained from many different sources. The main effort involved in acquiring secondary data is searching for and locating it, which is increasingly becoming a specialised and skilled task in the present context of information explosion and the advent of complex computer search systems.

acquiring secondary data
The main effort of acquiring secondary data is searching for and locating it. Acquiring secondary data is less expensive and less time consuming but has problems: it may not meet exactly the requirements of the research; details may not be available and validating the data may be difficult.

Acquiring secondary data is less expensive and less time consuming than collecting primary data. This is the biggest advantage with secondary data. But often problems arise while using secondary data.

- Secondary data may not meet the needs of the problem at hand for various reasons. Units of measurement may be different; aggregated data often does not provide the details required by the researcher; classifications of data may not match the requirements of the problem at hand; and the period for which the data are available may not suit the overall research needs.
- All the data required for research analysis may not be available. Matching part data obtained by primary data collection methods and part by secondary sources may become extremely difficult.
- The accuracies of data are not known and in some cases of rigorous research, analysis may cause difficulties in validation and reliability estimation.

We will examine the sources of secondary data and their search first, and then discuss the collection of primary data.

SOURCES OF SECONDARY DATA

The sources of secondary data are sources internal to a firm or industry and sources that are external.

(a) The internal sources are:

- company accounting records
- company reports

- in-house journals
- miscellaneous reports
- internal computer databases

(b) The external sources are:

- computerised data bases
- reports of associations
- reports and publications of government agencies
- other publications

Internal Sources

internal sources of secondary data
These constitute: Reports, accounting data, in house journal, computer database of the company and data warehouses.

Company accounting data These include accounting and financial details maintained in computers or ledgers; inventory, purchase, manufacturing activity logs; shop order files; worker files; payment ledger; cashbook; and so forth. When accessible, these provide data close to the primary data.

Company reports These consist of annual reports and regular reports submitted to the board of directors or statutory reports submitted to the government. A great deal of routine data can be obtained through these reports on operational and performance aspects.

In-house journal Most corporations usually support in-house journals and useful general data may be obtained from them.

Miscellaneous reports These include consultancy reports; special reports of research supported by the firm, special reports to the top management in specific areas of management when new methods are introduced or new activities are taken up, or when the report is needed for trouble shooting or for large improvements in the firms' operations.

Company computer databases The use of internal data for decision-making has increased so much in recent times that intranets (internal networks linking outward to the internet but forbidding access from outside) have begun to operate successfully. These are connected to the distributed organisational databases (Cooper & Schindler, 2000).

Enterprise data warehouses and data marts These have started coming up during the last 20 years, and seem to be gaining a competitive edge. The competitive edge seems to be coming more from using available information properly than by optimising approaches. A data warehouse is a collection of key pieces of information used to manage and direct business for the most profitable outcome and includes process managers who put the data into tables and the analysts make informal decisions from the tables (Anahory & Murray, 2000).

External Sources

external sources of secondary data
These constitute: Public computer databases, reports of industrial associations and syndicates, reports of government agencies and journals, computer databases and bibliographic services of professional and academic bodies.

Public computer databases These large databases, which can be accessed with desktop computers, are fast growing and cover the areas of financial information, product sales and marketing channels, performances, manufacturing and inventory values, employment, and so forth. (They include bibliographic services too.) Accesses to these databases are available at a charge. Software with updating services are also available. For a treatment of data accessing through internet and searching for computer networks of secondary data refer to Cooper & Schindler, 2000).

Reports of associations Associations of industries like the Electrical Manufacturers Association, Automobile Association, and so forth have developed their own annual reports, which provide details of industry's sales growth, operating characteristics, and the like. They also publish special reports and research statistics. Newspapers and magazines collect information from these associations and publish it. These are available on subscription.

Reports of government agencies Both central and state government departments provide large amounts of aggregated data and information on financial and operational activities and R&D activities in publications like the Reserve Bank of India (RBI) bulletin, details of industries in industrial classifications, census, industrial surveys and annual reports, economic surveys, and so on. The reports cover demographic details, housing, wages and income, production and sale of manufacturing and service organisations, agriculture and general employment. The relevant reports are surveys of current business, economic census, current industrial reports, census reports and the like.

Industrial syndicates These organisations also provide data on industrial services, plantwise/areawise information on manufactured products, inventories, sales and movement through marketing channels, financial ratios, and the like.

Other publications Other sources of useful data/information are academic publications such as books, professional journals, project reports, and dissertation abstracts. Computer search systems and computerised bibliographic services are also coming up fast in support of the individual researcher.

A sample list of secondary data sources is provided in Appendix B to this chapter, however, it is by no means exhaustive.

Computer Search for Secondary Data

There is an incredible potential source for research data in worldwide computer databases, electronic libraries and the internet (world wide web). For integrating the use of these sources into research efforts, a research scholar needs skills different from those required a decade ago.

computer search for secondary data
Specifying clearly the data needs and selecting an appropriate key-word, search can be made effective while accessing such computer data sources as electronic library, internet and electronic databases through a large number of search engines available.

The resources are not orderly arrays of files and documents and they cannot be considered as catalogues. Since a large quantum of information is changed and updated possibly every hour/every day, the researcher must be prepared for constant change. However, there are a number of ways to search these sources and find what is needed. Electronic searching sources also have to be used by the researcher along with electronic research sources.

The necessary information may be had from electronic databases, e-libraries, or the world-wide web. In finding and getting information or data for research purposes, it is desirable to follow some well planned procedures.

The following steps may be useful (Mckie, 1997).

1. Specify your data needs.
2. Select a keyword/search query.
3. Select a suitable electronic library search source/database/search engine for the internet search.
4. Save useful information resulting from the search.
5. If necessary, repeat steps (2) and (3) with modified keywords.

Step 1—Specify information/data needs The problem of research should be defined as clearly as possible in order to be specific about the data/information needed. Since electronic searching requires 'keyword' use, the more specific/clear the research objective, the more suitable a keyword would be for close search.

Step 2—Select keywords A keyword is used for querying the database or web. Single keywords give very general information, which is not very useful. To be more efficient in search, use an appropriate 'key phrase'.

Truncate the keyword Limit the data/information searched by specifying periods (1990–2000) or range (all people below a certain age) or type (technical manpower) or language (English) etc.

Use Boolean search ("AND", "OR", "NOT") For example, instead of using keyword 'scheduling semiconductor', you may use "scheduling AND semiconductor" for searching for information on scheduling particularly in semiconductor manufacturing.

Step 3—Select a library database/website (search engine)/business database In selecting a particular website for particular data, the user has to look for scope of the data/information and the authority of the source of the data/information.

Library searches Many university and college libraries have catalogues that can be searched electronically through an internet connection. Hytel net (a telenet connection) is useful to gain access to remote library catalogue systems. Using tools like sociofile, current contents, and silver platter, it is possible to conduct fast catalogue searches. Data sets of secondary sources and questionnaires are available to students and faculty members of universities (in easy use form with SAS/SPSS packages). CD-ROM based products are also available in many countries for this purpose.

Web searches There are a number of search engines available for web searches. They differ in matters of display/presentation, options for keywords, and speed of updating. These deal with web addresses, names of sites, and names of documents useful in generalised searches. There are a large number of competent search engines that connect a large number of websites. A special site *http://www.windweaver.com/index.htm* is useful for knowing what type of search engine is useful for a particular search (*http://www.Carleton.ca/~cmckie/research.htm* is also useful). Some of the useful sites are given in Appendix B of this book.

The specific types of information searches are:

Known item searches 'Where' searches (databases or websites), 'what' searches, for example, the Google item.

Where searches: Lycos system gives geographical locations.

What searches: Alta Vista, Yahoo are useful.

Who searches: These provide information on people (all sites provide this information).

Some of the search engines are listed at the end of this section.

Step 4—Store information The useful information obtained in each cycle of search should be saved and stored suitably so that at the end of the search phase, the several bits can be organised systematically into a meaningful review of literature or a researchable data set.

A number of cycles of this search procedure (steps 2 to steps 4) may be necessary to obtain the required information for research.

Web addresses of a few search engine.

www.google.com

www.lycos.com

www.yahoo.com

www.hotmail.com

(For additional search engines and websites, see Appendix B).

From the above discussions, it is clear that larger amounts of secondary data are available at present to the researcher than ever before and at a much quicker time. The computer has brought most libraries and data sources around the world nearer to every researcher. To be efficient at using such secondary data, the researcher needs to devote additional skills and care at every step of research.

PRIMARY DATA COLLECTION METHODS

Many methods and procedures have been developed to help in acquiring data. They make use of different means of describing and quantifying data. Each of these is suitable in specific situations of source and type of data. Too much dependence upon one method is not desirable. The recent trend in social science and management research is to use multiple methods. They serve two purposes; one of eliminating or minimising bias, the other of corroborating and, hence, providing greater reliability of data.

The primary data relevant to a problem is collected by one of the standard methods of research—experiments, surveys, field studies, case studies, system studies, and the like. The basic methods and tools for data collection for research include observation, questionnaire, interview, and projective technique.

The employment of any of these tools of data collection depends on the type of research that is being undertaken and the time and resources available to the researcher. Table 12.1 shows tools for data collection predominantly used in different types research.

Table 12.1 Tools for Data Collection Verses Types of Research

Type of Research	*Tools of Data Collection*				
	Observation	*Questionnaire*	*Interview*	*Projective Techniques*	*Records*
Experimental	X	X	X	X	–
Exploratory	X	X	X	–	X
Descriptive	X	X	X	–	X
Causal	–	X	X	–	–
Case Study	X	X	X		X
Model building	X	–	X	–	X

Observation

Observation is the most direct form of data collection. Usually data is gathered by observation when it can be gathered accurately only by this method. For example, behaviour of children (who cannot talk).

There is a considerable difference between casual observation and scientific observation. Scientific observation is well planned, recorded, and checked for validity and reliability. It has a research purpose and, therefore, has focus during its process (notwithstanding this, many haphazard observations have led to scientific discovery). Conditions under which data can be effectively collected are:

1. Data must be accessible to the observer (private activity, motivation, and attitudes). Some behaviours are communicated through facial expression and body language. These are observable when the activity is repetitive, frequent, and predictable.
2. They must be of short interval to reduce distortion due to recall.
3. It is desirable that the observational data is used to supplement the other methods of data collection.

Sampling The subjects are sampled randomly and followed up (cf. QC - control samples are taken at equal intervals of time). Alternatively, a particular place or position is sampled randomly for occurrence of any activity (cf. work sampling, where particular activities are observed at random intervals). For an example, see Atkins (1978) in which parent-child interactions are observed.

Observational approaches can be classified as follows:

Natural verses contrived Observing how many cars pass a circle every hour is a natural observation, which is useful when phenomena occur frequently. A store worker checked by an observer disguised as a customer is a contrived observation.

observation

This is the most direct form of primary data collection. This is effective when data is accessible by observation of facial expression and body language relating to activities, which are repetitive and frequent. This should be supplemented by other methods as a check.

observational approaches

Basically there are two approaches. Systematic observation and participant observation. In the former recording schedule are used in direct or indirect observation and non-behavioural and behavioural observations. In the latter insiders view point is obtained by the observer being embedded in the system, using analysis and collecting of data parallelly.

Open verses disguised An observation made on television or metering certain occurrences are examples of open observations. Observations in lab experiments are often disguised, that is, the participants are unaware of certain kinds of observations made by the experimenter.

Structured verses unstructured In structured observation what aspects are to be observed and recorded are exactly known. The others are ignored; an observation checklist is usually used (cf. questionnaire). When any aspect of a phenomenon, as in exploratory situations, is considered useful, the observation becomes unstructured.

Direct verses indirect When current behaviour or occurrence is observed, the observation is direct. When past behaviour is to be observed, it can only be done through effects (physical traces). In this case, the observation becomes indirect. Direct observation is time consuming and costly, particularly if specific aspects or events have to be sampled (due to large times of waiting for the events to occur). Direct observation is not suitable for phenomena of long duration or rarely occurring phenomena. Data gathered through direct observation is not generally quantified (though it can be).

Mechanical verses human When devices like televisions, meters, video cameras, and photographic analysis are used for observation, it becomes mechanical. All other observations are human.

Non-behavioural and Behavioural Non-behavioural observations are analysis of records (historical or current records)—written, sound recorded or video taped, photographs or computer records, personal records. Content analysis may be used in this context, physical condition analysis, process and activity analysis, work, study, and manufacturing system analysis, and the like. Behaviour observation includes observation of (i) non-verbal behaviour, body movements, gestures, facial expressions; (ii) linguistic behaviour, which includes vocal sounds made during interactions; (iii) extra lingual behaviour like pitch of talking or manner of talking; and (iv) spatial behaviour, in which how an individual behaves in close physical proximity to others is studied.

Basically, there are two kinds of observation. The first is systematic observation, which has recording schedules; the second is participant observation, in which the observer is embedded in the system, and collection and analysis of data take place simultaneously (for details, refer the section on participant observation in the Chapter 6).

Evaluation of Observations as Data Collection Procedures

Structuring observations reduces (potential) bias of observation and increases reliability but reduced search in structured observations reduces validity. The observer must assimilate the information obtained in the observation and make inferences from them. It is at once a strength and weakness of behavioural observation. Good training is, therefore, necessary for the observer.

Disguised observation is often difficult and may cause loss of information obtainable in undisguised observation. Observations in contrived settings (lab settings) allow greater control over extraneous influences, affecting the results, but the experimental set up itself may introduce differences in the behaviour of the subject. Mechanical contrivances used in observation will free the observation from the observers' selective process and bias but lacks the integrative and inferential powers of the human observer. Observation is not very useful for measuring attitudes, motivation, awareness, or knowledge. In such cases, the questionnaire mode is more appropriate.

questionnaire
This is the instrument for data collection in survey research for large samples. Impersonal and standard formats help in getting data objectively. Information on facts, attitudes, motivation and knowledge can be obtained easily.

Questionnaires

Questionnaires are preferred in most surveys because they are less expensive. Skills required to administer them are also less than what is required for interviewing. Large samples can be dealt with simultaneously in questionnaires as mailing is possible. Further, the impersonal and standardised formats of questionnaires has uniformity (which is absent in interviewing) and tends to be a little more objective. The anonymity of the responder (particularly in mailed questionnaires) gives greater freedom of expression. However, if answers of certain questions are related to emotions and feelings, they may be better handled by a skillful interviewer than through a questionnaire. One great disadvantage is the low response rates (sometimes as low as 5 to 10 per cent).

Design of questionnaire A questionnaire is a formalised set of questions aimed at eliciting information regarding facts, level of knowledge, attitudes, needs, and motivations. At the current level of standardisation of the design of questionnaires, it can be treated more as an art than as a science. The cardinal approach to developing a questionnaire is to make it simple and avoid the inclusion of ambiguous and leading questions. The design of a questionnaire can be taken up in several steps. These steps are only considered as a convenient approach to design a good questionnaire rather than as a strict procedure for it.

Steps in the design of a questionnaire

steps in questionnaire design

There are many steps in this. Major ones are selecting the type of questions, selecting the methods and form of responses and pre-testing and revision of questions.

Step 1—Information sought The first step in any questionnaire design is the specification of the information sought. The exact information required has to be stated. Target population has to be specified. The objectives of the questionnaire have to be spelt out and the respondents should be so chosen as to make them less diversified. In this step, an attempt must be made to reduce both surrogate information error as well as respondent errors.

Step 2—Type of questionnaire The type of questions to be included in the questionnaire has to be decided. The major decisions are whether one or more questions need to be designed for each item of information. Getting a few quick trial responses and analysing the answers can facilitate this. Questions useful to the research problem only should be included. However, if additional questions are 'thrown-in', their purpose must be clear to the researcher. In general, questions may demand choice or preference by the respondent through an agree-disagree format.

Example Innovative tasks are mostly restricted to the R&D and Production Departments.

Strongly agree		Neutral		Strongly disagree
5	4	3	2	1

Two or more questions can be asked as one question. These are called 'double-barreled' questions.

Example The extent to which you are satisfied regarding the remuneration package and recruitment policies of the organisation, to enable it to recruit managers, are:

Highly Satisfactory		Moderately Satisfactory		Highly Unsatisfactory
5	4	3	2	1

Questions

Demanding aggregations of several types of information should be avoided as far as possible.

The main issue involved in the design of questions is to specifically consider the respondent and his difficulties in answering. Some of the difficulties may arise because of the following reasons.

- *Uninformed respondent* Many simple questions are preferred to a single complex or composite question.
- *Forgetful respondents* When memory-based answers are required, aided recalls may be used to make the answers less error prone (errors are omission, creation, and telescoping).

- *Inarticulate respondents* When 'why' questions are used, the respondent may be unable to answer, though willing. In such situations, it is desirable to use projective techniques.
- *Personal and embarrassing questions* Preferably, either a random response method or counter-biasing statements should be used. In the random response method, the question is mixed with other questions and a single answer is elucidated.

Example A fairly unbiased percentage of rejection at the inspection stage can be obtained by asking the following questions.

(i) Acceptance rate at inspection for your product is _____ per cent.

(ii) The acceptance rates at inspection for your company/s in general, in your sector is _________ per cent (100 - answer given in question (a)) = per cent rejection). Question (b) is inconsequential.

(iii) Some respondents may be unwilling to answer and may deliberately distort the information. This can be verified by alternate questioning methods.

The content of the questions should be simple in meaning. Suggestive and leading questions introduce bias into the answers. When a question is designed, possible alternate answers must be kept in mind, particularly, if they are open ended. Assumptions must be clarified. The focus and reference of the questions should be such that the respondent tends to answer it objectively.

Example Clearly laid down policies are necessary for promoting innovation in industry.

Questions

(i) Policies and procedures for R&D in your organisation are:

Very Clear	Fairly Clear	Moderate	Ambiguous	Very Obscure
5	4	3	2	1

(ii) If you have answered the above question (i) as Ambiguous or Very Obscure to what extent, in your opinion, are absence of clearly defined policies the cause for the poor rate of innovation in your organisation.

Very Large Extent		Moderate Extent		Very Small Extent
5	4	3	2	1

Step 3—Method of administration When the questionnaire elicits information regarding behaviour—past and present—and intended attitudes and opinions, it is desirable to use an interview along with the questionnaire. Mail survey or telephone survey may be used, particularly for demographic properties like age, sex, income, occupation and the like, as in most survey research.

Step 4—Form of response The response format deals particularly with the freedom of the researcher and that of the respondent. The formats usually used are open-ended and multiple-choice questions.

- In the open-ended format, the respondent is free to give any reply. A wide range of answers is obtained in this type of question, that is, variance of the relevant variable tends to be rather high. But in certain cases, some special answers may be very useful. The researcher in no way influences the respondent for a particular type of answer. Errors due to lack of articulation are present and may decrease with probing.
- Multiple choice questions are easier to answer and reduce interviewer bias. Gradations of answers are possible, but involve greater design effort on the part of the researcher. Answers, other than those offered, are lost. Usually, the problems will be regarding the number of alternatives to give and to check whether the alternatives are balanced or

unbalanced. Balanced designs are universally preferred. To decide which method is better, a split ballot approach can be used. Two or more versions of the questions are offered to a small group of respondents. The best one is chosen.

Step 5—Wording and phrasing of questions In this regard, the basic principle is to make the questions simple and straightforward. Increasing the length of the questions for the same answer is desirable.

Example Capital productivity (where highly machine-oriented operations are involved), material productivity (when cost of material is a major portion of product cost) and labour productivity (when operations are mostly manual) are a few productivity indices used in manufacturing organisations.

Considering the most relevant one for your organisation, how would you rate your organisation's productivity?

	Very High		Moderate		Very Low
Capital productivity	5	4	3	2	1
Material productivity	5	4	3	2	1
Labour productivity	5	4	3	2	1

Step 6—Sequence of questions The sequence of questions may be as follows:

- Simple questions in the beginning to complex questions in the end, with increasing complexity.
- Questions must be free from bias in the beginning.
- Neutral questions in the beginning, sensitive ones in the middle, and controversial ones in the end are desirable because generally it has been found that the efficiency of response is high in the beginning and low at the end.

Step 7—Layout of the questions The format and layout of the questionnaire should be physically designed so as to eliminate recording errors. Branching questions (like in computer programmes) should be avoided, particularly on mailed questionnaires. Sometimes, it is desirable to include codes with the questions.

Step 8—Iteration Like in any design function, it may be necessary to go through steps one to seven in one or two iterations to eliminate undesirable features of questions.

Step 9—Pre-testing and revision of questions The pre-test is generally done on a small sample of respondents who are similar to the respondents of the main study (undergraduates in campus in place of senior executives is to be avoided!). The main questions involved in pre-test are the following:

- Which are the items to be pre-tested? The guiding factor is to choose questions, in which the interviewer's errors tends to be large.
- How is the pre-test conducted? It is essential to interview the respondents after answering the questionnaire and ascertain why the questions were answered the way they were. Alternatively, protocol analysing (loud thinking of the respondent during answering), and debriefing may also be used.
- Is the number of respondents sufficient? Adequate sample size should be determined for the pre-test (cf. Sample size determination).

Interviews

Interviews can be used in all segments of the population, whereas questionnaires can be used only with educated segments, particularly where the questions tend to become complex. The sample for interviews tends to be more representative than in the case of questionnaires as

interviews

Interviews can be used for data collection for all segments of population whereas questionnaire can be used only with the educated segment. They are the commenest method to get information on behaviour, attitudes, needs and characteristics of people. Interviews are in-depth in nature.

people are generally more inclined to talk than to write. Interviews are flexible and in this sense a little more customer-oriented than standard, which is the case with questionnaires. Questions not understood by respondents can be explained, which is not possible with questionnaires. A skillful interviewer can overcome unwillingness on the part of the respondent to answer emotionally laden or complex questions.

Depth interview Interviews are the most common methods of obtaining information on behaviour, attitudes, needs, and characteristics of people. One method of getting information is to ask directly. But direct questions may fail to elicit proper answers because the subject is unwilling, or the questions are embarrassing, or for other reasons. Depth interview is a technique used under these circumstances. There are two kinds of depth interviews—individual depth interview and focused group interview. Focused group interviews are most widely used in management research.

individual depth interview
The interviewer develops freely questions as he or she goes along the interviewing process and restrains from influencing the respondent who is free to respond as he or she likes.

Individual depth interview This may take anywhere between 1/2 an hour to 45 minutes. The interviewer asks no specific set of questions. There is freedom for the interviewer to create questions as he goes along with the interview. On the other hand, the respondent has the freedom of response, both with respect to content and with respect to manner. The interviewer should not try to influence the respondent in any way to change, either the content or the form. Ideas obtained through individual depth interview are generally of high quality (Fern, 1982). Individual depth interview is used:

- When detailed probing is necessary to elicit answers on behaviour, attitude, character, and needs.
- When the subject matter is confidential.
- When emotions or embarrassment may be evoked while answering the questions.
- When obtaining answers to questions which would be constrained in groups because of the subject's conformity to socially acceptable norms.
- When information on complex behaviour patterns is desired while interviewing professionals.
- When it may be desirable to allow the respondent to sketch anecdotes or tell stories.

Fern (1982) investigated into the assumptions of focus group for idea generation and obtained a few useful results.

Individual interviews produce higher quality and higher volume of ideas per individual, which are useful in exploratory research. One of the major disadvantages of individual depth interview is that it is tiring and only a small number of people can be interviewed per day, say five to six persons.

focused group interview
A group of individuals is interviewed by the researcher focusing on a given experience and its effects. Group is led by a moderator and is informed of topic in advance. Respondents are free to express their own lines of thought but are controlled only to the general direction of the responses to the subject under focus.

Focused group interview A group of 8 to 12 individuals is formed to reflect a particular behaviour or characteristic and is led by a moderator. The moderator must develop a rapport with the group, set structured group rules for interaction, and clarify objectives of the interview. He must evoke intense discussion. Finally, he must summarise the outcome of the interview.

The main function of the interviewer is to focus attention upon a given experience and its effects. What topics and what aspects of the topics are to be covered is known in advance to the interviewer. The topics or their aspects are derived from the research problem by the interviewer and/or based on the experience in which the respondent has participated, or both. The list of topics or aspects forms a framework for the interview but the manner in which the questions are framed and asked is left largely to the interviewer's discretion. The respondent is free to express his own line of thought; however, the interviewer controls the direction of the interview to achieve focus by confirming or guiding the respondents to give him the information he wants.

The persons interviewed are known to have been involved in the particular situation and the interviewer has analysed the theoretically significant elements, patterns, and structure of the situation. Also, the scientist has arrived at certain propositions or hypotheses regarding the situation. Based on these two premises, he develops a guide to the interview, setting forth the major areas of inquiry and the kind of data to be obtained. This enables the interviewer to get the situation defined as per the respondent group and modify or sharpen his hypothesis or proposition. A more pervasive definition of focused interview could include any interview in which the interviewer knows in advance what specific aspects of an experience he wishes to have the respondent group cover, whether or not the interviewer has observed or analysed the specific situation.

A focussed group has several advantages. Individuals can sharpen their opinions. More accurate information can be obtained by the focus group interview than by interviewing a single individual. Security in belonging to a crowd urges some inarticulate respondents to speak out. The answers in a focus group interview are more spontaneous and feel for the area represented by the group is much greater. Volume of ideas per individual may be smaller and the cost of interviewing will be lower for focus interviews. The determination of correct group sizes is very important for focus groups. Two groups of four persons each may help in getting more information than a single eight-person group. Its disadvantages are that it is difficult to ascertain a random sample for focussed group. Participants may play games, distorting the outcome of the interview. Strong individuals affect group reactions and moderator biases are present. Also, generalisation from group to population is generally risky. [Refer to chapter by Alan Hedgs in Walker, 1985.]

Projective Techniques

The underlying theory behind projective techniques is that the description of vague and fuzzy objects requires interpretations based on one's experience, attitudes, and values. The more vague the object is, the greater the revelation of the respondent. There are four types of projective techniques: (i) Association tests, (ii) Completion tests, (iii) Construction techniques, and (iv) Expression techniques. All have originated from clinical psychology.

projective techniques
These require a well trained interviewer. In this form of interview evaluations are obtained on vague and fuzzy objects or pictures and interpretations are made by the interviewer to measure attitudes feelings and experiences.

Association tests In these tests either the first thought or word that comes to mind when the researcher presents a word or phrase (free word association) or successive words or thoughts that come to mind (successive word organisation), is given by the respondent. The responses are analysed for measuring attitudes to certain category of stimuli.

Completion tests In sentence completion tests, the respondent completes an incomplete sentence with the phrase or word, that comes first to his mind (cf. open-ended question). In strong completion techniques, which are an extended version of the S.C.T., an incomplete sentence is completed based on the respondents' experiences and attitudes.

Construction techniques The respondent is asked to construct (that is, develop) a stray diagram or a description by just presenting a visual depiction of a context.

Cartoon techniques A cartoon or a drawing is shown to the respondent and the respondent writes a story or draws a picture. This will be the projection of the sub-conscious mind or socially unacceptable feelings.

Third person techniques The respondent is informed about what a third person possesses or does or which characteristic he has. The respondent is then asked to express his feelings towards these.

Vague pictures Details are as above.

Expression techniques This is mainly role-playing (by the respondents) of the behaviour of another person.

All these techniques require a highly trained interviewer. They tend to be expensive and since the samples are small and are non-probable in nature, the respondents are generally non-representative. Considerable measurement errors creep in. It has one advantage, however, that is, of uncovering aspects not given out by direct interviews. Often, this helps in hypothesis generation. (Anastasi, 1982.)

non-sampling errors
These errors relate to the data collection procedures of observation interview and survey. They are of two kinds. Non-observation errors which are due to some elements not having been studied and observation errors which are due to respondents not answering certain questions / answering deliberately wrongly.

NON-SAMPLING ERRORS

Sampling errors are statistical errors arising out of drawing inferences from sample to population. They can be estimated. It is obvious that in a complete enumeration census, sampling errors will be totally absent. But the data gathered will still have errors due to other reasons. These errors are called non-sampling errors. Non-sampling errors are common to both research sample surveys and complete enumerative surveys. Errors arise in the method of data collection, data processing, and in the responding elements. The following paragraphs briefly discuss the non-sampling errors related to sample surveys.

The sources of errors are (Murthy, 1967):

- Inadequate data specification.
- Inadequate or faulty methods of interview, observation, or measurement.
- Lack of trained investigators.
- Inadequate scrutiny of basic data.
- Errors in coding data entry and verification.
- Errors in presentation and printing.
- Non-coverage errors.
- Response errors.

These however could be treated as two errors, non-observation errors and observation errors.

Non-Observation Errors

These errors arise in sampling surveys because some population elements of interest are not studied. Non-inclusion may be due to an inadequate sampling frame in which some elements of interest are left out, either as a result of wrong procedure (incomplete listing) or deliberately, because of practical difficulties. These are termed non-coverage errors. Sometimes there may be over coverage, that is, the same items listed differently in different lists may get duplicated. For example, when a company manufacturing multiple family products is listed under different product classifications and product classification lists are used as frame, the same organisation may get duplicated in the sample.

The other major types of non-sampling errors are non-response errors. These arise because the subjects included in the sample did not respond. The non-response may be straightforward refusal to respond to the survey, delaying the response testing, or the persistence of the researcher to a point beyond acceptable time limit.

Observation Errors

These are field errors caused by the respondent not answering specific questions; or answering certain questions deliberately wrongly, ambiguously, or carelessly, which render the questionnaire one of doubtful utility. Interviews are much better than questionnaires from the point of view of observation errors.

Handling non-sampling errors Improving the sampling frame and adjusting the results appropriately can reduce non-coverage errors. Non-response errors can be reduced by making prior appointments, by follow-ups, and by convincing the respondent of the importance and value of his response to the research (for details see Churchill, 1987, Chapter 11).

factorial validity
This validity for a data collection procedure can be obtained by subjecting the data to confirmatory factor analysis to confirm whether theorized dimensions emerge from the data.

VALIDITY AND RELIABILITY OF DATA COLLECTION PROCEDURES

Validity and reliability in data collection relates not only to accuracy in the data items that are measured but its accuracy with respect to the purpose for which it was collected.

Factorial validity can be established by submitting the data to confirmatory factor analysis. The results of factor analysis (a multivariate technique) will confirm whether or not the theorised dimensions emerge. The measures are developed by first delineating the dimensions, so as to operationalise the concept. Factor analysis would reveal whether the theorised dimensions are indeed tapped by the items in the measure. Criterion-related validity can be established by methods, that are already discussed in section on validity is measurement in chapter 10.

The reliability of a measure is established by testing for both consistency and stability. Consistency indicates how the items measuring a concept hang well together as a set. Cronbach's alpha is a reliability coefficient that reflects how well the items in a set are positively correlated to one another. Cronbach's alpha is computed in terms of the average intercorrelations among the items measuring the concept. The closer Cronbach's alpha is to 1, the higher the internal consistency reliability (Kerlinger, 1986).

consistency
Split half reliability coefficient is obtained by splitting the total questions set into two half sets and correlating their scores. This tests the consistency of data collection procedure.

The methods to be followed for consistency, reliability and stability, as discussed in section on reliability in measurement in chapter 10, can also be applied to data collection procedures. The following sections discuss some additional aspects of validity and reliability of interviews, observation, and questionnaires.

Another measure of consistency (reliability) used in specific situations is the split half reliability coefficient. Since this reflects the correlations between two halves of a set of items, the coefficients obtained will vary depending on how the scale is split. Sometimes split-half reliability is obtained to test for consistency when more than one scale, dimension, or factor is assessed, and the items across each of the dimensions or factors are split based on some predetermined logic (Campbell, 1976). In almost every case, Cronbach's alpha is an adequate test of internal consistency/reliability.

As discussed earlier, the stability of a measure can be assessed through parallel form reliability and test-retest reliability. When a high correlation between two similar forms of a measure is obtained, parallel form reliability is established. Test-retest reliability can be established by computing the correlation between the same tests administered at two different time periods (Sekaran, 2000).

Validity and Reliability of Interviews

The key to an effective interview is establishing rapport. The relative status of the interviewer and his ethnic origin facilitate the establishment of rapport. Women and younger people generally seem to be more successful in eliciting information (Best and Kahn, 1986). Experience tends to increase interviewing skills. Interviews based on carefully designed structures are generally more valid. Critical judgement of experts is helpful in determining the questions. Restating questions in an altered form will ensure reliability or repeating the interview would also help in this. Danger of interview bias is constant, however, inexperienced researchers do not ordinarily possess bias.

Validity and Reliability of Observation

In order that observation is valid to a satisfactory degree, significant incident of behaviour must be identified. One way to ensure this is to supplement the knowledge and skill of the researcher with the judgement of experts in the field and the relationship of qualities in the incidents to establish theories. Researchers may tend to see what they expect to see and to overlook incidents that do not fit their theory (Best and Kahn, 1986). This may distort their observation. It is better to use independent observers trained in observing and recording. Observation try-outs may be used in the initial phase. Joint observation helps build reliability. Randomly selected time samples (5 seconds or 10 seconds) may help more in obtaining unbiased and representative samples of behaviour and would enhance both validity and reliability.

Validity and Reliability of Questionnaires

A possible procedure for validation and ensuring reliability of questionnaires is suggested below:

1. Ask the right questions.

2. Phrase them in the least ambiguous manner.
3. Clearly define the important terms.
4. Rate the content validity.
5. Obtain predictive validation by correlating questionnaire scores with observed behaviour or peer/superior ratings.
6. Administer the questionnaire to the same participants twice and compare the two responses.
7. Get the first four listed above checked by an expert.

SUMMARY

The two sources of data for a research problem are secondary data, which was already collected for some other purpose but useful for solving the research problem; and primary data, which has to be specially collected by the researcher through the use of tools of data collection. Secondary data can be internal to a company, like company reports and in-house journals, or external to it, like computer databases and government publications. The advantage of secondary data is the low cost and effort to obtain data. The researcher—using one or more tools like observation, questionnaire, interview and projective techniques—gathers primary data. The type of tool used depends on research design, but generally a combination of two or more needs to be used. Observation is the most direct method of data collection and is used when other methods are not feasible. Facial expression and body language can give to the observer rich information.

In most surveys, questionnaires are preferred because skills required for data collection are less, large samples can be handled easily and there is greater objectivity in the method. But the main limitation is low response rates. The *sine qua non* of questionnaire design is to keep it simple, unambiguous, and to carefully sequence the questions.

Interviews are best suited for obtaining information on attitudes, behaviour, needs and characteristics of people. Depth interviews by a trained and skillful interviewer are best suited for situations where information on emotionally-laden issues are being probed. Focused interviews are group interviews, that elicit information from a group on its experience in a specific problem area or situation. Projective techniques like completion test and cartoon techniques are intended to uncover subconscious feelings and opinions of the responder, which no other technique can provide.

Suggested Readings

- Bernard, Russel H. (2000). *Social Research Methods*. London: Sage.
- Cartwright, C. A. and G.P. Cartwright (1974). *Developing Observational Skills*. New York: McGraw-Hill.
- Peterson, Robert A. (2000). *Constructing Effective Questionnaires*. New York: Barnes and Noble.
- Walker, R. (1985). *Applied Qualitative Research*. Aldershot: Gower.
- Zimmerman, Donald and Muraski Michail Lynn (1995). *Elements of Information Gathering: A Guide for Technical Communicators, Scientists and Engineers*. Phoenix: Oryx Press.

QUESTIONS AND EXERCISES

1. What is the difference between (i) natural and contrived observation, and (ii) direct and indirect observation? Explain with examples.
2. When do you use the following?
   (a) Depth interview schedule
   (b) A mailed questionnaire
   (c) Focused interview
   (d) An unstructured interview
3. What is secondary data? When do you use it for research? Are there different types of secondary data? If yes, give examples.
4. What are the choices of tools available for collecting primary data? Give examples.
5. Study a few research reports or dissertations that use questionnaires. What types of questions were used? Was the choice of the question type adequate for the research undertaken? Comment.
6. Which type of data collection method would you use for the following situations? Justify your choice.
   (a) You are required to find out what kind of leadership exists in a large organisation.
   (b) There is a general feeling among researchers that technology development effort in an industrial scenario, like the Indian one, dominated by foreign collaborations, is low key. You have to verify it.
   (c) You have to assess what kind of training programmes are popular with industrial organisations.
   (d) Introduction of total quality management approaches are believed to be ineffective in some organisations. You have to find out whether it is a fact and if so why.
   (e) In implementing modern management techniques the research question is CEOs acceptance is less important than the acceptance of the lower level managers and workers.
7. Search for a few good field survey research studies. Get the details of the research framework and variables. Develop questionnaires/interview schedules for data collection. Check against the one actually used or discuss the merits of your questionnaire. Test it against a small sample and note its shortcomings.
8. How are tests different from questionnaires? When do you use tests and when do you generally design a questionnaire? Give some examples.
9. Choose a questionnaire from a thesis. Carefully study (i) the type of scales, (ii) the working of questions, (iii) the layout of questions, (iv) form of response. Do you agree with each for the research continued in the thesis? Comment in detail.
10. How do you reduce non-sampling errors during data collection in (i) questionnaires and (ii) interviews?
11. What is question layout? Why is careful consideration of layout important in questionnaire construction?
12. In what research situations are projective techniques useful? What are the disadvantages of projective techniques?
13. If repeatedly gathered data shows the same results over a number of replications, are the results valid? Or are they reliable, or both?
14. What would you do to validate and verify the reliability of a questionnaire when it consists of a mix of homogeneous and non-homogeneous questions? Explain your approach.
15. What would you do to validate a questionnaire that has only questions demanding yes/no responses?
16. If you have validated a questionnaire, is it necessary to validate the responses (data) obtained through it? Discuss. If your answer is yes, fully/partially, explain how would you do it?
17. Evaluate the following questionnaire portions from the point of view of format and wording of questions.

(A) Questionnaire Set (Mukund Mohan, 1986)

Instructions: The questionnaire set is a part of a study undertaken on implementation of production/operations management techniques in selected Indian industries. Your company is included in the sample required for the study.

Based on your experience and belief about the implementation project, which you have already discussed with the case worker, you are expected to rate the items on the scales given along with.

Every item begins with a Statement. Relate the Statement with the project under study, and then answer Query 1. Only if, the answer is 'Yes', proceed further, otherwise move onto the next item. It is important to keep in mind "For the project under study - -" while you answer Query 2. Answer the Query 3 in consonance with the Query 2.

Please note the following points, while you answer:

- Terms such as Adequacy, Efficiency, Sufficiency, Appropriateness, and Effectiveness should be taken only in a subjective sense.
- Do not consult anybody. Your cooperation is essential for the successful completion of the study.

IMPLEMENTATION CONTEXT

Item 101

Statement: The structuredness of a problem situation, in the sense that a standard or readymade solution or model is available for implementation and problem solving, is an important factor for successful implementation.

Query 1: Do you agree with the statement?

Agree __________ Disagree __________

Query 2: For the project under study, the degree of structuredness of the problem-situation was __________

Z1. Small __________ Z2. Do Not Know __________ Z3. Large __________
(Highly complex) (Highly Structured)

Query 3: The structuredness of the problem situation was to the extent of __________

0 1 2 3 4 5 6 7 8 9 10

_______ SMALL _______ Z2 _______ LARGE _______

Item 112

Statement: Participation of workers and other supervisory personnel in the design and implementation phases is an important factor for successful implementation.

Query 1: Do you agree with the statement?

Agree __________ Disagree __________

Query 2: For the project under study, the degree of participation was __________

Z1. Small __________ Z2. Do Not Know __________ Z3. Large __________
(Poor) (Excellent)

Query 3: The participation was to the extent of _______

0 1 2 3 4 5 6 7 8 9 10

_______ SMALL _______ Z2 _______ LARGE _______

Item 123

Statement: The modernity of the technology for production compared to the current state of the technology is an important factor for successful implementation.

Query 1: Do you agree with the statement?

Agree __________ Disagree __________

Query 2: For the project under study, a degree of modernity of the technology was ________

Z1. Small ________ Z2. Do Not Know ________ Z3. Large ________
(Poor) (Excellent)

Query 3: The modernity of the technology was to the extent of ________

0 1 2 3 4 5 6 7 8 9 10

________ SMALL ________ Z2 ________ LARGE ________

Item 201

Statement: The objective of problem solving and implementation should be well determined for successful implementation.

Query 1: Do you agree with the statement?

Agree ________ Disagree ________

Query 2: For the project under study, a the degree of clarity of the objective was ________

Z1. Small ________ Z2. Do Not Know ________ Z3. Large ________
(Poor) (Excellent)

Query 3: The clarity of objective was to the extent of ________

0 1 2 3 4 5 6 7 8 9 10

________ SMALL ________ Z2 ________ LARGE ________

Item 211

Statement: Resistance from shop-floor personnel should be sufficiently resolved for successful implementation.

Query 1: Do you agree with the statement?

Agree ________ Disagree ________

Query 2: For the project under study, the degree of sufficiency of resistance resolution was ________

Z1. Small ________ Z2. Do Not Know ________ Z3. Large ________
(Unresolved) (Resolved)

Query 3: The sufficiency of the resistance resolution was to the extent ________

0 1 2 3 4 5 6 7 8 9 10

________ SMALL ________ Z2 ________ LARGE ________

Item 301

Statement: Changes within the organisation should occur as per the plan, within a specified period, for successful implementation.

Query 1: Do you agree with the statement?

Agree ________ Disagree ________

Query 2: For the project under study, the degree of implementation success was ________

Z1. Small ________ Z2. Moderate ________ Z3. Large ________
(No change) (Temporary) (Permanent)

Query 3: The implementation success was to the extent of ________

0	1	2	3	4	5	6	7	8	9	10

________SMALL________________Z2________________LARGE__________

(b) Questionnaire Set (Jays, 1995)

Attachment to the firm

Q1. If you had your way, how many years would you remain with this company?

1–2 years # 3–4 years # >5 years # until retirement

Satisfaction

Overall job satisfaction

Q2. I rate my division/department higher, as a place to work than other organisations I know about.

strongly disagree # disagree # neither disagree nor agree # agree # strongly agree

Supervisor's consideration

Q3. How would you describe the leadership climate in your Division?
(Check the most correct option)

strongly task-oriented
moderately task-oriented
neither task nor people-oriented
moderately people-oriented
strongly people-oriented

Satisfaction about leadership climate

Q4. Do you find superiors willing to make time to discuss a problem that might be worrying you?

#almost always #often #sometimes #rarely #never

Psychological quits

Q5. Taking everything into account (the pay, the people you work with, supervision and the work you do) how do you feel about your job?

i love it # on the whole I like it # i am not really keen on it # i dislike it a good deal # i hate it

Q6. Given an opportunity to be the leader of a prestigious project of the organisation, what would you do?

grab it # try to get it # wait for it to come to you # try avoiding it # reject the offer

Q7. Would you recommend your son/daughter to join this organisation?

#very unlikely #unlikely #neither #likely ‘ #very likely

Q8. How would you like yourself to be identified as?

#an individual #a family man #a productive citizen #a member of an organisation #a part of a team

Q9. What was the last major development in the organisation?
(specify).......................

Q10. How would you describe your identity in the organisation?

like a bird whose wings have been clipped

like a bird with roadside astrologers
like a caged bird
like a free bird
like a bird living with an ornithologist

Q11. Please put these 5 things in order of importance.

having a job with high status
working with friendly people
adequate wages
security of employment
doing work that is personally satisfying

(c) Questionnaire Set (B.S.Chetty 1995)

Q1. When strategic plans are being formulated, or critical decisions are being made, some of the following factors may have to be taken into account. Indicate how important a consideration each of the following factors is in influencing the outcome of the strategic decisions that are made by members of the top management group in your firm. (Circle one number on each line.)

	Not Important at all	Only a little Important	Somewhat Important	Considerably Important	Extemely Important
a. Suppliers of parts and raw materials	1	2	3	4	5
b. Suppliers of equipment	1	2	3	4	5
c. Supply of labour	1	2	3	4	5
d. Distributors of your products	1	2	3	4	5
e. Actual users of your products	1	2	3	4	5
f. Competitors for your supply of raw materials and parts	1	2	3	4	5
g. Competitors for your customers	1	2	3	4	5
h. Government regulations controlling your industry	1	2	3	4	5
i. The public's political views and attitudes toward your industry	1	2	3	4	5
j. Your relationship with trade unions	1	2	3	4	5
k. Keeping up with new technological requirements in your industry in the production of goods	1	2	3	4	5
l. Improving and developing new products by implementing new technological advances in the industry	1	2	3	4	5
m. Your sources for financial resources	1	2	3	4	5

Q2. Please rate your firm's performance during 1988-92 on a scale of 1 to 5, given the national average for firms in your industry.

National Average for Your Industry during 1988-92

			Above average				Below average
a.	Average annual growth in return on total assets during 1988–1992 (explained below)		1	2	3	4	5
b.	Average annual rate[1] of growth in sales during 1988–92		1	2	3	4	5
c.	Average annual rate of growth in return on sales during 1988–92. (explained below)		1	2	3	4	5

1. Return on total assets $= \dfrac{\text{Net profits}^2}{\text{Total assets}}$

2. Return on Sales $= \dfrac{\text{Net profits}^2}{\text{Sales}}$

Q3. The response to this question, in certain cases, may be sensitive information. Since only year-to-year changes are important for the purpose of this study, the actual numbers may be disguised by multiplying throughout by any fraction (such as 0.72), or an integer not that is revealed.

Note: Please use the same integer or fraction throughout.

Year	1988	1989	1990	1991	1992
Sales Rs (in lakhs)					

Q4. Ratio of (Net profits/Total assets)

Note: The values for Net Profits and Total Assets from the corporate annual report or divisional reports may be used here. If these figures are not readily available, the following guidelines may be used.

Net Profits: Profit prior to deducing (a) income tax, (b) corporate assessment for interest on corporate debt, and (c) special and non-recurring costs.

Total Assets: Cash + other assets + net receivables + finished goods inventory + inventory of raw materials + work-in-process inventory + net book value of plant and equipment (net of depreciation).

or

Investment + short term borrowings + other current liabilities

Year	1988	1989	1990	1991	1992
Ratio					

1. Not adjusted for inflation (average annual rate of inflation 10.4%)
2. Profits before taxes

Q5. Ratio of (Net profits/Sales)

Year	1988	1989	1990	1991	1992
Ratio					

CHAPTER 13

Data Preparation and Preliminary Data Analysis

- Introduction
- Data Preparation
- Exploratory Data Analysis
- Statistical Estimation
- Content Analysis

Data Mining

LEARNING OBJECTIVES

Upon completion of this chapter, you will be able to:

- ✓ Understand the need to convert raw data into researchable data
- ✓ Learn about the various steps in data preparation
- ✓ Learn the need for coding categorisation and transcribing for computer processing
- ✓ Understand the ways of converting data into new variables
- ✓ Learn how to describe data and display it in suitable forms for efficient communication
- ✓ Familiarise yourself with tabulation, cross tabulation, and distribution
- ✓ Learn to summarize data
- ✓ Study a few techniques of exploratory data analysis
- ✓ Understand data mining
- ✓ Know about content analysis as a means of studying written communication

INTRODUCTION

Raw data from a research project cannot generally be directly used for analysis. It has to be prepared and converted into a suitable form. Then, it has to be subjected to preliminary analysis. The way raw data is prepared and the manner in which the preliminary data analysis is carried out can often make a substantial difference in the usefulness of a report.

Raw data of any type is in the form of source documents—completed questionnaires, interview schedules, observation sheets, or records of different types. In many cases, the raw data may be numbers and in others answers to questions. The initial database is usually in the form of a data matrix in which the rows are records of a particular study object and columns correspond to specific variables (a cell is the value of a specific variable in a specific case). The data is entered into the matrix, either directly (when they are mere numbers) or indirectly (after coding, for example, answers to open-ended questions). Some manual editing may have to be done to the source code and later, on the coded and entered data, also through the computer for correcting missing data errors and improving quality. Finally, the data base is organised.

initial database
This is usually in the form of a data matrix in which the rows are records of a particular study object and columns corresponds to specific variables or problem characteristics.

Description of data and exploratory data analysis (EDA) are analogous to exploratory study undertaken prior to the main research study. EDA plays a complementary role in the final analysis of data. In description basic measures of the data, like mean and dispersion, are computed; the characteristic of the distribution of the variables is obtained. In EDA one makes further graphical representations of the data for a qualitative appraisal. Special intuitive rearrangements of the descriptions obtained tend to reveal additional, and sometimes hidden, features and pattern, in the data.

Large databases, as in secondary data (public databases), or data gathered over years, as in longitudinal research are available. Massive qualitative data are generated in qualitative research methods, like large cases or participant observation. In such cases, initial deeper probing of the data using techniques of data mining yield underlying patterns, trends, and knowledge. This will be very useful to the researcher for final analysis and interpretation. The techniques can also serve to generate hypothesis, indirectly using AI methods.

In this chapter, we will first examine data preparation activities and then preliminary data analysis, which includes data displays and data mining methods.

DATA PREPARATION

preparation of data
The steps involved in data preparation are: editing data, coding data, transcription of data, generating new variables and frequency distribution tabulation.

The steps involved in the preparation of data are (i) editing data, (ii) coding, (iii) transcription of data (transcribing), (iv) generating new variables/functional combinations/splitting forms, and (v) tabulation of frequency distribution (Tull and Hawkins, 1987).

Editing Data

After getting the raw data, the first job is to edit the data in such a way that the data are presentable, readable, and accurate. The basic purpose of editing is to impose some minimum quality standard on the raw data. Editing involves the inspection and correction of each questionnaire or observation form. Data editing is often done in two stages—field edit and central office edit (Churchill, 1988). The field edit is a preliminary edit designed to detect the obvious omissions and inaccuracies in the data. Some of the items checked in this editing are completeness, legibility, comprehensibility, consistency, and uniformity of the data. The central office edit, which follows the field edit, involves more thorough and rigorous scrutiny and correction of completed returns. Most of the time, the questionnaires are pre-coded and are entered directly into the computer with little or no editing. Although this approach is economical, it often produces less accurate data. While entering the data into the computer, it is very important to decide what to do with unclear or wrong responses, missing data, or inconsistent responses. In addition, after the data are entered into the computer, computer editing should be conducted. The editor may also try to discern disinterest on the part of the respondent by careful scrutiny of the markings on the questionnaire. This means, data editing involves taking care of missing data and ambiguous answers, checking of accuracy and quality of the data, and, finally, computer editing.

Missing data It is very common for a questionnaire to be returned with one or more specific questions unanswered. This constitutes a 'no response'. It is very important to take a decision about what to do about such missing data. Often it is advisable to use the data as it is. That is, the unanswered questions could be assigned a 'missing' code, and entered into the computer. When multivariate analyses are being conducted, it is generally necessary to completely exclude any respondent with missing data on any variable in the analysis.

Ambiguous answers Many questionnaires contain one or more responses whose meaning is not clear. Under these circumstances, it is necessary to decide whether to 'guess' which answer is correct based on other responses in the questionnaire, or to discard the entire questionnaire, or to treat both answers as missing data, or to re-contact the respondent, or take other relevant action. Other kinds of ambiguities that may occur are illegible responses and marks between response categories.

Accuracy/Quality As the analyst reviews a number of questionnaires, he should note suspect responses. Respondents will sometimes rush through questionnaires in an almost random manner. This tends to produce a number of inconsistent responses. Questionnaires containing such inconsistencies should be examined carefully and deleted from the database if it appears that the respondents were haphazard in completing them. While editing, it is important to be alert for inconsistencies between responses obtained by different interviewers and individual questions that are frequently left unanswered or that produce ambiguous responses.

Computer editing Computer editing can be used instead of, or preferably in addition to, manual editing (Fellegi and Holt, 1976 and Hodges and Cosse, 1983). The computer can be instructed to examine each set of coded responses for values that lie outside the permissible range, or for conflicting responses to similar questions. It can also be used to run checks, and to detect variations in responses between interviewers.

Coding Data

coding data
Coding is conversion of raw data into symbols or numerals in order to facilitate tabulation, categorization and further processing.

Coding is 'the technical procedure by which data are categorised', that is, it involves establishing categories and assigning data to them. Through coding, the raw data is transformed into symbols, usually numerals, that may be tabulated and counted. However, the transformation is not automatic. It involves judgment on the part of the coder (Selltiz, Wrightsman and Cook, 1976).

Coding closed questions in most scaling devices is simple because the coding is established when the data collection instrument is designed. Respondents then code themselves with their responses, or the interviewer codes them in recording the responses on the checklist provided. Coding open-ended questions can be very difficult. The coder has to determine appropriate categories on the basis of answers that are not always anticipated (Schuman and Presser, 1979 and McDonald, 1982).

Establishing categories Categories for answers to multiple choice or dichotomous questions are established at the time when the question is formulated. Open-ended questions may also have response categories established at the time they are formulated. However, it is common to create some or all of the response categories to open-ended questions after at least some of the questionnaires have been returned. Since the computer analyses most of the studies, the common practice is to assign numerical values to the categories to distinguish between them. Common category values assigned for missing data are a 'blank', a 'constant', or a value that is one number larger than the largest response value.

Assigning data to categories After categories have been established and questionnaires or other measuring instruments have been completed by at least some respondents, the observations must be assigned to categories. This is typically done in a manner designed to allow computer analysis.

Transcription of Data (Transcribing)

Transcription of data is the process of physically transferring data from the measuring instruments onto cards, magnetic tape or disk, or directly into the computer. While the earlier standard for transcription was key punching into tab cards (IBM cards), this has largely been replaced by data entry via a keyboard onto magnetic tape or disk, or directly into the computer. Other methods of transcription used include the use of mark-sensed questionnaires and optical scanning. Mark sensing requires that the answer be recorded by marking it with a special pencil in an area that is coded for that answer; a machine 'reads' the answer by sensing the area in which it is recorded.

transcription of data
This is the process of physically transferring data from the measuring instruments on to computer media for making useable for computer analysis.

Optical scanning involves direct machine 'reading' of alphanumeric codes and transcription onto cards, magnetic tape or disk. These methods are usually too expensive and awkward to use except for very large or repeated studies in which the same collection form is used. In a sample survey, normally, data entry is done via keyboard to magnetic tape or disk, or into the computer.

New Variable/Functional Combination/Splitting Form

It is often necessary to create new variables as a part of the analysis procedure. The commonly used methods for generating new variables are as follows (Tull and Hawkins, 1987):

- New variables are often generated from combinations of other variables in the data. For, data on a person's age, marital status, and presence and age of children may be combined to generate a new variable called 'stage in the family life cycle'.
- It may be desirable to collect internally scaled data as such and later assign them to classes. For example, family income is often collected in rupees, and later classified by a convenient number of income brackets.
- New variables may be added from secondary data. For example, secondary information like median level of income, education, and employment in the country of residence of the respondent.

creation of new variables
New variables not contemplated prior to data collection can be developed using the coded data by combining two or more variables or converting scales or combining with the secondary data.

Data Description

Tabulation of Frequency Distribution Tabulation consists simply of counting the number of cases that fall into the various categories. The tabulation process starts with the preparation of basic data array. There are two types of tabulation procedures, namely, simple tabulation and cross tabulation. Simple tabulation involves counting a single variable. In cross tabulation, two or more of the variables are treated simultaneously. The next step in the tabulation process is the preparation of one-way and many-way frequency distributions.

The frequency distribution provides a much more concise portrayal of the data, which would be otherwise difficult to understand. Absolute frequency is simply the number of respondents who provided that particular value. Relative frequency is the percentage of all respondents who provide a particular value. Cumulative frequency is generally expressed as a per cent, though it can also be expressed as an absolute value. It is the percentage of all respondents who provide a response equal to or less than a particular value. When categorical data are being analysed, all of the categories are normally used in the construction of a frequency distribution. However, if there are a large number of categories, or if interval or ratio data are involved, it is useful to group the responses into a smaller set of categories. For example, a frequency distribution with 45 responses for 80 respondents would do little to clarify the nature of the response. In such situations, the researcher may use a smaller number of categories, determined either *a priori* or by the distribution of the data.

A one-way frequency distribution is a frequency distribution for a single variable. It is also called a simple tabulation. It is used, in addition to communicating the results of a study, (i) to determine the degree of item non-response, (ii) to locate blunders (errors that occur during editing, coding, or entering data into the computer), (iii) to locate outliers (observations so different in magnitude from the rest of the observations that the analyst chooses to treat them as special cases), (iv) to determine the empirical distribution of the variable in question, and (v) to calculate summary statistics (Churchill, 1988).

Example Frequency Table and Bar Chart for Nominal Data [Table 13.1 and Figs. 13.1 and 13.2]

Table 13.1 Nominal Data

Class of machines		*Number in class*	*Relative frequency per cent in each class*
1. Manually operated machines (MM)		75	37.5%
2. Semi-automatic machines (SAM)		93	46.5%
3. Fully automatic machines (FAM)		32	16.0%
	Total	200	100%

Fig. 13.1 Bar chart for Nominal Data

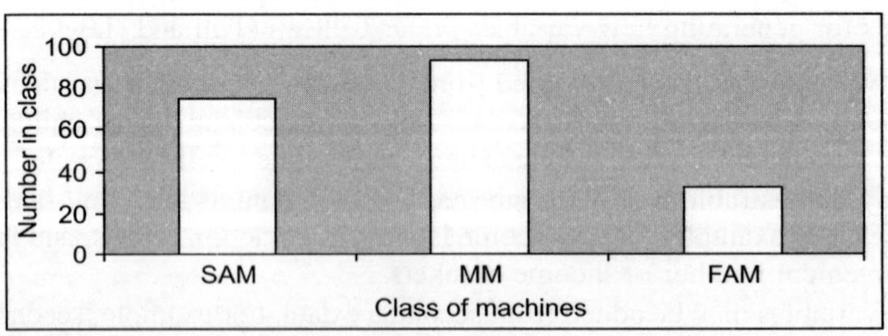

Fig. 13.2 Pie chart for Nominal Data

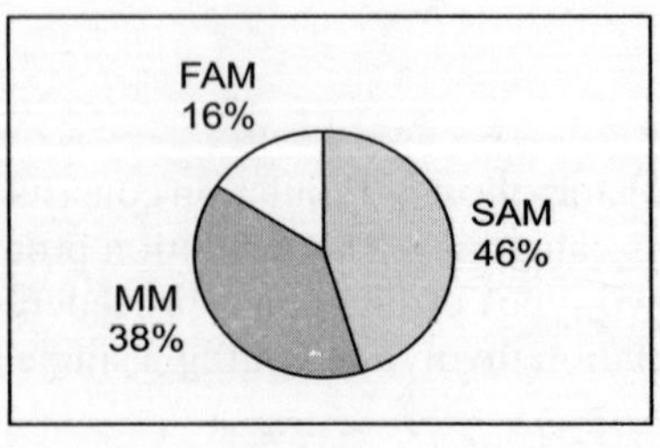

[A]. Nominal data:

[B]. Ordinal, interval and ratio data

Test scores obtained by a group of 100 candidates for admission to a training programme are shown in the Table 13.2a and 13.2b below. Make (i) a frequency table, (ii) a histogram, and distribution (Fig. 13.4) for the data, and (iii) find the mean and standard deviation.

(i) Cell interval = Highest – lowest number of classes

Table 13.2 (a)

57	70	75	78	82	84	86	88	89	94
62	70	75	78	82	84	86	88	90	94
62	71	75	79	82	84	87	88	90	95
64	72	76	79	83	84	87	88	90	95
65	72	76	79	83	85	87	88	91	96
67	72	76	80	83	85	87	88	92	96
67	73	77	80	84	85	87	88	92	98
68	73	78	81	84	86	87	89	92	98
68	74	78	81	84	86	87	89	93	99
69	74	78	81	84	86	88	89	93	99

Table 13.2 (b)

Test scores	*Frequency*
55 and under 60	1
60 and under 65	3
65 and under 70	6
70 and under 75	10
75 and under 80	15
80 and under 85	19
85 and under 90	27
90 and under 95	11
95 and under 100	8
Total	100

Frequency Table; [*Note*: Chosen number of classes = 8;]

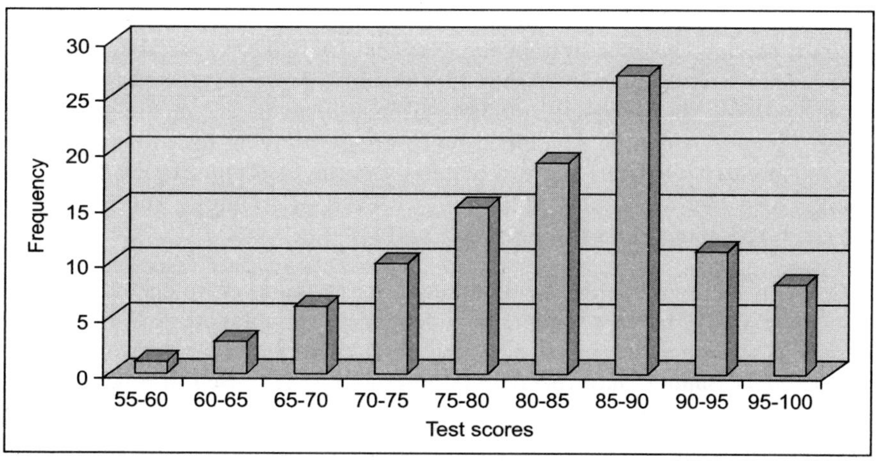

Fig. 13.3 Histogram for the data

Cell interval = (99–57)/8 = 5.25 (Rounded off to 5)

(ii) The histogram for the data is shown below:

Fig. 13.4 Frequency distribution

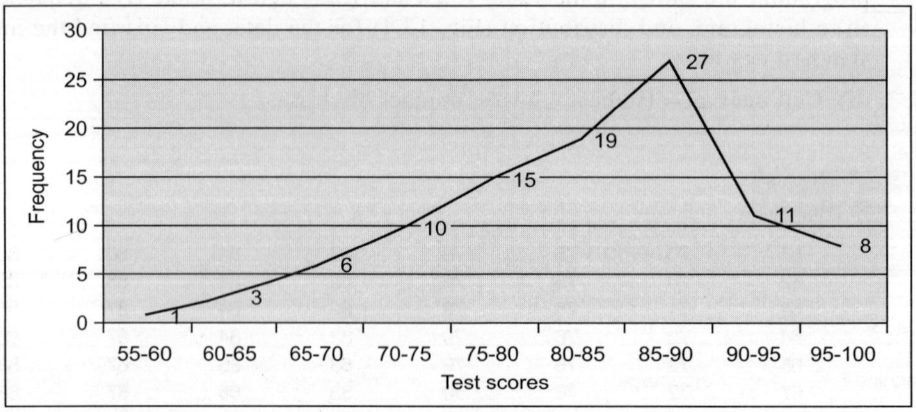

(iii) The frequency distribution is shown (Fig. 13.4). *Note*: The mid-points of the cell ranges are taken for drawing the curve (See next table).

One-way frequency distribution is to be distinguished from a two-way or n-way frequency distribution (two variables, n variables). There are two forms of n-way frequency distributions, one form of which is known as cross tabulation, and another form is banners.

cross tabulation
This is a method of tabulating relationships generally among two variables in which joint occurrences of the variables will be reflected as the cells in the table.

Cross tabulation Cross tabulation is a most important technique for studying the relationships among variables. It involves constructing a table so that one can see how respondents with a given value on one variable responded to one or more other variables. Constructing a two-way cross tabulation involves the following steps:

1. On the horizontal axis, list the value or name for each category of the first variable.
2. On the vertical axis, list the value or name for each category of the second variable.
3. For each respondent, locate the category on the horizontal axis that corresponds to his or her response.
4. Then find the value on the vertical axis that corresponds to his or her response on the second variable.
5. Record a 1 in the cell where the two values intersect.
6. Count the 1s in each cell.

Example In an inspection experiment, two machining operations are used to decide whether to accept material 1 or material 2. The number of items rejected after machining a sample of 200 separately on the machine is given in frequencies (Table 13.3). The cross tabulation developed for the same is shown in Table 13.4. Table 13.4 displays frequencies and row and column percentages successively so that quick comparisons may be made and any relational (association or causal) hypothesis can be developed by carefully studying the cross tabulation. The example shows only two machines and two materials. It can be easily extended to n machines and m materials in which case there will be n rows and m columns. The frequencies and percentages can be computed in a similar way.

Banners Banners are a way of displaying several cross tabulations in one table. In a banner the values for a variable of interest (preferably a dependent variable) are arrayed down the first column on the left and the values of potentially associated variables are arrayed in columns to the right in the table. Banners have become popular and widely used in reports prepared by research agencies. Banners allow data to be presented concisely so as to give depth to the data displayed in the table, which is not possible with the display of single cross tabulation. [See Maguire & Wilson 1983 for illustrations].

Table 13.3 Data

Treatment (Machining)		Inspection (Reject)	
	Material 1	Material 2	Total
Machine 1	72	48	120
Machine 2	56	24	80
Total	128	72	200

Table 13.4 Cross Tabulation

		Material 1	Material 2	Material 3
	Frequency	72	48	120
Machine 1	Percentage	36%	24%	60%
	Row percentage	60%	40%	100%
	Column percentage	56.25%	67.67%	
	Frequency	56	24	80
Machine 2	Percentage	28%	12%	40%
	Row percentage	70%	30%	100%
	Column percentage	43.75%	33.33%	
	Frequency	128	72	200
Total	Percentage column	64%	36%	100%
	Percentage	(100%)	(100%)	

Summarising Statistics

There are two major ways of summarising statistics. The first provides measures of the mid-point of the distribution and is known as measures of central tendency. The second gives an indication of the amount of variation in the data comprising the distribution and is known as measures of dispersion.

Central tendency The three primary measures of central tendency are the arithmetic mean, the median, and the mode. The arithmetic mean should be computed only from interval-scaled or ratio-scaled data. Adding all the observations and dividing the sum by the number of observations obtain it. Often, however, arithmetic means must be calculated from absolute frequency distributions. In these cases, the number of observations in that category multiplies the midpoint of each, the resultant category values are summed, and the number of observations divides the total.

$$\bar{x} = \frac{\sum_{i=1}^{n} f_i x_i}{n}$$

where f_i = the frequency of the ith class
x_i = the mid point of that class
h = the number of classes
n = the total number of observations

The median, which requires only ordinal data, is obtained by finding the value below which 50 per cent of the observations lie. If cumulative frequencies were calculated for the data array, it would be the value for which the cumulative frequency was 50 per cent.

The mode, requiring only nominal data, is found by determining the value that appears most frequently. In a relative frequency distribution, the mode is the class that has the highest frequency. Data can have more than one mode.

The three measures will not be the same for distribution of values that are not symmetrical and, when different, they are useful for different purposes. For obtaining an estimate of a population total, the sample arithmetic mean times the number of population units provides the best estimate. If one wants an estimate of the most representative amount, the mode should be used. If we want an average that is unaffected by extremes, the median is the best estimator.

Dispersion The standard deviation, variance, and range are measures of how 'spread out' the data is. The smaller these three values are, the more compact the data.

The formula for the standard deviation of a sample calculated from an array of the sample data is:

$$s = \sqrt{\left\{\frac{\sum_{i=1}^{n}(x_i - \bar{x})2}{n-1}\right\}}$$

Where s = sample standard deviation

x_i = the value of the ith observation

$\bar{x}$ = the sample mean, and

n = the sample size

m = mid range of cell value

f_i = frequency of x falling with m

The variance, the square of the standard deviation, is found by the same formula with the square root sign removed. The range is equal to the maximum minus the minimum value in the data array.

Example

Mean and standard deviation for the data of test scores.

$$\bar{X} = 82.7 \text{ (rounded)} = \frac{8270}{100}$$

$$S = \sqrt{\left\{\frac{\sum f(m-\bar{x})^2}{(n-1)}\right\}} = \sqrt{\{82.0505\}} = 9.06$$

Table 13.5

Test scores	*Frequency f*	*Midpoints m*	*(m – x̄)*	*(m – x̄)²*	*f (m – x̄)²*
55 and under 60	1	57.5	-25.2	635.04	635.04
60 and under 65	3	62.5	-20.2	408.04	1,224.12
65 and under 70	6	67.5	-15.2	231.04	1,386.24
70 and under 75	10	72.5	-10.2	104.04	1,040.40
75 and under 80	15	77.5	-5.2	27.04	405.60
80 and under 85	19	8.5	-0.2	0.04	0.76
85 and under 90	27	87.5	4.8	23.04	622.08
90 and under 95	11	92.5	9.8	96.04	1,056.44
95 and under 100	8	97.5	14.8	219.04	1,752.32
	100				Σ=8,123.00

EXPLORATORY DATA ANALYSIS

Exploratory data analysis is a logical extension of data description seen in the previous section. They are a collection of intuitive and theoretical tools for systematically exploring the data, understanding the data better, and a guide to patterns and trends underlying large amounts of data, either secondary as with large public databases, or primary, as with many qualitative research studies. In this section, we will study two statistically-oriented data display techniques, stem and leaf display and the box plots. We will also get a broad outline of the data mining technique, which uses a set of advanced statistical and AI techniques.

Stem and Leaf Display

Stem and leaf displays combine some of the characteristics of histograms and the general trend of a set of values as a whole. It can be manually derived or obtained in the computer by a software like Minitab. It displays individual data values highlighting distribution of values in each group as against a histogram, which gives only group aggregates.

stem and leaf display
This is a display used in exploratory data analysis. It displays individual data values highlighting the distribution in each group as against a histogram which gives group aggregates.

A manufacturing company wants to hold a finished stock inventory of at least 290 units for 25 items so that urgent orders can be filled quickly. A check on inventory levels of these items reveal the following number in stock. Are the stocks of these items adequate? Draw a stem and leaf diagram.

140, 270, 50, 0, 75, 150, 295, 70
500, 40, 0, 80, 140, 170, 170, 240
290, 15, 390, 660, 90, 310, 190, 320
200

	Stem and Leaf display		Histogram (Table)
0	00, 00, 15, 40, 50, 70, 75, 80, 90	(9)	0 – 99 9
1	40, 40, 50, 70, 70, 90	(6)	100 – 199 6
2	00, 40, 70, 90, 95	(5)	200 – 299 5
3	10, 20, 90	(3)	300 – 399 3
4		(1)	400 – 490 0
5	00	(1)	500 – 599 1
6	60		600 – 699 1
		(25)	(25)

Answer: only 7 of the 25 items in stock are equal to or greater than 290.

[*Note:* All displays are in terms of units].

The efficiency of this type of notation is obvious; for example,

0**| is used to record values between 0 and 99
3**|20 represents 320 and 6**|10 represents 610
[Leaves are arranged in ascending order, say,
0**|50, 00,75,70,40,00,80,15,90| (9)]

The leaf is a 2-digit leaf.

In a price system, if Rs 100/- is the unit Rs 6500/- would have been represented as 6*|5 and a stock out of 90 would have been represented as –0**|90 (0 to–99).

box plots
These are visual summaries of data displaying median, lower and upper quartiles, and largest and smallest values. Outliers are highlighted in box plots.

Box Plots

Box plots reduce the details present in stem and leaf displays and provides a visual summary of the data, which consists of median, lower, and upper quartiles of the largest and smallest values. Medians and quartiles are robust measures and insensitive to outliers and change very little for changes in small portions of the data (Tukey, 1977, Tufte, 1977). In summary, the box plot displays main features of data in terms of centre, middle half, range of data, and unusual observations.

Data table: Test scores obtained by candidates in an employment admission examination.

For the scores shown in table 13.6

- Number = 100
- Mean = 82.38
- Median = 84.00
- Standard deviation = √907.6 = 30
- Minimum = 57.00,
- Maximum = 99.00
- First quartile = 76.00 (Q_1)
- 3rd quartile = 88.00 (Q_3)

Table 13.6

57	70	75	78	82	84	86	88	89	94
62	70	75	78	82	84	86	88	90	94
62	71	75	79	82	84	87	88	90	95
64	72	76	79	83	84	87	88	90	95
65	72	76	79	83	85	87	88	91	96
67	72	76	80	83	85	87	88	92	96
67	73	77	80	84	85	87	88	92	98
68	73	78	81	84	86	87	89	92	98
68	74	78	81	84	86	87	89	93	99
69	74	78	81	84	86	88	89	93	99

Trimmed mean (TRMEAN) 5 per cent of the smallest values and 5 per cent of the largest values are 'trimmed' off and the mean is calculated and rounded off to the nearest integer value.

For the remaining 90 per cent of the values (after trimming 5 per cent lowest/highest values) the mean value is trimmed mean = 82.644.

Standard error of mean = 3

The box plot for the data in table is displayed in Figure below.

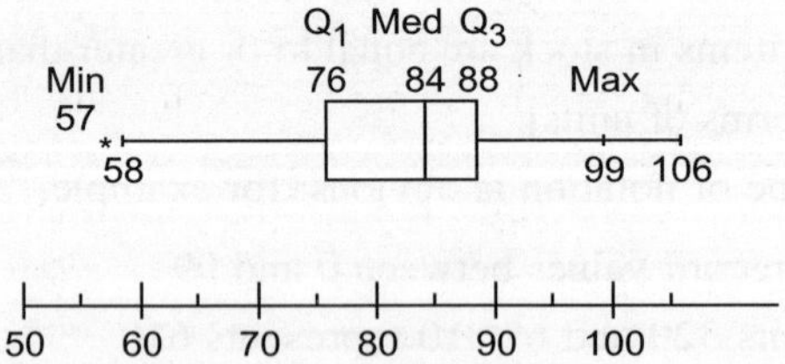

Note:

- The edges of box are 1st QRT and 3rd QRT values (Q_1 and Q_3).
- The box encloses Inter Quartile Region (IQR) or middle half of the data.
- Potential outliers are indicated by the symbol *.
- Potential outliers are values falling greater than 1½ IQRs below Q_1 or 1½ IQRs above Q_3.
- Serious outliers fall 3 IQRs above Q3 or 3 IQRs below Q_1.

For the problem:

- Value 57 is a potential outlier because it is more than 18 units below.
  76 (1½ (88-76) = 18) (Q_1) D; similarly 107 would bc an outlier
- Lines, called whiskers, extend from the box to the smallest and largest non-outlier values (58,106).

Data Mining

Computers deliver a flood of data, which with the advent of IT, are generated at great speeds. Sorting out relevant information from this mass of data is becoming increasingly difficult; for example, earth satellites generate terra-byte data every day. They are useful in many ways, but manual processing of such data is impractical and would lead to outdated results. This mind boggling volume of data may have a wealth of information, which needs to be unearthed. This is the motivation for data mining.

The purpose of data mining (DM) is knowledge discovery (KD). It extracts hidden information from large databases and helps in decision-making. Most business houses/corporations have databases on the computer giving minute details of the operations and transactions. Data mining can contribute significantly in deriving valuable information from these databases for detailed decision-making. Advances in storage and distribution have made centralised giant databases a reality. But it is the computational and analytic techniques that can render this data into patterns, trends, and useful information that DM provides. Data mining is an interdiscipli nary field with contribution from statistics, artificial intelligence, decision theory, and so on.

data mining
Data mining is a set of approaches which can identify and extract useful patterns from data stored in large real-world databases. There are two major approaches: general approach including models and techniques which can be used for any kind of data and domain specific approach for a particular problem situation. Data mining techniques consist of statistical analyses and heuristic search procedures involving learning.

However, data mining, as it is practiced at present, has evolved over nearly four decades, since the use of computers and accessories started being used for data collection and static data provision. Relational Databases Management System (RDBMS) and Structured Query Languages (SQL) were developed during the 80s and 90s for providing dynamic data at the level of the record. Subsequently, online data processing and multi-dimensional databases and data warehouses came to be used. Since the year 2000, data mining for prediction and prospective purposes, using algorithms from AI, statistics and massive databases in various fields have come up. Now, application of data mining to business data has made management decision-making accurate and quick and has rendered large business databases imperative. Marketing, customer service and financial analysis are some of the management functions using data mining approaches. Pattern discovery and predicting trends and behaviour are capable of being applied to management decision, say, for example: (1) retail purchase patterns and targeting marketing, credit marketing, locating loan defaulters by banks etc. (Cooper and Schindler 1999).

What is data mining? Data mining is a set of approaches that can identify and extract useful patterns from data stored in large real world databases (Apte, 2003). Data mining is done using data mining systems, which are computer software, as manual systems are just not practical with such massive databases.

Data mining requires human initiated queries. The person knows clearly what he is looking for. He must have a substantial amount of domain knowledge. Data mining is important for the following reasons.

- Provides more qualified answers, for example which searching for a list of those who buy spirulina a food supplement, but DM can give, answers for specific categories, like "urban men and women between the age of 50-70", which is better for planning the sales.
- Prunes questions for invalid or empty segments, for example, opting for search for information related to a particular TV channel will avoid all non TV owners and a full database search of the population.
- Summarises the content of the database, thus, enabling the segmentation of databases. Segmentation helps develop different policies for different segments. For example different strategies of house taxation for different types of houses in a city.
- Detects deviations in data and may indicate fraud. For example sudden increase in transactions on a credit card.
- Detection of relationship among records like association or dependence. For example yield of crop A and crop B increase or decrease together or almost all smokers have some lung disease.

- Detecting time dependent (sequential) patterns. For example a series of symptoms indicating a disease.

Effective DM application is a process involving the following steps H.E, NCST,

Identifying the problem/objective

A clear statement of the objective or problem must be made. This must indicate the way of measuring the (knowledge discovery) results. It should also include a cost-benefit statement of wrong/right predictions.

Data preparation

This is the most time consuming step. It includes: (i) Selection: selecting a part of the large database for a mining effort. This includes selecting the independent and dependent variables for the model. (ii) Data consolidation and cleaning by detecting unnecessary fields, treating missing values, and so forth. (iii) The required data may be in different databases or multiple sources. In these cases, it must be ensured that all data selected is measured in the same way. (iv) Transformation of data to a form suitable for the particular DM tool being used in the process, that is, conventional database to a universal one. (v) Build the particular model needed for pattern extraction. (vi) Apply the model to extract the pattern. This should depend upon the goal of the user.

Data mining modelling techniques

Data mining deals with large data and uses statistical analysis and heuristic search procedures involving learning. Therefore, a number of statistical databases and AI techniques are used for modelling. There are two approaches to data mining modelling at the first level[1].

- General approach—which includes models and techniques that can be used for any kind of data set irrespective of their problem nature.
- Domain specific approach—which includes models to meet the particular requirements of a particular problem (domain).

The general approach is of particular interest to researchers to explore possible diverse applications. The general approach itself is categorised based on its purpose into (i) predictive function, and (ii) descriptive function. The former deals with forecasting certain behaviour based on facts, for example, income, type of items purchased, and so on from a purchases database. Descriptive function describes patterns underlying the data sets to guide decision making. Predictive functions use the following type of models: (i) Classification models (ii) Clustering models, (iii) Associative models, (iv) Regression models. A brief review of the first three types follow.

Classification models A classification model assigns instances (cases) to one of a number of predefined classes based on specific attributes. These classes may come from historical databases (for example, an existing classification of investors database based on different securities, patients; medical diagnosis database, including symptoms, may be used to predict possible investigations based on symptoms etc.) a number of techniques like decision tree models, neural networks, and machine learning are used for classification models (discipline based models are called techniques). The basis of evaluating the classification models is the least classification error as performance measure. The best method is chosen after evaluating and considering the problem domain.

Some of the techniques used are now outlined.

- ***Statistical-method based techniques*** These use several classification rules like (i) assigning the subject to the group with the highest conditional probability (for a group

1 Much of the material in this sub-section is based on Sampath et al (2000). *Functions, Models and Techniques of Financial Data Mining.*

and an object), (ii) using the Baysean method for parametric data or assumed (nearly) parametric data, (iii) using the nearest neighbour method, which is a simple learning method for non-parametric data; and (4) using statistical pattern recognition methods.

- ***Neural network-based techniques*** They are termed non-parametric methods because they don't make assumption regarding on (1) mathematical/functional form of (data) density distribution of the data sets. These are used extensively in vision, speech recognition, and other human sensory processing areas. Their ability to make good classification needs to be empirically tested. Advanced learning techniques and improved implementation methods are their advantages. Neural networks are a collection of nodes that are connected. Each node operates on the local data and input received through connections. The result is a non-linear predictive model. These networks will have to be trained on a set of training data to adjust the weights of different inputs and to correct errors.
- ***Machine learning-based techniques*** A learning system is a computer programme, which makes decisions based on the cumulative experience of successfully solved cases. Decision trees or sets of classification rules may be used for learning. The set of rules may use conjunctive operations (logical AND), disjunctive operations (logical OR), or a combination of the two. Formulation of such rules is the key to these techniques. A number of decision tree algorithms are developed, like ID3 and CART, and are being used for comparatively smaller data sets. There is no guarantee a single method will work or any single method is the best, but, they are better than humans having experience beyond the data. Techniques based on classification models have to address the following: (i) feature set selection, (ii) order of preference assigned to attributes, (iii) good training data sets, (iv) computational time requirements.

Clustering model This is used to segment a database into several groups. *A priori* knowledge of classes of the database is not known (unlike in prediction models). It is a purely exploratory model used to identify different classes in a data set (it is also called automatic classification model). The goal is to find classes, which differ from one another and have similarities among members in a class. Though there are well known clustering methods available in statistics, some modifications are needed for use in data mining. One of the widely used clustering techniques is the Auto Class, which automatically classifies a data set. This has to be iteratively used to obtain a large number of detailed classes and their hierarchies.

Associative models These are aimed at densing correlations among a set of items of data. Several special purpose query languages for exploring association rules either as part of SQL or separately, are in use. A Fuzzy Association Rule Mine (FARM) is also used.

Data mining in research Data mining can be useful in the following ways.

- Collecting a specific class of data for hypothesis testing when a large database of mixed classes is available or a reclassification is required.
- Data segmentation can be done to generate refined hypotheses. Some creative guesses need to be made. The query (intense questioning) is still in the human domain and the process is inductive where AI methodologies can be used.
- Patterns of events (stolen credit card frauds, retail purchases) can be obtained. Trends, as required for regional target marketing, can also be obtained from past data and used for prediction.

STATISTICAL ESTIMATION

Statistical estimation involves the estimation of an unknown population value from a known sample value. There are two kinds of procedures for statistical estimation, point estimation, and interval estimation.

- *Point estimation:* A point estimate is a single number, or point, that is used to estimate a population value of interest. A point estimate may be made for any population value, but the estimates most commonly made are for the mean and the proportion of the population.

- *Interval estimation:* An interval estimate consists of two points between which the population value is estimated to lie with some stated level of confidence. As in point estimation, interval estimates are also made for the population mean and proportion.

CONTENT ANALYSIS

While carrying out *ex post facto* studies or field studies, it will often be necessary to analyse company documents, published newsletters, internal reports, company annual meeting proceedings, and other sources of information. A detailed and systematic way of getting the content of communication through these documents is by the use of content analysis. Content analysis is a systematic study of communication, content for the ideas, and propositions or symbols that are relevant to the subject of study. Usually the frequency of appearance of a particular idea/symbol is obtained as a measure of content. It is, however, possible to obtain more information, for example, whether the ideas appear with favourable, unfavourable, or of neutral connotation. The main objective is to obtain terms of themes or recurrent ideas or propositions that will be helpful for research. The output of the content analysis will serve as supplementary data in qualitative research situations and where interpretations are made of the analytical investigations.

content analysis
Content analysis is a systematic qualitative approach of getting the content of communication in the form of ideas and propositions through various documents used in an organization. Usually the frequency of appearances of a particular idea is obtained as a measure of content.

The basic problem of content analysis is selective reporting, which is a conscious or unconscious process of observing and noting only facts that fit some preconceived idea/ideas (Jahoda, 1958).

Some of the other problems of content analysis are detailed below.

1. ***Sampling problems:*** Representativeness of the sample is very difficult to achieve in content analysis situations. The representation of a sample of various groups of documents need not be equally weighted. More important documents must be given greater weightage, that is, the percentage in the sample will be higher. Representing all documents sometimes is also not necessary.

   Example Let us say, a company's corporate thrust over several years has to be obtained from various documents, like administrative reports; proceedings of the meetings of the board of directos; memos sent to various heads of the departments, with respect to policies and procedures; files maintained at the departments; and leaflets produced by the company. The chairmans reports must have the greatest weight in this situation. Next may be leaflets and third, the policy letters to the heads of the departments, whereas the last one may not be important at all for the purpose and may be left out of content analysis.
2. ***Analysis approach:*** Two approaches are possible. First is an *a priori* approach, in which the contents of documents and method of analysis will be laid down, like, for example, frequency, correlation, trends, and classifications. The second is a posterior approach in which the contents are perused, significant ideas and themes are segregated and the items are classified using induction. Both methods are equally useful, but in an *a priori* approach the researcher has to be sure of what he is looking for.
3. ***Quantification problems:*** The frequency of occurrence of the ideas and themes is in most cases the only quantification that is attempted. Many social scientists (Goode and Hatt, 1953) feel that qualitative classifications with simple counts is adequate in most cases and forced quantification should be avoided.
4. ***Reliability:*** Replication of results must be possible and to enable this a correct codification of the ideas and themes must be carefully done. Communication from all fields is treated as social relations data; material is organised in many ways, based on the structure of the ideas. Such organisation requires to be done with considerable amount of objectivity and using a coding system.

The steps involved in the technique are (Kidder, 1981):

(i) Choosing the phenomenon.
(ii) Selecting the media from which the observations are made.
(iii) Derivation of coding categorisation.
(iv) Development of sampling strategy.
(v) Analysing data.

In the analysis step, systematic features of variables are categorised as high, low, medium, or siginificant/insignificant, or in any other way.

While frequencies are noted, significance of ideas and themes, in the context of the information appearance, must also be carefully noted down. Usually, content analysis is weak from the point of view of generalisation. Cartwright (in Festinger and Katz, 1953) discusses certain types of variables employed in content analysis. These are listed below.

- Subject matter—What is the communication about?
- Direction—Is the treatment favourable or unfavourable toward the subject?
- Standard—What is the basis (or grounds) on which the classification of direction is made?
- Values—What goals are explicitly or implicitly revealed?
- Methods—What means or actions are employed to realise goals?
- Traits—What characteristics of persons are revealed?
- Actor—Who initiates actions?
- Authority—In whose name are statements made?
- Origin—What is the place or origin of the communication?
- Target—To whom is the communication particularly directed?
- Form of communication—Is it fiction, news, television, and so on?
- Form of statement—What is the grammatical or syntactical form of the unit of analysis?
- Intensity—How much strength or excitement value does the communication have?
- Device—What is the rhetorical or propagandistic character of the communication?

Some Recent Developments

In recent developments of content analysis methods, **matrix format data** is developed in order to capture the complexity of large amounts of qualititative data. In the matrix format, one axis represents constructs and the other occurrences (of patterns) of phenomena. A count of occurrences (frequencies) may be entered into the matrix or they may be indicated qualitatively (like large or small, high or low, and so on). Further, the occurrences (variables) may be ordered along the time dimension so that antecedents and consequences may be identified. The ordered sequences may signify causal relationship (see Miles and Hubermann, 1994).

The other methods of content analysis are (i) Conversation analysis and (ii) Discourse analysis.

Conversation analysis: Analyses of conversations in interviews and settings of schools examines how judgements are made. Conversation analysis assumes that conversations are made up of stable patterns in the context, are sequentially organised (in tune with the ongoing process), and are well grounded in data (Silverman, 2000 may be referred for details).

Discourse analysis: This deals not only with conversation but also texts of documents like newspapers, advertisements, conference proceedings, speeches in company bulletins, and transcripts of recorded discussions. It deals with the context of the discourse and, particularly, the aspects of power relations and ideologies (see Fairclough, 1995 for details).

Example of Content Analysis

Social and behavioural scientists have associated industrialisation/urbanisation with 'time' scarcity and a high value on time. In this context, Barbarat and Sheth (1989) examine the proposition that, as the United States of America has evolved from an agrarian to an advanced industrial/urban society, advertising themes have changed to reflect an increased concern with time.

Very little empirical evidence has been advanced until 1989, to test the assumption that consumers have become more concerned with time, even though several conceptual works and interdisciplinary review researches have appeared. Based on US census data, the lifestyles of the populace showed marked changes, often the late 1800s viewed towards the 'culture of consumption' triggered by the consumer revolution. During this period (the beginning of modern marketing era), advertising emerged as a social and a cultural force. As advertisers perceived consumer's concern with 'time', they appealed to their concern by providing time oriented benefits of their products.

Research hypotheses Using advertising as the testing base, the following hypotheses were formulated.

H1: In the United States of America, magazine advertising has made references to time oriented concerns and product benefits with increasing frequency during the succeeding decades, since the late 1800s (when the United States of America was largely an agrarian economy).

H2: Time-oriented appeals have been used as primary appeals with increasing frequency during succeeding decades since the late 1800s (in contrast to their use as secondary or tertiary appeals).

Research method, sampling, and measurement Contents of advertisements appearing in one publication (Ladies Home Journal)) over a period of 98 years were analysed to find the frequency of and emphasis on 'time', as evident from the advertising copy. Six coding categories were developed by two judges to classify magazine advertisements, as part of a pilot study.

To test H1, advertisements were coded (Yes or No), depending on whether each advertisement reflected an orientation towards time.

To test H2, all time-oriented advertisements were analysed to determine whether time appeals were used as primary appeals (copy of an advertisement has primary appeals, that is, fundamental or main appeal and a secondary appeal).

Since the judgments of two people were involved in sample codification, measurements had to be compared and tested to determine interactor reliability. High reliability coefficients of 96 per cent and 97 per cent have been reported in the papers (85 per cent being regarded as satisfactory).

Results and discussion Results indicate that the proportion of ads citing time-oriented concerns and benefits increased steadily from 1890 until just before World War II, then it increased sharply in 1943 as advertisers attempted to appeal to women. This is consistent with H1. It has also been observed that the proportion has been maintained at relatively high levels during the past decade.

There is an increased frequency of time-oriented appeals. Two possible explanations have been forwarded by the authors for the increased frequency. Firstly, measured frequency must be due to changing product-mix (for example, more personal care, fewer apparel advertisements, and so on). Secondly, consumers 'time concerns as a measure may reflect an overall change in the number of appeals per advertisement.

Further examination of the advertisements for confirming the above two explanations resulted in coming to the conclusion that changing product-mix do not appear to be the reason.

The authors further discuss decadewise, on the basis of pre- and post-war, how the evidence gathered by them, which supports the hypothesis, is consistent with those reported in other advertising and historical works.

SUMMARY

Raw data collected for a research project is rendered suitable for analysis by data preparation. The data is first edited so that minimum quality of data is imposed. Editing is first manually edited, in which omission and inaccuracies are detected, and completeness and uniformity of data are ensured. After entering the data in the computer it is computer-edited. Responses with missing data are best completely eliminated from analysis.

In the second step, the data is categorised by careful coding and symbols are given. Particular attention is given to open-ended questions. Often new variables are created by combining others, or obtained from secondary data and added, or scales are changed to suit particular kinds of analysis.

The next step in data preparation is tabulation of frequency distribution. In simple tabulation, counts of a single variable in various categories or frequency distributions are obtained. In cross tabulation, the percentage of responses against several variables are displayed, so that relationships among them can be obtained. In summarising statistics, measures are provided for central tendency and dispersion of data sets.

Exploratory data analysis will yield insights into the data. It includes simple visual techniques like stem and leaf analysis and box plots, and highly developed and complex data mining methods that use statistical and AI models for unearthing hidden trends and patterns in large private and public databases. Population parameter estimates are obtained as the last stage of data preparation. Finally, as a part of preliminary data analysis communication from documents, recorded speeches may be analysed to get general data to be used in the research.

Suggested Readings

- Apte, Chid (2003). "The Big Dig – Data Mining Analysis for Business Intelligence and Decision Support", *OR/MS Today*, February 2003.
- Foster, Jeremy (1999). *Data Analysis Using SPSS for Windows: A Beginners Guide*. Thousand Oaks, California: Sage.
- Tufte, Edward R. (1997). *Visual Explanations: Images and Quantities Evidence and Narratives*. Cheshire, CT: Graphics Press.
- Tukey, John W. (1977). *Exploratory Data Analysis*. Reading, MA: Addison-Wesley.

QUESTIONS AND EXERCISES

1. Distinguish between editing and coding.
2. Which is more important from the analysts' point of view, field editing or central office editing? Give reasons for your answer.
3. Discuss how would you treat missing items from questionnaires?

4. What are the bases of classifying collected data into categories?
5. In what way are banners of special use to the researcher?
6. Does cumulative distribution have more value than simple distribution?
7. What is data reduction? What are the steps involved in it?
8. Is validation a field control? Discuss.
9. What can be done to assess the accuracy or quality of data? Give examples to illustrate your answer.
10. Why should you generate new variables?
11. Explain the uses of cross tabulation.
12. When would you prefer to use interval estimates over point estimates?
13. A multinational firm has developed a new product that is particularly appropriate for use in developing countries. In order to meet the firm's sales potential requirements, the product will be introduced only in countries having one million or more households with an average annual income of Rs 6500 or more. Initial research uncovers the following data.

    In which country or countries, if any, should the product be introduced? In which countries should the product not be introduced?

Annual Household Income

Country	Mean	Median	Mode	Variance	No. of Households
A	Rs 12,000	Rs 6140	Rs 4000–5000	Rs 15,400	5,000,000
B	7000	7100	6000–7000	4680	3,500,000
C	8060	5040	4000–5000	6000	2,700,000
D	9300	7800	6000–7000	9000	2,000,000
E	10,340	6200	5000–6000	10,480	1,900,000

14. A social organisation was interested in determining if there were various demographic characteristics that might be related to people's propensity to contribute to charities. The organisation was particularly interested in determining if individuals above 40 were more likely to contribute larger amounts than individuals below 40. The average contribution in the population was Rs 15,000 and this figure was used to divide the individuals in the sample into two groups, those that have contributed large amounts or more than average versus those that contributed less than average. The table 1 presents a two-way classification of the sample of individuals according to contributions and age.

Table 1 Personal Contributions and Age

Personal Contribution	Age		
	39 or less	40 or more	Total
Less than or equal to Rs.15,000	79	50	129
More than Rs.15,000	11	60	71
Total	90	110	200

In addition, the social organisation wanted to determine if contributions were dependent on income and/or age. The following table presents the simultaneous treatment of age and income. The median income in the population was Rs.182,000 and this figure was used to split the sample into two groups. (Table 2)

Table 2 Personal Contributions by Age and Income

Personal Contributions	Income					
	Less than or equal to Rs 182,000		More than Rs 182,000		Total	
	Age		Age		Age	
	39 or less	40 or more	39 or less	40 or more	39 or less	40 or more
Less than or equal to Rs.15,000	63	22	16	28	79	50
More than Rs.15,000	7	18	4	42	11	60
Total	70	40	20	70	90	110

(a) Does the amount of personal contributions depend on age? Generate the necessary tables to justify your answer.

(b) Does the amount of personal contributions depend on age alone? Generate the necessary tables to justify your answer.

(c) Present the percentage learning for more than Rs 15,000 by age and income in tabular form. Interpret the table.

Part F

Data Analysis and Reporting

CHAPTER 14

Hypothesis Testing—Univariate Analysis

- Introduction
- Logic of Hypothesis Testing
- Identification of an Appropriate Test for Hypothesis Testing
- Parametric Tests
- Non-parametric Tests
- Chi-Square Test

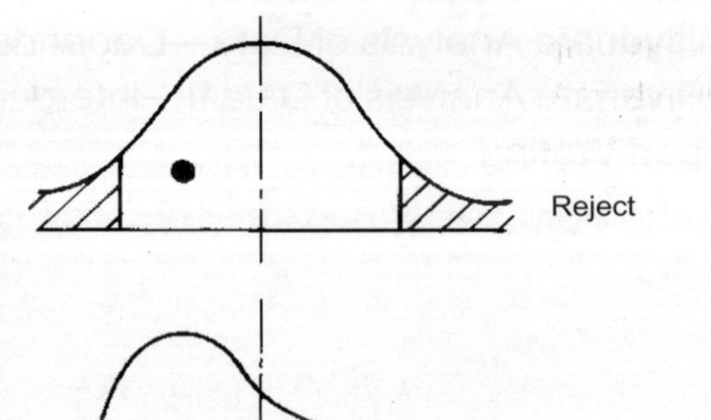

Learning Objectives

Upon completion of this chapter, you will be able to:

- ✓ Appreciate the significance of sampling in the overall research process
- ✓ Appreciate the pessimism of hypothesis testing as a basis of progress of science
- ✓ Understand why two hypotheses are needed to find the significance of a single relationship
- ✓ Understand why type II error is the main focus in hypothesis testing
- ✓ Learn how to choose a hypothesis test for a research problem
- ✓ Study a few typical univariate hypothesis tests to absorb the underlying principle of hypothesis testing
- ✓ Understand the difference between parametric and non-parametric hypothesis testing approaches
- ✓ Know about the process of hypothesis testing

Introduction

The process of hypothesis testing in research is analogous to the judicial processes by which an accused individual is judged in a court of law. The person brought before the judge is considered to be innocent. The responsibility of proving him guilty rests with the prosecution. Let us assume the person accused is innocent by R_I and that the person is guilty by R_G. If the judge or the jury finds the evidence provided by the prosecution is inconsistent with R_I they reject R_I and accept R_G that is, that the person is guilty. The possibilities of the judgement situation are:

1. The defendant is innocent (R_I is true) and the judge/jury judges that he is innocent (retains R_I). Therefore, the decision is correct.
2. The defendant is guilty (R_I is false) and judge/jury judges that he is innocent (retains R_I). Therefore, the decision is wrong.
3. The defendant is innocent (R_I is true) and the judge/jury judges he is guilty (rejects R_I). Therefore, the decision is wrong.
4. The defendant is guilty (R_I is false) and the judge/jury decides that he is guilty (rejects R_I). Therefore, the decision is correct.

The judgement process retains the prejudgement assumption of innocence or rejects the prejudgement assumption of innocence, based on the evidence. All the judgement effort is, therefore, directed to the assumption of innocence. Similarly, in hypothesis testing, all the testing effort is directed to H_O, the status quo hypothesis, that is null hypothesis. The entire legal approach is to avoid (condition 3 above) judging an innocent person as guilty, even if it means sometimes (incur the decision 2 above) leting go of the guilty. In hypothesis testing the probability of rejecting H_O is controlled and kept to a very small value because science would rather miss a true piece of knowledge at anytime than add a false one to the existing body of knowledge. Science, like law is pessimistic.

hypothesis testing
In hypothesis testing first a statement (research hypothesis) is made about a parameter of a population. A random sample is taken from the population and hypothesis tested with the appropriate sample statistic. A research hypothesis is accepted or rejected by rejcting or accepting a null hypothesis.

In classical hypothesis testing, first a statement (hypothesis) is made about a parameter of a population. This may be a conjecture or a guess. A random sample is taken from the population and the hypothesis is tested with the appropriate sample static. On the basis of the result from the sample, a decision concerning the validity of the hypothesis (acceptance or rejection) is made. In general, hypothesis may relate to one or more populations, involving comparisons or levels of parameters like the means, proportions, and variances of a population or differences between means, proportions, and variances of two or more populations. The methods used for classical hypothesis testing are essentially those of statistical estimation.

There is an alternative hypothesis testing approach to the classical one, that is, the Bayesian statistical approach. Bayesian approach also uses sampling procedures but reach beyond them. Subjective probabilities based on beliefs and experiences are used in the form of a distribution derived (from estimations by a number of experts) and are modified after the sample data is obtained. These modified estimates are known as posterior probabilities. (Such modifications can be made several times to get successive posterior probabilities). Expected outcomes are obtained in hypothesis testing using the posterior probabilities.

In this chapter, we consider hypothesis testing in univaraiate procedures. Hypothesis testing procedures in bivariate analysis are discussed in Chapter 15. Multivariate analysis is discussed in chapters 17 and 18.

LOGIC OF HYPOTHESIS TESTING

In hypothesis testing, two kinds of hypothesis are involved. The first kind is called null hypothesis, which can be evaluated in terms of probabilities provided by the sample statistics. The second is research hypothesis, which is intended to test the research prediction. The null hypothesis is the logical opposite of the research hypothesis. Thus, if the null hypothesis is rejected, then the research hypothesis is considered acceptable (note that there is a probability associated with it and, therefore, acceptance is only tentative).

Null Hypothesis

null hypothesis
This is a statement that the statistical differences or relationships have occurred purely due to chance operating in an unrestricted manner.

This is a statement that the statistical differences or relationships have occurred for no other reason than laws of chance operating in an unrestricted manner. Suppose we are testing the difference between the means μ_I and μ_{II} of two populations. The null hypothesis H_o is stated as,

$$H_0 : \mu_I = \mu_{II}$$

We take two samples, one from each population, and compute the statistic x, which is a function of x_1 and x_2. We also compute the probability of some observable difference between x_1 and x_2 that could occur due to sampling, which can be used in accepting/rejecting the null hypothesis.

Research Hypothesis

alternate hypothesis
This is the research hypothesis asserts that the observable differences or relationships are not just due to chance but also due to phenomenon.

This asserts that the observable difference between x_1 and x_2 is not just due to chance. This is a statement of differences or relationships among phenomena, the acceptance or rejection of which is based upon resolving the null hypothesis, which is its logical alternative. It is stated as,

$$H_a : \mu_I \neq \mu_{II}$$

The sampling statistics enable us to make a probability statement about the null hypothesis. If we find that this probability is very low, say 0.05 or less, then we may say that the difference between the two means could not be solely due to sampling error.

Choice of probability level Generally, a probability level α of 0.05 is taken as suitable for rejection of the null hypothesis. When the calculated probability is lower than this level, the null hypothesis is rejected. This is called rejection level or significance level. Statistical significance level is a level of probability set by the researcher as grounds for rejection of null hypothesis (usually represented by p). The value of p depends upon the type of error the researcher is willing to tolerate. If the test statistic falls within the acceptable region (if computed p is greater than acceptable level) then the test is considered inconclusive.

substantive significance
This refers to the strength of the relationship as explainable in a discipline where as statistical significance refers to permissible errors.

Substantive significance Statistical significance of a test refers to the permissible error of application of the test where as substantive significance refers to the strength of the relationship whose use, in practical application, is of greater concern to the researcher. A relationship may be statistically significant (beyond reasonable doubt) but of no value in practice (substantive significance).

Strong and weak testing Conceptually, however, both data and statistical techniques can be classified as strong and weak. Data is considered strong when it can be fitted to a distribution and is interval or ratio scaled (metric). Data is considered weak when it is non-metric (ordinal or nominal scale). Statistical techniques are strong when they can extract more information from the data and are termed parametric. These are distribution dependent. Statistical techniques called distribution free are weak tests and can extract less information from data. The various possibilities are strong when: (i) Strong technique is applied to strong data (appropriate traditionally), and (ii) weak technique to weak data (appropriate traditionally). However, strong techniques can be applied to weak data and weak techniques to strong data, according to the discretion of the researcher and, therefore, a wider variety of tests are available to him.

Degrees of freedom The concept of degrees of freedom (df) is important in all applications of hypothesis testing techniques. Degree of freedom refers to the number of bits of unconstrained information. It can be considered the number of bits of information used in calculating simple statistics like mean and variance of or a test statistic (as in χ^2 -tests, t-tests and F tests). Degrees of freedom give an indication of the sensitiveness of a statistical technique. It is represented as $(n-k)$ when n is the total number of bits of information and k is the number of linear constraints.

degrees of freedom
This refers to the number of bits of unconstrained information. These are important in calculating means and variance from the data sets.

Example n-1 degrees of freedom associated with a sample variance since 1 degree of freedom is lost in calculating $\bar{x}$, which is used in calculating variance. Similarly, in F ratio for two samples (n_1 and n_2) variance degrees of freedom = $(n_1 + n_2 - 2)$ since one bit of information is lost for each sample. This is particularly important in χ^2 test, t-tests, and F tests.

Errors in Hypothesis Testing

There are two types of error associated with hypothesis testing.

errors in hypothesis testing
There are two type of these errors: Type I error is an error of rejecting a null hypothesis that is true (probability of this error is α) and Type II error is the error of accepting a null hypothesis that is false (probability of this error is β).

Type I error In a statistical test, this is the error committed while rejecting null hypotheses that are true. The probability of making this error is represented by α.

Type II error In a statistical test this error is committed in accepting null hypotheses that are false. Probability of type II error is represented by β.

The goodness of a statistical test is measured by α and β. An increase in rejection region increases α and reduces β and a decrease in rejection region decreases α and increases β.

The power of a statistical testing in hypothesis testing is given by $(1-\beta)$, that is, the probability of rejecting a null hypothesis when it is false. This power increases as the distance between true and hypothesised values of the population parameter increases.

In practice, α is always known but β is often unknown because it is not always computed *a priori*. Thus, when the test indicates the null hypothesis in the acceptance region, instead of accepting the null hypothesis, the judgment must be withheld, that is, unless β is known, you should not accept H_0. While when H_0 is in the rejection region there is no inclusiveness associated, as α is known a *priori* and it is the probability of rejecting the null hypothesis when it is true. This is the reason for supporting the research hypothesis by rejecting the null hypothesis, and not by directly testing the research hypothesis.

Reducing type II error The probability of acceptance of H_o, which is false (type II error), cannot be determined, as the real population parameter is never known. There are several means of reducing this probability. They are:

- Increase the level of significance used as the standard for rejecting the null hypothesis (use $\alpha = 0.01$ in place of 0.05 or even lower).
- Use a one tailed test rather than a two tailed test if there is a basis for it.
- Decrease the standard error, that is, take a bigger sample.

Steps in hypothesis testing procedure (Fig. 14.1) The hypothesis testing procedure is simply a decision rule that decides whether the null hypothesis H_O should be rejected or retained for every possible value of a statistic that is observed in a sample of size *n*. The possible values of the statistic is termed sample space. This space is divided by the decision rule into mutually exclusive regions—a rejection region and an acceptance region.

A test in which it is intended to determine whether a population parameter has changed, regardless of the direction of change (not equal to), is referred to as a two tailed test (non-directional test) because there will be two rejection regions, one at each end of the appropriate sampling distribution (see Fig. 14.2a and 14.2b). A test in which intended determination of a population parameter change is focussed on the direction of change (less than or greater than) is known as a one-tailed (directional test) test. The rejection region will then be either at the lower end or at the higher end of the sampling distribution. The dividing point between acceptance region or rejection region is called the critical value of the population parameter which is determined in terms of the standard deviation of the random variable.

Fig. 14.1 Flow chart for hypothesis testing procedure

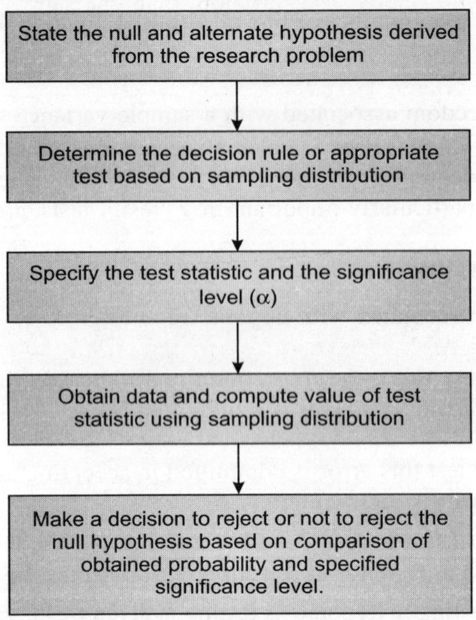

Five steps are to be performed for a typical testing of a hypothesis, as shown in the chart in Fig. 14.1. Generally, in any research, the first three steps are completed before collecting sample data.

In the statistical analysis of research data, the first and primary task of the researcher is to choose the appropriate test or method of analysis. There are a large number of well developed tools and techniques of statistics available to the researcher for this purpose. In order to make an appropriate choice of the technique in the second step, the following considerations should be kept in mind.

- *Type of analysis:* Whether the analysis is descriptive or inferential needs to be ascertained. Descriptive statistical analysis provides indexes of central tendency of scores or how they cluster, scatter, or disperse. These include mean, mode, median, range, variance and standard deviation, which characterise various aspects of the distribution of a variable. This analysis usually limits generalisation to the particular group being observed. Inferential analysis, on the other hand, involves conclusions that can be drawn about the measures as well as the estimates of parameters of the population *u* and *r*, based on the measures of the statistics of a suitably drawn representative sample.

- *Type of data:* Data are a set of measures related to a sample. When the data are nominally scaled, the objects or data are categorised. Normal arithmetical calculations are not made. Mean and median have no meaning. Mode is the only appropriate measure of central tendency; non-parametric tests are the only appropriate tests that can be used. When the scales are of the ordinal or interval type, there is a need to decide the appropriateness of parametric or non-parametric tests.
- *The size of the sample:* When interval scaled data is being analysed for inferential purposes, the size of the sample, whether large (> = 30) or small (< 30), determines if a z-test or t-test should be used. In certain cases of multivariate analysis (for example, factor analysis) the minimum size of the sample is dictated by the number of variables being considered.
- *Number of variables:* Depending upon whether a single independent variable is analysed (uni-variate) or two or more variables (multi-variate) are to be analysed, both in hypothesis testing and in determining relationships, the techniques adopted may be different.
- *Assumptions underlying samples:* When more than one sample is considered for purposes of comparison and testing (whether from the same population or different populations), it is important to know whether the samples are independent or dependent. The following questions are raised: Does selection of one sample limit the selection of the other ? Are the populations normally distributed? Are the variances of the populations same?
- *Nature of relationship:* In the analysis, whether the researcher is seeking a casual relationship or only an associative relationship will determine the type of technique to be used.
- *Number of groups:* Techniques for analysing a single group are different from those used for analysing multiple groups. While a single group may be explored for natural variables (for example, factor analysis), comparative analysis and relational analysis may be required for multiple groups.
- *Levels or differences:* While testing hypothesis, the level of a variable value may be of interest (as in a univariate analysis) or the significance of difference between levels of a variable in two or more groups or samples may be of interest as in multivariate analysis.

In most research, the choice of significance level is determined by the researcher at the time of selecting the test. A significance level refers to the probability $\alpha$of making type I error. Based on the significance level the critical value(s) of a test static is determined.

The actual value of the test statistic is compared with the critical value and a decision is made based on the hypothesis (obtained by meaning probability verses α).

IDENTIFICATION OF AN APPROPRIATE TEST FOR HYPOTHESIS TESTING

A large number of univariate tests are available for the hypothesis testing. Figure 14.3 gives an overview in a tree diagram of various univariate tests in relation to measurement scale, sample, and nature of test. Table 14.1 gives the main features of the tests. A complete and detailed discussion of all of them is beyond the scope of this book. The formulae for performing the various tests are given in the appendix of the book.

information for appropriate test
The information required to identify the appropriate test are the scale of measurement, nature of test (parametric/non-parametric), number of samples, dependence or independence of samples.

The user can identify the appropriate test for his research (univariate hypothesis testing) by providing the following information.

1. Whether the scale of measurement is nominal/ordinal or interval.
2. Whether the test is a parametric test or distribution free test.
3. Whether the sample involved is a single sample or multiple samples.
4. Whether the samples are dependent or independent when two or more samples are drawn.

Table 14.1 Univariate Statistical Tests

Type of test	*Type of measurement*	*Single sample*	*Multiple samples (K)*	
			Dependent	*Independent*
Non-parametric	Nominal	Chi-square	McNemar (for M = 2)* Cochran Q (for M > 2)*	Chi-square
Non-parametric	Ordinal	Kolmogorov-Smirnov	Wilcoxon (for M = 2)* Friedman two-way analysis of variance (for M > 2)*	Mann-Whitney (for M = 2) median test* Kruskal-Wallis one-way analysis of variance*
Parametric	Interval or Ratio	z test t test	t, test (for M = 2)	z test (M = 2) t test (M = 2) analysis of variance* (for M > 2)

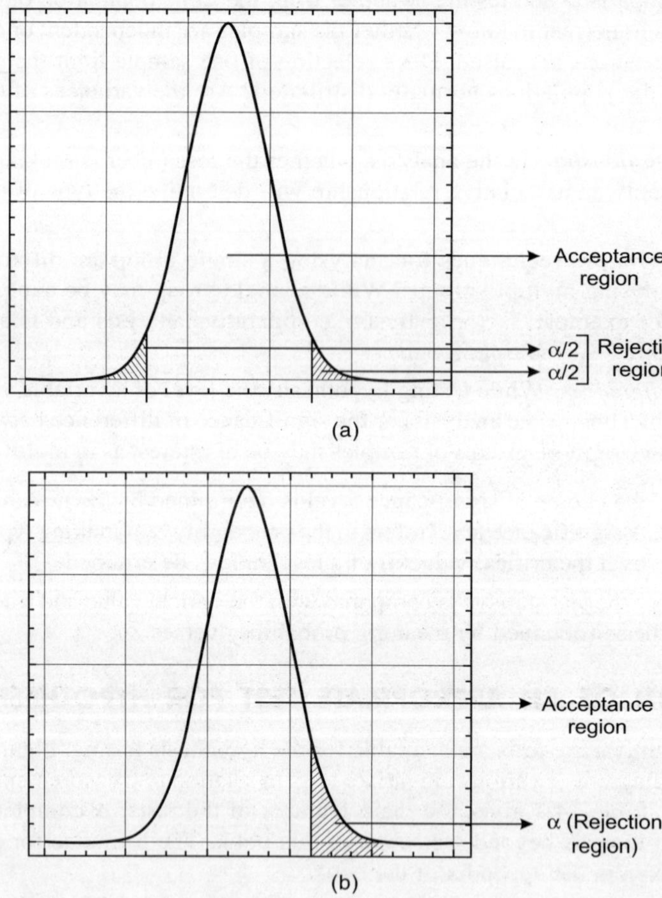

Fig. 14.2 (a) Two-tailed test (b) One-tailed test

Moving along the decision boxes in Fig. 14.3 appropriately, the user gets to a specific test. The tree diagram in Fig. 14.3 may indicate one or more tests, depending on other conditions or choice of the researcher (see examples below).

In the following sections some of the more common hypothesis testing procedures are detailed along with illustrations. (Green et al., 1988, Kanji, 1999, Sprent and Smeeton, 2001)

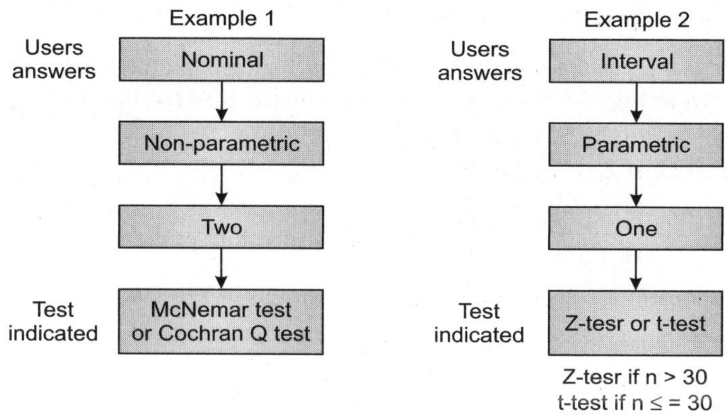

Fig. 14.3 Choice of a univariate statistical test

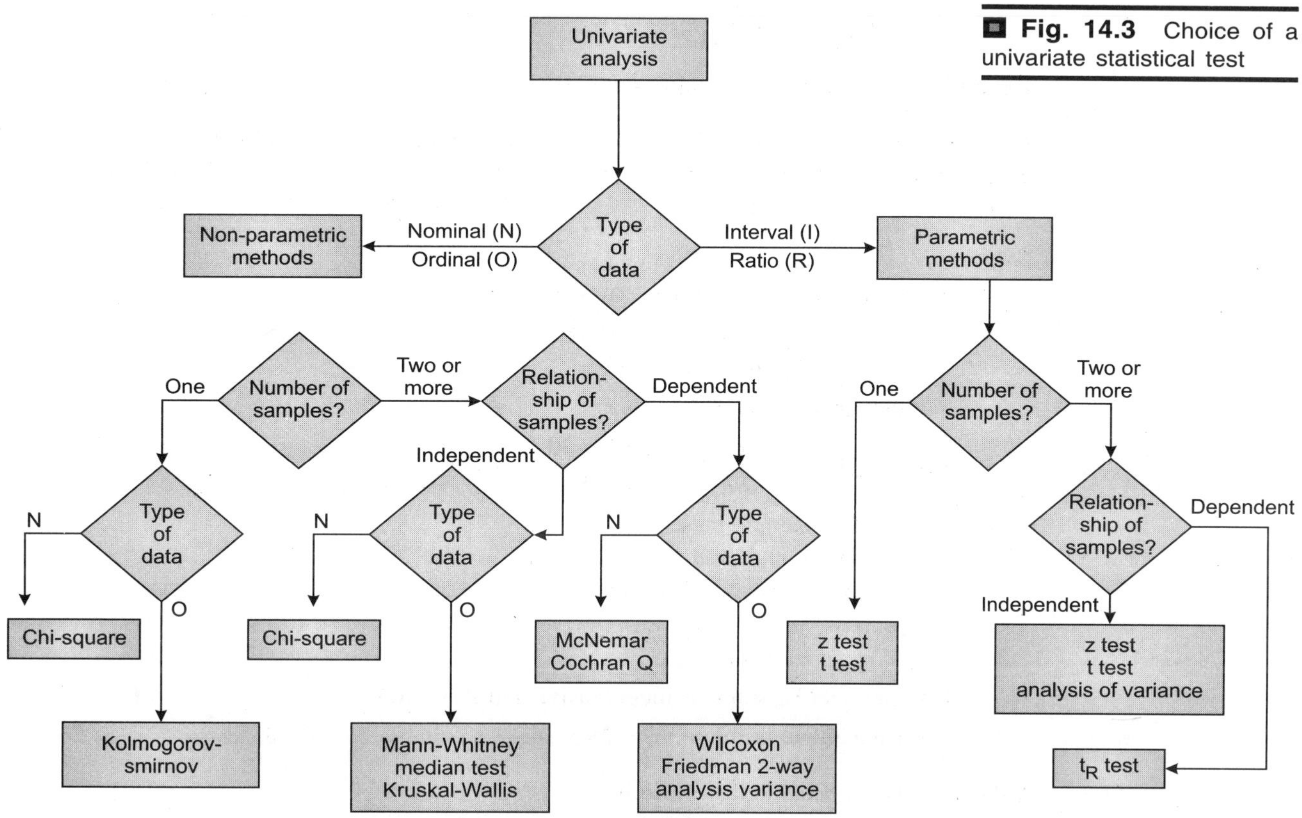

PARAMETRIC TESTS

Z-Test

Logic of Z-test: When samples are large (*n* greater than 30), tests for hypothesis concerning the levels of population parameters μ_p (for a single population), or differences in the population parameters, $(\mu_1 - \mu_2)$ or $(p_1 - p_2)$ [two populations] are all based on normally distributed test statistics and may be regarded as essentially the same test and is termed as the Z-Test.

Given that $H_0 : \mu = \mu_o$

When sampling distribution mean $= \mu_o$

parametric test

When the population distribution is known parametric test is employed. This includes z-test (normal distribution), t-test (student t distribution) and F-test. Z-tests are used with large samples (n > 30) and t-tests are used with small samples ($n \leq 30$). F-test is used in analysis of variance particularly with experimental data.

Two situations may be met with:

1. $H_a : \mu \neq \mu_o$ is the research hypothesis. The acceptable regions and rejection given are shown in Fig. 14.2(a)—a two tail test that is divided into two equal areas as shown.
   Test statistic is $Z_o = (\mu - \mu_o)/(\sigma_o)$
   Reject H_0 if $Z_o > Z_a/2$ or $Z_o < -Z_a/2$

2. If $H_a : \mu > \mu_0$ (1)
   If $H_a : \mu < \mu_0$ (2)
   } is the research hypothesis

The acceptance and rejection regions are shown in Fig. 14.2(b) and Fig. 14.2(a).

Test statistic is $Z_o = (\mu - \mu_o)/(\sigma_o)$

Reject H_0 if $Z_o > Z_a$ (See Fig. 14.2[b])

Therefore, accept $H_a : \mu > \mu_o$,

Reject H_o if $Z_o < Z_a$ (See Fig. 14.2[a])

Therefore, accept $H_a : \mu < \mu_o$

Example Z-test for mean (single sample)

Problem: The average shelf life of a deteriorable product is claimed by the manufacturers as 30 months. A random sample of 81 units had a mean of 28.7 months and a standard deviation of 8 months. Perform a hypothesis test using a significance level of 0.05.

Solution:

1. A one tail Z-test is used ($n > 30$)

$$H_0 : \mu = 30 \quad a = 0.05$$
$$H_a : \mu < 30$$

Sample mean, $\bar{x} = 28.7$

$$\text{Test statistic } Z_o = \frac{\bar{x} - \mu}{S/\sqrt{n}} = \frac{28.7 - 30}{8/\sqrt{81}} = -1.46$$

Where $\bar{x}$ = sample mean
μ = population mean
S = population variance

for $a = 0.05$, $Z_c = -1.65$.
Reject H_0 if $Z_c < -1.65$
Do not reject H_0 if test is inconclusive and $Z > -1.65$

2. If for the above problem, $\bar{x} = 28.5$, make a suitable hypothesis test.

Solution: Hypothesis to test again is;

$$H_0 : \mu = 30$$
$$H_a : \mu < 30$$

(a) In the one tail test $Z_o \dfrac{28.5 - 30}{8/\sqrt{81}} = 1.685$

Since $Z_o < -1.65$, reject H_0

(b) But let us take a two tailed list:

$H_0 : \mu = 30$, $H_a : \mu \neq 30$
as before $Z = -1.685$
$Z_c = Z_{(0.025)} = -1.96$ or $+1.96$
Do not reject H_0; test is inconclusive.

Thus, the results of the above example show that it is necessary to choose the two tail and one tail tests carefully. One tail tests are more appropriate where there is a bone of contention. Otherwise, it is desirable to use the two tail test.

Example Z-test for Proportion (Single sample)

Problem: A piston ring manufacturer has to produce them with not more than 3 per cent of rings defective. Large quantities of rings are manufactured and sold by the company. A purchaser samples random 300 rings and finds 12 defective. (Should he accept the lot or reject it)? Perform the hypothesis test using a significance .02 for the manufacturer's claim.

1. $H_o : \Pi = 0.03$
   $\alpha = 0.02 \quad Z_{cr} = 2.05$ (From tables for normal distribution)
2. $H_a : \Pi > 0.03$

$$Z_a = \frac{p-\pi}{\sqrt{\frac{\pi(p-\pi)}{n}}} = \frac{p-0.03}{\sqrt{\frac{0.03x0.97}{300}}}, p - \frac{12}{300} = .04$$

$$Z_o = \frac{0.04-0.03}{\sqrt{\frac{0.03x0.097}{300}}} = 1.015$$

Reject H_o if and only if $Z_0 > 2.05$

Do not reject H_o

Example Z-tests for difference between means of two large independent samples.

With usual notations:

$H_0 : \mu_1 - \mu_2 = 0$

$H_a : \mu_1 - \mu_2 \neq 0$

given

μ_1 = mean of the first population

μ_2 = mean of the second population

$\bar{x}_1$ = mean of the sample selected randomly from 1st population

$\bar{x}_2$ = mean of the sample selected from the second population, n_1 and n_2 are sample sizes for the first and second sample.

Since $\bar{x}_1 - \bar{x}_2 = D$ (difference of sample means) is a linear function of random variables x_1 and x_2 using expected value theorems for large samples (independent samples). Z-Test for difference between means of two large independent samples is as follows:

$$\mu_{\bar{x}_1 - \bar{x}_2} = \mu_1 - \mu_2$$

$$\sigma^2_{\bar{x}_1 - \bar{x}_2} = \sigma^2_{\bar{x}_1} + \sigma^2_{\bar{x}_2} \text{ (for large samples, the distribution is normal)}$$

$$\sigma^2_{\bar{x}_1 - \bar{x}_2} = \sqrt{\frac{\sigma_1^2}{n_1} + \frac{\sigma_2^2}{n_2}}$$

Where σ_1^2 and σ_2^2 are sample variances

$$\text{Test Statistic} = \frac{(\bar{x}_1 - \bar{x}_2) - (\mu_1 - \mu_2)}{\sqrt{\frac{\sigma_1^2}{n_1} + \frac{\sigma_2^2}{n_2}}} Z_0$$

Problem: Average life of the bulbs manufactured by two companies A and B are considered to be same. A random sample of 56 A bulbs has an average life 26.4 and $S_A = 6.4$ weeks and a random sample of 680 B bulb has an average life 28.9 weeks and $S_B = 5.3$ weeks. Test the hypothesis that the average lives are same at 5% significance level.

Solution:

$$n_A > 30,\ n_B > 30$$

$\therefore$ Z test is used.

Hypothesis to be tested are;

$$H_0 : \mu_A = \mu_B$$

$$H_a : \mu_A \neq \mu_B$$

$\alpha = 0.05$. Two tail test is used.

$$\text{Test Statistic} = Z_0 = \frac{\bar{x}_A - \bar{x}_B}{\sqrt{\frac{S_A^2}{n_A} + \frac{S_B^2}{n_B}}} = \frac{2.64 - 28.9}{\sqrt{\frac{6.42^2}{56} + \frac{5.3^2}{68}}}$$

$$Z_0 = -2.34 \text{ or } Z_0 = +2.34$$

Where

$$\bar{x}_A = 26.4$$

$$\bar{x}_A = 28.9$$

$$S_A = \text{Standard deviation of sample B} = 5.3$$

$$n_A = 56$$

$$n_B = 64$$

Z_c (from table for $\alpha = 0.05$) $= -1.96$

Two Tail test is used

$$< -2$$

$$Z_0 < Z_c$$

$\therefore$ Reject H_0.

The average life of the bulbs A and B are not the same.

t-Test

Logic of the t-test When the samples are small (n less than 30), the central limit theorem does not hold good and the test statistic as given in Z-test.

That is, $\dfrac{\bar{x} - \mu}{S/\sqrt{n}}$

does not follow a normal distribution, but follows a student's t-distribution.

Student's t-distribution gives greater variances for smaller values of n and approaches the normal distribution values (that is, Z) when n is very large. However, in t-tests also the population is assumed to be normally distributed. In testing the hypothesis with small samples t-distribution values are used (instead of Z values) from the tables.

$$\text{Test statistic } t = \frac{\bar{x} - \mu}{S/\sqrt{n}}$$

when differences between means are tested

$$t = \frac{(\bar{x}_1 - \bar{x}_2)}{\sigma_{differences}}$$

The numerator is almost always the same. If null hypothesis is true

$\mu_1 = \mu_2$ and $(\bar{x}_1 - \mu_1)(\bar{x}_2 - \mu_2)$, or $\{(\bar{x}_1 - \bar{x}_2) - (\mu_1 - \mu_2)$ becomes $(\bar{x}_1 - \bar{x}_2)\}$

The difference arises mostly in the denominator, that is, while using t-values, it is necessary to know the degrees of freedom that reflect the sample's size. If there is a single sample involved, degrees of freedom is $(n–1)$, if two samples are involved, (as finding the difference in means between two populations) the degree of freedom is $(n_1 + n_2 – 2)$ $[(n_1 – 1) + (n_2 – 1)]$. The degree of freedom associated with any statistic, refers to the number of components that are free to vary. $(n–1)$ degrees of freedom associated with a single sample of n is meant to reflect that if we know $(n–1)$ values, the nth one can be determined easily, hence $(n–1)$ values are free to vary. It reflects the number of squared deviations available for estimating variance. As in Z-tests, two tail and single tail tests can be used in t-tests too.

Example t-test for mean of a small sample

Problem: A worker demands an average time of 15 minutes for an operation. The industrial engineer feels the operation takes much less time than 15 minutes. He observes 16 randomly selected repetitions of the operation and calculates the average as 12.4 minutes with a standard deviation of 1.3 minutes. For a significance level of 0.01, how good is the case for the industrial engineer?

Solution:

Hypothesis $H_0 : \mu = 15$, $H_\alpha = \mu < 15$, $\alpha = 0.01$

$$\text{test statistic } t_o = \frac{\bar{x} - \mu}{S/\sqrt{n}} = \frac{(x - 15)}{S/\sqrt{n}}$$

degrees of freedom = df = n – 1 = 16 – 1 = 15

Reject H_0 if and only if $t_c < -2.602$ (table value for $\alpha = 0.01$)

$$t_o = \frac{13.4 - 15}{1.3/\sqrt{16}} = -4.92$$

Reject H_o.

Example t-Test for difference in means of two independent small samples

Problem: A customer wants to find out whether the cooking gas supplied by two suppliers is the same with regard to performance in stoves. Eight stoves were selected randomly. One stove was used on the cooking gas supplied by A and another on that supplied by B. The time the stoves worked on the same quantity of gas as supplied by A. Nine stoves were randomly selected.

Time for A—19.7, 18.1, 20.4, 22.6, 18.8, 19.2, 19.3, 21.5

Time for B—18.9, 23.2, 19.8, 22.4, 21.3, 22.2, 21.6, 20.3, 24.7

Are the two cooking gases equivalent?

Solution: Since both the samples are small, t–statistic is the appropriate test statistic. The conditions for t–statistic to be used are (i) populations are normally distributed, (ii) population variances are same, and (iii) the samples are selected independently.

Hypotheses are

$H_0 : \mu_1 = \mu_2$

$H_a : \mu_1 \neq \mu_2$

$(n_1, n_2 < 30)$

∴ A Two Tail 't' Test is used

$$\text{Test Statistic is } t_0 = \frac{\bar{x}_1 - \bar{x}_2}{\sqrt{\frac{(n_1-1)S_1^2 + (n_2-1)S_2^2}{(n_1-1)(n_2-1)}}} \times \frac{1}{\sqrt{\frac{1}{n_1^2} + \frac{1}{n_2^2}}}$$

Where

S_1^2, S_2^2 are variances

$\bar{x}_1$, $\bar{x}_2$ are means of the samples

n_1, n_2 are the sample sizes

degrees of freedom $= \upsilon = n_1 + n_2 - 2$

$= 9 + 8 - 2 = 15$

[From table t_c (for $\upsilon = 15$) $= -1.753$ $+1.753$]

Reject H_0 if $t_0 < -1.753$

or $t_0 > +1.753$

$$\text{Now,} \quad \bar{x}_1 = \frac{19.7 + 18.1 + --- + 19.3 + 21.5}{8} = 19.95$$

$$S_1^2 = \frac{\sum (x_2 - \bar{x})^2}{n-1} = \frac{(18.1 - 19.95)^2 + (18.1 - 18.1)^2 + --- (18.1 - 21.5)^2}{8-1}$$

$$= \frac{15.42}{7} = 2.2029$$

Similarly $\bar{x}_1 = 21.6$ and $S_2^2 = 3.185$

$$t_0 = \frac{19.95 - 21.6}{(8-1)2.209 + (9-1)3.185} \times \frac{1}{\sqrt{\frac{1}{8} + \frac{1}{9}}} = -2.056$$

$t_0 < t_c$

∴ reject H_0

∴ the performance of the two suppliers, A and B, are not the same.

Example *t*-test for two small dependent samples for difference in means (paired differences) - t_r test

Problem Supplies of bars from two suppliers affect the cycle time for producing a fabricated part in a machine shop. Seven bars of supplier I were randomly selected and assigned to seven different machines. The same seven machines were randomly assigned seven bars from supplier II. The number of minutes required to fabricate the parts are given in the table 14.2a. Can

Table 14.2(a)

Machine	*Time for 10 fabricated part*	
	Supplier I	*Supplier II*
M1	69	63
M2	75	72
M3	46	48
M4	61	57
M5	58	56
M6	83	78
M7	57	53

we conclude that different suppliers do affect the machining times of the parts fabricated? Use a significance level of 5 per cent.

Solution: Paired differences for the example (Table 14.2b)

$$\text{Machine}\begin{Bmatrix}\text{Time for Supplier I}\\ \text{minus}\\ \text{Time for Supplier II}\end{Bmatrix} = d_i$$

Table 14.2(b) **Paired differences and their squares**

Machine	d_i	d_i^2
M1	6	36
M2	3	9
M3	–2	4
M4	4	16
M5	2	4
M6	5	25
M7	4	16
	$\Sigma d_i = 22$	$\Sigma d_i^2 = 110$

$$d = \frac{\sum d_1}{7} = 3.14 \quad S_d^2 = \frac{\sum d_i^2 - \left(\frac{\sum d_i}{n}\right)^2}{n-1} = \frac{110 - (3.14)^2}{7-1} = 6.81$$

$$S_d = \sqrt{6.81} = 2.61$$

$$\text{Test Statistic} = t = \frac{\bar{d} - (\mu_1 - \mu_2)}{S_d / \sqrt{n}} \quad \text{For } H_o\ \mu_1 - \mu_2$$

$\therefore \quad t = \dfrac{\bar{d}}{Sd/\sqrt{n}}$ with df = 2 – 1 = 1

$H_o\ \mu_1 - \mu_2$

$H_a\ \mu_1 - \mu_2$

for $\alpha = 0.05$ $t_c = -2.447$ or $+2.447$ (from tables)

$\therefore$ reject H_o if and only if $t_o < -2.447$ or $t_o > +2.447$

Two-tail test is used

$$t_o = \frac{3.14}{2.61/\sqrt{7}} = 3.18 > +2.447$$

$\therefore$ reject H_o

The supplies of the two different suppliers do affect the machining times of the parts.

F-Test for Analysis of Variance

The F-test is used in testing the difference between two or more population means. Analysis of variance is employed when testing the hypothesis, incorporating two or more population means. If three means are involved,

Null hypothesis $H_o : \mu_1 = \mu_2 = \mu_3$

Research Hypothesis $H_a : \mu_1 \neq \mu_2 \neq \mu_3$

For a given alternative, we use F-test in this situation.

Logic of F-test: This test will give an overall statement of acceptance or rejection of H_0, that is, whether there is a significant variation among the means, but does not give a comparison of any two means, that is, whether or not all the samples involved represent the same population in terms of their means.

If the variance among their means is greater, logically it would mean that these groups would differ more. Such variance can be depicted in terms of the variability of group means about their grand mean. In testing hypothesis regarding significant difference between means, it is necessary to find the probability of occurrence of between-groups variance. If each group came from the same population, the variability we would expect is called within-groups variability. The central point in the analysis of variance is, if there is no difference among the groups, then the between-groups variance will be approximately equal to within-group variability. Therefore, F is defined as

$$F = \frac{\text{Variance between groups}}{\text{Variance within groups}}$$

The greater the ratio of F, the greater the probability that groups represent different populations. If sampling error were zero, $F = 1$ for a true null hypothesis. Since sampling error is a reality, we use sampling distribution of F to get this error for a stated significance. If actual level of F is calculated to be greater than this, then we reject the null hypothesis. As in the case of t-test, an appropriate degree of freedom is used to get the table value of F.

Sampling distribution of F is used to find the probability of occurrence of a particular value of F, under conditions of null hypothesis. The sampling distribution of F changes according to the degree of freedom (and reflects the number of groups and the size of the groups).

Thus, F statistic is the basis for obtaining probability statements with regard to null hypothesis. The larger the F, the smaller the probability of acceptance and the less we would expect the null hypothesis to be true. The derivation of F and its use in testing hypotheses about means is depicted in the following example.

The discussion of the simplest case of ANOVA given above is equivalent to a single factor completely randomised design of experiments. The assumptions are: (i) The net effect of all treatments is zero, (ii) There is an equal number of observations for each treatment.

A schematic representation of completely randomised design is given in Fig. 14.4.

Example The table 14.3a shows the times of performance of three independent samples of an operation in different conditions. There were eight subjects in the group. Are the mean times truly affected by the different conditions?

$$M_1 = 6 \ M_2 = 8 \ M_3 = 10$$
$$M_T = 8$$

Fig. 14.4 Schematic representation of completed randomized design

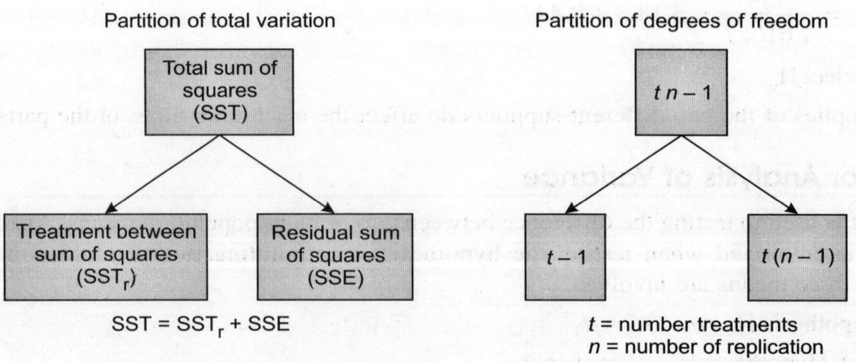

Table 14.3(a)

X_1	X_2	X_3
4	7	9
6	9	9
4	6	10
5	11	8
9	10	9
6	8	11
4	8	13
10	5	11
($\Sigma = 48$)	($\Sigma = 64$)	($\Sigma = 80$)

Where

M_1, M_2, and M_3 are group means and

M_T is the grand mean

Null Hypothesis

$$H_o : \mu_1 = \mu_2 = \mu_3$$

Alternate Hypothesis

$$H_a : \mu_1 \neq \mu_2 \neq \mu_3$$

Within group deviation, $d_{ij} = x_{ij} - M_i$ (Table 14.3b)

Between group deviation, $D_{ij} = x_{ij} - M_T$

$$M_1 = 6 : \quad d_{1j} = 0 : d_{1j}^2 = 38 : D_{1j} = -16 : D_{1j}^2 = 70 :$$

$$M_2 = 8 : \quad d_{2j} = 0 : d_{2j}^2 = 28 : D_{2j} = 0 : D_{2j}^2 = 28 :$$

$$M_3 = 10 : \quad d_{3j} = 0 : d_{3j}^2 = 18 : D_{3j} = 16 : D_{3j}^2 = 50 :$$

$$M_T = 8 \quad M_T = 8 \quad M_T = 8$$

Total variance SST $= \Sigma_j \Sigma_i (x_{ij} - M_T)^2$

$= 70 + 28 + 50 = 148$

Within group variance SSw $= \Sigma_j \Sigma_i (x_{ij} - M_i)^2$

$= 38 + 28 + 18 = 84$

Between group variance SSB $= \Sigma_j n_j (M_i - M_T)^2$

$= 8(6-8)^2 + 8(8-8)^2 + 8(10-8)^2$

$= 64$

Table 14.3(b)

X_1	d_{1j}	d_{1j}^2	D_{ij}	D_{1j}^2	X_2	d_{ij}	d_{2j}^2	D_{2j}	D_{2j}^2	X_3	d_{3j}	d_{3j}^2	D_{3j}	D_{3j}^2
4	-2	4	-4	16	7	-1	1	-1	1	9	-1	1	1	1
6	0	0	-2	4	9	1	1	1	1	9	-1	1	1	1
4	-2	4	-4	16	6	-2	4	-2	4	10	0	0	2	4
5	-1	1	-3	9	11	3	9	3	9	8	-2	4	0	0
9	3	9	1	1	10	2	4	2	4	9	-1	1	1	1
6	0	0	-2	4	8	0	0	0	0	11	1	1	3	9
4	-2	4	-4	16	5	-3	9	-3	9	13	3	9	5	25
10	4	16	2	4	8	0	0	0	0	11	1	1	3	9

Table 14.3(c)

Source	Sum of squares	Degrees of freedom	Mean sum of square	F - ratio	p
Between	64 (SSB)	(3–1)=2	32	8.00	0.01
Within	84 (SSW)	(8+8+8-3)=21	4		

Variance between group 32

Variance within group 4

$$F_{actual} = 8.00$$

$$F_{critical} \text{ (from table)} = 5.78.$$

Since $F_{actual} > F_{critical}$, the null hypothesis is rejected.

NON-PARAMETRIC TESTS

non-parametric test
Non-parametric tests are called distribution free tests and are used when the population distributions are not known (This happens when samples are very small and distribution can not be generated accurately). The more important non-parametric test are χ^2 test. Kruskal-Wallis test, Kendal's Coefficient of Concordance. These tests are used on ranked data or nominal data. These are also used when parametric tests fail by converting the data to ranked or nominal ones.

The non-parametric tests make less restrictive assumptions than parametric tests. They are easier to carry out and understand and are applicable in a wide range of situations. These tests are based on categories (as with nominally scaled data) or on ranks (sometimes even ordering is not required).

However, in these distribution-free tests there is a certain amount of ignoring of information (when ranks and not numerical data are used). Therefore, they are weak and less efficient than the relevant standard parametric tests, that is, β would be greater for the non-parametric test than for the parametric. But the analyst, it would appear, could be more confident with non-parametric tests when restrictive assumptions for parametric tests are not satisfied.

Chi-Square Test

When measurements relate only to assigning observations to categories (as in nominal scale data), a chi-square test is used. The researcher will be interested in comparing the various categories. "Chi-square is best thought of as discrepancy statistic" (Williams, 1968). Its computation is based on discrepancies between frequencies actually observed and those expected from a theoretical distribution. Chi-square has a sampling distribution. Chi-square as a random variable is given by $(n-1)S^2/r^2$ where n is the sample size, s^2 is sample variance, and r^2 is the population variance. The distribution of chi-square in repeated sampling is asymmetrical with a negative skew and the values are tabulated like t-statistic; $(n-1)$ indicates degrees of freedom and that the sample size is small. If H_o on variance of a population is true, then chi-square is close to $(n-1)$. The chi-square test can be applied to many situations. Situations in which it is most commonly used are detailed below.

- While curve fitting is used for testing a hypothesis of distribution, the values of chi-square are given by,

$$\text{Chi-square} = \sum_{i=1}^{n} \frac{(O_i - E_i)^2}{E_i^2}$$

  where

  O_i is the observed frequency of ith category and

  E_i is the expected frequency of ith category

- For testing difference among categories (within a sample). More than two samples can be used in a test of this kind.
- For finding the difference between samples, like, for example, persons with five different educational backgrounds trying to find a new curriculum. (In this case df = (n – 1)(c – 1), where n number of samples and c the number of categories.)

- When hypothesis of a population variance is to be tested. The test statistic in this case is

$$\text{Chi-square} = \frac{(n-1)\,S^2}{r^2}$$

Example A manufacturer desires to know customer preference for packaging his product. Four different package designs are available. A random sample of 113 customers gave the following information. (Table 14.4(a))

Table 14.4(a)

Package	*Number of customers preferring the package*
1	30
2	36
3	25
4	22

Test the hypothesis that there is differential customer preference for packaging.

$$H_0\colon p_1 = p_2 = p_3 = p_4$$

$H_{\acute{a}}$: H_0 is not true

$$\alpha = 0.05 \quad d\,f = 4 - 1 = 3$$

Reject H_0 if, and only if, chi-square (actual) > 7.815

[Critical value of chi-square = 7.815]

$$\text{Chi-square (actual)} = \sum \frac{(O_i - E_i)^2}{E_i}$$

$$\text{Chi-square (actual)} = [(30 - 28.25)^2 + (36 - 28.25)^2 + (25 - 28.25)^2 + (22 - 28.25)^2] \times \frac{1}{28.25}$$

$$= 3.99$$

Since Chi-square (actual) < Chi-square (critical), do not reject the hypothesis H_0. That is, there is no significant preference among the four categories.

Table 14.4(b)

p_i	$E_i = np_i$	O_i	
.25	28.25	30	
.25	28.25	36	
.25	28.25	25	
.25	28.25	22	n = 113

McNemar Test

This test is used for testing distribution by categories of two related samples (nominally scaled data).

In certain situations it may be required to determine the changes in individual categories due to some event. A classic example is the change of brands by consumers after seeing an advertisement on television. A marketing manager may like to know of the change in the number of consumers choosing certain brands. The McNemar test is suitable in such situations:

Table 14.5

		After treatment	
		Unacceptable	*Acceptable*
Before treatment	Acceptable	10 (AU)	40 (AA)
	Unacceptable	160 (UU)	40 (UA)

1. Make a null hypothesis that the event has no effect on the distribution of categories.
2. Make a 2×2 contingency table.
3. Compute chi-square value (shown in the example).
4. Check the significance of the chi-square using the critical value of chi-square at α.

Example Brass bars supplied to a processing shop have large proportion of unacceptable pieces. A special treatment operation is proposed. Prior to the treatment a sample of 250 bars has 200 unacceptable pieces. After special treatment 40 of the 50 acceptable bars have become unacceptable and others remain acceptable. Of the 200 bars unacceptable prior to the treatment, 30 have become acceptable and the other remain unacceptable. Is the special treatment effective in making greater proportion of the bars acceptable?

1. Null Hypothesis H_o: Special treatment has no effect on the proportion of the categories.
2. H_a : Null Hypothesis is not true.
3. Contingency table (Table 14.5)

   Ensure that the sum of the expected values in cells AU and UA under the null hypothesis is larger than 5 for using the χ^2 test

   $$E = 0.5\,(AU + UA)$$
   $$= 0.5\,(10 + 40) = 25$$

   Under null hypothesis the changes A to U and U to A have same probability, that is, 0.5.

4. Chi-Square $= \chi^2 = \dfrac{\{(AU - UA) - 1\}}{AU + UA} = \dfrac{\{(10 - 40) - 1\}^2}{10 + 40} = \dfrac{29^2}{50} = 16.82$
5. Critical value of χ^2 = for $0.001 = \alpha$ and df $= 2 - 1 = 1$
   (from tables) $= 10.83 < 16.82$

Therefore, the null hypothesis is rejected. We conclude that the special treatment has effect on the bars to become acceptable.

Kolmogorov-Smirnov Test

This test is used to determine if the rank ordering in a single sample obtained in research differs from a theoretical or hypothetical rank order. It tests the agreement between a set of observed rankings (sample values) and the values assigned in a null hypothesis. The procedure involves the following steps:

1. Make a cumulative frequency distribution (CFD) of proportions for each rank for the null hypothesis.
2. Find the cumulative frequency distribution of proportion for each rank for the sample observations (CF).
3. Find Kolmogorov-Smirnov D(KSD) – largest difference between CFS.
4. Check the significance of D using the KSD table.

Table 14.5(a)

Rank	*Process innovation*	*No. on the sample rating*
2	Very desirable	12
3	Desirable	10
1	Moderately desirable	13
5	Undesirable	7
4	Very desirable	8

Table 14.5(b)

	Observed No. for each category	*Observed proportion*	*Observed cumulative proportion*	*Null H proportion*	*Null H cumulative proportion*	*Absolute deviation*
Very desirable	12	.24	.24	0.20	.20	0.04
Desirable	10	.20	.44	0.20	.40	0.04
Moderately desirable	13	.26	.70	0.20	.60	0.10
Undesirable	7	.14	.84	0.20	.80	0.04
Very undesirable	8	.16	100	0.20	1.00	0.00
			Total 50			

Example Perception of process innovation, in small scale units as the objective of R&D, was studied with a five-point scale question.

Very desirable Desirable Moderately desirable Undesirable Very undesirable

The table 14.5(a) shows observed numbers in a sample of 50 SSI units.

Sample Rating

1. H_o : Proportion of sample rating each scale point = 0.2 (1/5), that is, there is no difference in assigning desirability to the rank.
2. H_a : H_o is not true.
3. Working table [Table 14.5(b)]

Max absolute deviation = 0.10 = Kolmogorov-Smirnov Deviation ($KSDH_o$)

For a sample >35 from tables of KSD, the critical value = $\frac{1.07}{\sqrt{50}}$ = 0.15134, at 0.20 significance and > 0.10

$$KSD_{cr} > KSDH_0$$

We cannot reject null hypothesis. Therefore, the test is inconclusive.

Kruskal-Wallis Test (For Ranked Data)

This can be used to test to compare whether three or more populations have identical distributions. If all the sample sizes are five or more, then the following test statistic has an approximately chi-square distribution.

$$\chi^2 = \frac{12}{n\,(n+1)} \sum_{j=1}^{m} \frac{R_j^2}{n_j} - 3(n+1)$$

With df = m – 1

Where

m = number of populations

R_j = sum of the ranks for the jth population

n_j = the number of observations in the sample from the jth population

$n = \sum_{j=1}^{m} n_j$; combined number of sample observations

Example Three groups of participants in a training programme were randomly sampled to determine whether the scores of tests conducted at the end of the programme were the same. The scores are as follows: [Table 14.6(a)]

Table 14.6(a)

Group 1	*Group 2*	*Group 3*
116	81	108
168	152	95
127	111	74
172	123	129
142	136	118
		132
$(n_1=5)$	$(n_2=5)$	$(n_3=6)$

If the null hypothesis (test score distribution is same for all groups) is not true then chi-square values tend to get large and the hypothesis is rejected. The ranks are from low value to high values of test scores. [see Table 14.6(b)]

G_1—Group 1

G_2—Group 2

G_3—Group 3

Table 14.6 (b)

	Ranks	*G1 Ranks*	*G2 Ranks*	*G3 Ranks*
74 G1	1			1
81 G2	2		2	
96 G3	3			3
108 G3	4			4
111 G2	5		5	
116 G1	6	6		
118 G3	7			7
125 G2	8		8	
127 G1	9	9		
129 G3	10			10
132 G3	11			11
136 G2	12		12	
142 G1	13	13		
152 G2	14		14	
168 G1	15	15		
173 G1	16	16		
	$\Sigma=136$	$\Sigma=59$	$\Sigma=41$	$\Sigma=36$

Test the hypothesis that the test scores are the same for all three groups; α = 0.05

1. H_o : The distribution of test scores is the same for all 3 groups
   H_a : H_o is not true
2. $$\chi^2 \frac{12}{16(16+1)}\left[\frac{59^2}{5}+\frac{(41)^2}{5}+\frac{36^2}{6}\right]-3(16+1)$$
   $$= 0.044\ [1248.4] - 51 = 4.05$$
3. Reject H_o if, and only if, chi-square $\chi^2 > 5.991$ (df = m – 1 = 3 – 1 = 2 from table of chi-square values).
4. Do not reject H_o.

Friedman's Two-Way ANOVA

Consider the example from the previous example (Kruskal-Wallis Anova). If the samples are related and matched, then Friedman's Two-Way Anova is the test to be used. The following table is used to match samples in this test. (Table 14.7)

Table 14.7

	Treatments		
Samples	*Ranking GP1*	*Ranking GP2*	*Ranking GP3*
1	3	1	2
2	3	2	1
3	3	2	1
4	3	1	2
5	3	2	1
	Σ=15	Σ=8	Σ=7

1. Place the sample observations in a table such that columns represent treatment (K) and rows as representative sample units.
2. Assign ranks to scores 1 to K, the smallest score representing rank 1.
3. Sum ranks for each column.
4. Calculate (chi-square) χ^2 using formula.

$$\text{Chi-square} = \frac{12}{nk(K+1)}\sum_{j=1}^{K} Rj^2 - 3n(K+1),\ df = m-1$$

Where n is the sample size
K = number of treatments
For our problem,

$$\text{Chi-square} = \frac{12}{5x3x4}\ [(15^2 + 8^2 + 7^2) - 3x5x4] = 7.5$$

degrees of freedom = 2
Significance at 0.05 level
Chi-square = 5.99 at $\alpha = 0.05$ (from tables)

Reject H_o, that is, we conclude that there is difference among the population distributions.

Kendal's Coefficient of Concordance (W)

This is a multivariate non-parametric technique. But it is included in this chapter as a part of the discussion on ranking methods. When there are m rankings of n objects and the general relationship between rankings are designed in a research situation, we compute the Kendal Coefficient of concordance denoted by W, which is given by

$$W = 12*S/m^2(n^3 - n),$$

Where S is the sum of the squares of deviation, given by

$$S = \sum_{i=1}^{n} [R_i - m(n + 1)/2]^2$$

Where R_i is the ith rank.

If all the ranks agree, W=1, and if they disagree W is very small and close to 0. Thus, W varies from 0 to 1. It is necessary to apply correlation for tied ranks (Kendall and Gibbons, 1990). For testing the significance of W, we may use tables of significant values of S (probability of S) when $n < 6$. For values $n > 7$, Fisher's Z-distribution test can be used (for details, see Kendall and Gibbons, 1990, chapter 6).

The details of the hypothesis testing in relation to each multivariate analysis is generally included in the outputs of commercially available statistical packages like SPSS/PC and are, therefore, not dealt with in this book. The principles of hypothesis testing, discussed earlier, could be generally sufficient for interpreting them. In special cases, the reader may refer to the Suggested Reading list at the end of the chapter.

SUMMARY

In statistical hypothesis testing, first a statement is made about a parameter of a population, a random sample is selected from it and based on the estimation of appropriate sample statistics, the hypothesis (statement) is accepted or rejected. Several considerations like type of data, size of the sample, number of variables, and number of groups determine the type of test to be used.

The method of hypothesis testing is one of rejecting or not rejecting a null hypothesis, which is the logical opposite of the research hypothesis. Such a rejection or non-rejection is always associated with a probability, which is termed as the significance level, by which the researcher generally sets his judgement. Type I error is committed in hypothesis testing when a true null hypothesis is rejected and type II error is committed when a false null hypothesis is accepted. Power of test is the probability of rejecting a null hypothesis when it is false.

There are well developed statistical hypothesis testing procedures. Among the univariate parametric tests, the prominent ones are Z-test for samples larger than or equal to 30, *t*-test for samples smaller than 30, and *F*-test for analysis of variance. Levels of parameters, like mean, proportion, and variance in a single normally distributed population, or differences in parameters across two or more normally distributed populations are tested in these tests.

Chi-square test is an important non-parametric test and is used for testing differences among categories within a sample and between samples. In cases of multivariate analyses like multiple regression, factor analysis, and discriminant analysis, the above tests are more often used under different conditions.

Suggested Readings

- Bernard, Russel H. (2000). *Social Research Methods*. London: Sage.

- Freund, Rudolph J. and William J. Wilson (1997). *Statistical Methods*, 2d ed. San Diego: Academic Press.
- Green, Paul E., Tull, D. S. and Albaum G. (1988). *Research for Marketing Decisions*, 5th ed. Englewood Cliffs: Prentice Hall.
- Kanji, Gopal K. (1999). *100 Statistical Tests*. New Delhi: Sage Publications.
- Sprent, P. and Smeeton, N. C. (2001). *Applied Non Parametric Statistical Methods*, 3d ed. London: Chapman and Hall.

QUESTIONS AND EXERCISES

1. Is it true that a hypothesis can only be rejected but not accepted? Give reasons to explain your answer?
2. Why is research hypothesis not directly tested?
3. What are the situations in which the following tests would be used? Give an example for each.
   (a) Z-test for two means
   (b) t-test for a mean
   (c) χ^2 test
   (d) Kolmogorov–Smirnov two sample test
   (e) Cochran Q test
4. Why is consideration of power of the test important in hypothesis testing?
5. Why are parametric tests considered more powerful than the non-parametric ones?
6. Why is it that type II error cannot be calculated *a priori*?
7. Suppose an analyst wanted to find if the observed frequencies correspond to some known pattern, what is the approach followed for hypothesis testing?
8. Why is it logical to reject a negative hypothesis rather than try to confirm a positive one?
9. What are the questions that lead to an appropriate univariate hypothesis testing?
10. What is the difference between Kendall's Coefficient of Concordance and Kendall's τ ? Explain with an example.
11. The rework percentage of a large machine having various machine groups shop is 30 per cent. On a particular machine group (turning machines) out of 400 jobs produced, 100 jobs are reworked. Does the rework proportion on turning differ significantly from that of the machine shop?
12. You are concerned that the mean time between failures of the radar system used at the municipal airport is less than the 150 hours claimed by the manufacturer of the system. A random sample of 78 time periods between failures had a mean value of 143.8 hours and a standard deviation of 12.6 hours. Test the manufacturer's claim against the alternative proposed by yourself at 1 per cent significance level.
13. A marketing executive of a shop wants to test the effect of background music on his customers. The average customer purchase was Rs 716 for the last few months. The executive changes the sound system to softer music with brief silent periods. The average of 125 purchases made during this period was Rs 755, with a standard deviation of Rs 206. Can we conclude that the experimental background music has a positive effect on the amount purchased per customer at 0.05 significance level?
14. A plastic injection mould is working properly if the average amount of plastic used per component produced is equal to 15 ounces. A sample of 100 components has an average weight of 15.3 ounces and a standard deviation of 2.0 ounces.
    (a) If the mould is injecting 15.4 ounces, what is the probability of a type II error if the hypothesis test is performed with the alternate hypothesis H_a: $\mu > 15$, and a = 0.02?
    (b) If everything is the same as in (a), except that the alternate hypothesis is H_a: $\mu \neq 15$, what is the probability of a type II error?
15. A retail and wholesale plumbing supply store has a large walk-in trade. The owner wants to try to determine whether the sales clerk tending the store on Saturdays, when 'do-it-yourself' customers make up the bulk of

the clientele, affects the amount sold per purchase. Fifty randomly selected sales from Saturdays, when Karthik was tending the store, had an average of Rs 639.3 with a standard deviation of 204. The 60 randomly selected sales when Mohan was tending the store had an average of Rs 739.4 with a standard deviation of Rs 237.9. Do these sample results indicate that there is a difference in the average amount sold per customer for the two sales clerks? (Use $\alpha = .03$).

16. A manufacturer producing 110 volt motors judges the quality of the motors produced by the minimum voltage required to start the motors running. New energy-efficiency requirements have tended to raise the minimum voltage required to start the motors. The design engineer wants to determine whether there is any difference in the minimum voltage requirements for two different energy efficient motor designs he is considering for mass production. A sample of nine prototypes of the first design required an average voltage of 91.2 volts to start with a standard deviation of 8.7 volts. The 11 randomly selected prototypes of the second design required 95.8 volts with a standard deviation of 9.3 volts. Is there a difference in the two designs with respect to the minimum amount of voltage required to start the motors? (Use a = .10).

17. A large executive recruiting firm randomly sampled 90 applicants rejected for top-level management jobs in large corporations and found that 37 were rejected because the 'personal factor' wasn't right; that is, they were not 'our kind of person'. Twenty-one of the 75 randomly selected job applicants for top-level positions in medium sized corporations were rejected because of the 'personal factor'. On the basis of these sample data, can the recruiting firm conclude at 10 per cent significance level that there is a difference in the importance of the 'personal factor' for the two sizes of firms?

18. The Vidhyut Manufacturing Company has set up quality control on the variance of the voltage (measured in square volts) as well as the mean voltage of its standard nine volt cell. Its control on variance is set up to test the hypothesis H_a: $\sigma^2 > .04$. If H_o is accepted, the variability of the battery voltages is assumed to be in control; if H_o is rejected, then the manufacturing process is stopped and all procedures are carefully checked. A sample of 15 nine volt cells yielded a sample s^2 of .25. Do you reject H_o, and what action, if any, do you recommend? What assumption was necessary regarding the distribution of *x*, the individual battery voltage?

19. Random samples of size 18 and 22 senior students, respectively, from East-West High and Central High School (both are very large) were given a standard mathematics aptitude test. For the East-West students, s^2 was 384, and for Central students, s_2^2 was 84. Test the hypothesis H_a: $\sigma_1^2 = \sigma_2^2$ against H_a : $\sigma_1^2 \neq \sigma_2^2$. Use a = .05. Interpret this result so that the two high school principals, both non-statisticians, would understand the implications of the conclusion you make.

20. The quality control engineer has determined that there is a higher than average percentage of defects of a particular component for components produced between the end of the lunch period and the beginning of the afternoon break. The quality engineer wants to determine whether the percentage of defectives is the same during this time period for all 5 operators. The following results were obtained for a randomly selected day (the operators were not aware of the engineer's special interest in that day's output).

	Operator				
	1	2	3	4	5
Good	286	242	244	264	246
Defective	16	4	30	10	12
Total Components	302	246	284	274	258

Can the quality control engineer conclude that the percentage of defectives is the same for all the five operators? Test at five per cent significance level. (Note that the hypothesis, "the percentage of defects is the same for the five operators", is the same as the hypothesis, "the classification of a component as good or defective is independent of the operator producing the component". This latter hypothesis suggests the use of the contingency table methodology).

21. The design department has proposed 3 different package designs for the company's product. The marketing manager believes the first design would be preferred twice as much as the second design and that the second design would be three preferred times more than the third design. Market test results show that 111 people preferred the first design, 62 preferred the second, and 40 preferred the third design. Are these results consistent with the marketing manager's appraisal of the relative preference for the 3 designs? Test at five per cent significance level.

22. The finance manager of a company would like to know whether the billing clerks differ with regard to the types of mistakes made on customer billing statements. Six hundred faulty statements were randomly selected and classified under the head of the clerk preparing the statement and the type of error made. The following tabulations resulted.

	Type of Mistake			
Billing Clerk Number	*Addition*	*Wrong Price*	*items Wrong*	*Combination and Misc.*
BC1	12	54	36	42
BC2	36	21	48	27
BC3	18	27	54	72
BC4	21	27	84	21

Are the clerks on par with regard to the types of billing errors they make? Test at 5 per cent significance level.

23. A large distributor of dairy products wants to determine whether there is a difference in the amount of milk consumed per week for three different age groups. The following sample results were obtained from independent random samples of each of the respective age groups.

Age in Years	21-30	31-45	46-65
Quarters per Week	3.75	2.25	1.00
	1.50	1.75	2.50
	2.00	6.50	1.75
	8.25	5.75	3.00
	4.25	6.25	1.50
	3.50	7.25	
	4.25		

Is there a difference in milk consumption patterns for the three age groups? Test at five per cent significance level.

24. A dice has three sides painted green, two sides painted yellow, and the remaining sides painted blue. The dice is tossed 150 times, and the colour of the top side is recorded.

Colour	***Sample Frequency***
Green	65
Yellow	43
Blue	42

Can it be concluded, at 1 per cent significance level, that the dice is not fair?

25. A large retailer is considering installing key duplicating machines in his stores. The machines require the sales clerks' to operate them. He is considering 2 different makes of key duplicating machines, and he would like to determine if the machines are the same with respect to the time it takes to duplicate keys. The table below shows the results obtained when independent random samples of various types of keys were duplicated. On the basis of these sample data, can the retailer conclude at the 1 per cent significance level that there is a difference between the 2 machines in the time required to duplicate keys?

(Machine times in seconds)	
Machine 1	Machine 2
5.6	7.2
11.3	3.1

(Machine times in seconds)	
4.1	2.7
3.4	4.1
15.8	3.8
9.2	2.6
5.4	5.6
3.4	2.9
	2.7
	3.2

26. Two samples of mathematics students took a standardised engineering aptitude test. Using a two-tailed test at the .05 level of significance, determine whether the two groups were random samples from the same population.

Group A	**Group B**
N = 25	N = 30
$\overline{X} = 80$	$\overline{X} = 88$
S = 8	S = 9

27. A consumer research agency tested two popular makes of automobiles with similar weight and horsepower. Eleven car A's provided 24.20 mean miles per gallon of fuel with an S of 1.40, while 11 car B's provided 26.30 mean miles per gallon of fuel with an S of 1.74. Using a two-tailed test at the .05 level, test the null hypothesis that there was no significant difference between the mean gasoline mileage of the two makes of cars.

28. Data representing monthly sales by ten sales representatives for one month period before and after a company's promotional campaign is given below. Use Wilcoxon matched pairs rank test to determine whether the promotional campaign did increase sales. Use $\alpha = 0.01$ and a one-tailed test.

Sales representative	*Monthly sales before campaign*	*Monthly sales after campaign*
R1	220	250
R2	100	140
R3	150	170
R4	210	310
R5	280	330
R6	270	270
R7	330	320
R8	180	190
R9	170	280
R10	160	220
150	220	

29. A simple random sample of 12 companies is selected from each of two industries, electronics and chemical. The forms R&D expenditures (million rupees) for the past year are recorded below.

Electronics: 125, 140, 50, 78, 112, 220, 107, 189, 170, 120, 139, 192

Chemical: 65, 85, 96, 80, 153, 191, 95, 41, 75, 100, 68, 77

Use the rank sum method to test that no difference exists between the average levels of R&D expenditure between the two industries (α - 0.05).

30. Toss a coin 40 times and record heads and tails as H and T, respectively. Test this data for randomness (α - 0.05).

31. A manufacturer purchased large batches of a product from four sub-contractors. The batch sizes were all the same. The table gives the number of defectives per batch. Can you conclude there was no difference in the number of defects per batch among the subcontractors (α - 0.01). Use Kruskal–Wallis Test.

Number of defectives per batch			
Sub-contractor A	*Sub-contractor B*	*Sub-contractor C*	*Sub-contractor D*
120	300	150	180
60	280	170	270
100	70	200	130
00	250	30	220
20	240	190	160
40	290	210	160
	310	80	230
	140		

CHAPTER 15

Bivariate Analysis and Hypothesis Testing

- Introduction
- Correlation
- Simple Linear Regression Model
- Non-Parametric Methods of Association

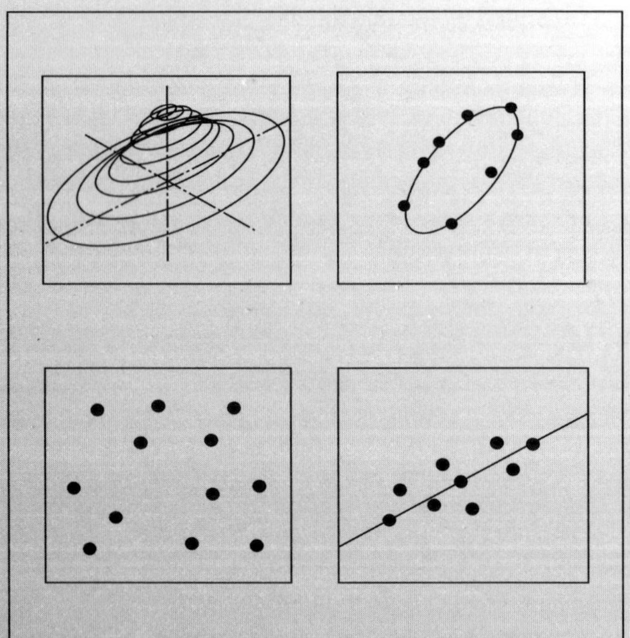

LEARNING OBJECTIVES

Upon completion of this chapter, you will be able to:

- ✓ Understand the associative relationship between two variables
- ✓ Study correlation analysis as a means of measuring association between two variables
- ✓ Understand regression as a means of prediction
- ✓ Learn how to determine the degree of correlation and its significance
- ✓ Understand the significance of regression in hypothesis testing
- ✓ Appreciate the differences between correlation and regression
- ✓ Know about different methods of non-parametric association and their relevant tests of significance

INTRODUCTION

In order to understand relationships of variables or factors to complex constructs such as productivity, motivation, social responsibility, and competitiveness, correlational studies are carried out. Variables found to be related can be causal or associative. When no association exists between a dependent variable (construct) and an independent variable, a causal study can be simplified by eliminating that particular variable. This is the main advantage of studying an association.

Most constructs are complex variables and are multivariable in nature. As a precursor to studying multivariate association, a bivariate association is studied and analysed. Bivariate association is useful in its own right for analysis of data, but it very often lays the foundation to a later more comprehensive multivariate study researchers.

The direction of relationship is not given by an analysis of association. It has to be carefully obtained by the researcher using a substantive understanding of the problem and a good knowledge of the phenomena or related research developments.

Correlation (or regression) analysis, as with any inferential study, is performed on a sample of data pertaining to the variables and the estimates of population measures are obtained in the usual methods of inferential statistics.

In general, the relationship between the dependent variable Y and independent variable X can be expressed as:

$$Y = f(X)$$

The relationship may be causal or associative. In most management research, it is typically hypothesised to be associative.

In a problem definition involving two variables, a researcher is usually faced with the question of whether there is an association between them and, if so, what strength and functional form it has. The forms of relationship may be many in general and need to be approached in a variety of ways. The form may be specified theoretically (for example, linear, logarithmic, and so on) and tested statistically. In most cases, however, the form of relationship is assumed to be linear. In this chapter, linear associative relationship between two variables, one dependent and another independent, is examined. Testing of hypothesis, concerning their significance, will also be detailed. The statistical significance of these relationships have to be confirmed before one affirms them. The further use of such relationships in research requires that they are not only strong but also statistically significant. The methods of obtaining such a relationship for continuous and intervally-scaled variables (parametric) will be discussed first. Subsequently, methods suitable for ordinally and nominally scaled data, in which the population is not necessarily normally distributed (non-parametric), will be dealt with along with relevant hypothesis testing.

Simple correlation and simple regression are the two bivariate parametric measures of association. In correlation analysis, the closeness of relationship between two variables, which jointly vary and are unrestricted by an experimenter, is determined. In regression, the fundamental equation that relates the criterion variable (dependent variable) to one (or more variables in multiple regression) predictor (independent) variable is derived. Regression considers the scatteredness of the dependent variable when the independent variable is held constant.

CORRELATION

correlation
Correlation is the degree of association among variables in a set of data. Statistically speaking simple correlation, measures a linear relationship between two variables. Correlation does not imply that any one of the variables causes the other.

Correlation is the degree of association between variables in a set of data. But, in a statistical sense, a correlation analysis usually produces a measure of the linear relationship between the two variables. Therefore, correlation analysis is closely related to regression analysis. Usually, there is a misunderstanding about the relationship between correlation and causality. Saying two variables are highly correlated does not necessarily mean that one of the variables 'causes' the other.

correlation coefficient (r)
Correlation coefficient (r) between two variables is the ratio of covariance of the two variables to corrections for the units in measurement and given by $r = \frac{COVXY}{S_x S_y}$ and is called Pearson Product Moment correlation coefficient. r lies between −1 and +1.

Correlation coefficient (r) The sample correlation coefficient between two variables X and Y is defined as the ratio of covariance of x and y to corrections for units in measurement.

$$r = \frac{COVXY}{S_X S_Y}$$

$COVXY$ indicates how strongly x and y vary together and also gives the direction of relationship (positive or negative) S_x S_y, the standard deviations of x and y, and standardises the value of r (which will now vary from –1 to +1).

For computational purpose r is given by,

$$r = \frac{\sum_{i=1}^{n}(x_i - \bar{x})(Y_i - \bar{Y})}{\sqrt{\left\{\sum_{i=1}^{n}(x_i - \bar{x})\right\}^2}\sqrt{\left\{\sum_{i=1}^{n}(Y_i - \bar{Y})\right\}^2}}$$

The above coefficient is called Pearson's product-moment correlation coefficient. It is one of the many measures of association. If the paired values of X and Y fall on a straight line with a positive slope, then $r = 1$. If the line has a negative slope then $r = -1$. If the points are scattered, $r = 0$. Generally, r lies between –1 and +1 ($-1 < r < 1$) (See Fig. 15.1). The figure gives the scatter diagram of x and y which represents their relationship in a factorial way. When $r = 0$ the variables are orthogonal (independent of each other); when $r = 1$ all points fall on a straight line with a positive slope x and y are directly related when $r = -1$; x and y are inversely related perfectly where $0 < r < 1$ positive relationship and $-1 < r < 0$ negative relationship are indicated.

scatter diagram
This represents the plot of two variables on x-y coordinate axes and qualitatively gives the relationship.

Inferences from sample correlation coefficient to population correlation coefficient The sample correlation coefficient r has an analogous population correlation coefficient, which is denoted by ρ. The population correlation coefficient ρ is given by,

inference from sample r
Sample r is theoretically an unbiased point estimator of population correlation coefficient ρ.

$$\rho = \frac{E[(X - \bar{X})(Y - \bar{Y})}{\sqrt{\{V(X)V(Y)\}}}$$

The numerator gives the 'average' (expected value) of the products $(X - \bar{X})$ $(Y - \bar{Y})$ in the population. $V(X)$ and $V(Y)$ are variances of X and Y, respectively, in the population. Theoretically, r is proved to be an unbiased point estimator of ρ, that is, $\rho = r$. Therefore, for all practical purposes r is used in its place without loss of generality.

It is to be kept in mind that (i) r is symmetric, that is, correlation of x with y is same as that of y with x. Therefore, in correlational analysis dependent or independent variable need not be specified. (ii) r provides indication of a linear relationship between x and y. (iii) The distributions

Fig. 15.1

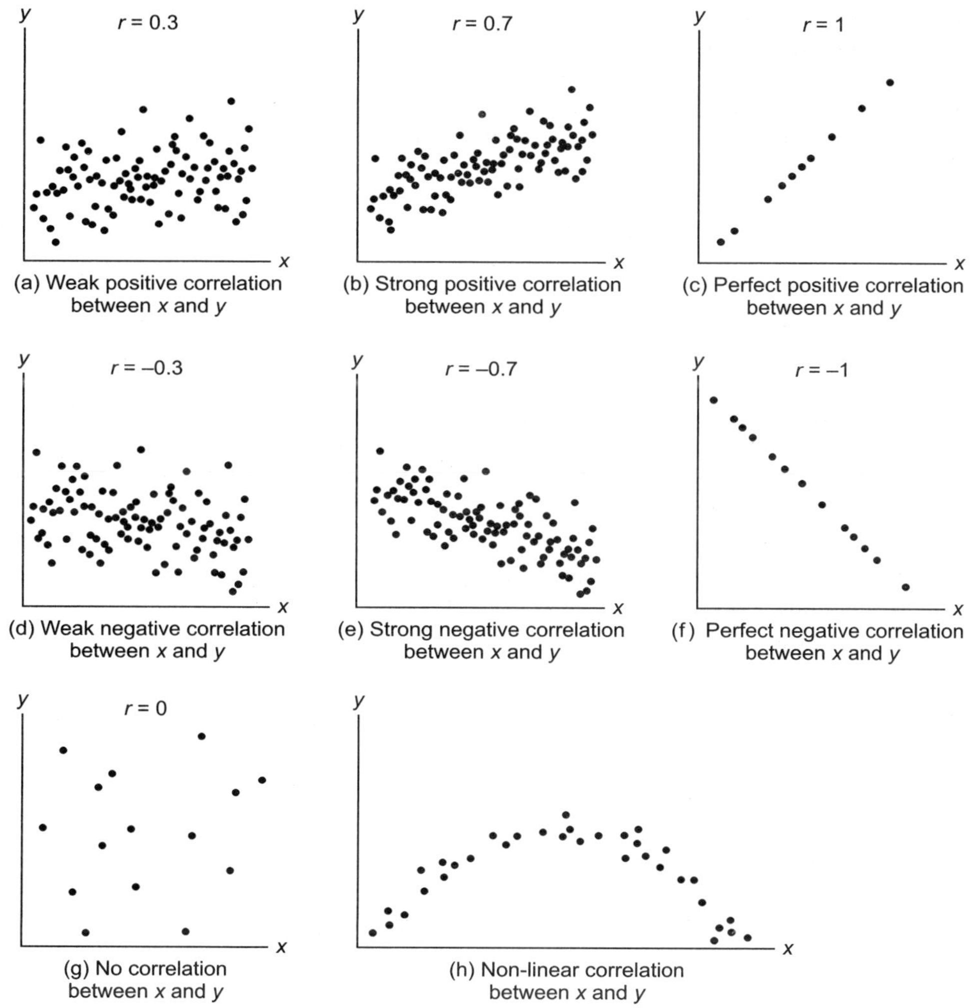

are same for both x and y and the variables are continuous. If the distributions are not the same r tends to be smaller and to underestimate ρ.

Hypothesis testing for bivariate parametric correlation

hypothesis testing for correlation
Significance of r is tested using at test and the significance test between r and ρ is tested using Fisher Z-transformation test.

[A] r can be used as an estimate of the population correlation coefficient ρ. If $\rho = 0$, there is no relationship between x and y in the population and it can be concluded that x and y are independent in the statistical sense.

The hypothesis $H_0 : \rho = 0$ is tested with the t-statistic having (n-2) degrees of freedom.

$$\text{Test statistic, } t_0 = \frac{r}{\sqrt{\{(1-r^2)/(n-2)\}}} = \frac{\text{Magnitude of relationship}}{\text{Appropriate estimate of stand error}}$$

The assumptions are that the samples are random and both x and y are normal variables (r depends upon distribution y only) and the relationship is linear. Either a two-tailed or one-tailed test can be used.

Null hypothesis $H_0 : \rho = 0$
Research hypothesis $H_a : \rho \neq 0$

$$\text{Test statistic, } t_0 = \frac{r}{\sqrt{\{(1-r^2)/(n-2)\}}}$$

If $t_0 > t_c$, then reject H_0
If $t_0 \leq t_c$, then suspend judgment (do not reject H_0)

Example A research correlation coefficient of 0.46 was derived between two normally distributed variables on the basis of the measurements on a sample of 258 study objects. Is the correlation coefficient significant at $\alpha = .01$?

$$H_0 : \rho = 0$$
$$H_a : \rho \neq 0$$

$$t_0 \frac{r}{\sqrt{1-r^2} / \sqrt{n-2}} = \frac{.46\sqrt{258-2}}{\sqrt{1-0.46^2}} = \frac{.46x.6}{.89} = 8.28$$

t_c for $\alpha = 0.01$

(for two-tail test $\alpha^1 = \frac{\alpha}{2} = .005$)

is 2.6. Since $-2.6 < 8.28 > +2.6$, H_0 is rejected. The relationship between the two variables is significant. (See also the example under regression analysis.)

[B] Z-test for a correlation coefficient to investigate the significance of difference between ρ (population correlation coefficient) and a specified value ρ_0.
The assumptions and limitations are as stated for the t-test above. We use Fisher Z-transformation on r as defined in the t-test.

$$Z_1 = ½ \log_e \{(1+r)/(1-r)\} = 1.1513 \log_{10}\{(1+r)/(1-r)\}$$

Z, is distributed approximately normally, with μ_{z1} as 1 mean and σ_{z1} as standard deviation.

$$Z_1 = ½ \log e \frac{1+r}{1-r} = 1.5131 \text{ Log}_{10} \frac{1+r}{1-r} \text{ and } \sigma_{z1} = \frac{1}{\sqrt{n-3}} \text{ - - -}$$

(Ref: Dowdy and Weardon, 1983)

$$\mu_{z1} = ½ \log e \frac{1+p}{1-p_0} = 1.5131 \text{ Log}_{10} \frac{1+p}{1-p},$$

$$\text{Test statistic} = \frac{Z_1 - \mu_{z1}}{\sigma_{z1}}$$

Using the data of Example II in section on fitting of a linear regression model later in this chapter.

$$r = 0.98,\ p_0 = 0.9,\ n = 15,\ \alpha = 0.10$$

We have, $$Z_1 = 1.5131 \text{ Log}_{10} \frac{1+.98}{1-.98} = 1.5131 \text{ Log } 99$$

$$\mu_{z1} = 1.5131 \text{ Log}_{10} \frac{1+0.9}{1-0.9} = 1.5131 \text{ Log } 19$$

$$\sigma_{z1} = \frac{1}{\sqrt{15-3}} = \frac{1}{\sqrt{12}}$$

$$Z_0 = \text{Test Statistic} = \frac{1.513\left[\log_{10} \frac{99}{19}\right]}{\sqrt{1/12}} = 6.7$$

$Z_c = 1.64$ (two-tail test), from Table of Z for $\alpha = 0.10$

$Z_o > Z_c$

Therefore, the null hypothesis is rejected.

SIMPLE LINEAR REGRESSION MODEL

A simple linear regression model is a mathematical way of stating the statistical relationship that exists between two variables. The two principal elements of a statistical relationship are:

1. The tendency of dependent variable *Y* to vary systematically with independent variable *X*.
2. The scattering of the points about the 'curve' that represents the relationship between *X* and *Y*. These two elements of a statistical relationship are represented in a simple linear regression model by assuming that:
   - There is a probability distribution of *Y* for each value of *X*.
   - The mean of the probability distribution of *Y* for each *X* falls on the line. The two assumptions are illustrated in the following figures.

heteroscadisticity
This is a condition in regression where the scatter diagram about the regression line has a pattern indicating variations in the distribution of y for various values of x (the regression line is $y = b_o + bx$) b is the regression coefficient.

A heteroscedastic pattern of scatter diagram is shown in Fig. 15.2. It should be noted from Fig. 15.2 that the distance of points being homoscadastic (no clear pattern of the scatter diagram about the regression line) is a precondition for use of Pearson's *r* (Bryman and Cramer, 1990).

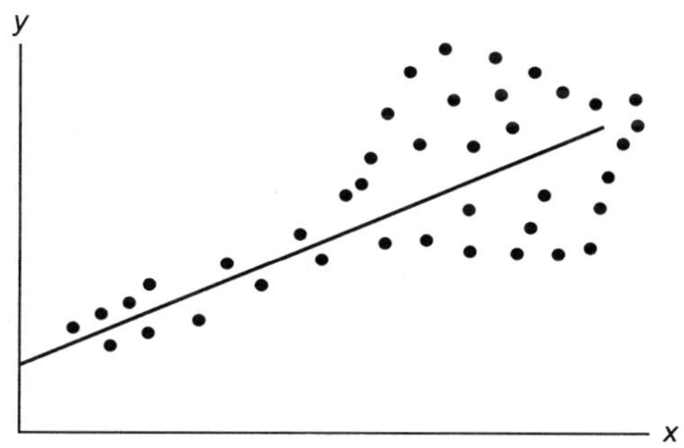

Fig. 15.2 Heterosedasticity

Example For the data presented in Table 15.1, regression equation fitted is $Y = -310.76 + 7.07X$

$$R^2 = 0.88$$

$$\text{Since } r = +\sqrt{R^2} \; r = +\sqrt{0.88} = +0.938$$

Since the slope of the regression line is positive, r = + 0.938.

Table 15.1 Details of Heights and Weights for Example I

Height (Inches) X	Weight (Pounds) Y
60	110
65	150
74	200
70	185
70	170
66	160
68	180
72	195
64	135
71	215

Now, assuming (X,Y) is a bivariate normal distribution the following hypothesis is tested using the standard t-test.

Null hypothesis is $H_o : r = 0$

Research Hypothesis H_a: r not equal to zero at significance level $\alpha = 0.05$.

In theory,

statistic $t = r * \sqrt{\{(n-2)/(1-r2)\}}$, follows

student's t-distribution with $(n-2)$ degrees of freedom.

Let, $$sr = \sqrt{\left\{\frac{1-(r)2}{n-2}\right\}} = \sqrt{\left\{\frac{1-(0.938)2}{10-2}\right\}}$$

$(n-2 = df = 10-2 = 8), = 0.122$

$$t = \frac{r}{sr} = \frac{0.938}{0.122} = 7.68$$

Critical value of t, t_c from table for $\alpha = 0.05$, is 2.36

Here, the $t > t_C$ $(7.68 > 2.36)$; hence, H_o:r = 0 is rejected.

Therefore, the correlation coefficient is significant.

The systematic way in which Y varies as a function of X is identified as a straight line (shown in Fig. 15.3), the regression line of Y on X. The regression line goes perfectly through all means of the conditional probability distributions of Y, given a value of X. The data is collected by taking random samples from the conditional probability distributions of Y for values of X. For example, in Table 12.1, when $X = 60$ inches, Y was observed to be 110 pounds. This particular value of Y represents a random sample of size 1 drawn from the conditional probability distribution of Y when $X = 60$. This value of Y, as shown in Fig. 15.4, is somewhat below the mean of conditional distribution.

Fig. 15.3 Regression line for example

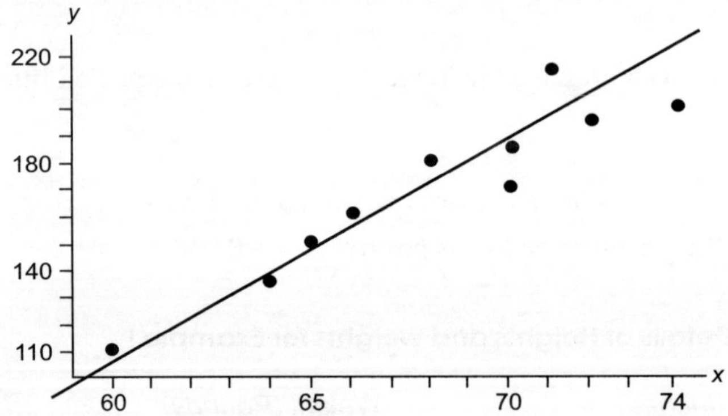

The formal statement of the simple linear regression model is

$$Y_i = \beta_0 + \beta_i X_i + e_i,\ i = 1,2,\ldots, n$$

Where

Y_i value of the dependent variable in the ith trial,

(0, 1 are the parameters in the model,

X_i is the value of the independent variable in the ith trial

e_i is the random error in the ith term.

By trial we mean an observed value of Y for a fixed value of X.

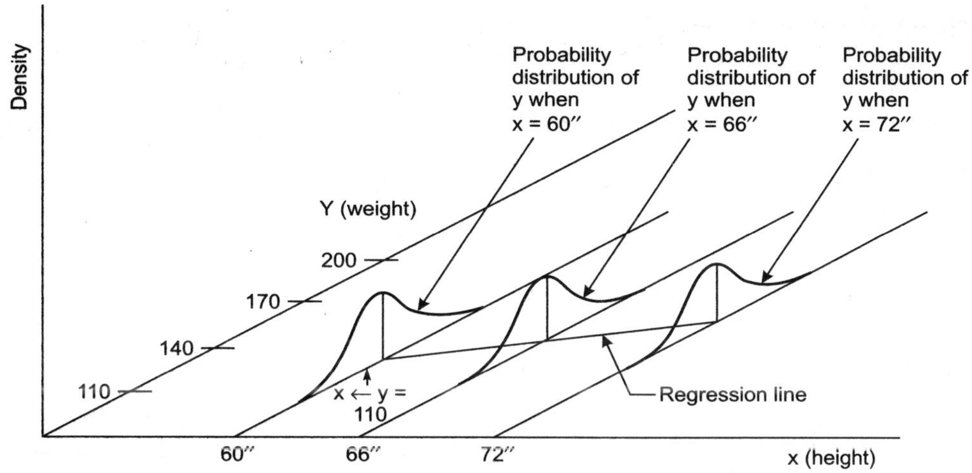

Fig. 15.4 Conditional probability distribution in regression

Assumptions: The assumptions of the simple linear regression model are :

- For the ith trial, the expected value of the error component e_i is zero ($E(e_i) = 0$), and the variance of the error component ($V(e_i)$) is r^2 [that is, $V(e_i)) = r^2$] and is constant for all values of i; $i = 1,2,\ldots,n$ (homoscadasticity).
- The error component in any pair of trials, say the ith and j^{th}, are un-correlated.
- The terms β_0 and β_1 are the model parameters, whose values are typically unknown and must, therefore, be estimated from the sample data. Further, X_i is considered to be a known constant in the model.

The consequences of the assumptions are:

The observed value of Y in the ith trial, Y_i, is the sum of two components, a 'constant' and a 'random' part.

$$Y_i = \underbrace{\beta_0 + \beta_1 X_1}_{\text{Constant part}} + \underbrace{e_i}_{\text{Random part}}$$

and $$E(Y_i) = \beta_0 + \beta_1 X_i.$$

Fitting of a Simple Linear Regression Model

Since B_0 and B_1 are generally not known in a regression problem, they must be estimated from sample data on X and Y, obtained either by experimentation or survey.

A scatter plot of these data will pictorially show the feasibility of the regression line that can be fitted to this data using the least squares criterion which requires that the sum of the squared vertical deviations between the line and scatter of points is minimised. It turns out that the values of B_0, B_1 which minimise least-squares are the solutions to the following two simultaneous equations, which are referred to as normal equations:

$$\Sigma Y_i = nb_0 + b_1 \Sigma X_i$$
$$\Sigma X_i Y_i = b_0 \Sigma X_i + b_i \Sigma X_i^2$$

Solving the above equations for b_0 and b_1 provides the point estimators of B_0 and B_1, respectively.

$$b_1 = \frac{\sum X_i Y_i - \left(\sum Y_i / n\right)}{\sum X_i^2 - \left(\sum X_i\right)^2 / n} \text{ and } b_0 = \overline{Y} - b_1 \overline{X}$$

where $\overline{X} = \left(\sum X_i / n\right)$, $\overline{Y} = \left(\sum \overline{Y}_i / n\right)$

coefficient of determination This is given by r^2 and indicates the strength of relationship between the two variables. This also is the ratio of amount of variation explained by the regression line to the total variation in Y.

Coefficient of determination, R^2 One measure of strength of the linear relationship between X and Y is given by the coefficient of determination. The coefficient of determination, R^2, gives the proportion of variability in the dependent variable Y, which is explained by the independent variable X through the fitting of the regression line. R^2 is a simple ratio of the amount of variation explained by the regression line to the total variation in Y, and the values of R^2 are bound between 0 and 1.

$$R^2 = \frac{SST - SSE}{SST} = \frac{\text{Explained Variation}}{\text{Total Variation}}$$

Where

SST = Total variation

SSE = Error variation

If $R^2 = 1$ and $SSE = 0$, the observations fall perfectly on the fitted regression line. If $R^2 = 0$, the fitted regression must have zero slope. Correlation coefficient r is directly related to coefficient of determination, R^2, in the simple regression model, $Y = B_0 + B_1 X$. If we write r in its calculating form,

$$r = \frac{\sum (X_i - \overline{X})(Y_i - \overline{Y})}{\sqrt{\left\{\sum X_i^2 - \left(\sum X_i\right)^2 / n\right\}} \sqrt{\left\{\sum Y_i^2 - \left(\sum Y_i\right)^2 / n\right\}}}$$

$$= \frac{\sum X_i Y_1 - \left(\sum X_i \sum Y_i\right) / n}{\sqrt{\sum X_i^2 - \left(\sum X_i\right)^2 / n} \sqrt{\sum Y_i^2 - \left(\sum Y_i\right)^2 / n}}$$

we can clearly see that $r = +\sqrt{\{R^2\}}$

Therefore, the square of 'correlation coefficient' measures the amount of variability in the Y variable when it is related linearly with the variable X. The regression line of Y on X is given by $Y = b_0 + b_1 x$; where b_1 is the slope of the line. Also, the sign of correlation coefficient r represents the slope (negative or positive). Hence, by mathematical manipulation the following relationship is obtained.

$$r = \{\sqrt{\{\Sigma X_i^2 - (\Sigma X_i/n)^2\}}/\sqrt{\{Y_i^2 - (\Sigma Y_i/n)^2\}}\ \} * b_1$$

A useful comparison between regression and correlation analysis is given in Table 15.2.

Table 15.2 Comparison of Regression and Correlation

Regression analysis	*Correlation analysis*
Dependent variable is assumed to be a random variable	Dependent variable is assumed to be a random variable
Independent variable is assumed to be fixed	Independent variable considered to be a random variable
For hypothesis testing, the dependent variable is assumed to be normally distributed	Assume (X, Y) to be jointly distributed as bivariate normal for hypothesis testing
A linear relationship between $X1$ and $Y1$ is established $(Y = a + bX)$	Association existing between X and Y is determined
A random sample of Y values is taken with the X's being fixed or given	A random sample of pairs of values is taken

Example The district wise advertising expenditure (X) and Sales (Y) of a company are given in the table 15.3(a). Find a linear equation for estimating sales given the advertising expenditure.

(n = 15)

Table 15.3(a) **Expenditure and Sales Figures for Example II**

Sales district	*Advertising expenditure ($ 1,000) X*	*Sales district Y*
1	1.814	55.420
2	1.112	45.819
3	0.718	16.940
4	1.421	35.818
5	3.085	85.090
6	2.119	65.025
7	0.525	17.918
8	1.108	32.845
9	1.621	41.180
10	2.645	62.910
11	2.927	87.013
12	0.847	22.150
13	0.621	16.660
14	0.981	27.050
15	1.394	39.121
Total	22.938	647.959

Table 15.3(b) **Regression Worksheet for Data Given in 15.3(a)**

District	X_i	Y_i	X_i^2	Y_i^2	X_iY_i	*Y (estimated)*
1	1.814	55.420	3.291	3071.376	100.532	50.870
2	1.112	45.819	1.237	2099.381	50.951	31.940
3	0.718	16.940	0.516	286.964	12.163	21.323
4	1.421	35.818	2.019	1282.929	50.897	40.279
5	3.085	85.090	9.517	7240.308	262.503	85.149
6	2.119	65.025	4.490	4228.251	137.788	59.101
7	0.525	17.918	0.276	321.055	9.407	16.119
8	1.108	32.845	1.228	1078.794	36.392	31.831
9	1.621	41.180	2.628	1695.792	66.753	45.672
10	2.645	62.910	6.996	3957.668	166.397	73.284
11	2.927	87.013	8.567	7571.262	254.687	80.889
12	0.847	22.150	0.717	490.622	18.761	24.801
13	0.621	16.660	0.386	277.556	10.346	18.707
14	0.981	27.050	0.962	731.703	26.536	28.415
15	1.394	39.121	1.943	1530.453	54.535	39.537
Total (Σ)	22.938	647.917	44.772	35864.113	1258.647	647.917

$$b_1 = \frac{\sum X_iY_i - \left(\sum X_i \sum Y_i\right)/n}{\sum X_i^2 - \left(\sum X_i\right)^2/n} = \frac{1258.647 - (22.938)(647.917)/15}{44.772 - (22.938)^2/15} = 26.965 \text{ (Table 15.3(a))}$$

$$b_0 = \overline{Y} - \mathrm{b}_1\,\overline{X} = (647.917/15) - (26.965)(22.938/15) = 1.962$$

$$R^2 = \frac{\left[\sum XY - \left(\sum X \sum Y\right)^2/n\right]^2}{\left[\sum X^2 - \left(\sum X\right)^2/n\right]\left[\sum Y^2 - \left(\sum Y\right)^2/n\right]} = \frac{261.4322^2}{(9.6952 \times 7492.90)}$$

$= 0.9408 =$ Coefficient of determination

The linear regression equation for estimating sales is given by $Y = 1.962 + 26.965{*}X$

t-test for regression coefficient b

A t-test can be used or an F test based on variance due to regression and residual variation, can be used.

t–test for the regression coefficient b We know the estimate of b is given by,

$$b = \frac{\sum x_i y_i - \frac{1}{n}\sum x_i \sum y_i}{\sum x_i^2 - \frac{1}{n}\left(\sum x_i\right)^2}$$

Variance of x's about regression line $= S_x^2 = \dfrac{\sum (x_i - \bar{x})^2}{n-1}$

Variance of y's about regression line $S_{y.x}^2$ is given by

$$S_{y.x}^2 = \frac{\sum \{y_i - \bar{y} - b(x_i - \bar{x})\}^2}{n-2}$$

Test statistic $t_o = \sqrt{(n-1)}$

Where $n - 2$ is degrees of freedom

If $t_o > t_c$

or $-t_o < -t_c$, then H_o is rejected.

Hypothesis testing in bivariate regression analysis

Example Test the significance of the regression coefficient b for the following data:

x: 1	2	3	4	5
y: 5	4	6	8	7

Solution:

x	y	x^2	xy
1	5	1	5
2	4	4	8
3	6	9	18
4	8	16	32
5	7	25	35
15	**30**	**55**	**98**

$$b = \frac{98 - 15 \text{ x } 30/5}{55 - 152/5} = 0.8; \; a = \bar{y} - b\bar{x} = 6 - 0.8 \text{ x } 3 = 3.6$$

Regression equation: $\dot{y} = 3.6 + 0.8$ x

Estimated $\dot{y}$ values for the above values of x are as follows.

x	$\dot{y}$	$(y - \dot{y})$ error	err^2
1	4.4	0.6	0.36
2	5.2	-1.2	1.44
3	6.0	0.0	0.00
4	6.8	1.2	1.44
5	7.6	-0.6	0.36
			$\Sigma = 3.60$

[$\dot{Y} = 3.6 + 0.8$ x 5] ← (for x = 5)

$$S^2_{y.x} = \frac{3.60}{5-2} = 1.2 \text{ standard error of } b$$

$$S^2_{x.x} = \frac{10}{4} = 2.5$$

Hypotheses:

$$H_0: \beta = 0$$
$$H_a: \beta \neq 0$$

at $\alpha = 0.01$; β = population regression coefficient

$$\text{Test statistic: } t_0 = \frac{b - \beta_0}{S_{y \cdot x} / \sqrt{S_{xx}}}$$

Standard error of $b = S_{yx}/\sqrt{S_{xx}}$

$$t_0 = \frac{0.8 - 0}{\sqrt{1.2}/\sqrt{2.5}} = 1.31$$

t_c = 4.541 (from table)

for $\alpha = 0.01$

Therefore, $t_0 < t_c$

H_0 cannot be rejected; the regression is not significant.

F-test for regression coefficient As an alternative to the t-test given in 15.3.2 we can use analysis of variance technique and compute F. The fundamental ANOVA identity is,

$$\sum_2 (y_2 - \bar{y})^2 = \sum (\hat{y}_2 - \bar{y})^2 + \sum_2 (y_2 - \hat{y})^2$$

with usual notations;

y_2- points $\hat{y}_2$ estimates of y_2

$\bar{y}$ - mean of all y_2S

The analysis of variance table is as follows: (Table 15.4)

Table 15.4

Variance due to	*df*	*SS*	*Mean SS*	*F-ratio*
Regression	1 $(n-1)$	$(\hat{y}_2 - \bar{y})$	$\frac{(\hat{y}_2 - \bar{y})^2}{1}$	$F = \frac{(\hat{y}_2 - \bar{y}_2)}{(y_2 - y_2)/n-2}$
Residual	$(n-2)$	$(\hat{y}_2 - \bar{y}_2)^2$	$\frac{(y_2 - \hat{y}_2)^2}{n-2}$	
Total	9 $(n-1)$			

Example The returns on two securities *A* and *B* in the market for the past 10 years are given in the table 15.5(a). *A* is taken as the independent variable. Carry out a regression analysis and list the significance of the regression coefficient at

$$\alpha = 0.05.$$

The regression equation is obtained as follows:

$$\bar{X} = \frac{\sum X}{n} = \frac{260}{10} = 26, \quad \bar{Y} = \frac{\sum Y}{n} = \frac{240}{10} = 24$$

Table 15.5(a) Returns on Securities A and B

Product	*Return on security A*	*Return on security B*
1	24	20
2	10	12
3	36	26
4	-16	-8
5	20	26
6	32	28
7	14	8
8	30	36
9	60	48
10	50	44

Table 15.5(b) Regression Equation for Data in 15.5(a)

Return on A	*Return on B*	*XY*	X^2
24	20	480	576
10	12	120	100
36	26	938	1296
-16	-8	128	256
20	26	520	400
32	28	896	1024
14	8	112	196
30	36	1080	900
60	48	2880	3600
50	44	2200	2500
260	240	9352	10848

$$\sum XY = 9352, \quad \sum X^2 = 10848 \text{ (Table 15.5(b))}$$

$$\overline{X}^2 = (26)(26) = 676$$

$$b = \frac{\sum XY - n\overline{X}\overline{Y}}{\sum X^2 - n\overline{X}^2} = \frac{9352 - (10)(26)24}{10848 - (10)(676)} = \frac{3112}{4088}$$

$$= 0.76$$

$$a = \overline{Y} - b\overline{X} = 24 - (0.76)(26) = 4.24$$

$$\hat{Y} = 4.24 + 0.76x$$

A table for sum of squares is set up as follows:

for $\alpha = 05$ $df_1=1$ $df_2=8$ $Fc_r=5.32$

F = 87.90 (Refer to tables 15.6 and 15.7)

∴ the regression coefficient is significant.

rank correlation (r_s)
Association between two sets of ranked data can be obtained using Spearman's rank correlation. The significance of r_s is tested using a t-test. Kendal's t is another measure of rank correlation.

contingency coefficient (c)
C is a measure of association between two categories (nominally scaled) of data based on χ^2 distribution, and is obtained using contingency tables.

NON-PARAMETRIC METHODS OF ASSOCIATION

We consider three prominent non-parametric methods of association; Spearman's rank correlation coefficient (r_s), Kendall's tau (t), and contingency coefficient (*c*).

Spearman's Rank Correlation Coefficient (r_s)

When two sets of rankings of ordinal data are available, then Spearman's rank correlation coefficient r_s is given by (Kendal and Gibbons, 1990).

Table 15.6

	(X)	(Y)	$(X-\bar{X})^2$	$(Y-\bar{Y})^2$	$(X-\bar{X})(Y-\bar{Y})$	$\hat{Y}$	$(Y-\hat{Y})^2$	$(\hat{Y}-\bar{Y})^2$
1	24	20	4	16	8.00	22.48	6.1504	2.5
2	10	12	256	144	192.00	11.84	0.0256	148
3	36	26	100	4	20.00	31.6	31.36	58
4	-16	-8	1764	1024	1344.00	-7.92	0.0064	1019
5	20	26	36	4	-12.00	19.44	43.0336	21
6	32	28	36	16	24.00	28.56	0.3136	21
7	14	8	144	256	192.00	14.88	47.3344	83
8	30	36	16	144	48.00	27.04	80.2816	9.20
9	60	48	1156	576	816.00	49.84	3.3856	670
10	50	44	576	400	480.00	42.24	3.0976	335
Total	260	240	4088	2584	3112.00	240	214.9888	2362.70
Mean covariance					345.78			
SD	21.3125	16.9443						
Variance	454.22	287.11						

Table 15.7 Analysis of Variance

Variance due to	*df*	*SS*	*Mean SS*	*F ratio*
Regression	1	2362.70	2362.70	$F=\frac{2362.70}{26.88}$
Residual	8 $(n-2)$	215.00	26.88	$=87.90$
Total	9 $(n-1)$			

$$r_s = 1 - \frac{6E_d^2}{n(n^2-1)}$$

Where n is the sample size, and

d is the difference in rankings of two variables

r_s is less subject to errors when sample sizes are small ($n < 30$). The significance of correlation can be tested using a t-test (when $n > 10$), the test statistic being

$$t = r_s\sqrt{\left\{\frac{n-2}{1-r_s^2}\right\}}$$

If the rank of one variable is the perfect opposite of the other (which can easily be verified) $r_s = -1$. If the ranks are same, $E_d = 0$ and $r_s = 1$. For ordinal data, the Pearson's product moment correlation for larger values of n is very close to the values of r_s and hence that procedure may be used not withstanding the nature of scale and tests conducted to test the significance of r_s.

Example Seven jobs ranked by two attributes, job difficulty and worker skill, are given in the following table. Find whether the ranks are correlated significantly.

Job	1	2	3	4	5	6	7	8	9	10	11	12
Rank on job difficulty	5	1	3	4	8	12	9	10	7	2	6	11
Rank on skill required	5	2	6	1	10	8	4	11	7	3	9	12
d	0	-1	-3	3	-2	4	5	-1	0	-1	-3	-1
d^2	0	1	9	9	4	16	25	1	0	1	9	1

$$E_d^2 = 71$$

$$r_s = 1 - \frac{6E_d^2}{n(n^2-1)} = 1 - \frac{6*71}{12(144-1)} = 0.752$$

Hypothesis testing for significance of r_s

$H_0: r_s = 0$

$H_a: r_s \neq 0;$

$\alpha = 0.05$ and degrees of freedom = n–2

$$t = 0.752/\frac{12-2}{1-(0.752)^2} = 3.606, \text{ 10 degrees of freedom}$$

$t_c = 1.812$ (0.05)

$t > t_c$.

Therefore, the null hypothesis is rejected and it is confirmed that the ranks are correlated strongly and significantly.

Kendall's Tau

Ranks of each pair of all possible pairs of two variables is made. If the rankings of the first variable is higher than that of the second, –1 is assigned, if the ranking of the second variable is higher +1 is assigned; when all pairs are completed, the total of all positive values is obtained (P) and total of all negative values is obtained (Q). Then Kendall's τ is given by,

$$\tau = \frac{2(P-Q)}{n(n-1)}$$

Like r_s, τ will lie between –1 and +1 and its significance can be established by the Z - test using the Z statistic given by (Kendall and Gibbons, (1990) (n > 30),

$$Z = \frac{38\sqrt{\{n(n-1)\}}}{\sqrt{\{2(2n+5)\}}}$$

Example The data used above for rank correlation is rearranged in the following way (ascending ranks for first variable).

Job difficulty	1	2	3	4	5	6	7	8	9	10	11	12
Skill required	2	3	6	1	5	9	7	10	4	11	12	8

For the first variable all values are positive. Contribution to P will arise only from pairs in the second variable in which natural order occurs.

2,3,6,1,5,9,7,10,4,11,12,8

P = (2,3,6,5,9,7,10,11,12) = 65;

Q = (1,4,8) = 13; (P–Q) = 52.

$$\tau = \frac{2s}{n(n-1)} = \frac{52*2}{12(12-1)} = 0.79$$

To assess the significance of τ we perform a hypothesis test.

N = 12 (>10), Z test will be used.

Hypotheses to be tested are:

$H_0: J = 0$

$H_a: J \neq 0$

$$\text{Test stastic} = \frac{S}{[n(n-1)(2n+5)/18]^{1/2}} = Z_0$$

Given $n = 12, \alpha = 0.05$

$$S = P - Q = 65 - 13 = 52$$

$$Z_0 = \frac{52}{[12(12-1)[12x12+5]/18]^{1/2}}$$

$$= 3.56$$

$$Z_{cr} = 1.64$$

$$Z_0 > Z_{cr}$$

∴ Reject H_0

$$S = 39;\ S_{cr} = 30 \text{ (Table for } S\text{)}$$

$$S > S_{cr}$$

∴ Reject H_0

∴ Kendel's τ is significant.

Contingency Coefficient

When the data is nominal and variables can only be classified into identified groups, it often becomes necessary to find out if there is a relationship between the classifications. The chi-square test using contingency tables is aimed at investigating the independence of the classified variables. Contingency coefficient, however, can be used to measure their association. It is denoted by C and given by,

$$C = SQRT\ \{X^2/(n + X^2)\}$$

Where

n is the sample size,

X^2 = computed chi-square in the normal way.

The difficulty with contingency coefficient is that there is no measure to indicate the strength of the relationship. In such cases, under the assumption of normal distribution for the variable, an index of predictive association can be calculated (for details see, Churchill, 1987).

Example The table below shows the frequency of occurrence of 3 categories of size of the organisations. Is the size of the skilled workforce (variables S) associated with the types of organisations (variables O)?

Size of the skilled workforce	Organisation type			Total
	01	02	03	
S1	9	12	4	25
S2	4	20	17	41
S3	3	14	17	34
Total	16	46	38	100

The table below displays the percentages in the contingency table computed from the given data (the expected frequencies).

Size of the skilled workforce	Organisation type			Total
	01	02	03	
S1	4*	11.5	9.5	25%
S2	6.56	18.86	15.58	41%
S3	5.44	15.64	12.92	34% Total
16%	46%	38%	100%	

*[Note: S1/O1 = (16 × 25)/100 = 4.00

S3/O1 = (34 × 16)/100 = 25.44
S2/O3 = (41 × 38)/100 = 15.58]

$$X^2 = \frac{(O_{ij} - E_{ij})}{E_{ij}} = \frac{(9-4)^2}{4} + \frac{(12-11.5)^2}{11.5} + \frac{(4-9.5)^2}{9.5}$$

$$= \frac{(4-6.56)^2}{6.56} + \frac{(20-18.86)^2}{18.86} + \frac{(17-15.58)^2}{15.58}$$

$$= \frac{(3-5.44)^2}{5.44} + \frac{(14-15.64)^2}{15.64} + \frac{(17-12.92)^2}{12.92}$$

$$X^2 = [6.25 + 0.022 + 3.18 + 1.00 + 0.07 + 0.13 + 1.09 + 1.09 + 0.17 + 1.29]$$

$$X^2 = 13.202$$

$$\text{Contingency coefficient} = C = \sqrt{\left\{\frac{13.202}{13.202 + 100}\right\}} = 0.34$$

$$\text{Upper limit for } C = \sqrt{\{(r-1)/r\}} = \sqrt{\{2/3\}} = 0.816$$

Thus, a value of C = 0.34 shows only a moderate association.

Note: For a detailed derivation of the non-parametric relationships and the test statistic the reader can refer to Kendall and Gibbons, 1990.

SUMMARY

Simple correlation and regression are the two measures of parametric bivariate association, in which a single dependent variable is related to a single independent variable. Correlation is the degree of closeness of relationship between the variables. Pearson product moment correlation coefficient *r* is a measure of this closeness between two sets of interval data, and assumes values between −1 and +1, and 0 when there is no association. A scatter plot graphically indicates whether a relationship exists between the variables. The significance of *r* is tested by using a Z-test.

A linear regression model is a mathematical way of stating the relationship and is represented by a straight line. The slope *b* of the line is related to the coefficient of determination, which is the square of the corresponding correlation coefficient. The significance of *b* can be tested using a t-test. In both regression and correlation, the dependent variable is assumed to be a random variable, which is normally distributed and the independent variable is assumed to be fixed. The regression equation can be used for estimating the dependent variable value given the value of the independent variable.

Three non-parametric measures of association are Spearman's rank correlation, Kendall's Tau and contingency coefficient. Spearman's rank correlation (r_s) and Kendall's Tau are used to determine the relationship between two sets of rankings of ordinal data. The significance of r_s is tested using t-tests. Kendall's Tau, using ranks of each pair of all possible pairs of two sets of variables, gives the degree of association between the two variables. The significance of Kendall's Tau is tested using a Z-test. The contingency coefficient is used with the data of two nominal variables for determining the association between different classifications of a set of nominal data.

Suggested Readings

- Bernard, Russel H. (2000). *Social Research Methods*. London: Sage.

- Freund, Rudolph J. and Wilson William J. (1997). *Statistical Methods*, 2nd ed. San Diego: Academic Press.
- Green, Paul E., D.S. Tull and G. Albaum (1988). *Research for Marketing Decisions*, 5th ed. Englewood Cliffs: Prentice Hall.

QUESTIONS AND EXERCISES

1. What is the meaning of the term 'strength of association'?
2. Is the regression model a deterministic model or a probabilistic model? Explain.
3. In regression analysis what is the assumption about error term? Why doesn't error term appear in the estimating regression equation?
4. What is thc mcaning of coefficient of determination?
5. For the problem worked out on simple regression analysis, carry out a t-test for finding the significance of the slope b_1. What does the test indicate?
6. For the data given in Table 1, find the coefficient of determination? Is *r* significant? How do you test it?
7. Demand during the last 10 months of the year was as follows:

J	F	M	A	M	J	J	A	S	O
5	19	18	15	31	22	27	39	38	44

Make forecasts for the months of November and December. What is the correlation coefficient? What are the errors in such a forecast?

8. The operation of a plating bath is studied. A particular plating operation requires a preparation time and the plating time for the job. The preparation time and plating time both fluctuate depending upon the job. The readings for ten jobs are given in the table. Make a scatter diagram and estimate the correlation coefficient. Can you conclude that the two are correlated? Explain your answer.

Preparation Time	Plating Time
12	38
10	88
1	50
1	65
2	56
3	62
3	65
4	60
6	50
5	75

9. In a painting operation the data on painting time and painting area are obtained and given in the table. Make a regression analysis. Can you conclude that painting times can be predicted by knowing required areas to be painted? If, yes, what is the accuracy? If, no, why?

Painting time (mts)	Painted area (square feet)
86	140
62	140
104	140
62	160
79	150
94	160
79	150
86	125
86	140
58	155

CHAPTER 16

Analysis of Experimental Data

- Introduction
- Analysis of Single Factor Experiments
- Single Factor Randomised Blocks Design
- Latin Square Design
- Completely Randomised 2 X 2 Factorial Design

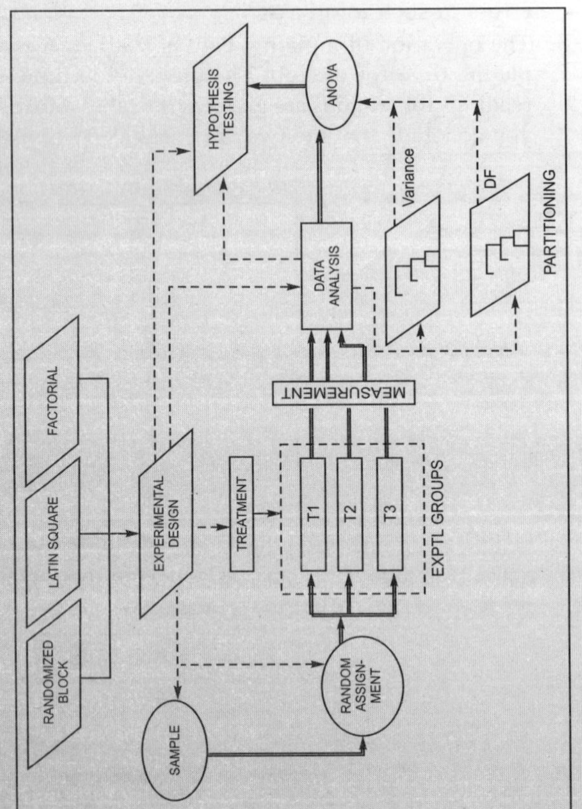

LEARNING OBJECTIVES

Upon completion of this chapter, you will be able to:

- ✓ Learn to differentiate between formal and informal experiments
- ✓ Understand the centrality of ANOVA in analysing experimental data
- ✓ Learn to apply F-tests to analysis of experiments
- ✓ Determine the influence of extraneous factors on the results of experiments
- ✓ Understand the meaning of interaction between factors of an experiment and its measure
- ✓ Understand the importance of hypothesis testing in experiments
- ✓ Each with the concept of blocking in experimental design
- ✓ Know the basics of statistical analysis of simple designs for mind expanding in experimental research

INTRODUCTION

In Chapter 6 the reader's attention was called to the basic principles of experimentation, inductive reasoning as the basis of experimental design, and the general features of experimental designs commonly used in research. In this chapter, we will detail the analytical steps in treating experimental data. We elaborate the data analysis of (i) single factor experiments—cases of randomised block design and Latin square design are dealt with (the case of completely randomised experimental design is dealt with in Chapter 14 on hypothesis testing in the section on analysis of variance), and (ii) fully randomised factorial experiments with two factors. There are a large number of variants and combinations (hybrids) of experimental research designs. Our aim in this chapter is to provide an understanding of the basic methods of analysis of experimental data, which will help the reader to grasp the analysis of more complex designs.

ANALYSIS OF SINGLE FACTOR EXPERIMENTS

In the analysis of single factor experiments one independent variable is manipulated and subjects are randomly assigned to the different treatment conditions. The analysis is presented for each experimental design giving details of (i) Neutralising the effects of nuisance (confounding) variables, (ii) obtaining the treatment index, and (iii) testing the relevant hypothesis.

Neutralising the nuisance variables Basically there are two ways of neutralising nuisance variables. The first is to hold them constant across treatments throughout the experiment. The second is to spread the effect of the nuisance variable randomly over the treatment conditions. The first method can be generally applied in the case of confounded variables such as testing environment, (that is, temperature, level of illumination, humidity noise, time of the day, and so on.). But this straightforward method is unfortunately not applicable to handle all potential nuisance variables because we may not be able to control them or even identify all of them. The effects of such remaining nuisance variables are neutralised or equalised over all levels of dependent variables through random assignment of subjects to the treatment conditions.

neutralizing nuisance variables
This is done by either holding them constant across treatments or by equally spreading their effects across the treatments using random assignment of subjects to treatments.

In many experiments in management (behaviourally and socially related experiments), variabilities of the subjects (persons) confound the independent variables. In such cases, some form of matching of subjects is considered. But since the subject's characteristics may not be known in most cases, matching becomes infeasible as a solution to the problem. In such cases, the subjects are assigned to the treatment condition randomly. Even when several variables of a single subject are considered, it can be shown that random assignment will ensure any difference among the subject groups will reflect only chance factors. The effect of nuisance variables will be more or less equally distributed among the treatment groups.

random assignment methods
Two methods are: (i) simple random assignment using random numbers and (ii) Blocking in which the elements are grouped into blocks based on matching characteristics.

Methods of random assignment

1. ***Simple random assignment*** When the subjects are unknown to the researcher (which is mostly the case), an equal chance is given to all the subjects selected in the sample. This is done as explained in a simple example that follows:

   Assume the sample size = 9 and number of treatments = 3. A series of nine single digit random numbers are selected from a table of random numbers (or generated on computer) such that the maximum number = number of treatments. In this case it is 3. They are assigned to the subjects identified as S_1, S_2, and so forth. as follows (T_1, T_2, T_3 are the treatment codes) (Table 16.1(a) and 16.1(b)).

Table 16.1(a)

Subject	*RN*	*Subject*	*RN*
S_1	3	S_6	3
S_2	2	S_7	2
S_3	1	S_8	3
S_4	1	S_9	1
S_5	2		

Table 16.1(b) Treatment Assignments

T_1	T_2	T_3
S_3	S_2	S_1
S_4	S_5	S_6
S_9	S_7	S_8

Note: The selection of RN should continue until the same number of subjects from the sample are assigned to each treatment.

2. ***Blocking*** In this method, the total number in the sample are grouped into blocks based on matching characteristics (variables) most relevant to the experiment (such as grade point average of students, IQ, age, educational background, and so on). This is suitable when the subjects are known in some way, to the researcher. Then the subjects in each block are randomly assigned to the treatment. See the example below:

   If, for the earlier example we have 3 blocks

Table 16.2(a)

	Subject	*RN3*
Block 1	S_1	3
	S_2	1
	S_3	2
Block 2	S_4	1
	S_5	3
	S_6	2
Block 3	S_7	2
	S_8	3
	S_9	1

Table 16.2(b)

T_1	T_2	T_3
1	2	3
S_2	S_3	S_1
S_4	S_6	S_5
S_9	S_7	S_8

index of treatment condition

This is defined as the ratio of between-group variability to within group variability. Between group variability is the sum of treatment effects and within group variability is due to chance factors (or experimental error). This index Is always greater than I. This is the same as F ratio.

Because in a randomised block one instance of each treatment occurs once in each block, the nuisance variable variance will be reduced further.

Index of treatment conditions Once the experiment is conducted, minimising the effect of nuisance variables, the data generated for each treatment will yield the means of the treatment conditions. The questions that are to be answered are: Are the differences in means due to treatment manipulations? How significant are these differences? Do they support research hypothesis?

To answer these questions, the differences in means of the treatment data will be expressed in terms of a measure of variability called between-group variability. This variability is composed of two components, as follows:

Between-group variability = Treatment effects + effect of chance factors

The effect of chance factors is the aggregate of all variability that is not controlled or accounted for in the experiment and constitute the experimental error. It consists of individual subject differences, variations in environmental conditions, and measurement errors. The chance variance in these groups is called experimental error (also as the group variability).

Treatment index is defined as the ratio of between-group variability to within-group variability

Between-group variability = Treatment effects + within-group variability

The treatment index is always greater than 1. If, however, there is no treatment effect then treatment index will be equal to 1. The treatment index is, therefore, same as the F ratio, which was dealt with in Chapter 14 on hypothesis testing.

Hypothesis testing The next step in the analysis of experimental data in statistically testing the significance of the F ratio and drawing appropriate conclusions. If $F > F_{cr}$ for a significant level specified by the researcher, then the null hypothesis (that is, there is no treatment effect) will be rejected.

Analysis of experimental data for simple single factor experiments is presented in the following section.

SINGLE FACTOR RANDOMISED BLOCKS DESIGN

In the analysis of completely randomised single factor design, detailed in Chapter 14, all nuisance variables were constant throughout the observation and the source of variation among sample results were only due to treatments. An improvement over this assumption is that at least one source of confounding variable distorts the results. The randomised blocks design (RBD) is employed to isolate such a variation from the residual error. As explained in the previous section, blocking will render the subjects in each block more homogenous and a smaller error mean will be obtained than in the case of a completely randomised design.

RBD Model

For a single observation in RBD

$$x_{ij} = \mu + \beta_i + t_j + e_{ij}$$

Where

$x_{ij} = j^{th}$ observation in i^{th} block.

$i = 1, 2\ldots i\ldots n$ (blocks)

$j = 1, 2..j..k$ (treatments)

μ = overall mean

e_{ij} = experimental error in the ith block subjected to j^{th} treatment

β_i = effect of ith block

t_j = effect of jth treatment

Assumptions

(i) The blocking variable and the treatment variable do not interact.

(ii) $\sum_{j}^{k} t_j = 0$. The net treatment effect is zero.

(iii) $\sum_{i}^{n} \beta_i = 0$. Net blocking effect is zero.

[Total sum of squares] = [Treatment sum of square] + [Block sum of squares] + [Residual error sum of squares]

$$A = \quad B \quad + \quad C \quad + \quad D$$

$$A \rightarrow SST = \sum_{i}^{n}\sum_{j}^{k}(x_{ij}-\mu)^2$$

$$B \rightarrow SST_r = n\sum_{j}^{k}(\bar{x}_j-\mu)^2$$

$$C \rightarrow SSB = k\sum_{i}^{n}(\bar{x}_i-\mu)^2$$

$$D \rightarrow SSE = k\sum_{i}^{n}\sum_{j}^{k}(x_{ij}-\bar{x}_j-\bar{x}_i+\mu)^2$$

To obtain the mean of the sum of each square we divide it by the appropriate degrees of freedom. The partitioning of the total variance and of the degrees of freedom is shown in the diagrams below (Fig. 16.1).

Fig. 16.1 Partitioning of sums of squares and degrees of freedom for RBD

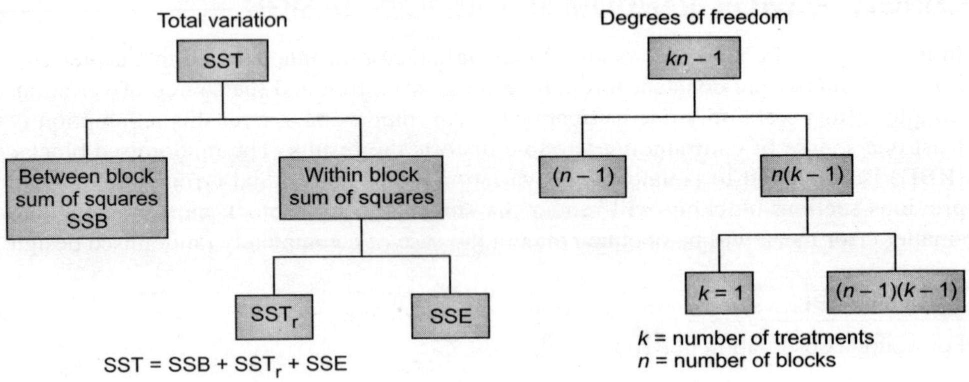

From the above sums of squares and degrees of freedom, a table of analysis of variance is developed (Table 16.3).

1. *For treatments* $H_o: t_1 = t_2 = t_j = t_k \rightarrow$ (Null Hypothesis)
   $H_a: H_o$ is not true $\rightarrow$ (Research Hypothesis)
2. *For blocks* $H_o: t_1 = t_2 = t_j = t_k \rightarrow$ (Null Hypothesis)
   $H_a: H_o$ is not true $\rightarrow$ (Research Hypothesis)

Table 16.3 Analysis of Variance Table for RBD

Source of variance	*Sum of squares*	*df*	*Mean squares*	*F ratio*
Between blocks	SSB	$n-1$	$MSB = \frac{SSB}{n-1}$	$\frac{MSB}{MSE} = F_B$
Between treatments	SST_r	$k-1$	$MST = \frac{SST_2}{k-1}$	$\frac{MST_r}{MSE} = F_{TR}$
Residual error	SSE	$(n-1)(k-1)$	$MSE = \frac{SSE}{(n-1)(k-1)}$	
Total	SST	$kn-1$		

If F_B (between block$_S$) > F_{cr} for $(n-1)$ degrees of freedom and the stated α,

If F_T (between treatment) > F_{cr} for $(k-1)$ degrees of freedom and the stated α,

reject the null hypotheses H_o for both treatments and blocks.

Example In a manufacturing situation consisting of single machining stations, castings of three different alloys (but of same size and shape) are processed. An experiment is conducted to test if there are significant differences among the three alloys in terms of their machining times. The process is tested over a month but the effect of external causes (like variation of plant efficiency shifts and so on.) may be high. The testing period is blocked into five hour twenty minute periods in a day of two eight hour shifts. The treatments (different materials) are assigned randomly to the blocks. The design is shown below in Table 16.4(a):

Table 16.4(a)

		Treatments		
		Aluminium 1	*Brass* 2	*Zinc alloy* 3
Blocks	Day 1	A	B	C
	Day 2	A	C	B
	Day 3	C	A	B
	Day 4	B	A	C
	Day 5	C	B	A

The first, second, and third periods in each day were named A, B, C and the alloys were assigned to these randomly in each block. Data collected in the experiment are shown in table 16.4(b). The machining times (in minutes) of the bars are given in the table.

Table 16.4(b)

	Treatments		
Block	*1*	*2*	*3*
1	22	16	31
2	16	15	11
3	32	29	44
4	16	21	26
5	14	19	18

Solution: Treatment totals and means, block totals and means, are calculated as shown in Table 16.4 (c).

Using the formulae given in the model:

$$A \rightarrow SST = 1098 = (22-22)^2 + (16-22)^2 + \text{- - -} (18-22)^2 = 1098$$

$$B \rightarrow SST_r = 5\ [(20-22)^2 + (20\text{-}22)^2 + (26-22)^2] = 120$$

$$C \rightarrow SSB = 3\ [(23-22)^2 + (14-22)^2 \text{ - - - } (17-22)^2] = 780$$

$$D \rightarrow SSE = (22-20-23+22)^2 + (16-20-23+22)^2 + \text{ - - - - } + (18-26-17+22)^2 = 198$$

Analysis of variance for the experiment is shown in Table 16.5.

Table 16.4 (c)

Block days	*Treatments* 1	2	3	*Block totals*	*Block means*
1	22	16	31	$\sum x_{1.} = 69$	$\bar{x}_{1.} = 23$
2	16	15	11	$\sum x_{2.} = 42$	$\bar{x}_{2.} = 14$
3	32	29	44	$\sum x_{3.} = 105$	$\bar{x}_{3.} = 35$
4	16	21	26	$\sum x_{4.} = 63$	$\bar{x}_{4.} = 21$
5	14	19	18	$\sum x_{5.} = 51$	$\bar{x}_{5.} = 17$
Treatment totals	100 $\sum x_{.1}$	100 $\sum x_{.2}$	130 $\sum x_{.3}$	330 $\sum x$	
Treatment means	$\frac{20}{x_{.1}}$	$\frac{20}{x_{.2}}$	$\frac{20}{x_{.3}}$		Total meanμ=22

Table 16.5 Analysis of Variance Table (RB Design)

Source of variation	*Sum of squares*	*df*	*Mean squares*	*F ratio*
Between treatments	$SST_r = 120$	$(n-1) = 2$	60	$\frac{MST_r}{MSE} = 2.42$*
Between blocks	SSB=780	$(t-1) = 4$	195	$\frac{MSB}{MSE} = 7.88$#
Residual error	SSE=198	$(n-1)(t-1) = 8$	24.75	
Total	SSB=1098	$tn-1 = .14$		

* Significant at 0.25 level
\# Significant at .01 level

F critical for 2 and 8 df at 5 per cent significance level = 4.46, 1.66

Between blocks variance is significant:

Variance across treatments is insignificant

It can be concluded that the variance across the days is significant but the machining times were not significantly affected by the casting materials. However, the times did vary across the different time periods of the day.

LATIN SQUARE DESIGN

In the randomised block design control of only one source of extraneous variable was considered. In many market research situations two extraneous variables are present. For instance, geographical locations, time periods, test scores, and types of stores may be major causes of concern to the researcher. The Latin square design is appropriate for statistically controlling the extraneous (nuisance) variables in such cases.

The randomisation procedure adopted in this design has been outlined in Chapter 6.

Latin Square Design Model

The model is similar to the RB design discussed in the previous section. However, it is necessary to include the effects of the second blocking variable (since there are two extraneous variables in this case). In the Latin square design, the two extraneous sources of variation are designated by rows and columns of the table of treatments. Consequently, the number of rows and columns must be equal to the number of treatments. On this table (with any assignment of treatments to rows and columns is used as a starting table), the randomisation procedure is used, and a randomised table of treatments is used for the computation of means, sums of squares, and the ANOVA.

A test observation in the Latin Square Design is,

$$x_{ijk} = \mu + R_i + C_j + T_k + E_{ijk}$$

Where

μ = Total mean

R_i = effect of ith row

C_j = effect of jth column

T_k = effect of kth treatment

E_{ijk} = effect of experimental error in the ith row and j^{th} column subject to k^{th} treatment

$k = 1, — t$

$j = 1, — t$

$k = 1, — t$

t = number of treatments

Assumption

(i) There are no interactions among treatment and extraneous variables.

(ii) $\sum_{i}^{t} R_i = 0; \sum_{j}^{t} C_j = 0; \sum_{k}^{t} T_k = 0$

Now, the sums of squares are computed.

[Total sum of squares] = [Row sum of squares] + [Column sum of squares] + [Treatment sum of squares] + [Residual sum of squares] (1)

$$\text{Row sum of squares} = SSR = t\sum_{i}^{t} (\bar{x}_{i.} - \mu)^2 \qquad \mu = \bar{x}\ \ldots$$

$$\text{Column sum of squares} = SSC = t\sum_{j}^{t} (\bar{x}_{.j} - \mu)^2$$

$$\text{Treatment sum of squares} = SST_r = t\sum_{k}^{t} (\bar{x}_{..k} - \mu)^2$$

$$\text{Residual sum of squares} = SSE = \sum_{i}^{t}\sum_{j}^{t} (x_{ikj} - \bar{x}_{.i.} - \bar{x}_{.j} - x_{..k} + 2\mu)^2$$

$$\text{Total sum of squares} = \sum_{i}^{t}\sum_{j}^{t} (x_{ijk} - \mu)^2$$

Analysis of variance In this experiment, the variance and degrees of freedom are partitioned as shown in Fig. 16.2.

Analysis variance for Latin Square design is shown in Table 16.6.

Hypothesis Testing

1. For treatments $H_o : \bar{\mu}_1 = \bar{\mu}_2 = ---- \bar{\mu}_t$ (null hypothesis)

   $H_a = H_o$ is not true

Fig. 16.2 Partitioning of variance and degrees of freedom in the latin square design

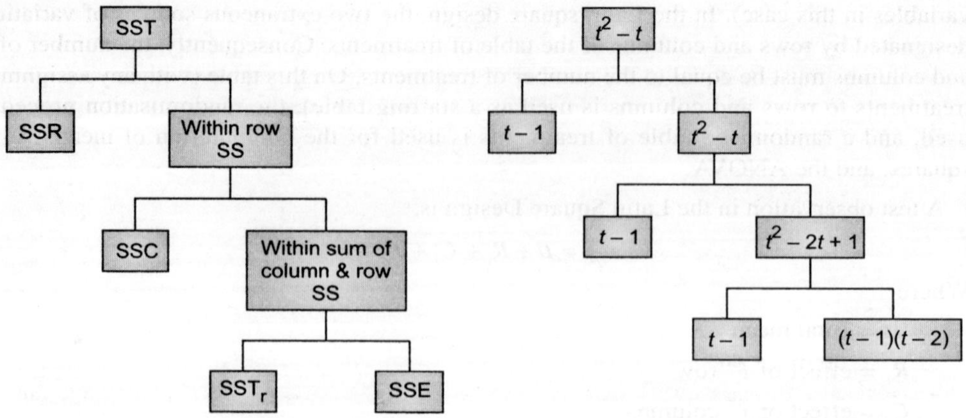

SST = SSR + SSC + SST_r + SSE

Table 16.6 Analysis of Variance Table for Latin Square Design

Source of variation	*Sum square*	*df*	*Mean square*	*F ratio*
Between rows	SSR	$t-1$	$MSR = \frac{SSR}{t-1}$	$MSR/MSE = F_R$
Between columns	SSC	$t-1$	$MSC = \frac{SSC}{t-1}$	$MSC/MSE = F_C$
Between treatments	SST_r	$t-1$	$MST_r = \frac{SST_r}{t-1}$	$MST_r/MSE = F_{TR}$
Residual error	SSE	$(t-1)(t-2)$	$MSE = \frac{SSE}{(t-1)(t-2)}$	
Total	ST	t^2-1		

2. For Rows $\quad H_o : \overline{R}_1 = \overline{R}_2 = - - - - \overline{R}_t$

   $H_a : H_o$ is not true

3. For Columns $\quad H_o : \overline{C}_1 = \overline{C}_2 = - - - - \overline{C}_t$

   For treatments F_T is compared with F_{cr} for $t - 1$, $(t - 1)(t - 2)$

   For columns F_C is compared with F_{cr} for t – 1, $(t - 1)(t - 2)$

   For rows F_r is compared with F_{cr} for $t - 1$, $(t - 1)(t - 2)$

For a given value of α

Example A food manufacturer had nine people rate three different varieties of a new food product developed by it. A 3 × 3 Latin square experiment was used to test it. The three test treatments of the new food product were labelled A, B, and C. The test results are shown in Table 16.7(a).

Table 16.7(a)

Ethnic Group	*AGE (Yrs)*		
	25–35	*36–50*	*Over 50*
Tamilian	C	B	A
Gujarati	A	C	B
Punjabi	B	A	C
Tamilian	29	41	32
Gujarati	36	30	39
Punjabi	40	31	38

Table 16.7(b)

Ethnic Group		*Design AGE GP*			*Scores*		
		1	2	3	1	2	3
	1	C	B	A	29	41	32
Ethnic Group	2	A	C	B	36	30	39
	3	B	A	C	40	31	38

(a) Compute an analysis of variance table.

(b) Discuss the possibility that the ratings of the products as a function of age and ethnic backgrounds (c).

Solution: Ethnic Group (rows) (Table 16.7(b))

1. $\bar{x}_{1..} = \sum_{j,k=1}^{3} \frac{x_{1jk}}{3} = \frac{29+41+32}{3} = 34$

2. $\bar{x}_{2..} = \sum_{j,k=1}^{3} \frac{x_{2jk}}{3} = \frac{36+30+39}{3} = 35$

3. $\bar{x}_{3..} = \sum_{j,k=1}^{3} \frac{x_{3jk}}{3} = \frac{40+31+38}{3} = 36.33$

Age Group (columns)

1. $\bar{x}_{.1.} = \sum_{i,jk=1}^{3} \frac{x_{i1k}}{3} = \frac{29+36+40}{3} = 35$

2. $\bar{x}_{.2.} = \sum_{ij,k=1}^{3} \frac{x_{i2k}}{3} = \frac{41+30+31}{3} = 34$

3. $\bar{x}_{1.3.} = \sum_{ij,k=1}^{3} \frac{x_{i3k}}{3} = \frac{32+39+38}{3} = 36.33$

Treatments

A. $\bar{x}_{..1} = \sum_{i,j=1}^{3} \frac{x_{ij1}}{3} = \frac{36+31+32}{3} = 33$

B. $\bar{x}_{..2} = \sum_{i,j=1}^{3} \frac{x_{ij2}}{3} = \frac{40+41+39}{3} = 40$

C. $\bar{x}_{..3} = \sum_{i,j=1}^{3} \frac{x_{ij3}}{3} = \frac{29+30+38}{3} = 32.33$

Total $\mu = \bar{x}_{...} = \frac{29+41+\ldots 38}{9} = 35.11$

From equations mentioned in the model

For rows $SS_R = r\sum_{i=1}^{r} (\bar{x}_{1..} - \mu_{...})$

$$= [(34-35.11)^2 + (35-35.11)^2 + (36.11-35.11)^2] = 2.684 \times 3 = 8.052$$

For columns $SS_C = r\sum_{i=1}^{r}(\bar{x}_{.j.} - \mu_{...})^2$

$= [(35 - 35.11)^2 + (34 - 35.11)^2 + (36.35 - 35.11)^2] = 2.752 \times 3$

$= 8.256$

For treatments $SS_{TR} = r\sum_{k=1}^{r}(.\bar{x}_{..k} - \mu_{...})^2$

$= 3\ [(33 - 35.11)^2 + (40 - 35.11)^2 + (32.33 - 35.11)^2] = 108.25$

Total SS $SS_T = r\sum_{i=1}^{r}\sum_{j=1}^{r}(\bar{x}_{ijk} - \mu_{...})^2$

$= [(29 - 35.11)^2 + (36 - 35.11)^2 + (40 - 35.11)^2] +$

$+ (41 - 35.11)^2 + 30 - 35.11)^2 + (31 - 35.11)^2$

$+ (32.11 - 35.11)^2 + (39 - 35.11)^2 + (38 - 35.11)^2$

$= 172.87$

SSE = Residual error sum of squares = $\sum_{i}^{t}\sum_{j}^{t}(x_{ijk} - \bar{x}_{t.} - \bar{x}_{.j} - \bar{x}_{..k} + 2\mu)$

$= [29 - 34 - 35 - 32.33 + 2 \times 35.11] + [41 - 35 - 34 - 40 + 2 \times 35.11]$

$+ \text{- - -} [38 - 36.33 - 32.33 + 2 \times 35.11]$

$= 48.37$

Check $SS_R + SS_C + SST_r + SSE = SST$

$2.684 + 2.752 + 108.25 + 48.37 = 172.87$

Table 16.8 Analysis of Variance Table for Latin Square Design Problem

Source of variation	*Sum of squares*	*Degree of freedom*	*Mean squares*	*F - ratio*
SSR (Ethnic groups)	8.052	$r-1=2$	4.026	$\frac{MSR}{MSE}=1.7$
SSC (Age groups)	8.196	$r-1=2$	4.098	$\frac{MSC}{MSE}=1.7$
SST (Treatments)	108.27	$r-1=2$	54.14	$\frac{MST_r}{MSE}=2.24$
SSE (Error)	48.27	$(r-1)(r-2)=2$	24.19	–
SST (Total)	172.87	$r^2-1=8$	–	–

F_{cr} for $df_1 = 2\ df_2 = 2$ is 19.00 at 0.05 and 3 at 0.25

$F_T, F_R\ F_C$ are all $< F_{cr.25}$

It is concluded that H_o for columns, rows, and treatments cannot be rejected as neither the food variety nor the extraneous variables (age or ethnic groups) affect the ratings of the new food product.

interaction effects
The interactions between two (or more) factors in an experiment are reflected as variance by suitably partitioning of total treatment (variance) sum of squares.

COMPLETELY RANDOMISED 2 × 2 FACTORIAL DESIGN

The previous two sections dealt with experimental designs for a single factor with different treatment levels and one and two extraneous variables. In this section, we will examine the analysis of data related to a factorial experiment, which is appropriate for two or more factors. Factorial experiments are designated by x^n where x is the number of factors and n is the number of treatments. Further, the interaction effects between the factors is also considered in the factorial experiments and analysed through a suitable partition of total treatments variance to factor treatments and interaction between them. We will present the model and illustrate it by a 2×2 (2^2) factorial experiment problem. Only the case of completely randomised design is dealt with.

A note on ANCOA is given in Appendix A2.

2 × 2 Factorial Design Model

Initially analysis of 2×2 factorial experiments is similar to the one for a single factor randomised design. Subsequently, the total effect of treatments is divided into parts for the factors and the precision of the design is improved. A 2×2 factorial design represented in Table 16.9.

Table 16.9 A 2 × 2 Factorial Design

		Levels of factor A	
		a_1	a_2
Levels of Factor B	b_1	$a_1 b_1$	$b_1 a_2$
	b_2	$a_1 b_2$	$a_2 b_2$

There are two levels of treatment for each factor.

j = Treatment

n = number of replication

X_{ij} = Score for j^{th} treatment in i^{th} replication

μ = overall mean score

$$\text{Treatment sum of square} = SST_R = n \sum_{j}^{k} (\bar{x}_{.j} - \mu)^2$$

$$\text{Residual sum of squares} = \sum_{i}^{n} \sum_{j}^{k} (x_{ij} - \bar{x}_{.j})^2$$

$$\text{Total sum of squares} = \sum_{i}^{n} \sum_{j}^{k} (x_{ij} - \mu)^2$$

The initial ANOVA for the experiment is shown in Table 16.9(a).

The significance of the F-test is checked and further examination of the results to determine treatment effects is decided.

To determine treatment effects and treatment interaction for the two-factor experiment,

$$T_j = a_m + b_1 + (ab)_{ml}$$

Table 16.9(a) Initial ANOVA Table for the Factorial Experiment

Source of variation	*Sum of squares*	*df*	*Mean square*	*F - ratio*
Between treatments	SST_r	$K-1$	$MST_r \dfrac{SST_r}{K-1}$	$\dfrac{MST_r}{MSE}$
Residual error	SSE	$K(n-1)$	$MSE \dfrac{SSE}{K(n-1)}$	
Total	SST	$nK-1$		

$$\alpha = \text{number of treatments of } a$$
$$\beta = \text{number of treatments of } b$$

Where

$$T_j = \text{net treatment effect of } j^{\text{th}} \text{ treatment}$$
$$a_m = \text{Treatment effect of } m^{\text{th}} \text{ level of factor } a$$
$$b_l = \text{Treatment effect of } l^{\text{th}} \text{ level of factor } b$$

$$\text{Total treatment sum of square} = SST_r = \sum_i^n \sum_j^k (x_{ij} - \mu)^2$$

$$\text{Treatment } a \text{ sum of squares} = SST_a = bn \sum_m^{\alpha} (\bar{x}_{am} - \mu)^2$$

$$\text{Treatment } b \text{ sum of squares} = SST_b = an \sum_l^{\beta} (\bar{x}_{bl} - \mu)^2$$

$$\text{Treatment interaction sum of squares} = SST_{ab} \sum_m^{\alpha} \sum_l^{\beta} (\bar{x}_{.j} - \bar{x}_{am} - x_{bl} + \mu)^2$$

$$\text{Check } SST_r = SST_a + SST_b + SST_{ab}$$

The partitioning of total variation and degrees of freedom is shown in Figure 16.3.

$$a = \text{number of levels of factor A}$$
$$b = \text{number of level of factor B}$$
$$K = \text{ab}$$

Fig. 16.3 Two factor factorial design

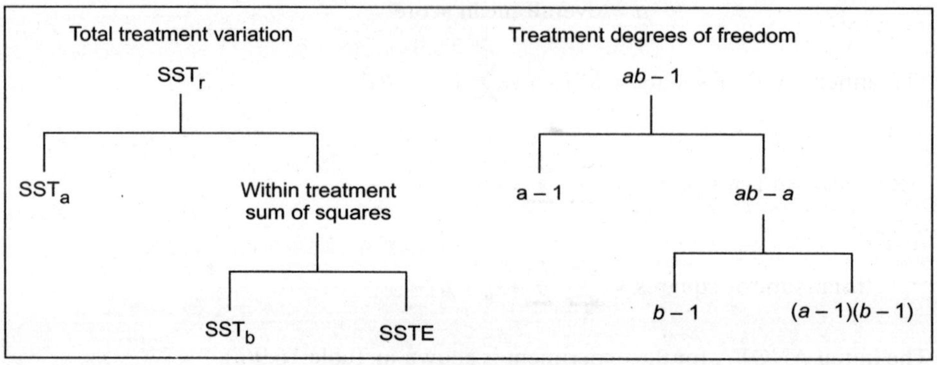

The final analysis of variance details for the two factor factorial design is displayed in Table 16.10.

Table 16.10 Final Analysis of Variance Table for 2 × 2 Factorial Experiment

Source of variation	*Sum of squares*	*df*	*Mean square*	*F ratio*
Treatment *a*	SST_a	$a-1$	$MS_a = \frac{ST_a}{a-1}$	MS_a/MSE
Treatment *b*	SST_b	$b-1$	$MS_b = \frac{SST_b}{b-1}$	MS_b/MSE
Interaction *ab*	SST_{ab}	$(a-1)(b-1)$	$MST_{ab} = \frac{SST_{ab}}{(a-1)(b-1)}$	MS_{ab}/MSE
Residual Error	SSE	$ab(n-1)$	$MSE = \frac{SSE}{ab(n-1)}$	
Total	SST	$(abn-1)$		

Example A manufacturing company tested a 2 × 2 factorial design for experiments at different levels of training programmes, as follows:

A_1 = Special outside academic programme

A_2 = Exposure to lectures within the plant

B_1 = Special outside training programme

B_2 = on the job training within the plant

The experiment was replicated three times and twelve different participants were used as test units. The results of their productivity, as output per day, are shown in the table below.

Productivity as output per day is shown in Table 16.11(a):

Analyse what the results mean.

Results of (Productivity Experiment) 2 × 2 Factorial Experiment

Table 16.11(a) Data

	A_1		A_2	
Replication	B_1	B_2	B_1	B_2
1	22	26	20	18
2	29	21	24	19
3	30	19	25	23

Table 16.11(b) 2 × 2 Factorial Experiment (Illustrative example): Initial Calculations

	Treatments				
Replication (i)	a_1		a_2		
	b_1	b_2	b_1	b_2	
1	22	26	20	18	
2	29	21	24	19	
3	30	19	25	23	
Treatment totals	$\sum x_{.1} = 81$	$\sum x_{.2} = 66$	$\sum x_{.3} = 69$	$\sum x_{.4} = 60$	$\sum x = 276$
Treatment means	$\bar{x}_{.1} = 27$	$\bar{x}_{.2} = 22$	$\bar{x}_{.3} = 23$	$\bar{x}_{.4} = 20$	$\mu = 23$

X_{ij} = number of participants i (1,2,3) receiving treatments j (1,2,3,4)

$$\text{Total sum of squares} = SST = \sum_{i=1}^{n}\sum_{j=1}^{k}(x_{ij}-\mu)^2$$

$$= (22-23)^2 + (26-23)^2 + (20-23)^2 + (18-23)^2$$
$$+ (29-23)^2 + (21-23)^2 + (24-23)^2 + (19-23)^2$$
$$+ (30-23)^2 + (19-23)^2 + (25-23)^2 + (23-23)^2$$
$$= 170$$

$$\text{Treatment sum of squares} = SST_R = \sum_{j=1}^{kn}(\bar{x}_{.j}-\mu)^2$$

$$= [(27-23)^2 + (22-23)^2 + (23-23)^2 + (20-23)^2]$$
$$= 78$$

$$\text{Residual error sum of squares} = SSE = \sum_{i}^{n}\sum_{1}^{k}(x_{ij} - \bar{x}_{.j})^2$$

$$= (22 - 27)^2 + (26 - 22)^2 + (20 - 23)^2 + (18 - 20)^2$$
$$+(29 - 27)^2 + (31 - 22)^2 + (24 - 25)^2 + (19 - 20)^2$$
$$+(30 - 27)^2 + (19 - 22)^2 + (25 - 25)^2 + (23 - 20)^2$$
$$= 92$$

Initial ANOVA is shown in Table 16.11(c)

Table 16.11(c) Initial ANOVA Table

Source of variation	*Sum of squares*	*df*	*Mean square*	*F - ratio*
Between treatments	78	$K-1=3$	28	$F = \frac{26}{11.5} = 2.26^*$
Residual error	92	$K(n-1)=8$	11.5	
Total	170	$nK-1=11$		
F_{cr}				$F_{cr} = 4.46$ at 0.05 $= 3.11$ at 0.10 $= 1.63$ at 0.25

* Significance at 0.25

Table 16.11(d) Training Programme vs Academic Programme

		b_1	b_2		
Academic programme	a_1	81	66	$\sum x_{a1} = 147$	$\bar{x}_{a1} = 24.5$
	a_2	69	60	$\sum x_{a2} = 129$	$\bar{x}_{a2} = 21.5$
		$\sum x_{b1} = 150$	$\sum x_{b2} = 126$		
		$\bar{x}_{b1} = 25$	$\bar{x}_{b2} = 21$		$\mu = 23$

Since there are two factors in the experiment, factor examination is necessary.

$$\text{Treatment } a \text{ sum of squares} = SST_a = bn\sum_{m}^{a}(\bar{x}_{ak} - \mu)^2$$

$$= 2 \times 3\,[(24.5 - 23)^2 + (21.5 - 23)^2] = 27.0$$

$$\text{Treatment } b \text{ sum of squares} = SST_b = an\sum_{l}^{b}(\bar{x}_{bl} - \mu)^2$$

$$= 2 \times 3\,[(25 - 23)^2 + (21 - 23)^2] = 48$$

Treatment interaction (ab) sum of squares

$$= SST_{ab} = n\sum_{m}^{a}\sum_{l}^{b}(\bar{Y}_{.j} - \bar{Y}_{am} - \bar{Y}_{bl} + \mu)^2$$

$$= 3\times[(27 - 24.5 - 25 + 23)2 + (22 - 24.5 - 21 + 23)2$$
$$+(23 - 21.5 - 25 + 23)2 + (20 - 21.5 - 21 + 23)2]$$

$$= 1 \times 3 = 3$$

$$\text{Check } SST_R = 78 = SST_a + SST_b + SST_{ab}$$
$$= (27 + 48 + 3) = 78$$

Final ANOVA table for the productivity experiment is shown in Table 16.11(e).

Table 16.11(e) Final ANOVA Table for the Productivity Experiment

Source of variation	*Sum of squares*	*df*	*Mean squares*	*F - ratio*
Treatment a	27	$a-1=1$	27	$27/11.5 = 2.35 F_a$
Treatment b	48	$b-1=1$	28	$48/11.5 = 4.17 F_b$
Interaction ab	3	$(a-1)(b-1)=1$	3	$3/11.5 = 0.26 F_{ab}$
Residual error	92	$ab(n-1)=8$	11.5	
Total	170	$(abn-1)=11$		

$$\alpha = .25,\ F_{cr} = 1.54 \text{ for df} = 1$$
$$\alpha = 0.10,\ F_{cr} = 3.46 \text{ for df} = 1$$
$$\alpha = 0.05,\ F_{cr} = 5.32 \text{ for df} = 1$$

treatment a is significant at $\alpha = 0.25$

treatment b is significant at $\alpha = 0.10$

interaction effect is insignificant

It is concluded that,

a) Training programmes are significantly effective at 0.10.
b) Academic programmes are significantly effective at $\alpha = 0.25$.
c) There is no interaction between the treatments.

SUMMARY

The description of models and examples illustrated show the power of formal experimental designs in comparison with basic (informal) designs. Formal experimental design allows the quantification of statistical significance of the differences in treatment errors, which is not possible with informal designs. Thus, the manager using formal experiments gets an idea of the amount of risks involved in making decisions based on them.

While using the completely randomised single factor experiment, the manager has to ensure the absence of even a single extraneous variable. Therefore, it is not preferred in practice. This provides an understanding of what is involved in experimentation.

The randomised block design highlights that when there is one major extraneous variable to contend with, low blocking techniques can reduce the experimental error and is practically more useful to the manager.

The Latin square design can handle two extraneous or confounding variables. With the replication of the experiment there is a potential danger of carryover effects (one period's observations may distort the next period's observations). A double change over design can be used. In case of three non-interacting extraneous variables, a Greco Latin square design can be used (see Ostle, 1962 and Banks, 1965).

Factorial designs present a comparison of different levels of two or more interacting factors. They provide precise information about treatment effects and the interaction of their effects by suitably partitioning the treatment sum squares.

Suggested Readings

- Anderson, Mark J. and Patrick J. Whitcomb (2000). *DOE Simplified—Practical Tools for Effective Experimentation*. New York: Productivity Inc.
- Barton, Russel R. (1999). *Graphical Methods for the Design of Experiments*. Lecture notes. New York: Springer Verlag.
- Hicks, C. R. (1982). *Fundamental Concepts in the Design of Experiments*, 3rd ed. New York: Holt, Rinehart and Winston.
- Winer B. J., D. R. Brown and K. M. Michels (1991). *Statistical Principles in Experimental Design*. New York: McGraw Hill.

QUESTIONS AND EXERCISES

1. A researcher is attempting to find the effects of various chemical additives on activity levels in children who are hyperactive. An experiment is designed by him for this purpose. The two conditions consist of food without additives and the same food with additives. Data for two groups of $n = 9$ each relates the response measures developed by the researcher and are given in the following table. Use $\alpha = 0.05/\alpha = 0.25$

No additives	With additives
$X_{1,1}$—31	$X_{2,1}$—30
$X_{1,2}$—33	$X_{2,2}$—28
$X_{1,3}$—25	$X_{2,3}$—36
$X_{1,4}$—28	$X_{2,4}$—41
$X_{1,5}$—24	$X_{2,5}$—29
$X_{1,6}$—30	$X_{2,6}$—32
$X_{1,7}$—31	$X_{2,7}$—27
$X_{1,8}$—26	$X_{2,8}$—35
$X_{1,9}$—30	$X_{2,9}$—36

Calculate:
   a. means of two treatment conditions.
   b. The basic ratios.
   c. The sums of squares for between treatments error and total.
   d. df statements for these sources of variability.
   e. The mean squares.

   Construct a summary table of variance. What do you conclude?

2. Suppose you determined that the power of the results produced by a particular experiment is 0.60. What does this value tell you about the type II error associated with this study? What can you say about your chances of obtaining a significant F under these circumstances?
3. Each of three turners was given one trade test on four different lathes. The results were recorded in the table below (number of pieces produced in an 8-hour shift).

Lathe	Turner A	Turner B	Turner C
I	120	116	109
II	112	100	97
III	125	110	101
IV	131	110	101

(i) Are there any significant differences among turners in the trade test?

(ii) Are there any significant differences among lathes as these machines react to turner skill? Assume that turners react psychologically differently to the specific machines.

4. A professor in a management school tested the effectiveness of three problem-solving techniques. Fifteen engineering students who registered for his course were divided into five engineering disciplines. They rated the effectiveness of the techniques. The results are shown in the table below.

Blocks (Engineering disciplines)	**Treatments**		
	A Creativity Techniques	**B Logical Techniques**	**C System Techniques**
Accounting	42	31	43
Finance	36	35	36
Marketing	40	52	44
Management	38	47	42
Economics	32	38	36
Industrial Engineering	29	35	30
Operations Research	52	50	54
Manufacturing Engineering	46	49	44
Computer Applications	40	44	40
Human Factors Engineering	38	36	35

a) Compute the analysis of variance table.

b) Interpret the results (at $\alpha = 0.05$).

5. The president of Gopalan Corporation has asked his financial analyst to compare the expected return and risk levels of nine investments in three industries. The analyst proceeds by comparing the ratios of the expected return to the corresponding standard deviation for these investments. These ratios were then tabulated, as shown below:

Industry A	**Industry B**	**Industry C**
0.5	0.3	0.7
0.6	0.4	0.8
	0.6	1.1
		1.2

Should the financial analyst conclude that there is no difference in the average ratios of expected return to standard deviation of the three industries? Use a 0.05 significance level.

6. Labour and management disagree over productivity of a machine shop with regard to labour time and machine time on a job. They have collected the following data regarding output times in minutes.

Machine	Worker			
	1	2	3	4
A	12	13	14	11
B	16	15	13	12
C	14	12	13	13
D	15	13	15	12

Perform a two-way analysis of variance at the 0.01 significance level.

7. An investment analyst wishes to compare the performance of three money market funds. To do so, he selects 30 observations, 10 corresponding to each fund. An index of performance is developed with a reference base of 100. The following results are obtained.

Fund I	71	60	83	70	90	62	73	74	65	88
Fund II	123	140	111	129	127	136	130	119	121	149
Fund III	133	118	141	132	127	138	133	129	122	144

Can you conclude that no real differences in performance exist among the three funds if $\alpha = 0.05$?

8. An advertising agency wanted to find out how effective price dealing was for a tonic. A 3 × 3 Latin square experiment was set up to measure these alternate price deals upon the tonics rates. The design is given below:

		Latin square design		
			Stores type	
		1	2	3
Time period	1	C	A	B
	2	A	B	C
	3	B	C	A

Treatment A = 5% discount on price

B = 2% discount on price

C = 1% discount on price

The test results are shown in the table below. Develop a table of analysis of variance and analyse the effectiveness of the discounts for the tonic at $\alpha = 0.05$.

Results (sales)

Time periods	Store type		
	1	2	3
1	102	118	134
2	64	132	98
3	74	104	74

9. The data for a 2 × 2 factorial design is given in the tables below. Are the treatment effects and the interaction effects significant at $\alpha = 0.05$

Data Matrix

	a_1b_1	a_1b_2	A_2b_1	a_2b_2
	3	9	8	2
	1	6	6	5
Sum	4	15	6	7

Data matrix

		Factor A		Sum
		a_1	a_2	
Factor B	b_1	4	14	18
	b_2	15	7	22
	Sum	19	21	

CHAPTER 17

Multivariate Analysis of Data—Dependence Analysis

- Multiple Regression
- Discriminant Analysis
- Canonical Correlation Analysis
- Path Analysis
- Other Methods

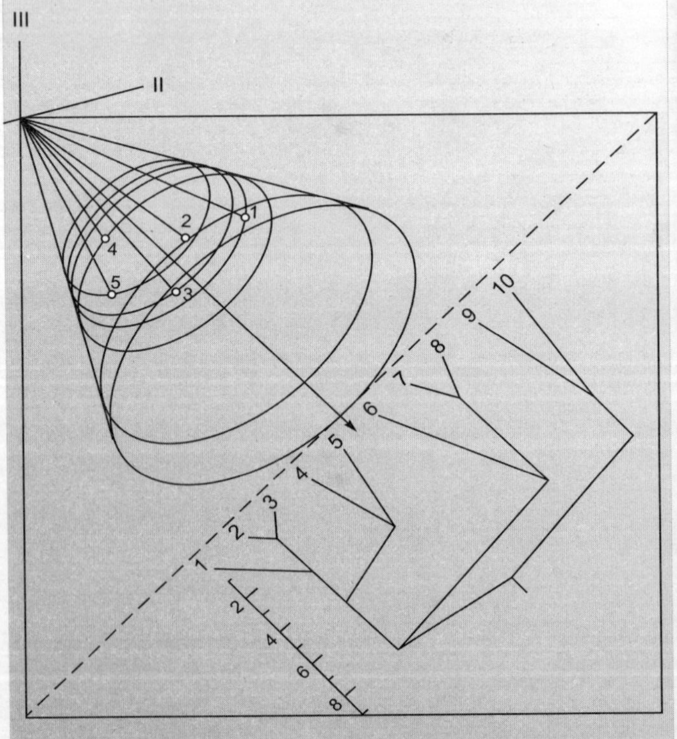

Learning Objectives

Upon completion of this chapter, you will be able to:

- ✓ Understand the basics of multiple regression for prediction
- ✓ Know the basic problems of multiple regression
- ✓ Learn to use the multiple discriminant analysis for differentiating between two or more groups with multiple measurements
- ✓ Know about the variants of linear regression analysis
- ✓ Understand the need for analysing the residuals in the linear regression model
- ✓ Test the statistical significance of the regression model
- ✓ Understand the statistical significance of discriminant function
- ✓ Learn to use cannonical analysis as a means of finding the correlational relationship between two sets of random variables
- ✓ Understand the basics of path analysis for casual relationships
- ✓ Learn the principles of conjoint analysis and automatic interactive detector

When more than two variables are considered in a relationship that is being studied, we use multivariate analysis techniques. In multivariate analysis, all the variables that have interrelationships that preclude the interpretation of the effect of each variate separately are considered random variates. Thus, multivariate analysis deals with relationships among weighted combinations of variables that are called variates. The choice of multivariate analysis procedures was explained in Chapter 2, where the procedures were placed in the perspective of the overall research process outlined there. These are procedures extensively used in experimental research, survey research, and when analysing large secondary data.

The techniques, objectives, type of data needed, and the interpretation of the results are dealt with using simple examples. Computer outputs using the SPSS package are provided and the results are interpreted. The treatment is only general and useful for a first understanding of the techniques. A detailed explanation of these techniques is beyond the scope of this book. The reader is referred to in-depth texts given in the references for further understanding of the techniques and their application.

In this chapter, multivariate methods of association among dependent and independent variables will be analysed. The methods discussed under this category, are multiple regression, multiple discriminant analysis, and canonical correlation. These are termed dependent techniques and are useful for prediction purposes. Finally, other dependent techniques like conjoint analysis, AID, and path analysis will be outlined briefly.

In the next chapter, techniques for analysing the interdependence among a set of variables will be discussed. These include factor analysis, multidimensional scaling, and cluster analysis.

Multiple Regression

Introduction

Multiple regression is a logical and mathematical extension of simple linear bivariate regression. It examines the relationship between two or more intervally scaled predictor variables and one intervally scaled criterion variable. Ordinal data that are near 'interval', such as semantic differential scale data can also generally be used (Darlington, 1968). Assume that Y is a dependent variable that depends on $X_1, X_2, \ldots, X_n$, and the relationship between Y and X_i's is linear, then a mathematical relationship between Y and X_i's can represented by the following equation,

multiple regression
It examines the relationship between two or more intervally scaled predictor (independent) variables and one intervally scaled criterion (dependent) variable.

$$Y = b_0 + b_1X_1 + b_2X_2 + \ldots + b_nX_n$$

Where

b_0 = constant derived from the analysis (parameter)

b_i = coefficients of association with the predictor variable (parameters)

X_i = predictor or explanatory variables that influence the criterion variable Y

Often, Y is referred to as the 'regressand' and X_1, X_2,..., X_n as the 'regressors'. The above equation is an exact relationship explaining the variations in Y as fully attributed to the changes in X_i's. However, in reality, the dependent variable is influenced by a large number of other factors. Hence, errors are likely to occur while estimating the parameters. The sources of errors are, (i) omission of certain variables from the function, (ii) errors of aggregation, and (iii) errors of measurement (refer Koutsoyiannis, 1977).

In order to account for all these sources of errors, one more variable u (error term) has to be introduced into the above equation. This is termed as the error component or the random component. Then the above equation becomes,

$$Y = (b_0 + b_1X_1 + b_2X_2 + \ldots + b_nX_n) + u$$

Assumptions and the Procedure

Similar to estimating the linear regression model, the Ordinary Least Squares (OLS) procedure is used for estimating the parameters of the equation (for details see Maddala, 1977). Some assumptions are made while applying the OLS procedure.

They are as follows:

1. u_i is a random variable. (where $Y_i = b_0 + b_{i1}x_1 + b_{i2}x_2 + \ldots. b_{in}x_n + u_i$)
2. The mean of the random variable u is zero for all X_i.
3. The variance of each u_i is the same (constant) for all the X_i values (homoscedasticity)
4. u_i is normally distributed with mean zero and variance.
5. The values of u_i (corresponding to X_i) are independent of any other u_j (corresponding to X_j) (absence of autocorrelation).
6. The explanatory variables are not perfectly linearly correlated (absence of multicolinearity).

coefficient of multiple determination
This is the square of multiple correlation coefficient (R^2) and indicates the proportion of variation in dependent variable explained by the entire set of independent variables. The reliability of estimates are tested using t and F tests on R^2.

Similar to the coefficient of determination R^2 in the linear (bivariate) regression analysis, here too we have the coefficient of multiple determination, which is denoted by the same symbol R^2. R^2 is nothing but the square of multiple correlation coefficient. The values of R^2 range from 0 to 1. R^2 indicates the percentage of the variation in the dependent variable, which is explained by the entire set of explanatory or predictor variables.

Whenever additional explanatory variables are included in the function, the coefficient of multiple determination does not reduce. It usually increases even though some of the additional variables may not contribute to the existing percentage of variation of the dependent variable. In order to correct this, R^2 is adjusted so as to take into account the degrees of freedom, which decreases as new regressors are introduced in the function. The expression for adjusted R^2 is given by,

$$\text{Adjusted } R^2 = 1 - \frac{(1 - R^2)(n - 1)}{(n - m - 1)}$$

where n is the number of samples and m is the number of predictor variables.

If n is large, both R^2 and adjusted R^2 will be the same, but in small samples (if the number of samples is small relative to number of independent variables), adjusted R^2 will be smaller than R^2 and may even take a negative value. In such cases, it should be interpreted as zero. Consequently, one possible criterion to select an optimum subset model is to choose the model that has the maximum adjusted R^2.

In addition to measuring the strength of association between the set of predictors and a criterion, in a multiple regression equation, it is important to assess the probability of error due to chance. Since the entry of variables into the equation is dependent upon this probability, the selected probability level should be appropriate to the problem at hand.

Verification

After the estimation of the parameters with the method of OLS [other methods like Generalized Least Square (GLS) or Weighted Least Square (WLS) may be used], the next step is to test for the validity of the estimates. The traditional statistical criteria used for assessing the reliability of the estimates are the coefficient of multiple determination R^2, the standard errors of the estimates and the related t and F statistics. The t test is used for testing the least squares estimates of the b coefficients. The F test is used for testing R^2, the overall significance of a regression. However, the reliability of the estimates obtained using the results of the above criteria are valid only if the stated assumptions are satisfied. The next question that arises is, 'What if one or more of the assumptions are violated?' Therefore, it is important to check whether the assumptions are satisfied, or not. Some insight for establishing the assumptions and problems that arise due to violating the assumptions are discussed in the next few sections.

Problems Encountered While Using Multiple Regression

As a pointer to the problems that may arise while using multiple regression it is normal practice to analyse the residuals. Most packages on MRA provide the plots of the residuals to enable the researcher to take remedial action.

study of residuals
Deviations of the actual values of residuals from predicted values can be used to determine (i) the presence of auto correlation, non-linearity of regression relationship outliers and heteroscedasticity.

Analysis of residuals As mentioned in the bivariate regression analysis, it is useful to study the residuals in the case of multiple regression too. We can analyse the deviations of actual values from predicted values to determine: (i) magnitude of prediction errors, (ii) the departure from model assumptions, and (iii) whether to continue the analysis. (Fig. 17.1)

(i) Violation of the assumption of independence of residual terms can be identified from a plot of the residuals $(Y - \hat{Y})$ for a time series data. A sum of positive residuals followed by a sum of negative residuals suggests the presence of autocorrelation (Fig. 17.1a).
(ii) A non-linear pattern of residuals indicate the need for functional transformation (log or polynomial) to the equation to get a non-linear regression (Fig. 17.1d).
(iii) The plots of residuals may show a good linear fit for most values except for a few outliers deviating much from the general trend. These can be examined for reasons and a decision can made to eliminate them or retain them in the regression model by running the regression with and without them (Fig. 17.1b).
(iv) There may be patterns in the residual values, many highly deviating from zero or many values close to zero, and so on. These may indicate omission of some independent variables from the regression, a high standard error of estimate, or a low R^2 value. (Fig. 17.1c)
(v) Constant variation of y may be indicated by the plots of the residuals against x showing high variability. This clearly indicates heteroscedasticity (for a detailed treatment of residual measures, refer Pindyek and Rubenfeld, 1981).

Three major assumptions that should be checked before interpreting the results of the OLS procedure are: (i) homoscedasticity, (ii) absence of autocorrelation, and (iii) absence of multicolinearity.

Assumption of homoscedasticity: This assumption is that the probability distribution of random variable u is the same over all observations of X. In particular, the variance of each u_i is the same for all the values of the explanatory variables. The violation of this assumption implies that the variance of each u_i is not the same. In that case, u_i's are heteroscedastic. This problem is encountered more often in cross-sectional data than in time series data. The consequences of the violation of this assumption are that (i) tests of significance are inapplicable, (ii) the minimum variance property of the OLS method does not hold, (iii) the estimates of the regression parameters will still be unbiased but inefficient, and (iv) the prediction would also be inefficient.

Fig. 17.1 Example residual plots

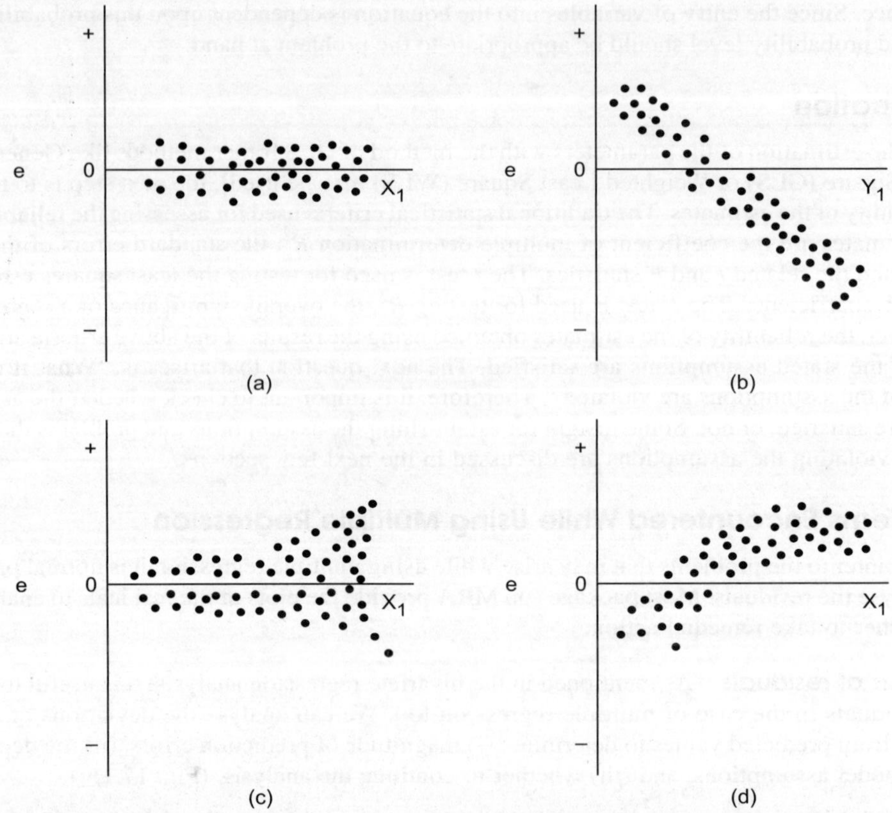

Many tests for homoscedasticity have been suggested, some of which are: (a) Spearman rank-correlation test, (b) Goldfeld and Quandt test, and (c) Glejser test [Koutsoyiannis (1977) and Maddala (1977)].

auto-correlation

Auto correlation exists in an independent variable when its value in one period is not independent of its variable in the previous period. This renders the predictions using regression equation inefficient.

Assumption of serial independence (absence of autocorrelation): This assumption states that the successive values of the random variable u are independent. That is, the value that u assumes in any one period is independent from the value that it assumed in any previous period. This assumption implies that the covariance of u_i and u_j is equal to zero. If this assumption is not satisfied, then the presence of autocorrelation or serial correlation in random variable u is established. The consequences of autocorrelation are: (a) the OLS variances of the parameter estimates are likely to be larger, (b) the variances of the random term u may be seriously underestimated, (c) the predictions based on OLS will be inefficient, and (d) OLS regression coefficients are still unbiased, but they are no longer minimum variance estimates. The presence of autocorrelation is higher in any time series data. Some tests for autocorrelation are: (i) Von Neumann Ratio, and (ii) the widely used Durbin-Watson Test. For a more detailed treatment of these test readers may refer to Maddala (1977) and Allison (2000).

multicollinearity

This is a problem in multiple regression. It indicates that several independent variables are nearly perfectly correlated ($r = 1$). This renders the regression coefficients indeterminate and regression equation cannot be used for prediction purposes.

Absence of multi-collinearity: While using multiple regression, one of the assumptions is that independent or explanatory variables are not perfectly linearly correlated. In many situations, it may be observed that the correlation coefficient among independent variables are nearly equal to unity. In this case, the regression coefficients (parameters) become indeterminate as the OLS method breaks down for the reason that it is impossible to obtain the numerical values for each of the parameters separately. In other words, the individual effects of each of the independent variables on the dependent variable cannot be isolated. This problem is referred to as the problem of multicolinearity. The consequences of multicolinearity are, if the intercorrelation between the explanatory variables is perfect, then ($r_{xi,xj} = 1$) then (a) the estimates of the coefficients are indeterminate, and (b) the standard errors of these estimates become infinitely large. One of the several procedures for detecting this problem is the Farrar-Glauber test, (Kennedy and Gentle, 1980). Multicolinearity is also detected by the following diagnostics: (i) large changes in the estimated regression coefficients when a variable is added or deleted, or when an observation is altered or deleted, (ii) non-significant results in individual tests on the regression coefficients for important independent variables, (iii) estimated regression coefficients with an algebraic sign that is the opposite of that expected from theoretical considerations or prior experience, (iv) large coefficients of correlation between pairs of independent variables in the correlation matrix, and (v) wide confidence intervals for the regression coefficients representing important independent variables.

Researchers have also proposed more complex approaches than variance inflation factors (see Kennedy and Gentle, 1980). Multicolinearity is not a problem in forecasting applications but is a very serious problem when analysis is used to gain an understanding of how predictor variables influence the dependent variable. The problem of overcoming multicolinearity is discussed in the next section.

Overcoming Multicolinearity

A variety of remedial measures may be employed to overcome the problem of multicollinearity. Some of them are discussed briefly in the following paragraphs.

Dropping variables The lack of sufficient information in the sample to provide an accurate estimation of the individual parameters is one of the reasons for encountering the problem of multicolinearity. In some cases, this problem can be overcome by getting estimates for a few parameters rather than estimating all of them. In other words, it is advisable, to discard some of the variables. This remedial measure has two limitations. Firstly, no direct information is obtained about the dropped independent variables. Secondly, the magnitude of the regression coefficients for the independent variables remaining in the model is affected by the correlated variables not included in the model.

Ridge regression The problem with the method of least squares is the requirement of unbiased estimates of the regression parameters with minimum variance. But there is no guarantee that this variance will be small. One of the ways to tackle this problem is to find a biased estimator with smaller variance compared to an unbiased estimator. By finding this type of an estimator, it may not be possible to provide a 'best fit' to the data, but it would obtain a stable set of parameter estimates. For a detailed discussion of ridge regression refer to Montgomery and Peck (1981).

Using principal components This is a purely statistical technique where the original variables are transformed into another set of variables, which are a linear combination of the original variables. This method helps to identify the number of independent sources of variation that is just enough to explain the total variation of the explanatory variables (*X's*).

For a detailed discussion on multicolinearity refer to Koutsoyiannis (1977), Maddala (1977, pp.183-194), Kennedy (1980) and Allison (1999).

Variable Selection and Model Building

Up to this point, the major focus of discussion was on the technicalities of the multiple regression model and the techniques to ensure that the underlying assumptions are not violated. One of the most difficult problems in regression analysis is the selection of the set of independent variables to be employed in the model. Past experience and theoretical considerations are helpful in selecting the explanatory variables (regressors) to be used. In most of practical problems, the researcher will have a large number of independent variables that should include all the influential factors, but the actual subset to be used in the model needs to be determined. The regression model that includes only a subset of regressors involves two conflicting conditions. One is that the model should have as many regressors as possible, which maximises the information content of these factors, which influences the predicted value of the dependent vari-

variable selection
One of the most difficult problems of regression model is the selection of variables to be included in the model. Mostly used procedure is the stepwise regression method. Its limitation is that it presumes that there is a single best set.

able. The other condition is that the model should include only a few regressors since the variance of the prediction increases with the number of variables. Also, a large number of regressors in the model leads to greater costs in data collection. Some of the computational techniques used in generating subset regression models are very briefly discussed below.

All possible regressions All possible-regression selection procedure comprehensively tests for the feasibility of all independent variables. However, its disadvantage is that researchers may not be interested in all possible independent variables. In many situations, they may be only interested in the feasibility of certain critical predictor independent variables. Another disadvantage of all possible selection is that the amount of computation required is very large.

Stepwise regression methods The stepwise regression procedure is probably the most widely used of all automatic search procedures. This procedure employs either a forward selection or backward elimination approach for the inclusion of a best fit model based on *F* limits. The *F* limits are not determined by the significance levels but in terms of error reduction. A limitation of stepwise regression is that it presumes there is a single 'best' subset of independent variables. In most cases there is no unique 'best' subset. Hence, some statisticians suggest that all possible regression models with a similar number of independent variables should be fitted to study whether some other subsets might be more suitable. The order of selection or elimination does not necessarily imply the order of importance of the regressor. All the stepwise procedures do not necessarily lead to the same choice of variables in the final model.

An Overview of Multiple Regression Analysis Procedure

The measures generally derived in multiple regression analysis can be summarised as follows:

1. A least squares function fitting the data, the regressor equation is obtained.
2. An *F* test is made for checking the significance of the overall regression model.
3. R^2, the coefficient of multiple determination (both sample based and population adjusted) is obtained.
4. Standard errors of regression coefficients are computed.
5. Partial hypotheses regarding the significance of the regression coefficients b_j (parameters) are tested using the *t*-test.
6. Selection of a subset of regressors is made if required (using the backward elimination procedure). See Flury and Riedwyl (1988).

A note on significance of regression

- Statistical significance of the overall regression model:

The hypotheses tested are $H_o : \beta_1 = \beta_2 = \beta_3 = \ldots \beta_n = 0$

H_a : Not all β's = 0 (β_o is not included)

F-test statistic is used.

$$F = \frac{\text{Sum of squares due to regression/df in regression}}{\text{Sum of squares of the residuals/df in residuals}}$$

If $F < F_{cr}$ for stated α do not reject H_o.

If $F > F_{cr}$ for stated α reject H_o

$$\text{Further} = F = \frac{R^2\,(n-p)}{(1-R^2)\,(p-1)}$$

where *p* is the number of parameters estimated by the model (including β_o).

Substantive significance of the model is:

(i) R^2 increases with a larger number of variables used in the regression.

(ii) R^2 increases as individual relationships r^2yk increases.

(iii) R^2 increases as correlation between independent variables decrease.

- Similar to simple linear regression analysis, the normal equations are (for a three-variable case):

$$\sum y = na + b_1\sum x_1 + b_2\sum x_2$$
$$\sum x_1 y = a\sum x_1 + b_1\sum x_1^2 + b_2\sum x_1x_2$$
$$\sum x_2 y = a\sum x_2 + b_1\sum x_1x_2 + b_2\sum x_2^2$$

The determination of b_1 and b_2 are cumbersome, but can be solved using standard computer software packages.

- Variance around the regression hyper plane (regression line in two-variable case, a plane in three-variable case)

$$S^2_{y.12...(k-1)} = \frac{\sum (y-\hat{y})^2}{n-k};$$

Standard error of estimation $= S_{y123...k-1} = \sqrt{\dfrac{\sum (y-\hat{y})^2}{n-k}}$

Where

n = number of variables,

k = number of constants,

$n - k$ = degrees of freedom.

This is an unbiased estimation of population variance. The subscripts 1,2 . . . . k–1 denote variables.

- Coefficient of multiple determination is given by,

$$r^2 = 1 - \frac{\sum (y-\hat{y})^2}{\sum (y-\bar{y})^2} = \left[\frac{\text{unexplained variance}}{\text{Total variation}}\right]$$

(compare for two variable case) $r^2 = 1 - \dfrac{s^2_{y.x}}{s^2_y}$

Where $S^2_{y.x} = \dfrac{\sum (y-\hat{y})^2}{n-2}$

and $S^2_y = \dfrac{\sum (y-\bar{y})^2}{n-1}$

- In an inference about population regression slope coefficients and overall regression, the slope coefficients b's are tested using the t-test.

$$H_o: B_1 = 0; B_2 = 0; B_3 = 0 - - - B_{k-1} = 0$$
$$H_a: B_1 \neq 0, B_2 \neq 0 - - - - B_{k-1} \neq 0$$

$$t_1 = \frac{b_1 - B_1}{Sb_1}; t_2 = \frac{b_2 - B_2}{Sb_2}; \text{——} ; t_{k-1} = \frac{b_{k-1} - B_{k-1}}{Sb_{k-1}}$$

In a three-variable case,

$$Sb_1 = \frac{S_{y12}}{\sqrt{\sum (x_1-\bar{x}_1)^2 (1-r_{12}^2)}} \qquad Sb_2 = \frac{S_{y12}}{\sqrt{\sum (x_2-\bar{x}_2)^2 (1-r_{12}^2)}}$$

If $t_1 > t_{cr05}$ and $t_2 > t_{cr05}$, then the null hypothesis is rejected.

- F-test for overall regression

  H_o; all B_i values equal zero

  H_a ; not all B_i values equal zero

Total variation = explained variation + unexplained variables (in regression)

$$\sum(y-\bar{y})^2 = \underset{\begin{bmatrix}(k-1)\text{ degrees}\\ \text{of freedom}\end{bmatrix}}{\sum(\hat{y}-\bar{y})^2} + \underset{\begin{bmatrix}n-k\text{ degrees}\\ \text{of freedom}\end{bmatrix}}{\sum(y-\hat{y})^2}$$

$$\therefore \qquad F^{(u_1u_2)} = \frac{\sum(\hat{y}-\bar{y})^2}{k-1} \Big/ \frac{\sum(y-\hat{y})^2}{n-k}$$

If $F(u_1u_2) > F_\alpha$, reject null hypothesis

$F(u_1u_2) < F_\alpha$, do not reject null hypothesis

Coefficient of multiple determination adjusted for degrees of freedom,

$$R^2_{adj} = 1-(1-R^2)\left(\frac{n-1}{n-k}\right)$$

Variants of Regression Analysis

A few of the variants of the basic multiple regression analysis are now discussed.

Multiple regression with nominal variables In some situations researchers may have to employ nominally scaled predictor variables, such as marital status, gender, or occupational category, in a multiple regression analysis. Maddala (1972) suggests the use of dummy or indicator variables as long as there are relatively few such variables. While natural dichotomies can be coded as 0 or 1, polynomous data (multiple categories), such as occupation and caste, in each category serve as variables. Dummy variables can also be used, (i) to measure the shift of a regression function over time, (ii) to measure the change of parameters over time, (iii) as proxies for the dependent variable, and (iv) for seasonal adjustment of time series (see Wonnacott and Wonnacott, 1981).

If, however, the dependent variable is an indicator variable, the shape of the response function will frequently be curvilinear. In these cases, transformations of non-linear function into log-linear (logit) or probit analysis is recommended. (For an excellent introduction to these topics refer to DeSarbo and Hilderbrand (1980), Cox (1970) and Finney (1971).

Multiple regression with rank order or rank transformed variables There are situations when the dependent and independent variables are rank orders and are best transformed into such ranking. To estimate the association between such sets of data, rank correlation techniques can be used. (Refer to Siegel 1986), Sprent and Smeeton (2001).

Multiple regression with lagged variables Often, instead of selecting different variables as the explanatory variables, it may so happen that the dependent variable is expected to be related to the lagged values of the dependent variables among the set of explanatory variables. For a detailed discussion refer Maddala (1977).

variable transformation

By using appropriate transformation to independent variables almost any type of nonlinear regression relationship can be studied by linear regression equation. Polynomial regression, log linear regression and a polynomial regression with interactions between variables are a few examples.

Non-linear multiple regression Often Y may be related to a function $f(x)$, which is not necessarily linear. Quite a few procedures are available to obtain the estimates of the parameters. For more details refer Maddala (1977). However, a note on non-linear regression is given below for general understanding.

Variable transformation The linear multiple regression model is very flexible. This flexibility gives it its power. By means of appropriate variable transformation, a researcher can analyse nearly any non-linear relationship between the dependent variable and the independent variables. The cases of polynomial regression, log-linear regression, and regression with variable interactions are outlined below:

Polynomial regression If the researcher considers the shape of the relationship to be non-linear approximating to a quadratic one (the simplest) then the regression equation becomes,

$$Y_i = b_o + b_1x_{1i} + b_2x^2_{1i} + u_i$$

For this equation x_1^2 is transformed to x_2 ($x_1^2 \rightarrow x_2$), which changes the polynomial-regression model to a linear one, as

$$Y_i = b_o + b_1x_{1i} + b_2x_{2i} + u_i$$

Similarly, cubic and higher order polynomial curves can be transformed to a linear function. It is to be noted, however, the points of inflection will be one for a quadratic curve, two for a cubic curve, and so on.

Log-linear regression Non-linear exponential or multiplicative models can be converted into linear models by the use of logarithmic transformation as follows.

Exponential model:

$$Y_i = ax_{1i}^{b1}\, x_{2i}^{b2} ------ x_{ni}^{bn}u_i$$

These can be represented as a linear model as:

$$Y_i = b_0 + b_1x^*_{1i} + b_2x^*_{2i} + --- b_nx^*_{ni} + u^*_i$$

Through logarithmic transformations of the form:

$$b_0 = \log a,\ x^*_{1i} = \log x_{1i}, ------ x^*_n = \log x_{ni}$$

and $\quad u^*_i = \log u_i$

Alternatively, if logarithms can be taken on both sides of the exponential model, we get

$$\text{Log } Y_i = \log a + b_1 \log x_{1i} + \text{- -}\ b_n \log x_{ni}$$

It is to be noted that scales change in the former case.

Regression with variable interactions Joint effect of two or more variables can also be dealt with by procedures of the linear regression model, by appropriate transformations. Consider the two-variable case:

$$Y_i = b_0 + b_1x_{1i} + b_2\, x_{2i} + b_3\, x_{1i} \,.\, x_{2i} + u_i$$

The variable transformation $x_1, x_2 \rightarrow x_3$ is applied such that

$$Y_i = b_0 + b_1x_{1i} + b_2\, x_{2i} + b_3\, x_{3i} + u_i$$

which is a linear regression model.

Applications

The multiple regression analysis has various applications such as: (i) Measuring the determinants of say, market structure, and demand; (ii) Forecasting sales; (iii) Determining the effect of a particular independent variable on the dependent variable, while the other predictor variables are held constant; (iv) Determining whether predictor variables, other than those being considered, are related to the criterion variable, adjusting data obtained from experiments for factors not controlled and believed not to be randomly distributed; (v) Estimating values for the missing data (item non-response) in surveys; and (vi) Comparing data obtained on the same data items (but from different respondents) by different interviewers, to determine if any bias exists.

Interpretation of coefficients When it is desirable to compare the relative effects of predictor variables, care must be taken to code these using the same measurement units. If it is not possible, standardised* regression scores must be developed to compare the relative changes in variables measured in different units.

* Standardising is the process of making the mean 0 and standard deviation 1, for the responses or data obtained; standardised$X$ = (original score of$X$ mean of$X$) std. dev. (X).

Causation One of the most 'naive' but highly resorted to abuse of multiple regression analysis is the assumption that the level of predictor variables causes the level of criterion variable. However, all they indicate is association between the variables. Association is evidence of causation, but not a proof of it.

Order of importance of predictor variables Most analysts have an urge to use measures such as squared partial correlations or squared beta coefficients to rank predictors in order of importance in accounting variation in the criterion. However, if the predictors are correlated, this urge should be tempered. In case of correlated predictors, there is no unambiguous measure of relative importance of predictor variables. Whether to partialise the effects or use partial correlation matrices for estimation depends upon the objective, (see Gorusch 1983).

Example A geographer developed a computer programme to locate facilities such as healthcare centres. In general, the problem considered was how best to choose the locations of X_1 facilities from X_2 possible sites ($X_2 > X_1$). In each problem there were X_3 demand centres; a demand centre could be a community, such as a town, or an artificial entity, such as an electoral district.

The programme considered transportation and building costs and the convenience of the populations in the demand centres in choosing the best set of locations for X_1 facilities. It was an iterative process; in other words, a set of locations was chosen and then improved, step by step, until the best solution was reached. The geographer wished to prove that his programme was capable of handling problems of a practical size. He expected that computer time would increase with the number of potential sites (X_2), the number of facilities to be located (X_1), and the number of demand centers (X_3). He hoped that his program would not take too much computer time, and hence, become too expensive to solve practical large sized problems.

Using his large research grant, he sent his assistant to 30 population centres in which problems of this kind were being considered or had recently been considered. Having obtained 30 observations of X_1, X_2, and X_3, as well as rough estimates of costs and convenience measures, he solved the 30 problems with his programme.

The geographer believed that X_1, X_2, and X_3 were the variables that mainly determined Y, the computer execution time, in seconds. He was satisfied to leave all other determinants of computer time to the error term. Table 17.1 presents his data.

Table 17.1 Data for Example

Number of locations (X_1)	*Number of potential sites (X_2)*	*Number of demand centres (X_3)*	*Central processor execution time (seconds) (Y)*
5	10	96	105
10	22	107	290
6	11	97	98
4	9	83	85
7	15	107	168
4	12	66	106
5	8	105	98
8	18	103	191
7	15	107	151
6	15	82	171
3	9	58	95
8	23	65	337
8	18	108	236
2	8	68	110
2	11	35	110
6	13	82	135
5	11	90	134

Contd.

Table 17.1 *(Contd.)*

Number of locations (X_1)	*Number of potential sites* (X_2)	*Number of demand centres* (X_3)	*Central processor execution time seconds in* (Y)
7	17	78	197
6	16	72	186
4	15	47	149
1	4	53	63
5	12	84	101
4	9	84	101
3	6	75	72
6	17	66	173
9	16	141	174
4	8	90	78
6	11	96	127
4	12	69	105
6	11	98	175

Table 17.2 **SPSS output; Multiple Regression**

REGRESSION/VARIABLES X_1 X_2 X_3 *Y/DEPENDENT Y/METHOD ENTER* X_1 X_2 X_3

* * * * * *M U L T I P L E   R E G R E S S I O N* * * * * *

	Mean	***Std Dev***
X_1	5.367	2.125
X_2	12.733	4.472
X_3	83.733	22.053
Y	144.033	62.992

N of Cases = 30

Correlation

	X_1	X_2	X_3	Y
X_1	1.000	.838	.704	.794
X_2	.838	1.000	.239	.926
X_3	.704	.239	1.000	.232
Y	.794	.926	.232	1.000

Multiple R	.92868
R square	.86246
adjusted R square	.84659
Standard error	24.67295

Analysis of variance

	DF	***Sum of Squares***	***Mean Square***
Regression	3	99245.34729	33081.78243
Residual	26	15827.61937	608.75459

F = 54.34338
Signif F = .0000

Variables in the Equation

Variable	***B***	***SE B***	***Beta***	***t***	***Sig t***
X_3	–.580246	.692875	–.203140	–.837	.4100
X_2	8.979020	4.446797	.637392	2.019	.0539
X_1	11.929255	12.795603	.402445	.932	.3598
(Constant)	14.266051	46.157093		.309	.7597

Obtain a fitted linear relationship with Y as depedent variable and X_1, X_2 and X_3, as the independent variables. What do standard errors of the coefficient measure? Test the hypotheses that the regressions coefficients are equal to zero against the hypothesis that they are not equal to zero separately for each of the coefficients. Check whether the regression computed is significant or not.

Solution: The SPSS output is presented in Table 17.2. The (least squares) estimate of Y can be obtained using the equation

$$Y = 14.266 + 11.9293\ X_1 + 8.979\ X_2 - 0.58\ X_3.$$

The coefficient of multiple correlation (R) is 0.929, determined first as in the bivariate case (equivalent to the simple correlation between X_i and Y_i). Coefficient of multiple determination is 0.863 (R^2). The beta coefficients 0.402, 0.637 and – 0.203 are partial correlation coefficients when variables X_1, X_2, X_3 and Y are standardised with $\mu = 0$ and unit standard deviation before the regression computation is carried out.

$$\text{Adjusted } R^2 = 1 - \frac{(1 - R^2)\,(n-1)}{(n-m-1)}$$

Where

n is the number of samples, and

m is the number of predictor variables

$$\text{Adjusted } R^2 = 1 - \frac{(1 - 0.863)\,(30 - 1)}{(30 - 3 - 1)} = 0.846$$

Adjusted R^2 gives a better estimate of R^2 of the universe whereas sample R^2 takes the chance variation in the sample data only (Flury and Riedwyl,1988). Before the multiple regression equation is made use of, it is necessary to validate it with a test of significance of the overall regression. The F-test is used for this purpose.

The critical values for $DF_1 = 3$, $DF_2 = 26$ from F tables are 4.64 (p = 0.01) and 2.98 (p = 0.05). Therefore, overall regression is significant even at 0.01 level. In order to test whether X_1, X_2, and X_3 significantly contribute to overall variance accounted by regression (this is not evident from the F test), it is necessary to apply the t-test to each b coefficient.

The t statistic is computed as (b_j/Standard Error of b_j) as follows:

$$t_{b1} = 0.932,\ t_{b2} = 2.019,\ t_{b3} = 0.837.$$

$$F = \frac{\text{Sum of squares due to regression/df in regression}}{\text{Sum of squares of the residuals/df in residuals}}$$

$$F = \frac{(99245/3)}{(15827/26)} = 54.34$$

It is noticed that only B_2 is significant and the other two variables X_1 and X_3 do not significantly contribute to variation in Y. Thus, the increments in R^2 produced by X_1 and X_3 are insignificant. The normalised beta values give partial correlation coefficients. In practices, we may employ a simple regression model.

$Y = 14.27 + 8.98\ X_2$ for prediction purposes.

DISCRIMINANT ANALYSIS

Introduction

The ordering of things into classes is a basic procedure of empirical science. The analyst uses multi-measurements for differentiating between two or more groups of individuals, things, or events. The traditional method is to compute the significance of the difference between the means of groups, taking each characteristic separately. However, the method is inefficient in that it does not make it possible to evaluate the relative amount of information for differentiation provided by several measurements taken together. Neither does it combine the information taking into account the interrelations, if they exist, between the characters dealt with. Hence, an alternative is to construct a linear combination of the variables, a weighted sum, in such a way that it best discriminates among the groups in some sense. Discriminant analysis is the method by which such linear combinations are determined. Discriminant analysis is similar to regression analysis, which involves the investigation of the criterion/prediction variable relationship; also a weighted sum of the measurements is needed as in multiple regression. The difference lies in the nature of the criterion, which is qualitative rather than quantitative as in the case of multiple regression. Multiple discriminant analysis is a generalisation of the method of discriminant analysis appropriate for only two groups. It is mainly used as a method for studying relationships among several groups or populations, and provides a basis for the classification of individuals among several groups. Discriminant analysis may be interpreted as a special type of factor analysis, which extracts orthogonal factors of the measurements, taking into account the differences among the criterion groups. The model derives the components that best separate the cells or groups. In many instances, the problem is one of studying group differences or classifying items into groups based on certain criteria.

discriminant analysis
This is an empirical method to construct a linear combination of several variables (multi measurements) in such a way that it best discriminates among the groups. This investigates relationship between criterion and predictor variables as in multiple regression but the criterion is qualitative (discriminant function).

Assumptions

In discriminant analysis, samples of individuals are assumed to be drawn from several different populations where different (p) quantitative scores are available for each individual. The p measurements are assumed to follow a multivariate normal distribution with equal variance-covariance matrices within the several populations.

The Method

Multiple discriminant analysis results in a reduction of the multiple measurements to one or more weighted combinations having maximum potential for distinguishing among members or different groups. The discriminant function will distinguish better than any other linear function between the specified groups on whom common measurements are available. In other words, it is the single weighted composite that, of all possible weighted composites, provides maximum average separation between the groups relative to variability within the groups. In the case of two groups, a single discriminant function will account for all differences; however, in the case of several groups, one weighted combination of the scores may not distinguish well between all the groups. Therefore, a second or even a third composite may be required to distinguish between groups that were not well separated by the first. The second discriminant function will be constructed with a weighted composite that of all possible weighted composites, is uncorrelated with the first (within groups) and provides for the maximum average separation among the groups. Similarly, the procedure is extended to larger number of discriminant functions.

Scope of multiple discriminant analysis The primary importance of multiple discriminant analysis is the study of relationships among several groups in terms of multiple measurements. This provides a basis for classification of individuals among the several groups. The approach provides tests of significance for certain important hypotheses for relationships among several groups; for example, a single composite score accounts for all significant differences among the groups. Some of the tests are discussed in the following section.

Testing Statistical Significance of Discriminant Functions

1. *Mahalanobis' distance:* The first step in a test of significance of a discriminant function is to measure the separation or distinctness of the two groups. This can be done by computing Mahalanobis' distance, which can be tested using a multivariate equivalent of the *t*-test for the equality of two means. Mahalanobis' d^2 statistic is a squared distance measure. It is equivalent to the standard Euclidian distance measure, and measures the distance from each case to the group mean.
2. *Wilk's lambda:* This is a statistical significance test of the discriminant function. The ability of the variables to discriminate among the groups, (beyond those from which the

testing significance of discriminant function
There are three tests: Mahalanobis' distance, Wilks Lambda and Canonical correlation coefficient.

information was extracted for the previously computed function) is measured by Wilk's lambda. This is a multivariate measure of groups' difference over discriminating variables and can be calculated in many ways. In general, it is calculated such that values of lambda near zero indicate high discrimination, and when it equals its maximum value of 1.0 there is no discrimination.

3. *Canonical correlations:* The canonical correlation coefficient is a measure of the association that summarises how the discriminant function is related to groups. Canonical correlation will be discussed in detail later in this chapter.

Interpreting dimensions of discriminant functions The problem of interpreting the nature of the dimensions of discriminant function is a difficult task. One easy way to characterise the dimensions is in terms of groups they separate most. In the past, the nature of the discriminant function was described by examining relative magnitudes of the weighting coefficients. This can be problematic, as the coefficients are dependent on the unit of measurement, which may be different for different original measures. Therefore, the effect of differences are largely removed by multiplying each discriminant function coefficient by the standard deviation of the particular variable to which the weight is applied. This is equivalent to dividing the weights by the square root of the pooled variance. This will render the within-group variance to unity. Following this, the relative magnitudes of the coefficients can be compared to determine which variables contribute most to the definition of the composite function. For more details on the interpretation of discriminant analysis refer Morrison (1969). A detailed discussion on discriminant analysis can be found in Klecka (1980).

Example of computer processing The credit firm of Maheswari and Rao Inc. has expressed interest in the possible use of discriminant analysis in the preliminary screening of credit applications. From past records the company has assembled information on two classes of married credit guarantees (a) poor risks and (b) good risks. Additional information about a sample of credit guarantees has also been obtained and is given in the Table 17.3. Compute linear discriminant functions for a two-way analysis. Which variables appear to discriminate best among the two groups?

Solution: For the example, let us consider the number of credit cards (NOC) as the grouping variable with less than five credit cards as group 0 and greater than or equal to five credit cards as group 1.

The SPSS/PC+ software gives the group means and groups standard deviation, as displayed in Table 17.4. The totals indicate means and standard deviations when all the 20 cases are considered.

Table 17.3 Data for the Problem

(a) Poor risk

Annual income (AI)	*No. of credit cards (NOC)*	*Age (AGE)*	*No. of children (NO CHILD)*
9.2	2	27	3
10.7	3	24	0
8.9	1	32	2
11.2	1	29	4
9.9	2	31	3
10.7	4	29	1
8.6	3	28	1
9.1	0	31	5
10.3	5	26	2
10.5	4	30	3

Contd.

Table 17.3 (*Contd.*)

(b) Good risk

Annual income (AI)	*No. of credit cards (NOC)*	*Age (AGE)*	*No. of children (NO CHILD)*
18.6	7	42	3
17.4	6	47	5
22.6	4	41	1
24.3	5	39	0
19.4	1	43	2
14.2	12	46	3
12.7	8	42	4
21.6	7	48	2
26.4	5	37	3
19.4	9	51	1

Table 17.4 SPSS Output; Discriminant Analysis—Group Means and Standard Deviations

Group means

NOC	*AI*	*AGE*	*NO CHILD*
0	11.89091	31.36364	2.27273
1	18.32222	42.00000	2.55556
Total	14.78500	36.15000	2.40000

Group standard deviations

NOC	*AI*	*AGE*	*NO CHILD*
0	4.63777	5.71442	1.48936
1	5.32418	7.48331	1.50923
Total	5.83368	8.38090	1.46539

(a) It can be seen from the Table 17.4 that the annual income (by 70 per cent), age (by 33 per cent) and number of children by (13 per cent) were higher for group 1, that is, the good work group.

(b) Wilk's lambda and the univariate F ratio within Table 17.5 shows that null hypothesis for the means for annual income and age is rejected at significance level <. 05. For this process, Wilk's lambda is considerably lower than 1 (except for no child = .9903). This means that on a univariate basis AI and age display significant difference between poor risk and good risk groups.

Table 17.5 SPSS Output; Discriminant Analysis—Wilks' Lambda (U-statistic) and Univariate F-ratio with 1 and 18 Degrees of Freedom

Variable	*Wilks' lambda*	*F*	*Significance*
AI	0.68336	8.340	0.0098
AGE	0.58038	13.01	0.0020
NOCHILD	0.99030	0.1764	0.6795

(c) The pooled within group correlation matrix given in Table 17.6 shows good correlation of 0.52 between AI and age, which can be anticipated. No child and AI are negatively correlated but not highly, in which, again, b) can be expected.

Table 17.6 SPSS Output; Discriminant Analysis—Pooled Within-Groups Correlation Matrix

	AI	*AGE*	*NO CHILD*
AI	1.00000		
AGE	0.52415	1.00000	
NOCHILD	-0.31796	0.05601	1.00000

Discriminant function The above univariate analysis gives an insight into the groups distribution and some differences but discriminant analysis considers variables and their relationships simultaneously. As already described, the linear discriminant function D is given by

$$D = a_o + a_1x_1 + a_2x_2 + ...+a_nx_n$$

This linear combination can be obtained by estimating the coefficients (weights) a's such that the value of D differs as much as possible between the two groups. The coefficients are obtained as follows (and these are displayed in Table 17.7):

Table 17.7 SPSS Output; Discriminant Analysis—Unstandardised Canonical Discriminant Function Coefficients

	FUNC 1
AI	0.9264180E-01
AGE	0.1036268
NOCHILD	–5.462513

Canonical Discriminant Functions evaluated at Group Means (Group Centroids)

Group	*FUNC 1*
0	–0.78249
1	0.95638

(a) Obtained within group sums of squares $\sum (X_1 - \bar{X}_1)^2 = \sum X_{11}^2$

$\left(\sum x_{11}^2, \sum x_{21}^2, \sum x_{31}^2\right)$ for the three variables

(b) Obtain cross products $\sum (X_1 - \bar{X}_1)(X_2 - \bar{X}_2) = \sum x_{11}x_{21}$

(c) Obtain Matrix S_1,

$$\begin{matrix} \sum X_{11}^2 & \sum X_{11}X_{21} & \sum X_{11}X_{31} \\ ------- & \sum X_{21}^2 & \sum X_{21}X_{31} \\ ------- & ------- & \sum X_{31}^2 \end{matrix}$$

Similarly, obtain Matrix S_2 and S_3

(d) Form S_1+S_2+S_3 = W

(e) Divide matrix W by degrees of freedom ($\sum ni - k$); ni is the number of objects in i^{th} group (total number of objects – total number of groups) to obtain within group covariance matrix, U.

(f) Inverse of U can be used to calculate weights using formula,

$$W_1 = \sum_{j=1}^{m1} u_j d_j$$

these are un-standardised coefficients a of the discriminant function.

(For detailed calculations, see the next example).

Now we can obtain the scores of the discriminant functions.

(i) Discriminant score for Group 0 = – 5.462513 + 0.092641 × (11.89091) + 0.1036268 × (31.36364) + 0.144566 × (2.27273) = – 0.78249

(ii) Discriminant score for Group 1
= – 5.462513 + 0.092641 × (18.32222) + 0.1036268 × (42.00) + 0.144566 × (2.55556) = 0.95638

Classification on the basis of discriminant function scores is as follows.

Using the discriminant function scores each case can now be classified into the two groups, 'poor risk' and 'good risk'. Actual class of the cases is compared with the classification obtained using discriminant function scores to find the efficiency of the discriminant function. Since the results of analysis are applied to the sample, using which the discriminant analysis was made, the efficiency thus obtained is somewhat optimistic. Figure 17.2 shows the distribution (normal) of the discriminant scores for group 1 (poor risk) and group 0 (good risk).

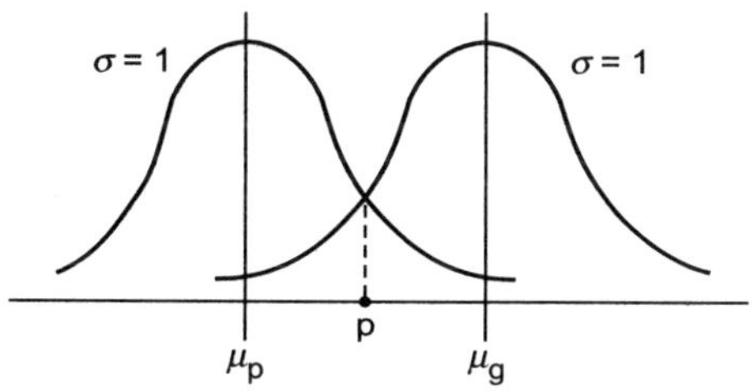

Fig. 17.2 Distribution of discriminants scores for two risk group

The two discriminant distribution groups, poor risk (μ_b) and good risk (μ_g), have unit standard deviations. A point p mid-way between μ_b and μ_g is chosen for purposes of classification. Discriminant scores of a particular case falling in between p and μ_g is classified as good risk and that falling between p and μ_b as poor risk. It can easily be seen that there will always be an error associated with such classification.

However, in the SPSS package, an alternate method based on the Bayesian posterior probability rule is used.

$$p(g/D) = \frac{p(D/g)\cdot p(g)}{Ep(D/g)\cdot p(g)}$$

$p(g)$ is the prior probability of a case belonging to group, say, 'good risk' $p(g)$ can be computed easily as a proportion of g in the sample. A case is classified in the group based on discriminant score for which the possession probability is the largest. Table 17.8 shows the classification of cases as per this rule (using Fisher's linear discriminant function given in Table 17.9).

Note: The second highest group has a probability (1-highest probability) because there are only two groups. Wrong classifications are shown with "**" and Table 17.8 also shows the results of classification. Finally, the significance of the discriminant function is obtained by Wilk's lambda and the Chi-square test, as shown in Table 17.10 (low Wilk's lambda of 0.546 and chi-square value of 9.985, which is significant at 0.02 level). The problem has been solved for the number of credit cards as a grouping variable. Similarly, the problem can be solved for other variables. The best discriminating solution is obtained by using age as the grouping variable where the classification is 100 per cent correct. The processing on SPSS for the other two cases is left as an exercise.

Example of hand calculations Technology transfer to India from an Asian country and an European country are rated on three variables scales of 0 – 10 degree of success (x_1), ease of transfer (x_2), and after transfer assistance (x_3). The scores for 11 transfers each are displayed

Table 17.8 SPSS Output; Discriminant Analysis—Classification of Cases

Discrim score	*Case number*	*Mis val*	*Actual sel group*	*Highest group*	*probability P(D/G)*	*P(G/D)*	*2nd group*	*highest P(G/D)*
–1.3789	1		0	0	0.5509	0.9275	1	0.0725
–1.9842	2		0	0	0.2295	0.9734	1	0.0266
–1.0330	3		0	0	0.8022	0.8752	1	0.1248
–1.8419	4		0	0	0.9526	0.8341	1	0.1659
–1.8996	5		0	0	0.9068	0.8475	1	0.1525
–1.3216	6		0	0	0.5898	0.9205	1	0.0795
–1.6198	7		0	0	0.4024	0.9511	1	0.0489
–1.6848	8		0	0	0.9221	0.7828	1	0.2072
–0.6848	9		0	0				
–1.5251	10		0	0	0.8689	0.8580	1	0.1420
0.9476	11		1	1	0.9283	0.8413	0	0.1587
1.0463	12		1	1	0.4320	0.9468	0	0.0532
1.7422	13		0**	1	0.9458	0.8362	0	0.1638
1.0243	14		1	1	0.8995	0.7845	0	0.2155
0.8301	15		0**	1	0.0919	0.8489	0	0.1511
1.0796	16		1	1	0.9229	0.8429	0	0.1571
0.0532	17		1	1	0.7549	0.7249	0	0.2751
0.6442	18		1	1	0.3980	0.9517	0	0.0483
1.8015	19		1	1	0.7684	0.8833	0	0.1167
1.2508	20		1	1	0.4192	0.9487	0	0.0513

Classification Results -

Actual group	*No. of cases*	*Predicted group 0*	*Membership 1*
Group 0	11	9	2
		81.8%	18.2%
Group 1	9	1	8
		11.1	88.9%

Percentage of "grouped" cases correlated classified : 85.00%

Table 17.9 SPSS Output; Discriminant Analysis—Classification Function Coefficients (Fisher's Linear Discriminant Functions)

NOCI =	*0*	*1*
AI	0.1099265	0.2710193
AGE	0.6730338	0.8532280
NOCHILD	0.9630235	1.2142160
(Constant)	–12.9954500	–22.6452700

Table 17.10 SPSS Output; Discriminant Analysis—Canonical Discriminant Functions

Fcn	*Eigenvalue*	*Percent of variance*	*Cum Pct*	*Canonical Corr*	*Wilks' Lambda*	*Chi-square*	*DF*	*Sig*
1*	0.8315	100.00	100.00	0.6738	0.5460	9.985	3	0.0187

* marks the 1 canonical discriminant function remaining in the area

below. Make a discriminant analysis to find if there is (i) a relationship between the country of origin of technology and the variables, and (ii) whether the countries can be correctly classified using these variables.

Table 17.11(a)

	Asian country (A)		
	x_1	x_2	x_3
1	8	7	9
2	7	6	8
3	7	6	7
4	7	6	7
5	5	4	5
6	7	6	6
7	8	7	7
8	5	5	5
9	7	5	7
10	9	7	9
11	7	6	7

Table 17.11(b)

European country (E)		
x_1	x_2	x_3
6	4	4
5	5	4
4	4	3
3	3	2
3	3	3
4	3	7
6	6	5
5	4	4
8	5	6
6	3	2
5	4	4

Solution: The following table of mean scores is set up.

	A	E	Difference (d)
Degree of success—x_1	7	4	3
Ease of transfer—x_2	7	5	2
After transfer assistance—x_3	6	4	2
$n =$	11	11	

See the calculations in the note below.

Matrix W (refer to model in the example with computer processing) developed using the results of the above calculation and is displayed in Table 17.12.

Referring to the model given in the example with computerised solution:

$$\text{Matrix } S_1 = \begin{vmatrix} \sum x_{11}^2 & \sum x_{11}x_{21} & \sum x_{11}x_{31} \\ & \sum x_{21}^2 & \sum x_{21}x_{31} \\ & & \sum x_{31}^2 \end{vmatrix}$$

$$= \begin{vmatrix} 18 & 14 & 10 \\ & 14 & 8 \\ & & 9 \end{vmatrix}$$

Similarly for matrix S_2:

$$S_2 = \begin{vmatrix} 24 & 19 & 13 \\ & 22 & 12 \\ & & 10 \end{vmatrix}$$

$$W = S_1 + S_2 = \begin{vmatrix} 42 & 33 & 23 \\ & 36 & 20 \\ & & 19 \end{vmatrix}$$

degrees of freedom $d_f = n_1 + n_2 - 2 = 11 + 11 - 2 = 20$

The weights w_j for the variables are computed as follows:

$$w_j = \sum_i u_{ji} d_i$$

Table 17.12 Mean Average Scores for Discriminant Analysis

Country A	x_1	x_2	x_3	x^2_{11}	x^2_{21}	x^2_{31}	$x_{11}x_{21}$	$x_{11}x_{31}$	$x_{21}x_{31}$
1	9	8	7	2^2	1^2	1^2	2	2	1
2	8	7	6	1^2	0	0	0	0	0
3	7	7	6	0	0	0	0	0	0
4	7	7	6	0	0	0	0	0	0
5	5	5	4	2^2	2^2	2^2	4	4	4
6	6	7	6	1^2	0^2	0^2	0	0	0
7	7	8	7	0	1^2	1^2	0	0	1
8	5	5	5	2^2	2^2	1^2	4	2	2
9	7	7	5	0	0^2	1^2	0	0	0
10	9	9	7	2^2	2^2	0	4	2	0
11	7	7	6	0	0	1^2	0	0	0
Total	77	77	66	=18	14	9	14	10	8
Mean	7	7	6						

Country E	x_1	x_2	x_3	x^2_{11}	x^2_{21}	x^2_{31}	$x_{11}x_{21}$	$x_{11}x_{31}$	$x_{21}x_{31}$
1	4	6	4	0^2	1^2	0^2	0	0	1
2	4	5	5	0^2	0	1^2	0	1	0
3	3	4	4	1^2	1^2	0^2	1	0	0
4	2	3	3	2^2	2^2	1^2	4	2	2
5	3	3	3	1^2	2^2	1^2	2	1	2
6	7	4	3	3^2	1^2	1^2	3	3	1
7	5	6	6	1^2	1^2	2^2	1	2	2
8	4	5	4	0^2	0	0	0	0	0
9	6	8	5	2^2	3^2	1^2	6	2	3
10	2	6	3	2^2	1^2	1^2	2	2	1
11	4	5	4	0^2	0	0	0	0	0
Total	4	5	4	= 24	22	10	19	13	12
Mean	4	5	4						

Table 17.13 Detailed Calculation for Discriminant Analysis Example

$V = \frac{W}{df} =$	2.1	1.65	1.15
	1.65	1.8	1
	1.15	1.0	0.95
$V^{-1} = U =$	2.25	−1.308	−1.3161
	−1.308	2.107	−0.635
	−1.3161	−0.635	3.3175

Note: The matrix inversion calculations are not given, but obtained through the computer.

$$w_1 = 2.225 \text{ x } 3 - 1.308 \text{ x } 2 - 1.316 \text{ x } 2 = 1.429$$

$$w_2 = -1.308 \text{ x } 3 + 2.107 \text{ x } 2 - 0.635 \text{ x } 2 = -0.98$$

$$w_3 = -1.316 \text{ x } 3 - 0.635 \text{ x } 2 + 3.314 \text{ x } 2 = 1.41$$

$\therefore$ mean discriminant function scores are:

$$\overline{Y}_1 = 7 \text{ x } 1.429 - 7 \text{ x } .98 + 6 \text{ x } 1.41 = 12.03$$

$$\overline{Y}_2 = 4 \text{ x } 1.429 - 5 \text{ x } .98 + 4 \text{ x } 1.41 = 6.456$$

unitising the standard deviation of the discriminant score:

$$v_y = \sum_i^n w_i d_i = 1.429x3 - 0.98x2 + 1.41x2$$

$$\sqrt{v_y} = 2.269$$

New weights for the discriminant function variables are:

$$w_1 = \frac{1.429}{2.269} = 0.63, \quad w_2 = \frac{.98}{2.269} = -0.432, \quad w_3 = \frac{1.41}{2.29} = 0.621$$

Modified $\bar{Y}'s$ are

$$\bar{Y}_1 = 7 \text{ x } 0.63 - 0.43 \text{ x } 7 + 6 \text{ x } 0.621 = 5.126$$

$$\bar{Y}_2 = 4 \text{ x } 0.63 - 0.43 \text{ x } 5 + 4 \text{ x } 0.621 = 2.854$$

$$P_{cr} = \frac{5.126 + 2.854}{2} = 3.99$$

Note: A figure similar to Fig. 17.2 can be drawn for pictorial representation.

The discriminant scores are computed using the new weights; companies whose scores are more than (equal to) 3.99 are grouped under A. Others are grouped under E. The results are shown below (detailed calculations are not given).

		Predicted		
		A	E	Total
Actual	A	9	2	11
	E	2	9	11

Only serial numbers 5 and 8 in A and 7 and 9 in E are errors. Correct classification per cent is:

$$\frac{18}{22} x 100 = 81.8\%$$

Significance of discriminant function: F test is used as follows.

$$F = \frac{n_1 n_2 (n_1 + n_2 - k - 1) v_y}{m(n_1 + n_2)(n_1 + n_2 - 2)} \qquad \text{df} = m + (n_1 + n_2 - m - 1)$$

$$F = \frac{11 x 11 (11 + 11 - 3 - 1)\, 5.14}{3(11 + 11)(11 + 11 - 2)}$$

$$= \frac{121 x 18 x 5.147}{22 x 60} = 8.493$$

$$F_{cr} = 3.16 \text{ for } \begin{cases} df_1 = 3 \\ df_2 = 22 - 3 - 1 = 18 \end{cases}$$

∴ F is highly significant.

CANONICAL CORRELATION ANALYSIS

Introduction

Canonical correlation analysis, or simply canonical analysis, is a multivariate statistical technique that characterises the independent statistical relationships that exist between two or possibly more sets of random variables. The interrelationships between two variable sets of measurements (with at least two variables in each variable set) made on the same subjects can be studied by the canonical correlation method. Alternatively, the regression analysis of data with k independent variables and m dependent variables is called canonical correlation analysis. Canonical correlation is the maximum correlation between linear functions of the two vector variables. The so called multiple regression analysis becomes a special case of canonical analysis, which can be considered a generalisation of multiple regression analysis.

canonical correlation analysis

This is multivariate statistical technique to characterize the statistical relationships between two or more sets of random variables by selecting a linear combination of the sets and maximizing the correlations between these combinations.

The Model

Suppose there are two sets of variables $Z^{(x)}$ and $Z^{(y)}$ with p and q variables within each set of variables, respectively. Two new linear combination of the each set of variables, $u_k = a_k z^{(x)}$ and $v_k = b_k z^{(y)}$, are such that the simple correlation coefficient r_k between the transformed variables u_k and v_k is maximised. The new variables u_k and v_k are called the canonical variates and r_k is called the canonical correlation coefficient between the canonical variates u_k and v_k. In all, there will be s pairs of such linear transformations, $k = 1,\dots,s$ where s is the smaller of p and q. As in the case of principal component analysis, successive pairs of canonical variates are required to be uncorrelated with the preceding variates.

Assumptions

The assumptions that must be met for applying canonical correlation analysis are as follows.

1. Measurement error of the variables is minimal.
2. Variance of variables are not restricted.
3. Magnitudes of the coefficients in the correlation matrix must not be attenuated by large differences in the shapes of the distributions for the variables.

Type of data: The variables need not be continuous or directly measured. Nominal scaled data, which is appropriate where a classificatory structure exists, can also be used. The use of differently coded dummy variables, principal components of either or both sets of observed variables, can also be made.

The Method

The canonical model selects linear functions that have maximum covariances between domains, subjected to the restrictions of orthogonality, that is, the functions in the new pair of linear functions must be uncorrelated with all previously located functions in each new domain. The mathematics involved in the extraction of these linear functions are similar to that of principal component analysis. The difference lies in the matrix that is subjected to the mathematical treatment. In principal component analysis, the variance-covariance matrix is used whereas in canonical analysis the correlation matrix is made use of in obtaining linear functions.

Significance Test

Several tests are available when the researcher wishes to test the statistical significance of a null hypothesis of no relationship between the criterion and the predictor variable sets. The most widely used is the Bartlett (1951) test, which tests for the significance of canonical correlations.

Interpretation

As a thumb rule, canonical correlations of 0.30 or less are treated as trivial. When a statistically significant canonical correlation is identified, the researcher desires to determine the extent to which the various variables contributed to the identified multivariate relationship. To facilitate this, several additional coefficients are calculated. They are structure coefficients, communality and adequacy coefficients, redundancy coefficients, and analysis and index coefficients. Details of each one of this and other supplementary techniques can be found in Thompson (1984). Even though canonical analysis is one of the 'major methods' of multivariate analysis, some difficulty is encountered in attempting to interpret a pair of canonical variables, both of which are linear combinations of the original variables.

Canonical analysis and regression analysis Canonical analysis is closely related to regression analysis. This involves the regression of a vector of response variables on a vector of predictors. However, a clear distinction can be noticed between them. In canonical analysis, the two sets of variables are treated symmetrically, this is not the case with multiple regression. Another important point is that, in multiple regression the fact of deciding a variable as a response is of great importance. But in canonical analysis, either set of variables can be used to predict the other, or more precisely, both sets of variables simultaneously predict each other.

Example For a group of 30 students studying in a certain class, four ability variables: (i) Reading Comprehension Test (RCT), (ii) Creativity Test (CT), (iii) Mechanical Reasoning Test. (MRT), and (iv) Abstract Reasoning Test (ART); and three motive measures such as: (a) Sociability Inventory (SI), (b) Physical Science Interest Inventory (PSII), and (c) Office Work Interest Inventory (OWII) were measured. The details of these are given in Table 17.14. Using the data given in Table 17.14, study the canonical relationships between four ability variables and three motive measures.

Solution: In SPSS, canonical correlation is included in multivariate analysis of variance (MANOVA). Most other softwares choose the correlation matrix as input from among dependent and independent variables. But SPSS generates these correlations and uses them in the analysis.

Table 17.14 Data for the Problem

RCT	*CT*	*MRT*	*ART*	*SI*	*PSII*	*OWII*
39	9	12	9	10	20	18
15	7	10	10	4	15	13
28	8	12	9	9	8	6
47	13	14	12	4	28	24
40	10	15	12	11	26	1
21	10	14	11	6	8	9
33	9	12	9	11	16	11
46	18	20	15	9	36	2
42	10	17	13	6	33	16
38	14	18	11	9	30	3
42	12	17	12	6	27	12
32	10	18	8	1	20	23
39	16	17	11	4	23	11
43	8	10	11	8	28	19
41	13	10	8	7	33	4
34	7	9	5	8	9	6
41	11	12	11	2	17	20
38	11	14	11	7	18	14
32	5	14	13	4	13	3
41	17	17	11	8	21	20
32	10	12	7	8	25	3
43	5	11	11	2	28	14
24	9	9	7	5	27	24
43	12	15	12	11	26	6
43	16	19	12	2	31	14
25	10	15	7	8	17	14
36	14	16	12	3	24	16
45	10	16	11	9	34	17
27	8	10	13	11	24	12
39	9	17	11	9	28	10

The motivating variables SI, PSII, and OWII are dependent variables (criterion variables) and the ability variables RCT, CT, MRT, and ART are independent (covariates in the SPSS) variables. Within the cells, regression is performed in the analysis of variance to extract three roots and canonical coefficients (weights) for the three dependent variables and displayed in Table 17.15 and 17.16. Table 17.15 shows the coefficients when raw scores are used and Table 17.16 when the variables are standardised (with mean = 0 and $\sigma = 1$). The structural correlations of dependent variables with the canonical function are displayed in Table 17.17. In order to choose the most efficient function, the variance explained by each canonical variables is obtained in the analysis of variance (Table 17.18), leading to a choice of canonical function number 1.

Similar procedure for criterion variables yields tables 17.19 to 17.22, leading to the choice of function 1. Again, canonical function 1 is chosen based on the variance (50.406). The final result is summarised in Table 17.23.

Table 17.15 SPSS Output; Canonical Correlation—Raw Canonical Coefficients for Dependent Variables

	Function no.		
Variable	*1*	*2*	*3*
SI	–.014	.309	.206
PSII	.130	–.007	.000
OWII	–.007	.144	–.081

Table 17.16 SPSS Output; Canonical Correlation—Standardised Canonical Coefficients for Dependent Variables

	Function no.		
Variable	*1*	*2*	*3*
SI	–.042	.935	.624
PSII	1.003	–.051	.003
OWII	–.045	.982	–.549

Table 17.17 SPSS Output; Canonical Correlation—Correlations between Dependent and Canonical Variables

	Function no.		
Variable	*1*	*2*	*3*
SI	.022	.489	.872
PSII	.999	.045	–.001
OWII	.031	.556	–.831

Table 17.18 SPSS Output; Canonical Correlation—Analysis of Variance (Variance Explained by Canonical Variables of Dependent Variables)

CAN. VAR.	*Pct Var DE*	*Cum Pct DE*	*Pct Var CO*	*Cum Pct CO*
1	33.313	33.313	15.503	15.503
2	18.320	51.633	1.085	16.589
3	48.367	100.000	.181	16.769

The linear composites (canonical functions) are as follows.

(i) Criterion composite (ability variables):

$$Va = -0.014\times SI + 0.130\times PSII - 0.007\times OWII$$

(ii) Predictor composite (motives, covariates):

$$V_m = 0.096\times RCT + 0.081\times CT + 0.011\times MRT + 0.093\times ART$$

The canonical correlation (simple correlation between the two composites) is 0.611 when these discriminant function scores are correlated. The structural correlations indicate that PSII is the dominant variable in the dependent canonical function (correlation = 0.999) and others

Table 17.19 SPSS Output; Canonical Correlation—Raw Canonical Coefficients for Covariates

	Function no.		
Covariates	*1*	*2*	*3*
RCT	.096	.081	–.017
CT	.081	.087	–.051
MRT	.011	–.320	–.238
ART	.093	–.166	.500

Table 17.20 SPSS Output; Canonical Correlation of Variance (Standardised Canonical Coefficients for Covariates

	CAN. VAR.		
Covariate	*1*	*2*	*3*
RCT	.760	.641	–.134
CT	.265	.288	–.167
MRT	–.035	–1.016	–.756
ART	.205	–.366	1.105

Table 17.21 SPSS Output; Canonical Correlation—Correlations between Covariates and Canonical Variables

	CAN. VAR.		
Covariate	*1*	*2*	*3*
RCT	.953	.183	–.051
CT	.651	–.222	–.366
MRT	.568	–.744	–.352
ART	.602	–.520	.602

Table 17.22 SPSS Output; Canonical Correlation—Analysis of Variance (Variance Explained by Canonical Variables of the Covariates)

CAN. VAR.	*Pct Var DE*	*Cum Pct DE*	*Pct Var CO*	*Cum Pct CO*
1	23.458	23.458	50.406	50.406
2	1.342	24.800	22.655	73.060
3	.058	24.858	15.580	88.640

Table 17.23 SPSS Output; Canonical Correlation—Summary of Results

Variables	*Canonical weights*	*Structure correlations*
Dependent		
SI	–0.014	0.022
PSII	0.130	0.099
OWII	–0.007	0.031
Independent		
RCT	0.096	0.953
CT	0.081	0.651
MRT	0.011	0.568
ART	0.093	0.602
Canonical correlation is 0.611		

are insignificant. Whereas in the covariate canonical function, RCT is highly correlated with the canonical function (0.953), but others are also fairly high.

PATH ANALYSIS

path analysis

This is a technique of obtaining causal relationshijp between a set of independent variables and a set of dependent variables using a path diagram. This relationship may be direct or indirect. This deals with non observable constructs, just like factor analysis (dealt with in chapter 18) and is therefore a latent variable analysis procedure.

LISREL

This is a standard software package of SPSS for carrying out path analysis. It carries out a series of regression analyses simultaneously.

Factor analysis and path analysis are two types of latent variable analysis that deal with non-observable constructs (for example, factors are non-observable and are therefore latent variables). Path analysis is a technique for testing and refining one's theory (Tull and Hawkins, 1988). Path analysis deals with the causal relations underlying a set of independent variables and a set of dependent variables. The causal relationship between two variables may be either direct or indirect. In path analysis, path diagrams are set up and the causal relationships between variables are attributed according to theory or hypothesis of a researcher [Kline, (1994); Hilton, (1972) and Swamidass & Newell, (1987)]. Then the path analysis is carried out to test these relationships. It is a series of regression analyses conducted simultaneously to determine a set of theorised relationships. In this process, confirmatory factor analysis is used and goodness of fit of relationships is tested. A standard software for doing path analysis is the LISREL package of SPSS. (LISREL stands for Linear Structural Relationship).

Following rules are relevant:

Path diagram: The following points must be kept in mind while developing a path diagram:

- Arrows connecting variables shows causality. Arrow head shows direction of causality.
- Independent variables are independent causally, that is, no arrow points towards them.
- Dependent variables are caused and, therefore, arrows point towards them.
- All independent variables are connected by curved arrows if they are correlated.
- Downstream or dependent variables are never connected by curved arrows.
- Residual arrows (origin not specified for these) represent the influence of extraneous variables not considered in the analysis and are unlabelled.
- Residual arrows are always attached to each downstream variable since they represent residual variance. Their absence means that all variance in the analysis is accounted for by independent variables.
- Significant causal relationships between two variables are shown as direct arrows between them.
- All relationships indicated by arrows are linear.
- Up and down arrows between two variables is possible.
- Looping via variables is possible, that is, A to B to C to A.
- It is desirable that standardised scores be used in path analysis (raw scores can also be used but analysis becomes more complex). Let us take the simplest case of three variables x_1, x_2 and x_3. x_1 and x_2 are independent variables and x_3 is the dependent variable.

A simple path diagram is shown in Fig. 17.3 for this situation. Note that there is no unlabelled arrow going into x_3. This indicates that no residual variance exists.

- Correlation between any two variables is the sum of the compound path correlations connecting these two points. In a path there are no loops, backtracking, or curved arrows.
- Paths can be reversed as they sum up to correlations.

The path values are called path coefficients and are partial regression coefficient between the variables.

Fig. 17.3 Path diagram

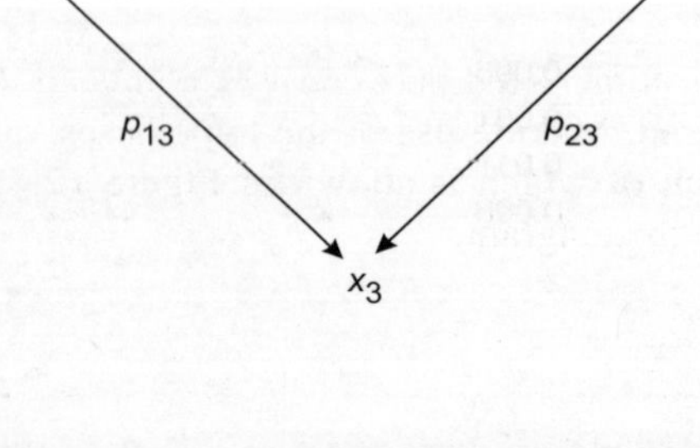

Let us assume the variables x_1, x_2 and x_3 are correlated as shown in the table below.

	x_1	x_2	x_3
x_1	1.0	0.1	0.3
x_2	0.1	1.0	0.5
x_3	0.3	0.5	1.0

The equation of path analysis, keeping the above rules in mind, are the following:

$$r_{x}1_{x}2 = r_{12}$$

$$r_{x}1_{x}3 = p_{13} + r_{12}\,p_{23}$$

$$r_{x}2_{x}3 = p_{23} + r_{12}\,p_{13}$$

$$r_{12} = 0.1$$

$$p_{13} + 0.1\,p_{23} = 0.3 \qquad (1)$$

$$p_{23} + 0.1\,p_{13} = 0.5 \qquad (2)$$

Solving 1 and 2, we get

$$p_{13} = 0.253 \text{ and } p_{23} = 0.475.$$

we can say now that causal influence of x_1 on x_3 is 0.253 and x_2 on x_3 is 0.475

$R^2{}_{x}1_{x}2_{x}3 = r_{x}1_{x}3 \times p_{13} + p_{23} \times r_{x}2_{x}3$, (in standard regression) is the variance accounted for by x_1 and x_2.

$$= 0.253\times0.3 + 0.475\times0.5 = 0.3134$$

Variance explained by x_1 and x_2 $= (0.253\times0.475\times1)\times2 + 0.253^2 + 0.475^2 = 0.3136.$

Example In a study of industrial patents a researcher hypothesised that the following variables were causally linked. The variables are related to industrial firms.

x_1 = type of industry—high technology or otherwise (dichotomous)

x_2 = age of the firm (continuous)

x_3 = policy of developing new products (5-point rating scale)

x_4 = whether formal R&D department exists (dichotomous)

x_5 = organisational flexibility (openness to change) measured on a questionnaire (5-point rating scale)

x_6 = number of patents produced (reports of the firm)

The operational linkages developed in the theory are:

1. x_1 and x_2 are exogenous variables.
2. x_6 is the final variable (criterion variable).
3. x_3, x_4, x_5 are endogenous variables caused by x_1 and x_2 and error variables (u, s). Hypothesis used were follows:

- Firms that are more aged produce a smaller number of patents than newer firms.
- High technology firms produce more patents than other firms.
- Older firms have formal R&D departments. Formalising R&D causes fewer productivity of patents.
- Older firms are less organisationally flexible than the newer ones. [Higher resistance to change (lower flexibility) causes barriers to innovation and, therefore, older firms produce fewer patents].

Hundred industrial organisations aged between 15 to 50 years were studied and regression/ multiple regressions were used. Making use of the hypotheses, a structural model was developed, (the graphical diagram of which is shown in Figure 17.4). The path coefficients (p_{ij} linking x_j to x_i) are shown in the diagram.

It is to be noted that arrow $x_j - x_i$ indicates the causal path between cause variable x_j and effect variable x_i (Example $p_{4.2} = 0.32$), a coefficient of 0.32 of path linking variable 2 and variable 4 p_{jj} = is the path coefficient of residual variable u_j. Each u_j is a variable of an endogenous variable unaccounted for the antecedent variables. All the coefficients are significant at $\alpha = 0.05$ level. Nearly 50 per cent of the variance in the number of patents produced is accounted for by hypothesised variables.

Fig. 17.4 Path diagram for patents

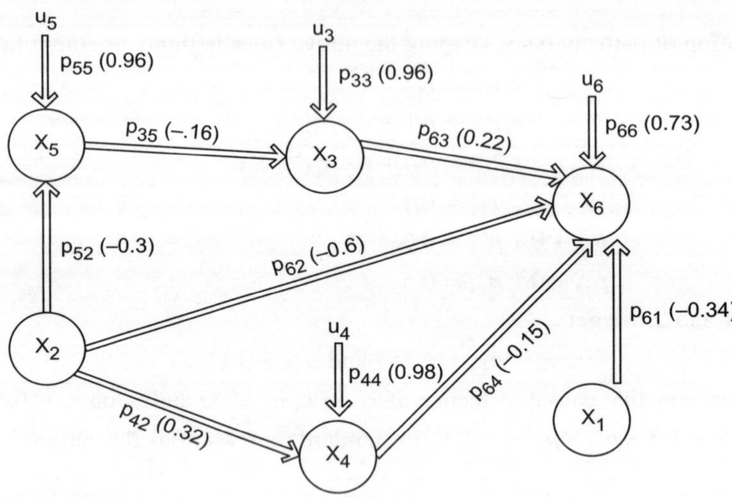

OTHER METHODS

Conjoint Analysis

Conjoint analysis has its base in experimentation. It deals with the measurement of judgments and preferences and is widely used in marketing research, particularly in consumer research. What conjoint analysis does is to decompose the overall value, as given by the respondent, into utilities (values) for each individual attribute (whose summation will yield the overall value). In other words, the contribution of each feature of the product to consumer's choice is obtained (Green et al, 1988).

The solution in metric conjoint analysis involves a type of analysis of variance in which overall preference is the criterion variable. The level of each stimulus (factorially designed) serves as the predictor variable, design variables are the dummy (valued) variables.

In non-metric conjoint analysis, the criterion variable is ordinal scaled. In non-metric conjoint analysis multiple factor approach is used in evaluations. A number of cards are made with different levels of attributes (like, for example, hot iron, whose attributes may be price, weight, the time of attaining the required temperature, the appearance, and warranty period). The respondent is asked to put them in three piles—like, neither like nor dislike. Thereafter, he is required to rank the cards in the order of most-liked to least-liked. Using the overall rating as the criterion variable, preference ratings and the levels of attributes as the predictor variables, and using ordinary dummy variable regression, the part worths are obtained.

These part worths, when properly added, gives the total utility for each combination. For a more detailed explanation, see Green et al (1988).

Automatic Interaction Detection Analysis

In the relationship between a criterion variable and the predictor variable, if the response of the criterion variable to changes in a predictor variable depends upon the level of another predictor variable, then interaction exists between the two predictor variables. In that case, the additive property of individual predictor variable contributions to changes in the dependent variable does not hold. Generally, such interactions are difficult to obtain. Automatic Interaction Detector (AID) is a sequential search procedure developed by Sonquist and Morgon of the Michigan

University. Criterion variable is interval scaled or dichotomous. The predictor variables will be converted to nominal using another scale. The basic procedure used in AID is to split the predictor variables into two groups in a sequential manner and then perform one way analysis of variance type computations to get the best split initially and then on each of the splits subsequently. Thus, a tree is generated such that at each split the best binary split, as also the elements of the groups so split, are obtained. Finally, predictor variables that most significantly explain criterion variable variation are obtained. There is no statistical inference or validation in AID. It can be used on large samples of 1000 or more units and the best use is as a screening device. For more details, the reader is referred to Green et al (1988).

SUMMARY

When more than two variables are considered in a relationship, multivariate techniques are used for analysis purposes. These techniques can be classified as dependence analysis techniques and interdependence analysis techniques. In this chapter, dependence analysis techniques like multiple regression, discriminant analysis, and canonical correlation are discussed. Other developments like path analysis, conjoint analysis, and automatic interaction detector briefly outlined. Simple non-statistical explanations of the techniques are presented and examples are illustrated through computerised analysis providing computer outputs. Some supplementary hand calculations are also made.

Linear multiple regression analysis examines the relationship between two or more intervally-scaled predictor variables and one intervally-scaled dependent (criterion) variable. It uses ordinary least squares fit to data to obtain the regression equation to be used in applications. The strength of the relationship is determined by the coefficient of multiple determination. The significance of the relationship is tested by the ANOVA (F) test. The violation of assumptions underlying the technique can be understood and remedied using the residual analysis. One of the major problems of using multiple regression analysis is the presence of multicolinearity, which is overcome by ridge regression. Non-linear relationships can be handled by the method of transformation of variables to convert them into linear relationships that can be solved by linear regression method.

Multiple discriminant analysis helps the researcher to understand and explain problems that involve a single categorical dependent variable and several metric independent variables. Several groups of items are analysed using the same variables. A discriminant function is derived using the common variables as a weighted linear combination of the variables (characteristics). A statistical test is applied (typically F test) to test whether mean scores of the discriminant function for the groups are significantly different (distanced). The capability of the discriminant function to classify items correctly into the groups is checked.

Canonical correlation analysis (or simply canonical analysis) is a powerful technique used to explore relationships among multiple criterion variables and multiple predictor variables. The technique selects linear combination of two sets of variables to maximise covariance between them. It provides the number of ways in which the two sets of variables are interrelated. This is particularly useful where a*priori* knowledge of the data is meagre. Multiple regression is a special case of canonical correlation. The mathematical basis of canonical analysis is similar to that of multiple discriminant analysis. The statistical test to assess the significance of the canonical correlation is the Bartlett's Test. An example (computerised analysis) is presented to give a basic understanding of the technique.

Path analysis is a multivariate technique used to test and refine one's theory. It deals with causal relationships. It uses a network of relationship among independent and dependent variables, which are displayed as a path diagram. Simultaneous simple and multiple regressions are used to derive the relationships. The software generally used is LISREL. The technique provides path coefficients, which are partial regression coefficients between the variables that are connected by the path. It tells us how much of the variance of the final dependent variable is accounted for by the other variables considered in the network. A simple computational feature and a small case application of path analysis are illustrated.

Conjoint analysis, an experimental approach to measuring preferences and judgements of marketing executives, and automatic interaction detector, which deals with the interactions of predictor variables and their influence on the dependent variable, are outlined.

Suggested Readings

- Allison, Paul (1999). *Multiple Regression—A Primer*. London: Pine Forge Press.
- Freund, Rudolph J. and William J. Wilson (1997). *Statistical Methods*, 2nd ed. San Diego: Academic Press.
- Harris, R. J. (2001). *A Primer on Multivariate Statistics*, 3rd ed. Orlando: Academic Press.
- Tacq (1999). *Multivariate Analysis Techniques in Social Science Research*. London: Sage.

QUESTIONS AND EXERCISES

Regression Analysis

1. What is the objective of multiple regression when it is used in exploratory research? Discuss.
2. Where there are a large number of independent variables it will be necessary to eliminate a number of variables from analysis for parsimony. How would you get the variables that are relatively important?
3. Can a multiple regression equation be statistically significant and of no use substantively? Give reasons for your answer.
4. If the independent variables are not correlated highly does it mean effect regression analysis ? If they are, will there be any problems for purposes of (a) estimation (b) understanding?
5. When do you use dummy variables in regression analysis? Discuss an application from research.
6. Take from research literature two examples of multiple regression. Present the method and results critically reviewing particularly the assumptions, problems of interpretation, and significance of results.
7. When is lagged regression analysis important? Give an example.
8. Suppose you are interested in the relationship of age, size, and annual sales turn-over of companies in a specific industrial sector having the following cross sectional data, use multiple regression and interpret the results.

Age (Years)	Size (100 employees)	Annual sale (turn over) (Rs 100,000)
31	67	32,000
29	68	13,000
35	76	20,000
45	75	29,000
37	70	40,000
17	72	50,000
21	73	15,000
42	67	31,000
18	64	8000
29	71	19,000

9. How does one use regression analysis to estimate a, b and c.
10. How is heteroscadasticity treated in multiple regression analysis? Can you discuss an example from research literature ?

11. In a random sample of 23 firms in the same industry, the following quantities were obtained for each:

X_1 = research and development expenditure (millions of rupees)
X_2 = advertising expenditure on television (millions of rupees)
X_3 = all other advertising expenditures (millions of rupees)
Y = annual sales (millions of rupees)

Regression analysis yielded the following results:

$$\hat{Y} = -2.3 + 5.8\,X_1 + 4.2\,X_2 + 7.4\,X_3$$
$$(1.20) \quad (1.31) \quad (1.56)$$

The quantities in parentheses are the standard errors of the net regression coefficients. The standard error of estimate $S_{Y.123}$ was 12.4. The standard deviation of the dependent variable S_Y was 25.

a. Interpret the net regression coefficient b_1.
b. Test at the 1 per cent level of significance whether each of the net regression coefficients is significantly different from zero.
c. What is the expected effect when highly correlated independent variables are included in a multiple regression equation?
d. Calculate the coefficient of multiple determination.
e. Estimate the average annual sales for a firm that has research and development expenditures of Rs 6 million, television advertising expenditures of Rs 10 million, and all other advertising expenditure of Rs 7 million.
f. Assume the following standard deviations:

$$Sx_1 = 15 \qquad Sx_2 = 10 \qquad Sx_3 = 5$$

Calculate the beta coefficients, β_1, β_2, and β_3. Interpret β_1.

12. A local real estate agent has decided to perform a multiple regression analysis on the prices of homes in her area. She feels that the 2 major variables that affect the value of the homes that she sells are the square footage of the total floor area and the age of the home. The agent gathers data on the 25 homes he sold in the last year; the 3 variables she measures for each house are the price the house sold for in ten thousand rupees (PRICE), the square footage of the house in hundreds of square feet (FLOOR), and the age of the house in years (AGE). The results are listed in the table below:

HOME	PRICE	FLOOR	AGE
1	62	11	21
2	63	10	12
3	65	10	18
4	67	11	10
5	68	8	17
6	70	9	13
7	74	15	10
8	74	18	21
9	75	12	26
10	76	15	21
11	77	17	14
12	78	27	22
13	79	23	20
14	80	22	15
15	80	18	14
16	82	22	12
17	82	18	18
18	86	20	17
19	87	23	9
20	88	26	17
21	90	24	14
22	91	16	17

Contd.

HOME	PRICE	FLOOR	AGE
23	94	19	16
24	95	23	17
25	100	19	2

a. Using a computer, fit the multiple linear regression model to the given data to predict the price of a house based on its floor area and age.
b. Interpret the slope coefficients (b values) in terms of the variables.
c. Test the significance of the slope coefficients, using $\alpha = 0.05$.
d. Test the overall significance of the model, using $\alpha = 0.05$. State your conclusion.

Discriminant Analysis

13. What are the differences between regression analyses, multiple discriminant analysis and analysis, of variance?
14. How do you validate the results of a discriminant analysis?
15. Researchwise what use can be there in obtaining the dominant variables in a discriminant function?
16. In a discriminant analysis the following classification was obtained.
    a. How good is the statistical analysis?
    b. What do the results show?

    The following are the lots produced in a production shop. The items were machined after heat treatment for a specific period of time. Twelve were accepted but eight were rejected, as shown in table below:

    (a) Accepted

Duration of heat treatment (Mts)	Hardness Score
70	20
40	50
30	20
60	70
40	60
50	40
60	60
60	50
50	70
60	30
60	40
60	40

(b) Rejected:

Duration of heat treatment (Mts)	Hardness Score
30	50
60	30
40	30
40	40
60	20
50	30
50	20
40	40

(i) Find the discriminant function and its validity.
(ii) How does the function discriminate between acceptable and non acceptable limits?

17. Choose two research papers in which discriminant analysis is used.
   a. What use were the results of the analysis put to?
   b. Do you think discriminant analysis can be used for hypothesis testing? Justify your answer with examples.

Canonical Correlations

18. When is canonical correlation analysis suitable for multivariate data analysis? Give examples.

19. What is the use of the canonical correlation coefficient? Answer the question keeping in view the difficulties of applying it in a particular case.

20. What is the advantage of using canonical loadings instead of weights in determining the structure of the relation between the dependent variable and the covariates.

21. How are canonical root and R^2 related in multiple regression analysis?

22. What are the main aspects of interpreting canonical correlation analysis?

23. The table below shows three attributes of quality control programme QA, QB, and QC, and three quality performance measures PA, PB, and PC. Use canonical correlation to investigate the relationship, if any, between the quality programme and quality performance.

QA	QB	QC	PA	PB	PC
4	5	1	48.7	1.5	16.8
11	13	4	6.7	1.3	35.8
17	6	5	2.7	1.4	3.2
6	6	5	34.7	2.1	30.1
7	10	3	3.1	2.5	25.7
9	5	3	9	0.5	22.4
14	10	5	23.2	1.0	20.7
5	12	3	21.7	3.1	29.7
10	3	3	41.4	0.6	17.6
10	5	3	13	0.4	25.9
8	6	2	23.6	1.9	32.3
14	9	4	3.3	0.9	27.6
18	10	3	10.8	0.8	27.5
10	11	3	16.5	2.9	35.5
6	4	1	27.8	0.3	24.5

CHAPTER 18

Multivariate Analysis of Data—Interdependence Analysis

- Introduction
- Factor Analysis
- Multidimensional Scaling (MDS)
- Cluster Analysis

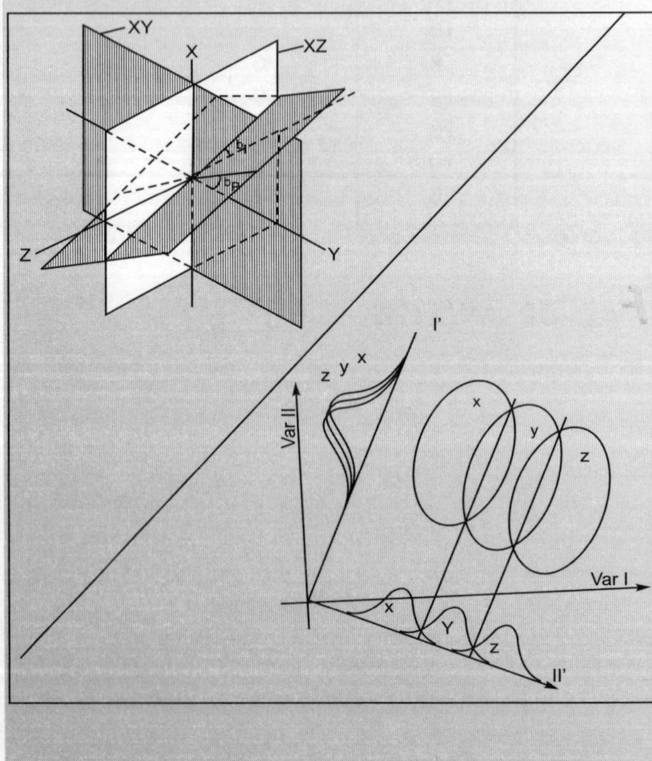

LEARNING OBJECTIVES

Upon completion of this chapter, you will be able to:

- ✓ Know about parsimony as central idea of factor analysis
- ✓ Study factor analysis as a correlational analysis
- ✓ Learn about principle component analysis
- ✓ Understand the meaning of factor rotation
- ✓ Learn to Interpret factors
- ✓ Determine the number of factors to be extracted
- ✓ Know about multidimensional scaling (MDS) as a measurement technique
- ✓ Learn the basics of MDS
- ✓ Learn testing of dimensions determined through MDS
- ✓ Compare MDS and factor analysis
- ✓ Learn to use cluster analysis as a classification technique
- ✓ Learn to implement cluster analysis using correlation
- ✓ Learn to implement cluster analysis using Euclidean measures
- ✓ Compare cluster analysis and factor analysis

INTRODUCTION

This chapter deals with multivariate analysis techniques to analyse the internal interdependence of a number of observations in a data set derived in research. The data are generally related to complex constructs whose internal patterns of relationships have to be explored or analysed. They are aimed at simplifying the understanding of phenomena using a parsimonious way of looking at the data. Three techniques are discussed. They are factor analysis, multidimensional scaling, and cluster analysis. These techniques employ correlational techniques or concepts of similarity and multidimensional Euclidean distances. The detailed mathematics of the techniques is beyond the scope of this book. Simplified explanations are given and generally an intuitive approach is taken for clarification. The techniques are illustrated by simple examples (or real research) that are explained with the help of computer outputs. In some places simple hand computations are made for extra elucidation. For a more thorough understanding of these techniques, the reader is advised to study the appropriate literature referred to in the suggested readings of this chapter.

FACTOR ANALYSIS

Introduction

Factor analysis is typically used for analysing survey data. In survey research, a researcher tries to obtain the description of the structure of a problem or a construct using a large number of variables (15 to 50). These variables are defined based on explanation, experience, or knowledge. They may be derived in exploration or qualitative research. The researcher would, in such cases, look out for a smaller number variables that can be used for describing the phenomena.

factor analysis
This is a set of analysis procedures to study internal dependence of a large number of observations as in a survey research. It derives a smaller number of composites or factors (linear combinations of original variables) generally orthogonal to each other, which account for most of the variance of the original variables.

The relationship among these variables can be represented by a table of correlations between each pair of variables. Starting from this relationship a set of composites (linear combinations of original variables) are derived in factor analysis such that, (i) the number of composites is smaller than the number of variables, (ii) most of the variance of the original variables are accounted for by the composites, and (iii) generally these composites are uncorrelated among themselves, that is, they are orthogonal to each other. The composites are called factors and several procedures developed over time to get these factors are called factor analysis procedures.

Factor analysis is a multivariate statistical procedure or technique attempting to reveal a simple underlying structure that is presumed to exist within a set of multivariate observations.

This structure is expressed in terms of variances and covariances between variables and similarities between observations. Factor analysis is a generic term for a variety of procedures developed for this purpose. In factor analysis, the relationship within a set of, say, *m* variables is regarded as reflecting the correlations of each of the variables with *p* mutually uncorrelated underlying factors ($p<m$). This technique tries to establish whether a variable, say X_i, could be generated by a linear combination of a minimum number of underlying factors (p). Therefore, variance in *m* variables is derived from *p* factors; also, a contribution is made by unique sources that independently affect the *m* original variables. Usually, the *p* underlying factors are referred to as common factors and sum of all the independent contribution as the unique factor. A variable can be a test score, an item, or a questionnaire response that is observable. The factor, on the other hand, is a non-observable construct, which is a linear combination of some of these observables.

It is interesting to note that this technique was developed by experimental psychologists in the 1930s and the very name 'factor' is attributed to hypothetical mental attributes, referred to as 'factors of mind'. Factor analysis is used, in a strict sense, to mean a statistical procedure by which a data matrix is decomposed into a prescribed number of uncorrelated factors and a residual set of 'unique' random variations.

Geometric Representation of Factor Analysis

Consider the correlation of three variables. The rank of the correlation matrix is three. The three variables, for example, A, B, and C can be represented geometrically as shown in Fig. 18.1 as three vectors, which is the true state of affairs. Variables A and B are in the plane of the paper and C projects up from the plane of the paper. Using any three uncorrelated (orthogonal) dimensions the vectors A, B, and C can be completely described. The solution is a full rank model in three dimensional spaces (Rank-3 model).

Fig. 18.1 Three vectors A, B, and C in three dimensional space

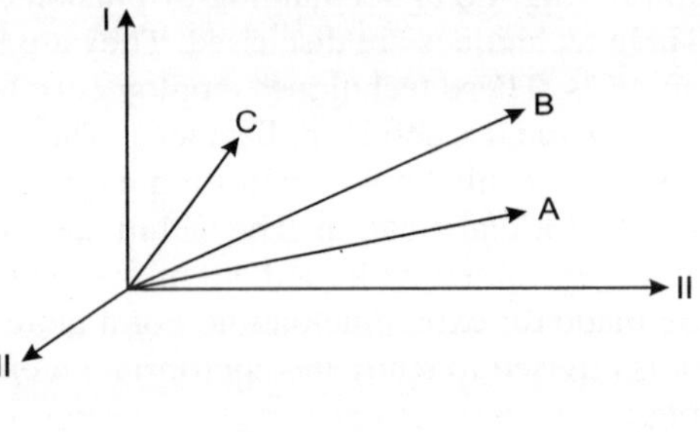

We can also construct Rank 1 and Rank 2 models as shown in Fig. 18.2. In a Rank 1 model we hypothesise that the relationship of the three variables can be represented by using a single dimension. In Rank 2, we hypothesise that the relationships can be represented by 2 dimensions, I and II. Both the Rank 1 and Rank 2 models are reduced rank models. In most applications of factor analysis, we attempt to fit a reduced dimensioned model, achieving parsimony. There are many methods available for this purpose.

One way of looking at factor analysis is to consider it as a kind of multiple correlation. If we may go on choosing the formation of composites one at a time in a sequence, we can impose the condition that the first composite be so formed that the average of its squared correlations with all the variables in the set is maximum. Next, the second composite is formed so that it is not correlated with the first and its average squared correlation with the remaining variables in the set is maximum. This is continued until the rank of the correlation matrix is completed. Such a process is called extraction of factors and the principle component method (Thorndike, 1978). The maximisation of squared multiple correlation ensures the maximisation of variance accounted for by the composite, and is central to the factor extraction process.

factor loading of a variable
This is the cosine of the angle between the variable and the factor. It is the simple correlation coefficient between them.

Let us look at the above process in a simple way with an example. A firm's investment (INVRD) in R&D and (TECL) in technology leadership strategy are two variables that are correlated with a correlation coefficient of 0.866 (factor loading). Can a single composite be

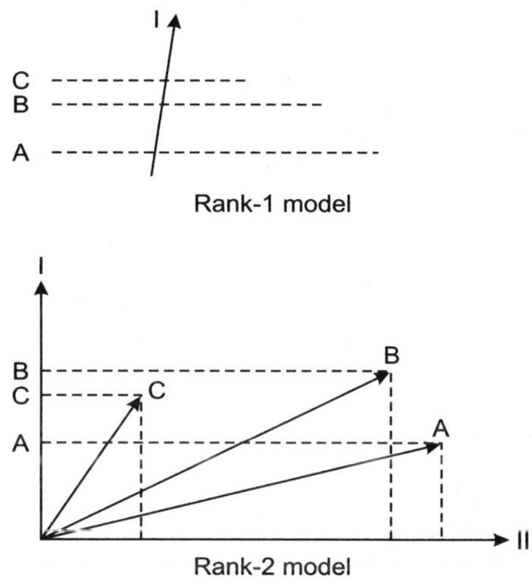

Fig. 18.2 Rank 1 and Rank 2 models

obtained which maximises the information about both? Representing their vectors we obtain Fig. 18.3. Can the two vectors INVRD and TECL be represented by a single reference vector (F1) that best summarises the two variables? The angle between the two vectors = 30° (cos 30° = 0.866). The reference vector is placed exactly on the bisector such that F1 makes 15° with each of INVRD and TECL.

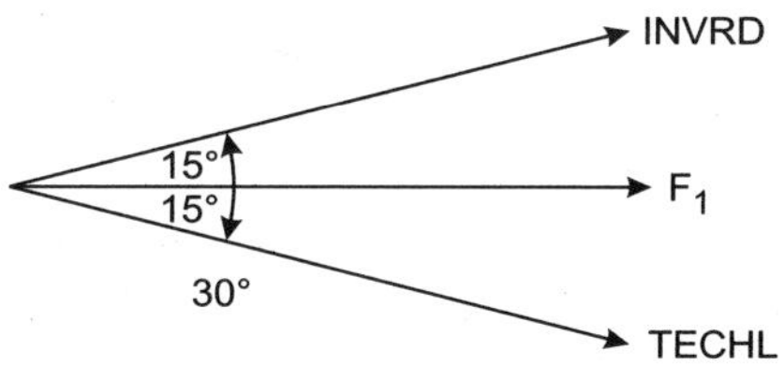

Fig. 18.3 One factor model

Now the percentage of variance accounted for by F_1 is given by,

square of the correlation between F_1 and INVRD $= \cos^2 15°$

square of the correlation between F_1 and TECHL $= \cos^2 15°$

square of the loadings of INVRD and TECHL on F_1 $= 2\cos^2 15$

$= 2 \times .933 = 1.866$

If each of the variables has a variance of 1 (standardised), then the

average squared loading (variance explained) = 0.933, which makes a good representation of INVRD and TECL

Now let us choose a second reference vector (composite) F_2, which is orthogonal to F_1, to maximise the squared loadings (in the way of extraction of factors until the rank of the matrix (2 in this case) is exhausted (See Fig. 18.4).

The squared loadings of INVRD and TECL on F_2 is now

$$= \cos^2 (90° - 15°) + \cos^2 (90° + 15°)$$
$$= \sin^2 15° + (-\sin 15)^2 = 2 \sin^2 15$$
$$= 2 \times 0.067 = 0.134$$

The table 18.1 shows the details of extraction of the factors.

communality of a variable
The communality of a variable is the sum of its squared loadings on all the factors.

Example to illustrate communality and per cent variance extracted An intercorrelation matrix of 5 variables A, B, C, D, and E is shown below. The two factors extracted by principle components analysis are also shown. Compute the communalities of the variables and the per cent of variance of factors extracted by factor analysis.

Fig. 18.4 2-Factor model

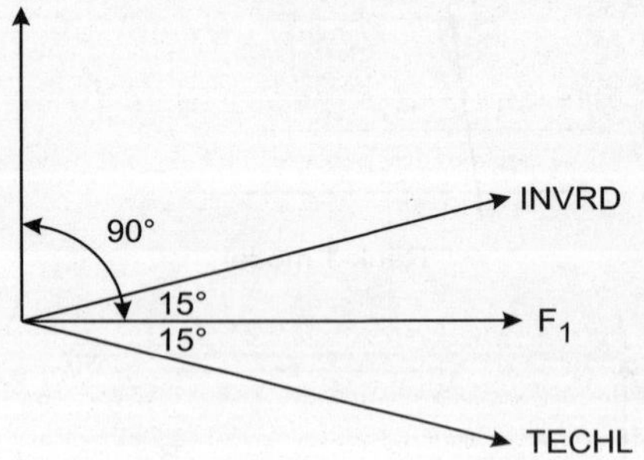

Table 18.1

Variable	Factor F_1	F_2	Communality
INVRD	0.933	0.067	1.0
TECHL	0.933	0.067	1.0
Extracted Variance	1.866	0.134	2.0
% Variance	93.3%	6.7%	100%

Intercorrelation matrix

	A	B	C	D	E
A	1	.65	.45	.54	.44
B		1	.33	.54	.41
C			1	.33	.42
D				1	
E					1

Factors extracted

	F_1	F_2
A	0.76	– 0.13
B	0.72	– 0.31
C	0.67	0.53
D	0.67	– 0.21
E	0.63	– 0.17

$$\text{Communality} = \sum_{1}^{m} (\text{Factor Loading})^2 \text{ for each variable}$$

$$\text{Communality of A} = .76^2 + (-.13)^2 = 0.5975\ (.60)$$
$$\text{Communality of B} = .72^2 + (-.31)^2 = 0.620\ (.62)$$
$$\text{of C} = 0.67^2 + 0.53^2 = .7279\ (.73)$$
$$\text{of D} = .67^2 + (0.21)^2 = .590\ (.59)$$
$$\text{of E} = .63^2 + (.17)^2 = .4258\ (.43)$$

proportion variance explained by a factor
This is the average of squared loadings for the variables grouped under it.

Variance extracted (for each factor) = variance explained by each factor

$$\text{Variance explained} = \frac{\sum_{1}^{m} (\text{Factor loading})^2}{\text{number of variables}\,(m)}$$

$$\text{Variance (explained) by } F_1 = \frac{.76^2 + .72^2 + .67^2 + .67^2 + .63^2}{5} = .501(50.1\%)$$

$$\text{Variance (explained) by } F_2 = \frac{(-.13)^2 + (-.31)^2 + (.53)^2 + (-.21)^2 + (-.17)^2}{5}$$

$$= .1127(11.3\%)$$

Total variance explained by F_1 and F_2 = 61.4 per cent

The Model

If there are n variables then a full rank model is given by

$$x_i = a_{i1}f_1 + a_{i2}f_2 + - + a_{ik}f_k + \ldots a_{in}f_n$$

Where

f_k is the kth common factor, and

coefficients a_{i1}, a_{i2}, a_{in} are loadings of ith variate on the n factors.

A more commonly employed model is given by

$$x_i = a_{i1}f_1 + a_{i2}f_2 + \ldots\ a_{ik}f_k + \ldots a_{im}f_m + u_i$$

where ($m < n$), that is, fewer factors than variables, and m is the specified number of factors and u_i is the random variation unique to the original (observable) variable x_i.

If we consider an individual score value of x_{ij} of ith variable on j^{th} factor, we have the following expression.

$$x_{ij} = a_{i1}f_{1j} + a_{i2}f_{2j} + \ldots .a_{ik}f_{kj} + \ldots .\ a_{im}f_{mj} + e_{ij}$$

Because each f has unit variance (standardised) and the contribution of each factor to the variation x_i is given by the square of the regression weight for predicting the variable (this weight is the loading of the variable I on the factor a_{ik} k). The sum of the factor loadings will give the proportion of variance of variable I and is called communality.

$$\text{Communality} = h_i^2 = \sum_{k=1}^{m} a_{ik}^2$$

$$= \text{Squared multiple correlation of the variable } x_i$$

Now, uniqueness of variable = $u_i^2 = 1 - h_i^2$

Total variable variance = common variance + unique variance

$$1 = h_i^2 + u_i^2$$

$$u_i^2 = s_i^2 + e_i^2 \ldots (s_i = \text{specific variance})$$

Since each variable is associated with an error (e_i), the reliability of a variable is,

$$r_{ii} = 1 + e_i^2$$

$$\therefore \quad \text{reliability}\, r_{ii} = h_i^2 + s_i^2$$

The factor analysis model can now be written as,

$$x_{ij} = a_{i1}f_{1j} + a_{i2}f_{2j} + --- + a_{ik}f_{kj} + ..a_{im}f_{mj} + s_{ij} + e_{ij}$$

Where

s_{ij} = specific portion of variance of x_{ij}, and

e_{ij} error portion of the variance

Factor loadings range from –1.00 to +1.00 through 0. They are interpreted similar to correlations between variables and the factors. Factor scores are composite variables that represent the status of individuals on factor dimensions. In other words, they are the measurements of the factor, defined as weighted combinations of several original variables. Alternatively, common factor and unique factor can be redefined in the following way: factors that are involved in the creation of more than one observed variable are called common factors and those that are used in creating only one observed variable are called unique factors. The square of the factor loadings (h^2) for that variable (or the square of the correlation between the variable and the common factor) is referred to as the communality and ($1 - h^2$) is known as the uniqueness component. If m factors are extracted from m variables (that is, $m \times m$ matrix of variances and covariances), then communalities are equal to the original variances. However, if we extract fewer number of factors, the communalities will be less than the original variances. These communalities provide an index to the efficiency of the reduced set of factors.

Assumptions

Assumptions underlying factor analyses are as follows:

1. *Postulate of factorial causation:* This imposes a particular causal order on the data—that observed variables are linear combinations of some underlying causal variables.
2. *Postulate of parsimony:* The principle of parsimony leads to a unique conclusion where there are infinite number of factors models possible, but there is only one particular configuration of factor loadings that is consistent with the one common factor model.

Methods of Factor Analysis

methods of factor analysis

There are two methods: R-mode which uses inter correlation matrix of variables as input and Q-mode which uses a matrix of similarity as input. Only R-mode methods are amenable for statistical analysis.

Most of the factor methods operate by extracting the eigenvalues and eigen vectors from a square matrix. Many factor methods have been developed. The widely used among these are R-mode and Q-mode techniques. The R-mode technique considers the interrelations between variables, and operates by extracting the eigen values and eigen vectors from a covariance or correlation matrix whereas Q-mode analysis extracts the eigen values and eigen vectors from a matrix of similarities between all possible pairs of objects. R-mode techniques are statistical procedures but Q-mode procedures focus on the similarities between individuals in the data set, and are not usually amenable to statistical analysis (Kline 1994).

In any factor analysis exercise, four steps are generally involved. They are:

(i) Preparation of a relevant correlation matrix to be used as input for the software used for extraction of factors
(ii) Extraction of initial factors
(iii) Rotation of initial set of factors to a terminal solution
(iv) Interpretation of the rotated factor solution

Generally, a large number of solutions (set of factors) are possible. A technique of extraction of factors gives only a feasible solution (like the initial solution in a linear programming technique). Therefore, there is a need to obtain the best statistical solution starting from this initial feasible solution. This is precisely what is done in rotation of factors. Usually, the second and third steps are performed by the computer. We shall now look into the details of the last three steps.

methods of extracting factors

These are: Principle component analysis (PCA), maximum likelihood method, alpha factoring, image factoring and least squares method. PCA is the most widely used one.

Extraction of initial factors Many methods of extracting factors have been developed. Some of them are listed below:

(a) Principal component analysis
(b) Maximum likelihood method (or canonical factoring)
(c) Alpha factoring
(d) Image factoring
(e) Least squares method

Some restrictions are imposed while obtaining the initial factors. They are: (i) there are p common factors, (ii) underlying factors are orthogonal, and (iii) the first factor contributes to as much variation as possible, the second factor accounts for as much of the residual variance left unexplained by the first factor, the third factor accounts for as much of the residual variance left unexplained by the first two factors, and so on. Here, only the widely used principal component analysis for extracting initial factors is discussed.

Principal component analysis: Principal component analysis (PCA) yields a mathematically unique solution of a factor problem. This method extracts the maximum amount of variance accounted for by a minimum number of factors. The factors are nothing but the eigen vectors of the variance-covariance or correlation matrix.

principle component analysis (PCA)
This is a mathematical manipulation. It reveals how several measures of a domain can be combined to produce maximum discrimination among individuals along a single dimension and that several dimension are needed to define the domain under investigation.

Suppose there are n original variables, PCA linearly transforms n original variables into m new variables, where the new variable is a linear combination of the old ones. For example, if $X_1, X_2, \ldots, X_n$ are the original variables, they are transformed to factors $Y_1, Y_2, \ldots, Y_m$.

$$Y_1 = a_1X_1 + a_2X_2 + \ldots + a_nX_n$$
$$Y_2 = b_1X_1 + b_2X_2 + \ldots + b_nX_n$$
$$Y_m = m_1X_1 + m_2X_2 + \ldots + m_nX_n$$

$$\begin{array}{lllll} & Y_1 & Y_2 & Y_3 & Y_m \\ X_1 = & a_1 & b_1 & c_1 & \ldots\ldots m_1 \\ X_2 = & a_2 & b_2 & c_2 & \ldots\ldots m_2 \\ \cdot\cdot & \cdot\cdot & \cdot\cdot & \cdot\cdot & \cdot\cdot \\ \cdot\cdot & \cdot\cdot & \cdot\cdot & \cdot\cdot & \cdot\cdot \\ X_n = & a_n & b_n & c_n & \ldots\ldots m_n \end{array}$$

and so on, where a's are the elements of the first eigen vector and b's are the elements of the second eigen vector, and so on.

The values $a_1, a_2, \ldots, a_n$ are the loadings of the original variables on the first factor. The vector $(a_1, a_2, \ldots, a_n)$ is called the eigen vector. The eigen value of the first eigen vector is Σa_i^2 and represents the variance explained by the first factor. The solution of factor analysis gives factors (eigen vectors) arranged from 1 to m, in a decreasing order of eigen values.

$$\text{Percentage variance accounted by the factor } j = \frac{\text{Eigen value of } j}{\sum_i (\text{Eigen value of } i)}$$

When correlation matrix is used as input,

$$\text{Percentage variance accounted by the factor } j = \frac{\text{Eigen value of } j}{\text{Number of variables}}$$

It is to be noted that the correlation between any two new variables will be zero (the new variables will be orthogonal to each other). The elements of the eigen vectors are termed as principal component loadings. With respect to factor analysis, these are known as factor loadings. The loadings of a variable on a factor (factor loading) is a simple correlation between the two. The eigen vectors and roots are derived by an iterative process.

Strictly speaking, PCA is not a statistical procedure but a mathematical manipulation. However, it assumes some characteristics of statistical procedures when decisions are made to discard some new variables that are inconsequentially small. In this technique, like some other statistical techniques, utility is judged by performance and not by theoretical considerations. This procedure, called principal component analysis, defines the factor or basic dimension two variables measure in common. If a third variable is included, the measure space is three dimensional, and as more and more variables are added the measure space becomes multidimensional. Thus, principal component analysis reveals how several measures of a domain can be combined to produce maximum discrimination among individuals along a single dimension. But it often reveals several independent dimensions are required to adequately define the domain under investigation.

rotation of factors
The factors are rotated such that the factor loadings change and can be interpreted in a meaningful way in a substantive sense.

Rotation of factors: Most of the factor analytic methods produce results in a form that is difficult or impossible to interpret. In many cases, even though factor analysis reduces the dimensionality of a problem to a great extent, the meaning of factors may be difficult to deduce. This may be the result of some extraneous factors (orthogonal axes). By rotating the factors, it is possible to find a better position for them, so that a more meaningful and interpretable result can be obtained. A variety of rotational procedures are available. Some of them are as follows:

(1) Kaiser's Varimax rotation
(2) Oblique rotation
(3) Quartimax rotation
(4) Equimax rotation

Rotation does not improve the degree of fit between the data and the factor structure but attempts a possible 'simplification'. A simple example will illustrate this point.

Consider part of a two-factor solution depicted in the Fig. 18.5.

Fig. 18.5 Factor rotation

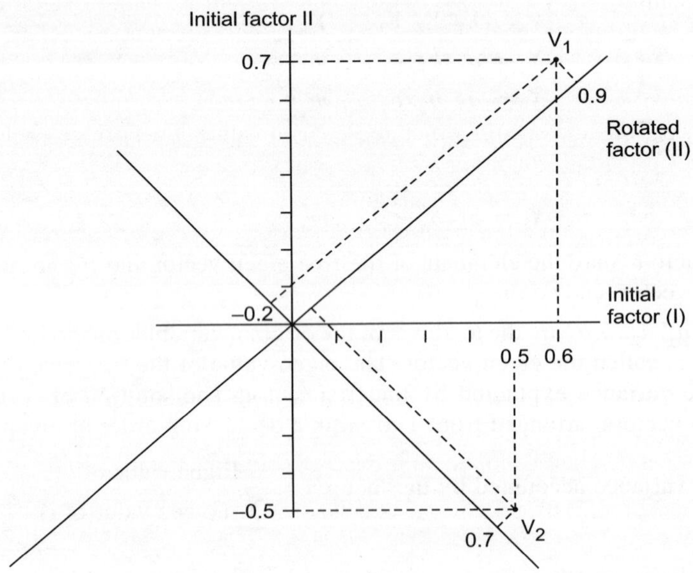

Two variables V_1 and V_2 are loaded on the factors (axes) as follows:

Loadings before rotation

	Factor I	Factor II
V_1	0.6	0.7
V_2	0.5	-0.5

Loadings after rotation

	Factor I	Factor II
V_1	-0.2	0.9
V_2	0.7	0.1

Variance explained before rotation

$$V_1 = 0.7^2 + 0.6^2 = 0.85$$

$$V_2 = 0.5^2 + 0.5^2 = 0.50$$

Variance explained after rotation

$$V_1 = -0.2^2 + 0.9^2 = 0.85$$

$$V_2 = 0.7^2 + 0.1^2 = 0.50$$

It is to be noted that (i) variance explained has remained the same, (ii) factor loading has changed, and (iii) new factor loading is easier to interpret. V_1 belongs to Factor II and V_2

belongs to Factor I. This could not be interpreted from the unrotated solution. For a more detailed explanation refer Cooley (1971), Kerlinger (1986), and Tacq (1999).

Problems encountered in factor analysis: Factor analysis involves a successive partitioning out of variance associated with successive factors. Determining the number of factors that should be extracted is very difficult.

One frequently used procedure is factoring the original correlation to determine the number of factors for which the sum of squares of loadings for all variables on each factor exceeds 1.0 separately (Kaiser Criterion). This is an eigen value specification, which sets a minimum. A factor explains at least the amount of variance that a truly independent variable could contribute (then each variable would be a factor).

Another meaningful way is to look for substantive significance by deciding on the minimum contribution a factor should make (say, 5 per cent or 10 per cent).

Scree test is employed in which the eigen values plotted against the factors can be used. This test employs the plot in the order of extraction of the factors and the eigen values sharply level off. All factors beyond the one for which these eigen values level off are excluded from consideration. (Refer Cattel and Vogelman, 1977)

Factors are conceived as primary dimensions of individual differences. Desirable properties of a good factor transformation include (i) parsimony, (ii) orthogonality or at least relative independence, and (iii) psychological or conceptual meaningfulness.

Scope of factor analysis: Factor analysis procedures can be employed to:

(i) Scale a set of responses that sample a particular sociological or psychological domain.
(ii) Reduce the dimensionality of a set of variables by taking advantage of their inter-correlations.
(iii) Identify fundamental and meaningful dimensions of a multivariate domain.

However, factor analysis need not be confined to exploring the underliysing dimensions of the data. It can be used to test specific hypotheses about the structure of a data set. When used for this purpose, it is referred to as confirmatory factor analysis. Statistical tests can be used to determine if the data being analysed are consistent with the imposed constraints reflected by the hypotheses or, whether the data confirm the substantively generated model (see Tacq 1999).

confirmatory factor analysis (CFA)

This is a factor analysis procedure to test the hypothesis regarding how well the data fits a specified pattern of factor loadings. CFA works best when the results of a prior exploratory factor analysis are available.

Interpretation of factors Interpretations of a set of factors with various loadings are a subjective issue. The primary factor loadings provide a picture of the correlations to be expected between the composite factor variates and the original variables, and the primary-factor cosine matrix provides an indication of the degree and nature of correlations to be expected among the several factor scores. Objectives of the investigation may necessitate oblique primary structure in some cases (especially when a multidimensional correlated variable system is under study) or an oblique reference structure (when the objective is to develop a composite measure or index from a correlated system). A problem with oblique primary structure is that all variables tend to project substantially on all factors. In these situations, source of higher variation within a factor matrix may lead to an acceptable factor structure (for details, see Overall and Klett, 1972).

Extensions of basic factor analysis models One relatively new development that has taken place in the factoring procedure is **confirmatory factor analysis**. In confirmatory factor analysis hypotheses about how well the data fits certain specified patterns of factor loadings is tested. Exploratory factor analysis is used to make sense of a data set as to how many factors are there and what they are. Exploratory factor analysis can be considered as a technique for data reduction. In confirmatory factor analysis hypotheses about how well a data fits certain specified pattern of factor loadings is tested. These patterns may include the number and nature of factors corresponding to prior theoretical notions. Also, complex hypotheses, like equality of factor matrices across populations can be tested. In confirmatory factor analysis one may know the measures and propositions related to the measures (Kline, 1994).

Parameters in exploratory factor analysis are estimated using ordinary least squares (OLS). The solution minimises the sum of squared errors. In confirmatory factor analysis, the parameters (factor pattern, factor correlation, and uniqueness) are typically estimated by maximum likelihood (ML). ML estimates are preferred because they are consistent and efficient and allow statistical tests of hypothesis, which OLS does not. The solution is deemed to be obtained in confirmatory factor analysis when a single best-fitting solution is obtained. In order to get this, the researcher has to specify the number of factors to solve for. The programme starts estimating the elements of the factor pattern and arrives at the solution when the expected correlation is equal to the factor loadings. It is, therefore, necessary to identify the problem (how many factors are to be solved and tested) before using ML to estimate the parameters. Confirmatory factor analysis works best when the researcher has the measures that have been carefully developed and have been subjected to prior exploratory factor analysis. (http://luna.cas.usf.edu). In confirmatory factor analysis, all common factors are assumed to be uncorrelated; however, some unique factors may be correlated, an observed variable may not have a unique factor associated with it, and the observed variables are affected only by some of the common factors. An illustration of confirmatory factor analysis carried out in actual research is presented in Annexure 18.1.

One other important development of factor analysis is in using two or more factor loading solutions to extract a fixed pattern or test the congruence of factor extractions between original factor structure and subsequent extractions (especially in causal analysis, see Goldberger and Duncan, 1973). These methods may be useful in testing the validity of factor solutions when factor analysis has been carried out on split-half sample and cross-validated with factor extractions from the other half.

Factor analysis for prediction Factor analysis can sometimes be used in multiple regression and other analyses where the predictors are both numerous and highly correlated. If the predictors are first factor-analysed and the criterion variable is regressed on the full set of factor scores, R^2 will be identical to that obtained from the usual multiple regression analysis.

Factor analysis with non-interval data Although factor analysis is typically applied to interval-scaled data, some analysts have employed dichotomous data or mixtures of interval scaled and dichotomous variables. In situations where the data is nominal-scaled, latent-structure analysis may be employed (for an excellent introduction to the method, refer Lazarsfeld and Henry, (1968).

Example In a study of technology transfer, the following variables were considered and the scores for these variables were obtained by using a questionnaire in 73 firms.

VARIABLE	SYMBOL
1) Technological experience of the organisation	TECHEXPR
2) Familiarity with the transferred technology	FAMITECH
3) Customer focus in technology transfer	CUSTFOCS
4) Investment in R&D	RDINCS
5) Investment in technology transfer process	USERINVO
6) Technological leadership of the organisation	TECHLEAD
7) Extent of technical training adopted in the organisation	EXTETRAI

The table of inter-correlations among these variables are displayed in the Table 18.2. Perform a factor analysis and comment on the factors extracted.

Solution: For the problem given, by using the inter-correlation matrix as an input in the SPSS package and using varimax rotation, the results are obtained in the following outputs.

- Initial Factor Matrix—Factor loading (Table 18.3).

Table 18.2 Data for the Problem

Inter correlation among variables

1	1.000						
2	0.886	1.000					
3	0.502	0.688	1.000				
4	0.341	0.501	0.456	1.000			
5	0.175	0.411	0.828	0.422	1.000		
6	0.153	0.322	0.308	0.320	0.124	1.000	
7	0.081	0.150	0.446	0.718	0.233	0.292	1.000

Table 18.3 SPSS Output; Factor Analysis—Initial Factor Matrix (Factor Loading)

	Factor 1	*Factor 2*	*Factor 3*
TECHEXPR	0.67194	–0.61594	0.29005
FAMITECH	0.83803	–0.48370	0.17259
CUSTFOCS	0.88588	–0.04354	0.35566
RDINVS	0.75645	0.40690	0.17076
USERINVO	0.68112	0.06652	–0.68141
TECHLEAD	0.45475	0.23884	0.50125
EXTETRAI	0.56402	0.70223	0.14635

- Initial statistics (Table 18.4).
- Rotated Factor Matrix (Final)—Factor loadings (Table 18.5).
- Final statistics (Table 18.6).
- Reproduced correlation matrix communalities and residuals (Table 18.7).

The output are now explained.

The most important output of factor analysis is the final rotated matrix of factors, which displays the factor loading (Table 18.5) while the input matrix (Table 18.2) contains simple pairwise inter-correlations among variables. The factor variable correlations (Table 18.5) are derived by the use of the principal component analysis on the input matrix of correlations.

For example, 0.94648 is the correlation between the factor 1 and variable 'technical experience' and 0.95490 is the correlation between factor 3 and variable 'user involvement'. These correlations are called factor loadings. An examination of Table 18.5 shows that the variables TECHEXPR and FAMITECH load heavily on factor 1; variables RDINVS, TECHLEAD, and EXTETRAI load heavily on factor 2 and CUST FOC and USERINVOL load heavily on factor 3.

Table 18.4 SPSS Output; Factor Analysis—Initial Statistics

Analysis Number 1 Matrix input

Extraction 1 for Analysis 1, Principal—components Analysis (PC)

Initial Statistics:

Variable	*Communality*	*	*Factor*	*Eigen value*	*Pct of Var*	*Cum Pct*
TECHEXPR	1.00000	*	1	3.49965	50.0	50.0
FAMITECH	1.00000	*	2	1.33541	19.1	69.1
CUSTFOCS	1.00000	*	3	1.00657	14.4	83.5
RDINVS	1.00000	*	4	0.77001	11.0	94.5
USERINVO	1.00000	*	5	0.31930	4.6	99.0
TECHLEAD	1.00000	*	6	0.06459	0.9	99.9
EXTETRAI	1.00000	*	7	0.0047	0.1	100.0

Table 18.5 SPSS Output; Factor Analysis—Rotated Factor Matrix (Final) Factor loadings

	FACTOR 1	*FACTOR 2*	*FACTOR 3*
TECHEXPR	0.94648	0.07647	0.11549
FAMITECH	0.90731	0.20343	0.31850
CUSTFOCS	0.42685	0.28576	0.80581
RDINVS	0.22010	0.77526	0.34276
USERINVO	0.10711	0.09683	0.95490
TECHLEAD	0.28246	0.64982	-0.11426
EXTETRAI	-0.11468	0.86341	0.27210

Table 18.6 SPSS Output; Factor Analysis—Final Statistics

Variable	*Communality*	*	*Factor*	*Eigen value*	*Pct of Var*	*Cum Pct*
TECHEXPR	0.91501	*	1	3.49965	50.0	50.0
FAMITECH	0.96605	*	2	1.33541	19.1	69.1
CUSTFOCS	0.91318	*	3	1.00657	14.4	83.5
RDINVS	0.76695	*				
USERINVO	0.93267	*				
TECHLEAD	0.51510	*				
EXTETRAI	0.83267	*				

Table 18.7 SPSS Output; Factor Analysis—Reproduced Correlation Matrix Communalities and Residuals

TECHEXPR	*FAMITECH*	*CUSTFOCS*	*RDINVS*	*USERINVO*	
TECHEXPR	.91501*	–.02510	–.01692	.03381	–.0440
FAMITECH	.91110	.96605*	–.01407	.03442	–.0100
CUSTFOCS	.51892	.70207	.91318*	–.13568	–.0148
RDINVS	.30719	.46658	.59168	.76695*	–.0039
USERINVO	.21906	.42102	.84285	.42594	.9326
TECHLEAD	.30384	.35208	.21418	.52678	–.0159
EXTETRAI	–.01109	.15826	.41703	.73739	.3311

	TECHLEAD	EXTETRAI
TECHEXPR	–.15084	.09209
FAMITECH	–.30084	–.00826
CUSTFOCS	.09382	.02897
RDINVS	–.20678	–.01939
USERINVO	.13993	–.09815
TECHLEAD	.51510*	–.20557
EXTETRAI	.49757	.83267*

The lower left triangle contains the reproduced correlations matrix the diagonal communalities; and the upper right triangle, residuals between the observed correlations and the reproduced correlations.

There are 8 (38.0 per cent) residuals (above diagonal) that are > 0.05.

The square of any correlation (loading) indicates the proportion of variance of the variable accounted for by the factor, thus:

$$(0.07647)^2 = .00585$$

$$(0.20343)^2 = .04138$$

$$(0.28576)^2 = .08166$$

$$(0.77526)^2 = .60103$$
$$(0.09683)^2 = .00094$$
$$(0.64982)^2 = .42227$$
$$(0.86341)^2 = .54749$$

These are proportions of variance in variables TECHEXPR to EXTTRAI, accounted for by the factor 2.

The substantive interpretation of the factors involves the identification of the constructs that underlie the variables in a particular factor. The principal component analysis only reduces the data to achieve parsimony of variable, but may not provide the best solution from the interpretive point of view. This will be the task of the researcher. The main question is whether the variables grouped into a factor have something in common.

In our example (Table 18.5) factor I includes technical experience and familiarity of technology. From the technology transfer point of view, these two variablcs havc similar cxpcricncc in technology and, therefore, are from a theoretical standpoint, acceptable as a group and the factor could be termed as technology preparedness.

R&D investment, technological leadership, and technical training point to a focus on technology management through investments in both R&D and human resources and a commitment to technology through the managerial objective. The factor is termed technology management.

The third factor includes customer focus and user involvement in technology transfer, which clearly shows customer (market) orientation. The factor could be named Customer Orientation.

Estimated correlations and communalities and residuals If we compute the correlations between the variables using the factor loadings, we would get an estimate of the original correlations. For example (from Table 18.5), assume estimated correlation between TECHEXPR and FAMITECH (say Γ12), multiply corresponding factor loadings on each factor, then in summing we get,

$$\Gamma_{12} = 0.94684 \times 0.90731 + 0.07647 \times 0.20343 + 0.11549 \times 0.31850 = 0.9110$$

which is value shown in column 1 and row 2 of Table 18.7. This, as can be seen, will not be exactly the same as the original correlation coefficient but close enough to it (0.886). In general,

$$\Gamma_{\text{ij}} = \sum_{k=1}^{m} L_{ik} . L_{jk}$$

Where L stands for loading and only the m factors are used.

The communalities are the proportions of variance of the variables extracted by their factors. h_j^2 is the communality for variable j

$$h_j^2 = \sum_{k=1}^{m} L_{jk}^2$$

and in our example; $\text{hTECHEXPR}^2 = 0.94648^2 + 0.07647^2 + 0.11549^2 = 0.91501$, which is shown in the first row on the diagonal of the matrix in Table 18.7. From an observation of the Table 18.7, we can see the best captured variable is FAMITECH ($h^2 = 0.96605$) and the poorest ones are TECHLEAD ($h^2 = 0.5151$) and RD INV ($h^2 = 0.76695$).

The right hand upper triangle of the matrix gives the residuals or differences between actual and estimated correlations. Consider, for example, the pair 'FAMITECH and CUSTFOCS'. Original correlation is 0.6880; estimated correlation = 0.70207 (refer to Table 18.2 and Table 18.7), and Residual = (0.6880–0.70207) = –0.0147 (Table 18.7, II row, III column, Residual = 0.0147).

One of the important uses of reproduced correlations and residuals is that if there are too many residuals that are greater than 0.05, the factor model does not fit the data and it should be reconsidered because the residuals show how well the model fits the data.

Table 18.6 gives details of communalities eigen values and percentage variance are explained.

The first factor accounts for 50 per cent of the variance, the second 19.1 per cent, and the third 14.4 per cent and in all the three-factor solution accounts for 83.5 per cent of the total variance. This percentage generally helps determine how many factors we should go in for. We can use a criterion on a first approximation of 10 per cent or less of variance, explained by adding a factor. But, it is better to use Kaiser's criterion (Harmon, 1967 and SPSS PC+ Manual, 1990). The output uses Kaiser's criterion to extract three factors.

Rotation of factor axis Table 18.3 shows a factor solution that is unrotated. It is to be noted that orthogonal rotation of factor axes is only to facilitate substantive interpretation of factors. Orthogonal rotation does not alter the communality of each variable (except for rounding errors) and the total variance explained by the factors is the same. Only the loadings change and similar variables tend to be grouped together under a factor.

Further, in the first factor all the loading will be positive and substantial. In the other factors they become bipolar. In Table 18.3 for factor 2, the first three variables are negatively loaded and the last four positively loaded. In factor 3, the third and fifth are negatively loaded and the remaining are positively loaded. This may happen because certain variables in a group may be uncorrelated with one another. This would be against the principle of grouping variables having similar characteristics. One way of achieving this similarity is to rotate the factor axes such that (i) each variable exhibits at least one non-significant loading, (ii) for each pair of factors there should be several non-significant loadings in one but significant on the other, and (iii) for every pair of factors there should only be a small fraction of significant loadings on both. This is precisely what has been done so that the rotated final Factor Matrix is obtained as in Table 18.5.

MULTIDIMENSIONAL SCALING (MDS)

Introduction

When measuring a single predetermined attribute, characteristic, property, or opinion, uni-dimensional scaling techniques, as dealt with in Chapter 10, are adequate. Uni-dimensional scaling techniques are inappropriate when a researcher has to measure or understand difficult to measure complex constructs such as technological transformation, management competencies, and so on, which have multidimensional attributes or characteristics. Further, the same stimulus object can be perceived and cognitively mapped differently by different individuals and ascribe different properties to it. Thus, a multidimensional approach to scaling becomes necessary. In MDS, as against uni-dimensional scaling, the dimensions of a construct (attributes) are not predefined by the researcher, but originate from the scalers. The major objectives of MDS are to determine (i) what dimensions (attributes or characteristics) scalers employ when judging a stimulus object (construct), (ii), how many dimensions are employed, (iii) the relative importance of the stimulus objects and how they are perceptually related.

multidimensional scaling (MDS)
This is a scaling technique which is a mathematical procedure using similarity (or dissimilarity) metric or non metric measures of a stimulus object (construct). It determines what objects the scalers employ and how many dimensions are employed (in other words locating spatially multidimensional points given the distances between every pair of points).

Multidimensional scaling (MDS) is a powerful mathematical procedure that can systematise data by representing the similarities of objects spatially as in a map (Schiffman et al, 1981). In multidimensional scaling models, the existence of an underlying multidimensional space is assumed. This term describes a set of techniques that deal with property space in a more general way than does the semantic differential. With multidimensional scaling, it is possible to scale objects, individuals, or both, with a minimum of information.

Multidimensional scaling procedures, which use direct similarity (or dissimilarity) measures as input, have the advantage of being low in experimenter contamination. They do not require *a priori* knowledge of the attributes of the stimuli to be scaled. Rather, they provide a space that reveals dimensions relevant to subjects. Multidimensional scaling is characterised by respondent judgments concerning the degree of similarity of pairs of stimuli on a similarity or distance basis. The scale value assigned to each stimulus pair may be either metric, that is, interval or ratio scaled, or non-metric, that is, nominally or ordinally scaled. In either case, the scale value reflects the psychological similarity (or dissimilarity) of each stimulus pair. And this concept of psychological distance is central to the theory behind multidimensional scaling as a measurement technique.

Multidimensional scaling techniques are commonly used in market segmentation analysis, product life cycle analysis, advertising evaluation, vendor evaluation, test marketing, and attitude measurement.

Fundamentals of MDS

"The problem of multidimensional scaling, broadly stated, is to find 'n' points whose interpoint distances match, in some sense, the experimental dissimilarities of 'n' objects" (Kruskal, 1964).

Instead of dissimilarities, the experimental measurements may be similarities, confusion probabilities, interaction rates between groups, correlation coefficients, or other measures of proximity or dissociation.

measures of proximity
These are similarities, confusion probabilities, interaction rates between groups and correlation coefficients.

In MDS the following terminology is used.

Object	:	A thing or event, for example, an orange.
Stimulus	:	A perceived object, for example, a tasted orange.
Attribute	:	A perceived characteristic of a stimulus, for example, sweet.
Proximity	:	A number that shows the amount of similarity or difference between a pair of stimuli.
Symbol	:	S_{ij}, where i and j stand for stimuli.
Data Matrix	:	Arrangement of data into a table where the first column shows the proximities between stimulus 1 and each of the succeeding stimuli and so on. This matrix is square and symmetric.
Point	:	A position in a space that is an abstract representation of a stimulus.
Dimension	:	A characteristic that serves to define a point in a space; an axis through the space.
Space	:	The set of all potential points defined by a set of dimensions (or axes).
Configuration	:	A particular organisation of a set of points, for example, a map.
Euclidean distance	:	Distance is calculated using the Pythagorean theorem. If A (x_1, x_2) and B (y_1, y_2) are two points in two dimensional space then, distance between A and B is $d_{1,2} = [(x_1 - x_2)^2 + (y_1 - y_2)^2]^{1/2}$

In general, if there are r dimensions, then the Euclidean distance is given by,

$$d_{zj} = \left[\sum_{k=1}^{r} (x_{zk} - x_{jk})^2 \right]^{1/2} \quad \text{if } r = 2, \text{ only two dimensions are involved;}$$

For example, in a two-dimensional space, the Euclidean distance between j and z can be obtained by:

1) Projecting their points on to the axis (1) and squaring.
2) Projecting the points on to the axis (2) and squaring.
3) Taking the square root of the sum of the two squared differences.

It is easy to get these distances between any pair of points working from axis (1) and (2). The problem of MDS is similar to obtaining the axes and their projections given the distances between a number of points in two dimensions. While deriving interpoint distance was easy, deriving the number of dimensions and the configurations (pattern of points) in these dimensions so that the interpoint distances match the ones given initially is difficult. The problem is analogous to metric MDS. When these interpoint distances are ranked, the smallest being 1, next smallest being 2, and so on, then finding the number of dimensions (axes) and the pattern of points, with respect to these axes, such that the original ranks closely match the derived ranks, then the problem is analogous to the non-metric MDS.

The pattern can be rotated, shrunk or elongated, or reflected to match the target (original pattern) but the relative distances of points will not change. (For a more detailed treatment of MDS the reader can refer to the references listed at the end of the chapter.)

Process of MDS

The types of data required are dependent on the area of research. An ideal multidimensional scaling experiment involves gathering four types of data: (a) similarity judgments among all pairs of stimuli, (b) ratings of stimuli on descriptors such as adjectives, (c) objective measures (such as physicochemical parameters) relating to the sensory properties of the stimuli, and (d) information about the subjects (Schiffman, 1981).

Multidimensional scaling (MDS) represents the objects as points in a multidimensional (n) space. The number of dimensions used may be 1 to (n–1), but typically 1 to 5 dimensions are used. Distance between objects created in multidimensional space is based on rank order similarities and is known as stress. The objective of the process is to decide on the fewest dimensions with which the low stress value will be created. Like in factor analysis, the dimension must be named by the researchers.

MDS can be thought of as a process having a variety of procedures to plot stimulus objects as points in a multidimensional geometric perceptual space where dimensions are interpreted as attributes through which stimulus objects are differentiated from each other by the respondents. Depending upon the nature of input and output data, MDS can be classified as doubly metric (both data metric), doubly non-metric (both data non metric), or non-metric (input data metric, output data non-metric). The MDS process consists of three steps, (i) data collection (ii) data analysis, and (iii) data interpretation.

MD-SCAL

This is a computer routine to carry out multidimensional scaling analysis in two stages. First is to transform ordinal input data when used into distance measures and the second is to determine the relationship among stimulus objects. The fewest dimensions with acceptable stress is the solution.

stress

Stress is the ability of distances between the stimulus objects created in an MDS analysis to reflect the original rank order similarities data. Zero stress gives perfect fit.

MDS data collection There are many methods of data collection, but generally two kinds of data are obtained; consonance data and dominance data. In the former, the scalers make judgments on similarities or differences among stimulus objects. These similarities may be perceived or actual. MDS of consonance data results in a geometric map of the stimulus objects, as determined by their distances with reference to the dimensions. Data collection is by paired comparison.

The second type of MDS uses dominance data, which gives the order of the stimulus objects by ranking them. In practice a number of viable alternatives exist for MDS data collection and none is superior to the others for all research needs (Coombs, 1984 and Cox and Cox 2001).

MDS data analysis This is done with the help of computers, using routines like TORSCA, INDSCAL, and M-D-SCAL (Kruskal [1978]; SPSS/PC Package). The procedure is data reduction, consisting of two phases. The first is transforming the ordinal input data when used into distance measures, the second step is to determine the relationship among the stimulus objects. As in factor analysis, the goal of MDS is to achieve parsimony of dimensions to represent the stimulus objects. To assist in determining the proper number of dimensions, an index of stress is computed. Stress is the ability of distances between the objects created in the multidimensional space to reflect the original rank order similarities data. The software provides stress figures ranging from 0 to 10. Zero shows the perfect fit. The number of dimensions range from one less than the number of stimulus objects. The fewest number of dimensions with an acceptable (figure of stress) fit is the preferred solution.

Example In a study of technological transformation process (TTP) the similarities/proximities of the following nine attributes were asked to be rated by 73 company executives. The data obtained was metric data.

1. Changes in manufacturing control
2. Technological changes in adoption
3. Changes in input system
4. Successful indigenous collaborations
5. Manufacturing system performance changes
6. Manufacturing system changes
7. Adoption
8. Adaptation
9. Innovation

The objective was to arrive at a parsimonious representation of the attributes and to find the best number of dimensions to represent it. The data from 73 company executives was subjected to analysis through the M-D-SCAL software package (Krishnaswamy et al., 1997).

Results: In all, five dimensions emerged in the output with the details as shown in Table 18.8.

The stress loadings shown in Table 18.8 indicate the ratio of the sum of squares of the difference between the actual and estimated similarity coefficients over the sum of the squares of actual similarities. The lower the stress, the more appropriate the number of dimensions, that truly generate the coordinate points. Zero stress indicates perfect reproduction of the similarity coefficients. Stress less than 5 per cent is considered excellent. A look at the table shows that any one of these cases (number of dimensions) indicated is a good solution to the specific problem. The solution chosen should finally be corroborated by theoretical considerations.

Table 18.8 Multidimensional Scaling Number of Dimensions and Stress Loadings

Number of dimensions	*Stress loadings*
5	0.008
4	0.004
3	0.01
2	0.009

The results, with respect to each solutions shown in the table, were obtained separately under the headings: (i) final configuration of points in the dimensions, (ii) the Sheperd diagram that shows the scatter of the scale points against the regressed ones, and (iii) the plots against possible combinations of dimensions. The Sheperd diagrams were almost linear, bearing out the low stress factors for all cases.

However, the stress in the case of four dimensions is 0.004, which is half of the next lowest, number of dimension that is five. However, only the cases of four dimension solution and two dimension solution will be discussed here. In the four dimension solution the nine factors are grouped into four dimensions as follows:

MDS dimension 1 includes attributes 1 and 2

MDS dimension 2 includes attributes 3, 5, and 7

MDS dimension 3 includes attributes 4 and 8

MDS dimension 4 includes attributes 6 and 9

Dimension 1 now highlights manufacturing control and technical changes in adoption. This dimension is termed manufacturing system control. Dimension 2 includes changes in the input system, changes in manufacturing system performance, and adoption. This is termed as system adoption and relates to efforts, both in the input as well as in the manufacturing, to achieve a satisfactory degree of adoption. Dimension 3 indicates the attribute's indigenous collaboration and adaptation, which would mean that whatever indigenous collaborations are needed and ultimately obtained are for the purpose of adaptations, that is, modifications to products and their performance. This would be termed as collaboration for adaptation. Finally, the fourth dimension included the attribute's manufacturing system changes and innovation, indicating that innovative tasks are more common to changes in some aspects of the manufacturing system than to changes in products. This fourth dimension is termed as manufacturing innovation.

A two-dimensional solution is also close to theoretical arguments found in literature. Figures 18.6(a) and 18.6(b) shows the plot of DIST and DHAT versus data for 2 dimension(s). The plot of dimension 1 against dimension 2 and the attributes that are considered in this analysis would indicate two clusters, the first with attributes 1, 2, 3, 5, and 7 and second with attributes 4, 6, 8, and 9. The details of the variables against attributes would yield the names of these two dimensions. The first dimension is named as production system changes and the second is named product changes. The former is related more to the manufacturing control system. The latter is related to changes in materials, product performances, indigenous collaborations, and innovative efforts directed to product changes or new products.

Factor Analysis versus Multidimensional Scaling

According to Schiffman (1981), multidimensional scaling differs from factor analysis in the following ways.

Fig. 18.6(a) DIST and DHAT versus data for two dimension(s)

```
            STRESS =     .0094
                      .     .1869.     .7978.    1.4088.    2.0197.    2.6306.
                    -.1186      .4924     1.1033     1.7142     2.3252     2.9361
                    *.****.****.****.****.****.****.****.****.****.****.*
         88.55      ..                                                       ..  88.55
         85.66      ..                                                  X    ..  85.66
         82.76      ..                                                X      ..  82.76
         79.87      ..                                                       ..  79.87
         76.98      ..                                          X            ..  76.98
      S  74.09      ..                                          X            ..  74.09
      H  71.19      ..                                                       ..  71.19
      E  68.30      ..                                         X             ..  68.30
      P  65.41      ..                                         X             ..  65.41
      A  62.52      ..                                    X                  ..  62.52
      R  59.62      ..                                  0X                   ..  59.62
      D  56.73      ..                                  0X                   ..  56.73
         53.84      ..                             X     X                   ..  53.84
         50.95      ..                                                       ..  50.95
         48.05      ..                             X                         ..  48.05
         45.16      ..                         X                             ..  45.16
      D  42.27      ..                                                       ..  42.27
      I  39.38      ..                   X      X                            ..  39.38
      A  36.48      ..                  +X                                   ..  36.48
      G  33.59      ..                  X                                    ..  33.59
      R  30.70      ..                                                       ..  30.70
      A  27.81      ..           X  X                                        ..  27.81
      M  24.91      ..           X0                                          ..  24.91
         22.02      ..           X                                           ..  22.02
         19.13      ..           X                                           ..  19.13
         16.24      ..        0X                                             ..  16.24
         13.34      ..   X                                                   ..  13.34
         10.45      ..                                                       ..  10.45
                    *.****.****.****.****.****.****.****.****.****.****.*
                          .1869.     .7978.    1.4088.    2.0197.    2.6306.
                    -.1186      .4924     1.1033     1.7142     2.3252     2.9361
```

```
CONFIGURATION PLOT DIMENSION 2 (Y-AXIS) VS. DIMENSION 1
(X-AXIS)
test
          .*....*....*....*....*....*....*....*....*....*....*....*....*
  3.000**                                                        **3.000
  2.769**                                                        **2.769
  2.538**                                                        **2.538
  2.308**                                                        **2.308
  2.077**                                                        **2.077
  1.846**                                                        **1.846
  1.615**                                                        **1.615
  1.385**                                                        **1.385
  1.154**                                                        **1.154
   .923**                                                        **.923
   .692**                                                        **.692
   .462**               1                                        **.462
   .231**                               ;  9                     **.231
   .000**--------------------3----0--------6---------------------**.000
  -.231**                    2     7                             **-.231
  -.462**                       5                                **-.462
  -.692**                                                        **-.692
  -.923**                                                        **-.923
 -1.154**                                                        **-1.154
 -1.385**                                                        **-1.385
 -1.615**                                                        **-1.615
 -1.846**                                                        **-1.846
 -2.077**                                                        **-2.077
 -2.308**                                                        **-2.308
 -2.538**                                                        **-2.538
 -2.769**                                                        **-2.769
 -3.000**                                                        **-3.000
          .*....*....*....*....*....*....*....*....*....*....*....*....*
          .  -3.3333. -2.0000. -.6667.  .6667.  2.0000.  3.3333.
     -4.0000  -2.6667  -1.3333   .0000   1.3333   2.6667   4.0000
```

■ **Fig. 18.6(b)** DIST and DHAT versus data for two dimension(s)

Multidimensional scaling refers to a collection of data analysis procedures (not a single procedure), factor analysis refers to a family of procedures used to analyse multivariate data sets, such as various attribute ratings for a number of stimuli.

The multidimensional scaling model is based on distances between points, whereas the factor analysis model is based on the angles between vectors.

- Both models generally use Euclidean space, but multidimensional scaling has an advantage in that it is easier to interpret distances between points than angles between vectors.
- Factor analysis often results in a relatively large number of dimensions, mainly because most procedures are based on the assumption of linear relationships between the variables. This is a severe assumption with regard to perceptual data. The multidimensional scaling approach does not contain this assumption, and the result is that it normally provides more readily interpretable solutions of lower dimensionality.
- Data for multidimensional scaling, when collected by direct judgment of dissimilarities, are least subject to experimenter contamination and most likely to contain relevant structure. Data for factor analysis generally contain scores for each stimulus on a list of attributes that may or may not be relevant.

CLUSTER ANALYSIS

Introduction

clustering analysis
This is the name of a set of classificatory techniques used to assign observations to several groups so that each group is more or less homogeneous and distinct from others.

Cluster analysis is the name given to a bewildering assortment of techniques designed to perform classification by assigning observations to groups so that each group is more or less homogeneous and distinct from others. Given the multivariate nature of data, the researcher is posed with the problem of identifying natural grouping of the objects. Cluster analysis deals with the process of assigning objects to groups so that similarity within and difference among groups is restored. Cluster analysis is a pre-classificatory method, where groups of objects have been formed on the basis of profile resemblance in the data matrix itself. Many of these procedures are relatively simple but are usually not supported by an extensive body of statistical reasoning. Different procedures are available and will generate different solutions to the same data set.

Another way of looking at cluster analysis is to consider that when several variables are positively correlated they form a cluster. When highly correlated they form more tight clusters than when their correlations are lower. The most important principle of cluster analysis is the coefficient of belonging. This coefficient is called the b coefficient and is given by

$$b = \frac{\bar{r}_{ii}}{\bar{r}_{io}}$$

$$= \frac{\text{mean of correlations among variables within the cluster}}{\text{mean of correlations between variables within the cluster to those outside the cluster}}$$

(using the correlation matrix as in factor analysis)

Cluster analysis is performed as follows.

1. The largest off-diagonal element in the correlation matrix (the highest correlation between two variables) gives two variables to form the nucleus of the cluster.
2. Each of the remaining variables is to the cluster in turn and the b coefficient for the cluster with that variable included is calculated.
3. The variable whose inclusion yields the highest b coefficient for the new cluster (of three variables) is added to the cluster.
4. Steps 2 and 3 are repeated for a fourth variable, adding to the cluster the variable that yields the highest b coefficient.
5. Continue adding variables by the above procedure until there is a sharp drop in the b coefficient or until the b coefficient falls below some predetermined value. What constitutes a sharp drop or a minimum acceptable value of b is a matter for the individual investigator to decide. If a loose clustering is satisfactory, a low criterion value for b may be used.
6. When the decision is reached that the first cluster is complete, a new cluster may be started by searching among the variables that have not been clustered for the most highly correlated pair and proceeding as above, being careful not to include already clustered variables in the new cluster.
7. Variables are added to the second cluster until the b coefficient for that cluster becomes too low.
8. Additional clusters may be formed from among the remaining variables until all variables have been placed in one or another cluster or until there is no pair of variables remaining that yields a satisfactory b coefficient, at which point clustering is complete.

The principal difference between cluster analysis and factor analysis is that a variable is assigned to one cluster only whereas in factor analysis the variance of a variable is broken additively and the variable is assigned to several factors (groups). While in a factor analysis the factors are orthogonal, in cluster analysis the cluster will almost always be correlated. Cluster analysis is a technique of synthesis and factor analysis is analytic in the sense of variance. Each technique has its special uses. (Thorndike, 1978)

cluster extraction

This is done on the basis of pair wise measures of proximity or similarity or resemblance. Either distance (Eucledian) type measures or matching-type measures between objects are used.

Extraction

Cluster analysis methods use pairwise measures of proximity, similarity, or resemblance for cluster extraction. The choice of which objects and variables to use in the first place is largely a matter of the researcher's judgment. Distance is a measure of how far apart the objects are, whereas similarity is a measure of how close they are. Generally, these measures are classified into (i) distance-type measures and (ii) matching-type measures.

In distance-type measures, usually the Euclidean measure between points is used. In distance type measures, there is an inherent disadvantage. If variables have different measurement units, then the distance calculations using Euclidean measure vary widely with varying units. This disadvantage is overcome by expressing all variables in standardised form (mean = 0, and standard deviation = 1). The Euclidean measure assumes metric measures of variables and the space of variables is orthogonal, that is, the variables are uncorrelated.

When the researcher has a nominally scaled or categorical data, then it is necessary to employ attribute matching coefficients. Similarity is measured by the extent to which two objects share common attributes. Let us say that, we wish to determine similarities among wrist watch customers. The attributes of the wrist watch are dual shape (square 1, circular 2), finish, (steel 1, plated 2) and letter type (English 1, Roman 2, no letters 3) for three customers the details of preferences are shown in Table 18.9.

Table 18.9 Customer's Preferences

Customer	*Dual shape*	*Finish*	*Letter type*
1	1	2	1
2	2	2	2
3	2	1	2

Matching coefficients indicate number of matches between any two types.

$$s_{ij} = \sum_{c=1}^{p}$$

Where

s_{ij} = similarity between two (customers) objects i and j

c = attribute

p = number of attributes measured

$$m_c = \begin{cases} 1 \text{ if } x_{ic} = x_{jc} \\ 0 \text{ if } x_{ic} \neq x_{jc} \end{cases}$$

$$s_{12} = 0 + 1 + 0 = 1$$

$$s_{13} = 0 + 0 + 0 = 0$$

$$s_{23} = 1 + 0 + 1 = 2$$

weights for dual shape = 2

finish = 2

letter type = 3

These are unweighted similarities and may be dominated by attributes that have very few categories in them. Weighting is usually done by the number of categories in the attribute as follows.

$$s_{ij} = \sum_{c=1}^{p} W_c m_c$$

(W_c = weight for attribute c)

$$s_{12} = 2(0) + 2(1) + 3(0) = 2$$

$$s_{13} = 2(0) + 2(0) + 3(0) = 0$$

$$s_{23} = 2(1) + 2(0) + 3(1) = 5$$

Some of the measures of proximity are squared Euclidean distance, Euclidean distance, city block distance, Chebychevs distance, and cosine or correlation measure.

For any two objects i and j having coordinates x_{ik} and x_{jk} in an n dimensional space (slopes of x_{ik} and y_{ik} in k^{th} characteristics) the Euclidean distance d_{ij} is given by

$$d_{ij} = \left\{ \sum_{k=1}^{n} (x_{ik} - x_{jk})^2 \right\}^{1/2}$$

City block distance is the sum of the distances along the axes. In a two-dimensional case, city block distance from point $x1(2,3)$ to $x2(8,9)$ is given by,

$$\text{City Block Distance} = (8 - 2) + (9 - 3) = 12.$$

In most managerial research, the proximity measure used in cluster analysis is the inter-correlation, as in factor analysis.

Methods of Clustering

Once having decided the measure of similarity coefficient, the researcher may draw upon a variety of clustering programmes, which can be grouped under the following three categories (Green, Tull and Albaum, 1988).

Dimensionalising methods These approaches use principal-components or other factor-analysis methods to find a dimensional representation of points from inter-object association measures. Clusters are then developed based on grouping their component scores.

Nonhierarchial methods These methods, based on the proximity matrix methods, use (a) a sequential threshold to develop clusters one by one by successively determining cluster centres, (b) parallel threshold to develop several clusters simultaneously, and (c) partitioning methods where the clusters are formed on the basis of optimising some overall criterion measure for a given number of clusters.

hierarchical method of clustering
In this each point is started as a cluster at the first level. Two nearest points are placed in a cluster at the second level. This is continued until all points are grouped into single cluster.

Hierarchial methods In these procedures, a hierarchy or tree-like structure is constructed starting from each point as a cluster. At the next level the two closest points are placed in a cluster. At the following level, a third point joins the first two, or else a second two-point cluster is formed, based on various criterion functions for assignment. Eventually, all points are grouped into one large cluster.

A hierarchical algorithm starts with each point as its own cluster and eventually ends up with all points in one undifferentiated cluster. For building up the clusters, there are many grouping rules. Some of them are as follows:

Single linkage or minimum distance This rule finds two points with the shortest Euclidean distance. These are placed in the first cluster. Then the third point with the shortest distance to the members of the cluster (smaller than the two closest un-clustered points) joins this cluster. Otherwise two closest unclustered points are placed in a cluster.

Complete linkage This also starts in a similar way as the single linkage. But the criterion for joining points to clusters or clusters-to-clusters is maximum distance rather than minimum.

Average linkage This rule is similar to the previous rules; however, the distance between two clusters is the average distance from points in the first cluster to the points in the second cluster.

Centroid method The two clusters are joined for which the distance between the two centroids (points with mean values on each clustering variable) is smallest.

Median method This is same as centroid method, except that when two clusters are joined, the centroid of the new cluster is computed giving equal weight to the two component clusters.

Ward's method The two clusters are joined to yield the smallest increase in the overall sum of squared within-cluster distances.

The results of the cluster analysis are presented as a dendrogram, which is the most common method. A dendrogram is a 'tree' that indicates the groups of objects forming at various similarity (distance) levels.

dendrogram
This is a tree like diagram that indicates groups of objects (clusters) at various similarity distance levels.

Reliability

In spite of many attempts to construct procedures for the statistical reliability of clusters, there are no defensible procedures. As a result, these procedures should be used for pre-classification, where the objective is to formulate rather than test categorisations of data. More reliable techniques like discriminant analysis should be employed to get optimal weights for variables after performing cluster analysis. Clustering techniques are useful as systematic procedures for use in factor analysis.

For more detailed discussions on cluster analysis the reader may refer to Tryon and Bailey (1970), Anderberg (1973), Bejinen (1973), and Hartigan (1975).

Example The data matrix shown in Table 18.10 was obtained from a study of potential benefits of using shampoo. Nineteen benefits are shown in three dimensions and are derived from free association techniques using a cluster analysis programme to cluster the 19 benefits. How would you interpret the clusters?

Table 18.10 **Data for the Problem**

Benefit	*Coordinate*		
	1	*2*	*3*
1 Body	–0.768	–0.274	–0.315
2 Fullness	–0.857	–0.249	–0.228
3 Holds	–0.116	–0.489	–0.23
4 Bouncy	–0.113	–0.322	–0.769
5 Notlimp	–0.794	0.058	0.189
6 Manageable	0.541	0.018	0.247
7 Zesty	0.651	–0.229	–0.425
8 Natural	0.088	0.782	–0.168
9 Clean	–0.006	0.381	–0.045
10 Sheen	0.289	0.248	–0.312
11 Curly	0.257	–0.427	–0.178
12 Long	0.386	0.495	–0.433
13 Grooming	0.48	–0.189	0.631
14 Soft	0.007	0.904	–0.216
15 Nice	0.317	–0.217	0.926
16 CombsEa	–0.456	–0.229	0.504
17 Healthy	0.035	–0.344	0.349
18 Alive	0.707	–0.444	–0.129
19 Pretty	0.432	0.52	0.053

Solution: Since the data are coordinate points on a 3-dimensional space we can use a distance measure. The most commonly used squared euclidean measure is chosen to represent the distance (dissimilarity). The problem is solved using the agglomeration hierarchial clustering method and complete linkage method.

Using the SPSS PC+ package on the given data, we obtain:

- Squared Euclidean distance coefficient matrix - (Table 18.11).
- An agglomeration scheduling using complete linkage (Table 18.11).
- Dendogram using complete linkage of the 20 benefits (Figure 18.7).

Table 18.11 SPSS Output; Hierarchical Cluster Analysis -Agglomeration Schedule Using Average Linkage (Between Groups)

	Clusters combined			*Stage cluster 1st appears*		
Stage	*Cluster 1*	*Cluster 2*	*Coefficient*	*Cluster 1*	*Cluster 2*	*Next stage*
1	1	2	0.016646	0	0	11
2	8	14	0.023749	0	0	12
3	3	17	0.057987	0	0	9
4	10	12	0.085059	0	0	10
5	13	15	0.114378	0	0	13
6	7	18	0.136977	0	0	8
7	9	19	0.211229	0	0	10
8	7	11	0.230319	6	0	15
9	3	16	0.268304	3	0	14
10	9	10	0.237475	7	4	12
11	1	5	0.315789	1	0	18
12	8	9	0.332233	2	10	17
13	6	13	0.380234	0	5	14
14	3	6	0.662131	9	13	16
15	4	7	0.768257	0	8	16
16	3	4	1.192721	14	15	17
17	3	8	1.309297	16	12	18
18	1	3	1.649916	11	17	0

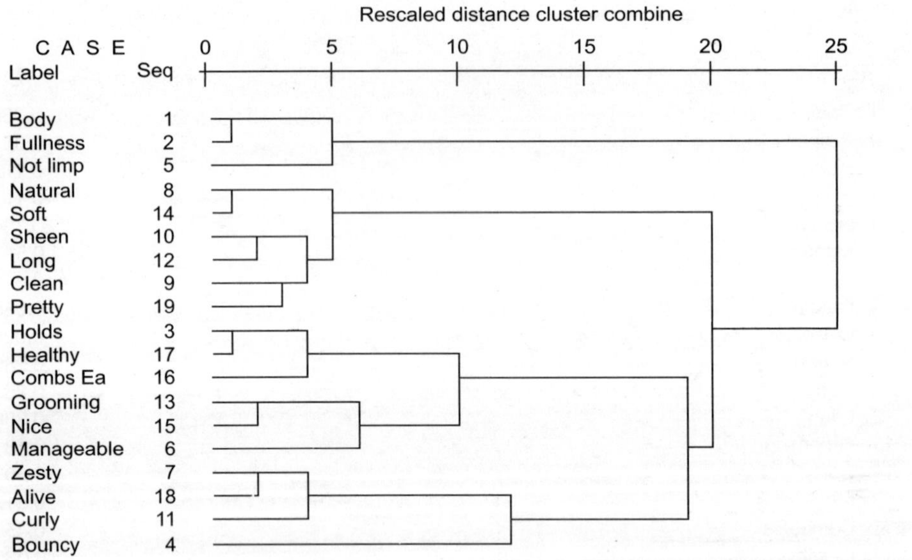

Fig. 18.7 Dendrogram using average linkage (between groups)

The squared Euclidean distance coefficients are obtained as follows. Say, body fullness distance is d_{12} then from the data for 1 and 2,

$$d_{12}^2 = \{0.768-(-0.857)\}^2+\{-0.274-(-0.249)\}^2+\{-0.315-(-0.228)\}^2$$
$$= (+0.089)^2 + (-0.034)^2 + (-0.087)^2$$
$$= .016646$$

which is shown at the top of the squared Euclidean distance coefficient matrix.

The agglomeration schedule (Table 18.11) and dendrogram (Figure 18.7) are derived as follows:

Since the smallest value of distance corresponds to $d_{12} = 0.016646$, the smallest coefficient 0.016646 corresponds to a rescale value of 1 and the largest coefficient 1.64991 corresponding to a rescale value of 25 (values of 1 and 25 are true for any dendrogram obtained on the SPSS package).

The rescaled distance for any cluster can be obtained using the formula,

Rescaled value for cluster X = $RSV_X = \{(C_{max} - C_{min})*R + 1\}$

Where

C stands for distance coefficient from the table and

$R = (25 - 1)/(C_{max} - C_{min})$.

For the dendrogram in the example,

$$R = (25 - 1)/(1.64991 - 0.01664) = 14.694$$

$$\text{RSV}_{7\text{-}11} = \{14.694\ (0.230319 - 0.016646) + 1)$$

$$= 4.13 \text{ (Say 4) [See Dendogram]}$$

$$\text{RSV}_{4\text{-}7} = [14.694\ (0.768257\quad 0.016646) + 1)$$

$$= 12.04 \text{ (Say 12)} \qquad \text{[See Dendrogram]}$$

This kind of clustering affords the researcher the choice of the number of clusters by specifying a rescaled maximum distance (or a Euclidean maximum distance) within a cluster. With the rescale, it is easy to compute the percentage of the maximum distance in the data. Say, at 20 per cent of the maximum distance (dissimilarity) we obtain six clusters.

In a similar manner, the entire dendrogram is generated. From the dendrogram, using a rescaled value of 6 we get six clusters, as shown below.

(1) 1,2, and 5 - (Body, Fullness, Not limp)
(2) 8,9,10,12,14, 19 - (Natural, Soft, Sheen, Long, Clean, Pretty)
(3) 3,16,17 - (Holds, Healthy, Combs easy)
(4) 6,13,15 - (Grooming, Nice, Manageable)
(5) 7,11,18 - (Zesty, Alive, Curly) and
(6) 4 - (Bouncy)

Observation The clusters (1), (2), (4), and (5) seem to have highly compatible characteristics. Cluster (6) could go into cluster (5) from the point of view of similarity. In cluster (3) 'healthy' seems a little out of place, (3) and (4) could be partly combined and are done so at a distance of around 10.

The clusters seem quite reasonable and practically meaningful.

SUMMARY

In this chapter, multivariate analysis techniques of interdependence are dealt with. They are used when the structure of relationships among variables of a construct are internally studied. Three techniques are discussed, namely, factor analysis, multidimensional scaling, and clustering analysis.

In factor analysis, large numbers of variables derived from a survey are analysed. The objective of factor analysis is (i) to determine the latent structure (made up of non-observable natural variables) of a data set obtained, and (ii) to describe the data set parsimoniously using fewer latent variables (factors) than original variables, which tend to be large in surveys. Factor analysis typically uses correlational techniques and extracts the factors one by one, starting with the one that can account for the largest variance of the data set. The subsequent factors are extracted using the same principle, but with the condition that newly extracted factors are orthogonal to the earlier ones. In order to make the description of data set using factors meaningful, a rotation of the factors is made in the multidimensional space. There are many methods of factor analysis. Only the principal component analysis is detailed and a problem is illustrated through computer printouts.

Multidimensional scaling (MDS) is used when measuring an object (stimulus) with multiple attributes or characteristics. MDS is used when a number of subjects rate an object on several attributes. To get a meaningful scaling of the entity on the attributes, MDS first determines (i) what dimensions are used by scalers, (ii) how many dimensions are used, and (iii) the relative importance of the stimulus objects. In MDS (which is a computerised technique), first the ordinal data (that is generally used for MDS) is converted into distance measures and then the relationships are determined. The objective is parsimony (as in factor analysis). An index of stress is used to obtain the proper dimensions. Fewest number of dimensions with an acceptable index of stress is usually the preferred solution.

Cluster analysis is the name of a set of techniques intended to classify a set of observations, in which data is put into groups or clusters, so that the data in each group is more or less homogeneous and distinct from others. The groups are mutually exclusive, that is, one observation finds place only in one group. The groups here have some correlation among themselves. There are a number of techniques available for cluster analysis using Euclidean distance coefficients and complete linkage analysis is illustrated using an example with computer outputs.

ANNEXURE 18.1

Confirmatory Factor Analysis to Test Research Hypothesis (Narasimha Murthy, 1995)

In a study of manufacturing strategy in Indian industrial organisations, the influence of environment on manufacturing strategy was modelled using an appropriate theoretical framework derived from earlier literature. It was considered that three components—supply factor, technology factor, and market factor—influenced the manufacturing strategy of a firm. Further, several variables were grouped under each factor on the basis of earlier research and theory. A hypothesis was formulated to confirm these groupings as follows and tested using confirmatory factor analysis.

Testing of hypothesis H_1

Research hypothesis H_1 and the corresponding null hypothesis are stated below:

H_1: The environmental factors grouped on theoretical basis as supply, market, and technology factors are the same as represented by data.

H_O: Null hypothesis: The environmental factors grouped on theoretical basis as supply, market, and technology factors are not the same as represented by data.

The theoretical groupings of the environmental variables into factors is shown in Exhibit 18.1.

Factors supported by theory		Considered under the factor
1. Supply	1	Suppliers of parts and raw materials (V1)
	2	Suppliers of equipments (V2)
	3	The supply of labour (V3)
2. Market	1	Distributors of products (V4)
	2	Actual users of products (V5)
	3	Competitors for the customers (V6)
3. Technology	1	Keeping up with new technological requirements (V7)
	2	Implementing new technologies to develop and improve new products (V8)

Exhibit 18.1 Details of factors supported by theory

Contd.

A confirmatory factor analysis (Wood C.H., 1991) is carried out using the statistical package LISREL7 to test hypothesis H_1. The decision rule used for this hypothesis is the validity [significance of Goodness of Fit Index (GFI)] of the confirmatory factor analysis.

The LISREL output giving estimates of the factor loadings is given in Table 18.2. The factor loadings of the variables-suppliers of raw materials and parts, suppliers of equipment, and suppliers of labour on the supply factor are 0.816, 0.387, and 0.422, respectively. The loadings of the variables 'distributors', 'actual users of the product', and 'competitors' who are customers on the 'market' factor are 0.741, 0.481, and 0.485, respectively. The loadings of the variables keeping up with new technological requirements and implementing new technologies to develop and improve new products on the technology factor are 0.847 and 0.676, respectively. These loadings are high, indicating a significant result.

Exhibits 18.2 and 18.4 give the results of validity of the factor analysis. The coefficient of determination of X variables is very high (0.998), indicating a good fit. The chi-square test for the goodness of fit is 32.01 at P = 0.015, which is greater than 0.01 for 17 degrees of freedom (degrees of freedom is calculated as ½(p + q)(p + q + 1) – t. Where p + q = number of variables and t = number of parameters estimated. T = (8(factors) + 3(factor covariances) + 8 (error covariances)) = 19)) indicates that the derived correlations and the observed correlations are from the same population and the differences are due to sampling error. Therefore, this also shows a good fit. The residual of

LISEREL ESTIMATES (MAXIMUM LIKELIHOOD)			
	SUP	MKT	TECH
VAR 1	.816	.000	.000
VAR 2	.387	.000	.000
VAR 3	.422	.000	.000
VAR 4	.000	.741	.000
VAR 5	.000	.481	.000
VAR 6	.000	.485	.000
VAR 7	.000	.000	.847
VAR 8	.000	.000	.676

Exhibit 18.2 The factor loadings obtained by using LISREL7

Total Coefficient of Determination for X – Variables is .998	
Chi-square with 17 degrees of freedom	= 32.01 (P = .015)
Goodness of fit index	= 0.904
Adjusted Goodness of fit index	= 0.797
Root mean square residual	= 0.094

Exhibit 18.3 The factor loadings obtained by using LISREL7

T Values for the factor loadings			
	SUP	MKT	TECH
VAR 1	2.828	.000	.000
VAR 2	4.106	.000	.000
VAR 3	2.697	.000	.000
VAR 4	.000	3.805	.000
VAR 5	.000	2.930	.000
VAR 6	.000	4.576	.000
VAR 7	.000	.000	2.730
VAR 8	.000	.000	3.068

Exhibit 18.4 Details of t values obtained

0.094, which is very small, also indicates that confirmatory factor analysis is valid. From the Table 18.4 the *t* values for all the variables are significant, indicating that the factor analysis is valid. Hence, the null Hypothesis H_O is rejected.

Note: In LISREL analysis for confirmatory factory analysis (CFA), the following points may be kept in mind.

1. The input correlation matrix is the data to be analysed.
2. LISREL requires what model to analyse, that is, hypothesised factor loading of variables and the number of factors.
3. The CFA has three matrix parameters programmed:
   (a) LX or Lambda X is the factor pattern matrix. It shows regression coefficients that relates factors (columns) and variables (rows). The factor pattern can be modified to fit any CFA hypothesis.
   (b) PH or Phi is the factor correlation matrix. It shows the correlations of factors with one another.
   (c) TD or Theta-delta is the matrix of uniqueness.

LISREL Output

1. Prints back the matrix supplied by the researcher.
2. Iteration history, indicating how long it took to get the solution or whether there was any problem.
3. Results with measures of goodness of fit along with the coefficient of determination for the variables.

Suggested Readings

- Freund, Rudolph J. and William J. Wilson (1997). *Statistical Methods*, 2nd ed. San Diego: Academic Press.
- Harris, R. J. (2001). *A Primer on Multivariate Statistics*, 3rd ed. Orlando: Academic Press.
- Kline, Paul (1994). *An Easy Guide to Factor Analysis*. London: Routledge.
- Tacq (1999). *Multivariate Analysis Techniques in Social Science Research*. London: Sage.

QUESTIONS AND EXERCISES

1. What is the purpose of factor analysis ? What is variable recovery?
2. What does the table of factor loadings signify? How does it help in arriving at factors? Give an example.
3. How is principal component analysis different from factor analysis? Is 'substantive interpretation' different from statistical interpretation? Why is substantive interpretation held to be central to factor analysis?
4. What is the difference between confirmatory factor analysis and exploratory factor analysis?
5. What is the difference between Q-factor analysis and cluster analysis?
6. How can factor analysis be used with multiple regression? Explain giving an example from research literature.
7. It is seen that factor analysis results can be used in subsequent hypothesis testing. Can you choose two examples from research literature and explain?
8. Compare the methods available for determining the number of factors to be extracted. Are they all subjective methods? If 'yes', why are they so? If 'No', which are objective methods?
9. Can you factor analyse the data in Table 18.10? If your answer is 'No', explain your answer and if your answer is 'Yes', interpret the factors.
10. Use a standard factor analysis package and factor analyse the following correlation matrix. Interpret the results.

	v1	v2	v3	v4	v5	v6	v7	v8	v9
v1	1	0.88	0.44	0.52	0.55	0.29	–0.3	0.32	–0.36
v2		1	0.38	0.44	0.48	0.24	–0.26	0.41	–0.31
v3			1	0.84	0.74	0.44	–0.47	0.24	–0.32
v4				1	0.75	0.46	–0.45	0.25	–0.33
v5					1	0.35	–0.38	0.24	–0.29
v6						1	–0.34	0.67	–0.36
v7							1	–0.4	0.58
v8								1	–0.38
v9									1

11. What are the stages in cluster analysis?
12. How is cluster analysis different from factor analysis?
13. Since both cluster and factor analysis are grouping techniques will there be a difference in result if a particular inter-correlation matrix is used as input in both? Give reasons to explain your answer.
14. Since MDS and cluster analysis use similarity coefficients and inputs, is there any difference between the two? Explain.
15. Identify an example of cluster analysis application to group technology from research literature, say from international journal for production research. Explain the similarity coefficient used. Could factor analysis have been used instead of cluster analysis? If 'Yes' indicate how, if 'No' say why not and draw inferences to the distinctiveness of cluster analysis in certain data situations.
16. How do you decide which method of cluster analysis to use, hierarchical or non-hierarchical? Elucidate through examples from research.
17. Is there a problem of selection of the best number r of clusters? if 'Yes' (as in the case of factors in factor analysis), how is the best selection accomplished?
18. Perform a cluster analysis for the data given in question 12. Compare these results with the factor analysis results and interpret the difference.
19. The intercorrelation matrix of 9 variables is given below.

A	B	C	D	E	F	G	H	I	
A	1								
B	0.04	1							
C	–0.67	0.45	1						
D	–0.4	0.41	0.39	1					
E	–0.54	0.03	0.5	0.06	1				
F	–0.74	–0.4	0.2	0.2	0.36	1			
G	–0.22	–0.44	–0.16	0.11	0.02	0.37	1		
H	–0.75	–0.28	0.15	0.13	0.16	0.57	0.11	1	
I	–0.57	0.16	0.35	0.38	0.39	0.19	0.25	0.57	1

a) Make a cluster analysis. Interpret the clusters.
b) Perform a factor analysis and compare the results with the results of cluster analysis.
c) Obtain a dendogram and interpret it.

20. Why is a path analysis associated with confirmatory factor analysis? Explain.
21. Identify an example of path analysis from research literature and check whether the points given in the text have been explicitly followed. Interpret the paths.

CHAPTER 19

Report Writing

- Introduction
- Pre-writing Considerations
- Format of Reporting
- Briefing
- Rules for Typing or Word Processing

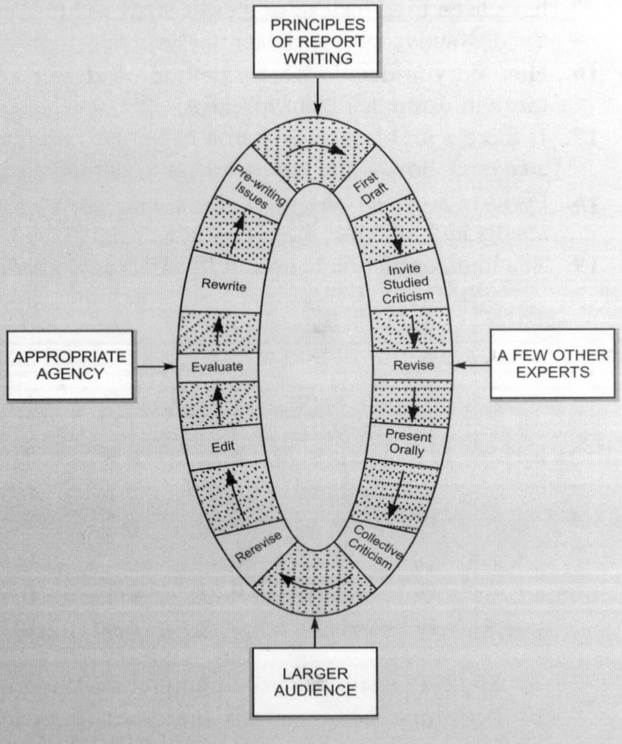

LEARNING OBJECTIVES

Upon completion of this chapter, you will be able to:

- ✓ Differentiate between the various research reporting methods
- ✓ Know the different formats of research reporting
- ✓ Learn the principles of theses writing
- ✓ Learn how to communicate research results in written and oral presentations
- ✓ Understand how to develop a good research report/thesis

INTRODUCTION

Research reports vary in scope and treatment. Each university might set its own format and style of thesis writing for its research students. The funding organisations supporting research may demand a certain way of reporting. The editorial board of each research journal may lay down guidelines for research papers published by them. While there may be minor changes in these, their main intention is to enable the researcher to communicate his ideas and results efficiently to the readers. In order to achieve efficient communication there are certain conventions followed in form and style. In this chapter, issues and matters common to such reporting are discussed. The user, however, is advised to consistently follow whichever format and style he chooses for research reporting throughout the report.

Research reports can be broadly classified into:

classification of research reports
The broad classifications are: Dissertations, research reports to sponsorers, research journal publications and contract research reports.

- Dissertations submitted for obtaining research degrees like M.Sc. and Ph.D. in a university.
- Reports of research submitted to the organisation sponsoring the research (organisational research reports, reports to the Department of Science and Technology, the University Grant Commission, and the Council for Scientific and Industrial Research).
- Publications in the form of research papers in research journals.
- Reports of research to a client organisation (contract research or consultancy research).

In each of the above cases, there is need for some form of acceptance of the report. The university sets up panels of examiners, who are outstanding scientists, to examine the thesis and recommend its acceptance for the award of the degree. In addition, an oral defence, open to public, is arranged. The sponsoring authority or the client organisation will evaluate the research report. The research journals set up referees from among outstanding scientists and peers to rigorously evaluate whether the research can be published.

PRE-WRITING CONSIDERATIONS

Dissertations/Theses

It is a good practice on the part of the student to prepare for writing a thesis. A good starting point is to read some of the standard books on the subject given in the bibliography. While these books treat the formatting and the structure of writing to be observed in detail, they are not very explicit on some of the difficulties faced by the students in composing the thesis.

Some helpful points to be kept in mind while writing the thesis are:

- It is important for the researcher to put himself in the position of a reader. Since the subject matter and the details of the thesis are intimately known to the student he may unconsciously assume the same on the part of the reader, who does not have the benefit of familiarity with the subject matter. This attitude on the part of the writer will create problems concerned with scientific communication in the thesis.

- While preparing drafts, particularly if they are supported by well structured outlines, it is better to put in efforts and care to make the draft as close as possible to the finished product. It is better to avoid the 'to be added later', 'to be modified later' type of writing. This saves a lot of time in the later stages of completion of the thesis.
- While developing a synopsis, when the university wants it as short as three to four pages, it is better to initially develop a longer one, say 10 pages and clip the unimportant portions.
- Footnotes should be given for more important references which are close to the thesis subject matter or from which the researcher has drawn inspiration for his work.

basic issues of reporting
These are: the purpose of the report, to whom addressed and time available for development of the report.

Some basic issues regarding the report have to be considered before writing the report. These issues, however, may not be important in dissertations. These are related to:

- The purpose of the report—What is being communicated must be well understood.
- To whom is the report addressed—The answer to this question will help understanding the background, the needs, and view points of the reader. The report can then be fashioned suitably in a proper style, with adequate elaborations, emphasising the uses which the reader will be most interested in.
- Time available for developing the report. Scope and detail will then be defined accordingly.

Having given consideration to these issues, the researcher must develop an outline of the research report immediately after completing the preliminary analysis of the data. A useful guideline for developing an outline would be to develop a content type heading list that will include chapter headings, section headings, and sub-section headings. Thereafter, under each sub-section, heading phrases or short sentences indicating the sequence of ideas or information units have to be developed keeping in mind "the woods and not the trees". This has to be done in such a way that no major item of planned information or logic is missed. Such misses may occur during the writing phase, unlike in the case where the trees and not the wood are focused upon. In the outline, what to write is mainly determined. During report-writing, how to write is emphasised. Of course there may be additions, modifications, and deletions in the later stages of development of the report.

Style and Composition of the Report

style of reporting
The report should be written in a clear and logical manner in a straight forward simple language. It should convey precise information in a reader friendly manner.

The research report should be written in a clear, logical, and concise manner. The style adopted should be open, straightforward, and dignified; pedantic phraseology, bombastic, flowery, elegant, and folk style language should be avoided. The style should be simple, with short sentences, the main objective explanation and description. Emphasis on such word usage as in essays (humour, proverbs, figures of speech etc.) should be avoided. The writing should be in third person as far as possible, but first person can be sparingly used where the author's personal beliefs and opinions are expressed. In referencing only the last name used should be included, like 'Emory' and not 'C William Emory'. Application to names should be avoided. Abbreviations should be used only after they are spelt out first. There may be some exceptions to this rule.

Figures, charts, and tables should be captioned carefully and concisely and must be numbered serially from the first to the last. Statistics are best presented using (i) semi-tabular presentation (for very small ones no caption is needed), (ii) tabular presentation, and (iii) graphs. Graphs include line graph, area charts, pie charts, and 3D charts.

In presenting quantitative terms, fractions and numbers less than ten should be left out. Generally, in reports, statistical formulae and computations are not presented. Errors of spelling, agreement of the subject with predicate, wrong use of articles, inconsistency in tense should be avoided by revising the manuscript.

The research report should convey precise information shorn of multiplicity of meaning and ambiguity. It should be presented in an organised manner, properly captioned so as to develop the research themes in well-defined sections. The report must be such that the reader can easily understand it. Gunning (1952) discussed this aspect and developed the Fog index, which is a standard of readability.

Principles of Thesis Writing

Based on the authors' experience of guiding management-research students, the following principles of thesis writing have been developed. These would be of considerable help to the student in checking and evaluating him/her own thesis.

principles of thesis writing
There are fifteen principles which will be helpful in developing a thesis. They relate to consistency, connectivity, indentation, highlighting, openness, clarity, ordering, self sufficiency, synthesis and analysis.

Consistency There should be consistency: (i) in the objectives of the research stated, in the introduction, results obtained, and conclusions drawn in the last chapter; (ii) in the location, typing, and format of captions for tables and figures; (iii) in the referencing format employed in the text; (iv) in the structure of each reference under books, reports and journals, in bibliography; and (v) in the indentation used in each chapter.

Connectivity The text of the thesis should not have abrupt and ragged beginnings and endings. Section to section and chapter to chapter transition should be logical. Linking sentences have to be developed. This is complementary to the principle of indentation and helps to keep up continuity in the report.

Indentation The thesis should be indented or cut into meaningful chapters and sections depending upon the structure and content of the various aspects of presentation. This indentation can be tried at the outline stage to enable clear organisation of the material into meaningful groups. This will help in writing the thesis in a modular way.

Continuity The flow of the thoughts and ideas in each section (or sub-section or paragraph if necessary) should be carefully maintained so that it becomes one continuous coherent bit of presentation, suitably linked to the next.

Highlighting It is necessary for the student to emphasise and highlight the major aspects or points that are significant in his work. The minor, less consequential ones should be toned down. This should be followed while introducing the problem, or discussing its usefulness, while observations are made on literature, while presenting results, and asserting contributions. This gives a proper perspective to his work. The most important objective should be dwelt upon in greater detail, likewise the most important result.

Openness Every research has limitations and errors. A tacit appreciation of this is a frank and open approach to putting down the errors and limitation in data, in method, and even in the tools used (of course major errors should not be tolerated, they should be corrected during the study or analysis itself). Inadequacies of sample size and tentativeness or weakness of results should also be stated. Defending these is one thing in science, but deliberately obliterating them is another.

Clarity In a thesis, the student is trying to communicate, and not impress, or confuse the examiner. Simple language, and concise and direct statements should be used. Ambiguous words, phrases, and sentences should be avoided. The most important portions of the thesis, like statement of hypothesis, validation, and assertions of the result, should be particularly monitored for clarity.

Asserting When assertions are made, particularly when they are strong, the student should enunciate the support of earlier research for such assertions or of the facts obtained and of analysis made in the research work. Assertions without support are highly detrimental to scientific approach.

Ordering When discussing objectives, variables, and results, it is necessary that different objectives, variables, and results are ordered in the same way (even if they are chronologically different (in the sense of the students discovering them). This makes the presentation and communication more orderly, and checking by the examiner easy.

Compatibility (Boundedness) When discussing results or presenting conclusions, it is essential that the results are confined to the data or what the techniques can give. In other words, conclusions and inferences must be compatible with the data and techniques of analysis, and must not transgress them. The results are obtained through the tools and techniques of statistics, or otherwise. However, they are not bounded by techniques.

Jargon Every discipline has its own special words, modes of expression, and phraseology. The student would do well to use them, that is, the jargon of the discipline, to let the examiner know of his 'soaking' in the knowledge-area or of his 'immersion', as a scholar in the subject matter.

Elaboration/brevity One of the most difficult things while developing a thesis is to appreciate where or at what point in the thesis the student has to compress a considerable amount of research material, and where there is a need to elaborate. The student should develop discernment in this regard. Elaborate treatment of aspects close to the thesis and concise outlining of the distant ones, and concise treatment of what is already known in his presentation, and elaboration of what is new is indicated by this principle.

Self-sufficiency Whenever tables, graphs, figures, and illustrations are presented in the text, it is desirable to make these as complete as possible, to be read and understood by themselves without the need to look into the text. Details, captions, and legends should ensure this.

Enrichment Usually the researcher collects wider information than is necessary to answer the research questions. After the main objective of the thesis is achieved, the student should exploit the opportunity of enriching his work by presenting by-products and related results from any additional data or information not directly relevant to the objective, but which would add to knowledge. This is especially important if the additional effort required is only marginal. For example, some additional hypothesis not examined critically in the thesis may be enunciated for future work.

Synthesis-analysis-synthesis In writing the thesis, the *sine qua non* is to employ synthetic and analytic approaches in cycles. Get an overview (outline/content) of the thesis (synthesis). Delve into the details and structure the parts (analysis). Then once again get an overview by standing away and looking at the totality (synthesis). Many errors, inadequacies, and incongruencies will surface in such an approach.

FORMAT OF REPORTING

Format of Dissertations

typical format of dissertations

There are many variants. The typical one is preliminary information on problem, introduction, literature review, research design, results, concluding remarks, bibliography, appendix.

The contents of all theses are not uniformly the same. There are many variants and orderings used while presenting research material. However, we will discuss a somewhat typical format. A typical format for a dissertation is displayed in Table 19.1.

Main body of the dissertation The main body of the dissertation will have five major components—introduction, literature review, the research design with details of the research study, and conclusions.

Introduction The introduction should clearly and logically bring out the background of the problem addressed in the research, and how the researcher identified the problem. Any general observation made for the purpose must be outlined. Whether the problem emerged from a review of research literature must be stated. The theoretical and practical importance of the problem should be highlighted, the rationale of the problem should be enunciated, and broad and comprehensive statement of the problem (hypothesis or model) and the scope of research should be given.

The literature review A comprehensive review of the research literature referred to must be made. It must be borne in mind that, for any problem, there may be portions of literature that are

Table 19.1 Format of a Dissertation

1. PRELIMINARY
    - Title
    - Acknowledgment
    - Abstract or synopsis
    - Table of contents
    - List of tables
    - List of figures
2. MAIN BODY OF THE REPORT
    - Introduction
    - Background of the problem
    - Statement of the problem
    - Brief outline of the chapters
3. LITERATURE REVIEW
4. THE RESEARCH DESIGN/METHOD
    - The theoretical framework (variables)
    - Hypothesis/model
    - Instrument for data collection
    - Reliability and validity of the instrument
    - Data Collection
5. RESULTS
    - Pilot study
    - Descriptive analysis
    - Hypothesis testing
    - Model testing
    - Data analysis techniques
    - Tables and figures
6. CONCLUDING REMARKS
    - Summary
    - Support for hypothesis/use of models
    - Contributions
    - Shortcomings
    - Direction for further research
7. BIBLIOGRAPHY
    - Appendix (if appropriate)

Note It must be noted that there may be changes in specific cases.

somewhat distantly or generally relevant. These should be abridged considerably. Some portions of the literature (usually a small portion) are closely related to the dissertation, from the point of view of variables, logic of methodology, and substantive thinking. These should be critically and elaborately dealt with. A good approximation may be 80:20 rule—80 per cent of the literature review must dwell on specifics and 20 per cent on the general.

Development of tables similar to Table 19.2 will be helpful in presenting the relative aspects of several studies. Procedures of natural reconstruction, Papineou's Tree and network theory of models, as discussed by Ryan et al (1992), may be useful in structuring the literature review.

Research design or method This chapter should provide an overview of the design of the research undertaken. It should include the sample of subjects/organisations; a separate section on the instrument/questionnaire, its design and appropriateness; and one on the methods of analysis employed for solving the research problem. If a pilot study is planned to be used, its purpose should also be given in the research design. Schematic/flow charts are particularly suitable for this purpose (see Table 19.3).

This chapter should also give details of the experiments, the treatments in experiments, data collection methods, standard battery of tests used, if any, assumptions in models, and so forth. If a mathematical model or a statistical model is used, a separate section should be dedicated for going into the details and formulation of the model (Table 19.4).

Table 19.2 A Sample Literature Survey

Name	*Control strategy*	*Structure*	*Reference*
ISIS	Constraint-directed reasoning	3-level hierarchy	Fox, 1983
PEPS	Rule based	4-level hierarchy	Robbins, 1985
OPAL	Meta-rules and constraint based analysis	—	Bensana et al, 1986
MASCOT	Meta-rules and constraint based analysis	—	Erschler & Esquirol, 1986
—	Backward chaining	—	Alexander, 1987
OPIS	Opportunistic reasoning	3- level hierarchy	Ow & Smith, 1987
DR	—	—	Brown, 1989
ESCH	—	—	Alpar and Srikanth, 1989
MOPPS	—	—	Walters & Warwick, 1990
IKONMAN	—	—	Wilcox, 1990
ISA	—	—	Bonsignorio & Mazzarello, 1990
KBSS	Forward chaining	Tandem architecture	Kusiak, 1990

Table 19.3 A Sample Research Design

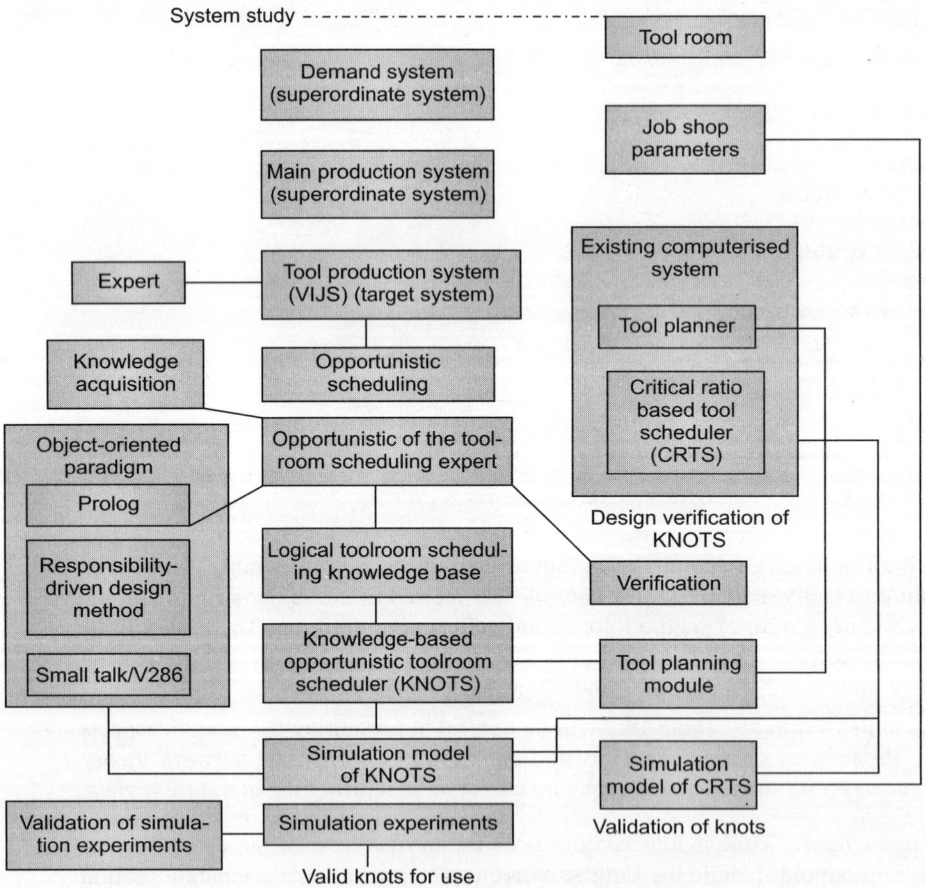

Results In this chapter, the data, the reliability and validity of the results of the statistical analysis are presented, usually in the form of tables, figures, and equations. An open and frank presentation of all results, those that support the hypothesis or indicate the model and those that do not, is a very important requirement of this chapter. Tables should be clear and should be complementary. All redundancy in the data/results presented should be eliminated. Levels of significance of the results should be included in the tables (See Table 19.5). Additional results

Table 19.4 A Sample Model

The complete integer linear goal programming model is summarised below:

Minimise

$$z = p1\sum_i dm_i + p2\sum_j dF_j + p3\sum_j dv_j + p4\sum_i d_i \quad \text{.... objective function} \quad (1)$$

Subject to

$$\sum_j \sum_{kj} \frac{h_{ijkj}}{p_{ij}} Y_{ijkj} + dm_i - Y_i = M_i \quad \text{.... Man-hours} \quad (2)$$

$$\frac{1}{nj}\sum_{kj}\sum_i \frac{Y_{ijkj}}{r_{jkj}} + dF_j - dF_j = DF \quad \text{.... Demand} \quad (3)$$

$$\frac{1}{nj}\sum_{kj} v_{ij}\sum_i \frac{Y_{ijkj}}{r_{jkj}} + dv_j - dv_j = V_j \quad \text{.... Value added} \quad (4)$$

$$Y_i - d_i + d_i = OT_i \quad \text{.... Overtime} \quad (5)$$

$$\sum_i \frac{Y_{ijkj}}{r_{jkj}} - \sum_i \frac{Y_{ijmj}}{r_{jmj}} = 0; kj \neq mj \quad \text{.... Proportionality} \quad (6)$$

$Y_{ijkj} > 0$ and integer

where

Y_{ijkj} = number of sub-assemblies (components) assembled by worker i.
h_{ijk} = hours required by a particular worker 'i' to perform unit k^{th} sub-assembly operation of the jth assembly
p_{ij} = efficiency of worker i working on j^{th} assembly
r_{jkj} = number of sub-assemblies Kj required per assembly j
v_j = value added per assembly
V_j = aspired level of value added
dm = negative deviation on the man hours
dF = positive deviation on the demand
DF = demand for the assemblies
dv = negative deviation on the value added
nj = number of sub-assemblies in j such that Kj = 1,2,3,....nj
kj = number indicating the position of the sub-assembly.

The premptive priority factors are :

P1 : minimise the underutilisation of man hours
P2 : minimise the final assembly inventories
P3 : minimise the deviation from the aspired level of value added
P4 : minimise excess of overtime above the desired value

Table 19.5 Sample Results

Correlation between superior's score and superior's rating

Sl. No.	*Sample size*	*Variables*	*r' value*	*Significance level*
1	29	ASCSUP & ARASUP	0.43197	0.05
2	29	HSCSUP&HRASUP	0.27153	0.05

beyond what was originally contemplated, should also be given to enrich the value of the dissertation.

Concluding remarks The chapter on concluding remarks should discuss the results obtained in the earlier sections, as well as their usefulness and implications. It may be worthwhile to give a brief summary of the dissertation before presenting the contributions. The weaknesses in the research should be frankly depicted. The future directions of research based on the work completed should also be logically outlined.

References and bibliographies Usually in dissertations, a bibliography is provided. This includes publications that are referred to in the dissertation text and those that are studied by the student but not referenced. In research reports usually only references are given. The bibliography should follow standard formats for books, research reports, and journal publications. A sample is shown in Table 19.6.

Appendices These are for the purpose of providing detailed information that would be too cumbersome/inappropriate within the main body of the dissertation. For example, questionnaires, derivation of certain equations, record of interviews, data obtained for statistical calculations, any forms used, computer programmes, and so on (refer sample Appendices in Table 19.7 and 19.8).

Table 19.6 A Sample Bibliography

Boot, John CG and Cox Edwin B (1979). *Statistical Analysis for Managerial Decisions*, 2nd ed., (International Student Edition). (New Delhi: Tata McGraw-Hill.).

Burdick, RK (1983). "Statement of Hypothesis in the Analysis of Variance". *Journal of Marketing Research* 20, issue no August. 320-324.

Churchill, Gilbert A (1987). *Marketing Research Methodological Foundations*, 4th ed. (New York: The Dryden Press).

Clarke, R.B., A.P. Coladarci and John Cofferry (1965). *Statistical Reasoning and Procedures.* (Ohio: Charles, E. Merril Books Inc).

Edwards, Allen (1967). *Statistical Methods*, 2nd ed. (New York: Holt, Reinhart and Winston).

Fergusson, G.A. (1959). *Statistical Analysis in Psychology and Behavioural Sciences.* (New York: McGraw-Hill).

Fisher, R.A. (1958) *Statistical Methods for Research Workers*, 13th ed. (New York: Halfner Publishing Co).

Gibbons, Jean Dickinson. (1985). *Non-parametric Statistical Inference*, 2nd ed. (New York: Marcel Dekker Inc).

Mendenhall, W. and J.E. Reimuth (1986). *Statistics for Management and Economics.* (New York: Duxbury Press).

Ostle, B. and R.W. Marsing (1973). *Statistics in Research.* (London: George Allen and Unwin Limited).

Sawyer, Alan G. and Pald J Peter (1983). "The Significance of Statistical Significance Tests in Marketing Research". *Journal of Marketing Research* 20 (May, 1983): 122-133.

Siegal, S. (1956). Non-Parametric Statistics. (New York: Mcgraw-Hill).

Tull, D. and D.I. Hawkins (1987). *Marketing Research, Measurement and Method*, 4th ed. (New York: Macmilian Publication Co).

Williams, F. (1968). *Reasoning with Statistics.* (Holt, Rinehart and Winston).

Yamanne, T. (1973). *Statistics: An Introductory Analysis*, 3rd ed. (New York: Harper and Row).

Table 19.7 Sample Appendix-B_1

Growth of total, internal and external manpower of organisation E

Year	*Total No. of employees*	*No. of external employees*	*No. of internal employees*	*Sq. rt. of employees external*	*Cu. rt. of internal employees*
1968	9	1	8	1.00	2.00
1969	17	1	16	1.00	2.52
1970	12	3	9	1.73	2.08
1971	24	9	15	3.00	2.47
1972	34	9	25	3.00	2.95
1973	72	8	64	2.83	4.00
1974	90	16	74	4.00	4.20
1975	121	16	105	4.00	4.72
1976	142	21	121	4.76	4.95
1977	220	28	192	5.29	5.77
1978	248	28	220	5.29	6.04
1979	250	30	220	5.48	6.04
1980	265	36	229	6.00	6.12

Table 19.8 Sample Appendix–B_2

1. Brief descriptions of variables of the environments for manpower planning.
   The variables given in the Table 3.6 are mostly self-explanatory. However, a few of the variables will be described in the following paragraphs in order to clarify their meanings.
2. Size of Occupational Categories
   This variable refers to a number that can be considered adequate for consideration as a separate category, to set policies for promotion and recruitment, and also to compute turnover and absenteeism. This has great influence on the MPP system. Larger numbers facilitate more systematic and numerate treatment of manpower. Subjective judgment is involved in deciding the size.
3. Changes in Product
   This includes all kinds of changes, that is, design changes, material changes, feature changes, and performance changes that affect their selling and manufacture, mechanisation of operation, changes in methods, and changes in the production rate. They give the proportions of operations mechanised, of changes in methods of production, and of changes in the production rate. All the three variables depict the extent (pervasiveness) of change in the operations.

Format of Research Reports

In the cases of reporting research, either sponsored, in-house or contract, the format shown in Table 19.9 is used. It is a modified version of the most commonly adopted American Psychological Association (APA) publication manual format. It will be noted that the main difference in thesis/dissertations and the research project reports is that the former tends to be more comprehensive and complete and the latter succinct and brief. The literature review tends to be more exhaustive in dissertations. A brief one will be given in the introduction for research reports. Instead of a bibliography, only references are given in research reports.

Table 19.9 Format of the Research Report

I. TITLE PAGE
   A. Title
   B. Author's name and affiliation
   C. Running head
   D. Acknowledgements (if any)

II. ABSTRACT

III. TABLE OF CONTENTS

IV. INTRODUCTION (no head used)
   A. Statement of the problem
   B. Background/review of literature
   C. Purpose and rationale/hypothesis

V. METHOD
   A. Subjects/Sampling design/Research design
   B. Apparatus or instrumentation (if any)
   C. Procedure for data collection and data analysis

VI. RESULTS
   A. Tables and figures (as appropriate)
   B. Statistical presentation
   C. Limitations

VII. DISCUSSION
   A. Support or non-support of hypotheses
   B. Practical and theoretical implications
   C. Conclusions

VIII. REFERENCES/BIBLIOGRAPHY

IX. APPENDIX (if appropriate)

Note: The format given here is a modified version.

Format of Publication in a Research Journal

All reputed journals require a particular general format and style from authors. These differ from journal to journal. But a typical format is, introduction; the case; the method; results; and conclusions. Material for publication is far more difficult to write than reports or dissertations. The reason is that the former have to be more concise than either of the latter and the communication and readability has still got to be extremely good. Rigorous peer evaluation in a detailed evaluation report format almost always makes it necessary to revise papers.

Reporting of Qualitative Research

reporting of qualitative research
The general format is same as for all research reports but there will be emphasis on research setting, presentation of data, interpretation of data, validation and verification of findings.

Earlier attempts at presentation of research reporting have been mainly influenced by quantitative researches. The approaches to these presentations have, more or less, clear conventions. But in reporting qualitative research, the approaches are less clear and seem to be still evolving. In this section, we will examine reporting of qualitative research, emphasising its special aspects. Some of these aspects are listed below.

1. Since most qualitative research is not dependent on a theoretical framework (filling a void in the literature) the reference to literature is more for comparisons and in defence of the research in a later part of the report, rather than in the introduction. The research question is more critical and is dwelt upon initially.
2. The richness of data obtained in qualitative research has its advantages and disadvantages. Too much description muddles the presentation. Too little may entail omissions that blur the interpretations. The correct balance between description and explanation is important but difficult.
3. Qualitative research is based primarily on empirical data and not on previous research. Therefore, the setting (context of research) has to be clearly conveyed to the reader through "thick descriptions" for the reader to understand and feel the sensitivity and complexity of the phenomenon and the environment. This communication is challenging, particularly to one who is not familiar with the research context.
4. A lot of "showing" and "telling" about the research process is required. Recordings of conversations and write up of stories are required for this purpose.
5. Biases of the researchers, derived from the past experience, may be mixed up with reporting subjectively (qualitative research uses a lot of perceptions and viewpoints of the researcher and participants in data gathering and analysis). These should be declared and explained, which is again a difficult task.
6. The verification of findings by a few experts is also subjective. Presentation of these logically must build up credibility of the findings.
7. Establishing credibility (internal validity) and transferability (external validity) of findings must be done by finding exceptions and by triangulation.
8. The sample size is established on the basis of "saturation" (information overlap, redundancy or confirmation of data), as against *a priori* sample size determination in statistical methods of quantitative research.
9. The findings of research need to be supported by quotes or phrases (metaphors) with multiple perspectives of the participants. These have to be described in the researcher's own language and kept confidential.
10. The logical "trace" of the emergence of concepts, themes, categories, and typologies should be clearly explained using tables, flow charts, mind maps, and so on.

Keeping these in view, a general report format needs to be developed. A typical format for reporting qualitative research is given in Table 19.10. The format is developed based on the recommendations of Patton (1980), Golden-Biddle (1997), and Margo Rowan et al (1997). This format can be used for thesis writing, practical research reporting, and journal papers, with minor variations in emphasis and content. The format is presented in detail in the Table 19.10.

Table 19.10 Detailed Format of Qualitative Research Report

1. PRELIMINARY
   Title
   Acknowledgement
   Abstract or synopsis
   Table of contents
   List of tables
2. INTRODUCTION
   - o Purpose of Research
     - Importance and relevance of research topic
     - Origin of the research problem
     - Research finding
     - Documentation of ethical approval
   - o Focus of Research
     - Research questions
     - Why are the questions important?
     - What are the consequences of answering the questions?
3. METHODS OF RESEARCH
   - o Setting
     - Context of research
     - Role of researcher
   - o Approach
     - What are the methods employed for research?
     - What are the questions asked for data collection?
     - How are the methods and questions appropriate for the research questions and the setting?
     - What are the strengths and weaknesses of the methods employed?
   - o Sampling
     - Description of the sampling method
     - Rationale of the choice of the sampling method
     - Sample size
     - Situations, time periods, and people to be sampled
4. PRESENTATION OF DATA
   - o Organisation and description of data
     - Detailed data collection to understand the details of the process
     - Description of information based on observation and/or interviews
     - Description of whatever information is needed to take the reader to the setting being interpreted
     - Description of findings around the research questions
     - Issues and concerns generated by the researchers and participants the in research
5. ANALYSIS OF DATA
   - o Analysis of Data
     - Patterns, themes, tendencies, trends, and motifs that logically emerge from data
     - Categories, classification systems and typologies
     - Participant (in research) generated typologies to explain their world
     - Researcher generated typology
   - o Interpretation and explanation of data
     - Linkages between categories and dimensions
     - Relationships
       * Things that go together
       * Things (parts) that are interdependent
       * Enquiry and speculation about causes and consequences
       * Hypotheses arising out of the enquiry
6. VALIDATION AND VERIFICATION OF FINDINGS
   - o Methods used for validation
   - o Credibility of findings
     - Discussion of rival hypothesis/Alternate explanations
     - Analysis of negative or deviant cases
     - Triangulation
       * of methods
       * of sources
       * of investigators
   - o Personal perspectives of the researcher
   - o Transcriptions of recorded reactions of participants and experts who have examined the study
7. CONCLUSIONS
   - o Basic findings
   - o Implication of basic findings
   - o Recommendation of participants/staff
   - o Recommendations of the researcher

A few comments to help qualitative report writing are:

1. Qualitative research report writing requires the researcher's unique experience.
2. Usually qualitative research reporting is a collective work of the researcher, staff, and participants, integrating all their views.
3. Interdisciplinary interests and endeavours are important in reporting. The report may be made up of examples and quotes drawn from psychology, education, sociology and other disciplines to present a clear picture to the reader.
4. Negotiating with the support group and mentors and co-authoring with participants are very useful in reporting (Ely, Vinz, Anzul and Downing, 1997).

BRIEFING

briefing

This is a condensed version of the report in an oral presentation. The briefing should be tailor made for the audience and the delivery should balance speed, gestures and use of visual aids.

Briefing is a condensed version of the report presented orally. While the oral presentation of dissertations is made to the academic community and/or the examiners, research reports may be orally presented to a group of executives and it could take about 20-30 minutes, generally. Briefing is as much an art as a science. What should be presented to the audience must be clearly understood. The objectives and nature of the project should be clearly stated, key points should stand out, delivery must be fluent, and the focus must be on the audience. The delivery should be restrained. Speed, clarity, pauses, and gestures do play a part in holding the attention of the audience and making the presentation interesting. Adequate visual aids should be used and eye contact should be established often with the audience. Mere reading from notes should be avoided.

The briefing should preferably have the following contents, in the given order.

- A brief statement of the nature of the project.
- Presentation of the organisation of the project and what is done in it (10 to 15 per cent of the presentation time).
- Conclusions and discussions.
- Recommendations.
- A question-answer session.

A good rule for oral presentation is to fix the main points in the mind and keep some cards/ notes for connecting information. Use of transparencies/power point slides for this purpose is also effective.

To be effective, the briefings require good pre-planning and practice-briefing (Anthony, 1970).

RULES FOR TYPING OR WORD PROCESSING

- Good quality bond paper that is 82" × 11" and 13 to 16 pound weight should be used.
- If any special symbol is not available on the typewriter or word processor, it should be carefully and clearly written in black ink.
- All margins should be 12", at the top, bottom, left, and right.
- All pages should be double spaced. Single spacing should not be used anywhere.
- Referencing in text should have last name(s) of the author(s) and the year of publication; for example; Best and Kahn (1986). Listed references or bibliography should have a standard format, which should be consistently used throughout (shown in Table 19.6).
- Parts of the text that contain listings, long quotations, examples, or cases or problems should be indented.
- Headings and sub-headings should be used for dividing the report into major sections/ topical portions.
- Vertical listings of points should be used.

SUMMARY

Research reports vary in scope and content. Their main purpose is to clearly communicate research ideas, methods, and results to the reader. They are broadly classified into university dissertations, research reports, and journal papers. Their formats follow a general pattern, which include a chapter or section, each on introduction, research method, results, and conclusions. In the report are included tables, schematic diagrams, graphs, and exhibits to make the communication clear. The main difference between research reports and dissertations are that in the former, literature review is brief and the presentation of results is concise, while in the latter they tend to be elaborate. Journal papers have to be very concise, but still have to communicate adequately.

Some important prewriting considerations like outlines are recommended. While writing the dissertation, the student is advised to keep in mind principles relating to aspects like consistency, clarity, continuity, openness, and a synthesis-analysis approach.

For the physical preparation of the report, certain standards relating to spacing of material, margins and referencing in text, and bibliography have to be followed. When the research details have to be orally briefed, the briefing period should be around 30 minutes, and clearly cover the objectives and key points. While briefing, the delivery should be fluent, adequate visual aids should be used, and the focus must be on the audience.

Suggested Readings

- Anthony, Jay (1990). *Effective Presentation*. London: British Institute of Management.
- Tufte, Edward R. (1992). *Visual Display of Quantitative Information*. Cheshire, CT, UK: Graphics Press.
- Turabian, Kate L. (1971). *A Manual for Writers of Term Papers, Thesis, and Dissertation*, 3rd ed. Chicago: University of Chicago Press.

QUESTIONS AND EXERCISES

1. How should a research report be organised?
2. Why is "focusing on the audience" important in research report writing or briefing?
3. What are the differences between reporting and briefing a research project? (Your answer must include differences in content, emphasis, and length.)
4. How is a research report evaluated?
5. Is there any difference in style desirable while writing the introduction and discussion of results?
6. What is the Gumming Fog Index? Apply it to a piece of writing in a thesis or research report. Discuss the findings.
7. Take an abstract of a thesis and study it well. Now rewrite the abstract in your own way. If necessary, consult the thesis. Discuss the improvements you have made with your group.
8. Use a standard format of research report evaluation. Evaluate a thesis and discuss the findings.
9. Study the literature for a given problem area of research. Develop a Papineou's Tree.
10. Why should one use a logical approach in developing a research report and not a chronological approach?
11. Analyae a piece of your own research writing. What are the problems you face in developing a good research report or thesis?

APPENDIX A1

Systems Concept

CHARACTERISATIONS OF A SYSTEM

A system is characterised by the following:

1. Elements, such as worker, machine, and material.
2. Conversion process such as machine operation.
3. Inputs and outputs, such as raw material and product.
4. Environment, namely, competitor, labour market, and taxation policy.
5. Goals and objectives, such as minimise rejection of a product, and on time delivery.
6. Purposeful function, such as scheduling orders so that in process inventory is minimised.
7. Properties of attributes, such as quality of product, and skill of a worker.
8. Transactions across boundaries, such as purchase order, trade enquiry, and labour turnover.
9. Structure, that is, centralised R&D, and decentralised production.
10. States and flows, that is, inventory level, delivery of material, and cash transaction.

The basic attributes of any system is its complexity arising out of multiplicity of components and a large number of interrelations among them. A system is generally made up of other systems. Several examples of the first six characteristics will be discussed later. A quick review of the properties of the system is made in this section.

"A system is an organised or complex whole; an assemblage or combination of things or parts forming a complex or unitary whole" Johnson et al (1980). Daily, we come in contact with such systems as economic systems, transportation systems, communication systems, and social systems. Each one of these systems has specific objectives to fulfill and consist of minor parts (sub-systems) that, interact among themselves in a harmonious manner, enabling the aggregate system to achieve its objective (for example, transportation system is made up of railways, roadways, airways; communication system consists of the postal system, telegraph system, telephone system, wireless system, and the Internet). Therefore, we can define system as an organised set of parts or elements so interrelated as to achieve desired objectives or goals. A physical entity is considered as a system if the outcome of its behaviour is conceptualised as a product of the interaction of its parts. Thus, the definition of the system is a researcher's choice.

At the level of the factory system we have many sub-systems, like the personal system, engineering design system, accounting system, operating (man-machine) system, material handling system, and many others. The systems design function at the factory level will consist of integrating all these sub-systems under the restrictions of factory policies and plans, so that its objectives are achieved. The environment of the system is the set of all objects, a change in whose attributes affects the system and also of those objects whose attributes are changed by the behaviour of the system. When we partition a system into its sub-systems, we do so for convenience. It is correct to assume that such a sub-division is arbitrary. In order to distinguish between the management activity and business environment, it is necessary to find out whether the management activity can control the environment.

IMPORTANCE OF THE SYSTEMS CONCEPT

The modern industry is characterised by enormous growth and information explosion. Growth has resulted in a multiplicity of products and activities, which has, in turn, resulted in complexity. Modern information technology has introduced new kinds of systems like decision support systems, data warehouses, worldwide webs, teleconferencing systems, and so on. Complexity has been tackled by functional specialisation. With functional specialisation, diversity of objectives among various functions has arisen. Diversity has resulted in conflicting interests among the functions or sub-systems. This conflict necessitates two major functions of management, integration of sub-systems for optimum realisation of system objectives and coordination among the sub-systems.

This is accomplished through generalisation across system analysis, synthesis, modelling, and simulation. There are four categories of work applicable to systems approach:

1. Systematic and descriptive factors, dealing with classification of systems, their organisation and environment, with particular reference to openness and closeness, using concepts of centralisation, differentiation, and interaction.
2. Regulation and maintenance, using concepts of equilibrium and feedback.
3. Dynamics and change, dealing with adaptation, learning, growth, and goal-seeking in given environments.
4. Decline and breakdown, dealing with entropy and decay.

Checkland (1972) details a methodology, which makes use of the complete analysis and synthesis using the planning and design of system concepts. The general guidelines for analysis provided by Checkland are shown succinctly in Figure A.1.

Fig. A.1 System Methodology

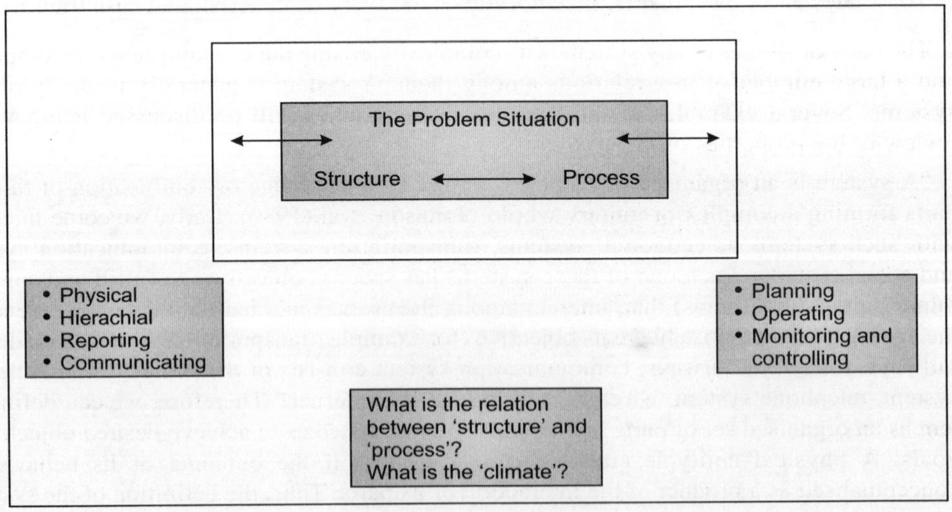

WAYS OF LOOKING AT A SYSTEM

Closed verses open Systems The theory of systems has drawn considerable inspiration from the theory of biology (for examples, see Bertalanffy, 1968). Living organisms are all open systems, that is, there is a transaction of information between the organism and its environment. When a system is not open to its environment it is called a closed system. A clock-monitored street light switching system is a closed system, whereas a system monitored by a photoelectric device is an open system, because the switching of the lights take place depending upon the intensity of light in the street.

The system concepts that are applicable to management are the concepts of open systems. Central to this idea is that goal-directed behaviour of the open system causes any of its actions to move the system towards achieving the goal for which it exists. In this movement, if there is any intervention from outside (for sensing which the system has the ability), that is, the environment, the open system reacts to this intervention and regulates itself so that it accomplishes the goal.

Any living organism has a fundamental goal of self preservation, that is, when an environmental condition threatens to destroy/harm it, it tends to self-regulate and evade the danger. A classical property of open systems is homeostasis, for example, when the temperature outside varies widely, the internal temperature is kept constant. There are other properties like steady state, equifinality, hierarchy of goals, and directive correlations. Of these, three properties—(i) span of foresight, (ii) adaptation and learning, and (iii) back reference period—are of particular interest to management researchers.

All open systems exhibit the property of span of foresight (looking ahead). As the reference time in future increases the ability of the organisation to identify changes in the environment becomes weaker, the reactions tend to be those of keen awareness than of action of adjustment. As the time span reduces, the reactions become more action oriented.

Adaptation is a long term adjustment of the organism to the environment over periods, comparable to several orders of its life span. Self regulation, on the other hand, deals with short-term fluctuations in the environment, and in this context, the back reference period is very important. The back reference period is the time required for the organisation to cause a certain change in its action consistent with environmental fluctuations. If the organism is in a situation in which the change is needed in a time span shorter than the back reference period, then the organism fails to self regulate and sustains harmful consequences. This is of particular importance to designing organisational systems, which must be capable of responding to the environmental changes, and this lag period should be clearly appreciated by the decision maker.

Organisations operate in environments consisting of social, economic, political, informational, and technological components. The environment may be (see Trist, 1963): (i) simple (for example, classical markets), (ii) complicated but placid (for example, imperfect competition), (iii) disturbed (for example, perfect competition), and (iv) turbulent fields (in which continued cut-throat competition exists, economic and government restrictions will be severe, and the general industrial climate is one of R&D).

When a system study is made, it is necessary to keep in mind the environment in which the whole organisation is operating. When we think of economic organisations, two other systems: (i) cooperative systems and (ii) socio-technical systems (Trist, 1963), assume importance. The organisation is not looked at as just a social system in which groups and individuals participate in a directed way. It is, in fact, considered as one that may consist of systems in which some sub-systems may cooperate (cooperative systems), causing the conventional organisational approaches to be modified accordingly. The concept of a socio-technical system goes one step further and treats any industrial system as essentially a combination of social and technical systems in which the technological component influences the social system and its behaviour. Analysis of such aspects should be given due consideration in system studies.

Some examples of systems related to the control function in a business or an industrial organisation are shown in Fig. A.2 and A.3. They are self explanatory.

In a complex system, feedback loops are arranged in a hierarchical way and feedback at each successively higher level gives greater understanding of the control process in the system.

Types of Systems Checkland (1981) classifies systems into four types, as under:

1. *Natural systems:* These are physical systems that make up the universe in a hierarchy, from the sub-atomic system through the systems of ecology to galactic systems.

Fig. A.2 Information decision systems

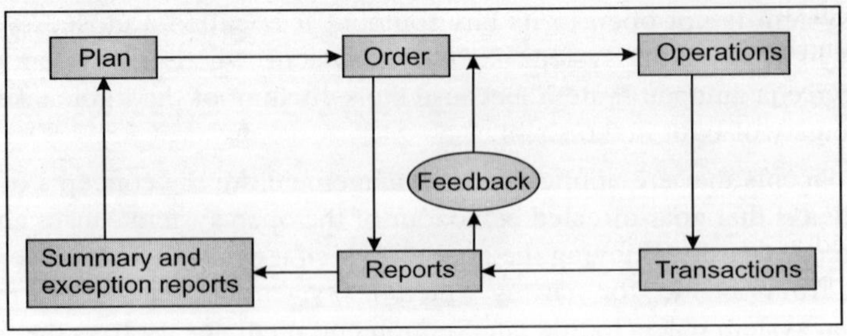

Fig. A.3 Control system—concept of cybernetics as applied to industry

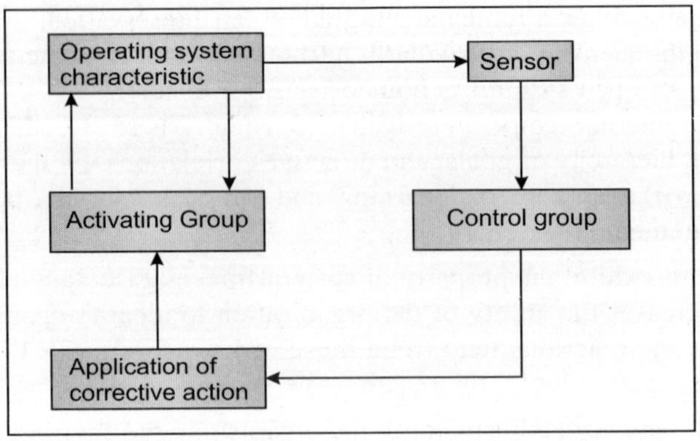

2. *Designed systems:* These can be both physical (for example, tools, bridges, and automated complexes) and abstract (for example, mathematics, languages, and philosophy).
3. *Human activity systems:* These are designed by human beings to undertake purposeful activity (such as man-machine systems, industrial systems and political systems).
4. *Social and cultural systems:* Most human activity will exist within a social system where the elements will be human beings and the relationships will be interpersonal. This differs in nature from the other three classes in that it spans the interface between natural and human activity systems. Examples of social systems would be a family, a community, and a boy scout movement, as well as the set of systems formed by groups of human beings getting together to perform some other purposeful activity, such as an industrial concern, a choral society, or a conference.
5. *Information systems:* (Ref. Marakas, 1999) Currently the influence an information system has on social and the cultural systems, not to speak of technical and administrative systems, is phenomenal. It has affected every aspect of human activity, as well as cultural and social systems.

In applied research, particularly where operations research methodologies are employed, the problem of the researcher is one of integrating the social aspects of the system into his model. In a way, the researcher uses the method of synthesis.

The aspect of synthesis is connected with the stage of development of scientific approach itself. Over the centuries, scientists have concentrated on analytical approaches, where in a complex system or problem is broken down into smaller fragments and each fragment is attempted to be solved. This was necessary at each step because of the quest for detailed knowledge. Now, with the growing inventory of knowledge in any area of human interest, more complex problems need to be tackled only through an approach of synthesis of the earlier detailed knowledge gained. Thus, the system philosophy and viewpoint have been more appreciated in research investigations in many physical sciences. OR, being similar to physical science, is also going through this phase. In the process of synthesis, the concentration is on interrelationships among the components and the total behaviour, rather than on detailed component knowledge or its structure. This analysis/synthesis process is exemplified by the following illustration (Fig. A.4).

Economies of division of labour leads to mass production and increased productivity, but lower job satisfaction because of the effect of monotony on the worker. This causes an increase in the industrial relations problems and subsequently reduces productivity. This was the analysis phase for job design. Subsequently, job enlargement, reduced specialisation, and job rotation were used as organisational means of improving productivity and evolving a concept of management of socio-technical systems. This phase has the characteristics of systems synthesis.

With the increase in complexity of systems, analytical procedures have yielded place to procedures of simulation and heuristics in problem solving. Currently, the turn is from heuristics to artificial intelligence procedures, in which knowledge of experts is used to solve complex problems. Underlying this change in approach is an attempt to ensure satisfactory performance of the system instead of an optimal one. This is known as satisficing, as against optimisation, which uses accurate analytical methods to get the best solution to the problem.

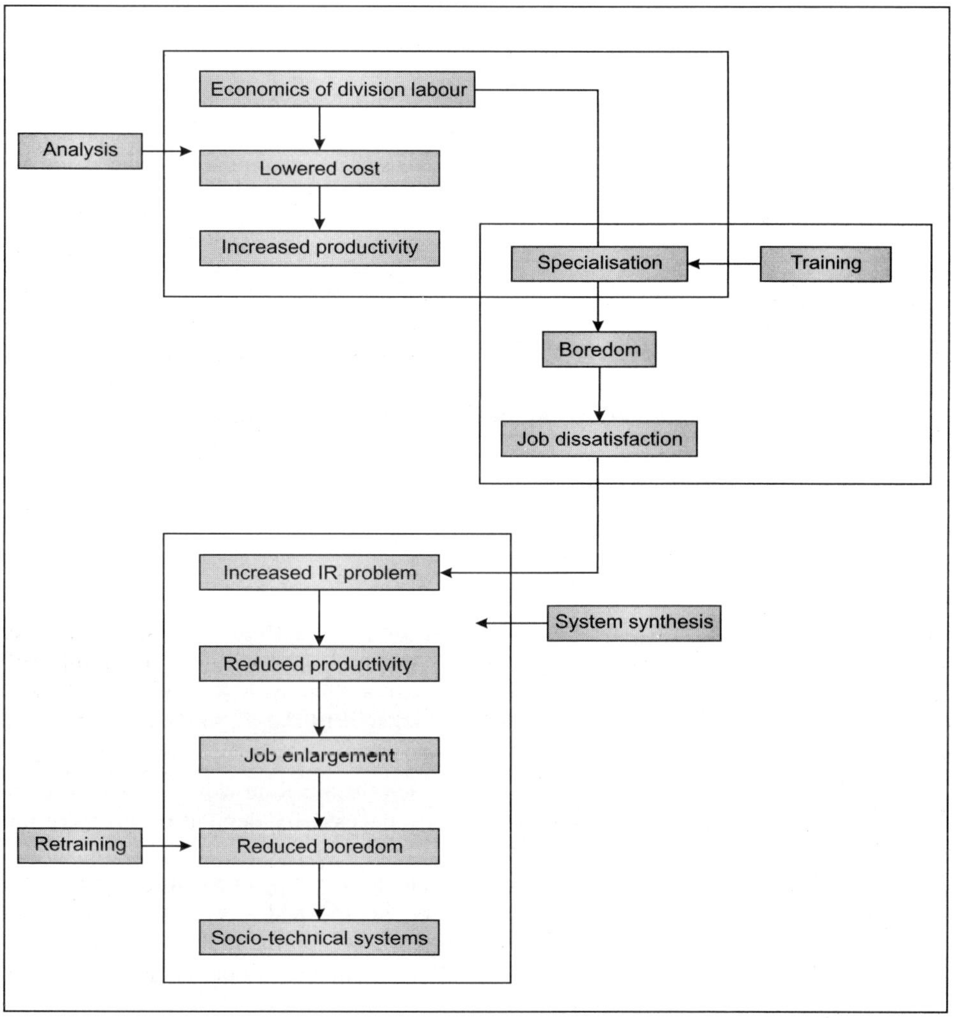

Fig. A.4 Socio-technical systems (job enlargement)

APPENDIX A2

Analysis of Covariance (ANCOVS)

Analysis of variance deals with the influence of manipulated variables on the dependent variables in an experimental situation. It is a technique that combines the features of analysis of variance and regression. For example, a typical analysis of variance model for the value Y_{ij} of the jth observation in the ith class is,

$$Y_{ij} = u_i + e_{ij} \qquad ...(1)$$

Where

u_i = the population means of the classes, and

e_{ij} = the residuals. Now, suppose variable X_{ij} is linearly related to Y_{ij}, it is better to remove the possible sources of variance in the criterion variable that may be attributable to factors not being controlled by the researcher (linear dependency with the predictor variable or covariate).

This covariance analysis increases the precision of the experiment. Therefore, the model that could be set up will be,

$$Y_{ij} = u_i + \beta(X_{ij} - \overline{X}) + e_{ij} \qquad (2)$$

Where

β = regression coefficient of Y on X_{ij}, and

$\overline{X}$ = grand mean of X_{ij}'s

If X_{ij}'s and Y_{ij}'s are closely related, the above model will fit the Y_{ij} values better than the original analysis of variance model, as in Equation (1).

A rule of thumb (Cochran and Cox, 1957) suggests that the absolute value of this correlation should be more than 0.3 even though the results may necessarily depend on error variance without covariate adjustment and the degrees of freedom associated with the error variance. Blocking (subdividing the test units into more homogeneous subgroups) helps in situations where there is some departure from linear relations between Y and X, and it also permits researchers to explore the possibility of block *Vs* treatment level interactions. Some assumptions made in the ANCOVA model are: all of the individual treatment level slopes are equal and differences in intercept terms measure the effect of various treatment levels.

The main objective of ANCOVA is to test the equality of covariate adjusted treatment level effects and to test whether, within treatment level regression slopes, are equal. Acceptance of the latter hypothesis is a precondition for carrying out the main test of covariate adjusted treatment differences. The covariates will be included in an experimental design to remove extraneous influences from the dependent variable, which increases measurement precision. Procedures such as linear regression are used to remove variation in dependent variables associated with one or more covariates. Then, a conventional ANOVA is carried out on the adjusted dependent variable. An effective covariate in ANCOVA is one that is highly correlated with the dependent variable, but not correlated with the independent variables. Thus, variance in the dependent variable forms the basis of an error term in ANCOVA. If the covariate is correlated with a dependent variable, it explains some of the variance (through regression) and leaves behind only the residual variance in the dependent variable. This residual variable provides a smaller error term for the F-statistic and a more efficient test of treatment effects.

Now, let us very briefly look at how the covariance model is developed and analysed in a completely randomised design (CRD). In CRD, the covariance model is given by Equation (2) in which u_i represent the treatment effects. The ith treatment mean will be,

$$\overline{Y} = u_i + \beta(\overline{X}_i. - \overline{X}..).$$

Where $\overline{Y}_{i.}$ is an unbiased estimate of $\beta(\overline{X}_i. - \overline{X}..)$..

Therefore, an estimate of u_i is given by

$$u_i = \overline{Y}_{i.} - \beta(\overline{X}_i. - \overline{X}..) \tag{3}$$

The second term of (3) is the adjustment factor introduced by the covariance analysis. The problem now remains in estimating β. The previous results, derived in CRD, continue to hold except for the fact that β is estimated from the error in the analysis of variance. Explicitly, β is calculated using

$$\beta = \frac{\text{Error sum of products of } X \text{ and } Y}{\text{Error sum of squares of } X}$$

The other computations are similar of those to ANOVA procedures, which was explained earlier in detail.

It is very important to mention here that it is possible to test the same hypotheses by carrying out within the model comparison approach of the regression model by including dummy predictor variables. For example, the full regression model is given by

$$\begin{aligned} Y_{ij} &= B_o + B_1\, W_{i1} + B_2\, W_{i2} + \ldots + \\ &\quad B_i\, W_{i1}\, (X_{ij} - \overline{X}..) + \\ &\quad B_{i+1}\, W_{i2}\, (X_{ij} - \overline{X}..) + \ldots + \overline{e}_{ij} \end{aligned}$$

Where W_{i1} and W_{i2} are zero-one dummies.

The major difference between the standard regression model and this model is that the new cross product terms and their associated partial regression coefficients are introduced.

The analysis of covariance helps in many ways, two of which are listed below.

ANCOVA increases precision in randomised experiments; that is, if X is a covariate measured in an experiment before the treatments are applied, it predicts, to some degree, the final response Y on the unit. Adjustment to the treatment mean results in removing the differences in yielding ability, which leads to lower experimental errors and more precise comparisons among the treatments.

ANCOVA adjusts bias that occurs due to different sources in observational studies. In many observational studies if Y and X are linearly related, researchers introduce the term in order to nullify for a possible source of bias in the comparisons to be made by him. It enables the researcher to study the nature of treatment effects in randomised experiments by observing whether treatment differences in the response remain or whether they shrink insignificantly after adjusting for dependency on Y. It can be used to study regression in multiple classifications, to assess whether it is the same in different classes across time or whether the relation is linear or curved.

APPENDIX A3

Some Research Findings on Creativity

PROCESS CREATIVITY

Creative activity, according to Newell, Shah and Simon, (1962),* is a special class of problem solving activity characterised by novelty, unconventionality, persistence, and difficulty in problem formulation. They emphasise the importance of richness of imagery and heuristics, but caution against basing conclusions on imagery systems. In addition to accumulating enormous knowledge, they recommend acquiring 'additional clues' to differentiate parts of the problem in order to be creative. Catherine (1938) found that the first stage of preparation was marked by frequent thought and idea changes, more frequently in the earlier part of preparation. With repetitions of an idea, modifications occurred in later periods of preparation.

COGNITIVE FACTORS IN CREATIVITY

Dealing with cognitive factors in creativity, Guilford (1959) summarises his thinking and research findings by stating that the following intellectual (traits) aptitudes are related to creativity.

- Ability to see problems
- Fluency of thinking—word fluency, expressional fluency, associational fluency, and ideational fluency
- Flexibility of thinking, in being spontaneous and adaptive
- Originality
- Capability of redefinition
- Elaboration

However, he opines that creativity goes beyond the domain of intelligence. Intelligence and creative talents are regarded as different areas of aptitude. Intelligence is not information itself but a collection of different abilities to process information of different kinds to produce different mental constructs (Guilford, 1980, p219). Information is of different kinds: figural, symbolic, semantic, and behavioural. The five basic operations that can be carried out on the basis of these kinds of information are: (i) cognition or simply knowing, (ii) memory or storing, (iii) structuring and coding, (iv) retrieving information, (v) divergent production, which is a broad search or scanning for generating alternatives; and (vi) convergent production, which is a focussed search for logical imperatives.

The products of information can be units or classes, implicit relations or systems, or transformations. Units or classes connote partitioning of information; implicit relations and systems have logical connotations. Among these products, the transformation process has a special significance in creativity as it produces a new kind of information.

Among the above operations, divergent production has the greatest implication for creativity as it connotes fluency of thinking (ready flow of ideas). Transformation ability provides flexibility of thinking. The higher levels of creativity can be attributed to intersection of these abilities depicted as segments of a cube of structure of intellect model, as propounded by Guilford (1980). The segments relate to divergent production and transformation ability.

Other relevant traits are (i) motivational qualities, which provide higher energy levels and effective work habits; (ii) unusually strong curiosity; (iii) reflective thinking, less tied to realities; (iv) risk taking behaviour; and (v) tolerance of ambiguity.

Problem solving, as envisaged by Dewey (1938), proceeds with awareness of the existence of the problem, understanding of the problem, structuring it, searching for solutions, and evaluating the method of solution. Guilford* (1980, pp.229) has developed a creative problem solving model, which is quite useful in trying to understand the process. 'Seeing the problem', a series of divergent-convergent productions along with transformation and evaluation, followed by a storing is what goes on during the creative problem solving process, according to the above model.

Rational thinking and metaphorical thinking (thinking in pictures) are two different forms of thinking. In rational thinking, the heart of scientific method, a concept is abstracted from a number of individual experiences and qualities are established based on classification defined accurately. They are then verified. Logical thinking processes are at the heart of rational thinking. They tend to be linear, one following the other. The metaphorical thinking on the other hand shows wide "lateral ramifications" and emotively effected. The results tend to be inaccurate interpolation or extrapolation of enormous amounts of information towards a finality (Daucher, 1967). However, both types of thinking are complementary and are not contrary. In the creative phase of any activity, be it painting or music or science, the metaphorical thinking dominates. That is all that is important to us in the context of research.

Some Tools for Stimulating New Ideas

- *Forced relationship* The problem solver deliberately forces some kind of relationship among entities or attributes without trying to evaluate them.
- *Idea search* Checklists of question are used as exhaustively as possible on the problem situation. Osborne (1963) suggested the key steps, namely, adapt, modify, magnify, minify, substitute, rearrange, reverse, and combine using questioning approaches so familiar in work study (ILO, 1978).
- *Using analogies* According to Gordon (1961), there are four types of analogies, namely, personal, direct, symbolic, and fantasy analogies. In personal analogy, the problem solver assumes to be the "object" of his investigation and tries to experience in imagination what it would be like. In direct analogy, the problem at hand is compared with a similar one in another related or unrelated field, even if the knowledge of the "similar" problem is approximate. Symbolic analogy is used when the essence of the problem situations are same. For example, in all problems of inventory in manufacturing, cash in bank, wastes in dust bins, and water in tanks. The essence of the situation is that there is filling up and then emptying. So the models representing them could be similar* (see Ramasastry (1974) and Shekdar (1988)). In fantasy analogy, one ignores all laws governing the problem situation, like the physical, organisational, scientific, cultural, and political, one tries to engage in wishful thinking and generate ideas for solutions, however, fantastic they are. Then they are evaluated within the constraints of those laws, which were ignored initially while generating new ideas.

APPENDIX A4

Some Further Group Problem-Solving Techniques

ISSUE BASED INFORMATION SYSTEM (IBIS)

IBIS was developed to serve as an argumentative procedure for decision making groups to use in coordination and support of debate over decisions that are politically influenced and those that sometimes occur in planning and design. The IBIS can be used as a procedure for arguing, designing, planning, and policymaking decisions on any topic. The IBIS procedure rests on the assumption that these activities are political in nature and serves to develop a discourse over an initially unstructured topic or problem area. The procedure structures, monitors, records debates and develops a database as the debate proceeds. The core components of IBIS are issues, the positions that people take on issues, arguments offered in support of or in opposition to positions, and references cited to support arguments. A secondary set of components includes questions of fact or consensus answers and evidence, positions and arguments, respectively. A further set of components includes topic norms, tables, matrices and trees, which are means of recording and interrelating the core components and the secondary components. The operational procedure includes:

1. Deciding upon rules of procedures.
2. Deciding upon a decision rule. The main purpose of this step is that no decision is made but the purpose of this discussion is explained to be the exploration of the problem and familiarisation of participants with various aspects of the problem.
3. The choice of form of procedure.
4. Illustrations of the progress of the argument. The last step is to construct a matrix illustrating the structure of the argument over the initial issue. These steps may be repeated.

IBIS's prime disadvantage is that it involves heavy paperwork. The positive aspect is the systematic method of familiarising the participants with the problem landscape* (Grant, 1982).

NOMINAL GROUP TECHNIQUE (NGT)

The NGT is particularly well suited for problem identification/analysis of problem situations, new idea generation and selection and consideration of alternatives. The NGT is a structured group meeting for the consideration of a single critical issue take for example, 'what do you think are the most important elements of a successful research education?' There are 4 basic steps in the NGT process[+] (Gill and Delbceq, 1982).

1. Silent generation (independent thinking and listening) of ideas in writing.
2. Round robin listing from group members to record each idea in a terse manner on a flip chart.
3. Serial discussion of each recorded idea for classification and evaluation.
4. Individual voting on priority of ideas with group decision being mathematically derived through rank ordering.

The first step is characterised by independent thinking without any interaction.

The second one provides each participant, in turn, the same consistent sequence and non-conflicting opportunity for alternative perspectives to be presented. This guarantees equal participation. Discussion being absent, the ideas can be explored in silence.

In the third step, each idea is discussed. Serially, all questions and comments that serve to classify are discussed. This provides the true first opportunity for individuals to discuss these ideas. There is no norm for the time limit for discussing an idea. The group takes its own time to move to the next idea. Differences of opinion are retained.

In the fourth step, after all the discussions are over, a voting will be done by the individuals by selecting a limited set from the total list of ideas. The individually selected and unanimously recorded ballots provide the most important feedback to the group. Diverse opinions are highlighted. Low ranking and high ranking items are further discussed in order to validate the outcome.

SYNECTICS

Synectics represents the dynamics of group problem solving and theories about individual difficulties with speculative, as opposed to routine, thinking. Syntactically the word synectics means the joining together of diverse elements. It applies where, in order to obtain synergy of creative efforts, a diverse group of individuals must join and cooperate in the accomplishment of a solution to the problem at hand. This process leads to new insights by bringing the together of elements that are normally unrelated. The basic assumption behind synectics is that few people use more than a fraction of their potential for creative thinking. By making the thinking operations and the various forces that keep the people thinking routinely explicit, both as individuals and in groups, skills may be developed to use latent capacities.

The objectives of synectics are:

1. To generate insightful and inventive solutions to a problem
2. To increase the probability of success of creative effort by using more of the latent potential of both individuals and groups

In the operational procedure, there are two preliminary activities. The first is to clarify objectives of the meeting and selection of expert participants. (Cf. Brainstorming). The second is to acquaint the group with the process of synectics. The session proceeds along the steps—Briefing, presention, and explaination. The participants may note down goals and wish clues. The team generates more goals and wish clues. A goal wish that appeals to the client is selected. The team develops immediate ideas for these goals and wish clues. The facilitator takes the team on an excursion to develop more ideas (making the thinking explicit).

Ideas are finally tested and tuned into possible solutions by the client, a session for evaluating the feasibility of the solution follows. There are some limitations of synectics. There may be some mental discomfort among the participants; high expectations may cause failure of the sessions; and the long time required for the sessions often discourages participants[*] (Gordon, 1961).

APPENDIX B

Sources of Information of Management and Social Sciences

The main sources of research material has been obtained from functional and non-functional literature and arranged in order of priority, with particular reference to the documentation services available in India.

Types of Sources

1. Bibliographies
2. Indexes
3. Abstracts
4. Statistical sources
5. Directories and Yearbooks
6. Encyclopedias
7. Dictionaries
8. Other sources
9. Websites

BIBLIOGRAPHIES

Bibliographies constitute the most important sources of research material. A bibliography may contain particulars of books as well as articles, but usually, articles published in daily newspapers are not included.

1. *International Bibliography of Social Sciences:* This bibliography is published in four parts—sociology, political science, economics, and anthropology—by the UNESCO in collaboration with the Committee for Social Science Documentation. It is an annual publication that has been published regularly since 1952. This bibliography is truly international in its coverage and lists the most important publications in the four disciplines irrespective of the form in which they are published. Unpublished motional and articles published in dailies are Bibliography excluded from this. Particular attention is paid to the official publications of national governments. This authoritative bibliography is presented in bilingual form (English-French) and includes both author and subject indexes and a list of periodicals consulted along with their official abbreviations.
2. *Asia Social Science Bibliography: With Annotations and Abstracts 1967.* This bibliography has been published by Vikas, Delhi (1974) and is edited by N. K. Gopi.

It is a continuing project of the Institute of Economic Growth. It covers: (a) social science-social data; (b) education and communication; (c) political science, (d) economics; (e) sociology, social anthropology, and social psychology; (f) demography.

This bibliography is a selected work, but includes almost all significant contributions, in English language, pertaining to the social sciences disciplines referred to above. References have been taken from 264 journals (local and foreign). It also includes contributions made in the countries of the region by both local and foreign authors, and even those published outside the region. The countries covered are Afghanistan, Burma, Ceylon, India, Indonesia, Iran, Laos, Malaysia, Nepal, Pakistan, Philippines, Singapore, South Korea, Taiwan, Thailand, and South Vietnam.

Author, subject and geographical indexes are provided.

3. *Documentation on Asia:* This bibliography has been originally edited by Girija Kumar and V. Machwe and published by Vikas, Delhi, in 1974, under the auspices of the Indian Council of World Affairs. This is a subject bibliography of articles and documents on Asia. The literature surveyed is indicative of political economic, and social developments and international relations of the countries in Asia. Documents covered include in full text or in summary, speeches, statements, resolutions, white papers, agreements, and reports from official and non-official sources. A variety of sources such as official gazettes, parliamentary debates, committee and commission reports, press releases, embassy bulletins, publications of international organisations, political party publications, newspapers, periodicals, and press agency bulletins, books and pamphlets have been provided.

   The series is essentially intended and designed for students of international relations and area studies. The coverage of Indian and Chinese materials is fairly comprehensive, almost exhaustive, particularly with respect to Chinese sources. It will also become a definite source of reference for work on India's foreign relations.

   Other unique features are the coverage of parliamentary debates of several countries and proceedings of the UN organs like the General Assembly and the Security Council. The coverage makes the *Documentation on Asia Series* a unique source of reference on Asian developments.

4. *Indian National Bibliography:* The INB is an authoritative bibliographical record of current publications in the major Indian languages received by the National Library, Kolkata, under the provisions of the Delivery of Books (Public Libraries) Act, 1954.

   Books in all languages are arranged in a sequence under subject groups. They are transliterated into Roman script, annotations are written in English.

   The INB consists of two parts, the first dealing with general publications and the second with Indian official publications. Each part has an exhaustive alphabetical index containing author, title, and subject entries.

5. *Bibliography of Bibliographies on India:* This bibliography has been compiled by D. R. Kalia and M. K. Jain and published by the Concept Publishing Co., Delhi in 1975.

   For the first time in India, an effort has been made in this volume to identify and publish bibliographical material on India in a consolidated form. Even though the compilation cannot claim to be exhaustive, it is indeed comprehensive and provides the most useful handbook of material on India.

   The book contains a total number of 1245 titles, comprising bibliographies, library catalogues, documentation lists, abstracts, dissertation lists, serial catalogues, and so on. Most of the titles included are in English but quite a good collection of material in Indian languages has been made available. Entries have been arranged subjectwise, giving bibliographical details about each title. The arrangement of entries within the subject is alphabetical.

INDEXES

Indexes usually contain the documentation of articles in periodicals and books and can hardly be distinguished from bibliographies. These do, however, concentrate more on periodical literature.

1. *Social Sciences Citation Index:* This is an international multidisciplinary index to literature on social, behavioural, and related sciences. It is published by the Institute of Scientific Information, Philadelphia, USA.

   The SSCI indexes approximately 70,000 new articles and significant editorial items from every issue of over 1000 of the world's most important social sciences journals. The SSCI also selectively covers 2000 other journals, indexing articles that are deemed to be relevant to the social sciences. All these journals belong to 26 disciplines, which include anthropology, archaeology, area studies, business and finance, communication, community health, criminology and penology, demography, economics, educational research, ethnic group studies, geography, history, information and library science, international relations, law, linguistics, management, marketing, political science, psychiatry, psychology, sociology, statistics and urban planning and development.

   The most important and notable feature of this indexing service is that it also cites the references cited in a particular article while it was written by its author. Generally, the indexed items consists of the author, title, journal, its volume and issue numbers, year of publication, and pagination of a particular article. Here the references of other publications referred to in the articles are also indexed. So, it is a very useful source in searching for periodical articles in the field of social sciences.
2. *Index to Scientific Reviews:* This index is also published by the Institute for Scientific Information, Philadelphia, USA.

   Every year, it indexes review articles and over 16,000 reviews selected from more than 2,700 of the world's most important journals. This is the first multidisciplinary guide to review articles.

   Among the different areas of sciences, it also includes social and behavioural sciences and this area alone covers over 100 disciplines.

   The Index to Scientific Reviews makes it easy to identify and locate review articles. They can be searched for by author names, title words and phrases, and organisations. It also provides a citation index, which has references of previously published material relevant to a subject cited in recent articles.
3. *Social Sciences Index:* Its coverage is also international and is published by H.W. Wilson Co., New York, USA. Previously, it was known as *Social Sciences and Humanities Index*, but has recently been bifurcated into two parts, the (i) *Social Sciences Index* and (ii) *Humanities Index*.

The most important indexing services in India are:

1. *Index India:* This index is published by the Rajasthan University Library, Jaipur. It is a quarterly of social sciences on Indian publications. It combines in one sequence indices pertaining to separate author and subject indexes—Indian newspapers, Indian periodicals, foreign periodicals, composite publications, biographical profiles, book reviews, and index to theses and dissertations.
2. *Guide to Indian Periodical Literature Quarterly of Social Issues:* This is author-subject index to articles, research papers, notes, conference proceedings, and book reviews from about 300 Indian journals in social sciences and humanities. It also covers the daily *Times of India* for news, signed articles, and significant editorials. The entries are arranged in alphabetical order, in the dictionary pattern. It is a basic reference tool on social sciences literature in India.

[*Indexing Services in India*. Published by the Indian Documentation Service, Gurgaon, India.]

ABSTRACTS

Abstracts are selective references and give a gist of the content of an article, book, dissertation, and research writings.

1. *Social Science Abstracts:* This is a comprehensive abstracting and indexing journal of the world's periodical literature in the social sciences. It was published between 1929

and 1933 by the Social Science Abstracts Inc., New York, and was discontinued for lack of funds.

2. *Dissertation Abstracts International:* This reference list was first published in 1938 as Micro Film Abstracts. It is published monthly by Xerox University Microfilms, Ann Arbor, Michigan, USA. It is a compilation of abstracts of doctoral dissertations submitted to Xerox University Microfilms by more than 350 cooperating institutions in the United States of America and Canada. Now it also includes dissertations from European universities.

   Dissertation Abstracts International is published in two sections:

   (a) Humanities
   (b) Sciences

   The Humanities section is further sub-divided into five main areas: These are:

   - Communications and thc arts
   - Education
   - Language, literature, and linguistics
   - Philosophy, religion and theology
   - Social sciences

   Keyword, title, and author indexes are also provided.

3. *Indian Behavioural Science Abstracts (Quarterly):* Published by Behavioural Science Centre, Delhi, this is a comprehensive journal containing detailed abstracts of behavioural science literature produced in India, or abroad, regarding India.

   It covers such fields as psychology, sociology and social anthropology, and behavioural aspects of economics, education, management, political science, public administration, extension education, social work, history, and human geography.

   It provides abstracts of articles, books, and research publications as well as unpublished doctoral, masters, and diploma theses. It gives all relevant details such as date of research, area, details of sample, methodology, and results of research.

4. *Indian Dissertation Abstract (Quarterly):* Published by the ICSSR, New Delhi, in collaboration with the Inter-university Board, it provides abstracts of doctoral dissertations accepted by Indian universities in the social sciences. The disciplines included within the scope of this journal are—economics (including commerce), education, management (including business administration), political science (including international relations), psychology, public administration, sociology (including criminology and social work), and social science aspects of anthropology, demography, geography, history, law, and linguistics.

   Each abstract included in the IDA contains information regarding the university, year of submission, supervision, title of the dissertation, methodology adopted and main findings of the study.

STATISTICAL SOURCES

The most important sources of data for any research scholar are statistical abstracts. The most frequently consulted of these publications are:

1. *United Nations Statistical Yearbook:* Published annually by the UN Department of Economic and Social Affairs, New York, it contains countrywise statistics of the world on population, national income, agricultural and industrial production, energy, external trade, and transport.
2. *Production Yearbook:* This is an annual publication, published by FAO Rome. It contains annual data on all important aspects of food and agriculture, including population, index numbers of agricultural and food production, prices, freight rates, and wages.

   Miscellaneous papers or monographs (ad hoc)

3. *Statistical Abstract India:* This publication serves as an important source material for data on different sectors of the Indian economy. It is published by the Central Statistical Organisation, Department of Statistics, Ministry of Planning, Government of India.
4. *Statistical Outline of India:* This is an annual publication, published by the Tata Industries Private Limited Bombay. This serves as a source of Industrial Statistics.
5. *Labour Statistics:* This annual publication is brought by the Ministry of Labour, Government of India. Source of information in all aspects of labour and manpower in India.

DIRECTORIES AND YEARBOOKS

Directories are normally lists of persons or organisations arranged alphabetically. Yearbooks and directories provide recent information, and the main trends in subjects of common interest, and are useful sources of general information.

1. *Yearbook of International Organisations:* This book has been published by the Union of International Associations, Brussels, since 1948. It is a reliable up-to-date source of information on international organisations. Information for each entry includes the name, address, brief history, membership, officers, finances, current activities, and list of publications of each listed organisation.
2. *Directory of Social Science Research Institutions in India:* This directory has been compiled by the ICSSR, which functions as a clearing house of information with respect to all research in the field of social sciences. The Directory covers social sciences research institutions that are outside the university system. But a few institutions (for example, Agricultural Economic Research Centres) have been included even though they are functioning within the university system. The Directory lists institutions/organisations in an alphabetical order.
3. *Learned Societies and Institutions in India—Activities and Publications:* Published by the Metropolitan Book Co., Delhi, this directory is intended to provide a reference tool that would facilitate building up the research collection in a library and also promote interchange of ideas among scholars engaged in similar academic pursuits. To fulfill this objective, it is designed to include aspects relating to various institutions, such as nature and scope of institutional publications, a brief descriptive introduction of each institution, including its publications, and latest address of each institution.

It is includes an index to institutional journals, an author index, and subject classification of institutions.

This discovery covers 375 institutions and over 4000 titles published by them.

ENCYCLOPEDIAS

Encyclopedias contain informational articles on subjects in every field, usually arranged in alphabetical order. Subject encyclopedias are useful reference tools in their respective fields. Listed below are two encyclopedias in the field of social sciences:

1. *International Encyclopaedia of the Social Sciences:* Edited by David L. Sills. and published by the Macmillan Co. and the Free Press in New York (1968), this encyclopaedia consists 16 volumes. 17th volume is the index.
2. *Encyclopaedia of the Social Sciences:* Edited by Edwin R.A. Soligman and published by Macmillan Co., in 1930 (1957). 16 volumes in 8.

DICTIONARIES

Dictionaries are used for definitions, spellings, abbreviations, symbols, foreign terms, usage of the words and phrases. Apart from general language dictionaries, there are also dictionaries that define terms of a technical and specialised nature. Subject dictionaries are useful sources of information as they give definitions of terms and new subdivisions for a clear understanding and proper perspective of the subject.

1. *Dictionary of the Social Sciences:* This distionary has been edited by Julius Gould and William L Kolb, compiled under the auspices of the UNESCO and published by the Free Press, New York, in 1964. It is designed to describe and define approximately one thousand basic concepts used in the social sciences. About 270 social scientists were consulted for its compilation.
2. *Dictoninary of Behavioural Science:* Compiled and edited by Benjamin B Wolman and published by Van Nostrand Reinhold Co., New York, in 1973, this dictionary is an up-to-date, comprehensive, and authoritative reference work covering every meaningful aspect of behavioural science. It defines approximately 20,000 terms in the fields of psychology, psychiatry, psychoanalysis, neurology, psychopharmacology, biochemistry, endocriminology, and related disciplines.
3. *Indian Economic Diary (Weekly):* This is a weekly reference publication, presenting an accurate and authentic record of significant economic events in India. It is a digest of news and features prepared from 50 different Indian newspapers and periodicals by a group of specialists in various economic disciplines.
4. *Data India (Weekly):* This periodical is published by the Press Institute of India, New Delhi.

It is the most important and useful reference source for data on all social and economic activities in India. The references are listed subject wise.

OTHER SOURCES

1. *Monthly Review of Indian Economy*: *Economic Intelligence Science:* This is published by the Centre for Monitoring Indian Economy Pvt. Ltd., Mumbai. This periodical provides a wide variety of economic information on agriculture, energy, industrial, finance banking, and statewise economic profiles. (Website: *www.cmie.com*).
2. *Survey of Social Science Research* published by Delhi.
3. *Economic and Political Weekly (EPW):* ICSSR, Research foundation publications.
4. *Management Information Guide:* This offers bibliographic references in many business areas.
5. *Human Resource Management Abstracts:* This is an index of articles that deal with management of people and organisational behaviour.
6. *Psychological Abstracts:* This publications summarises literature in psychology, covering several hundred journals, reports, monographs, and other scientific documents.
7. ABI/INFORM Global and ABI/INFORM provide the capability to search most major business, management, trade and industry, and scholarly journals from 1971 onwards. The information search can be made by keying in the name of the author, periodical title, article title, or company name. Full texts from journals and business periodicals are also available on CD-ROMs and electronic services.
8. INFOTRAC has a CD_ROM with an expanded academic, business, and investment periodicals index covering over 1000 periodicals in social sciences and business, which are updated monthly.
9. *Human Resources Abstract* is a quarterly abstracting service that covers human, social, and manpower information in journals and Govt. Publications.
10. The *Wall Street Journal Index* is available in full text at the Dow Jones News/ Retrieval Service. This index covers corporate news as well as general economic and social news. The Dow Jones News/Retrieval Service offers full texts of articles.
11. *Guide to Dissertation Abstracts*
12. Conference Papers
13. Conference Proceedings
14. Operations Research/Management Science
15. *Periodicals Abstract*
16. *Personnel Management Abstract*
17. *Social Science Citation Index*

SOME USEFUL WEBSITES ON MANAGEMENT RESEARCH METHODOLOGY

Social Science

Research methods in the social sciences: An internet resource list—*http://www.library.miami.edu/netguides/psymeth.html*

Resource for methods in evaluation and social research—*http://gsociology.icaap.org/methods/*

Social science data archives—*http://www2.fmg.uva.nl/sociosite/databases.html*

Social science research network—*http://www.ssrn.com/ern/*

General

Research methods links
http://www.msu.edu/course/prr/844/methlk.htm

Research methods links
http://www.msu.edu/course/prr/844/methlk.htm

Research methods knowledge base
http://trochim.human.cornell.edu/kb/index.htm

Research methodology sites and gateways
http://www.geocities.com/orgscience/gateway.htm

Scientific method links
http://kosmoi.com/Science/Method/links.shtml

Basic business research methods
http://www.mapnp.org/library/research/research.htm

Website of research methods Division of Academy of Management
http://www.aom.pace.edu/rmd/

Research methods knowledge base—Powerpoint lectures
http://trochim.human.cornell.edu/lectureshows/directory.htm

Primary, secondary, and tertiary sources
http://www.library.jcu.edu.au/LibraryGuides/primsrcs.shtml

World Bank research—Working papers
http://econ.worldbank.org/view.php?id=2382

Dr. Arsham's web page
http://home.ubalt.edu/ntsbarsh/

TSPBIB home page
http://www.ing.unlp.edu.ar/cetad/mos/TSPBIB_home.html

Research methods Division of the Academy of Management
http://allserv.rug.ac.be/~flievens/meth.htm

Research centres, groups, and institutes
http://www.lse.ac.uk/departments/researchCentresGroupsAndInstitutes/

Research methods division
http://aom.pace.edu/rmd/

Internet public library
http://www.ipl.org/div/subject/browse/soc00.00.00

Academy of Management
aom@academy.pace.edu

All business network
http://www.webcom.com/-garnet/labor/aa_eeo.html

(This site offers articles, publications, and government resources related to human resources management.)

AT&T Business Network

http://www.bnet.att.com

(This site gives access to good business resources and offers the latest business news and information.)

Business information resources

http://www.eotw.com/business_info.html

(Links small business researchers to magazines and journals, government and law, financial services, and other entrepreneurial organisations.)

Business management

http://www.lia.co.za/users/johannh/index.htm

(This page offers sources dealing with project management, total quality management (TQM), continuous improvement, productivity improvement, and related topics.)

Business researcher's interests—*http://www.brint.com/interest.html*

Dow Jones Business Directory—*http://www.Business directory.dowjones,com*

Entrepreneur's Resources Center—*http://www.herring.com/forum*

Harvard Business School Publishing—*http://www.hbsp.harvard.edu*

MBA page—*http://www.cob.ohio-state.edu/dept/fin/mba/htm*

(Designed by Ohio State University to help MBA Students.)

Multinational companies—*http://web.idirect.com/~tiger/worldbea.htm*

Wall Street Journal—*http://www.wsj.com*

Wall Street research net—*http://www.wsrn.com*

Operations Research Statistics and Mathematics

Statistical package resources—*http://dpls.dacc.wisc.edu/types/stat_pack_table.htm*

Statistical terminology—*http://www.nsf.gov/sbe/srs/help/helpterm.htm*

Internet glossary of statistical terms—*http://www.animatedsoftware.com/statglos/statglos.htm*

Statistics glossary—*http://www.cas.lancs.ac.uk/glossary_v1.1/main.html*

The Math Forum—Math Library—*http://www.mathforum.org/library/topics/operations_research/*

Institute for Operations Research and Management Science—*http://www.informs.org*

OR/MS Today—*http://lionhrtpub.com/orms/*

Operational Research Society—*http://www.orsoc.org.uk/*

Mathematical programming glossary—*http://carbon.cudenver.edu/~hgreenbe/glossary/index.php*

OR library—*http://www.brunel.ac.uk/depts/ma/research/jeb/info.html*

Michael Trick's operations research page—*http://mat.gsia.cmu.edu/*

A compendium of NP optimisation problems—*http://www.nada.kth.se/~viggo/problemlist/compendium.html*

The VRP web—*http://neo.lcc.uma.es/radi-aeb/WebVRP/index.html?links.html*

Research funding sources for OR/MS researchers—*http://www.informs.org/Funds/funding.html*

News and useful websites on OR—*http://www.ntut.edu.tw/~bmcchen/homepage/english/main a11.htm*

Optimisation and operations research sites—*http://www.rpi.edu/~mitchj/sites_or.html*

Decision Sciences Institute and useful links—*http://www.decisionsciences.org/links.htm*

Simulation links and information—*http://www.informs-cs.org/geninfo.html*

Operations research/Management science categories—*http://www.business.com/directory/management/operations_management/operations_research_management_science_or_ms/*

Statistics on the web—*http://my.execpc.com/~helberg/statistics.html*

Research journals in or/qm—*http://www.unisa.ac.za/Default.asp?Cmd=ViewContent&ContentID=1509*

The Pacific Optimization Research Activity Group—*http://www.polyu.edu.hk/~ama/links/pop/an1.html*

Dynamics for business policy—*http://web.mit.edu/15.87/www*

Marketing and Marketing Research

Marketing research and information systems—*http://www.fao.org/docrep/W3241E/w3241e00.htm#Contents*

List of secondary data sources for marketing research—*http://elab.vanderbilt.edu/curriculum/courses/novak/mktres98/seccondary_ data_guide.html*

Secondary research sources for marketing and advertising decisions—*http://jmc.ou.edu/FredBeard/Secondary.html*

Knowledge source for marketing research—*http://www.knowthis.com/research/methods.htm*

Marketing research – Interested Links—*http://www.educationindex.com/market/*

Data Related

Benchmark data set of the set covering problem—*http://math.josai.ac.jp/~kiwamura/en/*

Research methodology—secondary data sources—*http://www.nrf.ac.za/yenza/research/data.htm*

Other secondary data sources—*http://www.chicagofed.org/economic_research_and_data/other_secondary_ data_sources.cfm*

Information/Information Technology

Data Mining—*http://dm.section.informs.org/*

Department of Information Technology, India—*http://www.mit.gov.in/other.asp*

Operations Management

Institute of Operations Management and useful sites—*http://www.iomnet.org.uk/*

OM related organisations—*http://www.mhhe.com/omc/organizations.jsp*

Operations and supply chain management—*http://www.library.hbs.edu/guides/operations/index_print.html*

Institute for Supply Chain Management—*http://www.ism.ws/*

Logistics and supply management—*http://www.summitconnects.com/Online_Procurement_Links/Logistics_Supply_ Management.htm*

Integrated SCM and useful links—*http://web.mit.edu/supplychain/overview/*

Inventory management and warehouse operations—*http://www.inventoryops.com/toc.htm*

Creativity and Heuristics

Links to creativity related websites—*http://www.greggfraley.com/Links.htm*

Creativity—*http://www2.latech.edu/~dalea/instruction/creativity.html*

Heuristic—definition, meaning, explanation and information—*http://www.free-definition.com/Heuristic.html*

Heuristics—*http://www.nist.gov/dads/HTML/heuristic.html*

Heuristic evaluation—*http://www.useit.com/papers/**heuristic**/*

Heuristic paradigm—*http://www.heuristicparadigm.com/*

Meta-heuristic—*http://www.nist.gov/dads/HTML/metaheuristic.html*

Meta-Heuristics Books—*http://www.tabusearch.net/Resources/Books/Books_main.ASP*

Memetic Algorithms' home page—*http://www.ing.unlp.edu.ar/cetad/mos/memetic_home.html*

Finance and Accounting

Finance site list—*http://fisher.osu.edu/fin/journal/jofsites.htm*

CNN Financial Network—*http://cnnfn.com/index.html*

Fidelity Investment—*http://www.fid-inv.com*

I.O.M.A—*http://www.ioma.com/ioma/direct.html*

(This site links to business resources that include financial management, legal resources, small business, human resources, and internet marketing.)

Organisational Behaviour and HRM

Resources for organisational research—*http://www.uwec.edu/Sampsow/Links/ORM.htm*

Sources in Industrial/Organisational Psychology and organisational behaviour—*http://sorrel.humboldt.edu/~campbell/iolinks.htm*

HR portal—HR links—*http://www.adecco.com/Channels/adecco/human+resources/useful+websites/hr+professional+body/default.asp*

ASTD—*http://www.astd.org*

(ASTD (American Society for Training and Development) has information on shifting paradigms from training to performance.)

Human resources management on the internet—*http://members.gnn.com/hrmbasics/hrinet.htm*

Society for Human Resource Management—*http://www.shrm.org*

Economics

Research papers in economics—*http://repec.org/*

Economics links—*http://www.szarka.org/econ.html*

Internet resources for economists—*http://www.oswego.edu/~economic/econweb.htm*

Economics departments, institutes and research centers—*http://edirc.repec.org/continents.html*

Economics working papers archive *http://econwpa.wustl.edu/*

Methodology and history of economics—*http://cepa.newschool.edu/het/essays/method.htm*

Index to business topics—*http://www1.usal.com/~ibnet/iccindex.html*

(Covers a vast range of subjects for companies engaged in international trade.)

International Business Directory—*http://www.et.byu.edu/-eliasone/main.html*

(This site offered by BYU has valuable sources for international business.)

APPENDIX C

Formulae for Hypothesis Testing

1. Large sample statistical test

θ may equal μ p, $(\mu_1 - \mu_2)$, or $(p_1 - p_2)$

$H_o : \theta = \theta_o$

$H_a : \theta > \theta_o$ or $H_a : \theta < \theta_o$ (One-tailed test)

$H_a : \theta \neq \theta_o$ (Two-tailed test)

$$\text{Test Statistic} : z = \frac{\theta - \theta_o}{\sigma\theta}$$

Reject H_o if $Z > Z_\alpha$ or if $Z < -Z_\alpha$ (One-tailed test)

Reject H_o if $Z > Z_{\alpha/2}$ or if $Z < -Z_{\alpha/2}$ (Two-tailed test)

2. Small-sample test for a population mean

$H_o : \mu = \mu_o$

$H_a : \mu > \mu_o$ or $\mu < \mu_o$

$$\text{Test Statistic} : t = \frac{x - \mu_o}{s/\sqrt{n}}$$

Reject H_o if $t > t_\alpha$ or if $t < -t_\alpha$ (One-tailed test)

Reject H_o if $t > t_{\alpha/2}$ or if $t < -t_{\alpha/2}$ (Two-tailed test)

3. Small-sample test for the difference between two means based on independent random samples

$H_o : \mu_1 - \mu_o = D_o$

H_a : One or two-tailed hypothesis determined by the experimenter.

$$\text{Test Statistic} : t = \frac{(\bar{x}_1 - \bar{x}_2 - D_o)}{s\sqrt{(1/n_1 + 1/n_2)}} \quad \text{df} = n_1 + n_2 - 2$$

Reject H_o if $t > t_\alpha$ or if $t < -t_\alpha$ (One-tailed test)

Reject H_o when $t > t_{\alpha/2}$ or if $t < -t_{\alpha/2}$ (Two-tailed test)

4. Small-sample statistical test for the difference between two means based on a pair-difference experiment

$$H_o : \mu_1 - \mu_2 = \mu_d = D_o$$

$$\text{Test Statistic} : t = \frac{\bar{d} - D_o}{S_d/\sqrt{n}}$$

n is the number of paired differences and

$$S_d = \frac{\sum_{i=1}^{n} (d_i - \bar{d})^2}{n-1}$$

Standard deviation of paired differences.

Alternative hypothesis H_a and α are specified by the experimenter.

5. Test of an hypothesis about a population variance

$$H_o : \sigma^2 = \sigma^2_o$$

$$H_a : \sigma^2 \neq \sigma^2_o \qquad \text{(Two-tailed test)}$$

$$H_a : \sigma^2 > \sigma^2_o \text{ or } H_a : \sigma^2 < \sigma^2_o \qquad \text{(One-tailed test)}$$

$$\text{Test statistic} : X^2 = \frac{(n-1)S^2}{\sigma_o^2} \qquad \text{df} = (n-1)$$

$$\text{Reject } H_o \text{ if } X^2 < X^2_{1-\alpha/2} \text{ with } (n-1) \text{ df} \qquad \text{(Two-tailed test)}$$

$$\text{Reject } H_a : \sigma^2 > \sigma^2_o \text{ or } \sigma^2 < \sigma^2_o \qquad \text{(One-tailed test)}$$

6. Test of hypothesis about equality of two population variances

$$H_o : \sigma^2_1 = \sigma^2_2$$

$$H_a : \sigma^2_1 \neq \sigma^2_2 \qquad \text{(Two-tailed test)}$$

$$\text{Test statistic} : F = S^2_1/S^2_2$$

$$\text{df} = (n_1 - 1) \text{ and } (n_2 - 1)$$

$$\text{Reject } H_o \text{ if } F > F_{\alpha/2} \qquad \text{(Two-tailed test)}$$

7. Test of a hypothesis concerning the slope of a line

$$H_o : \beta_1 = \beta_{1o}$$

H_a : Specified by the experimenter

$$\text{Test Statistic } t = \frac{\beta_1 - \beta_{1o}}{s/\sqrt{s_{\beta 1}}}$$

$$\text{df} = (n-2)$$

Reject H_o, if $t < t_e$.

8. The Sign Test ($n < 25$)

H_o: The two population distributions are identical and P(A exceeds B for a given pair) $= p = .5$.

H_a: The two population distributions are not identical and $p \neq .5$, or

H_a: The population of A/B measurements is shifted to the right of the population of B/A measurements and p > .5*.

Test statistic: The number of times that (A – B) was positive

Rejection region: Reject H_o if $X \leq X_L$ or $X \geq X_U$

Where X_L and X_U are the lower and upper-tailed values of a binomial distribution, for a two-tailed test.

Reject H_o if $X \geq X_U$

Where X_U is the upper-tailed value of a binomial distribution, for one-tailed test.

9. Sign Test for large samples ($n \geq 25$)

$H_o : p = .5$

$H_a : p \neq .5$ (Two-tailed test)

$H_a = 0.5$ or $H_a < 0.5$ (One-tailed test)

$$\text{Test statistic} : z = \frac{x - .5n}{.5\sqrt{n}}$$

Reject H_o if $z \geq z_{\alpha/2}$ or $z \leq z_{\alpha/2}$

10. Mann–Whitney U Test

H_o: The population relative frequency distributions for A and B are identical.

H_a: The two population relative frequency distributions are shifted with respect to their relative locations (a two-tailed test), or

H_a: The population relative frequency distribution for A is shifted to the right of the relative frequency distribution for population B (one-tailed test).*

Test statistic: Use U, the smaller of U_A and U_B (two-tailed test).

$$U_A = n_1 n_2 + n_1 (n_1 + 1)/2 - T_A, \text{ and}$$
$$U_B = n_1 n_2 + n_2 (n_2 + 1)0/2 - T_B$$

Where T_A and T_B are the rank sums for samples A and B, respectively.

Use U_A for a one-tailed test.

Reject H_o if $U \leq U_o$,

Where $P(U \leq U_o) = \alpha/2$. (two tailed test).

For a one-tailed test and a given value of α, reject H_o if $U_A \leq Uo = \alpha$.

11. Mann–Whitney U Test for large samples ($n_1 > 10$ and $n_2 > 10$)

H_o: The population relative frequency distribution for A and B are identical.

H_a: The two population relative frequency distributions are not identical two-tailed test

H_a: The population relative frequency distribution for A/B is shifted to the right (or left) of the relative frequency distribution for population B/A. (One-tailed test)

$$\text{Test statistic} : z = \frac{U - [(n_1 n_2)/2]}{\sqrt{[n_1 n_2 (n_1 + n_2 + 1)/12]}}, \text{ and}$$

Let $U = U_A$.

---

* For the sake of convenience, we will describe the one-tailed test as the one designed to detect a shift in the distribution of the A measurements to the right of the distributions of the B measurements. To detect a shift in the B distribution to the right of the A distribution, just interchange the letters A and B in the discussion.

Reject H_o if $z \geq z_{\alpha/2}$ or $z \leq z_{\alpha/2}$ (Two-tailed test)

Reject H_o when $z < -z_\alpha$ (One-tailed test)

12. Kruskal–Wallis test for comparing t, more than 2 population distributions

H_o : Distributions of all populations are identical.

H_a : At least two of the t relative frequency distributions differ.

$$\text{Test statistic : } H = \frac{12}{n(n+1)} \sum_{j=1}^{t} \frac{R_j^2}{n_j} - 3(n+1);\ \text{df} = (t-1)$$

Reject H_o if $H > X^2_\alpha$

13. Calculation of the test statistic and the Wilcoxon Signed-Rank Test

(i) Calculate the differences $(X_A - X_B)$ for each of the n pairs. Differences equal to zero are eliminated and the number of pairs n, is reduced accordingly.

(ii) Rank the absolute values of the differences, assigning 1 to the smallest, 2 to the second smallest, and so on. Tied observations are assigned the average of the ranks that would have been assigned with no ties.

(iii) Calculate the rank sum for the negative differences and label this value T^-. Similarly, calculate T^+, the rank sum for the positive differences.

(iv) For a two-tailed test we use the smaller of these two quantities, T, as the test statistic to test the null hypothesis that the two population relative frequency histograms are identical.

14. Wilcoxon Signed-Rank for a paired experiment

H_o: The two population relative frequency distributions are identical.

H_a: The two population relative frequency distributions are not identical, in a two-tailed test

H_a: The relative frequency distribution for population A is shifted to the right (or left) of the relative frequency distribution for population B, in a one tailed test.

Test statistic: T, the smaller of the rank sum for positive differences and the rank sum for negative differences.

Reject H_o if $T \leq T_o$, where T_o is the critical value in tables.

15. Large-sample Wilcoxon Signed-Rank test for a paired experiment (n ≥ 25)

H_o: The two population relative frequency distributions for A and B are identical.

H_a: The two population relative frequency distributions differ in location, in a two-tailed test

H_a: The population relative frequency distribution for A is shifted to the right (or left) of the relative frequency distribution for population B – a one tailed test.

$$\text{Test statistic: } z = \frac{T - [n(n+1)/4]}{\sqrt{([n(n+1)(2n+1)/24)}}, \text{ and}$$

T can be either T^+ or T^-.

Reject H_o if $z \geq z_{\alpha/2}$ or $z \leq -z_{\alpha/2}$ (Two-tailed test)

Place all α in one tail of the z distribution. To detect a shift in the distribution of the A observations to the right of the distribution of the B observations, let $T=T^+$ and reject H_o when $z > z_\alpha$.

To detect a shift in the opposite direction, let $T=T^-$ and reject H_o if $z < -z_\alpha$ (One-tailed test).

16. Friedman Test for randomised block designs

H_o: The probability distributions for the t treatments (populations) are identical.

H_a: At least two of the t treatments have different probability distributions.

$$\text{Test statistic}: \chi^2 = \frac{12}{bt(t+1)} \sum_{j=1}^{t} R_j^2 - 3b(t+1); \qquad \text{df} = (t-1)$$

Reject H_o if $\chi^2 > \chi^2_\alpha$.

17. Runs Test

H_o: The sequence of elements call them S's and F's, has been produced in a random manner.

H_a: The elements have been produced in a non-random sequence (a two-tailed test)

H_a: The process is non-random owing solely to overmixing (an upper one-tailed test) or solely to undermixing (a lower one-tailed test).

Test statistic: R is the number of runs.

Reject H_o if $R \le k_1$ or $R \ge k_2$

Where $P(R \le k_1) + P(R \ge k_2) = \alpha$ and k_1 and k_2 are obtained from the tables (Two-tailed test).

Reject H_o if $R \le k_1$, where $P(R \le k_1) = \alpha$ and k_1 is obtained from the tables (Two-tailed test)

Reject H_o if $R \ge k_2$, where $P(R \ge k_2)$ is obtained from the tables (One tailed test).

18. Large-Sample Runs Test (n_1 > 10 and n_2 > 10)

H_o: The sequence of elements has been produced in a random manner.

H_a: The elements have been produced in a non-random sequence.

$$\text{Test statistic}: z = \frac{R - (2n_1n_2/n_1 + n_2) - 1}{\sqrt{\left[\dfrac{2n_1n_2(2n_1n_2 - n_1 - n_2)}{(n_1+n_2)^2(n_1+n_2)-1}\right]}}$$

Reject H_o if $z \ge z_{\alpha/2}$ or if $z \le -z_{\alpha/2}$ (Two-tailed test)

Reject H_o if $z \ge z_\alpha$ or $z \le -z_\alpha$ (One-tailed test)

19. Chi-Squared test of independence

H_o: row and column variables are independent

H_a: row and column variables are associated (dependent)

Test statistic : $\chi^2 = \Sigma(\text{Obs} - \text{Exp})^2/\text{Exp}$, where the sum if taken over all cells of the table.

df = (R – 1).(C – 1)

Reject H_o if $\chi^2 > \chi^2_\alpha$

Selected Statistical Tables

Table D-1 Lower Tail Areas of Standard Normal Distribution

z	0.09	0.08	0.07	0.06	0.05	0.04	0.03	0.02	0.01	0.00
–3.40	0.0002	0.0003	0.0003	0.0003	0.0003	0.0003	0.0003	0.0003	0.0003	0.0002
–3.30	0.0003	0.0004	0.0004	0.0004	0.0004	0.0004	0.0004	0.0005	0.0005	0.0005
–3.20	0.0005	0.0005	0.0005	0.0006	0.0006	0.0006	0.0006	0.0006	0.0007	0.0007
–3.10	0.0007	0.0007	0.0008	0.0008	0.0008	0.0008	0.0009	0.0009	0.0009	0.0010
–3.00	0.0010	0.0010	0.0011	0.0011	0.0011	0.0012	0.0012	0.0013	0.0013	0.0013
–2.90	0.0014	0.0014	0.0015	0.0015	0.0016	0.0016	0.0017	0.0018	0.0018	0.0019
–2.80	0.0019	0.0020	0.0021	0.0021	0.0022	0.0023	0.0023	0.0024	0.0025	0.0026
–2.70	0.0026	0.0027	0.0028	0.0029	0.0030	0.0031	0.0032	0.0033	0.0034	0.0035
–2.60	0.0036	0.0037	0.0038	0.0039	0.0040	0.0041	0.0043	0.0044	0.0045	0.0047
–2.50	0.0048	0.0049	0.0051	0.0052	0.0054	0.0055	0.0057	0.0059	0.0060	0.0062
–2.40	0.0064	0.0066	0.0068	0.0069	0.0071	0.0073	0.0075	0.0078	0.0080	0.0082
–2.30	0.0084	0.0087	0.0089	0.0091	0.0094	0.0096	0.0099	0.0102	0.0104	0.0107
–2.20	0.0110	0.0113	0.0116	0.0119	0.0122	0.0125	0.0129	0.0132	0.0136	0.0139
–2.10	0.0143	0.0146	0.0150	0.0154	0.0158	0.0162	0.0166	0.0170	0.0174	0.0179
–2.00	0.0183	0.0188	0.0192	0.0197	0.0202	0.0207	0.0212	0.0217	0.0222	0.0228
–1.90	0.0233	0.0239	0.0244	0.0250	0.0256	0.0262	0.0268	0.0274	0.0281	0.0287
–1.80	0.0294	0.0301	0.0307	0.0314	0.0322	0.0329	0.0336	0.0344	0.0351	0.0359
–1.70	0.0367	0.0375	0.0384	0.0392	0.0401	0.0409	0.0418	0.0427	0.0436	0.0446
–1.60	0.0455	0.0465	0.0475	0.0485	0.0495	0.0505	0.0516	0.0526	0.0537	0.0548
–1.50	0.0559	0.0571	0.0582	0.0594	0.0606	0.0618	0.0630	0.0643	0.0655	0.0668
–1.40	0.0681	0.0694	0.0708	0.0721	0.0735	0.0749	0.0764	0.0778	0.0793	0.0808
–1.30	0.0823	0.0838	0.0853	0.0869	0.0885	0.0901	0.0918	0.0934	0.0951	0.0968
–1.20	0.0985	0.1003	0.1020	0.1038	0.1056	0.1075	0.1093	0.1112	0.1131	0.1151
–1.10	0.1170	0.1190	0.1210	0.1230	0.1251	0.1271	0.1292	0.1314	0.1335	0.1357
–1.00	0.1379	0.1401	0.1423	0.1446	0.1469	0.1492	0.1515	0.1539	0.1562	0.1587
–0.90	0.1611	0.1635	0.1660	0.1685	0.1711	0.1736	0.1762	0.1788	0.1814	0.1841
–0.80	0.1867	0.1894	0.1922	0.1949	0.1977	0.2005	0.2033	0.2061	0.2090	0.2119
–0.70	0.2148	0.2177	0.2206	0.2236	0.2266	0.2296	0.2327	0.2358	0.2389	0.2420
–0.60	0.2451	0.2483	0.2514	0.2546	0.2578	0.2611	0.2643	0.2676	0.2709	0.2743
–0.50	0.2776	0.2810	0.2843	0.2877	0.2912	0.2946	0.2981	0.3015	0.3050	0.3085
–0.40	0.3121	0.3156	0.3192	0.3228	0.3264	0.3300	0.3336	0.3372	0.3409	0.3446
–0.30	0.3483	0.3520	0.3557	0.3594	0.3632	0.3669	0.3707	0.3745	0.3783	0.3821
–0.20	0.3859	0.3897	0.3936	0.3974	0.4013	0.4052	0.4090	0.4129	0.4168	0.4207
–0.10	0.4247	0.4286	0.4325	0.4364	0.4404	0.4443	0.4483	0.4522	0.4562	0.4602
–0.00	0.4641	0.4681	0.4721	0.4761	0.4801	0.4840	0.4880	0.4920	0.4960	0.5000

Table D-1 Lower Tail Areas of Standard Normal Distribution (Contd.)

z	*0.00*	*0.01*	*0.02*	*0.03*	*0.04*	*0.05*	*0.06*	*0.07*	*0.08*	*0.09*
0.00	0.5000	0.5040	0.5080	0.5120	0.5160	0.5199	0.5239	0.5279	0.5319	0.5359
0.10	0.5398	0.5438	0.5478	0.5517	0.5557	0.5596	0.5636	0.5675	0.5714	0.5753
0.20	0.5793	0.5832	0.5871	0.5910	0.5948	0.5987	0.6026	0.6064	0.6103	0.6141
0.30	0.6179	0.6217	0.6255	0.6293	0.6331	0.6368	0.6406	0.6443	0.6480	0.6517
0.40	0.6554	0.6591	0.6628	0.6664	0.6700	0.6736	0.6772	0.6808	0.6844	0.6879
0.50	0.6915	0.6950	0.6985	0.7019	0.7054	0.7088	0.7123	0.7157	0.7190	0.7224
0.60	0.7257	0.7291	0.7324	0.7357	0.7389	0.7422	0.7454	0.7486	0.7517	0.7549
0.70	0.7580	0.7611	0.7642	0.7673	0.7704	0.7734	0.7764	0.7794	0.7823	0.7852
0.80	0.7881	0.7910	0.7939	0.7967	0.7995	0.8023	0.8051	0.8078	0.8106	0.8133
0.90	0.8159	0.8186	0.8212	0.8238	0.8264	0.8289	0.8315	0.8340	0.8365	0.8389
1.00	0.8413	0.8438	0.8461	0.8485	0.8508	0.8531	0.8554	0.8577	0.8599	0.8621
1.10	0.8643	0.8665	0.8686	0.8708	0.8729	0.8749	0.8770	0.8790	0.8810	0.8830
1.20	0.8849	0.8869	0.8888	0.8907	0.8925	0.8944	0.8962	0.8980	0.8997	0.9015
1.30	0.9032	0.9049	0.9066	0.9082	0.9099	0.9115	0.9131	0.9147	0.9162	0.9177
1.40	0.9192	0.9207	0.9222	0.9236	0.9251	0.9265	0.9279	0.9292	0.9306	0.9319
1.50	0.9332	0.9345	0.9357	0.9370	0.9382	0.9394	0.9406	0.9418	0.9429	0.9441
1.60	0.9452	0.9463	0.9474	0.9484	0.9495	0.9505	0.9515	0.9525	0.9535	0.9545
1.70	0.9554	0.9564	0.9573	0.9582	0.9591	0.9599	0.9608	0.9616	0.9625	0.9633
1.80	0.9641	0.9649	0.9656	0.9664	0.9671	0.9678	0.9686	0.9693	0.9699	0.9706
1.90	0.9713	0.9719	0.9726	0.9732	0.9738	0.9744	0.9750	0.9756	0.9761	0.9767
2.00	0.9772	0.9778	0.9783	0.9788	0.9793	0.9798	0.9803	0.9808	0.9812	0.9817
2.10	0.9821	0.9826	0.9830	0.9834	0.9838	0.9842	0.9846	0.9850	0.9854	0.9857
2.20	0.9861	0.9864	0.9868	0.9871	0.9875	0.9878	0.9881	0.9884	0.9887	0.9890
2.30	0.9893	0.9896	0.9898	0.9901	0.9904	0.9906	0.9909	0.9911	0.9913	0.9916
2.40	0.9918	0.9920	0.9922	0.9925	0.9927	0.9929	0.9931	0.9932	0.9934	0.9936
2.50	0.9938	0.9940	0.9941	0.9943	0.9945	0.9946	0.9948	0.9949	0.9951	0.9952
2.60	0.9953	0.9955	0.9956	0.9957	0.9959	0.9960	0.9961	0.9962	0.9963	0.9964
2.70	0.9965	0.9966	0.9967	0.9968	0.9969	0.9970	0.9971	0.9972	0.9973	0.9974
2.80	0.9974	0.9975	0.9976	0.9977	0.9977	0.9978	0.9979	0.9979	0.9980	0.9981
2.90	0.9981	0.9982	0.9982	0.9983	0.9984	0.9984	0.9985	0.9985	0.9986	0.9986
3.00	0.9987	0.9987	0.9987	0.9988	0.9988	0.9989	0.9989	0.9989	0.9990	0.9990
3.10	0.9990	0.9991	0.9991	0.9991	0.9992	0.9992	0.9992	0.9992	0.9993	0.9931
3.20	0.9993	0.9993	0.9994	0.9994	0.9994	0.9994	0.9994	0.9995	0.9995	0.9995
3.30	0.9995	0.9995	0.9995	0.9996	0.9996	0.9996	0.9996	0.9996	0.9996	0.9997
3.40	0.9997	0.9997	0.9997	0.9997	0.9997	0.9997	0.9997	0.9997	0.9997	0.9998

Table D-2 Upper Percentage Points of Student Distribution

	Area on upper tail = a								
V(df)	*0.4000*	*0.2500*	*0.1000*	*0.0500*	*0.0250*	*0.0100*	*0.0050*	*0.0025*	*0.0010*
1	0.325	1.000	3.078	6.314	12.706	31.821	*	*	*
2	0.289	0.816	1.886	2.920	4.303	6.945	9.925	14.089	23.326
3	0.277	0.765	1.638	2.353	3.182	4.541	5.841	7.453	10.213
4	0.271	0.741	1.533	2.132	2.776	3.747	4.604	5.598	7.173
5	0.267	0.727	1.476	2.015	2.571	3.365	4.032	4.773	5.893
6	0.265	0.727	1.440	1.943	2.447	3.143	3.707	4.317	5.208
7	0.263	0.711	1.415	1.895	2.365	2.998	3.499	4.019	4.785
8	0.262	0.706	1.397	1.86	2.306	2.896	3.355	3.833	4.501
9	0.261	0.703	1.383	1.833	2.262	2.821	3.250	3.690	4.297
10	0.260	0.700	1.372	1.812	2.228	2.764	3.169	3.581	4.144

Contd.

Table D-2 Upper Percentage Points of Student Distribution (Contd.)

	Area on upper tail = a								
V(df)	*0.4000*	*0.2500*	*0.1000*	*0.0500*	*0.0250*	*0.0100*	*0.0050*	*0.0025*	*0.0010*
11	0.260	0.697	1.363	1.796	2.201	2.718	3.106	3.497	4.025
12	0.259	0.695	1.356	1.782	2.179	2.681	3.055	3.428	3.930
13	0.259	0.694	1.350	1.771	2.160	2.650	3.012	3.372	3.852
14	0.258	0.692	1.345	1.761	2.145	2.624	2.977	3.326	3.787
15	0.258	0.691	1.341	1.753	2.131	2.602	2.947	3.286	3.733
16	0.258	0.690	1.337	1.746	2.120	2.583	2.921	3.252	3.686
17	0.257	0.689	1.333	1.74	2.110	2.567	2.898	3.222	3.646
18	0.257	0.688	1.330	1.734	2.101	2.552	2.878	3.197	3.610
19	0.257	0.688	1.328	1.729	2.093	2.539	2.861	3.174	3.579
20	0.257	0.687	1.325	1.725	2.086	2.528	2.845	3.153	3.552
21	0.257	0.686	1.323	1.721	2.080	2.518	2.831	3.135	3.527
22	0.256	0.686	1.321	1.717	2.074	2.508	2.819	3.119	3.505
23	0.256	0.685	1.319	1.714	2.069	2.500	2.807	3.104	3.485
24	0.256	0.685	1.318	1.711	2.064	2.492	2.797	3.091	3.467
25	0.256	0.684	1.316	1.708	2.060	2.485	2.787	3.078	3.450
26	0.256	0.684	1.315	1.706	2.056	2.479	2.779	3.067	3.435
27	0.256	0.684	1.314	1.703	2.052	2.473	2.771	3.057	3.421
28	0.256	0.683	1.313	1.701	2.048	2.467	2.763	3.047	3.408
29	0.256	0.683	1.311	1.699	2.045	2.462	2.756	3.038	3.396
30	0.256	0.683	1.310	1.697	2.042	2.457	2.750	3.030	3.385
60	0.254	0.679	1.296	1.671	2.000	2.390	2.660	2.915	3.232
120	0.254	0.677	1.289	1.658	1.980	2.358	2.517	2.860	3.160
Inf	0.253	0.674	1.282	1.645	1.960	2.326	2.576	2.807	3.090

* Application of these values not recommended

Table D-3 Upper Percentage Points of X^2 DISTRIBUTION

	Area on upper tail = a								
V	*0.9950*	*0.9900*	*0.9750*	*0.9500*	*0.5000*	*0.0500*	*0.0250*	*0.0100*	*0.0050*
1	0.000	0.000	0.001	0.004	0.452	3.841	5.024	6.625	7.879
2	0.010	0.020	0.051	0.103	1.386	5.991	7.378	9.210	10.597
3	0.072	0.115	0.216	0.352	2.371	7.815	9.348	11.345	12.838
4	0.207	0.297	0.484	0.711	3.364	9.488	11.143	13.277	14.860
5	0.412	0.554	0.831	1.145	4.350	11.070	12.832	15.086	16.750
6	0.676	0.872	1.237	1.635	5.351	12.592	14.449	16.612	18.548
7	0.989	1.239	1.690	2.167	6.353	14.067	16.013	18.475	20.278
8	1.344	1.646	2.180	2.733	7.344	15.507	17.535	20.090	21.955
9	1.735	2.088	2.700	3.325	8.337	16.919	19.023	21.666	23.589
10	2.156	2.558	3.247	3.940	9.339	18.307	20.483	23.209	25.188
11	2.603	3.353	3.816	4.575	10.341	19.675	21.920	24.725	26.757
12	3.074	3.571	4.404	5.226	11.343	21.026	23.337	26.217	28.300
13	3.565	4.107	5.009	5.892	12.344	22.362	24.736	27.688	29.819
14	4.075	4.660	5.629	6.571	13.335	23.685	26.119	29.141	31.319
15	4.601	5.229	6.262	7.261	14.337	24.996	27.488	30.578	32.801
16	5.142	5.812	6.908	7.962	15.340	26.296	28.845	32.000	34.267
17	5.697	6.408	7.564	8.672	16.341	27.587	30.191	33.409	35.718
18	6.265	7.015	8.231	9.390	17.343	28.869	31.526	34.805	37.156
19	6.884	7.633	8.907	10.117	18.344	30.144	32.852	36.191	38.582
20	7.434	8.260	9.591	10.851	19.335	31.410	34.170	37.566	39.997

Contd.

Table D-3 **Upper Percentage Points of X^2 DISTRIBUTION**

	Area on upper tail = a								
V	*0.9950*	*0.9900*	*0.9750*	*0.9500*	*0.5000*	*0.0500*	*0.0250*	*0.0100*	*0.0050*
21	8.034	3.397	10.283	11.591	20.340	32.671	35.479	38.932	41.401
22	8.643	9.542	10.982	12.338	21.339	33.924	36.781	40.289	42.796
23	9.260	10.196	11.689	13.091	22.341	35.172	38.076	41.638	44.181
24	9.886	10.856	12.401	13.848	23.346	36.415	39.364	42.980	45.558
25	10.520	11.524	13.120	14.611	24.340	37.652	40.646	44.314	46.928
26	11.160	12.198	13.844	15.379	25.340	38.885	41.923	45.642	48.290
27	11.808	12.879	14.573	16.151	26.340	40.113	43.194	46.963	49.645
28	12.461	13.565	15.308	16.928	27.340	41.337	44.461	48.278	50.998
29	13.121	14.256	16.047	17.708	28.342	42.557	45.722	49.588	52.336
30	13.787	14.953	16.791	18.493	29.340	43.773	46.979	50.892	53.672
60	35.531	37.476	40.481	43.188	59.333	79.083	83.301	88.384	91.946

Table D-4 **Upper Percentage Points of F Distribution**

F0.10

DF Denominator V_2	*DF Numerator V_1*									
	1	*2*	*3*	*4*	*5*	*6*	*7*	*8*	*9*	*10*
1	39.86	49.50	53.59	55.83	57.24	58.20	58.91	59.44	59.86	60.19
2	8.53	9.00	9.16	9.24	9.29	9.33	9.35	9.37	9.38	9.39
3	5.54	5.46	5.39	5.34	5.31	5.28	5.27	5.25	5.24	5.23
4	4.54	4.32	4.19	4.11	4.05	4.01	3.98	3.95	3.94	3.92
5	4.06	3.78	3.62	3.52	3.45	3.40	3.37	3.34	3.32	3.30
6	3.78	3.46	3.29	3.18	3.11	3.05	3.01	2.98	2.96	2.94
7	3.59	3.26	3.07	2.96	2.88	2.83	2.78	2.75	2.72	2.70
8	3.46	3.11	2.92	2.81	2.73	2.67	2.62	2.59	2.56	2.54
9	3.36	3.01	2.81	2.69	2.61	2.55	2.51	2.47	2.44	2.42
10	3.29	2.92	2.73	2.61	2.52	2.46	2.41	2.38	2.35	2.32
11	3.23	2.86	2.66	2.54	2.45	2.39	2.34	2.30	2.27	2.25
12	3.18	2.81	2.61	2.48	2.39	2.33	2.28	2.24	2.21	2.19
13	3.14	2.76	2.56	2.43	2.35	2.28	2.23	2.20	2.16	2.14
14	3.10	2.73	2.52	2.39	2.31	2.24	2.19	2.15	2.12	2.10
15	3.07	2.70	2.49	2.36	2.27	2.21	2.16	2.12	2.09	2.06
16	3.05	2.67	2.46	2.33	2.24	2.18	2.13	2.09	2.06	2.03
17	3.03	2.64	2.44	2.31	2.22	2.15	2.10	2.06	2.03	2.00
18	3.01	2.62	2.42	2.29	2.20	2.13	2.08	2.04	2.00	1.98
19	2.99	2.61	2.40	2.27	2.18	2.11	2.06	2.02	1.98	1.96
20	2.97	2.59	2.38	2.25	2.16	2.09	2.04	2.00	1.96	1.94
21	2.96	2.57	2.36	2.23	2.14	2.08	2.02	1.98	1.95	1.92
22	2.95	2.56	2.35	2.22	2.13	2.06	2.01	1.97	1.93	1.90
23	2.94	2.55	2.34	2.21	2.11	2.05	1.99	1.95	1.92	1.89
24	2.93	2.54	2.33	2.19	2.10	2.04	1.98	1.94	1.91	1.88
25	2.92	2.53	2.32	2.18	2.08	2.02	1.97	1.93	1.89	1.87
26	2.91	2.52	2.31	2.17	2.08	2.01	1.96	1.92	1.88	1.86
27	2.90	2.51	2.30	2.17	2.07	2.00	1.95	1.91	1.87	1.85
28	2.89	2.50	2.29	2.16	2.06	2.00	1.94	1.90	1.87	1.84
29	2.89	2.50	2.28	2.15	2.06	1.99	1.93	1.89	1.86	1.83
30	2.88	2.49	2.28	2.14	2.05	1.98	1.93	1.88	1.85	1.82
60	2.79	2.39	2.18	2.04	1.95	1.87	1.82	1.77	1.74	1.71
120	2.75	2.35	2.13	1.99	1.90	1.82	1.77	1.72	1.68	1.65
Inf	2.71	2.30	2.08	1.94	1.85	1.77	1.72	1.67	1.63	1.60

Table D-4 Upper Percentage Points of F Distribution

Values of $F_{0.10}$

DF Denominator V_2	DF Numerator V_1 12	15	20	24	30	60	120	Inf
1	60.71	61.22	61.74	62.00	62.26	62.79	63.06	63.33
2	9.41	9.42	9.44	9.45	9.46	9.47	9.48	9.49
3	5.22	5.20	5.18	5.18	5.17	5.15	5.14	5.13
4	3.90	3.87	3.84	3.83	3.82	3.79	3.78	3.76
5	3.27	3.24	3.21	3.19	3.17	3.14	3.12	3.10
6	2.90	2.87	2.84	2.82	2.80	2.76	2.74	2.72
7	2.67	2.63	2.59	2.58	2.56	2.51	2.49	2.47
8	2.50	2.46	2.42	2.40	2.38	2.34	2.32	2.29
9	2.38	2.34	2.30	2.28	2.25	2.21	2.18	2.16
10	2.28	2.24	2.20	2.18	2.16	2.11	2.08	2.06
11	2.21	2.17	2.12	2.10	2.08	2.03	2.00	1.97
12	2.15	2.10	2.06	2.04	2.01	1.96	1.93	1.90
13	2.10	2.05	2.01	1.98	1.96	1.90	1.88	1.85
14	2.05	2.01	1.96	1.94	1.91	1.86	1.83	1.80
15	2.02	1.97	1.92	1.90	1.87	1.82	1.79	1.76
16	1.99	1.94	1.89	1.87	1.84	1.78	1.75	1.72
17	1.96	1.91	1.86	1.84	1.81	1.75	1.72	1.69
18	1.93	1.89	1.84	1.81	1.78	1.72	1.69	1.66
19	1.91	1.86	1.81	1.79	1.76	1.70	1.67	1.63
20	1.89	1.84	1.79	1.77	1.74	1.68	1.64	1.61
21	1.87	1.83	1.78	1.75	1.72	1.66	1.62	1.59
22	1.86	1.81	1.76	1.73	1.70	1.64	1.60	1.57
23	1.84	1.80	1.74	1.72	1.69	1.62	1.59	1.55
24	1.83	1.78	1.73	1.70	1.67	1.61	1.57	1.53
25	1.82	1.77	1.72	1.69	1.66	1.59	1.56	1.52
26	1.81	1.76	1.71	1.68	1.65	1.58	1.54	1.50
27	1.80	1.75	1.70	1.67	1.64	1.57	1.53	1.49
28	1.79	1.74	1.69	1.66	1.63	1.56	1.52	1.48
29	1.78	1.73	1.68	1.65	1.62	1.55	1.51	1.47
30	1.77	1.72	1.67	1.64	1.61	1.54	1.50	1.46
60	1.66	1.60	1.54	1.51	1.48	1.40	1.35	1.29
120	1.60	1.55	1.48	1.45	1.41	1.32	1.26	1.19
Inf	1.55	1.49	1.42	1.38	1.34	1.24	1.17	1.00

Table D-4 Upper Percentage Points of F Distribution (Contd.)

Values of $F_{0.05}$

DF Denominator V_2	DF Numerator V_1 1	2	3	4	5	6	7	8	9
1	*	*	*	*	*	*	*	*	*
2	18.50	19.00	19.20	19.20	19.30	19.30	19.40	19.40	19.40
3	10.10	9.55	9.28	9.12	9.01	8.94	8.89	8.85	8.81
4	7.71	6.94	6.59	6.39	6.26	6.16	6.09	6.04	6.00
5	6.61	5.79	5.41	5.19	5.05	4.95	4.88	4.82	4.77

Contd.

Table D-4 **Upper Percentage Points of F Distribution (Contd.)**

Values of $F_{0.05}$

DF Denominator V_2	DF Numerator V_1: 1	2	3	4	5	6	7	8	9
6	5.99	5.14	4.76	4.53	4.39	4.28	4.21	4.15	4.10
7	5.59	4.74	4.35	4.12	3.97	3.87	3.79	3.73	3.68
8	5.32	4.46	4.07	3.84	3.69	3.58	3.50	3.44	3.39
9	5.12	4.26	3.86	3.63	3.48	3.37	3.29	3.23	3.18
10	4.96	4.10	3.71	3.48	3.33	3.22	3.14	3.07	3.02
11	4.84	3.98	3.59	3.36	3.20	3.09	3.01	2.95	2.90
12	4.75	3.89	3.49	3.26	3.11	3.00	2.91	2.85	2.80
13	4.67	3.81	3.41	3.18	3.03	2.92	2.83	2.77	2.71
14	4.60	3.74	3.34	3.11	2.96	2.85	2.76	2.70	2.65
15	4.54	3.68	3.29	3.06	2.90	2.79	2.71	2.64	2.59
16	4.49	3.63	3.24	3.01	2.85	2.74	2.66	2.59	2.54
17	4.45	3.59	3.20	2.96	2.81	2.70	2.61	2.55	2.49
18	4.41	3.55	3.16	2.93	2.77	2.66	2.58	2.51	2.46
19	4.38	3.52	3.13	2.90	2.74	2.68	2.54	2.48	2.42
20	4.35	3.49	3.10	2.87	2.71	2.60	2.51	2.45	2.39
21	4.32	3.47	3.07	2.84	2.68	2.67	2.49	2.42	2.
22	4.30	3.44	3.05	2.82	2.66	2.55	2.46	2.40	2.34
23	4.28	3.42	3.03	2.80	2.64	2.53	2.44	2.37	2.32
24	4.26	3.40	3.01	2.78	2.62	2.51	2.42	2.36	2.30
25	4.24	3.39	2.99	2.76	2.60	2.49	2.40	2.34	2.28
26	4.23	3.37	2.98	2.74	2.59	2.47	2.39	2.32	2.27
27	4.21	3.35	2.96	2.73	2.57	2.46	2.37	2.31	2.25
28	4.20	3.34	2.95	2.71	2.56	2.45	2.36	2.29	2.24
29	4.18	3.33	2.93	2.70	2.55	2.43	2.35	2.28	2.22
30	4.17	3.32	2.92	2.69	2.53	2.42	2.33	2.27	2.21
60	4.00	3.15	2.76	2.53	2.37	2.25	2.17	2.10	2.04
120	3.92	3.07	2.68	2.45	2.29	2.18	2.09	2.02	1.96
Inf	3.84	3.00	2.60	2.37	2.21	2.10	2.01	1.94	1.88

* Application of these values not recommended

Table D-4 **Upper Percentage Points of F Distribution (Contd.)**

(Values of $F_{0.05}$)

DF Denominator V_2	DF Numerator V_1: 10	12	15	20	24	30	60	120	Inf
1	*	*	*	*	*	*	*	*	*
2	19.40	19.40	19.40	19.40	19.50	19.50	19.50	19.50	19.50
3	8.79	8.74	8.70	8.66	8.64	8.62	8.57	8.55	8.53
4	5.96	5.91	5.86	5.80	5.77	5.75	5.69	5.66	5.63
5	4.74	4.68	4.62	4.56	4.53	4.50	4.43	4.40	4.36
6	4.06	4.00	3.94	3.87	3.84	3.81	3.74	3.70	3.67
7	3.64	3.57	3.51	3.44	3.41	3.38	3.30	3.27	3.23
8	3.35	3.28	3.22	3.15	3.12	3.08	3.00	2.97	2.93
9	3.14	2.07	3.01	2.94	2.90	2.86	2.79	2.75	2.71
10	2.98	2.91	2.84	2.77	2.74	2.70	2.62	2.58	2.54

Contd.

Table D-4 Upper Percentage Points of F Distribution (Contd.)

(Values of $F_{0.05}$)

DF Denominator V_2	DF Numerator V_1								
	10	12	15	20	24	30	60	120	Inf
11	2.85	2.79	2.72	2.65	2.61	2.57	2.49	2.45	2.40
12	2.75	2.69	2.62	2.54	2.51	2.47	2.38	2.34	2.30
13	2.67	2.60	2.53	2.46	2.42	2.38	2.30	2.25	2.21
14	2.60	2.53	2.46	2.39	2.35	2.31	2.22	2.18	2.13
15	2.54	2.48	2.40	2.33	2.29	2.25	2.16	2.11	2.07
16	2.49	2.42	2.35	2.28	2.24	2.19	2.11	2.06	2.01
17	2.45	2.38	2.31	2.23	2.19	2.15	2.06	2.01	1.96
18	2.41	2.34	2.27	2.19	2.15	2.11	2.02	1.97	1.92
19	2.38	2.31	2.23	2.16	2.11	2.07	1.98	1.93	1.88
20	2.35	2.28	2.20	2.12	2.08	2.04	1.95	1.90	1.84
21	2.32	2.25	2.18	2.10	2.05	2.01	1.92	1.87	1.81
22	2.30	2.23	2.15	2.07	2.03	1.98	1.89	1.84	1.78
23	2.27	2.20	2.13	2.05	2.00	1.96	1.86	1.81	1.76
24	2.25	2.18	2.11	2.03	1.98	1.94	1.84	1.79	1.73
25	2.24	2.16	2.09	2.01	1.96	1.92	1.82	1.77	1.71
26	2.22	2.15	2.07	1.99	1.95	1.90	1.80	1.75	1.69
27	2.20	2.13	2.06	1.97	1.93	1.88	1.79	1.73	1.67
28	2.19	2.12	2.04	1.96	1.91	1.87	1.77	1.71	1.65
29	2.18	2.10	2.03	1.94	1.90	1.85	1.75	1.70	1.64
30	2.16	2.09	2.01	1.93	1.89	1.84	1.74	1.68	1.62
60	1.99	1.92	1.84	1.75	1.70	1.65	1.53	1.47	1.39
120	1.91	1.83	1.75	1.66	1.61	1.55	1.43	1.35	1.25
Inf	1.83	1.75	1.67	1.57	1.52	1.46	1.32	1.22	1.00

* Application of these values not recommended

Table D-4 Upper Percentage Points of F Distribution (Contd.)

Values of $F_{0.025}$

DF Denominator V_2	DF Numerator V_1								
	1	2	3	4	5	6	7	8	9
1	*	*	*	*	*	*	*	*	*
2	38.50	39.00	39.20	39.20	39.30	39.30	39.40	39.40	39.40
3	17.40	16.00	15.40	15.10	14.90	14.70	14.60	14.50	14.50
4	12.20	10.60	9.98	9.60	9.36	9.20	9.07	8.98	8.90
5	10.00	8.43	7.76	7.39	7.15	6.98	6.85	6.76	6.68
6	8.81	7.26	6.60	6.23	5.99	5.82	5.70	5.60	5.52
7	8.07	6.54	5.89	5.52	5.29	5.12	4.99	4.90	4.82
8	7.57	6.06	5.42	5.05	4.82	4.65	4.53	4.43	4.36
9	7.21	5.71	5.08	4.72	4.48	4.32	4.20	4.10	4.03
10	6.94	5.46	4.83	4.47	4.24	4.07	3.95	3.85	3.78
11	6.72	5.26	4.63	4.28	4.04	3.88	3.76	3.66	3.59
12	6.55	5.10	4.47	4.12	3.89	3.73	3.61	3.51	3.44
13	6.41	4.97	4.35	4.00	3.77	3.60	3.48	3.39	3.31
14	6.30	4.86	4.24	3.89	3.66	3.50	3.38	3.29	3.21
15	6.20	4.76	4.15	3.80	3.58	3.41	3.29	3.20	3.12

Contd.

Table D-4 **Upper Percentage Points of F Distribution (Contd.)**

Values of $F_{0.025}$

DF Denominator V_2	DF Numerator V_1 1	2	3	4	5	6	7	8	9
16	6.12	4.69	4.08	3.73	3.50	3.34	3.22	3.12	3.05
17	6.04	4.62	4.01	3.66	3.44	3.28	3.16	3.06	2.98
18	5.98	4.56	3.95	3.61	3.38	3.22	3.10	3.01	2.93
19	5.92	4.51	3.90	3.56	3.33	3.17	3.05	2.96	2.98
20	5.87	4.46	3.86	3.51	3.29	3.13	3.01	2.91	2.84
21	5.83	4.42	3.82	3.48	3.25	3.09	2.97	2.87	2.80
22	5.79	4.38	3.78	3.44	3.22	3.06	2.93	2.84	2.76
23	5.75	4.35	3.75	3.41	3.18	3.02	2.90	2.81	2.73
24	5.72	4.32	3.72	3.38	3.15	2.99	2.87	2.78	2.70
25	5.69	4.29	3.69	3.35	3.13	2.97	2.85	2.75	2.68
26	5.66	4.27	3.67	3.33	3.10	2.94	2.82	2.73	2.65
27	5.63	4.24	3.65	3.31	3.08	2.92	2.80	2.71	2.63
28	5.61	4.22	3.63	3.29	3.06	2.90	2.78	2.69	2.61
29	5.59	4.20	3.61	3.27	3.04	2.88	2.76	2.67	2.59
30	5.57	4.18	3.59	3.25	3.03	2.87	2.75	2.65	2.57
60	5.29	3.93	3.34	3.01	2.79	2.63	2.51	2.41	2.33
120	5.15	3.80	3.23	2.89	2.67	2.52	2.39	2.30	2.22
Inf	5.02	3.69	3.12	2.79	2.57	2.41	2.29	2.19	2.11

* Application of these values not recommended

Table D-4 **Upper Percentage Points of F Distribution (Contd.)**

Values of $F_{0.025}$

DF Denominator V_2	DF Numerator V_1 10	12	15	20	24	30	60	120	Inf
1	*	*	*	*	*	*	*	*	*
2	39.40	39.40	39.40	39.40	39.50	39.50	39.50	39.50	39.40
3	14.40	14.30	14.30	14.20	14.10	14.10	14.00	13.90	13.90
4	8.84	8.75	8.66	9.60	9.36	9.20	9.07	8.98	8.90
5	6.63	6.52	6.43	7.39	7.15	6.98	6.85	6.76	6.68
6	5.46	5.37	5.27	6.23	5.99	5.82	5.70	5.60	5.52
7	4.76	4.67	4.57	5.52	5.29	5.12	4.99	4.90	4.82
8	4.30	4.20	4.10	5.05	4.82	4.65	4.53	4.43	4.36
9	3.96	3.87	3.77	4.72	4.48	4.32	4.20	4.10	4.03
10	3.72	3.62	3.52	4.47	4.24	4.07	3.95	3.85	3.78
11	3.53	3.43	3.33	4.28	4.04	3.88	3.76	3.66	3.59
12	3.37	3.28	3.18	4.12	3.89	3.73	3.61	3.51	3.44
13	3.25	3.15	3.05	4.00	3.77	3.60	3.48	3.39	3.31
14	3.15	3.05	2.95	3.89	3.66	3.50	3.38	3.29	3.21
15	3.06	2.96	2.86	3.80	3.58	3.41	3.29	3.20	3.12
16	2.99	2.89	2.79	3.73	3.50	3.34	3.22	3.12	3.05
17	2.92	2.82	2.72	3.66	3.44	3.28	3.16	3.06	2.98
18	2.87	2.77	2.67	3.61	3.38	3.22	3.10	3.01	2.93
19	2.82	2.72	2.62	3.56	3.33	3.17	3.05	2.96	2.88

Contd.

Table D-4 Upper Percentage Points of F Distribution (Contd.)

Values of $F_{0.025}$

DF Denominator V_2	DF Numerator V_1								
	10	12	15	20	24	30	60	120	Inf
20	2.77	2.68	2.57	3.51	3.29	3.13	3.01	2.91	2.84
21	2.73	2.64	2.53	3.48	3.25	3.09	2.97	2.87	2.80
22	2.70	2.60	2.50	3.44	3.22	3.06	2.93	2.84	2.76
23	2.67	2.57	2.47	3.41	3.18	3.02	2.90	2.81	2.73
24	2.64	2.54	2.44	3.38	3.15	2.99	2.87	2.78	2.70
25	2.61	2.51	2.41	3.35	3.13	2.97	2.85	2.75	2.68
26	2.59	2.49	2.39	3.33	3.10	2.94	2.82	2.73	2.65
27	2.57	2.47	2.36	3.31	3.08	2.92	2.80	2.71	2.63
28	2.55	2.45	2.34	3.29	3.06	2.90	2.78	2.69	2.61
29	2.53	2.43	2.32	3.27	3.04	2.88	2.76	2.67	2.59
30	2.51	2.41	2.31	3.25	3.03	2.87	2.75	2.65	2.57
60	2.27	2.17	2.06	3.01	2.79	2.63	2.51	2.41	2.33
120	2.16	2.05	1.94	2.89	2.67	2.52	2.39	2.30	2.22
Inf	2.05	1.94	1.83	2.79	2.57	2.41	2.29	2.19	2.11

* Application of these values not recommended

Table D-4 Upper Percentage Points of F Distribution (Contd.)

Values of $F_{0.01}$

DF Denominator V_2	DF Numerator V_1								
	1	2	3	4	5	6	7	8	9
1	*	*	*	*	*	*	*	*	*
2	*	*	*	*	*	*	*	*	*
3	34.10	30.80	29.50	28.70	28.20	27.90	27.70	27.50	27.30
4	21.20	18.00	16.70	16.00	15.56	15.20	15.00	14.80	14.70
5	16.30	13.30	12.10	11.40	11.00	10.70	10.50	10.30	10.20
6	13.70	10.90	9.78	9.15	8.75	8.47	8.26	8.10	7.98
7	12.20	9.55	8.45	7.85	7.46	7.19	6.99	6.84	6.72
8	11.30	8.65	7.59	7.01	6.63	6.37	6.18	6.03	5.91
9	10.60	8.02	6.99	6.42	6.06	5.80	5.61	5.47	5.35
10	10.00	7.56	6.55	5.99	5.64	5.39	5.20	5.06	4.98
11	9.65	7.21	6.22	5.74	5.32	5.07	4.89	4.74	4.63
12	9.33	6.93	5.95	5.41	5.06	4.82	4.64	4.50	4.39
13	9.07	6.70	5.74	5.21	4.86	4.62	4.44	4.30	4.19
14	8.86	6.51	5.56	5.04	4.70	4.46	4.28	4.14	4.03
15	8.68	6.36	5.42	4.89	4.56	4.32	4.14	4.00	3.89
16	8.53	6.23	5.29	4.77	4.44	4.20	4.03	3.89	3.78
17	8.40	6.11	5.18	4.67	4.34	4.10	3.93	3.79	3.68
18	8.29	6.01	5.09	4.58	4.25	4.01	3.84	3.71	3.60
19	8.18	5.93	5.01	4.50	4.17	3.94	3.77	3.63	3.52
20	8.10	5.85	4.94	4.43	4.10	3.87	3.70	3.56	3.46
21	8.02	5.78	4.87	4.37	4.04	3.81	3.64	3.51	3.40
22	7.95	5.72	4.82	4.31	3.99	3.76	3.59	3.45	3.35
23	7.88	5.66	4.76	4.26	3.94	3.71	3.54	3.41	3.30

Contd.

Table D-4 Upper Percentage Points of F Distribution (Contd.)

Values of $F_{0.01}$

DF Denominator V_2	DF Numerator V_1 1	2	3	4	5	6	7	8	9
24	7.82	5.61	4.72	4.22	3.90	3.67	3.50	3.36	3.26
25	7.77	5.57	4.68	4.18	3.86	3.63	3.46	3.32	3.22
26	7.72	5.53	4.64	4.14	3.82	3.59	3.42	3.29	3.18
27	7.68	5.49	4.60	4.11	3.78	3.56	3.39	3.26	3.15
28	7.64	5.45	4.57	4.07	3.75	3.53	3.36	3.23	3.12
29	7.60	5.42	4.54	4.04	3.73	3.50	3.33	3.20	3.09
30	7.56	5.39	4.51	4.02	3.70	3.47	3.30	3.17	3.07
60	7.08	4.98	4.13	3.65	3.34	3.12	2.95	3.82	2.72
120	6.85	4.79	3.95	3.48	3.17	2.96	2.79	2.66	2.56
Inf	6.63	4.61	3.78	3.32	3.02	2.80	2.64	2.51	2.41

* Application of these values not recommended

Table D-4 Upper Percentage Points of F Distribution (Contd.)

Values of $F_{0.01}$

DF Denomiator V_2	DF Numerator V_1 10	12	15	20	24	30	60	120	Inf
1	*	*	*	*	*	*	*	*	*
2	*	*	*	*	*	*	*	*	*
3	27.20	27.10	26.90	26.73	26.61	26.50	26.34	26.20	26.13
4	14.50	14.40	14.20	14.02	13.90	13.84	13.74	13.60	13.54
5	10.10	9.89	9.72	9.55	9.47	9.38	9.20	9.11	9.02
6	7.87	7.72	7.56	7.40	7.31	7.28	7.06	6.97	6.88
7	6.62	6.47	6.31	6.16	6.07	5.99	5.82	5.74	5.65
8	5.81	5.67	5.52	5.36	5.28	5.20	5.03	4.95	4.86
9	5.26	5.11	4.96	4.81	4.73	4.65	4.48	4.40	4.31
10	4.85	4.71	4.56	4.41	4.33	4.25	4.08	4.00	3.91
11	4.54	4.40	4.25	4.10	4.02	3.94	3.78	3.69	3.60
12	4.30	4.16	4.01	3.86	3.78	3.70	3.41	3.41	3.36
13	4.10	3.96	3.82	3.66	3.59	3.51	3.34	3.25	3.17
14	3.94	3.80	3.66	3.51	3.43	3.35	3.18	3.09	3.00
15	3.80	3.67	3.52	3.37	3.29	3.21	3.05	2.96	2.87
16	3.69	3.55	3.41	3.26	3.18	3.10	2.93	2.84	2.75
17	3.59	3.46	3.31	3.16	3.08	3.00	2.83	2.75	2.65
18	3.51	3.37	3.23	3.08	3.00	2.92	2.75	2.66	2.57
19	3.43	3.30	3.15	3.00	2.92	2.84	2.67	2.58	2.49
20	3.37	3.23	3.09	2.94	2.86	2.78	2.61	2.52	2.42
21	3.31	3.17	3.03	2.88	2.80	2.72	2.55	2.46	2.36
22	3.26	3.12	2.98	2.83	2.75	2.67	2.50	2.40	2.31
23	3.21	3.07	2.93	2.78	2.70	2.62	2.45	2.35	2.26
24	3.17	3.03	2.89	2.74	2.66	2.58	2.40	2.31	2.21
25	3.13	2.99	2.85	2.70	2.62	2.54	2.36	2.37	2.17
26	3.09	2.96	2.82	2.66	2.58	2.50	2.33	2.23	2.13
27	3.06	2.93	2.78	2.63	2.55	2.47	2.29	2.20	2.10
28	3.03	2.90	2.75	2.60	2.52	2.44	2.26	2.17	2.06

Contd.

Table D-4 Upper Percentage Points of F Distribution (Contd.)

Values of $F_{0.01}$

DF Denomiator V_2	DF Numerator V_1								
	10	12	15	20	24	30	60	120	Inf
29	3.00	2.87	2.73	2.57	2.47	2.41	2.23	2.14	2.03
30	2.98	2.84	2.70	2.55	2.47	2.39	2.21	2.11	2.01
60	2.63	2.50	2.35	2.20	2.12	2.03	1.84	1.73	1.60
120	2.47	2.34	2.19	2.03	1.95	1.86	1.66	1.53	1.38
Inf	2.32	2.18	2.04	1.88	1.79	1.70	1.47	1.32	1.00

* Application of these values not recommended

Table D-4 Upper Percentage Points of F Distribution (Contd.)

Values of $F_{0.005}$

DF Denominator V_2	DF Numerator V_1								
	1	2	3	4	5	6	7	8	9
1	*	*	*	*	*	*	*	*	*
2	*	*	*	*	*	*	*	*	*
3	*	*	*	*	*	*	*	*	*
4	31.32	26.27	24.29	23.24	22.53	22.03	21.64	21.37	21.12
5	22.81	18.28	16.46	15.64	14.91	14.50	14.22	14.04	13.81
6	18.56	14.54	12.91	12.02	11.52	11.14	10.82	10.58	10.44
7	16.22	12.36	10.93	10.30	9.52	9.16	8.89	8.68	8.51
8	14.73	11.04	9.60	8.81	8.30	7.95	7.69	7.50	7.34
9	13.61	10.11	8.72	7.96	7.47	7.13	6.88	6.69	6.54
10	12.78	9.43	8.08	7.34	6.87	6.54	6.30	6.12	5.97
11	12.16	8.91	7.60	6.88	6.42	6.10	5.86	5.68	5.54
12	11.84	8.51	7.23	6.52	6.07	5.76	5.52	5.35	5.20
13	11.36	8.19	6.93	6.23	5.79	5.48	5.25	5.08	4.94
14	11.13	7.92	6.68	6.00	5.56	5.26	5.03	4.86	4.72
15	10.83	7.70	6.48	5.82	5.37	5.07	4.85	4.67	4.54
16	10.59	7.51	6.30	5.64	5.21	4.91	4.69	4.52	4.38
17	10.36	7.35	6.16	5.50	5.07	4.78	4.56	4.39	4.25
18	10.22	7.21	6.03	5.37	4.96	4.66	4.44	4.28	4.14
19	10.07	7.09	5.92	5.27	4.85	4.56	4.34	4.18	4.04
20	9.94	6.99	5.82	5.17	4.76	4.47	4.26	4.09	3.96
21	9.83	6.89	5.73	5.09	4.68	4.39	4.18	4.01	3.88
22	9.73	6.81	5.65	5.02	4.61	4.32	4.11	3.94	3.81
23	9.63	6.73	5.58	4.95	4.54	4.26	4.05	3.88	3.75
24	9.55	6.66	5.52	4.89	4.49	4.20	3.99	3.83	3.69
25	9.48	6.60	5.46	4.84	4.43	4.15	3.94	3.78	3.64
26	9.41	6.54	5.41	4.79	4.38	4.10	3.89	3.73	3.60
27	9.34	6.49	5.36	4.74	4.34	4.06	3.85	3.69	3.56
28	9.28	6.44	5.32	4.71	4.30	4.02	3.81	3.65	3.52
29	9.23	6.40	5.28	4.66	4.26	3.98	3.77	3.61	3.48
30	9.18	6.35	5.24	4.62	4.23	3.95	3.74	3.58	3.45
60	8.49	5.80	4.73	4.14	3.76	3.49	3.29	3.13	3.01
120	8.18	5.54	4.50	3.92	3.55	3.28	3.09	2.93	2.81
Inf	7.88	5.30	4.28	3.72	3.35	3.09	2.90	2.74	2.62

* Application of these values not recommended

Table D-4 Upper Percentage Points of F Distribution (Contd.)

Values of $F_{0.005}$

DF Denominator V_2	DF Numerator V_1 10	12	15	20	24	30	60	120	Inf
1	*	*	*	*	*	*	*	*	*
2	*	*	*	*	*	*	*	*	*
3	*	*	*	*	*	*	*	*	*
4	21.02	20.67	20.44	20.21	20.03	19.94	19.61	19.47	19.28
5	13.56	13.44	13.13	12.91	12.84	12.70	12.43	12.32	12.06
6	10.18	10.02	9.81	9.59	9.47	9.36	9.12	9.00	8.88
7	8.38	8.18	7.97	7.75	7.64	7.53	7.31	7.19	7.08
8	7.21	7.01	6.81	6.61	6.50	6.40	6.18	6.06	5.95
9	6.42	6.23	6.03	5.83	5.73	5.62	5.41	5.30	5.19
10	5.85	5.66	5.47	5.27	5.17	5.07	4.86	4.75	4.64
11	5.42	5.24	5.05	4.86	4.76	4.65	4.44	4.34	4.23
12	5.09	4.91	4.72	4.53	4.43	4.34	4.12	4.01	3.90
13	4.82	4.64	4.46	4.27	4.17	4.07	3.87	3.76	3.65
14	4.60	4.43	4.25	4.06	3.96	3.86	3.66	3.55	3.44
15	4.42	4.25	4.07	3.88	3.79	3.69	3.48	3.37	3.26
16	4.27	4.10	3.92	3.73	3.64	3.54	3.33	3.22	3.11
17	4.14	3.97	3.79	3.61	3.51	3.41	3.21	3.10	2.98
18	4.03	3.86	3.68	3.50	3.40	3.30	3.10	2.99	2.87
19	3.93	3.76	3.59	3.40	3.31	3.21	3.00	2.89	2.78
20	3.85	3.68	3.50	3.32	3.22	3.12	2.92	2.81	2.69
21	3.77	3.60	3.43	3.24	3.15	3.05	2.84	2.73	2.61
22	3.70	3.54	3.36	3.18	3.08	2.98	2.77	2.66	2.55
23	3.64	3.47	3.30	3.12	3.02	2.92	2.71	2.60	2.48
24	3.59	3.42	3.25	3.06	2.97	2.87	2.66	2.55	2.43
25	3.54	3.37	3.20	3.01	2.92	2.82	2.61	2.50	2.38
26	3.49	3.33	3.15	2.97	2.87	2.77	2.56	2.45	2.33
27	3.45	3.28	3.11	2.93	2.83	2.73	2.52	2.41	2.29
28	3.41	3.25	3.07	2.89	2.79	2.69	2.48	2.37	2.25
29	3.38	3.21	3.04	2.86	2.76	2.66	2.45	2.33	2.21
30	3.34	3.18	3.01	2.82	2.73	2.63	2.42	2.30	2.18
60	2.90	2.74	2.57	2.39	2.29	2.19	1.96	1.83	1.69
120	2.71	2.54	2.37	2.19	2.09	1.98	1.75	1.61	1.43
Inf	2.52	2.36	2.19	2.00	1.90	1.79	1.53	1.36	1.00

* Application of these values not recommended

Table D-5 Critical Values of D in the Kotmogorov-Smirnov One-Sample Test

Sample Size N	Level of Significance for O=Maximum IFo(X)–S_n(X)1 .20	.15	.10	.05	.01
1	.900	.925	.950	.975	.995
2	.684	.726	.776	.842	.929
3	.565	.597	.642	.708	.828
4	.494	.525	.564	.624	.733
5	.446	.474	.510	.565	.669
6	.410	.436	.470	.521	.618
7	.381	.405	.438	.486	.577

Contd.

Table D-5 Critical Values of D in the Kotmogorov-Smirnov One-Sample Test (Contd.)

Sample Size N	*Level of Significance for O=Maximum IFo(X)–S_n(X)1*				
	.20	*.15*	*.10*	*.05*	*.01*
8	.358	.381	.411	.457	.543
9	.339	.360	.388	.432	.514
10	.322	.342	.368	.410	.490
11	.307	.326	.352	.391	.468
12	.295	.313	.338	.375	.450
13	.284	.302	.325	.361	.433
14	.274	.292	.314	.349	.418
15	.266	.283	.304	.338	.404
16	.258	.274	.295	.328	.392
17	.250	.266	.286	.318	.381
18	.244	.259	.278	.309	.371
19	.237	.252	.272	.301	.363
20	.231	.246	.264	.294	.356
25	.21	.22	.24	.27	.32
30	.19	.20	.22	.24	.29
35	.18	.19	.21	.23	.27
Over 35	$\frac{1.07}{\sqrt{N}}$	$\frac{1.14}{\sqrt{N}}$	$\frac{1.22}{\sqrt{N}}$	$\frac{1.36}{\sqrt{N}}$	$\frac{1.63}{\sqrt{N}}$

Source: F.J. Massey,Jr., "The Kolmogorov-Smirnov Test for Goodness of Fit", *Journal of the American Statistical Association* 46, : 70.

Table D-6 Critical Values of T in the Wilcoxon Matched-Pairs Test

N	*Level of Significance for One-Tailed Test*		
	.025	*.01*	*.005*
	Level of Significance for Two-Tailed Test		
	.05	*.02*	*.01*
6	0	—	—
7	2	0	—
8	4	2	0
9	6	3	2
10	8	5	3
11	11	7	5
12	14	10	7
13	17	13	10
14	21	16	13
15	25	20	16
16	30	24	20
17	35	28	23
18	40	33	28
19	46	38	32
20	52	43	38
21	59	49	43
22	66	56	49
23	73	62	55
24	81	69	61
25	89	77	68

Table D-7 Critical Values of 0 in the Kolmogorov-Smirnov Two-Sample Test (Small Samples)

N	One-Tailed Test*		Two-Tailed Test#	
	$\alpha = .05$	$\alpha = .01$	$\alpha = .05$	$\alpha = .01$
3	3	—	—	—
4	4	—	4	—
5	4	5	5	5
6	5	6	5	6
7	5	6	6	6
8	5	6	6	7
9	6	7	6	7
10	6	7	7	8
11	6	8	7	8
12	6	8	7	8
13	7	8	7	9
14	7	8	8	9
15	7	9	8	9
16	7	9	8	10
17	8	9	8	10
18	8	10	9	10
19	8	10	9	10
20	8	10	9	11
21	8	10	9	11
22	9	11	9	11
23	9	11	10	11
24	9	11	10	12
25	9	11	10	12
26	9	11	10	12
27	9	12	10	12
28	10	12	11	13
29	10	12	11	13
30	10	12	11	13
35	11	13	12	
40	11	14	13	

Table D-8 Critical Values of D in the Kolmogorov-Smirnov Two-Sample Test for Large Samples (Two-tailed test)

Level of Significance	*Value of D So Large As to Cell for Rejection of H_o at the Indicated Level of Significance where $D = \text{Maximum} \lvert S_{n1}(X) - S_2(X) \rvert$*
.10	$1.22\sqrt{[n_1 + n_2)/n_1 n_2]}$
.05	$1.36\sqrt{[n_1 + n_2)/n_1 n_2]}$
.025	$1.48\sqrt{[n_1 + n_2)/n_1 n_2]}$
.01	$1.63\sqrt{[n_1 + n_2)/n_1 n_2]}$
.005	$1.73\sqrt{[n_1 + n_2)/n_1 n_2]}$
.001	$1.95\sqrt{[n_1 + n_2)/n_1 n_2]}$

Table D-9 Partial Table of Critical Values of U in the Mann-Whitney Test Critical Values for One-tailed Test at $\alpha = .025$ or a Two-tailed Test at $\alpha = .05$

n_2 / n_1	9	10	11	12	13	14	15	16	17	18	19	20
1												
2	0	0	0	1	1	1	1	1	2	2	2	2
3	2	3	3	4	4	5	5	6	6	7	7	8
4	4	5	6	7	8	9	10	11	11	12	13	13
5	7	8	9	11	12	13	14	15	17	18	19	20
6	10	11	13	14	16	17	19	21	22	24	25	27
7	12	14	16	18	20	22	24	26	28	30	32	34
8	15	17	19	22	24	26	29	31	34	36	38	41
9	17	20	23	26	28	31	34	37	39	42	45	48
10	20	23	26	29	33	36	39	42	45	48	52	55
11	23	26	30	33	37	40	44	47	51	55	58	62
12	26	29	33	37	41	45	49	53	57	61	66	69
13	28	33	37	41	45	50	54	59	63	67	72	76
14	31	36	40	45	50	55	59	64	67	74	78	83
15	34	39	44	49	54	59	64	70	75	80	85	90
16	37	42	47	53	59	64	70	75	81	86	92	98
17	39	45	51	57	63	67	75	81	87	93	99	105
18	42	48	55	61	67	74	80	86	93	99	106	112
19	45	52	58	65	72	78	85	92	99	106	113	119
20	48	55	62	69	76	83	90	98	105	112	119	127

Table D-9 Critical Values for One-tailed Test at $\alpha = .05$ or a Two-tailed Test at $\alpha = .10$

n_2 / n_1	9	10	11	12	13	14	15	16	17	18	19	20
1												
0	0											
2	1	1	1	2	2	2	3	3	3	4	4	4
3	3	4	5	5	6	7	7	8	9	9	10	11
4	6	7	8	9	10	11	12	14	15	16	17	18
5	9	11	12	13	15	16	18	19	20	22	23	25
6	12	14	16	17	19	21	23	25	26	28	30	32
7	15	17	19	21	24	26	28	30	33	35	37	39
8	18	20	23	26	28	31	33	36	39	41	44	47
9	21	24	27	30	33	36	39	42	45	48	51	54
10	24	27	31	34	37	41	44	48	51	55	58	62
11	27	31	34	38	42	46	50	54	57	61	65	69
12	30	34	38	42	47	51	55	60	64	68	72	77
13	33	37	42	47	51	56	61	65	70	75	80	84
14	36	41	46	51	56	61	66	71	77	82	87	92
15	39	44	50	55	61	66	72	77	83	88	94	100
16	42	48	54	60	65	71	77	83	89	95	101	107
17	45	51	57	64	70	77	83	89	96	102	109	115
18	48	55	61	68	75	82	88	95	102	109	116	123
19	51	58	65	72	80	87	94	101	109	116	123	130
20	54	62	69	77	84	92	100	107	115	123	130	138

TABLE D-10 Critical Values of T in the Wilcoxon Matched-Pairs Test

n	*Level of Significance for One-Tailed Test*		
	.025	.01	.005
	Level of Significance for Two-Tailed Test		
	.05	.02	.01
6	0	—	—
7	2	0	—
8	4	2	0
9	6	3	2
10	8	5	3
11	11	7	5
12	14	10	7
13	17	13	10
14	21	16	13
15	25	20	16
16	30	24	20
17	35	28	23
18	40	33	28
19	46	38	32
20	52	43	38
21	59	49	43
22	66	56	49
23	73	62	55
24	81	69	61
25	89	77	68

Table D-11 Cumulative Binomial Probabilities: P (r < r | n,p)

n	r_o	.10	.25	.40	.50
1	0	.9000	.7500	.6000	.5000
	1	1.0000	1.0000	1.0000	1.0000
2	0	.8100	.5625	.3600	.2500
	1	.9900	.9375	.8400	.7500
	2	1.0000	1.0000	1.0000	1.0000
5	0	.5905	.2373	.0778	.0313
	1	.9185	.6328	.3370	.1875
	2	.9914	.8965	.6826	.5000
	3	.9995	.9844	.9130	.8125
	4	.9999	.9990	.9898	.9687
	5	1.0000	1.0000	1.0000	1.0000
10	0	.3487	.0563	.0060	.0010
	1	.7361	.2440	.0463	.0108
	2	.9298	.5256	.1672	.0547
	3	.9872	.7759	.3822	.1719
	4	.9984	.9219	.6330	.3770
	5	.9999	.9803	.8337	.6230
	6	1.0000	.9965	.9452	.8281
	7	1.0000	.9996	.9877	.9453
	8	1.0000	1.0000	.9983	.9892
	9	1.0000	1.0000	.9999	.9990
	15	1.0000	1.0000	1.0000	1.0000

Contd.

Table D-11 Cumulative Binomial Probabilities: $P(r < r \mid n,p)$ (Contd.)

n	r_o	.10	.25	.40	.50
12	0	.2824	.0317	.0022	.0002
	1	.6590	.1584	.0196	.0031
	2	.8891	.3907	.0835	.0192
	3	.9740	.6488	.2254	.0729
	4	.9963	.8424	.4382	.1937
	5	.9999	.9456	.6652	.3871
	6	1.0000	.9857	.8418	.6127
	7	1.0000	.9972	.9427	.8064
	8	1.0000	.9996	.9847	.9269
	9	1.0000	1.0000	.9972	.9806
	10	1.0000	1.0000	.9997	.9977
	11	1.0000	1.0000	1.0000	1.0000
	12	1.0000	1.0000	1.0000	1.0000
20	0	.1216	.0032	.0000	.0000
	1	.3917	.0243	.0005	.0000
	2	.6768	.0912	.0036	.0002
	3	.8669	.2251	.0159	.0013
	4	.9567	.4148	.0509	.0059
	5	.9886	.6171	.1255	.0207
	6	.9975	.7857	.2499	.0577
	7	.9995	.8981	.4158	.1316
	8	.9999	.9590	.5955	.2517
	9	1.0000	.9861	.7552	.4119
	10	1.0000	.9960	.8723	.5881
	11	1.0000	.9990	.9433	.7483
	12	1.0000	.9998	.9788	.8684
	13	1.0000	1.0000	.9934	.9423
	14	1.0000	1.0000	.9983	.9793
	15	1.0000	1.0000	.9996	.9941
	16	1.0000	1.0000	1.0000	.9987
	17	1.0000	1.0000	1.0000	.9998
	18	1.0000	1.0000	1.0000	1.0000
	19	1.0000	1.0000	1.0000	1.0000
	20	1.0000	1.0000	1.0000	1.0000

Table D-12 Selected Critical Values of S in the Kendall's Coefficient of Concordance

Values at 5% level of significance

k	*N*					*Some additional values for N = 3*	
	3	4	5	6	7	*k*	*s*
3			64.4	103.9	157.3	9	54.0
4		49.5	88.4	143.3	217.0	12	71.9
5		62.6	112.3	182.4	276.2	14	83.8
6		75.7	136.1	221.4	335.2	16	95.8
8	48.1	101.7	183.7	299.0	453.1	18	107.7
10	60.0	127.8	231.2	376.7	571.0		
15	89.8	192.9	349.8	570.5	864.9		
20	119.7	258.0	468.5	764.4	1158.7		

Contd.

Table D-12 Selected Critical Values of S in the Kendall's Coefficient of Concordance (Contd.)

Values at 1% Level of Significance

k	N					Some additional values for N = 3	
	3	4	5	6	7	k	s
3			75.6	122.8	185.6	9	75.9
4		61.4	109.3	176.2	265.0	12	103.5
5		80.5	142.8	229.4	343.8	14	121.9
6		99.5	176.1	282.4	422.6	16	140.2
8	66.8	137.4	242.7	388.3	579.9	18	158.6
10	85.1	175.3	309.1	494.0	737.0		
15	131.0	269.8	475.2	758.2	1129.5		
20	177.0	364.2	641.2	1022.2	1521.9		

Table D-13 Critical Values of 'A' Statistic For any Given Value of n-1, Corresponding to Various Levels of Probability

(A is significant at a given level if it is the value shown in the table)

n–1*	Level of Significance for One-Tailed Test				
	0.05	0.25	0.01	0.005	0.0005
	Level of Significance for Two-Tailed Test				
	0.10	0.05	0.02	0.01	0.001
1	2	3	4	5	6
1	0.5125	0.5031	0.50049	0.50012	0.5000012
2	0.412	0.369	0.347	0.340	0.334
3	0.385	0.324	0.286	0.272	0.254
4	0.376	0.304	0.257	0.238	0.211
5	0.372	0.293	0.240	0.218	0.184
6	0.370	0.286	0.230	0.205	0.167
7	0.369	0.281	0.222	0.196	0.155
8	0.368	0.278	0.217	0.190	0.146
9	0.368	0.276	0.213	0.185	0.139
10	0.368	0.274	0.210	0.181	0.134
11	0.368	0.273	0.207	0.178	0.130
12	0.368	0.271	0.205	0.176	0.126
13	0.368	0.270	0.204	0.174	0.124
14	0.368	0.270	0.202	0.172	0.121
15	0.368	0.269	0.201	0.170	0.119
16	0.368	0.268	0.200	0.169	0.117
17	0.368	0.268	0.199	0.168	0.116
18	0.368	0.267	0.198	0.167	0.114
19	0.368	0.267	0.197	0.166	0.113
20	0.368	0.266	0.197	0.165	0.112
21	0.368	0.266	0.196	0.165	0.111
22	0.368	0.266	0.196	0.164	0.110
23	0.368	0.266	0.195	0.163	0.109

Contd.

Table D-13 Critical Values of 'A' Statistic For any Given Value of n-1, Corresponding to Various Levels of Probability (Contd.)

(A is significant at a given level if it is the value shown in the table)

*n–1**	*Level of Significance for One-Tailed Test*				
	0.05	*0.25*	*0.01*	*0.005*	*0.0005*
	Level of Significance for Two-Tailed Test				
	0.10	*0.05*	*0.02*	*0.01*	*0.001*
1	*2*	*3*	*4*	*5*	*6*
24	0.368	0.265	0.195	0.163	0.108
25	0.368	0.265	0.194	0.162	0.108
26	0.368	0.265	0.194	0.162	0.107
27	0.368	0.265	0.193	0.161	0.107
28	0.368	0.265	0.193	0.161	0.106
29	0.368	0.264	0.193	0.161	0.106
30	0.368	0.264	0.193	0.160	0.105
40	0.368	0.263	0.191	0.158	0.102
60	0.369	0.262	0.189	0.155	0.099
120	0.369	0.261	0.187	0.153	0.095
	0.370	0.260	0.185	0.151	0.092

**n* = number of pairs

Bibliography

1. Abraham K (1964). *The Conduct of Inquiry—Methodology for Behavioural Science*. (Aylesbury: Bucks: International Text Book Company Limited.
2. Ackoff, R.L. (1953). *Design of Social Research*, (Chicago: University of Chicago), xi, p 420.
3. Ackoff, R.L. (1971). "Towards a System of System Concepts". *Management Science* 17, no. 11.
4. Ackoff, R.L. (1978). *The Art of Problem Solving*. (John Wiley: Chichester).
5. Ackoff, R.L. (1981). "The Art and Science of Mess Management" Interfaces 11, no. 1.
6. Ackoff, R.L. and Maurice W. Sasieni (1963). *Fundamentals of Operations Research*. (New York: John Wiley and Sons Inc).
7. Ackoff, Russel L (1962). *Scientific Method: Optimising Applied Research Decisions*. (New York: John Wiley and Sons, Inc.).
8. Adams, J.L. (1979). *Conceptual Block Bursting – A Guide to Better Idea*. 2nd ed. (CA: Stanford Alumni Association,).
9. Adams, R.N. and J.J. Preiss (1960). *Human Organisation Research; Field Relations and Techniques*. (Homewood: Dorsey Press) p 456 (ed.).
10. Afifi, A.A. and S.P. Azen (1972). *Statistical Analysis – A Computer Oriented Approach*. (New York: Academic Press).
11. Aggrawal. J.C. (1966). *Educational Research: An Introduction*. (New Delhi: Arya Book Depot), IV. p 260.
12. Aigner, D.J. (1972). 'A Note On Verification of Computer Simulation Models'. *Management Science* 18, no. 11, pp:615–619.
13. Allen, T.J. (1977). Managing the Flow of Technology. Cambridge: The M.I.T Press.
14. Allison, Paul (1999). *Multiple Regression*. A Pine Forge Press Publication. (London: Sage Publication).
15. Almack, J.C. (1930). *Research and Thesis Writing*, (Boston: Houghton), p 310.
16. Alreck, Pamela L and Robert B Settle (1995). *The Survey Research Handbook*. (Bura Ridge IL: Irwin), Chapter 5.
17. Anahory, Sam and Dermis Murray (2000). *Data Warehousing in the Real World—A Practical Guide for Building Decision Support Systems*. Addison-Wesley, Pearson Education Limited, Essex, United Kingdom: Indian Reprint.
18. Anastasi, A. (1982). *Psychological Testing*. 5th ed. (New York: Macmillan).
19. Anderberg, M.R. (1973). *Cluster Analysis for Applications*. (New York: Academic Press).
20. Anderson, Mark J and Patrick J Whitcomb (2000). *DOE Simplified—Practical Tools for Effective Experimentation*. New York (Productivity Inc.).
21. Anderson, Janathan H Durston and Millicent Poole Berry (1971). *Thesis and Assignment Writing*. (New Delhi: Wiley Eastern).
22. Anderson, R.L. and Bancroft (1952). *A Statistical Theory in Research*. (New York McGraw-Hill), p 399.
23. Anthony, Jay (1990). *Effective Presentation*. (London: British Institute of Management).
24. Arbib, M.A. and M.B. Hesse (1986). *The Construction of Reality*. (London: Cambridge University Press).
25. Argyris, C (1976). "Problems and New Directions for Industrial Psychology". In M.D. Dunnettes (ed.) *Handbook of Industrial and Organisational Psychology* (Chicago: Rand McNally).
26. Argyris, C. (1980). *Inner Contradictions of Research*. (London: Academic Press).

27. Ashby, W.R. (1956). *An Introduction to Cybernetics*. (John Wiley and Sons, New York).
28. Assael, H. and J. Keon (1982). "Non-Sampling versus Sampling Errors in Survey Research". *Journal of Marketing* 46 : 114–123.
29. Assmus, G., John U. Farhley, and Donald R. Lehmann (1984). "How Advertising Affects Sales: Meta-analysis of econometric result". *Journal of Marketing Research*, 21 : 65–74.
30. Atkins, C.K. (1978). "Observation of Particular Child Interaction in Marketing Decision-Making, *Journal of Marketing*, (October,) : 41–45.
31. Baker, K.R. (1999). "Heuristic Procedures for Scheduling Job Families with Setups and Due Dates. *Naval Research Logistics* 46 : 978–991.
32. Baker, S. (1996). "Consumer Cognitions: Mapping Personal Benefits Relating to Perfume Purchase in UK and Germany. Paper presented at the 20th ESOMAR Seminar, Amsterdam data.
33. Baldwin, Maynard M. (ed.) (1975). *Portraits of Complexity: Applications of Systems Methodologies to Societal Problems*. (Columbus, Ohio: Battelle Memorial Institute).
34. Ball, M. and M. Magazine (1981). "The Design and Analysis of Heuristics". *Networks*, 11, 215–219.
35. Banks, E. (1990). "Verifying and Validating Complex Simulation Models by Analogy". *Simulation*. 54, no. 1 : 33–366.
36. Banks, Jerry and J.S. II. Carson (1984). *Discrete-Event System Simulation*. (Englewood Cliffs, New Jersey: Prentice Hall Inc.).
37. Barbara, I Gross and Jagdish N Sheth (1989). "Time Oriented Advertising: A Content Analysis of United States Magazine Advertising (1980 –1988)". *Journal of Marketing*, 53 : 76–83.
38. Barish, N.N. (1951). *Systems Analysis for Effective Administration*. (New York: Funk and Wagnalls Company).
39. Barlas, Yaman (1989). "Multiple Tests for Validation of System Dynamics Type of Simulation Models. *European Journal of Operations Research* 42, 1, no. : 59–87.
40. Barlas, Yaman (1990). "An Autocorrelation Function Test for Output Validation. *Simulation* 55, no. 1 : 7–166.
41. Barr, Richard, S Bruce L Golden, James P Kelly, Mauricio G C Rosende, and William R Stewart (1995). Designing and Reporting on Computational Experiments with Heuristic Methods. *Journal of Heuristics*1: 9–32.
42. Bartlet, M.S. (1951). "The Goodness of Fit of a Single Hypothetical Discriminant Function in the Case of Several groups". Ann. Eugen. 16, 199–214.
43. Barton, Russel R (1999). "Graphical Methods for the Design of Experiments". Lecture notes, Springer Verlag.
44. Behling O. and M. Shapiro (1974). "Motivation Theory: Source of the Solution on Part of the Problems?" *Business Horizons* : 59–66.
45. Bell, Pitere (1999). *Management Science and Operations Research*. (Cincinnati, Ohio: South Western College Publication).
46. Bell, J (1987). *Doing Your Research Project*? (Milton Keynes: Open University Press).
47. Benjinen, (1973). Cluster Analysis—*Survey and Evaluation Techniques*. (Groningen The Netherlands: Tilburg University Press.
48. Bennet R (1991). "How Is Management Research Carried Out?" *The Management Research Handbook,* Smith Craig N and Paul Dainty, ed. (London: Routledge).
49. Bennet, Spencer and David Bower's, (1976). An *Introduction to Multivariate Techniques for Social and Behavioural Sciences*. (London: Macmillan Press).
50. Benson, George P, Jayant, V Saraph and Roger G Schroeder (1991). "The Effects of Organisational Context on Quality Management: An Empirical Investigation." *Management Science*, 37 no. 9 : 1107–1124.
51. Bentz, Valarie Malhotra and Jeremy J Shapiro (1998). *Mindful Enquiry in Social Science Research*. (New Delhi: Sage Publications).
52. Bernard, Russel H (2000). *Social Research Methods*. (London: Sage).
53. Berson, John and Peters Geoff, eds. (1981). *System Behaviour*. Open University Set Book, (London: Harper and Row).
54. Bertalanffy, Von (1981). *General System Theory - A Critical Review*, in *Open Systems Group: System Behaviour*, 3rd ed. (London Harper and Row). Chapter 4.
55. Bertalanffy, Von. (1956). "General Systems Theory". *Year Book of the Society for Advancement of General System Theory* : 1–10.
56. Bertalanffy, Von. (1968). *General Systems Theory*. (Brazilier).
57. Best, J. W. and J V Kahn (1986). *Research in Education*, 5th ed. (New Delhi: Prentice-Hall of India Private Limited), pp 204–252.

58. Beveridge, W.I.B. (1961). *Art of Scientific Investigation*, 3rd ed. (Melbourne, Heinemann) p 177.
59. Bhandari, Narendra C (1974). "Case Research in the Indian Background." *Behavioural Sciences and Community Development* 8, 2 : Sept 129–135,.
60. Bilde, O and Vidal R.V.V. (1973). On the Connections Between Locations and Scheduling Problems in *Simulation Councils,* Johnson M. and S. Ashour (eds.), Proc. Ser. 3(2).
61. Billings, R.S. et al. (1977). "Impact of a Change in Technology on Job Characteristics: A Quasi-Experiment. *Administrative Science Quarterly* 22(2–4) : 318–339.
62. Bitner, Mary J, Jody D Myquist, and Bernard H Booms (1995). "The Critical Incident as a Technique for Analysing the Service Encounter in Services Marketing in a Changing Environment", ed. Thomas M Black, Gregory Dilpah and Valori Zeithaml, (Chicago: American Marketing Association).
63. Blalock, H.M, ed. (1971). *Casual Models in the Social Sciences.* (London: Macmillan), p 515.
64. Blalock, Hubert M (1970). *Introduction to Social Research.* (Englewood Cliffs: Prentice-Hall), p 120.
65. Blanchard, BS (1977). *Engineering Organisation and Management.* (New Delhi: Prentice-Hall of India).
66. Bogdan, R. and S.J. Taylor (1975). *Introduction to Qualitative Research Methods.* (New York: John Wiley).
67. Boot, John CG and Edwin B Cox (1979). *Statistical Analysis for Managerial Decisions*, 2nd ed., (New Delhi: McGraw-Hill, International Student Edition).
68. Boulding, Kenneth E (1956). "General System Theory: The Skeleton of Science". *Management Science*, no. 3, 2 April: 197–208.
69. Boyd, Harper W. and Ralph Westfall (1972). *Marketing Research*, 3rd ed. (Homewood, Illinois: Richard D. Irvin Inc.)
70. Bracht, G. and G. Glass (1968). "The External Validity of Experiments". *The American Educational Research Journal* 5, 437–474.
71. Braithwaite, A.R. (1973). *Scientific Explanation.* (London Cambridge University Press).
72. Breman, Robert E (2001). *Generalisability Theory.* (New York Barnes and Noble).
73. Brewer, J. and A. Hunter (1989). "Multi-Method Research: A Synthesis of Styles". Sage Library of Social Research 175, (Calif: Sage).
74. Brown, C.W. and E.E. Ghiselli (1955). *Scientific Method in Psychology.* (New York McGraw-Hill) p 368.
75. Browne, J. and B.J. Davies (1984). "The Design and Validation of a Digital Simulation Model for Job Shop Control Decision Making". *International Journal of Production Research* 22, no. 2 : 323–334.
76. Bryman, Alan and Duncan Cramer (1990). *Quantitative Data Analysis for Social Scientists.* (London: Routledge).
77. Buckley, W., ed. (1968). *Modern System Research for the Behavioural Scientist: A Source Book.* (Chicago: Aldine Publishing Company).
78. Budnick, F.S. Mcleavey D., and Mojena R. (1988). Principles of Operations Research for Management, 2nd ed, (Homewood, Illinois: Richard D.Irwin, Inc,).
79. Bullock, Alan, Oliver Stallybras, and Stephen Trombley ed. (1990), *Dictionary of Modern Thought*, 2nd ed. U.K. London Fontana Press : pp 64–65.
80. Bunge, Mario (1967). "Scientific Research I - Search for System. Berlin Springer Verlag.
81. Bunge, Mario (1967). "Scientific Research II - Search for Truth". Berlin Springer Verlag.
82. Burdick, R.K. (1983). "Statement of Hypothesis in the Analysis of Variance". *Journal of Marketing Research*, 20, pp 320–324.
83. Burgess, R.G. (1984). *In the Field: An Introduction to Field Research.* (London: Allen & Unwin).
84. Burgess, R.G. and M. Bulmer (1981). "Research Methodology Teaching: Trends and Developments." *Sociology* 15, pp 477–89.
85. Burgoyne, J. and V.E. Hodgson (1983). "Natural Learning and Managerial Action: A Phenomenological Study in Field Setting. *Journal of Management Studies,* 20 (3): 387–9.
86. Burrell, G and G. Morgan (1979). *Sociological Paradigms and Organisational Analysis.* (London: Heinemann).
87. Bwad, (1923). *Scientific Thought.* (London) p 18.
88. Calder, B.J. (1977). "Focus Groups and the Nature of Qualitative Marketing Research". *Journal of Marketing Research* 14, pp. 353–364.
89. Campbell, D.T and G. Katona (1953). "The Sample Survey—A Technique for Social Science Research in *Research Methods in the Behavioral Sciences,* L Festinger and D Kartz, (New York: The Dryden Press).
90. Campbell, D.T. (1976). "Psychometric Theory" in *MO Handbook of Behavioural and Organisational Psychology,* Dunnette (ed.) (Chicago: Rand McNally).
91. Campbell, D.T. and Fiske D.W. (1959). Convergent and Discriminant Validation by the Multitrait - Multi-Method Matrix. Psychological Bulletin, Vol.56, pp. 81–85.

92. Campbell, D.T. and S.S. Stanley (1966). *Experimental and Quasi-Experimental Design for Research*. (Chicago: Rand McNally).
93. Campbell, J.P., R.L., Daft and C.L. Hulin (1982). *What to Study: Generating and Developing Research Questions*. (London: Sage Publishers).
94. Campbell, N.R. (1952). *Foundations of Science*. (New York: Dover Publications).
95. Bailey, Carol A (1995). *A Guide to Field Research*. (Thousand Oaks, California: Pine Forge Press).
96. Cartwright, C.A. and Cartwright G.P. (1974). *Developing Observation Skills*. (New York: McGraw-Hill).
97. Cartwright, Dorwin P (1953). "Analysis of Qualitative Material" in D. Katz, Festinger, L. and *Research Methods in the Behavioral Sciences*, (New York: The Dryden Press).
98. Casley, D.J. and Lury D.A. (1981). *Data Collection Methods in Developing Countries*. (Oxford: Clarendon Press).
99. Catherine, Patrick (1938). "Scientific Thought". *Journal of Psychology* 5 : 55–83.
100. Cattel, R.B. and Vogelman S. (1977). "A Comprehensive Trial of the Scree and the KG Criteria for Determining the Number of Factors". *Journal Multivariate Behavioural Research* 12 : 289–325.
101. Cattel, R.B. (1952). *Factor Analysis*. (New York: Harper and Row)
102. Caws, Peter (1965). *Philosophy of Science*. (Van Northrand Co.)
103. Charmaz, K. (1983). "The Grounded Theory Method: An Explication and Interpretation" in *Contemporary Field Research*, Emerson R. ed., (Boston: Little Brown).
104. Checkland, P.B. (1972). "Towards a System-Based Methodology for Real World Problem Solving. *Journal of Systems Engineering* 3 no. 2, 1972.
105. Checkland, P.B. (1981). *System Thinking, Systems Practice*. (John Wiley). Chapter 2 and 3 (2000). 4th Edition.
106. Checkland, Peter B and J. Scholes (2000). *Soft System Methodology in Action*. (Chichester: John Wiley).
107. Chein, Isidon (1976). "An Introduction to Sampling" in Sellitz et al *Research Methods in Social Relations*, 4th ed. (Holt, Reinhart and Winston) pp 520–521.
108. Cherns, A.B. (1972). "Models for the Use of Research". *Human Relations* 25 no. 1 (month 1972).
109. Chetty, B.S. (1995). Manufacturing Planning and Control in Batch Manufacturing Organisations in India – An Exploratory Study. (Ph d. thesis, Department of Management Studies, Indian Institute of Science, Bangalore).
110. Chid, Apte (2003). "The Big Dig—Data Mining Analysis for Business Intelligence and Decision Support. February, 2003 OR/MS Today .
111. Child, D. (1970). *The Essentials of Factor Analysis*. (Holt, Rine-Hart and Winston).
112. Church, J.G. (1973). Sure Staff : A Computerised Staff Scheduling System for Telephone Business Offices. *Management Science*, Vol. 20(4), Part II.
113. Churchill, G.A. Jr. (1987). *Marketing Research: Methodological Foundations*. 4th Ed., (Chicago: Dryden Press).
114. Churchman, C West, Ackoff R.L., and Arnoff E.L. (1957). *Introduction to Operations Research*. (John Wiley and Sons) Chapter 2 to 5.
115. Churchman, C.W. (1971). *The Design of Inquiring Systems*. (New York: Basic Books).
116. Cicourel, A. (1964). *Method and Measurement in Sociology*. (Glencoe: Free Press).
117. Clarke, I and W. Mackaness (2001). Management Intuition and Interpretive Account of Structure and Content Using Cognitive Maps. *Journal of Management Studies* 38 no. 2.
118. Clarke, Peter A (1972). *Action Research and Organisational Change*. (London: Harper and Row).
119. Clarke, R.B., A.P. Coladarci, and John Cofferry. (1965). *Statistical Reasoning and Procedures*. (Ohio: Charles E Merril Books Inc).
120. Cochran, W.G. (1977). *Sampling Techniques*. (New York: John Wiley).
121. Cochran, W.G. and G.M. Cox (1957). *Experimental Designs*. 2nd ed. (New York: John Wiley).
122. Coghlan, David and J. Mcdonagh (1997). "Doing Academic Research in Your Own Business Organization" in *Business Research Methods, Strategies, Techniques and Sources*, ed. by David Coghlan and Teresa Bannik, (Dublin Oak Tree Press) 139–161.
123. Cohen, Marris R and Earnest Nagel (1934). *An Introduction to Logic and Scientific Method*. (New York: Harcourt, Brace Co.)
124. Connoly, Terry, Leonard M Jessup, and Joseph S Valacich "Effects of Anonymity and Evaluative Tone on Idea Generation in Computer-Mediated Groups". *Management Science* 36, no. 6 : 689–703.
125. Conoley, J.C. and J.J. Kramer (1989). *Tenth Mental Management Year Book*. (Lincoln NB: Nebraska Press).
126. Conway, R.W. (1965). "Priority Dispatching and Work-in-Process Inventory" in a Job Shop. JL of Indust. Engrg. XVI, 123–130.

127. Conway, R.W., B.M. Johnson, and W.L. Maxwell (1959). "Some Problems of Digital System Simulation. *Management Science* 6: 92–100.
128. Cook, T.D. (1983). "Quasi-Experimentation: Its Ontology, Epistemology and Methodology" In Morgan.
129. Cook, T.D. and D.T. Campbell (1979). *Quasi Experimentation, Its Design and Analysis Issues for Field Settings*. (Chicago: Rand McNally).
130. Cool, Karel O and Dan. Schendel (1987). "Strategic Group Formation and Performance: The Case of the US Pharmaceutical Industry 1963–1982". *Management Science*, 33 no. 9.
131. Cooley, William W (1971). *Multivariate Data Analysis*. (New York John Wiley Sons).
132. Coombs, C.H. (1960). "A Theory of Data". *Psychological Review* : 43–159.
133. Coombs, Clyde H (1984). *Theory of Data*. (New York: John Wiley).
134. Cooper, D.R. and P.S. Schindler (2000). *Business Research Methods*, 7th ed. (New Delhi: Tata McGraw-Hill).
135. Copper, H.M. (1989). "Integrating Research : A Guide for Literature Reviews". *Applied Social Research Methods Series 2*, In 2nd ed. (London: Sage Publishers).
136. Cornuejols, G., Fisher M.L., and Nemhauser G.L. (1977). "Location of Bank Accounts to Optimize Float: An Analytic Study of Exact and Approximate Algorithms". *Management Science* 23, 789–810.
137. Cox, T F and Cox, M A. (2001). *Multidimensional Scaling*. 2nd edition. (London: Chapman & Hall).
138. Cox, D.R. (1970). *The Analysis of Binary Data*. (London: Methuen and Co. Ltd.).
139. Cox, K.K., J.B. Higgenbotham and J. Burton (1976). "Application of Focus Group Interviews in Marketing". *Journal of Marketing Research* : 187–80
140. Crespi, I. (1961). "Use of Scaling Technique in Surveys". *Journal of Marketing* 25, (July, 1961) : 71.
141. Creswell, John W (2002). *"Research Design—Quantitative and Qualitative Methods*. (John Wiley).
142. Cronbach, L.J. 1951 September. "Coefficient a and the Internal Structure of Tests". *Psychometrica*, 16 (September, 1951).
143. Cryer, P. (1996). *Research Students Guide to Success*. (UK: Buckingham Open University Press).
144. Csikszentmihalyi, Mihaly (1996). *Creativity Flow and Psychology of Discovery and Invention*. (New York: Harper Collins Publishers).
145. Curle, A. (1949). "A Theoretical Approach to Action Research". *Human Relations* 2.
146. Darden, William R, Et Al. (1983). *Research Methods and Causal Models in Marketing*. (Chiag American Marketing Association).
147. Dasgupta, A.K. (1968). *Methodology of Economic Research*. (Bombay: Asia Publishing House) p 169.
148. Dasgupta, Sugata (1967). *Methodology of Social Science Research*. (New Delhi: Impex India) p 172.
149. Daucher, Hans (1967). *Creativity as a Structural Problem of Thinking*. (New York: McGraw-Hill), pp. 79–82.
150. David, L. (1991). *Handbook of Genetic Algorithms*. (New York: Van Nostrand).
151. De Bono, F (1971). *Lateral Thinking for Management*. (London: McGraw-Hill).
152. De Greene, Kenyon B (1970). ed. *System Psychology*. (New York McGraw Hill).
153. De Porter, Bobby and Mike Hernaski (1992). *Quantum Learning: Unleashing the Genius in You*. (New York: Dell Publishing)
154. Denzin, N.K. (1978). *The Research Act*, 2nd ed. (New York: McGraw-Hill).
155. Desarbo, W.S. and D.K. Hildebrand, (1980 summer). "A Marketers' Guide to Log-Linear Models for Qualitative Data Analysis". *Journal of Marketing* : 40–51.
156. Devellis, Robert, F. (2002). *Scale Development – Theory and Applications*. N.Y.: Sage.
157. Devpura, A., J.W., Fowler M.W., Carlyle and I. Perez (2000). "Minimising Total Weighted Tardiness on Single Batch Process Machine With Incompatible Job Families". *http://www.Uni-Duisburg.De/FB5/BWL/WI/Or2000/Sektion10/Fowler.Pdf*
158. Dewey, John (1938). *Logic: The Theory of Enquiry*. (New York: Henry Holt and Company).
159. Doll, W.J. and G. Torkzadeh (1990). "The Measurement of End-User, Software Involvement". Omega 18 no. 4 : 399–406.
160. Doyal, L. and R. Harris, (1986). *Empiricism, Explanation and Rationality*. (London: Routledge).
161. Draper, N.R and Smith H (1981). *Applied Regression Analysis*, 2nd ed. (New York: John Wiley).
162. Dubinskas, F.A. (ed.) (1988). *Making Time: Ethnographies of High-Technology Organisation*. (Philadelphia: Temple University Press).
163. Easterby, Smith Mark, Thorpe Richard, and Lowe Andy (2000). *Management Research – An Introduction*, 2nd ed. (London: Sage).
164. Eden, C., S. Junes, and D. Sims (1983). *Messing about in Problems*. (Oxford: Pergamon).
165. Edwards, A.L. (1957). *Techniques of Attitude Scale Construction*. (New York: Appleton-Century-Crofts Inc).

166. Edwards, Allen L (1968). *Experimental Design in Psychological Research*, 3rd ed. (New York Rinehart and Winston), pp 175–177.
167. Edwards, Allen (1967). *Statistical Methods*, 2nd ed. (New York: Holt, Reinhart and Winston).
168. Egelese, R.W. (1990). "Simulated Annealing A Tool for Operational Research". *European Journal of Operations Research* 46 : 271–281.
169. Eglese, R.W. (1986). "Heuristics in Operational Research" in *Recent Developments in Operational Research*, eds. Belton V. and R.M. O'Keefe, (*Operational Research Society*) pp 46–67.
170. Eilon, S. (1979). "Seven Faces of Research". *Omega* volume, no. 1 : 1–9.
171. Eisenhardt, K.M. (1989). "Building Theories from Case Study Research". *Academy of Management Review* 14 no. 4 : 532–550.
172. Ely, M., R., Vinz M Anzul and M. Downing (1997). *On Writing Qualitative Research: Living by Words*. (PA: The Falmer Press).
173. Emery, F.E and E.L. Tryst. (1960). "Socio-Technical Systems" in *Management Sciences Models and Techniques,* Verschuer Vol. 2, (Oxford Pergamon Press).
174. Emery, F.E. (ed) (1969). *Systems Thinking*. (London: Penguin).
175. Emory, William C (1976). *Business Research Methods*. (Homewood, Illinois: Richard D Irwin, Inc.)
176. Epstein, Robert. (1993). "How to Get a Great Idea". *Readers Digest* 142, (Massachusetts: Cambridge Center for Behavioral Studies) : (1993) 39.
177. Ettlie, J.E. and W.P. Bridges. (1982). "Environmental Uncertainty and Organizational Technology Policy." *IEEE Transactions on Engineering Management* 29, no. 1 (1982).
178. Evan, William M ed. (1971). *Organisational Experiments; Laboratory and Field Research*. (New York: Harper and Row) p 274.
179. Evered, R. and M. R. Lewis (1991). "*The Management Research Handbook*. In, Smith and Dainty (ed), (London: Routledge), pp. 7–22.
180. Evered, R. and M.R. Lewis (1981). "Alternative Perspectives in the Organizational Sciences: Inquiry from the Inside and Inquiry from the Outside". *Academy of Management Review*, 6, no. 3, (1981) pp. 385–95. Field Research, New York, viii, p 274. (ed).
181. Everitt, B. (1978). *Graphical Techniques for Multivariate Data*. (New York: North-Holland).
182. Eysenhardt, K. (1989). "Building Theories from Case Study Research". *Academy of Management Review*, 14 no. 4 : 385–95.
183. Fairclough, N. (1995). *Critical Discourse Analysis: The Critical Study of Language*. (London: Sage).
184. Fayyad, U.M., Shapir O.G., and Fratetskey P. Smyth (1996). "The KDD Process of Extracting Useful Knowledge from Volumes of Data", *Communication of the ACM* 39–11, pp. 27–34.
185. Fellegi, I.P. and Holt D. (1976). "A Systematic Approach to Automatic Edit and Imputation, *Journal of the American Statistical Association* volume : 17–35.
186. Fergusson, G.A. (1959). "Statistical Analysis in Psychology and Behavioral Sciences". (New York: McGraw-Hill).
187. Fern, E.F. (1982, February). "The Use of Focus Groups for Idea Generation". *Journal of Marketing Research*, (February, 1982) pp. 1–13.
188. Festinger, Leon and Daniel Katz (1953). *Research Methods in the Behavioral Sciences*. (New York: The Dryden Press).
189. Fetterman, D.M. (1989). "Ethnography: Step by Step". *Applied Social Research Methods Series* 17, (Beverly Hills California: Sage Publishers).
190. Fink, Arlene (1998). *Conducting Research Literature Reviews—From paper to internet*. (California: Sage).
191. Finley, Paul N (1985). *Mathematical Modelling in Business Decision Making*. (London: Croom Helm).
192. Finney, D.J. (1971). *Probit Analysis*. (Cambridge: Cambridge University Press).
193. Fishburer, Peter C. and John D.C. Little (1988). "An Experiment in Approval Voting". Management Science 34, no. 5.
194. Fisher, M.L., (1980). "Worst-Case Analysis of Heuristic Algorithms". *Management Science* 26, no. 1 : 1–17.
195. Fisher, R.A. (1958). *Statistical Methods for Research Workers*, 13th ed. (New York: Halfner).
196. Fisher, R.A. (1960). *Design of Experiments*. (New York: Halfner) p 248.
197. Fisherman (1971). "Estimating Sample Size in Computing Simulation Experiments". *Management Science* : 21–38.
198. Flanagan, John C (1954). "Critical Incident Technique". *Psychological Bulletin*, 51, no. 4 : 327–358.
199. Flury, Bernhand and Hans Riedwyl (1988). *Multivariate Statistics: A Practical Approach*. (London: Chapman and Hall).

200. Forester, M (1972). "An Inroduction to the Theory and Practice of Action Research in Work Organisations. *Human Relations* 25, no. 6.
201. Forrester, J.M. (1961). *Industrial Dynamics*. (Massachussets: MIT Press).
202. Forsythe, J.B. (1977). "Obtaining Cooperation in a Survey of Business Executives". *Journal of Marketing Research* 14 : 370–373.
203. Foster, Jeremy (1999). *Data Analysis Using SPSS for Windows: A Beginners Guide*. (Thousand Oaks, California: Sage).
204. Foulds, L.R. (1983). "The Heuristic Problem-Solving Approach". *The Journal of the Operational Research Society* 34, no. 10 : 927–934.
205. French, Wendell L and Cecil H. Bell Jr. (1978). *Action Research and Organisation Development* in *'Organisation Development'*. (New Jersey: Prentice-Hall Inc).
206. Freund, Rudolph J and Wilson William J (1997). *Statistical Methods*, 2nd ed. (San diego Academic Press).
207. Fruchter, Benjamin (1967). *Introduction to Factor Analysis*. (New Delhi: East-West Press), p 280.
208. Gareia, Diaz Alberto and Don T. Phillips (1995). *Principles of Experimental Design and Analysis*. (London: Chapmand and Hall).
209. Garfinkel, H (1967). *Studies in Ethnomethodology*. (Englewood Cliffs, New Jersey: Prentice-Hall).
210. Gash, S. (2000). *Effective Literature Searching*. (Gower: Aldershot).
211. Gay, L.R. and P.L. Dehl (1992). *Research Methods for Business and Management*. (New York: Macmillan International) pp 93–122.
212. Gee, Wilson (1950). *Social Science Research Methods*. (New York Appleton century Croffs.), p 390.
213. Geoffrion A.M (1987). "An Introduction to Structured Modelling". *Management Science* 33, no. 5 : 547–588.
214. Gibbons, Jean Dickinson (1985). *Non-parametric Statistical Inference*, 2nd ed. (New York: Marcel Dekker Inc).
215. Giddens, A. (1979). *Positivism and Sociology*. (London: Heinemann Educational).
216. Gigch, John Van (1987). *Applied General Systems Theory* 2nd ed. (New York: Harper and Row).
217. Gill, Sandra L and Andre L Delbecq (1982). "Nominal Group Technique (NGT)" in *Group Planning and Problem-Solving Methods in Engineering Management*, Olsen Shirley A, ed. Wiley Series, "Construction Management and Engineering". (New York: John Wiley and Sons), pp 271–287.
218. Gladwin, C.H. (1989). "Ethnographic Decision Tree Modelling". Sage University Paper Series, *Quantitative Research Methods* 19 (Beverly Hills, California: Sage Publishers).
219. Glaser, B.G. (1995). *Grounded Theory (1984–1994)*. Mill Valley Ed. A Sociology Press.
220. Glaser, B.G. and A.L. Strauss (1967). *The Discovery of Grounded Theory*. (Chicago: Aldine Publishing Company).
221. Glass, G.V., B., McGaw and M.L. Smith (1981). *Meta Analysis in Social Research*. (Beverly Hills, CA: Sage Publications).
222. Glover, F. (1993). *Genetic Algorithms and Scatter Search: Unsuspected Potentials*. (University of Colorado, Boulder, CO School of Business CB419).
223. Glover, F. (1989). "Tabu Search: Part I." *ORSA Journal of Computing* 1, no. 3 : 190–206.
224. Glover, F. (1990). "Tabu Search: A Tutorial". *Interfaces* 20, no. 4 : 74–94.
225. Glover, F. "Artificial Intelligence, Heuristics Frameworks and Tabu Search. *Managerial and Decision Economics* 11, no. 5 (1990) : 365–375.
226. Glover, F "A. Tabu Search: Part II. *ORSA Journal of Computing* 2, no. 1 (1990) 4–32.
227. Glover, F and M. Laguna (1997). *Tabu Search*. (Hingham, MA: Kluwer Academic Publishers).
228. Glover, F. J.P. Kelley and M. Laguna (1993). *Genetic Algorithms and Tabu Search: Hybrids for Optimisation*. (University of Colorado at Boulder CO Graduate School of Business and Administration).
229. Glover, F., E., Taillard and De Warra (1993). "A User's Guide to Tabu Search". *Annals of Operational Research* 41(1–4) : 3–28.
230. Goldberg, D (1989). *Genetic Algorithms in Search, Optimization and Machine Learning*. (Addison Wesley Publishing Company).
231. Goldberg, S.M. and C.P. Duncan (1983). *Structural Equations Models in Social Sciences*. (New York: McGraw-Hill).
232. Golden, B.L. and A. Assad (1988). *Vehicle Routing: Methods and Studies*. (B.V. North-Holland: Elsevier Science Publishers).
233. Golden-Biddle, K., and K.D. Locke (1997). *Composing Qualitative Research*. (Thousand Oaks: Sage).
234. Gomm, Roger and Peter Foster (2000). *The Case Study Method*. (Hammersley).

235. Goode, William J. and Paul K Hatt (1952). *Methods in Social Research*. McGraw-Hill: Chapter 5 and 6,).
236. Goodman, Leo A (1961). "Snowball Sampling", *Annals of Mathematical Statistics* 32 : 148–170.
237. Gopal, M.H (1964). *Introduction to Research Procedure in Social Sciences*. (Bombay: Asia Publishing House), p 214.
238. Gordon, G. (1992). *System Simulation*, 2nd ed. (New Delhi: Prentice-Hall of India Private Limited).
239. Gordon, William JJ (1961). *Synectics*. (New York: Harper and Row).
240. Gorsuch, R.L. (1983). *Factor Analysis*, 2nd ed. (Hillsdale: Earlbaum).
241. Graham, RJ and M. Johani, (1982). "People Problems and Planning: A System Approach to Problem Identification. *Interfaces* 8, no. 1, (1982) : 67–71.
242. Grant, Donald P (1982). "Issue-Based Information System (IBIS) in *Group Planning and Problem-Solving Methods in Engineering Management*. Olsen Shirley A, ed. Wiley Series "Construction Management and Engineering". (New York: John Wiley and Sons), pp 203–246.
243. Green, P.E. (1978). *Analysing Multivariate Data*. (Englewood cliffs, New Jersy Prentice-Hall).
244. Green, P.E. and V.R. Rao (1972). *Applied Multidimensional Scaling*. (Hinsdale, Illinois: the Dryden Press).
245. Green, Paul E, Tull D., and G Albaum (1988). *Research for Marketing Decisions*. 5th ed. (Englewood Cliffs, New Jersey: Prentice-Hall).
246. Greig, I.D. (1979). *Validation, Statistical Testing and the Decision to Model Simulation* 33, no. 2 : 55–60.
247. Greiner, Donna (1997). *The Basics of Idea Generation*. (New York: Quality Resources Books).
248. Guilford, J.P. (1959). *Traits of Creativity*. In Creativity and Its Cultivation Anderson H.H., ed., (New York: Harper and Row) pp 104–161.
249. Guilford, J.P. (1954). *Psychometric Methods*. (New York: McGraw-Hill), Chapters 2 and 10.
250. Guilford, J.P. (1967). *Nature of Human Intelligence*. (McGraw-Hill).
251. Guilford, J.P. (1980). "Creativity: Dispositions and Process" in *Creative Research—International Perspectives*. Raina M.K. ed. (New Delhi: National Council of Educational Research and Training) pp 218–235.
252. Guilford, J.P. and B. Fruchter (1978). *Fundamentals of Statistics in Psychology and Education*. (New York McGraw-Hill).
253. Gulliksen, H. and S. Messick eds. (1960). *Psychological Scaling: Theory and Applications*, (New York: John Wiley).
254. Gummeson, Eveved (2000). *Qualitative Methods in Management Research*, 2nd ed. (New Delhi: Sage Publications).
255. Gunning, Robert (1952). "Fog Index" in *Write Clear Reports: A Readability Index*. Swanson Dan H. *Supervisory Management*. (September, 1980) : 27–33 (AMACOM, A Division of American Management Association).
256. Guttman, L. (1950). "The Basis for Scalogram for Analysis". In *Measurement and Prediction*. Stouffer S.S. and Others, (New Jersey: Princeton University Press).
257. Hair, J.F., R.E. Anderson and R.L. Tatham (1990). *Multivariate Data Analysis with Readings*, 2nd ed. (New York: Macmillan Publishing Company).
258. Haire, M. (1950). "Project Team in Marketing". *Journal of Marketing*, (April, 1950) : 648–656.
259. Hall, N.G. M.E. "Posner Generating Experimental Data for Computational Testing with Machine Scheduling Applications". *Operations Research*, 49, no. 7 : 845–865.
260. Hamburg, Morris and Peg Young (1994). *Statistical Analysis for Decision Making*. 6th ed., International Edition, (Florida: The Dryden Press, Harcourt Brace College Publishers).
261. Hanson, N.R. (1958). *Patterns of Discovery*. (London: Cambridge University Press).
262. Harary, F., R. Z Norman and D. Cartwright (1965). *Structured Models: An Introduction to the Theory of Directed Graphs*. (New York John Wiley).
263. Harmon, H. H. (1967). *Modern Factor Analysis*, 2nd ed. (Chicago: University of Chicago Press).
264. Harris, R. J. (2001). *A Primer on Multivariate Statistics*, 3rd ed. (Orlando: Academic Press).
265. Hartigan, J. A. (1975). *Clustering Algorithms*. (New York: John Wiley and Sons).
266. Hassard, J. S. (1979). "Multiple Paradigm Analysis: A Methodology for Management Research". Smith and Dainty, ed. (1991). in *The Management Research Handbook*. (London: Routledge) pp 22–41.
267. Hicks, C. R. (1982). *Fundamental Concepts in the Design of Experiments*, 3rd ed. (New York: Holt, Rinehart and Winston).
268. Hicks, Michael J (1991). *Problem Solving in Business and Management: Hard, Soft, and Creative Approaches*. (London: Chapman and Hall).
269. Hilton, Gordan (1972). "Causal Inference Analysis: A Seductive Process". *Administrative Science Quarterly* Vol 17, no. 1 : 44–57.

270. Hindess, B (1977). *Philosophy and Methodology in Social Science*. (Harvester, Hassocks).
271. Hinsdale, H., J.F. Gubrium, and D. Silverman, (1989). *The Politics of Field Research*. ed. (London: Sage Publishers).
272. Hitchings, G.G. and M. Cottam, (1976). "An Efficient Heuristic Procedure for Solving the Layout Design Problem", *OMEGA* 4, (1976) : 205–214.
273. Hockey, G.R.J. and Westerman (1974). *Human Factors Engineering – An Introduction*. (University of Hull: Department of Psychology).
274. Hodges, III, B.D. and T.J. Cosse (1983). "Computer Code, Edit Open-Ended Questions to Improve Survey Accuracy and Efficiency. *Marketing News*, special Marketing Research issue, Section 1, Jan 21, pp 10.
275. Holbook, M.B., and W.L. Moore, (1982). "Using Canonical Correlations to Construct Product Spaces for Objects with Known Feature Structures. *Journal of Marketing Research* 19 : 87–98.
276. Holland, J. (1975). *Adaptation in Natural and Artificial System*. (University of Michigan Press).
277. Hollander, Myles and Douglas A Wolfe (1999). *Non-parameteric Statistical Methods*. New York John Wiley).
278. Horst, P. (1965). *Factor Analysis of Data Matrices*. (New York Holt, Rinehart and Winston).
279. Hotelling, H. (1936). "Relations Between Two Sets of Variables". *Biometrica* 28, (1936) : 321–377.
280. House, R.J. "Scientific Investigation in Management". *Management International Review* 4/5, no. 10 : 139–50.
281. Howard, K. and J.A. Sharp (1983). *The Management of a Student Research Project*. (Aldershot, Gower).
282. Hull, Frank et al (1988). "Suggestion Rates and Socio-Technical Systems in Japanese vs. American Factories: Beyond Quality Circles". *IEEE Transactions on Engineering Management* 35(1).
283. Hutchinson, E.D. (1949). *How to Think Creatively*. (New York: Abingdon Cokesbury), pp 237.
284. Huxley, Thomas (1953). "Scientific Research" in *Readings in Philosophy of Science*. Wiener P.P., ed, (New York: Chas. Screbner's Sns).
285. Hymes, D.H. (1978). *What Is Ethnography*? Socio-Linguistics Working Paper No. 45. (Austin, Texas: South-west Educational Development Laboratory).
286. Sasikumar M, NCST Mumbai :- *http://staff*.nest.evnet.in/1/1/sasi/dm log.html
287. ILO (1978). *Introduction to Workstudy*, 3rd ed. (Geneva, Switzerland: ILO Publications).
288. Indian Council of Social Science Research, New Delhi. (1972). *Survey of Research in Psychology*. (Bombay: Popular), p 454.
289. Indian Council of Social Science Research, New Delhi. (1973). *Survey of Research in Management*. (Delhi: Vikas), p 502.
290. Jackson, Michael C. (1991). Systems Methodology for Management. (New York: Plenum).
291. Jahoda, M., M. Deutsch, and W. Cook, (1958). *Research Methods in Social Relations*. (New York: The Dryden Press).
292. Jays, C. (1995). "Executive Turnover: Intentions, Desires and Psychological Quits". M.Tech. project report, Department of Management Studies, Indian Institute of Science.
293. Jenkin, G.M. (1969). "The Systems Approach". *Journal of System Engineering,* 1, no. 1.
294. Jenkyns, T.A. (1976). "The Efficacy of the Greedy Algorithm". Proc. of 7th S.E. Conference on Combinatorics, Graph Theory and Computing, 341–350.
295. Jerome, D. Wiest "Heuristic Programmes for Decision Making". *Harvard Business Review* : 129–143.
296. Jick, T.J. "Mixing Qualitative and Quantitative Methods: Triangulation in Action". *Administrative Science Quarterly* 24, (1979, December) : 602–11.
297. John, G. and T. Reve "The Reliability and Validity of Key Informants Data from Dyadic Relationships in Marketing Channels". *Journal of Marketing Research*, 19, (1982) : 517–524.
298. Johnson, R.A., F.E. Kast, and J.E. Rosen Weigh (1980). *Theory and Management of Systems*, 2nd ed. (New York McGraw-Hill).
299. Johnston, J. (1972). *Econometric Methods*, 2nd ed. (New York: McGraw-Hill).
300. Judd, C M and GH Mclleland (1998). "Measurement in *Handbook of Social Psychology,* Gilbert D.T. S T Fiske, and G Lindzey, eds. 4th ed. pp 180–232. (McGraw-Hill).
301. Kahn, R.L. and C.F. Cannell (1957). *The Dynamics of Interviewing*. (New York: John Wiley).
302. Kaiser, H.F. (1958). "Varimax Criterion for Analytic Rotation in Factor Analysis". *Psychrometrica* 23 : 187–200.
303. Kanji, Gopal K (1999). *100 Statistical Tests*. (New Delhi: Sage Publications).
304. Kaplan, A. (1964). *The Conduct of Enquiry: Methodology for Behavioural Science*. (San Francisco: Chandler).
305. Kaposi, Agnes and Margaret Myers (2000). *Systems for All*. (London: Imperial College Press).
306. Karthikeyan, G. and K.N. Krishnaswamy (1990). "Assembly Manpower Allocation under Proportionality Constraints". *European Journal of Operations Research*. 44, (1990) : 39–46.

307. Karthikeyan, G. "Allocation of Skilled Assembly Manpower under Proportionality Constraints". M.Sc. thesis, Department of Management Studies, Indian Institute of Science (1986).
308. Katona, G. and J.N. Morgan (1952). "Quantitative Study of Factors Affecting Business Decisions. *Quarterly Journal of Economics* 66 : 67–90.
309. Kelle, Udo (1995). *Computer Aid Qualitative Data Analysis – Theory, Methods and Practice*. (London: Sage Publications).
310. Kelly, J. (1955). *The Psychology of Personal Constructs*, vol.1 and 2. (New York: Norton).
311. Kelly, J. (1964). "The Study of Executives by Activity Sampling". *Human Relations* 17 : 227–87.
312. Kempf, K.G., R. Uzsoy and C.S. Wang (1998). "Scheduling a Single Batch Processing Machine with Secondary Resource Constraints. *Journal of Manufacturing Systems* 17, no. 1 : 37–51.
313. Kendall and Gibbons in Jack Dickenson (1990). *Rank Correlation Methods*. New York: Oxford University Press, 5th ed. Chapters 2, 3 and 4.
314. Kennedy, W. J. Jr. and J.E. Gentle (1980). *Statistical Computing*. (New York: Marcel Dekker).
315. Kepner, Charles H., Tregoe, and B. Benjamin (1981). *The New Rational Manager*. (London: John Martin Publishing).
316. Kerlinger, Fred N (1986). *Foundations of Behavioural Research*, 3rd ed. (New York: Holt, Rinehart and Winston Inc.).
317. Keyser, D.J. and R.C. Sweetland (1986). *Tests: A Comprehensive Reference for Assessments in Psychology*. Education and Business, 2nd ed. Kansas City Test Corporation of America.
318. Kidder, Louise H Sellitz, Wrightman and T.D. Cook (1981). *Research Methods in Social Relations*. 4th ed.
319. Kidder, L.H. and C.M. Judd (1986). *Research Methods in Social Relations*, 8th ed. (London: Holt, Rinehart and Winston).
320. Kim, J. and J. Curry (1977). "The Treatment of Missing Data in Multi-Variate Analysis". *Sociological Methods and Research* 6 : 215–240.
321. Kirca, O. and A. Satir (1990). "A Heuristic for Obtaining an Initial Solution for the Transportation Problem. *Journal of Operational Research Society* 41, no. 9 : 86 5–871.
322. Kish, J.L. (1965). *Survey Sampling*. (New York: John Wiley).
323. Klecka, (1980). *Discriminant Analysis*. (Beverly Hills, California: Sage Publications).
324. Kline, P. (1994). *An Easy Guide to Factor Analysis*. (London: Routledge).
325. Kling, J.W. and L.A. Riggs (1971). *Experimental Psychology*. (New York: Holt, Rinehart and Winston).
326. Klopfer, W.G. and E.S. Tanlbee (1976). "Projective Tests". *Annual Review of Psychology*, (1976) : 543–567.
327. Kolb, D.A., I.M. Rubin, and Mcintyre J.M. (1979). *Organisational Psychology: An Experiential Approach*. (London: Prentice-Hall).
328. Kothari, C.K. (1990). *Research Methodology, Methods, and Techniques*, 2nd ed. Viswa Prakashana, New Delhi.
329. Koutsoyiannis (1977). *Theory of Econometrics*. (London: English Language Book Series).
330. Krathwohl, David R. (1988). *How to Prepare a Research Proposal*, 3rd ed. (Syracuse University Press).
331. Krausz, E. and S.H. Miller (1974). *Social Research Design*. (London: Longman).
332. Krick, V (1962). *Methods of Engineering*. (New York: John Wiley).
333. Krik, Jerome and Marc L. Miller, (1986). *Reliability and Validity in Qualitative Research*. (Beverley Hills, CA: Sage).
334. Krikpatrik, S, C.D. Gelatta Jr, and M.P. Vechhi (1983). "*Optimisation by Simulated Annealing Sciences*." 220, 671–680.
335. Krishnaswamy, K.N. (1983). "Studies in Manpower Planning Practices in Manufacturing Organisations - An Indian Experience. Ph.D. dissertation, Department of Management Studies, Indian Institute of Science.
336. Krishnaswamy, K.N. (1985, September). "Manpower Planning Practices in Indian Manufacturing Organisations. *ASCI Journal of Management* 15, no. 1.
337. Krishnaswamy, K.N. (1998). Case Study Developed on the Data Obtained in the Project, "Technology Transformation, Its Relation to Imported Technologies – An Assessment, vol. II by Srinivasan M.N., K.B. Akhilesh, and K.N. Krishnaswamy of Department of Management Studies, Indian Institute of Science (1997).
338. Krishnaswamy, K.N. and T. Ganguly (1987, January). "Models of Reserve Manpower". *International Journal of Production Research*.
339. Krishnaswamy, K.N. and B.G. Raghavendra". (1992). Analysis and Model Development for Optimum Inventory and Distribution Policy". Project report, Department of Management Studies, Indian Institute of Science (1992).

340. Krishnaswamy, K.N., K.B. Akhilesh, and M.N. Srinivasan (1997). "Technology Transformation, in Relation to Imported Technologies – Case of Indian manufacturing companies". Quantitative Indicators, vol. 3, Project report of Department of Management Studies, Indian Institute of Science.
341. Krishnaswamy, K.N., Nagaraj G. Kulkarni and M.Mathirajan (1995), "Inventory Models with System Constraints and Changing Transportation Cost Structure. *International Journal of Management and Systems* 11, no. 1, (1995) : 91–110.
342. Kruskal, J.B. (1964). "Non-Metric Multi Dimensional Scaling: A Numerical Method". *Psychometrics* 29, (1964) : 115–129
343. Kruskal, Joseph B and Myron Wish (1978). *Multi Dimensional Scaling*. (Beverley Hills, California: Sage Publication).
344. Kuder, G.F., M.W. Richardson (1937). "The Theory of Estimation of Test Reliability". *Psychometrika* 2, (1937) : 151–160.
345. Kuhn, T. (1970). *The Structure of Scientific Revolution*, 2nd ed. (University of Chicago Press).
346. Lambert, Z. and R. Duaand (1975). "Some Precautions in Using Canonical Analysis". *Journal of Marketing Research* 3, (1975) : 467–475.
347. Latour, B. and S. Woolgar (1979). *Laboratory Life: The Social Construction of Scientific Facts*. (Sage Publication).
348. Law, A M and D W. Kelton (1991). *Simulation Modelling and Analysis*. (New York: McGraw-Hill).
349. Lawler, E. (1976). *Combinatorial Optimisation* (New York: Holt, Rinehart and Winston).
350. Lawrence, P. and J.W. Lorch (1967). *Organisation and Environment*. (Boston: Harvard University Press).
351. Lazarsfeld, P.F. and N.W. Henry (1968). *Latent Structure Analysis*. (Boston Houghton Mifflin).
352. Lazarsfeld, P.F. and M. Rosenberg (1953, 1957). *Language of Social Research: A Reader in the Methodology of Social Research*. (Free Press, p 590).
353. Leedy, Paul D. (1996). *Practical Research Planning and Design*, 6th Edition, (New Jersey: Prentice-Hall).
354. Lefferts, Robert 1990 *How to Write Successful Grant Proposals*. (Englewood cliffs, New Jersey: Prentice-Hall).
355. Lehman, D.R. (1989). *Market Research and Analysis*, 3rd ed. (Boston: Homewood, Illinois).
356. Lehman, D.R. and J.M. Hulbert (1975, January). "Reducing Error in Question and Scale Design – A Conceptual Framework. *Decision Sciences* 6 : 166–173.
357. Lewin, K. (1951). *Field Theory in Social Sciences*. (New York: Harper and Row).
358. Liebrand, Wim B.G, Nowak, Andrej and Hegselman Rains, ed. (1998). *Computer Modelling for Social Processes*. (London Sage Publication).
359. Likert, R. (1967). *The Human Organisation: Its Management and Values*. (New York: McGraw-Hill).
360. Lin, S., and B.W. Kernighan, (1973). "An Effective Heuristic Algorithm for the Traveling-Salesman Problem. *Operations Research* 21, no. 2, (1973) : 498–516.
361. Linda, Argote (1982). "Input Uncertainty and Organisational Co-ordination in Hospital Emergency Units. *Administrative Science Quarterly* 27) : 420–434.
362. Lindzey, G. (1959). "On the Classification of Projective Technique" : 158–168.
363. Little, J.D. (1970). "Models and Managers: The concept of a decision calculus". *Management Science* 16, no. 8 (1970) : 466–85.
364. Locke, Karen (2001). *Grounded Theory in Management Research*. (London: Sage).
365. Locke, Lawerence, F. Spiduso, Warren Wynck and Silverman, J. Stephen (2000). Proposals that Work: A guide to Planning Dissertations and Grant Proposals, 5th ed. (New York: Sage).
366. Lundberg, C.C. (1976). "Hypothesis Creation in Organisational Behaviour Research. *Academy of Management Review* 1 : pp. 5–12.
367. Luthans, F. (1973). *Organisational Behaviour.* (New York: McGraw-Hill).
368. Maanen, J.V., Jm. Dabbs Jr. and F.R. Faulkner (1982). *Varieties of Qualitative Research*. (Beverly Hills California: Sage).
369. Madan, Mohan T.R. (1991). "Technology Support Systems (TSS) - A New Concept for Analyzing Technological Transformation Process - An Analysis in the Indian Manufacturing Organisations". Ph.D. thesis, Department of Management Studies, Indian Institute of Science.
370. Madan, Mohan T.R. (1999). "Multiple Case Analysis – A Useful Tool for Exploratory Policy Studies. Course material, Management Development Institute Gurgaon, India (1999).
371. Maddala, G.S. (1972). *Econometrics*. (McGraw-Hill).
372. Maguire, R and T.C. Wilson "Banners or Cross Tabs? Before Dending Weight Data-Format Pros, Cons. *Marketing News*, (May 13), 10.

373. Malinowski, B. (1972). *Argonauts of the Western Pacific* (London: Routledge, Kegan and Paul).
374. Malone, D.W. (1975). "An Introduction to the Application of Interpretive Structural Modelling". *Proceedings of IEEE* 63, no. 3 : 397–404.
375. Mangione, Thomas W (1995). *Mail Surveys—Improving Quality*. (London: Sage).
376. Manly, B.F.J. (1992). *Design and Analysis of Research Studies*. (Cambridge: Cambridge University Press).
377. Manly, B.F.J. (1994). *Multivariate Statistical Methods—A Primer*, 2nd ed. (Chapman and Hall).
378. Marakas, George M (1999). *Decision Support Systems in the 21st century*. (New Jersey: Prentice-Hall).
379. Maranell, G.M., (1974). *Scaling: A Sourcebook for Behavioural Scientists*. (Chicago: Aldine).
380. March, James G and Herbert A Simon (1958). *Organisation*. (New York: John Wiley and Sons, Inc.).
381. Mathirajan, M and B. Meenakshi. "Experimental Analysis of Some Variants of Vogel's Approximation Method. *Asia Pacific Journal of Operations Research*, 21 (2004).
382. Mathirajan, M, A.I. Sivakumar and V. Chandru (2004). "Scheduling Algorithms for Heterogeneous Batch Processors with Incompatible Job-Families. *Journal of Intelligent Manufacturing* 15, no. 16.
383. Mathirajan, M, A.I. Sivakumar and P. Kalaivani (2004). "An Efficient Simulated Annealing Algorithm for Scheduling Burn-In Oven with Non-Identical Job-Sizes". International Journal of Applied Management and Technology, volume No. 2, 117–138.
384. Mathirajan, M. (1995). "Some PC-Based Heuristics for Employee Pick-Up Vehicle Routing Problem and Influence of Spatial Demand Distribution". M.Sc dissertation, Department of Management Studies, Indian Institute of Science.
385. Mathirajan, M (2001). "Heuristic Scheduling Algorithms for Parallel Heterogeneous Batch Processors. Ph.D dissertation, Department of Management Studies, Indian Institute of Science.
386. Mathirajan, M., K.N., Krishnaswamy and B.G. Raghavendra (1994). "An Evaluation of Some PC-Based Heuristic Computer Algorithms for Routing of Vehicles for Employee Pickup. *Journal of Transport Management* 18, no. 3 : 177–190.
387. Mathirajan, M., and A.I., Sivakumar (2002). A Literature Review, Classification and Simple Meta Analysis on Scheduling of Batch Processors uc Semi Conductor manufacturing, Forthcoming in (2006), International Journal of Advanced Manufacturing Technology (Springer).
388. Mccall, G.J. and J.L. Simmons (1969). *Issues in Participant Observation*. (Wokingham: Addison-Wesley).
389. Mcdonald, C. (1982). "Coding Open-Ended Answers with the Help of a Computer". *Journal of the Market Research Society* 24, (9–27).
390. Mcgrath, J.E. Martin, J. and Kulka, R.A. (1982). Judgement Calls in Research. (London: Sage Publishers).
391. McIver, J.P. and E. G. Carminer (1981). *Unidimensional Scaling*. (New Delhi: Sage).
392. Mckie, Craing (1997). *Using the Web for Social Research*. (New York: Mcgraw-Hill, Ryerson Ltd.)
393. Mcmillan, Claude and Richard F Gonzalez (1965). *System Analysis*. (Richard D. Irwin Inc.).
394. McNamara, Gerry and Jack Whitehead (2002). *Action Research: Principles and Practice* 2nd ed. (London: Routledge).
395. Meclintock, Charles B, D., Brannon Maynord Mody S. (1979). "Applying the Logic of Sample Survey to Qualititative Case Studies: The Case Cluster Method. *Administrative Science Quarterly* 24 : 612–629.
396. Mehan, H. and H. Wood (1975). *The Relativity of Ethnomethodology*. (London: John Wiley).
397. Mehta, S.V., and R. Uzsoy (1998). "Minimising Total Tardiness on a Batch Processing Machine with Incompatible Job Families. *IIE Transactions* 30, (1998) : 165–178.
398. Meier, R.C, T.N. William, and L.P. Harold (1969). *Simulation in Business and Economics*. (Prentice-Hall).
399. Mendenhall, William, James Reinmuth and Robert Beaver (1989). *Statistics for Management and Economics*. 6th ed. (Boston: PWS Kent Publishing Company) pp 813–868.
400. Merbach, Muller H (1981). "Heuristics and Their Design—A Survey. *European Journal of Operations Research* 8 : 1–23.
401. Merton, R.K., M. Fiske and P.L. Kendall (1956). *The Focused Interview*. (New York Free Press).
402. Michalewez, Z and Janikow (1991). "Genetic Algorithms for Numerical Optimization". *Statistics and Computing* 1, (1991) : 75–91.
403. Miles, N.B. and A.M. Huberman (1994). *Qualitative Data Analysis: A Source Book of New Methods*, 2nd ed. (London: Sage).
404. Mill, J.S. (1990). *A System of Logic*, 8th ed. (New York: Longmans).
405. Miller, D. and P.H. Friesen (1982). "The Longitudinal Analysis of Organisations". *Management Science* 28, no. 9 (1982) : pp. 1013–34.
406. Miller, Danny and Cornelva Drose (1986). "Psychological and Traditional Determinants of Structure. *Administrative Science Quarterly* 31 : 539–560.

407. Mitchell, J.V. Jr, ed. (1983). *Tests in Print III, An Index to test reviews, and the Literature on Specific Tests.* (Lincoln, N.B: The University of Nebraska Press).
408. Mitchell, J.C. (1983). "Case and Situational Analysis". *Sociological Review* 31 : 187–211.
409. Mitroff, I.I. (1974). *The Subjective Side of Science.* (Amsterdam: Elsevier Publishers).
410. Mizerski, R.W., N.K. Allison, and S. Calvert (1980). "A Controlled Field Study of Corrective Advertising Using Multiple Exposures and a Commercial Medium". *Journal of Marketing Research* 17, (1980) 341–348.
411. Mohan, A.V. (1995). "Marketing Programs and Technological Developments Across Product Life Cycle: An Exploratory Study in Indian Machine Building Sector". Ph.D. dissertation, Management Studies Department, IISc.
412. Montgomery, D.B. and Peck (1981). *Linear Regression Analysis.* (New York: John Wiley).
413. Montgomery, D.C. (1999). *Design and Analysis of Experiments,* 3rd ed. (New York: John Wiley).
414. Morris, W.T. (1967) "On the Art of Modeling". *Management Science :* 707–711.
415. Morrison, D.F. (1969). "On the Interpretation of Discriminant Analysis. *Journal of Marketing Research* 6 : 156–163.
416. Morrison, Donald F (1967). *Multivariate Statistical Methods.* (New York McGraw-Hill).
417. Morrissey, E.R. (1982). "Sources of Error in the Coding of Questionnaire Data". *Sociological Methods and Research Society* 1 : 75–76.
418. Morton, T.E. and D.W. Pentico (1993). *Heuristic Scheduling System: with Applications to Production Systems and Project Management.* (New York: John Wiley and Sons, Inc.).
419. Mouly, V.S. and E. Ramani (1990). "Survey Research and Ethnographic Research: An Appraisal of Two Research Methodologies. Indian Institute of Management-Bangalore (IIM-B) *Management Review* no. 5 (1990) : 31–51.
420. Mouly, V.S. (1990). "A Study of an R&D Team in an Indian Research Organization: An Ethnographic Approach". Ph.d. dissertation, Department of Management Studies, Indian Institute of Science.
421. Moustakas, C. (1992). *Heuristic Research: Design, Methodology and Applications.* (New Delhi: Sage Publications).
422. Moyser, B. and M. Wagstaffe, eds. (1987). *Research Methods for Elite Studies.* (London: Allen and Unwin).
423. Mukund, Mohan (1986). "Development of Implementation Support Systems for Operations Management Techniques-A Systems Method of Problem-Solving". Ph.D dissertation, Department of Management Studies, Indian Institute of Science.
424. Muller-Merbach, H. (1974). "Heuristic Methods: Structures, Applications, Computational Experience in *Optimisation Methods for Resource Allocation.* Cottle R. and J. Krarup, eds., (London English Universities Press,) pp 401–416.
425. Muller-Merbach, H. (1975). "Modeling Techniques and Heuristics for Combinatorial Problems" in *Combinatorial Programming: Methods and Applications.* B. Roy, ed. (Reidel, Dordrecht,) pp 3–27.
426. Mumford, E.E., R., Hirschheim G. Fitzgerald and A.T. Wood-Harper eds. (1985). *Research Methods in Information Systems.* (Amsterdam: Elsevier Science Publishers Bv).
427. Murthy, M.N (1967). *Sampling Theory and Methods.* (Calcutta: Statistical Publishing Society).
428. Narasimha, Murthy K.V. (1995). "Manufacturing Strategy in Indian Industrial Organizations: An Exploratory Study of Two Sectors." M.Sc. thesis, Department of Management Studies, Indian Institute of Science.
429. Narver, John C and Stanley F Slater (1990). "The Effect of Market Orientation of Business Profitability". *Journal of Marketing* 54 : pp. 20–35.
430. Naylor, T.H. and J.M. Finger (1967). "Verification of Computer Simulation Models." *Management Science* 14, no. 2, (1967) : 92–101.
431. Neter, J., W. Wasserman and M.H. Kutner (1990). *Applied Linear Regression Models*, 2nd ed. (Homewood, Illinois: Richard D Irwin).
432. Newell, A., J.C. Shah and H.A. Simon (1958). "Elements of A Theory of Human Problem Solving." *Psychological Review* 65, no. 3 : 151–166.
433. Newell, A., J.C. Shaw, and H.A. Simon (1962). "The Process of Creative Thinking" in *Contemporary Approaches to Creative Thinking*, Gruber H.E., G. Terrell and M. Wertheimer, ed. (New York: Atherton) pp 63–119.
434. Nie, N.H., C.H. Hull and Others. (1975). *Statistical Package for the Social Science*, 2nd ed. (New York: McGraw-Hill).
435. Norman, Richard (1971). "Organisational Innovation-Product Orientation and Re-Orientation". *Administrative Science Quarterly* 16, no. 2.

436. Northrop, F.S.C. (1931). *Science and First Principles.* (New York Meridian Books, WPC).
437. Northrop, F.S.C. (1967). *Logic of the Sciences and the Humanities.* (New York: Meridian Books, World Publishing Company).
438. Norusis, Manja J (1990). *SPSS/PC+ 4.0 User Manuals*, Chicago, Illinois.
439. Nunally, J.C. (1959). *Tests and Measurements Assessment, and Prediction.* (New York: McGraw-Hill), p 446.
440. Nunnally, J.C. (1967). *Psychometric Theory.* (New York: McGraw-Hill Inc.).
441. Olsen, Shirley A., ed. (1982). Group Planning and Problem-Solving Methods in Engineering Management. Wiley Series on *Construction Management and Engineering* (New York: John Wiley and Sons).
442. Oppenhein, A.N. (1986). "Analogy in Science". *American Psychologist* 11, 27–35.
443. Oppenhein, A.N. (1966). *Questionnaire Design and Attitude Measurement.* (New York: Basic Books).
444. Oren, T.I. (1981). "Concepts and Criteria to Assess Acceptability of Simulation Studies: A Frame of Reference". *Communications of the ACM* 24, no. 4, pp. 131–137.
445. Osborne, Alex F (1963). *Applied Imagination*, 3rd ed. (New York: Charles Schribner's and Sons).
446. Osgood, C.E., G.J. Suci and P.H. Tannenbaum (1957). *The Measurement of Meaning*, (Urbana: University of Illinois Press).
447. Osman, I.H. and J.P. Kelly (1996). "Meta-Heuristics: An Overview" in *Meta-Heuristics Theory and Applications*". I.H. Osman and J.P. Kelly, eds. (Boston: Kluwer Academic Publishers). Chapter 1, pp 1–21
448. Ostle, B. and R.W. Marsing, (1973). *Statistics in Research.* (London: George Allen and Unwin Limited).
449. Overall, J.E. and J. Klett (1972). *Applied Multivariate Analysis.* (New York McGraw-Hill).
450. Pacifico, Carl (1966). *Creative Thinking in Practice.* (New Jersey: Nayes Press) pp 26.
451. Pareek, Udai and S.R. Mittal Comp. (1966). *Guide to the Literature of Research Methodology in Behavioural Sciences.* (Delhi: Sterling Publishers) p 64.
452. Parnaby, (1979). "Concepts of A Manufacturing System". *International Journal of Production Research* 17, no. 2.
453. Parnes, Sidney J (1964). *Creativity: Unblocking Human Potential* (Creative Education Foundation. Dok Publisher).
454. Parnes, Sidney J (1964). "Research on Developing Creative Behaviour" in *Widening Horizons of Creativity.* Taylor Calwin W, ed. (John Wiley).
455. Pasmore, Williom and Friedlander (1989). "An Action Research Programme for Increasing Employee Involvement in Problem Solving". *Administrative Science Quarterly* 27, no. 3.
456. Patel, N.R. (1979). "On Locating Rural Service Centres". *Management Science,* 25, no. 1.
457. Patton, M.Q. (1980). *Qualitative Evaluation Methods.* (London: Sage).
458. Payne, S. (1951). *The Art of Asking Questions.* (New Jersey: Princeton University Press).
459. Peter, Kennedy (1979). *A Guide to Econometrics.* (Massachussets: M.I.T Press).
460. Peterson, Robert A. (2000). *Constructing Effective Questionnaires.* (Barnest and Noble).
461. Phillipps, E.M. and D.S. Pugh (1987). *How to Get a Ph.D.* (Milton Keynes: Open University Press).
462. Phillips, B.S. (1971). *Social Research*, 2nd ed. (New York: The Macmillan Company).
463. Pindyck, R.S. and D.L. Rubenfeld (1981). *Econometric Models and Econometric Forecasts.* (New York; McGraw-Hill) pp 142–146.
464. Polya (1957). *How to Solve It*, 2nd ed. (Garden City NJ: Double-day Anchor Books).
465. Popper, K.R. (1972). *The Logic of Scientific Discovery.* (London: Hutchinson).
466. Popper, Karl (1959). *Logic of Scientific Discovery.* (Cambridge University Press).
467. Premkumar, G. and W.R. King (1990). "Strategic Telecommunications Planning - A Descriptive Model. *Omega* 18, no. 5 : pp 447–462.
468. Prince, George M (1970). *The Practice of Creativity.* (New York: Collier Book, Macmillan Publisher).
469. Pugh, D.S. (1968). *The Aston Research Program–The Organisation in Its Context.* (Farnborough Saxon House).
470. Punj, G. and D. Stewart (1983). "Cluster Analysis in Marketing Research: Review and suggestions for application". *Journal of Marketing Research* 20 : 134–148.
471. Raghavendra, A., T.S., Krishnakumar R., Muralidhar D. Sarvanan and B.G. Raghavendra (1992). "A Practical Heuristic for a Large Scale Vehicle Routing Problem". *European Journal of Operational Research* 57 : 32–38.
472. Raghavendra, B.G. (1989). "An Introduction and Optimization Model for Media Planning". *International Journal on Management and System* 5, no. 1 : 1–16.
473. Raghavendra, B.G. and M. Mathirajan (1992). *Efficiency and Effectiveness in Advertising Media Planning in OR in India: A retrospective.* Silver Jubilee Publication of ORSI. Wiley Eastern Limited.

474. Ramachandran, P (1971). Training in Research Methodology in Social Science in India. (New Delhi: Indian Council of Social Science Research). p 117.
475. Ramasastry, A.S. (1974). "Materials Management Contributions to Banking". Ph.D. dissertation, Department of Management Studies, Indian Institute of Science.
476. Randolph, P., G. Swinson and C.E. Ellingsen (1973). "Stopping Rules for Sequencing Problems". *Operations Research*. 21 : 1309–1315.
477. Ranjitkumar, (1999). *Research Methodology: A Step By Step Guide for Beginners*. (Delhi: Sage India).
478. Rao, K.S.P., B.G. Raghavendra and K.N. Krishnaswamy (1993). "Experimental Evaluation of System Configurations of an Industrial Processing System Using a Markovian Approach". *Applied Mathematical Modeling*, 17 : 577–585.
479. Rapoport, R.N. "Three Dilemmas in Action Research. *Human Relations* 23, no. 6, (1970) : 499–513.
480. Rardin, R.L. and R. Uzsoy (2001). "Experimental Evaluation of Heuristic Optimisation Algorithms : A Tutorial". *Journal of Heuristics* 7, no. 3, (2001) 261–304.
481. Ravi, Rammurthy (1987). "Performance Evaluation of State-Owned Enterprise (SOE's) in Theory and Practice". *Management Science* : 876–893.
482. Rawlinson, Jeffery (1994). *Creative Thinking and Brain Storming*. (Hampshire, United Kingdom: Gower Publishing Co., Ltd.).
483. Ray, Michael and Rachel Myers (1986). *Creativity in Business*. (New York: Doubleday).
484. Renty, Joseph O, Fred D Reynolds, and Roy C Stout (1983). "Analysing Changing Consumption Pattern with Cohort Analysis". *Journal of Marketing* 20 : 12–20.
485. Rivett, Pabrick (1994). *The Craft of Decision Modelling*. (New York John Wiley).
486. De, Vellis Robert F (2002). *Scale Development—Theory and Applications*. (New Delhi: Sage).
487. Robinson, W.S. (1951). "The Logic and Structure of Analytic Induction". *American Sociological Review* 16 : 812–18.
488. Sapford, Roger (1990). *Survey Research*. (New Delhi: Sage Publications).
489. Romesburgh, H. C. (1984). *Cluster Analysis for Researchers*. (Belmont, California: Lifetime Learning Publications).
490. Rosenberg, M.J. (1968). *The Logic of Survey Analysis*. (New York: Basic Books).
491. Rosenthal, R. and R.L. Rosnow (1975). *Primer on Methods for the Behavioral Science*. (London: John Wiley).
492. Rowan, Margo and Patricia Houston" Qualitative Research Articles: Information for Authors and Peer Reviewers. *Canadian Medical Association Journal*, (November, 1999).
493. Rummel, R.W. and W.C. Ballaine (1963). *Research Methodology in Business*. (New York: Harper and Row).
494. Russel, Betrand (1951). *The Scientific Outlook*. (Glencoe: Illinois, Free Press).
495. Rutman, Leonard (1984). *Evaluation Research Methods – Basic Guide*, 2nd ed. (New Delhi: Sage).
496. Ryan, Bob, Robert W Scapens, and Michael Theobald (1992). *Research Method and Methodology in Finance and Accounting*. (New York: Academic Press).
497. Saaty, Thomas L (1959). *Mathematical Methods of Operations Research* (New York: McGraw-Hill).
498. Sampath, D., K.W., Ho W.J., Hsu, and C.E. Prakash (2000). "Functions, Models and Techniques for Financial Data Mining". Working paper, Centre for Financial Engineering, Nanyang Technological University.
499. Saunders, Mark, Phillip Levis, and Adam Thornhill (2003). *Research Methods for Business* New York; Prentice-Hall.
500. Saville-Troike, M (1982). *The Ethnography of Communication: An Introduction* (Great Britain: Basil Blackwell).
501. Sawyer, A.G., Worthing P.M., and P.E. Sendak (1979). "The Role of Laboratory Experiments in Test Marketing Strategies". *Journal of Marketing* 43, no. 3, (1979) : 60–67.
502. Sawyer, Alan G. and Peter Pald J (1983). "The Significance of Statistical Significance Tests in Marketing Research". *Journal of Marketing Research* 20 : 123–133.
503. Schiffman, S.S., L.M. Reynolds and F.W. Young (1981). *Introduction to Multidimensional Scaling- Theory, Methods, and Applications*. (New York: Academic Press Inc.).
504. Schrage, Linus (1991). *LINDO on Optimisation Modelling System*. 4th ed. (San Francisco Scientific Press) Chapter 4..
505. Schruben, L.W. "Establishing the Credibility of Simulations". *Simulation* 34, no. 3, (1980) : 101–105.
506. Schuman, H. and Presser, S. (1979). The Open and Closed Question. American Sociological Review, Vol.44, pp. 692–712.
507. Schutz, A. (1970). "*Reflection on the Problem of Relevance*" in M. Zander (ed) *The Way of Phenomenology*, New York: Pegasus.

508. Sekharan, Uma. (1992). *Business Research Methods—A Skill Building Approach*. 2nd ed., Chapter 2 and 3, John Wiley. (7th ed. (2000)).
509. Selltiz, C., M., Jahoda M. Deutsch and S.W. Cook, (1959). *Research Methods in Social Relations*, rev. ed. (New York: Holt, Rinehart and Winston, Inc.).
510. Selltiz, C., L.S. Wrightsman and S.W. Cook (1981). *Research Methods in Social Relation*, 4th ed. (New York: Holt, Rinehert and Winston).
511. Sevarance, Frank L (2002). *System Modelling and Simulation: An Introduction*. (New York John Wiley).
512. Shalley, C.E. (1991). "Effects of Productivity Goals, Creativity Goals and Personal Discretion on Individual Creativity". *Journal of Applied Psychology* 76, no. 2 (1991) :
513. Shekar, G.L. (1999). "Planning and Scheduling Systems for Steel Casting Production – A New Paradigm". Ph.D. dissertation, Department of Management Studies, Indian Institute of Science.
514. Shekdar, A.V. (1988). "Systems Analysis of Solid Waste Management - Some Studies in the Indian Context". Ph.D thesis, Indian Institute of Science.
515. Shekdar, A.V., A.D. Bhide and K.N. Krishnaswamy (1986). "An Inventory Theoretic Approach to Dust Bin Capacity". *Asian Environment* 8, no. 1.
516. Shenoy, S. (1975). "A Study of Context, Structure and Performance of Organisations. Ph.D. dissertation, Department of Industrial Management, Indian Institute of Science, India (April).
517. Sieber, S.D. (1973). The Integration of Felid Work and Survey Methods. "*American Journal of Sociology* 78 : 1335–1359.
518. Siedl, P.S., (1974). "Coding" in *Handbook of Marketing Research*. Robert F, ed. (New York: McGraw-Hill), pp 2–178 and 2–199.
519. Siegel, Sidney (1986). *Non-parametric Statistics for the Behavioural Science*, 2nd ed. (New York: McGraw-Hill).
520. Silver, Edward A., R., Victor V. Vidal, and Dominique De Werra A (1980). "Tutorial on Heuristic Methods. *European Journal of Operational Research* 5 : 153–162.
521. Silverman, David (2000). *Doing Qualitative Research – A Practical Approach*. (London: Sage).
522. Simon, H.A., and A. Newell (1958). "Heuristic Problem Solving: The Next Advance in Operations Research. *Operations Research* 6, no. 1 : 1–10.
523. Simon, Herbert A (1960). *The New Science of Management Decision*. (New York: Harper and Row).
524. Slama, and Taschchian, (Winter, 1985). "Socio-Economic and Demographic Characteristic Association in Purchasing Involvement. *Journal of Marketing Research* 49.
525. Smith, Craig and Paul Dainty (1991). *Management Research Handbook*, (London: Roultedge).
526. Smith, H.W. (1975). *Strategies of Social Research, the Methodological Imagination*. (London: Prentice-Hall International).
527. Snider, J.G. and Osgood C.E., eds. (1969). *Semantic Differential Technique*. (Chicago: Aldine Publishing Company).
528. Spradley, J.P. (1979). *The Ethnographic Interview*. (New York: Holt, Rinehart and Winston).
529. Sprent, P and N.C. Smeeton (2001). *Applied Non-Parametric Statistical Methods*, 3rd ed. (Chapman and Hall).
530. *Staff.nest.ernet.in/sasi/dmlong.htool*. Datamining.
531. Stanely, S.S., ed. (1951). *Handbook of Experimental Psychology*. (New York: John Wiley).
532. Stein, Morris I and Shirley J Heinze (1960). *Creativity and Individual*. The Free Press of Glencoe, University of Chicago.
533. Stevens, S.S. (1946). Oh the Theory of Scales of Measurement. *Science* 103 (2684) : 677–680.
534. Stevens, S.S. (1956). "Problems and Methods of Psychophysics". *Psychological Bulletin* 55 : 177–196.
535. Stevens, S.S. (1968). "Measurement, Statistics, and the Schemapiric View". *Science* 161 : 849–856.
536. Stewart, R. (1982). *Choices for the Managers: A Guide to Managerial Work and Behaviour*. (London: McGraw-Hill)
537. Stewart, D.W. (1982). "Filling the Gap: A Review of the Missing Data Problem" in *An Assessment of Marketing Thought and Practice*. Walker B.J. et al., eds. (Chicago: American Marketing Association) pp 395–399.
538. Stewart, R. (1965). "The Use of Diaries to Study Managers Jobs". *Journal of Management Studies* 2, (1965) : 228–35.
539. Strauss, A.L. and J. Corbin (1998). *Basics of Qualitative Research Techniques and Procedures for Developing Grounded Theory*. 2nd ed. (Thousand Oaks: Sage).
540. Sudman, S. (1976). *Applied Sampling*. (New York: Academic Press) pp 87.
541. Sueilby, Kaul Erik (1997). *The New Organisational Wealth*. (San Francisco, Berret – Koehler).

542. Summers, G.F., ed. (1970). *Attitude Measurement.* (Chicago: Rand McNally and Company).
543. Suresh, Babu E (1990). "An Analytical Study of Astra Ole: Diffusion Performance". M.Tech dissertation, Department of Management Studies, Indian Institute of Science.
544. Susman, Gerlad I and Roger D Evered (1978). "An Assessment of the Scientific Merits of Action Research. *Administrative Science Quarterly* 23, no. 4 : 582–602.
545. Sutcliffe, C. and J. Board (1990). "Optimal Solution of a Vehicle Routing Problem: Transporting Mentally Handicapped Adults to an Adult Training Centre". *Journal of Operational Research Society* 41, no. 1 : 61–67.
546. Swamidass, Paul M and W. T. Newell (1987). "Manufacturing Strategy, Environmental Uncertainty and Performance: A Path Analytic Model. *Management Science* 33, no.4 : 509–524.
547. Tacq. (1999). *Multivariate Analysis Techniques in Social Science Research.* (London: Sage).
548. Tatsuoka, M.M. (1971). *Multivariate Analysis.* (New York: John Wiley).
549. Taylor, Calvin W (1964). *Widening Horizons in Creativity.* (John Wiley and Sons).
550. Thakur, M and T.K. Das (1991). "Managing the Growth share Matrix Management". *International Review* 31, no.2, (October) : 139–150.
551. Thapan, M. (1986). "Lifting the Veils - Field Work in a Public School in South India". *Economic and Political Weekly* 21, no. 49 : 2133–2139.
552. Thierauf, Robert J. and Robert C Klekamp (1975). *Decision Making Through Operations Research.* (New York: John Wiley and Sons).
553. Thompson, J. (1984). *Canonical Correlation Analysis: Uses and Interpretation.* (Beverly Hills, California: Sage Publication.
554. Thorndike, Robert M (1978). *Correlational Procedures for Research.* (New York: John Wiley).
555. Thurstone, L.L. (1947). *Multi Factor Analysis.* (University of Chicago Press).
556. Thurstone, L.L. (1959). *Measurement of Values.* (University of Chicago Press).
557. Tinker, T. and Lowe T (1982). "The Management Science of the Management Sciences". *Human Relations* 35, no. 4 : 331–347.
558. Tonge, F.M. (1961). "The Use of Heuristic Programming in Management Science". *Management Science* 7, no. 3 : 221,
559. Tonge, F.M., (1961). "The Use of Heuristic Programming in Management Science: A Survey of the Literature. *Management Science* 7, no. 3 : 231–237.
560. Torgenson, W. (1958). *Theory and Methods of Scaling.* (New York: John Wiley and Sons, Inc.).
561. Tortora, T.D. (1978, August). "A Note on Sample Size Estimation for Multinormal Populations". *The American Statistician* : 100–102.
562. Trist, E.L. (1963). *Organisational Choice* (London: Tavistick Institute).
563. Tryon, R.C. and D.E. Bailey (1970). *Cluster Analysis.* (New York: McGraw-Hill).
564. Tufte, Edwad R (1992). *Visual Display of Quantitative Information.* (Graphics Press).
565. Tufte, Edwad R (1997). *Visual Explanations*—Images and quantitative evidence and narrative. CT Graphics Press).
566. Tukey, John W (1977). *Exploratory Data Analysis.* Reading, MA: Addison-Wesley.
567. Tull, D. S. and D.I. Hawkins (1987). *Marketing Research Measurement and Method*, 4th ed. (New York: Macmillan Publishing Company).
568. Tull, D.S. and G.S. Albaum (1973). *Survey Research - A Decisional Approach.* New York International Textbook Company Limited.
569. Turabian, Kate L (1971). *A Manual for Writers of Term Papers, Theses and Dissertations.* 3rd ed. (Chicago: Chicago University Press).
570. Turban, Effraim (1990). *Decision Support and Expert Systems: Management Support Systems.* 2nd ed. (New York: Macmillan Publishing Company).
571. Tyagi, M. (1968). "A Practical Method for the Truck Dispatching Problem". *Journal of the Operations Research Society of Japan* 10 : 76–92.
572. UNESCO, *Main Trends of Research in the Social and Human Sciences - Part I: Social Sciences.* (Paris, 1970) xivii : 819.
573. Uzsoy, R. (1995). "Scheduling Batch Processing Machine with Incompatible Job Families". *International Journal of Production Research* 33, no. 10 : 2685–2708.
574. Van, De Vall M., C. Bolas and T.S. Kang (1976). "Applied Social Research in Industrial Orgnanisats: An Evaluation of Functions, Theory, and Methods". *Journal of Applied Behavioural Science* 12, no. 2 : 158–77.
575. Van, Horn R.L. (1971). "Validation of Simulation Results". *Management Science* 17, no. 5 (1971) : 247–258.

576. Van, Maannen J. (1983). *Qualitative Methodology.* (London:Sage).
577. Van, Maannen J. and V.E. Hodgson (1983). "Natural Learning and Managerial Action: A Phenomenological Study in the Field Setting". *Journal of Management Studies* 20, no. 3 : 387–9.
578. Van, Gundy Jr, B. Arthur, (1988). *Techniques of Structured Problem Solving*, 2nd ed. (New York: Van Nortrand Reinhold).
579. Vasudevan, J. and D.J. Victor (1987). "Analysis of Bus Accidents Data From Three Transport Corporations". *Indian Highways* 15, no. 1 (1987) : 5–15.
580. Vasumathi, B.V. (2000). An Analytical Study of the Silk Reeling Operations in Karnataka. A P.hd Thesis, Department of Management Studies, Indian Institute of Science.
581. Vickers, Sur Geoffery (1965). *The Art of Judgement: A Study of Policy Making*. (London: Chapman and Hall).
582. Vijyakumar, P., Shanthamani V.S. and K.N. Krishnaswamy (1990). "Decision Making Styles of Manufacturing Executives—An Instrument for Classification. *ASCI Journal of Management.* 19, no. 2.
583. Wagner, H.M. (1975). *Principles of Operations Research* 2nd ed. (Englewood Cliffs, NJ: Prentice-Hall).
584. Wagner, R.F. (1951). "Using Critical Incidents to Determine Selection Test Weights". *Personnel Psychology* 4 : 373–381.
585. Walker, R. (1985). *Applied Qualitative Research*. Aldershot, Given By Alan Hedges.
586. Warfield, J.N. (1972). A Unified System Engineering Concept, *Battele Monograph No. 1* (Columbus, Ohio: Battele Memorial Institute).
587. Warfield, J.N. (1973). "A Binary Matrices in System Modeling". *IEEE Transactions on Systems, Man, and Cybernatics*, SMC-3, no.5 : 441–448.
588. Warfield, J.N. (1973). "An Assault on Complexity." *Battelle Monograph Number 8*, Battele Memorial Institute, Columbus, Ohio.
589. Warfield, J.N. (1974). "Developing Interconnection Matrices in Structural Modeling". IEEE *Transactions On Systems, Man, and Cybernatics*, SMC 4, no.1 : 81–87.
590. Warfield, J.N. (1974). Structuring Complex Systems, *Battelle Monograph No. 4*, (Columbus, Oh: Battelle Memorial Institute).
591. Waters, CDJ. (1988). "Expanding the Scope of Linear Programming Solutions for Vehicle Scheduling Problems". *Omega* 16, no. 6 : 577–583.
592. Weatherall, M. (1968). *Scientific Method*. (London: English University Press).
593. Webb, E.J., D.T., Campbell R.D. Schwartz, and L. Sechrest (1966). *Unobtrusive Measures: Non-Reactive Research in Social Science*. (Chicago: Rand McNally).
594. Weber, Max, E. Shilla and H.A. Finch, (1949). *Methodology of the Social Sciences*, (Free Press), xvii, p 188.
595. Weiers, R.M. (1983). *Marketing Research*, 2nd ed. (New Jersey: Prentice-Hall Inc.).
596. Weiner, P (1975). "Heuristics". *Networks*, 5 : 101–103.
597. Weiss, R.S. (1968). *Statistics in Social Research; An Introduction*. (New York: Wiley) p 369.
598. Weist, J.D. (1966). "Heuristic Programs for Decision Making". *Harvard Business Review* (Sept-Oct).
599. Wendell, G.R. and C.D. Creelman (1967). "Problems and Methods of Psychological Scaling" in *Contemporary Approaches to Psychology*. Helson Harry and William Bevan, eds. (New York: Van Nostrand).
600. White, (1969). D.J. "Problems Involving Infrequent but Significant Contingencies". *Operational Res. Quart.* 20 : 45–57.
601. White, D.J. (1975). *Decision Methodology* (New York: Wiley).
602. Whitley, R (1984). "The Scientific Status of Management Research as a Practically Oriented Social Science. *Journal of Management Studies* 21, no. 3, (1984) : 331–48.
603. Whitney, F.L. (1961). *The Elements of Research*. (New Delhi: Asia Publishing House; (New York: Prentice-Hall, 1950)
604. Williams, Lawrence K and others (1975). "On Administering Questionnaires in Organizational Settings". *Personnel Psychology* 28, no. 1 : 93–104.
605. Williams, F. (1968). Reasoning With Statistics, Astin Texas (Holt, Rinehart and Winston).
606. Wilson, B. (1984). *Systems Concepts, Methodologies, and Applications*. (John Wiley New York Chapter 2 and 3).
607. Wilson, E.B. Jr. (1952). *An Introduction to Scientific Research*. New York McGraw-Hill.
608. Winer, B.J, D.R. Brown, and K.M. Michels (1991). *Statistical Principles in Experimental Design*.
609. Wonnacott, T.H. and R.J. Wonnacott (1981). *Regression: A Second Course in Statistics*. (New York: John Wiley).
610. Wood, C.H. (1991). "Operations Strategy: Decisions, Patterns and Measurements". Ph.d. dissertation, Ohio University.

611. Woolsey, L.K. (1986). "An Innovative Qualitative Method of Research". *Canadian Journal of Counseling* 20, no. 4 : 242–254.
612. Yamanne, T. (1967). *Elementary Sampling Theory*. (New York: Prentice-Hall).
613. Yamanne, T. (1973). *Statistics: an Introductory Analysis*, 3rd ed. (New York: Harper and Row).
614. Yin, Robert K (1994). *Case Study Research*. (Thousand Oaks, CA : Sage).
615. Yin, R.K (1981). "The Case Study Crisis: Some Answers". *Administrative Science Quarterly* 26 : 58–65.
616. Yin, R.K. (1984). Case Study Research: Design and Methods, vol. 5, *Applied Social Research Series* (Beverly Hills, California: Sage Publishers).
617. Young, Pauline V (1966). *Scientific Social Surveys and Research*, 4th ed. (Prentice-Hall of India).
618. Yu, J. and H. Cooper (1983). "A Quantitative Review of Research Design Effects on Response Rates to Questionnaires. *Journal of Marketing Research* 20 : 36–44.
619. Zanakis, S.H. and J.R. Evans (1981). "Heuristic 'Optimization': Why, When and How to Use It". *Interfaces* 11, no. 5 : 84–91.
620. Zanakis, S.H., E.R. James and V.A. Alkis (1989). "Heuristic Methods and Applications: A Categorised Survey". *European Journal of Operational Research* 43 : 88–110.
621. Zanakis, S.H., J.R., Evans and A.A. Vazacopoulos. (1989). "Heuristic Methods and Applications: A Categorised Survey". *European Journal of Operational Research* 43 : 88–110.
622. Zelany, Gene (1991). *Say it with Charts*. (Homewood, Ill: Business One IRWIN).
623. Zelditch, M (1962). "Some Methodological Problems of Field Studies". *American Journal of Sociolology* 67 : 556–576.
624. Zikmund, W.G. (1997). *Business Research Methods*, 5th ed. New York The (Dryden Press). Harcourt publishers.
625. Zimmerman, Donald and Michael Lynn Muraski (1995). *Elements of Information Gathering – A Guide for Technical Communications Scientists and Engineers*. (Phoenix, Arizona Oryx Press).
626. Fritz, Zwicky (1969). *Discovery, Invention, Research*. (New York: Macmillan).

Glossary

Accessible population—A subset of a target population that is reachable by the researcher and from which the sample is drawn.

Adaptation—The process by which an organisation, system, or organism is fitted to its environment.

Ad hoc sample—Sample of participants drawn from an accessible population. Characteristics of the ad hoc sample must be described to define the limits of generalisability.

Alpha level (α level)—Level of type I error (the probability of rejecting the null hypothesis when the null hypothesis is true).

Alternate courses of action—Different ways of finding solutions to a problem in the process of decision-making.

Alternative hypothesis—Opposite of null hypothesis (notation: H_A).

Analysis of covariance (ANCOVA)—Statistical procedure, similar to analysis of variance, used to evaluate whether two or more groups have different population means. Analysis of covariance statistically removes the effects of extraneous variables on the dependent variable and, hence, increases the power of the statistical test.

Analysis of variance (ANOVA)—Statistical procedure used to analyse mean differences between two or more groups. ANOVAs compare the variability among groups with the variability within groups. Many variations of analysis of variance are possible, including repeated measure ANOVAs and factorial ANOVAs.

Applied research—Research to provide solutions to practical problems.

Area sampling—A type of cluster sampling applied to a population having well defined boundaries but without a sample frame.

Artifact—In research, any apparent effect of a major conceptual variable that is actually the result of a confounding variable that has not been properly controlled. Artifacts threaten the validity of research conclusions.

Artificial intelligence—Machines that are designed to evaluate and respond to situations in an appropriate manner. Most artificial intelligence machines are computer based and many of them have achieved remarkable levels of performance in specific areas.

Association—Relationship or correlation.

Authority—A way of acquiring knowledge. New ideas are accepted as valid because some respected authority has declared the idea to be true.

Automation—Use of equipment to conduct most or all aspects of presenting stimuli and recording participants' responses. Automation can minimise the work required of the researcher, increase precision in data gathering, and minimise experimenter bias in gathering and recording data.

Average deviation—The sum of the deviations from the mean divided by the number of scores.

B variance—It is the sum of the squared deviation scores from data mean and is a measure of dispersion.

Bar chart—It is a statistical presentation technique that represents frequency data as horizontal or vertical bars. Bar charts are used to represent time series and quantitative data.

Basic research—Fundamental or pure research that is carried out to add to knowledge but without applied or practical goals. Basic research is often contrasted with applied research.

Behaviour—Any observable act from any living or non-living organism. Behaviour is the subject matter of psychology.

Behaviourism—A philosophical perspective in psychology, which argues that scientific psychology should base its theories on observable events only (such as behaviour). This perspective challenged the introspective methodologies that dominated the early discipline of psychology.

Beta (β)—The probability of making a type II error (see Type II error).

Between-groups variance—Index of variability among group means.

Between-subjects factors—Independent variables in factorial designs in which participants are assigned to conditions so that each participant appears only in one condition.

Between-subjects design—Research design using two or more groups, in which each participant appears in only one of the groups.

Blind—When the researcher and/or participant is not aware of information that would, if available, increase the likelihood of biasing the experimental results (see single-blind procedure).

Box-Plot—An exploratory data analysis technique that gives a visual image of a variable's distribution, spread, shape, and outliers.

Branching questions—A technique used to direct respondents to different places in a questionnaire, based on the response to the question at hand.

Cannonical correlation—This is correlation between two sets of variables. The first canonical correlation is derived by computing the linear combination of each set of variables that will give the highest possible correlation. Additional canonical correlations can be computed using different linear combinations of the variables in each set. This technique helps scientists to understand complex relationships between constructs that cannot be easily trapped by a single measure.

Carry-over effects—These effects occur when a participant's involvement in one condition affects his or her performance in all subsequent conditions. Carry-over effects occur only when each participant appears in more than one experimental condition (that is, in within-subjects designs).

Categorical data—This kind of data is synonymous with nominal data.

Categorical variable—Synonymous with discrete variable, a categorical variable can have only a finite number of values.

Causal hypothesis—A form of research hypothesis in experimental research. It states that the independent variable has a causal relationship to the dependent variable. To accept this hypothesis, one must have rejected the null hypothesis and all confounding variable hypotheses.

Causal inference—Conclusion that changes in the independent variable resulted in a change in the dependent variable. It may be drawn only if all potential confounding variables are properly controlled.

Central tendency—Average or typical score in a distribution. Three measures of central tendency are the mean, medium, and mode.

Chi-square (χ^2)—A statistical distribution that forms the basis for inferential statistics used with nominal data.

Classification variables—Organismic or subject variables used to classify participants into discrete groups. Classification variables are used for assigning objects to groups in differential research.

Cluster analysis—A technique that identifies homogenous subgroups or clusters of subjects or study objects.

Cluster sampling—A sampling procedure in which the population is divided into clusters or subgroups. The sample is then drawn from each subgroup.

Coding data—Process by which numerical or classification scores are assigned to a set of responses from a respondent. The coded data are usually in a form that can be statistically analysed more easily.

Coefficient alpha—An index of (internal consistency) reliability.

Coefficient of determination—The square of the Pearson product moment correlation. It represents the proportion of variability in one variable that can be predicted on the basis of information about the other variable.

Cognitive mapping—A pictorial representation of how a manager models, thinks about, and perceives his problems and situations. This is developed from group interview.

Cohort groups—People of a given chronological age in a given culture, who behave similarly throughout their lives and differently from people of other ages because of shared life experiences.

Computer modelling—Using a computer to simulate a process where the intention is to have the computer mimic a process as closely as possible to the way in which it actually occurs.

Confidence interval—An interval in which we predict the population parameter to fall with a specified level of confidence (for example, a 95 per cent confidence interval will contain the population parameter 95 per cent of the time).

Confidentiality—An ethical requirement in most research information, particularly sensitive and personal information, provided by participants as part of a research study should be protected and made unavailable to anyone other than the researchers.

Confounded—Two independent variables are said to be confounded if they vary simultaneously during a study, thus, not allowing us to determine which of these variables was responsible for the observed change in the dependent variable.

Confounding variable—Any uncontrolled variable that might affect the outcome of a study. A potential confounding variable exists only if (i) there is a mean difference between the groups on the variable, and (ii) there is a correlation between the variable and the dependent measure.

Constants—Parameters that do not vary are called constants.

Constraints—Restrictions placed on research in an effort to increase the precision of the research and enhance the validity of the conclusions (also, limitations of resource/time).

Construct—An idea constructed by the researcher to explain events observed in a particular situation. Constructs are not necessarily direct representations of reality, they are not facts. They are explanatory fiction because, in most cases, we do not know the real reason for a particular event. Once formulated, constructs are used as if they are true (that is, analogically) to predict relationships between variables in situations that had not previously been observed.

Construct validity—Validity of a theory is also known as construct validity. Most theories in science present broad conceptual explanations of relationship between variables and make many different predictions about the relationships between particular variables in certain situations. Construct validity is established by verifying the accuracy of each possible prediction that might be made from the theory. Because the number of predictions is usually infinite, construct validity can never be fully established. However, the more independent predictions for the theory verified as accurate, the stronger the construct validity of the theory.

Consultancy research—Research carried out for an organisation by specialist consultant.

Content analysis—An analysis tool used for measuring the semantic content of messages or communications like speeches, advertisements, editorials.

Content items—In questionnaires and interviews, content items focus on the issues studied, such as respondents opinions, attitudes, and knowledge, in contrast to factual items, which can be independently verified (for example, age, gender, and so on).

Contingency—A particular relationship between two or more variables, where, given that the first event occurs, the second event is highly probable. The relationship between the variables is a probabilistic one and does not necessarily imply a causal connection between them.

Continuous variable—Any variable that can theoretically take on an infinite number of values. These are often contrasted with discrete or categorical variables.

Control group—A group of participants, used in either differential or experimental research, that serves as a basis for comparison of other (experimental) groups. The ideal control group is similar to the experimental group on all variables except the variable that defines the group (independent variable).

Controlled research—This includes any research that employs adequate control procedures to rule out competing hypotheses. Well-controlled research permits scientists to draw causal conclusions.

Convenience sampling—A non-probability sampling procedure in which the sample is unrestricted but accessible and available.

Correlated t-test (or direct-differences t-test or matched-pairs t-test)—statistical procedure used to test for mean differences between two groups in a within-subjects or matched-subjects design.

Correlation—The degree of association between two or more variables.

Correlation coefficient—A statistic that quantifies the degree of association between two or more variables. There are many kinds of correlation coefficients, depending on the type of data and relationship predicted.

Correlational research—Research that seeks to measure the relationship between variables, without trying to determine causality. The term is sometimes used broadly to include any non-experimental research design.

Criterion—In a regression analysis, the criterion is the variable that one attempts to predict.

Crossover effects—In quasi-experimental research, a finding where two non-equivalent groups show one pattern of scores before the manipulation and the reverse pattern of scores after the manipulation. The name derives from the crossing of lines when such a result is shown on graph.

Cross-sectional design—A design that compares the performance, attitudes, or histories of people of different ages or at different times in history. The groups are defined by the age range of the people in the groups or the historical time in which participants were tested. In a cross-sectional study, participants appear in only one group. This design is often contrasted with longitudinal designs.

Cross-sectional research—Research in which a cross-sectional research design is used.

Cross-tabulation—Procedure for organising frequency data that displays the relationship between two or more nominal variables. A cross-tabulation table contains individual cells, with the number in each cell representing the frequency of participants who show that particular combination of characteristics.

Data—Plural noun that refers to information gathered in research. Research conclusions are drawn on the basis of an evaluation of the data gathered as part of a study.

Data analysis—Research phase in which data gathered from observing participants are analysed, usually with statistical procedures.

Data mining—The process of extracting meaningful knowledge from large volumes of data contained in data warehouses.

Data warehouse—Electronic storehouses where vast amounts of data are arrayed, integrated, categorised, stored, and sold.

Decision tree—An organised pathway of ideas leading to a defined goal, in which at various points, a decision is made about which of two 'branches' of ideas to follow to the next decision point.

Deductive reasoning—Reasoning from the general to the particular. In deductive reasoning, specific predictions are made about future events.

Deductive theory—A theory that emphasises constructs and the relationship between constructs and seeks to make predictions, from the theory which can be tested through empirical research.

Degrees of freedom (df)—This is a statistical concept. One degree of freedom is lost each time a population parameter is estimated on the basis of a sample of data from the population. The distribution of most statistics (t, F.., and so on) are tabled by degrees of freedom (df).

Demographic variables—Data that describe the participants in a study (for example, their age, gender, occupation, and so on). This information should be routinely collected and reported in research.

Dependence analysis—Problem in multivariate analysis in which one (or more) of the variables is to be considered separately and to investigate how it depends upon others.

Dependent variable—Variable that is hypothesised to have a relationship with the independent variable.

Depth interview—A type of interview that is unstructured and made in a free environment in which the respondent shares information freely.

Descriptive statistics—Those statistics or statistical procedures that summarise and/or describe the characteristics of a sample of scores.

Discrete variable—A discrete variable can take on only a finite number of values. It is often contrasted with continuous variable.

Dispersion (variability)—This illustrates how spread out the scores are in a sample.

Double-barrelled questions—A question that calls for two responses, thereby creating confusion in the respondent.

Effectiveness function—An equation representing objectives of a model. It indicates in quantitative terms how effective an alternative course of action is in achieving the objectives.

Empirical—Based on observed data. A relationship between variables is empirically established if it has been observed to occur.

Empiricism—System of learning that is based solely on observation of the events around us.

Equivalence—A measure of reliability that is applied to both single instruments and measurement situations.

Experimentation—Process by which a researcher studies the relationship between independent and dependent variables by systematically manipulating the independent variable, assigning participants without bias to each level of the independent variable, and observing the effects of the independent variable on the dependant variable.

Experimenter bias—Any effect that the expectations of the researcher might have on the measurement and recording of the dependent variable. Uncontrolled experimenter expectancies can create powerful experimenter effects.

Experience survey—Interviews with people knowledgeable about the general subject being investigated.

Exploratory data analysis—Process in which data patterns guide the analysis or suggest revisions to the preliminary data analysis plan.

External validity—Extent to which the results of a study accurately indicate the true nature of a relationship between variables in the real world. If a study has external validity, the results are said to be generalisable to the real world.

Extraneous variable—Any variable other than the independent variable that might affect the dependent measure in a study. Extraneous variables are potentially confounding and must be controlled.

Extraneous variance—Variability in scores on the dependent measure that can be accounted for by the effects of extraneous variables.

Factor analysis—Body of techniques concerned with the study of interrelationships among a set of variables, none of which is a criterion variable.

Factorial design—Research designs employing more than one independent variable simultaneously. The major advantage of a factorial design is that it can measure the joint (interactive) effects of two or more independent variables.

Factor—In a factorial design, each of the independent variables is a factor.

Facts—Empirically observed events.

Factual items—In questionnaires and interviews, factual items are questions that can be independently verified, such as the respondent's age, gender, and occupation. In contrast, content items cannot be factually verified.

Fields (in computer files)—In data files, the field represents a variable that has a score for each participant in the study. Normally, the fields are shown as columns in a data matrix, where the rows represent records.

Focus group—An information collection approach widely used in exploratory research. A panel of subjects are met by a moderator for obtaining feelings, perceptions, and experiences on a specific topic.

Formal science—Science that uses formulation rules (automatic in nature, having theorems, axioms) and pure deductive systems.

Grounded analysis—An analysis approach based on grounded theory, to extract a problem structure from the data in qualitative data analysis. It is considered as a creative process, having as its components reflection, conceptualisation and cataloging.

Heuristics—Rules of thumb derived by experience, intuition, and simple logic.

Hypothesis—A declarative statement or a proposition that describes the relationship of two or more variables or the characteristic of a variable (like mean or variance).

Hypothetico-deductive method—A scientific procedure in which hypothesis are accumulated on specific observations and thereafter generalised by deductively testing them on larger observations.

Ideographic knowledge—Knowledge gained by studying particular cases, social groups, or situations.

Inductive theory—Inductive theories are built on a strong empirical base and tend not to stray far from that empirical base. It is often contrasted with deductive theory and functional theory.

Inference—Any conclusion drawn on the basis of some set of information. In research, we draw inferences on the basis of empirical data we collect and ideas we construct.

Inferential statistics—Statistical procedures that computes the probability of obtaining the particular pattern of data in a study if all participants were actually drawn from the same population. If the probability of obtaining such a pattern of scores is low, we reject the hypothesis that all participants were drawn from the same population (null hypothesis) and conclude that there were meaningful differences between groups or conditions.

Informed consent—Critical principle in the ethical treatment of participants. Participants have the right to know exactly what they are getting into and to refuse to participate.

Instrumentation—Potential confounding variable involving any change in the measuring instrument over time, which causes the instrument to give different readings when no change has occurred in the participant.

Interaction—Combined effect of two or more independent variables on the dependent variable. Interactions can be measured only in factorial designs.

Interdependence analysis—Problem in multivariate analysis to determine the relationship of a set of variables among themselves (no variate is a dependent variable).

Internal consistency reliability—Index of how homogeneous the individual items of a measure are. If the individual items are homogenous, they will tend to correlate strongly with one another, suggestions that all items are measuring the same characteristic.

Internal validity—Accuracy of the research study in determining the relationship between independent and the dependent variables. Internal validity can be assured only if all potential confounding variables have been properly controlled.

Intervening variable—A variable that affects a phenomena or system but cannot be seen, measured, or manipulated. Its effects are determined by its effects on independent or moderator variables.

Interpretation—Results of statistical analyses of data are interpreted in the light of (i) the adequacy of control procedures in the research design, (ii) previous research, and (iii) existing theories about the study.

Interrater reliability—Index of consistency between two or more ratings made by separate raters. It is indexed by the correlation between the ratings of the two raters.

Interrupted time-series design—Type of research design suitable for either single participants or groups in which multiple measures of the dependent variable are taken before and after some experimental manipulation. Time-series designs provide some degree of control for history and maturation.

Interval scale—Scale of measurement in which the distance between any two adjacent scores is the same as the distance between any other two adjacent scores, but zero is not a true zero. An example of an interval scale is temperature measured in either Celsius or Fahrenheit.

Interview schedule—A standardised interview, with each question and procedure spelled out for the interviewer. Interview schedules provide consistency in interviews, which are a part of research projects.

Intuition—A way of acquiring knowledge. In intuition, ideas come to people, supposedly, without intellectual effort or sensory processes.

Latin square design—A procedure used to provide a measure of counterbalancing in a within-subjects design. Instead of using all possible orders of presentation (as in counterbalancing), a Latin square design uses a set of orders that ensure that every experimental condition appears equally often in every position in the order.

Likert scale items—In Likert scales, each item is presented on a continuum, with extreme positions at the end points. For example, the scale may range from "strongly agree" to "strongly disagree".

Linear programming—An optimisation technique of operations research in which the objective function and constraints are linear functions.

Linear relationship—Relationship between two or more variables that, when plotted in a standard coordinate system, tend to cluster around a straight line. Most correlation coefficients are sensitive only to linear relationships between variables.

Logic—Set of operations that can be applied to statements and conclusions drawn from those statements to determine the internal accuracy of the conclusions.

Longitudinal (panel) design—A research design in which a group of participants is observed over time, with the dependent measures repeated during follow-up testing. Longitudinal designs are frequently used in the study of developmental aspects and historical research. This design is often contrasted with cross-sectional designs.

Magnitude—A characteristic of the abstract number system and of some measurement scales in which the numbers have an inherent order (for example, low to high).

Main effects—In a factorial design, main effects refer to the individual effects of the independent variables. In contrast, interaction effects are the combined effects of two or more independent variables on a dependent variable.

Manipulated factors—Independent variables in a factorial design in which the levels of the factors are determined by active manipulation by the experimenter.

Manipulated independent variable—Type of independent variable found in an experimental research study. When manipulated independent variables are used, participants are assigned to groups or conditions without bias.

Manipulation—Explicit control of the independent variable by the researcher.

Mann-Whitney U-test—A non-parametric inferential statistic used to test the difference between two groups when the dependent measure produces ordinal data.

Matched-pairs t-test—See correlated t-test.

Maturation—Potential confounding factor involving changes in participants on the dependent measure during the course of the study, which results from normal growth processes.

Mean—Arithmetic averages of scores. The mean is the most commonly used measure of central tendency, but should be computed only for score data.

Mean square—In analysis of variance (ANOVA), the mean square is a variance estimate. Several different mean squares are computed in any ANOVA. It is the ratio of mean squares that is the F-ratio and constitutes the inferential statistical test.

Measurement error—Any inaccuracy found in the measurement of a variable. Although it is impossible to determine the precise degree and direction of measurement error for a given participant, it is possible to specify the average error associated with a particular measure.

Median—Middle score in a distribution.

Meta-analysis—A procedure that allows the statistical averaging of results from independent studies of the same phenomena. Meta-analysis essentially combines studies on the same topic into a single large study, providing an index of how strongly the independent variable affected the dependent variable on an average in the set of studies.

Mode—Most frequent score in a distribution.

Metaphors—Metaphors are a way of communicating classification systems of qualitative analysis. They reveal the special properties of an object or event (for example, a teacher may be classified as a "Traffic cop", in an "Ostrich role", and so on.)

Models—In science, models are representations of the complex reality of the real world.

Moderator variable—Any variable that has an effect on the observed relationship between two or more other variables. When a moderator variable is operating, it is best to measure the relationship between variables separately in sub-groups defined by the moderator variable. For example, relationships between variables are often evaluated separately in males and females (a commonly used moderator variable).

Monte Carlo study—A procedure that evaluates the effectiveness of statistical tests by simulating with a computer the repeated sampling of participants from a population with known parameters. The characteristics of the populations can be systematically varied to see what effect these variations have on the accuracy of the statistical decision. This process allows one to empirically determine the probability of type I and type II errors, to see the strength of the impact of violations of the assumptions of statistical procedures.

Multidimensional scaling—A group of statistical methods that are used to simplify data by finding a small number of dimensions or factors that collectively account for most of the variability in a group of scores.

Multiple choice items—In a questionnaire, each question or item is presented with several answers, from which the respondent chooses one.

Multiple correlation—A correlation where one variable (say, *X*) is correlated with a set of variables. The correlation is computed by finding the linear combination of the set that will provide the highest possible correlation with the *X* variable.

Multiple observers—Control used to evaluate the accuracy of observations made by two or more independent observers.

Multivariate analysis of variance (MANOVA)—Extension of analysis of variance where two or more dependent measures are simultaneously evaluated.

Multivariate correlational designs—Correlational designs that include more than two variables.

Natural sciences—Branches of organised knowledge concerned with the material aspects of existence.

Negative correlation—Relationship between two variables in which an increase in one variable predicts a decrease in the other.

Nominal data—Data produced when a nominal scale of measurement is used. Nominal data are frequencies of participants in each of the specific categories.

Nominal fallacy—The tendency to confuse a label for a behaviour as an explanation for the behaviour. For example, labelling people as kind because they do many kind things for other people is reasonable, but it is unreasonable to say that they do those kind things because they are kind people.

Nominal scale—Scale of measurement in which only categories are produced as scores. Examples are diagnostic classification, sex of the participant, and political affiliation.

Nomothetic knowledge—Knowledge gained by studying and applying general laws and theories.

Nonequivalent control group design—Quasi experimental design used in field settings. In this design, two or more groups, which may not be equivalent at the beginning of the study, are compared on the dependent measure.

Non-experimental design—Any research design that fails to provide adequate controls for typical confounding.

Non-linear relationship—Any relationship between two or more variables that is characterised by a scatter plot where the points tend to cluster around a curved instead of a straight line. Most correlation coefficients are insensitive to non-linear relationships.

Non-manipulated independent variable—Pre-existing variable that determines group membership in a differential research study.

Non-parametric statistics—Inferential statistical procedures that do not rely on estimating population parameters such as the mean and variance.

Non-probability sampling—Any sampling procedure in which some participants have a higher probability of being selected than other participants or where the selection of a given participant changes the probability of selecting other participants. Often contrasted with probability sampling.

Normal distribution—Distribution of scores that are characterised by a bell-shaped curve in which the probability of a score drops off rapidly from the midpoint to the tails of the distribution. A true normal curve is defined by a mathematical equation and is a function of two variables (the mean and variance of the distribution).

Null hypothesis—Theory that States that the samples from each group are drawn from populations with identical population parameters. The null hypothesis is tested by inferential statistics.

Objective measure—Any measure that requires little or no judgment on the part of the person making the measurement. Objective measures are more resistant to experimenter biases than subjective measures.

Observation—Empirical process in which data about the phenomenon of interest is gathered and reported. Careful observation is a central task in all research.

Observational variable—Any variable that is observed and not manipulated in research. The term is usually used in low constraint research where the independent and dependent variable distinction does not apply.

One-way ANOVA—Statistical procedure that evaluates differences in mean scores of two or more groups where the groups are defined by a single independent variable.

Open-ended items—Items or questions on a questionnaire for which the respondent writes the answer (for example, an essay).

Operational definition—Detailed set of procedures used to measure or manipulate the level of a variable.

Ordered data—Data produced by ordinal scales of measurement.

Ordinal scale—Scale of measurement in which scores can be rank-ordered, but the distance between any two adjacent scores will not necessarily be the same as the distance between any other two adjacent scores.

Organismic variable—Any characteristic of the participant that can be used for classification. An organismic variable may be either directly observed (observed organismic variable) or may be inferred on the basis of the responses of the participant (response inferred organismic variable).

Panel design—See longitudinal design.

Paradigm of research—A framework within which all thinking and theories of science are ordered (Kuhn).

Parametric statistics—Inferential statistical procedures that rely on sample statistics to draw inferences about population parameters, such as mean and variance.

Parsimony—A guiding principle in science where a simple theory is preferred to a more complex theory if both theories explain the data equally well.

Partial correlation—A correlation between two variables (say *X* and *Y*) where the effects of a third variable (*Z*) are statistically removed from one of the two original variables before computing the correlation. Conceptually, it is the correlation between *X* and *Y* if *Z* were constant.

Participant observer—Any researcher gathering data in a setting in which the researcher is an active part. Participant observation tends to be less obtrusive than other observational procedures. However, the possibility for experimenter reactivity in participant observation is quite high.

Participant variable—Synonymous with organismic variable.

Partition—In an ANOVA calculation, the total sum of squares is divided (partitioned) into the between-groups sum of squares and the within-groups sum of squares.

Path analysis—A procedure that seeks to unravel causal links between variables from strictly correlational data by hypothesising detailed causal models and factoring the correlation matrix to see how closely the pattern of observed relationships fits the hypothesised causal model.

Pearson product-moment correlation—Index of the degree of linear relationship between two variables where each variable represents score data.

Percentile—Normative score that converts the raw score earned by a participant into a number from 0 to 100, which reflects the percentage of participants who scored lower than the participant in question.

Perfect correlation—Correlation of a +1.00 or a –1.00. When two variables are perfectly correlated, knowing the score on one variable permits perfect prediction of the score on the other. In a scatter plot, a perfect correlation is shown by all points falling on a straight line (but not a horizontal or vertical line).

Phases of research—Every research project develops through phases in which certain types of questions are asked and answered. These phases are idea-generating, problem-definition, procedures-design, observation, data-analysis, interpretation, and communication.

Pie chart—Statistical representation technique that uses sections of a circle to represent 100 per cent of a frequency distribution.

Placebo effect—In a treatment study, any observed improvement in response to a sham treatment. Placebo effects are probably the result of participants' expectations regarding treatment effectiveness.

Population—Any clearly defined set of objects or events (people, occurrences, animals, and so on). Populations usually represent all events in a particular class (for example, all college students, all boys between the ages of 10 and 12, all headache sufferers).

Population parameters—Any summary statistic computed on the entire population.

Positivism—View that all true knowledge is scientific, in the sense of describing observable phenomena.

Post hoc tests (or comparisons or analyses)—Secondary analyses that evaluate relationships between variables, not specifically hypothesised by the researcher prior to the study.

Power of statistical test—Ability of an inferential statistical procedure to detect differences between groups when such differences actually exist.

Practical significance (substantive)—Often contrasted with statistical significance. Practical significance refers to whether the observed difference between two groups or conditions in a study is large enough to have a meaningful impact on the observed situation and/or subject of study.

Predictor—Variable in regression that is used to predict the scores on the criterion measure. For example, a test score (the predictor measure) might be used to predict future performance in a job.

Pretest—Use of a questionnaire (observation form) on a trial basis in a small pilot study to find out how well the questionnaire works.

Pretest-post-test design—Set of research designs in which participants are tested at two points in time—before and after the administration of the independent variable.

Pretest-post-test, natural control group design—Non-experimental research design in which pre-existing groups are each measured before and after the manipulation of an independent variable. These naturally occurring groups are assigned to different levels of the independent variable.

Probability—The ratio of specific events to the total number of possible events. For example, the probability of rolling snake-eyes (two ones) on one roll of a pair of dice is 1/36.

Probability sampling—A sampling procedure in which all participants have an equal probability of being selected and the selection of any participant does not change the probability of selecting any other participant. Often contrasted with non-probability sampling.

Problem definition (phase of research)—Research phase where vague and general research ideas are converted into precise questions to be studied.

Process of inquiry—Perspective taken by this text, which views research as a dynamic process focussed on formulating questions and systematically answering those questions through carefully controlled observation/studies.

Programme evaluation research—Specific area of field research for evaluating the effectiveness of a programme in meeting its stated goals.

Projective techniques—Various tests used to disguise the study objective and to allow the respondent to transfer or project attitudes and behaviour on sensitive subjects to the researcher.

Protocol analysis—Qualitative research method in which an episode of a manager's work is analysed as it occurs or immediately after it has occurred. The method uses the trust and confidence of the manager and gets the viewpoint of the manager about the episode.

Pseudoscience—Popular distortions of scientific knowledge and procedures that appear on the surface to be scientific, but in reality lack critical scientific procedures. Some fields such as astrology, extrasensory perception, the study of alien abductions, and medical quackery, have traditionally relied on pseudoscience to make them appear legitimate.

Psychology—Scientific study of the behaviour of organisms.

Pure research—Another term for basic or fundamental research (see basic research).

p-value—The probability of obtaining the statistic (for example, t or F) or a larger statistic, by chance, if the null hypothesis is true. Statistical analysis programmes routinely compute p-values in addition to the test statistic.

Q-Sort technique—General methodology for gathering and processing data. The subjects are asked to sort a number statements. The aim is to determine their relative ranking.

Quasi experiential design—Research design that, although not a true experimental design with all experimental controls built in, provides experiment-like controls to minimise threats to internal validity.

Questionnaire—An instrument that lists questions to be asked of participants.

Quota sampling—Purposive sampling in which relevant characteristics are used to stratify the sample to improve representativeness.

Random-number generator—A computer function that generates an endless sequence of random numbers.

Random sampling—Procedure for the selection of participants to be included in a research study, where each participant in the population has an equal chance of being selected and where the selection of any one participant will not affect the probability of selecting any other participant. In most research, random sampling from the population is not carried out because the procedure is not feasible. Instead, researchers rely on sampling from an accessible population.

Randomisation—Any procedure that assigns a value or order in an unpredictable or random way, such as by use of tables of random numbers. Randomisation procedures may be used for selecting participants, assigning participants to groups or conditions, or assigning the order in which a participant will experience a number of successive conditions.

Range—Distance between the lowest score and the highest score, inclusive of the scores.

Ratio scale—Scale of measurement in which the intervals between scores are equal (as in the interval scale) and the zero point on the scale represents some of the quality being measured (a true zero). Examples of ratio scales are height, weight, and frequency of an event.

Rationalism—One of the approaches to study about the universe, rationalism relies on systematic logic and a set of premises from which logical inferences are made.

Regression—A statistical procedure that produces an equation for predicting a variable (the criterion measure) from one or more other variables (the predictor measures).

Regression equation—Mathematical equation that predicts the value of one variable from one or more other variables. Most regression equations are linear regression equations.

Relationship—Any connection between two or more variables. In research, there are many types of relationships, from simple contingencies to established causal relationships.

Reliability—Index of the consistency of a measuring instrument in repeatedly providing the same score for a given participant. There are many different types of reliability, each referring to a different aspect of consistency. Types of reliability include interrater reliability, test-retest reliability, and internal consistency reliability.

Repeated measures ANOVA—Statistical procedure to evaluate the mean differences between two or more conditions, where the same participants contribute scores in each condition. The repeated measures ANOVA takes into account the fact that the same participants appear in all conditions.

Repeated-measures design—Any research design in which participants are tested more than once. Examples of such designs are pretest-post-test designs within-subjects designs, and time series designs.

Replication—A repeat study with either no changes at all in the procedure exact replication) or carefully planned changes in the procedure (systematic or conceptual replication).

Representative sample—Sample of participants that adequately reflects the characteristics of the population from which the sample is drawn.

Representativeness—Degree to which a sample is representative of the population from which it is drawn.

Research design—A map or a blueprint for achieving research objectives.

Research ethics—Set of guidelines designed to protect human and non-human participants from the risks of participating in research.

Research hypothesis—Precise and formal statement of a research question. The research hypothesis is constructed by adding operational definitions for each of the variables to the statement of the problem.

Research setting—Any characteristic of the situation and/or surroundings in which a research project is carried out. Settings may vary from natural, real-world settings to highly constrained and carefully controlled laboratory situations.

Reversal (ABA) design—Research design often used with single participants, where the effects of an independent variable on a dependent variable are inferred from observations made first without the independent variable being present, then with the independent variable being present, and again without the independent variable present.

Rival hypothesis—Any feasible alternative hypothesis to the causal hypothesis.

Robust—Term used in reference to statistical procedures. A statistical test is said to be robust to the violation of the assumptions on which the test is based if the test consistently leads to accurate conclusions in spite of the assumption violations.

Sample—Any subset drawn from a population. Researchers work with samples of participants and draw inferences about the larger population.

Sample statistic—Descriptive index of some characteristic of the sample of participants. Population parameters are estimated on the basis of statistics.

Sampling—Process of drawing a sample from a population. Many sampling techniques are available, including random sampling, stratified random sampling, and various non-random sampling techniques.

Sampling error—Chance variation among different samples drawn from the same population.

Sampling frame—In survey research, a sampling frame is a list of all participants from an available population. The sampling frame is a subset of a larger population from which a representative sample is drawn.

Scales of measurement—Characteristics of the scores produced by a particular measurement instrument. Scales of measurement vary depending on how closely scores match the real number system. There are four generally recognised scales of measurement: nominal scale, ordinal scale, interval scale, and ratio scale.

Scatter plot—Graphic technique that illustrates the relationship between two or more variables. In a two-variable situation, the scatter plot is constructed by labelling the x-axis with one of the variables and the y-axis with the other variable and plotting each participant's part of scores in the xy coordinate system.

Science—Way of knowing about the universe around us, which combines rationalism and empiricism to form a system that places great demands or procedures, data, and theories.

Score data—Data produced by interval or ratio scales of measurement.

Selection—Potential confounding variable in any research project. Selection represents any process that may create groups not equivalent at the beginning of the study.

Sensitivity analysis—An analysis used in mathematical modelling, where the sensitivity of model results to variations in a particular variable is studied.

Simple random sampling—See random sampling.

Single-blind procedure—Research procedure in which the researcher is unaware of the condition assigned to each participant. The purpose of the single-blind procedure is to minimise measurement biases.

Single-group, post-test only design—Nonexperimental research design in which the researcher manipulates the independent variable and then takes a postmanipulation measure on the dependent variable. The difference between this design and an ex post facto design is the actual manipulation of the independent variable by the researcher.

Single-group, pro-test-post-test design—Non-experimental design in which a group of participants is measured on a dependent variable. The independent variable is manipulated, and a second measure on the dependent variable is taken.

Skepticism—Unwillingness to accept information as valid knowledge without some documentation to confirm the information. Skepticism is one of the strongest tools available to a scientist.

Snowball sample—Judgement sample that relies on the researcher's ability to locate an initial set of respondents with desired characteristics, who will help in locating other similar respondents.

Solomon's four-group design—Sophisticated experimental design that combines the randomised, post-test only, control group design and the randomised pre-test-post-test control group design.

Spearman rank-order correlation—Correlation coefficient that indexes the degree of relationship between two variables, each of which is measured on an ordinal scale of measurement.

Spread—Synonymous with variability.

SPSS for Windows—A computer package (statistical package for the social sciences) for statistical data analysis on a Windows-based computer.

Standard deviation—Square root of variance. The standard deviation is an index of variability in the distribution of scores.

Standard error of the differences between means—In statistics the denominator in a t-test.

Standard score—A score that gives the relative standing in a distribution. A standard score is computed by subtracting the distribution mean from the score and dividing the value by the standard deviation from the distribution.

Statement of the problem—First major refinement of initial research ideas, in which a clear statement of the expected relationship between conceptual variables is made. The statement of the problem is refined into one or more research hypotheses by specifying the operational definitions of each conceptual variable in the statement.

Statistical Analysis Systems (SAS)—Computer package for statistical data analysis.

Statistical hypothesis—Synonymous with null hypothesis.

Statistical Package for the Social Sciences (SPSS)—Computer package for statistical data analysis.

Statistical significance—A finding is said to achieve statistical significance if it is unlikely that such a finding would have occurred by chance alone (see statistically significant differences).

Statistical validity—Accuracy of conclusions drawn from a statistical test. To enhance statistical validity, one must meet the critical assumptions and requirements of a statistical procedure.

Status survey—A simple survey designed to provide a description of the current status of some population characteristic.

Stem and leaf display—It is an explorative data analysis technique to reveal frequency distribution for each data value.

Stimulus variable—Any variable part of the environment to which an organisation reacts. A stimulus variable may be a natural part of the environment and observed by the researcher, or may be actively manipulated by the researcher.

Strata—Sub-populations within populations from which we draw samples based on the base rates in the population of the factor(s) that determine the strata.

Stratified random sampling—Variation of the random sampling procedure in which a population is divided in narrow strata along some critical dimension. Participants are then selected randomly from each of the strata in the same proportion that the strata are represented in the population. Stratified random sampling can increase the representativeness of the sample and is used extensively in sophisticated survey research.

Stress—Measure of 'badness of fit' of configuration determined in multidimensional scaling analysis when compared with original input data.

Structuralism—A philosophical perspective in which the scientist seeks to identify the structure of the underlying mechanisms that control behaviour, such as consciousness. This approach was popularised by Wundt. Often contrasted with functionalism.

Structural modelling—Method of scenario generation of a problem space to help develop a mathematical model.

Subject effects—Any response by participants in a study that does not represent the way they would normally behave if not under study. Two powerful participant effects are the placebo effect and a participant's response to the demand characteristics of the study.

Subject selection—See participant selection.

Subjective measures—Measures based primarily on uncorroborated opinions, feelings, biases, or judgements. Subjective measures, as contrasted with objective measures, are more prone to distortions due to subject or experimenter effects.

Summary statistics—Descriptive statistics that provide some general characteristic of the sample in a single number. Typical summary statistics are the mean, median, variance, and standard deviation.

Sum of squares—Sum of the squared differences from the mean. The sum of squares is the numerator in the variance formula.

Survey—A set of one or more questions posed to a group of participants about their attitudes, beliefs, plans, life-styles, or any other variable of interest. Surveys may be conducted over the phone, in person, or through the use of a written form.

Survey research—Research that seeks to use survey procedures to identify relationships among the variables being surveyed.

Systematic replication (or conceptual replication)—Situation where a study is repeated with small, theory-based changes in the procedures. Systematic replication is more common than exact replication, because it verifies original findings while also expanding knowledge of the phenomena.

System study—Study of decision makers, information systems, decision-making procedures, and the environments of a decision-making system before modelling a particular decision problem.

Table of random numbers—A table containing a long list of randomly generated numbers. Such tables are used frequently in research for random selection and assignment of participants. A table of random numbers is included in Appendix D of this text.

Target population—Population to which we hope to generalise the findings of a research study. In most research, the entire target population is not accessible to the researcher.

Testing—Potential confounding variable in research. Testing represents any change in a participant's score on a dependent measure, which is a function of the participant that has been tested previously in the research project.

Test-retest reliability—Index of consistency in scores over time. Test-retest reliability is computed by calculating the Pearson's product-moment correlation between scores from two testings, separated by some specified time interval.

Theoretical concept—Abstraction (thought or idea) that defines the relationship between two or more variables.

Theory—In science, theory is the collection of ideas about how and why variables are related to one another. Theory is usually built on empirical observations and is validated by making predictions deduced from the theory, which are then empirically tested.

Transcription of data—It is the conversion of recording of interviews or conversations into a readable document. It is widely used in qualitative research.

Treatment—See manipulation.

True zero—Characteristic of a measurement scale where zero represents none of the concepts being measured.

t-test—Statistical procedure designed to test for mean differences between two groups of participants.

t-test for independent groups—Statistical procedure designed to test for mean differences between two groups of participants, all participants in the study appear in one and only one group.

Two-group, posttest-only design—A design in which two groups of participants are compared once after some manipulation of the independent variable.

Two-way ANOVA—Statistical procedure for the analysis of a factorial design with two independent variables.

Typologies—Classification systems used in qualitative research for description purposes. They are made up of categories of the world or a phenomenon particularly of the behaviour of people.

Type I error—Probability of rejecting the null hypothesis when the null hypothesis is true.

Type II error—Probability of not rejecting the null hypothesis when the null hypothesis is false.

Univariate—Having to do with one variable. For example, a univariate distribution would provide the distribution for a single variable.

Univariate designs—See single-variable designs.

Univariate Analysis—Statistical analysis of single variables, mainly hypothesis testing.

Unobtrusive measure—Any measure that can be taken of participants without their being aware that they are being measured.

Unobtrusive observer—Anyone who is able to observe the behaviour of participants without their being aware they are being observed.

Validity—Major concept in research that has several specific meanings (internal validity, external validity, construct validity, and statistical validity). In a general sense, validity refers to the methodological and/or conceptual soundness of research (for example, in the case of an experiment, a question regarding the validity of an experiment is, "Does this experiment really test what it is supposed to test?")

Variability—Differences among participants on any given variable.

Variable—Any characteristic that can take on different values. Variables are sets of events measured in research. Research is aimed at defining the relationships between variables.

Variance—Summary statistic that indicates the degree of variability among participants for a given variable. The variance is essentially the average squared deviation from the mean and is the square of the standard deviation.

Within-group variance—Variability among participants within a particular group or condition. Provides a basis for comparing mean differences between groups in most statistical procedures.

Index